Civics
for Americans

PATRICK and REMY

Teacher's Annotated Edition
prepared by L. JoAnne Buggey

SCOTT, FORESMAN AND COMPANY
Editorial Offices: Glenview, Illinois
Regional Sales Offices: Palo Alto, California •
Tucker, Georgia • Glenview, Illinois •
Oakland, New Jersey • Dallas, Texas

ISBN: 0-673-13317-6
Copyright © 1980
Scott, Foresman and Company, Glenview,
Illinois.
All Rights Reserved.
Printed in the United States of America.

12345678910 KPK 89888786858483828 18079

TO THE TEACHER

Civic education is teaching and learning the rights and responsibilities of citizenship. American citizens have the *right* to participate in decisions about governance, such as making rules, setting goals, and distributing resources within groups. They also have the *responsibility* to become thoughtful, capable decision makers. Thus, civics for Americans ought to focus on decision making in the lives of citizens.

INSTRUCTIONAL PURPOSE

The main purpose of *Civics for Americans* is helping students acquire knowledge and skills needed to carry out their responsibilities and protect their rights as citizens of a free society. To this end, lessons emphasize basic knowledge of governmental institutions, decision making of public officials, economic policies and processes that affect the decisions of citizens, and practical political decisions in the daily lives of citizens. Lessons also stress doing as well as knowing; they allow for practice of basic skills in finding and using information and in making, judging, and influencing decisions.

As students work through *Civics for Americans,* they continually make and judge decisions, and they analyze decision making by government officials and those seeking to influence government. Thus, the text combines facts about governmental institutions and the duties of public officials with instruction about how citizens might influence public decisions.

All American citizens—young and old, rich and poor, male and female—may be involved in three essential tasks of decision making. All may make decisions, try to influence decisions of others, and judge their own decisions as well as those of public officials and other citizens. Thus, skills in decision making are fundamentals of civic education.

Responsible decision making involves careful assessment of alternatives and their consequences in light of values and goals. Responsible decision makers consider the effects of their choices on themselves and various others. They judge the fairness of their choices in terms of both individual and group goals. Before choosing an alternative, the responsible citizen asks: (1) How will my decision affect me and (2) How will it affect various others? The responsible citizen tries to make decisions that balance the needs of the individual and of society.

INSTRUCTIONAL DESIGN

Civics for Americans reflects sound principles of teaching and learning.

Every chapter begins with a dramatic episode to capture student attention and introduce the content focus and purposes. Telling students at the outset of instruction what they are expected to achieve enables them to learn more effectively and efficiently. Knowing the point of a lesson helps the learner to stay on track, to attend to what is relevant to the assigned task.

Each chapter concludes with an originally written case study featuring current topics, issues, and events. Each case is carefully designed to develop one or more decision-making skill and to highlight important content presented in the chapter.

Abstract ideas about civics are made tangible and illustrated through descriptions of the personal experiences of citizens and leaders in government. Lessons highlight decision-making experiences learners have encountered in daily life and will encounter again. Students are motivated to learn when they see clearly that what is learned in school is linked to life outside the school. For example, students who are shown that decision-making skills can help them achieve goals they value are likely to strive to acquire these competencies.

Skills in decision making and information processing are patterned into the textbook in a variety of ways. Students continually work with these skills in different lessons and have the opportunity to apply what they have learned to questions, case studies, and a variety of other activities. This provides for cumulative reinforcement of skill learning without boring repetition.

Questions and activities challenge students to use information, ideas, and skills. These application exercises allow students to move from lower to higher cognitive levels. For instance, students move from finding and comprehending information to organizing and evaluating it. They move from identifying alternatives to inferring consequences and defending choices. Higher-level thinking skills learned in the process of making, analyzing, or judging a decision can be applied, or transferred, to other occasions for decisions. Ability to apply skills to a wide range of decisions demonstrates the highest cognitive capacity—competence to think and learn independently.

As with any set of skills, the more opportunities students have to practice, reflect upon, and demonstrate citizenship competencies, the more likely it is they will develop proficiency. Thus, *Civics for Americans* presents repeated opportunities to develop and practice basic competencies. For example, students not only read about making decisions, they practice making and judging decisions. They continually use skills in finding, comprehending, organizing, evaluating, and communicating information and ideas. Through regular application of these skills, students may demonstrate competence.

INSTRUCTIONAL OUTCOMES

The minimal outcome of civic education in our schools ought to be a significant increase in citizenship competencies among Americans. One main facet of competent citizenship is basic knowledge of societal realities—the way, for instance, our governmental and economic institutions work. A second main facet of competent citizenship has to do with skills in thinking, deciding, and acting.

Americans cherish the ideal of freedom. This ideal entails the right, responsibility, and capability to decide and to implement decisions concerning governance. Thus, the aim of civic education for Americans, a free people, ought to be the development of knowledge about social, political, and economic realities and ability to think independently and constructively about governance and the rights and responsibilities of citizens.

Civics for Americans has been designed to help students learn basic knowledge and skills needed to become competent citizens. The reward for learning the lessons in this text will be to make significant progress in the lifelong pursuit of becoming a good citizen in a free society.

CONTENTS OF THE TEACHER'S GUIDE
AUTHORS' PREFACE	G2
PROGRAM OVERVIEW	G4
LESSON PLANS	G5
BIBLIOGRAPHIES	G30

PROGRAM OVERVIEW

MATERIALS

- *Civics for Americans,* a 576-page, hardbound student text.
- Teacher's Annotated Edition with answers, teaching notes, lesson plans, and bibliography.
- Tests on Duplicating Masters, 39 masters provide 1-page Chapter Tests and 2-page Unit Tests. Tests are easily graded; questions add up to 100 points.
- Duplicating Masters Activities, 50 masters, 2 for each chapter, reinforce learnings and provide for application of skills.

CONTENT

Seven units, divided into twenty-five chapters, cover citizenship, national government, citizen influence, state government, local government, our free enterprise system, and foreign policy. Chapters are divided into sections to make study and review easy. A Resource Section at the back of the student text contains Flag Etiquette, the Declaration of Independence, and charts of facts about states and Presidents. The Constitution is included in its original text with explanations students can understand.

SKILLS

Three areas of skill development are stressed in the program: basic social studies skills, decision-making skills, and life skills.

The **basic social studies skills** are the skills students need for using information:

- finding information
- comprehending information
- organizing information
- evaluating information
- communicating information and ideas

Finding information has to do with locating facts or opinions within a reading assignment. For example, students use the headings within a chapter section to find details about a person, place, or event. They get information from charts, tables, graphs, and pictures in the text or from the back matter. They use library resources such as an encyclopedia or "facts-on-file" to find certain kinds of information. They read newspapers to find information and learn to ask good questions.

Comprehending information refers to understanding what one reads, sees, and hears. It includes such skills as getting the main idea or recognizing contrasting points of view in paragraphs, maps, charts, graphs, cartoons, and pictures; making inferences; recognizing point of view, bias, and propaganda; extrapolating information. Recognizing social studies vocabulary, knowing the literal meanings of words, summarizing the main idea in a sentence or paragraph, reading graphic information critically, relating details from one source to another, "reading between the lines"—these are all comprehension activities.

Organizing information is classifying. It involves the use of ideas or definitions to put information in certain categories. For example, students classify events in terms of a definition and arrange data in order.

Evaluating information is making judgments about its worth. It is deciding whether or not information is valid. It involves detecting flaws in reasoning, analyzing an argument to see if it is consistent with the facts, determining what the facts are.

Communicating information and ideas is writing and speaking. Students frame questions, tabulate information, write paragraphs that summarize information, write arguments for or against a point of view, write letters to gain information and express opinions.

Questions and activities call for students to practice these skills. Each chapter test includes a part which reviews these skills.

The skills in **decision making** include:

- identifying an occasion for decision
- identifying and clarifying alternatives
- inferring the consequences that are likely to result from particular alternatives
- evaluating the consequences
- choosing an alternative in the light of goals

- judging choices with reference to criteria about practicality and fairness

These skills are introduced in Chapter 2. Each subsequent chapter provides opportunities to practice these skills.

Life Skills are those practical skills frequently measured on competency tests and called variously *life skills, applied skills,* or *minimum essential skills.* These include such everyday activities as filling out forms and using checks as well as civic activities such as casting a ballot or using a small claims court.

FEATURES
- Case Studies at the end of every chapter give students a real-life example of the institutions, officials, and decision-making process described in the chapter.
- People & Government, illustrated feature pages in each unit, focus on the actual work individuals in given civic jobs do.
- Skills for Life, one in each unit, help students gain competency in practical matters they face as citizens—filing income tax, voting, balancing a checkbook, and the like.
- Words in heavy print. Throughout the book, the special social studies words, terms for government institutions and officials, and concept words appear in heavy print. These words are included in the vocabulary lists in Section Reviews. They all appear in the Glossary, with dictionary-style pronunciations and social studies definitions.

REVIEW AND ASSESSMENT
Opportunities for review and assessment are provided throughout the program. Sections end with Section Reviews that include vocabulary lists, questions to review main ideas, and exercises that provide for application of skills. Chapter Test and Activities pages give in-book tests of vocabulary, information, and skills. The activity suggestions include recommendations of outside reading as well as various individual and group projects. Unit Tests pull together vocabulary, ideas, and skills from the whole unit. Where the Tests on Duplicating Masters are available for assessment, the in-book test can be used as open-book tests for review.

TEACHING PLAN
Civics for Americans is designed for a year's course in civics. The primary plan for using the book is to work through the units and chapters according to the sequence presented in the book. However, there are alternative combinations of units which can be recommended.

ONE YEAR COURSE
Alternative Plan
This sequence emphasizes the political behavior of citizens before examining the institutions of government.
Unit 1—Government and Citizenship
Unit 3—How Citizens Influence Government
Unit 2—Making Decisions in National Government
Unit 4—Making Decisions in State Government
Unit 5—Making Decisions in Local Government
Unit 6—Our Free Enterprise System
Unit 7—America and the World

ONE-SEMESTER COURSE
A. Focus on Government Institutions
Unit 1—Government and Citizenship
Unit 2—Making Decisions in National Government
Unit 3—Making Decisions in State Government
Unit 4—Making Decisions in Local Government
B. Focus on Citizenship Skills and National Government
Unit 1—Government and Citizenship
Unit 2—Making Decisions in National Government
Unit 3—How Citizens Influence Government
C. Focus on National Government
Unit 1—Government and Citizenship
Unit 2—Making Decisions in National Government
Unit 6—Our Free Enterprise System
D. Focus on Citizenship Skills and State and Local Governments
Unit 1—Government and Citizenship
Unit 3—How Citizens Influence Government
Unit 4—Making Decisions in State Government
Unit 5—Making Decisions in Local Government

UNIT 1 GOVERNMENT AND CITIZENSHIP

CHAPTER 1 CIVICS IN YOUR LIFE   PAGES 4–19

OVERVIEW
Civics is a part of every person's life. Therefore, the kinds of decisions governments make are examined. The reasons we have governments are also examined.

OBJECTIVES
Each student will be able to:
1. Explain how civics is a part of daily life.
2. Identify important kinds of decisions governments make.
3. State reasons for having governments.

TEACHING IDEAS
1. Before beginning the unit divide the class into small groups. Have each group skim the illustrations in the book. Ask each group to write a list of at least ten topics to be studied in this course. Share the results and come up with a definition of civics.
2. Have each student begin a civics dictionary. Include the words in the vocabulary part of each Section Review. Label a page for each letter of the alphabet. Have each student design a civics coat of arms for the cover.
3. Begin a class timeline for use throughout this unit. Start at 1776 and go to the present.
4. Have each student write a brief summary of what it means to be a citizen of the United States. Put these away and share them with the students at the end of the course.
5. Discuss: The authors state, ". . . . your country's future is up to you to decide." What do they mean?
6. Have the class form into three groups. Assign places around the room. Change the groups several times. Possible groups might be based on eye color (brown, blue, other), age (under 13, over 16, other), children in the family (1, 2–4, 5 or more), food choice (chocolate, vanilla, strawberry ice cream), spare time activity (read, watch TV, play), or favorite sport (football, baseball, golf). Discuss what students find out about groups as a result of this activity (groups may change, we belong to many groups, we choose to belong to some groups, etc.).
7. Have students make a list of all the groups they belong to. Have them put an "X" by all groups where they help to make the rules.
8. Choose one public service from these examples. Describe what your community would be like without it.
9. Research topics: life in 1620; Mayflower Compact; Plymouth Colony; public services; U.S. Coast Guard; territorial waters.

EVALUATING OBJECTIVES
1. Have each student make a cartoon showing how civics is a part of daily life.
2. Ask students to write a letter to a friend who isn't taking this course, explaining why civics is an important part of daily life.
3. Ask students to write a poem of at least four lines about the importance of civics.
4. Have each student list the three main kinds of decisions governments make and give one example of each.
5. Have each student divide a paper into six parts. In each box draw an example of a decision a government might have to make. Put an "X" by the two that students feel are most important to them.
6. Have each student write three descriptions of government decisions. Divide the class into small groups. Have each student read the three statements. Have other class members say whether it is a decision about rules, goals, or who will receive benefits.
7. Write a paragraph summarizing the main reasons for having governments.

OVERVIEW

All individuals make decisions. They must also be able to judge the decisions they make.

OBJECTIVES

Each student will be able to:

1. State the questions to ask when making a decision.
2. Apply the questions to decision-making situations.
3. State the questions that help you to judge a decision.
4. Apply the questions to decisions.
5. Make and explain a decision tree.

TEACHING IDEAS

1. Before beginning the chapter have the students examine the illustrations. Working in pairs have them prepare a list of any decisions citizens must make.
2. Add to the civics dictionaries.
3. Have each student make a decision wheel. Draw a circle the size of a quarter. Label it Decisions I Make. Draw at least ten lines extending out from the circle like the spokes on a wheel. On each line name one decision you have made or might make.
4. Complete the following outline:
   I. Making Decisions
      A. (Use the chapter subheads)
      B. (and C.)
   II. Judging Decisions
      A.
      B. Guidelines for Judging Decisions
         1. (2, 3, and 4.)
      C.
5. Discuss: You have found $100. What should you do? Apply each of the three questions the authors suggest.
6. Discuss: You must have plenty of time to make a good decision. Do you agree or disagree? Why? Find evidence to support your answer in the chapter.
7. Divide the class into small groups. Explain that they had a group assignment due today. It isn't done. What should they do? Apply the decision-making questions.
8. Have students list at least five school rules. Put an "X" by the two they think are best. Have them explain how they made the decision.
9. Work in small groups. Identify a problem your community has solved. Briefly explain how the guidelines for judging decisions might be used in this situation. Share your ideas with another group.
10. Have students divide a paper into two columns. Make a list of all arguments for the Black Mesa Mine Decision in one column and arguments against it in the other.
11. Research topics: Sierra Club; articles on decision making; Navajo; geologists.

EVALUATING OBJECTIVES

1. A friend has a problem. List the three questions he or she should ask to help in making a decision. Briefly explain each.
2. Describe a decision you have made recently. Write three paragraphs. In the first explain the alternatives, in the second the consequences, and in the third tell which consequence you prefer.
3. Write a summary of the guidelines for judging decisions.
4. Your community has decided to build a domed sports stadium. Apply the guidelines to this situation.
5. State a problem. Apply the questions for making decisions. When you have made a choice then apply the guidelines for judging decisions.
6. Make a decision tree for an important American you have read about. Explain your decision tree in writing.

OVERVIEW
In the years after the signing of the
Declaration of Independence major problems
developed that led to the need for a
Constitutional Convention. Many important
decisions were made at the Convention. Not
all delegates agreed and some states were not
willing to ratify the Constitution immediately.

OBJECTIVES
Each student will be able to:
1. Identify the major national problems that
led to the Constitutional Convention.
2. State the main decisions made at the
Convention.
3. Summarize the main ideas of the
Federalists and Anti-Federalists about the
Constitution.

TEACHING IDEAS
1. Continue the class timeline and individual
dictionaries.
2. You are a reporter. Write an article on life
in 1787 and how it led to the need for a
Constitutional Convention.
3. Make a class list of the reasons for needing
a Constitutional Convention.
4. Divide a sheet of paper into two columns.
In the first column list the key points of the
Articles of Confederation. In the second
explain how the Constitution handled the
same problem. Complete the second column
in Chapter 4.
5. Develop a class Constitutional Convention
Hall of Fame.
6. Discuss: How does what you have read
support the following: George Washington
favored a strong central government. Give
page numbers to support your answer.
7. Make an outline map of the U.S. in 1787.
Match the names of the delegates to the
Convention with their home states.
8. Make a bar graph to show the occupations

of the delegates to the Constitutional
Convention. Begin with the data on page 41.
9. As a class make a list of the main points of
the Virginia Plan. Do the same for the New
Jersey Plan. Put an "X" by any ideas found
in both.
10. Have each student make a chart
comparing the Virginia Plan, the New Jersey
Plan, and the Great Compromise.
11. Research topics: life in 1787; Articles of
Confederation; delegates to the Constitutional
Convention; Federalists; Anti-Federalists.

EVALUATING OBJECTIVES
1. Write a summary of the Articles of
Confederation. Explain why the Articles made
the Convention necessary.
2. List three weaknesses of the Articles.
Explain how each one influenced the nation in
1787.
3. Write a short story called "Life in 1787."
4. Write a "Who's Who" of leaders in 1787.
5. Discuss: What were the main decisions
made at the Constitutional Convention?
6. Discuss: You are from New Jersey. What
are your views on the importance of the size
of your state? Your friend is from New York.
What are his or her views?
7. Explain the rules of the Convention to a
new delegate.
8. Discuss: How did the Great Compromise
affect the decisions made at the Convention?
9. If you had attended the Convention would
you have been a Federalist or Anti-Federalist?
Why? Give a two minute speech expressing
your views.
10. Summarize the Table on page 50.
11. Make a poster to convince a delegate to
sign the Constitution.
12. Choose to be a Federalist or
Anti-Federalist. Explain your views about the
Constitution to two other class members.

OVERVIEW

The Constitution is the plan for government in the United States. It is divided into three main sections.

OBJECTIVES

Each student will be able to:

1. Define the main purposes of the Constitution.
2. Describe the main parts of the Constitution.
3. Name the three branches of government and summarize the main purpose of each.
4. Identify roles of state and national governments.
5. Reinforce chart-reading skills.

TEACHING IDEAS

1. Before reading the chapter discuss anything the students might already know about the Constitution. Record their ideas. Reexamine these ideas at the end of the chapter.
2. Continue the class time-line and individual dictionaries.
3. Discuss: Has anyone ever read the Constitution? Why did President Truman suggest that everyone should read it over and over? Do you agree? Why?
4. Discuss: Why do we have a Constitution?
5. Make a diagram showing the parts of the Constitution.
6. Write a letter to the editor. Explain why we have a Constitution.
7. Complete the chart comparing the Articles and the Constitution begun in Chapter 3.
8. Some students might want to learn the Preamble.
9. Make a chart. Have one column for each branch of government. List powers of each.
10. Name the three branches of government. Write a paragraph summarizing the purposes of each branch of government.

11. Where in the Constitution does it explain the three branches of government? Where does it explain the roles of state and national government?
12. Discuss: Can the Constitution be changed? How? How many times has it been changed?
13. Discuss: What is the third section of the Constitution? Describe its purpose.
14. Begin a class list. Put powers of state government in one column. Put powers of national government in the other. Keep this to add to and for future reference.
15. Research topics: treason; Richard Nixon; Watergate; impeachment.

EVALUATING OBJECTIVES

1. Discuss: What reasons can you give for having a Constitution?
2. Write a poem about the purposes of our Constitution.
3. Discuss: What are the main parts of the Constitution? What is the purpose of each?
4. Write a brief summary of the goals as stated in the Preamble. Put an "X" by the one you feel is most important. Put an asterisk by the one you feel is least important. Explain your choices.
5. Discuss: Which article(s) are most important?
6. Name the three branches of government established in the Constitution. Write a one sentence summary of the purpose of each.
7. Discuss: What are three roles of state government? What are three roles of national government? How do they relate?
8. Summarize the part(s) of the Constitution that help to define the roles of state government.
9. Summarize the chart on page 62. Use words or a visual presentation.

OVERVIEW

The Constitution has been amended in order to extend the rights and liberties of citizens. Most people living in the United States are citizens. Citizens have certain responsibilities to preserve their Constitutional rights.

OBJECTIVES

Each student will be able to:

1. Identify the main ways the Constitution has been amended to extend citizens' rights and liberties.
2. State the ways a person gains and loses citizenship.
3. Describe the responsibilities of citizens in order to preserve their rights under the Constitution.
4. Reinforce chart-reading skills.

TEACHING IDEAS

1. Before beginning the chapter discuss what it means to be a citizen. Record all ideas. Revise as necessary at the end of the chapter.
2. Complete the unit timeline and continue individual dictionaries. The dictionaries should be continued throughout the course.
3. Discuss: What is the Bill of Rights? Where is it? What is its purpose?
4. Look at the chart on page 96. Give examples from life today to explain each of the five First Amendment rights.
5. Discuss: If you were to write your own Bill of Rights for today and the future, would you make any changes?
6. Which five amendments (not including the Bill of Rights) do you feel are most important?
7. Make an amendments outline. Begin with number 11. Include at least two points about each amendment.
8. Take a poll of any twenty adults. Are they citizens by birth or naturalization? Share your data and make a class tabulation.
9. Work in small groups. Prepare a handout to be given to someone who wants to know about becoming a citizen.
10. Use the chart on page 103. Explain the steps in becoming a citizen to a friend who is interested.
11. Discuss: Could you ever lose your citizenship? Explain your answer.
12. Use the subheads in this chapter to complete an outline titled "Citizens' Responsibilities."
13. What are the main duties of citizenship? Briefly describe each one. Which is most important to you? Why?
14. Describe a "responsible citizen."
15. Research topics: amendments; search warrants; citizenship procedures; voting procedures; immigration; immigrants.

EVALUATING OBJECTIVES

1. List the five amendments you think are most important. Explain why.
2. Discuss: What does it mean to amend the Constitution? How often has it happened?
3. What is the Bill of Rights? Answer in a poem, skit, song, poster, or cartoon.
4. Write a paragraph explaining which amendment has the greatest impact on your life.
5. Discuss: Ways of becoming a citizen and how a person could lose the privileges.
6. Make a picture story of the steps involved in becoming a citizen.
7. How did you become a citizen? How else would it be possible?
8. According to the authors, "The first duty of citizens is to respect and obey their laws." Explain what that means.
9. Describe several other responsibilities of a good citizen.
10. Write a summary of one of the charts in this chapter.

UNIT 2   MAKING DECISIONS IN THE NATIONAL GOVERNMENT

CHAPTER 6   DECISION MAKING IN CONGRESS   PAGES 118–141

OVERVIEW
Congress is divided into two parts, the Senate and the House of Representatives. Each has its separate and important roles, one of the most important being law making.

OBJECTIVES
Each student will be able to:
1. Name the two main groups that make up Congress and the powers of each.
2. Examine the main roles of members of Congress.
3. Identify the steps in a bill becoming a law.

TEACHING IDEAS
1. Before beginning Unit 2 discuss what NATIONAL GOVERNMENT means.
2. Divide into small groups. Make a list of ways life is different now than in 1787. Combine two groups. Share lists and agree on the four most important changes. Share these with the total class.
3. Begin an individual or class list of ways national government influences their lives and the lives of others in their community. Continue the list throughout the unit. Use it as a unit summary.
4. Continue individual dictionaries begun in Unit 1.
5. Discuss: How are Congressional districts set up? How many are there in your state? Why does each state have two Senators? How long is a Senator's term? How does this compare to the term of a Representative?
6. Write a summary of the map on page 120.
7. Write a summary statement to go under the cartoon on page 125.
8. Summarize the four main jobs of Representatives once they are elected.
9. Make a class list of federal programs in your community.
10. Discuss: All bills that become laws begin in the White House. Agree? Why?
11. Diagram possible presidential actions regarding a bill that has been approved by Congress.
12. Make a poster or radio script to convince people to support your views on how to best use our national forests.
13. View a filmstrip on the Congress.
14. Research topics: chart U.S. population at ten year intervals; number of Senators and Representatives in the past; map showing when each state joined the Union; current Speaker of House; majority and minority floor leaders and party whips.

EVALUATING OBJECTIVES
1. Divide a paper into two columns. Put the name of a main group that makes up Congress at the top of each column. List three key powers of each.
2. Divide a sheet of paper into two parts. On each side name a major group that makes up the Congress and illustrate the major powers of each.
3. Discuss: What are the major powers of Congress and how are they allocated?
4. Role-play: Divide the class into small groups. Have each group role-play one of the main roles of Congressmen. Have other groups identify the role.
5. Write a summary of the two roles of members of Congress you feel are most important.
6. Make your own diagram of a bill becoming a law.
7. Divide the class into small groups. Have them scramble the steps in a bill becoming a law. Exchange lists and arrange the steps in the correct order.

OVERVIEW

The national government must have money in order to enforce rules, and provide services and benefits. The federal budget is a plan for how the money is to be gathered and spent.

OBJECTIVES

Each student will be able to:

1. Summarize how the national government gets its money and how it spends it.
2. Explain the role of the federal budget.

TEACHING IDEAS

1. Before reading have students list any ways they are aware of that show how we pay for the national government.
2. Continue the list of ways national government influences their lives.
3. Make an outline showing the major ways the national government gets money.
4. Make a class list of the ways the national government gets money.
5. Change the pie graph on page 143 to a bar graph or pictorial pie graph.
6. Plan the questions necessary to survey what deductions people make on their income tax and how they feel about taxes. Have each student survey ten adults. Compile the data.
7. Discuss: Have tax forms available. Find out how much Benson and Green would pay this year. Give other examples and have students refer to tables to establish the tax.
8. Discuss: Is it fair for some organizations to be tax free? A class debate could also be held.
9. Divide the class into small groups. Have each group look for examples of excise taxes (grocery, garage, pharmacy, department store, etc.).
10. Invite an auto dealer to class. Plan questions to find out about the protective tariff.
11. Make up a person and figures following the model on Skills for Life.

12. Write a summary statement to go with the graph on page 151.
13. Make a poster showing who receives government money.
14. You represent the national government. Prepare a news summary of how the national government spends its money.
15. Refer to the national budget on page 154. Summarize the data or present it in some other way.
16. Work in pairs. List national priorities. Combine with two other groups. Agree on the three top priorities. Make a class summary.
17. List at least ten projects the federal government is spending money on. If they cut back, which two would you give up most easily? Which two would you defend longest?
18. Explain the national debt to someone who isn't in this course.
19. Discuss: Balancing the budget would eliminate the national debt.
20. Research topics: customs duties; excise taxes; tariffs; national debt (over time); current military spending; Medicare or Medicaid; food stamps; current budget.

EVALUATING OBJECTIVES

1. Make a booklet explaining how the national government makes and spends its money.
2. Write two paragraphs. In one summarize the ways the national government raises money. In the other, the ways it spends it.
3. Divide a sheet in two parts. In column one list ways the national government raises money. In column two list ways federal money is spent.
4. Write a letter to the editor, a three minute radio script, or draw a cartoon explaining the role of the federal budget.
5. Discuss: Why do we need a federal budget?

OVERVIEW

Getting elected President is a complicated process. Once elected the President has many responsibilities. Advisors help in many ways. The President responds to various influences before making important decisions.

OBJECTIVES

Each student will be able to:
1. Describe the steps in becoming President.
2. Summarize the major roles of the President.
3. Identify the key people who help the President.
4. Examine how the decisions a President makes may be influenced.

TEACHING IDEAS

1. Before reading this chapter begin a class list of roles of the President. List any activities the President is currently involved in. Continue the list throughout the chapter. At the end of the chapter group them according to the seven key roles.
2. Continue the list of ways national government influences their lives.
3. Make a poster "ad" including the formal and informal requirements for President.
4. Work in small groups. Rank order the formal and informal requirements for President. Join with two other groups. Try to agree on the top two requirements. Form a class list.
5. View a filmstrip on the national convention. Students could work in small groups to devise their own script.
6. Discuss: What are the main responsibilities of the President?
7. Work in pairs. One person list the four constitutional powers of the President. The other person list the three non-constitutional powers. Give examples of each.
8. Look for illustrations in the text that include the President. Identify the page number and the role demonstrated in each picture.
9. Vice-Presidents are usually invisible figures. Write a paragraph, or poem, or make a cartoon to explain what it means.
10. Complete an outline titled "Influences on a President's Decisions."
11. Divide a sheet into four sections. Illustrate each of the key influences on a President's decisions.
12. Make a list of pros and cons of the B-1 Bomber. Then discuss the decision.
13. Research topics: past Presidents (make a timeline); map the electoral votes of each state; any of the five wars Congress has declared; Vice-Presidents who have become President; the last State of the Union speech.

EVALUATING OBJECTIVES

1. Make a chart showing the steps in becoming President.
2. Summarize the steps in becoming President (either in words or pictures).
3. Write a letter to a friend explaining steps a person must go through before becoming President.
4. Outline the key roles of the President.
5. Prepare a brief hand-out on roles of the President to explain them to interested voters.
6. Work in pairs. List the roles of the President. Give at least three examples of each.
7. Discuss: Who are the key advisors of the President.
8. Identify three illustrations in your book that show people who aid the President.
9. Discuss: What are the main ways a President's decisions are influenced?
10. Make a cartoon or other visual showing the many influences on a President's decisions.

OVERVIEW
There are many federal agencies involved in making numerous kinds of decisions. They are influenced in the decisions they make in varied ways.

OBJECTIVES
Each student will be able to:
1. Identify the main roles of the key federal agencies.
2. List decision makers in federal agencies.
3. Examine how federal agencies are influenced.

TEACHING IDEAS
1. Before reading skim the chapter. Look at the subheads and visuals to try to decide what federal agencies there are. Begin a list to be continued throughout the chapter.
2. Continue the list of ways national government influences students' lives.
3. Discuss: What does bureaucracy mean?
4. Discuss: What do federal agencies do?
5. Write a summary statement of the chart on page 188.
6. Complete an outline titled "Cabinet Members."
7. Make a booklet on the cabinet departments. Make a section for each department. Write reports or poems, draw pictures or cartoons, or find articles or headlines relating to the work of each department.
8. Make a news bulletin board on the cabinet members.
9. Divide into small groups. Prepare a ten statement True or False activity for the various cabinet departments and their roles. Exchange with at least two other groups.
10. Discuss: Compare cabinet departments, independent agencies, and regulatory agencies.
11. Look in your local telephone book for names of federal agencies. List any you find.
12. Make a chart entitled "Decision Makers in Federal Agencies."
13. Make a list of the top leaders in federal agencies. Explain their roles.
14. Write a job "ad" for a top leader in a federal agency of your choosing.
15. Discuss: Compare career workers and political appointees.
16. Divide a paper into four columns. Title them Congress, the President, Client Groups, and Others. List ways each influences federal agencies.
17. Discuss: Where is the Concorde used today?
18. Research topics: when each cabinet department was established; ERA; NASA; CIA; U.S. Postal Service; FCC; Civil Service Commission; Concorde.

EVALUATING OBJECTIVES
1. Write a one sentence summary of the key role(s) of each cabinet department.
2. Work in pairs. Divide a paper into twelve columns. Write the name of one cabinet department in each column. List five examples of roles of each department.
3. Discuss: Why are the cabinet departments necessary?
4. Discuss: What other federal agencies are there besides cabinet departments?
5. Discuss: Who are the key decision makers in federal agencies? What do they do?
6. List five political appointees and five career workers.
7. Complete the statement "I learned . . ." about the key decision makers in federal agencies.
8. Write a paragraph to summarize the four main influences on federal agencies.
9. Divide a paper into four parts. In each section illustrate one of the main influences on federal agencies.

OVERVIEW
Laws and courts serve the people in a variety of ways. As a result, a number of federal courts are necessary. The Supreme Court plays special roles within the federal court system.

OBJECTIVES
Each student will be able to:
1. Identify the main roles of the courts.
2. Explain how federal courts are organized.
3. Examine how the Supreme Court works.
4. List ways Supreme Court decisions are influenced.

TEACHING IDEAS
1. Before reading start a list of what federal courts do. Add to the list throughout the chapter.
2. Begin a news chart on federal courts.
3. If students are not already keeping a civics dictionary make one for this chapter.
4. Complete the list of how the national government influences their lives. Discuss the list at the end of this unit.
5. Discuss: Compare the four kinds of laws and give examples of each.
6. Make an outline entitled "Kinds of Laws."
7. List the kinds of cases heard in federal courts.
8. Make a chart showing the kinds of cases heard in federal courts.
9. View a filmstrip on federal courts.
10. Write a summary of the chart on page 213.
11. List at least five special courts.
12. Locate three illustrations in your text that explain something about each of the main types of courts. Give the page numbers.
13. Work in pairs. Devise a ten item matching exercise on types of courts and their responsibilities.
14. Discuss: How is the attorney general connected to the courts?
15. Diagram the Supreme Court.
16. Make a Supreme Court timeline of one year.
17. Discuss: How do you get to be a Supreme Court justice?
18. Write a summary of the kinds of cases that are originally handled by the Supreme Court. Look for examples of real cases.
19. Make a timeline or decision tree on *Brown* v. *Board of Education*.
20. Research topics: location of Courts of Appeals; Supreme Court justices; current Supreme Court cases; Thurgood Marshall; John Marshall.

EVALUATING OBJECTIVES
1. Discuss: What kinds of cases are handled in federal courts?
2. Work in pairs. Make up ten fill-in-the-blank questions about cases that are handled in federal courts. Exchange with one other pair.
3. Find a visual to illustrate any three kinds of cases that can be handled in federal courts.
4. Outline the section entitled "Cases Heard in Federal Courts."
5. Diagram the levels of federal courts on a poster.
6. Write a summary of the kinds of federal courts.
7. Discuss: How do judges get appointed?
8. Discuss: What is the role of the Supreme Court?
9. Make a poster explaining the roles of the Supreme Court.
10. Diagram the steps in a case being reviewed by the Supreme Court.
11. List the kinds of cases that can be handled directly by the Supreme Court.
12. List the four main influences on Supreme Court decisions.

UNIT 3 HOW CITIZENS INFLUENCE GOVERNMENT

CHAPTER 11 TAKING PART IN INTEREST GROUPS PAGES 234–251

OVERVIEW
Citizens join interest groups for a number of reasons in order to influence government. They take part in interest groups in a variety of ways.

OBJECTIVES
Each student will be able to:
1. Explain what an interest group is.
2. List reasons why people join interest groups.
3. Identify who interest groups influence and how they do it.
4. Summarize how citizens can take part in interest groups.

TEACHING IDEAS
1. Before beginning the unit refer back to the list of ways government influences our lives. Begin a list for this unit of ways we influence government.
2. List reasons why it is important to vote. Add ideas throughout the unit.
3. Before beginning the chapter discuss what an interest group is. Skim the chapter for visual clues.
4. Begin a news bulletin board or booklet on interest groups.
5. Work in pairs. Choose an interest group. Write for information about the group and how to join it. Prepare a report for the class.
6. Make a poster to try to get someone to join an interest group.
7. List reasons for public interest groups.
8. Invite to class a speaker who represents an interest group active in your community. Plan the interview carefully.
9. The authors suggest five questions to ask to help you decide whether or not a group deserves your support. Present these questions visually.

10. Complete an outline entitled "Political Resources."
11. Divide a paper into four parts. Illustrate one political resource in each section.
12. Discuss: Which political resource is most important? Why?
13. Discuss: Who do interest groups try to influence?
14. Invite a lobbyist to class. Plan questions to find out how he or she influences others.
15. View a filmstrip on lobbyists.
16. Make a visual showing what Americans throw away each year. Discuss the interest groups that might be willing to try to change this.
17. Research topics: articles on retirement age; gun control; smoking or other contemporary problems; any interest groups listed in this chapter or others that are relevant.

EVALUATING OBJECTIVES
1. Define interest group.
2. List three interest groups and briefly describe the purpose of each.
3. Write a paragraph or poem, or draw a cartoon or other visual explaining what an interest group is.
4. Name five reasons why people join interest groups.
5. Name an interest group. List reasons why an individual might join.
6. Convince a person to join an interest group of your choosing.
7. Write a summary of who interest groups influence and give examples of how they do it.
8. Discuss: What is a lobbyist?
9. Change the guidelines for effective group action into a checklist to use when trying to judge if a person or group is effective.

OVERVIEW
The United States has a two-party political system. Deciding whether to support a particular party is a difficult decision. Political parties play an important role in our government.

OBJECTIVES
Each student will be able to:
1. Explain how political parties are organized.
2. Compare the political parties.
3. Identify the role of political parties.

TEACHING IDEAS
1. If this is an election year consider as much student involvement as possible in all aspects of the election.
2. Before reading, discuss what students already know about ways to get involved in political parties. Keep a class list of ideas throughout the chapter.
3. Continue the lists of ways we influence government and reasons for voting.
4. Begin a political parties news bulletin board or individual booklet.
5. Discuss: What is a political party? What is a two-party system?
6. Contact local political party headquarters. Request all information available. Arrange for a speaker to come to class or plan a fieldtrip to the party headquarters.
7. Discuss: What is the role of third parties?
8. Discuss: What roles have minor parties had in politics over time.
9. Discuss: How did political parties develop?
10. Summarize the diagram on page 254.
11. Work in pairs. Make a chart comparing the major political parties.
12. Illustrate the Republican or Democratic party platform for the last Presidential election. Have any parts of it been accomplished? Explain.
13. Illustrate the chart on page 260. Write a summary of the data.
14. List pros and cons of the major parties.
15. Write a summary of the arguments for or against major parties.
16. A recent article on political parties is called, "The Decline of the Parties." Explain what this might mean. Do you agree? Why?
17. Complete an outline entitled "How Parties Nominate Candidates."
18. Discuss: Compare open vs. closed primaries. Which is best? Why?
19. Make a list, diagram, or pamphlet on ways individuals can work to support candidates.
20. Make a decision tree on California Frontlash.
21. List pros and cons of using Frontlash.
22. Research topics: any political party; past political campaigns; posters; buttons; slogans; or memorabilia on parties.

EVALUATING OBJECTIVES
1. Write a paragraph explaining the two-party system.
2. Discuss the meaning of major parties, minor parties, and third parties.
3. Select six illustrations to explain how parties are organized. Write a caption for each.
4. Work in pairs. Make a ten-question matching exercise on the political parties. Exchange with another group.
5. Name two political parties. List four ways they are the same and four ways they are different.
6. List three reasons for supporting a major political party. Which do you feel is most important? Why?
7. Divide a paper into four sections. Illustrate a role of political parties in each section.
8. Discuss: What are the key roles of political parties?

OVERVIEW
There are rules that govern who can vote.
Once you are eligible to vote you must decide
how to vote. There are many ways that voters
are influenced.

OBJECTIVES
Each student will be able to:
1. Know rules governing who can vote.
2. Examine how citizens decide to vote.
3. Explain how to judge the campaign appeal
of candidates.

TEACHING IDEAS
1. Before beginning to read, skim the chapter
to find out who can vote. Begin a list that can
be added to throughout the chapter.
2. Begin a voters/election news bulletin
board.
3. Continue the lists of ways we influence
government and reasons for voting.
4. Work in pairs. Make an illustrated
summary of who can vote. Include errors.
Exchange materials and look for errors.
5. Have local voter registration forms
available. Discuss how they are used.
6. Summarize the voter qualifications
described in Section 1. Compare to
qualifications in your community.
7. Have sample ballots available to examine.
8. Arrange for someone to show students
how local voting machinery works.
9. Summarize the four key considerations
when trying to decide for whom to vote.
Which is the most important? Why?
10. Find examples of ways used to influence
voters.
11. Make up a speech about a local
candidate. Include all the propaganda
techniques. Then rewrite the speech without
any propaganda.
12. Summarize the chart started at the
beginning of the unit listing ways we influence

government. Have each student copy the list
down the left side of a sheet of paper. To the
right of the list make six columns. In the first
column check ways students have already
tried to influence government. In the second
column check ways students would like to try
to influence government this year. In the third
column check ways adults that students know
have influenced government. In the fourth
column check ways students think they might
want to influence government ten years from
now. In the fifth column check ways students
think they could influence government without
having to spend more than one dollar. In the
last column check ways students could
influence government without the help of
anyone else. Have students review their
findings and write a summary statement.
13. Research topics: chart voter turnout over
time (include major elections and off-year
elections); local groups' feelings about
candidates; propaganda.

EVALUATING OBJECTIVES
1. Summarize the rules for voting.
2. Discuss: Who can vote?
3. Write a letter to a friend explaining who
can vote.
4. Work in pairs. Devise six case studies of
people who can vote. Exchange with another
group. Have that group explain why each
person can vote.
5. Discuss: How do citizens decide who to
vote for?
6. List the four key considerations when
trying to decide for whom to vote. Give two
examples of each.
7. Write an editorial summarizing the four
key considerations when trying to decide on
the best candidate. Explain which of the four
is most important.
8. Discuss: What are the three most
influential propaganda techniques? Why?

UNIT 4   MAKING DECISIONS IN STATE GOVERNMENT

CHAPTER 14   STATES AND STATE LEGISLATORS   PAGES 298–315

OVERVIEW
State governments have varied powers, some exclusively, others shared. The legislature is a state's chief lawmaking body. The role of the state legislator is important and diverse. As a result they are influenced in many ways.

OBJECTIVES
Each student will be able to:
1. Summarize the powers of state governments.
2. Identify the powers of state legislatures.
3. Examine the main roles of state legislators.
4. Explain how state legislators are influenced.

TEACHING IDEAS
1. Before beginning the unit discuss with the class any laws they are aware of that have been made at the state level. List ideas and check the accuracy of the list throughout the chapter.
2. Begin a two column class list. Title the first column "How State Government Influences Us." Title the second column "How We Influence the State Government." Continue the listing throughout the unit.
3. Have a copy of your state constitution available to examine. Outline its key points. Compare it to the federal constitution.
4. Work in three groups. Have each group complete one section of a visual presentation of "Powers in Our Federal Government."
5. Outline the state government section of the diagram on page 301.
6. Examine the diagram on page 300. Summarize each section.
7. Summarize in written form the way state government is organized.
8. Outline "Activities of State Legislatures."

9. Get a copy of your state budget. Make a circle graph showing how the money is spent. Compare it to last year's budget. Compare it to the national budget.
10. Work in small groups. Give each group one role of a state legislator to research. Have each group prepare a report and display.
11. Invite a state legislator to class. Plan the interview carefully.
12. Choose a bill that has recently become a law in your state. Explain the steps involved in written form or visually.
13. Chart, outline, diagram, or summarize the ways a governor may influence state legislators.
14. Research topics: laws in neighboring states; pay of state legislators; system of government in other countries.

EVALUATING OBJECTIVES
1. List three powers exclusively belonging to state governments. Write a summary of each.
2. Work in pairs. Devise ten true or false statements about powers of state governments. Exchange with another group.
3. Choose up to six illustrations to summarize the powers of state government. Write a summary to go with them.
4. List the key powers of state legislatures.
5. Write a letter to the editor explaining what you think are the two most important powers of state legislatures and why.
6. Name five key roles of a state legislator. Rank them from most to least important. Write a paragraph explaining why your first and second choices are so important.
7. Make an outline titled "Key Roles of Legislators." Give at least two examples under each role.
8. Name the three most important ways state legislators are influenced.

OVERVIEW

The main role of the executive branch of state government is to enforce laws. The governor is the chief executive and has many duties. The executive branch is composed of the governor, executive officers, state agencies, and departments.

OBJECTIVES

Each student will be able to:

1. Identify the key roles in the executive branch of state government.
2. Identify the key roles of a state governor.
3. Explain how the executive branch is influenced in the decisions it makes.

TEACHING IDEAS

1. Before reading have the class work in small groups to list the roles of the governor. Skim the chapter for examples. Compile a class list and add to it throughout the chapter.
2. Continue unit list, bulletin board, or booklets begun in Chapter 14.
3. Begin a class news bulletin board or individual news booklet on the governor.
4. Check your state constitution for any statements about the requirements for becoming governor.
5. Summarize the role of governor in various plans for state government.
6. Write an editorial voicing your opinion on whether the governor should have more or less power.
7. Have an "executive branch" spelldown.
8. Work in small groups. Devise a biographical description of an "ideal" governor.
9. Begin a list of the governor's aides (include officials, departments, and agencies). Have students work in pairs to research one of the aides listed. Share reports with the class at the end of the chapter.
10. Invite an executive officer or his or her representative to class or plan to visit at the office. Plan the interview carefully to clarify executive branch roles.
11. Make a timeline for your present governor.
12. Plan to interview the governor or an aide.
13. Match the following examples to the key roles of the governor: enforces state laws, proposes state legislation, prepares the state budget, represents the state at official functions, may call a special session of the state legislature. Have students give other examples for the class to identify.
14. Summarize or outline the factors in a governor's decision making.
15. Choose a problem in your community. Identify ways you or your class could influence the appropriate people.
16. List the pros and cons of Governor Dukakis's plan.
17. Plan an interview with Governor Dukakis.
18. Research topics: past governors; current pay for governors and other executive branch workers; roles and requirements of governors of other states.

EVALUATING OBJECTIVES

1. Name the two most important roles in the executive branch of state government.
2. Who are the key workers in the executive branch of state government?
3. List the five key roles of the governor. Give two examples of each.
4. Prepare a poster entitled "Roles of the Governor."
5. Identify at least five illustrations to represent the roles of the governor.
6. Discuss: What are the key ways a governor is influenced.
7. Describe how you, your friends, or your family could influence decisions made by the governor and his or her officers.

CHAPTER 16 STATE COURTS PAGES 336–355

OVERVIEW
Each state has its own court system. The courts handle civil and criminal cases. Lawyers are an important part of the court system.

OBJECTIVES
Each student will be able to:
1. Explain how state courts are organized.
2. Compare civil and criminal cases.
3. Identify the main roles of lawyers.

TEACHING IDEAS
1. Before reading have the class discuss what they know about state courts and the kinds of cases they handle. Skim the chapter for examples.
2. Continue unit list, bulletin board, or booklets begun in Chapter 14. Use data to summarize the unit.
3. Work in small groups. Begin news booklets on state courts. Have students look through back issues of papers if available.
4. Divide a paper into two columns. List civil cases in one column and criminal cases in the other. Compare.
5. Make a civil or criminal case montage.
6. Work in pairs. Make a ten point matching activity. Describe ten cases. Exchange with another pair. Identify each case as civil or criminal.
7. Visit a local court, or invite someone from the court system to visit the class. Plan the interview carefully. Find out if your courts are crowded, have long delays, etc.
8. Arrange for several students to visit a small claims court. Have them report on the visit to the class.
9. Invite someone from a small claims court to class.
10. Write a "Letter to the Editor." Propose ways to speed up the court system.
11. Outline "Criminal and Civil Cases."

12. Invite someone to class to discuss jury duty.
13. Illustrate a timeline of a court case. Make up or use a real case.
14. Work in small groups. Choose a court case. Explain each step in the case to other class members.
15. Plan a class debate on the pros and cons of plea bargaining.
16. Work in small groups. Arrange for each group (or one member of each group) to visit a lawyer. If this is not possible invite a lawyer to visit the class.
17. List the characteristics of a good lawyer.
18. Make a poster showing times a person might need a lawyer.
19. Summarize "You Be the Jury." Are there any other questions you would like to ask?
20. Research topics: local court cases; history of local courts; famous civil or criminal cases; examples of injunctions; number of lawyers in your community.

EVALUATING OBJECTIVES
1. Name and summarize the roles of each of the four main state courts.
2. Look at the diagram on page 339. Write a summary statement to go with it.
3. Make up ten true or false statements about the roles of state courts. Exchange papers.
4. Give three examples of civil cases and three examples of criminal cases.
5. List three ways civil and criminal cases are different.
6. Divide a paper into two parts. Illustrate a civil and criminal case. Exchange papers. Explain how they are the same and different.
7. List five reasons why a person might need the services of a lawyer.
8. You are a lawyer. Make up a brochure so people will know how you can help them.
9. Make a cartoon or write a poem. Include as many roles of lawyers as possible.

UNIT 5   MAKING DECISIONS IN LOCAL GOVERNMENTS

CHAPTER 17   LOCAL GOVERNMENTS   PAGES 360–377

OVERVIEW
Local governments are organized in varied ways. Large numbers of local government workers provide needed services. These services are paid for in a variety of ways.

OBJECTIVES
Each student will be able to:
1. Identify the main ways local governments are organized.
2. Examine the key roles of local government.
3. Name the ways local government gets the money it needs.

TEACHING IDEAS
1. Before beginning the unit discuss examples of influences of local government. Use the index, skim the unit, and use the unit opener. Begin a list of influences. Continue the list through the unit.
2. Begin individual unit notebooks. Include one·section for each chapter. Organize with the same outline (chapters, subheads) as this unit. Do something to summarize each section of each chapter.
3. Divide a paper into three sections. List ways local government is influenced by state government, national government, and others.
4. Summarize the Table on page 362.
5. View a filmstrip that compares local, state, and national government.
6. Discuss: What is the role of each unit of local government?
7. Summarize the roles of each unit of local government in your own state.
8. Make a class list of special districts in your area.
9. Discuss: How are your local school districts organized? Have any districts consolidated in your state?

10. Compare the roles of the Board of Commissioners and other elected officials.
11. Outline: "How Local Governments Provide Services."
12. Make a mobile on roles of your county office.
13. Find out who holds each county position in your area.
14. Make a "local taxes" montage.
15. Invite a speaker to class to discuss local taxes.
16. Work in small groups. Rank order taxes other than property tax in order of importance. Explain your ordering to another group. Form a class list.
17. Research topics: location of townships; local government organization in neighboring states; county names; local ordinances; consolidation in your area; local taxes; revenue sharing and grants-in-aid.

EVALUATING OBJECTIVES
1. Summarize roles of each unit of local government.
2. Work in small groups. Write riddles about each unit of local government. Exchange with another group.
3. List three examples of local government that influence you and your family.
4. Make up a ten point activity matching roles with the county official that handles each role.
5. Name three key roles of local government. Explain each.
6. Divide a paper into three parts. In each section illustrate one service local government provides in your area.
7. Name five ways of raising money for local government.
8. Make a poster showing how local government raises money.

CHAPTER 18   CITY GOVERNMENT   PAGES 378–397

OVERVIEW

Cities are created by state governments. City governments are run by selected key officials. Many groups influence the decisions they make.

OBJECTIVES

Each student will be able to:

1. Examine the structure of local government.
2. Identify the key roles in local government.
3. Name ways local government can be influenced in the decision-making process.

TEACHING IDEAS

1. Before beginning to read have the class develop a list of roles of mayors that they know about. Add to the list throughout the chapter.
2. Continue unit list, or notebooks begun in Chapter 17.
3. Work in small groups. Divide paper into three parts. Compare mayor-council plan, council-manager plan, and commission plan.
4. Summarize the diagrams of plans for city government.
5. Which plan for city government do you think is best? Why?
6. Divide the class into four groups. Assign each group one plan for city government. Plan a speech to convince someone your plan is best.
7. Choose the plan you feel is best. Write a "Letter to the Editor" stating its key features and why you feel it is best.
8. Divide a paper into two columns. In the first column list the characteristics of a "weak mayor." In the second column do the same for a "strong mayor." Compare.
9. Work in small groups. Prepare a ten point matching activity. Describe activities of a mayor and match each to one of the key roles identified by the authors.

10. Write a summarizing statement comparing the roles of a mayor and a city manager.
11. Discuss: How are the roles of mayor, governor, and President the same? Different?
12. Check back papers and magazines for information about your city government chief executive.
13. Visit the chief executive of your area.
14. Invite someone from the chief executive's office to speak to the class. Plan the interview carefully to clarify roles of the chief executive.
15. Make a list of city officials in your city or the city nearest to you.
16. Work in twelve groups. Have each group look through one month of back issues of papers for any examples of how city government is influenced.
17. Research topics: percent of population in your state living in cities or towns; current and past leaders in local government; examples of local strikes.

EVALUATING OBJECTIVES

1. Name the four main types of city government. Write a one sentence summary about each.
2. List three key points in each type of city government.
3. What type of city government do most cities have? Write a paragraph about it.
4. Name five leaders in city government. Give one role of each.
5. List two ways the roles of mayors and city managers are the same. Different.
6. Discuss: What is the role of the city council?
7. Name the major ways local governments are influenced.
8. Divide a paper into three sections. Illustrate the key ways local government is influenced.

OVERVIEW
Cities in recent years have grown rapidly.
This growth has caused problems we are now
trying to solve.

OBJECTIVES
Each student will be able to:
1. Explain how cities grow.
2. Identify key problems of cities.
3. Examine how Washington helps cities.

TEACHING IDEAS
1. Before beginning to read take a poll. Find
out how many class members feel cities are
good places to live, good places to work, and
good places to visit. Compare the findings to
data in the chapter opener.
2. Before reading have each student list the
five best and five worst things about cities.
Make a class list. Compare the findings to the
data in the chapter opener.
3. Continue unit list or notebooks begun in
Chapter 17.
4. Work in small groups. Begin a list of all
reasons for living in a city. Continue to add to
the list. At the end of the chapter rank order
all the reasons, and summarize the findings.
5. Work in small groups. Each group should
prepare a population timeline of a city in your
state.
6. Discuss: What does it mean when we say
cities grow from the inside out?
7. Summarize the diagram on page 401.
8. Change the diagram on page 401 to a
visual presentation. Illustrate each circle.
9. Choose a city problem. Prepare a three
minute speech to convince people to try to
help solve it.
10. Work in pairs. Take pictures of a city
problem in your area. Organize them and
write a summary to explain the problem.
Display.
11. Show a filmstrip on city problems.

12. Invite a city planner to visit your class.
Plan the interview carefully to clarify his or
her roles.
13. Prepare before/after pictures of cities.
14. Describe and illustrate a future solution to
an urban problem.
15. Work in small groups. Look at papers
and magazines for examples of cities being
helped by the federal government.
16. Discuss: Which type of federal aid do you
feel is most helpful to cities? Why?
17. Design a "Big Apple" poster illustrating
its problems.
18. Summarize the problems of New York
City.
19. Research topics: six largest cities; cities
in 1787 (Boston, New York, Philadelphia,
Baltimore); immigration in 1900; megalopolis;
growth of metropolitan areas in your state;
growth of car ownership; rapid transit; city
planners; Buckminster Fuller.

EVALUATING OBJECTIVES
1. Write a summary of how cities grow.
2. Make a diagram of the growth of a city.
3. Cities grow from the inside out. Explain
what this means.
4. Discuss: What are the three key problems
of cities?
5. What do you feel is the most important
problem cities face? Explain your answer to
two other class members.
6. Make an illustration with as many
examples of pollution as possible.
7. Divide a sheet into four parts. Illustrate
one city problem in each top section and a
solution to the problem in the section below.
8. List three ways the federal government
helps cities.
9. Write a "Letter to the Editor" suggesting
how the federal government could best aid
your community.

CHAPTER 20   TAKING PART IN COMMUNITY LIFE   PAGES 418–431

OVERVIEW

There are many voluntary groups, some large and others small. In order to achieve their goals most voluntary groups meet regularly and have officers. They provide important services to communities.

OBJECTIVES

Each student will be able to:
1. Identify different types of voluntary groups.
2. Explain how voluntary groups are organized.
3. Examine the contributions of voluntary groups.

TEACHING IDEAS

1. Before beginning to read discuss the meaning of the chapter title. Skim the chapter for examples.
2. Continue unit list or notebooks begun in Chapter 17. Use them to summarize the unit.
3. Throughout the chapter build a collection of folders on voluntary groups. Work in pairs. Write for literature from as many groups as possible. Post a list so students can record where letters have been sent in order to avoid duplication. Organize display areas separating large and small voluntary groups.
4. Make a list of all voluntary groups in your community.
5. Invite a speaker to class to talk about voluntary groups in your community.
6. Make a check list of voluntary groups. Have each student contact ten adults. Ask what voluntary groups they have participated in. Compile a class list.
7. Organize a volunteer week. Have each student donate a certain amount of time to helping others. It could be a class organized, or individually organized, or even become a continuous project. Some schools have set up on-going interactions with a local nursing

home or a senior citizens' residence. Others have worked with an elementary school, the park board, or set up projects in their own school.
8. Work in small groups. Describe a voluntary group that you could form to provide a service for your community.
9. Plan to attend a meeting of a voluntary group. This could be done as a class or in small groups with parent supervision.
10. Describe a volunteer.
11. Explain to a friend how you get a leadership role in a voluntary group.
12. View a filmstrip that compares a democracy and a totalitarian society.
13. Divide a paper into four parts. Make four scenes including volunteers. Exchange papers and write a caption for each scene.
14. Research topics: Alexis de Tocqueville; any voluntary groups mentioned; Helen Keller; China; totalitarian countries.

EVALUATING OBJECTIVES

1. Name two large and two small voluntary groups.
2. Make an illustration of people involved in voluntary groups.
3. Write a newspaper article on the role of large and small voluntary groups.
4. Discuss: What role do meetings play in voluntary groups?
5. Describe the role of leadership in voluntary groups.
6. Write a summary of how voluntary groups are organized.
7. Name two important contributions of voluntary groups.
8. Write three headlines you might find in your paper about the importance of voluntary groups.
9. Write a three sentence summary of why we need voluntary groups.

UNIT 6   OUR FREE ENTERPRISE SYSTEM

CHAPTER 21   THE ECONOMY   PAGES 434–451

OVERVIEW
People are continuously faced with making economic decisions. The way these decisions are made depends on the economic system of a country. A number of factors must be considered when evaluating an economy's performance.

OBJECTIVES
Each student will be able to:
1. Identify the major economic decisions nations make.
2. Examine alternative economic systems.
3. Name key factors to consider in judging an economy's performance.

TEACHING IDEAS
1. Before beginning the unit discuss what students think a free enterprise system is. Skim the unit, chapter opener, illustrations, and index for ideas. Record suggestions. Use as unit review.
2. Begin a unit list of ways citizens participate in the economy.
3. Work in pairs. Make two lists to review goods and services. Save for reference in Chapter 22.
4. Work in small groups. Divide a paper into two columns. List all the natural and human resources you can. Save for reference in Chapter 22.
5. Summarize the meaning of scarcity.
6. Write a summary in response to each of the three questions the authors suggest should be asked when making economic decisions.
7. Divide a sheet into three parts. Illustrate each key decision maker (producers, consumers, and governments) making decisions.
8. Write a comparison of command and market economies.

9. View a filmstrip comparing a command and market economy.
10. Where is competition most important, in a market economy or a command economy?
11. Explain why people refer to the United States economic system as capitalistic.
12. Discuss: Why does the United States have such a large share of the world GNP?
13. Summarize the tables and graphs in Section 3.
14. Compare depression, recession, and inflation.
15. Explain the law of supply and demand.
16. Make a Decision Tree for Southwest Airlines.
17. Research topics: type of economic systems in other countries; economic systems of China and the USSR; capitalism; GNP; the Depression.

EVALUATING OBJECTIVES
1. List three key questions to ask when dealing with goods and services.
2. Every decision about what to produce is also a decision not to produce something else. Give two examples that illustrate this.
3. Write a statement explaining "unlimited wants" and "limited resources."
4. Discuss: Do all nations make economic decisions?
5. List three ways command and market economies are the same and three ways they are different.
6. Choose one. Explain how producers, consumers, or governments are involved in economic decisions.
7. List three questions you could ask about how an economy is doing.
8. Discuss: What is the importance of GNP?
9. Summarize how inflation and depression are related.

OVERVIEW
Organizing and managing a business is a complex process. Labor unions influence businesses in many ways.

OBJECTIVES
Each student will be able to:
1. Examine the main kinds of business organizations.
2. Identify the principal factors of production.
3. Examine the role of labor unions in business.

TEACHING IDEAS
1. Before reading make a list of small businesses in your community. Locate them on a map.
2. Continue citizen participation list from Chapter 21.
3. Divide a paper into four columns. List examples of each type of business within two miles of your school.
4. Work in small groups. Each group should choose one business. Find any material on its organization and make a display for the class.
5. Which type of business would you most like to be involved in? Why?
6. Work in pairs. Choose a stock from a corporation. Graph its progress throughout the unit.
7. Work in small groups. Interview the owner of a small business. Or, have the owner of a small business come to class. Find out how the business compares to the one the authors describe.
8. Work in small groups. Make a list of examples of each of the factors of production.
9. List examples of monopolies.
10. Discuss: Are there any examples of monopolies in your community?
11. Write a "Letter to the Editor" expressing your views about the role of monopolies.

12. Plan a pictorial account of union development. List the pictures you would need.
13. Invite a union member to class. Plan the interview carefully to find out the role of the union.
14. Summarize the charts on pages 455 and 462.
15. Make a poster titled "Union membership fringe benefits."
16. Discuss: How has the Taft-Hartley Act affected this country?
17. Summarize the key roles of unions either visually or in written form.
18. Discuss: What was Kroc's idea? Could we build on it?
19. Research topics: local businesses; labor unions; monopolies; antimonopoly laws; labor union leaders; Taft-Hartley Act; other acts listed.

EVALUATING OBJECTIVES
1. Name three main kinds of business organizations and write two statements about the benefits of each.
2. Name a corporation in your area. Explain what it means to be a corporation.
3. What is a cooperative? How does a cooperative help to meet community needs?
4. List the four factors of production. Give one example of each.
5. Divide a paper into four sections. In each section illustrate one factor of production. Exchange papers and have someone else caption each section.
6. Devise a matching activity. List ten resources. Exchange papers. Identify each as a natural resource or a human resource.
7. List two important roles of labor unions.
8. Draw a cartoon showing the influences of labor unions.
9. Make up a ten statement True or False activity on labor unions. Exchange papers.

CHAPTER 23   CONSUMER DECISIONS   PAGES 470-491

OVERVIEW
It is important to plan carefully before buying goods or services. It is also important to plan how to save and when to borrow. Even with careful planning it is necessary to have ways to protect consumer rights.

OBJECTIVES
Each student will be able to:
1. Identify the role of the consumer in the purchase of goods and services.
2. Examine how a consumer decides about saving and borrowing.
3. Name ways of protecting consumer rights.

TEACHING IDEAS
1. Before reading, list examples of consumer decisions. Skim the chapter. Compare ideas to chapter opener.
2. Add to the citizen participation list from Chapter 21. Use the list to summarize the unit.
3. Summarize the graph on page 473.
4. Work in small groups. Describe a family and its income. Explain how it uses its money.
5. Divide a paper into two parts. In one part list fixed expenses. In the other list flexible expenses.
6. Write ten True or False statements about budgets. Exchange papers.
7. Discuss: What is involved in keeping a budget?
8. Discuss: What is included in the budget on page 476?
9. Work in small groups. Illustrate a pamphlet on "Tips for Smart Shoppers."
10. Work in small groups. Choose a product. Follow the steps in section "Looking for a Sleeping Bag." Report to the class.
11. Work in pairs. Choose a food product. Check it out in several stores. Report your findings.
12. Collect samples of sales receipts. What information do they give? When should you keep them?
13. Check the labels on five food items and five clothing items. What data do they give?
14. Find examples of literature or ads offering "free" items when you later have to pay. Discuss how to avoid the trap.
15. Prepare a poster to encourage saving.
16. Divide a paper into two columns. List reasons for saving and borrowing.
17. Invite a speaker from a bank and a savings and loan association to class. Plan the interview carefully to find out how they compare.
18. Divide into five groups. Have each group choose one government agency that helps consumers. Plan a display and report to the class.
19. Invite a speaker from the Better Business Bureau to explain its roles.
20. Research topics: consumer aids; aid local stores give consumers; history of banking; government consumer agencies.

EVALUATING OBJECTIVES
1. Name two reasons for having a budget.
2. Give three examples of tips for shoppers.
3. Make a "tips for shoppers" comic strip.
4. Name two reasons people give for saving money.
5. Make a visual showing as many reasons as possible for borrowing money. Exchange papers and identify the reasons.
6. List one way banks and savings and loans are the same and one way they are different.
7. Name two government organizations that might help a consumer.
8. Name two private groups that aid consumers.
9. Discuss: How can you get help if you are unfairly treated as a consumer?

UNIT 7   AMERICA AND THE WORLD

CHAPTER 24   MAKING FOREIGN POLICY   PAGES 494–511

OVERVIEW
American foreign policy influences the whole world. Many people are involved in making American foreign policy. Foreign policy has changed over time.

OBJECTIVES
Each student will be able to:
1. Define the role of foreign policy.
2. Examine who makes foreign-policy decisions.
3. Identify key events in American foreign-policy since World War II.

TEACHING IDEAS
1. Before reading begin a unit list of examples of American involvement around the world. Add to it throughout the unit. Locate areas of involvement on a world map.
2. Begin a unit news bulletin board or booklet entitled "Foreign Policy and World Involvement."
3. Before beginning the chapter discuss ideas on what current American foreign policy is.
4. Work in small groups. Research foreign policy in 50 year blocks.
5. Devise a foreign policy timeline: 1787–1900.
6. Summarize what it means to say "The President is the nation's chief diplomat."
7. Discuss: What departments make up the foreign-policy bureaucracy?
8. Work in four groups. Have each group be responsible for reporting on one of the key groups in the foreign-policy bureaucracy.
9. Look for news items on the role of the State Department.
10. Write a news article on the roles of the Department of Defense.
11. Make a poster illustrating the roles of the National Security Council.
12. Work in pairs. List all the roles of Congress in foreign policy.
13. Illustrate a pamphlet on the roles of Congress in foreign policy.
14. Work in pairs. List decisions the President must have congressional approval to make.
15. Write ten True or False statements about foreign-policy bureaucracy. Exchange papers.
16. Write a newspaper article on the role of the proletariat. Find one illustration you could use.
17. Work in pairs. Divide a paper in two columns. Compare communism and democracy.
18. Create a Panama Canal timeline.
19. Research topics: Henry Kissinger or other government officials involved in international relations; isolationism; current diplomatic relations with China and the Soviet Union; foreign-policy bureaucracy groups; Cold War; SALT; Panama Canal.

EVALUATING OBJECTIVES
1. List three goals of American foreign policy.
2. Find ten illustrations to help someone else understand the meaning of foreign policy.
3. Write a brief statement about American foreign policy toward one other country.
4. Name four groups involved in foreign policy. List one role of each.
5. Discuss: How is the President involved in foreign policy?
6. Prepare a ten point matching activity on the foreign-policy bureaucracy.
7. Identify three key events in foreign policy since World War II.
8. Define containment.
9. Name three tools of containment. Which do you think is most important? Why?

OVERVIEW

Changes in the world are bringing people closer together. As a result of global interdependence the United States faces new foreign-policy decisions. The UN plays an important role in global interdependence.

OBJECTIVES

Each student will be able to:

1. Examine the meaning of global interdependence.

2. Identify new foreign-policy decisions as a result of global interdependence.

3. Examine the role of the UN.

TEACHING IDEAS

1. Before beginning the chapter have students list any examples of goods or services influenced in some way by other countries.

2. Continue the list and news bulletin board or booklets begun in Chapter 24. Use them to summarize the unit.

3. Define global interdependence.

4. Work in pairs. Describe three examples of global interdependence.

5. Choose a product that is an example of global interdependence. Make a diagram showing how the interdependence works. Use a map if necessary.

6. Summarize the map or table on oil producing countries.

7. Work in small groups. Look for examples of other nations that are dependent on the United States.

8. Work in small groups. Study the chart on page 515. List other examples of how interdependence is bringing people together.

9. Translate the chart on page 514 into a visual summary.

10. Work in pairs. Collect ten pictures of rich and poor. Describe why each is either an example of rich or poor.

11. Work in small groups. Divide a paper into two columns. List developing countries in one column and developed countries in the other.

12. Work in small groups. Make a report on a developed or developing country.

13. Work in pairs. List characteristics of developed and developing countries.

14. Make a hidden word puzzle of either developed or developing countries. Exchange puzzles.

15. List all ways oceans are important.

16. Devise a poster on how people can help others who are hungry.

17. Work in pairs. List examples of global pollution.

18. Work in small groups. Look for other examples of global pollution in newspapers, magazines, or books.

19. Discuss: Who originated the United Nations? When did this occur?

20. Compare the six main parts of the UN.

21. Make comparisons between Columbus, Ohio, and your town or city or the city nearest you.

22. As a summary, plan a Good Citizen Day. Share it with other classes.

23. Research topics: UN; oil rich countries; developing nations; hunger; global pollution; weapons; ocean use.

EVALUATING OBJECTIVES

1. Write a definition of global interdependence.

2. List three examples of global interdependence.

3. Name three changes in the United States as a result of global interdependence.

4. List three problems facing the rich and poor nations in the world.

5. Discuss: Where is hunger a problem?

6. List two roles of the UN.

7. What are the main agencies of the UN?

BIBLIOGRAPHY FOR STUDENTS

UNIT 1

Archer, Jules. *You and the Law*. Harcourt, 1978.

Bates, Elizabeth. *The Making of the Constitution*. Viking Press, 1973.

Bova, Ben. *Exiled From Earth*. Dutton, 1971.

Cleaver, Vera and Bill. *Where the Lilies Bloom*. Lippincott, 1969.

Commager, Henry S. *Great Constitution*. Bobbs, 1961.

Fincher, E. B. *The Bill of Rights*. Watts, 1978.

Fleming, Thomas, ed. *Benjamin Franklin: A Biography in His Own Words*. Newsweek (distributed by Harper, Row), 1972.

Kohn, Bernice. *The Spirit and the Letter: The Struggle for Rights in America*. Viking Press, 1974.

Langdon-Davies, J. *Mayflower and Pilgrim Fathers*. Viking Press, 1972.

Loeb, Robert H. and Maloney, John P. *Your Legal Rights as a Minor*. Watts, 1978.

Smith, Page. *The Constitution: A Documentary and Narrative History*. Morrow, 1978.

Starr, Isidore. *The Idea of Liberty: First Amendment Freedoms*. West, 1978.

Stevos, Joyce L. *The Constitution*. Scott, Foresman, 1978.

Swiger, E. P. *The Law in Your Everyday Life*. Prentice-Hall, 1978.

UNIT 2

Fenderson, Lewis. *Thurgood Marshall, Fighter for Justice*. McGraw-Hill, 1969.

Fincher, E. B. *The Presidency: An American Invention*. Abelard-Schuman, 1977.

Gray, L. L. *How We Choose a President; the Election Year*. St. Martins, 1976.

Habenstreit, Barbara. *Changing America and the Supreme Court*. Messner, 1974.

Josephy, A. M., Jr. *The American Heritage History of the Congress of the United States*. American Heritage, 1975. Distributed by Simon and Schuster.

Liston, Robert. *We the People? Congressional Power*. McGraw-Hill, 1975.

May, Charles Paul. *Warning! Your Health Is at Stake: The Story of the Fight for Pure Food and Drug Standards*. Hawthorn, 1975.

McCall, Virginia. *Civil Service Careers*. Watts, 1977.

Parker, Nancy W. *President's Cabinet: And How It Grew*. Parents, 1978.

Percy, Senator Charles. *I Want to Know About the United States Senate*. Doubleday, 1976.

Stevens, Leonard A. *How a Law Is Made: The Story of a Bill Against Air-Pollution*. Crowell, 1970.

Switzer, Ellen. *There Ought to Be a Law! How Laws Are Made and Work*. Atheneum, 1972.

UNIT 3

Booth, Alice Lynn. *Careers in Politics for the New Woman*. Franklin Watts, 1978.

Choosing the President. League of Women Voters Education Fund, 1976.

Cook, Fred J. *American Political Bosses and Machines*. Franklin Watts, 1973.

Hoopes, Roy. *Getting with Politics*. Dell.

Hoopes, Roy. *Primaries and Conventions*. Franklin Watts, 1978.

Levy, E. *The People Lobby: The SST Story*. Delacorte, 1973.

Liston, Robert A. *Getting in Touch with Your Government*. Messner, 1975.

Liston, Robert A. *Politics-From Precinct to Presidency*. Dell.

Loeb, R. H. *Your Guide to Voting*. Franklin Watts, 1977.

Murphy, William and Schneier, Edward. *Vote Power: How to Work for the Person You Want Elected*. Anchor Books, 1974.

O'Donnell, J. *Every Vote Counts: A Teen-Age Guide to the Electoral Process*. Messner, 1976.

Sagstetter, Karen. *Lobbying*. Watts, 1978.

Wolf, Alvin. *Lobbies and Lobbyists: In Whose Best Interest?* Allyn and Bacon, 1976.

UNIT 4

Bentley, Judith. *State Government*. Watts, 1978.

Bloomstein, Morris J. *Verdict: The Jury System*. Dodd, 1972.

Brindze, Ruth. *All About Courts and Law*. Random, 1964.

Cline, Graham, and Lilies. *Practical Law*. Holt, Rinehart and Winston, 1978.

Deming, Richard. *Man Against Man: Civil Law at Work*. Dell.

Deming, Richard. *Man and Society: Criminal Law At Work*. Dell.

Halacy, D. S., Jr. *Government by the States: A History*. The Bobbs-Merrill Company, 1973.

Heaps, Willard. *Juvenile Justice*. Seabury, 1974.

Levy, Elizabeth. *Lawyers for the People: A New Breed of Defenders and Their Work*. Dell, 1979.

Linder, Bertram. *Youth and the Law*. Sadlier-Oxford, 1977.

Phillips, Margaret. *Governors of Tennessee*. Pelican, 1978.

Sueling, Barbara. *You Can't Eat Peanuts in Church and Other Little-Known Laws*. Doubleday, 1975.

UNIT 5

Archer, Jules. *Washington vs. Main Street*. Crowell, 1975.

Brady, Marion and Howard. *Habitat*. Prentice-Hall, 1977.

Cutler, Irving. *Law and Government*. Merrill, 1978.

Cutler, Irving. *Urban Geography*. Merrill, 1978.

Eichner, James. *The First Book of Local Government*. Watts, 1976.

Liston, Robert A. *Downtown: Our Challenging Urban Problems*. Dell.

Liston, Robert A. *The American Poor*. Dell.

Peter, Laurence J. *The Peter Plan,* Bantam.

Schwartz, Alvin. *Central City/Spread City*. Macmillan, 1973.

Tarr, Joel. *Patterns in City Growth*. Scott, Foresman and Company, 1975.

UNIT 6

Benedick, Jeanne and Robert. *The Consumer's Catalog of Economy and Ecology*. McGraw-Hill, 1974.

Chabe, Alexander M. *Democracy and Communism*. Benefic.

Clawson, Elmer. *Our Economy: How It Works*. Addison-Wesley, 1979.

Ebenstein, William. *Today's ISMs: Communism, Fascism, Capitalism, Socialism*. Prentice-Hall.

Forman, James. *Inflation*. Franklin Watts, 1977.

George, Richard. *The New Consumer Survival Kit*. Little, Brown and Company, 1978.

Keeping Our Money Healthy. Federal Reserve Bank of New York, 1977.

Leinwand, Gerald. *The Consumer*. Pocket Books.

Morris, Richard B. *The U.S. Department of Labor History of the American Worker*. U.S. Government Printing Office, 1978.

Saalbach, William. *The Consumer and the American Economy*. Laidlaw. Five pamphlets.

Weinstein, Grace W. *Money of Your Own*. E. P. Dutton, 1977.

Wilson, Harmon and Warmke, Roman. *Life on Paradise Island*. Scott, Foresman.

UNIT 7

Archer, Jules. *Hunger on Planet Earth*. Crowell, 1977.

Brown, Lester R. *The Twenty-ninth Day: Accommodating Human Needs and Numbers to the Earth's Resources*. Norton, 1978.

Cook, Fred J. *The U-2 Incident, May, 1960: An American Spy Plane Downed Over Russia Intensifies the Cold War*. Franklin Watts, 1973.

Ford, Barbara. *Future Food: Alternate Protein for the Year 2000*. William Morrow, 1978.

Linder, Bertram et al. *Futuring*. Beacon Books, 1979.

Pratt, Francis. *The U.S. in World Affairs: What Is Its Role?* Allyn and Bacon, 1976.

Sheckley, Robert. *Futuropolis: Impossible Cities of Science Fiction and Fantasy*. A & W Visual Library, 1978.

Civics
for Americans

★★

John J. Patrick
Richard C. Remy

Civics
for Americans

★★

John J. Patrick
Indiana University

Richard C. Remy
Ohio State University

Scott, Foresman and Company

Editorial Offices: Glenview, Illinois
Regional Sales Offices: Palo Alto, California •
Tucker, Georgia • Glenview, Illinois •
Oakland, New Jersey • Dallas, Texas

Authors

John J. Patrick is Professor of Education at Indiana University in Bloomington and directs projects at the Social Studies Development Center there. He was a high-school social studies teacher for eight years. Dr. Patrick has authored books for teachers about social studies curriculum and instruction. He has also authored high-school social studies textbooks. His articles on curriculum and instruction have appeared in numerous professional journals. He has also served as a consultant to many school systems, development centers, and to national ministries of education in Europe and Asia.

Richard C. Remy is Associate Professor at Ohio State University, where he holds appointments in the Political Science and Humanities Education Departments. Dr. Remy is also Director of the Citizenship Development Program at Ohio State University's Mershon Center. He began his career as a classroom teacher in the Chicago Public Schools. His articles about topics in political science, curriculum, and instruction have appeared in many professional journals. He has written extensively for young students on citizenship and decision making. He has also served as a consultant to numerous school systems and state departments of education.

Contributing Author

L. JoAnne Buggey provided the in-book tests and the chapter-by-chapter lesson plans, annotations, and bibliography for the teacher's annotated edition of *Civics for Americans*. Dr. Buggey teaches social studies methods courses in the Department of Education at the University of Minnesota. She began her career as an elementary school teacher and subsequently co-directed the Social Studies Service Center for the Twin Cities area in Minnesota. She has assisted schools and communities to develop their curriculum resources.

Teacher-Consultants

The authors and publisher would like to thank the following teachers who read and critiqued *Civics for Americans* during its developmental stage. They contributed valuable comments, chapter by chapter, on both the content and the level of difficulty. Their assistance has helped make *Civics for Americans* a practical classroom text.

Marsha C. Lyons, Social Studies Coordinator Intern
Austin Independent School District, Austin, Texas

Morton C. Teitelbaum, Social Studies Teacher
Sanderson High School, Wake County Schools, Raleigh, North Carolina

Steven S. Toda, Social Studies Department Chairperson
Thomas Jefferson High School, Los Angeles Unified School District, Los Angeles, California

Acknowledgments: The Decision-Tree device used on page 31 was developed by Roger LaRaus and Richard C. Remy. The device is used in this text with their permission. Further acknowledgments for quoted matter and illustrations appear on pages 563–564. The acknowledgments section there is an extension of the copyright page.

ISBN: 0-673-13316-8

Table of Contents

Unit 1 Government and Citizenship   2

★★★

Chapter 1   **Civics in Your Life**   **4**
1/How Civics Is Part of Your Life   5
2/The Kinds of Decisions Governments Make   9
3/Why We Have Governments   12
Case Study: Fish Patrol   16

Chapter 2   **Citizens Make Decisions**   **20**
1/Making Decisions   21
2/Judging Decisions   27
Case Study: The Black Mesa Mine Decision   33

Chapter 3   **Citizens Make a Constitution**   **38**
1/The Background of the Constitutional Convention   39
2/Decision Making at the Constitutional Convention   43
3/How the Constitution Was Approved   49
Case Study: The Whiskey Rebellion   52

Chapter 4   **The Constitution—Our Plan for Government**   **56**
1/The Purpose of the Constitution   57
2/Three Branches of Government   60
3/How State and National Governments Are Linked   65
Case Study: The Constitution Works!   68

The Constitution of the United States (with explanations)   **74**

Chapter 5   **Rights and Responsibilities of Citizenship**   **94**
1/Extending Citizens' Rights and Liberties   95
2/Gaining and Losing Citizenship   103
3/Citizens' Responsibilities   106
Case Study: Deciding to Lower the Voting Age   110

Skills for Life: Registering to Vote   **24**
People and Government: Reporting the News   **98**
Unit Test   **114**

Unit 2 Making Decisions in the National Government 116

★★

Chapter 6	**Decision Making in Congress**	**118**
	1/How Congress Is Organized	119
	2/The Job in Congress Today	126
	3/Making Laws	132
	Case Study: To Cut or Not to Cut?	136
Chapter 7	**Paying for National Government**	**142**
	1/Where the Money Comes From	143
	2/How the Money Is Spent	151
	3/Making the Federal Budget	154
	Case Study: Housing in Saul Hollow	159
Chapter 8	**The Presidency**	**164**
	1/Getting Elected	165
	2/The President's Job	170
	3/Presidential Advisers	175
	4/How Presidential Decisions Get Made	178
	Case Study: The B-1 Bomber	181
Chapter 9	**Decision Making in the Federal Agencies**	**186**
	1/The Work and Organization of the Federal Agencies	187
	2/Decision Makers in Federal Agencies	195
	3/Those Who Influence the Decision Makers	198
	Case Study: The Fight over Concorde	202
Chapter 10	**Decision Making in the Federal Courts**	**208**
	1/How Laws and Courts Serve the People	209
	2/How the Federal Courts Are Organized	213
	3/What the Supreme Court Does	218
	Case Study: *Brown* v. *Board of Education*	225

Skills for Life: Filing an Income Tax Return	**146**
People and Government: At Work for the Forest Service	**190**
Unit Test	**230**

Unit 3 How Citizens Influence Government 232

★★

Chapter 11   **Taking Part in Interest Groups**   **234**
1/Why Citizens Join Interest Groups   235
2/How Interest Groups Influence Government   239
3/How Citizens Can Take Part in Interest Groups   244
Case Study: Conflict over Bottles   248

Chapter 12   **Taking Part in Political Parties**   **252**
1/Political Parties in the United States   253
2/Deciding Whether or Not to Give Support   258
3/The Role of Political Parties   263
Case Study: California Frontlash   270

Chapter 13   **Voting**   **274**
1/Rules for Voting   275
2/Deciding How to Vote   281
Case Study: The Winner   289

People and Government: Campaign Workers   **266**
Skills for Life: Casting a Ballot   **278**
Unit Test   **294**

Unit 4 Making Decisions in State Government 296

★★

Chapter 14   **States and State Legislatures**   296
1/The Powers of State Government   299
2/How State Legislatures Work   305
3/State Lawmakers   307
Case Study: Decision on a State Tax   312

Chapter 15   **Governors and State Agencies**   316
1/The State Executive Branch   317
2/The Governor's Job   321
3/State Agencies   325
Case Study: Governor Dukakis's Roadblock   332

Chapter 16   **State Courts**   336
1/State Court Systems   337
2/Criminal and Civil Cases   344
3/Lawyers   348
Case Study: You Be the Jury   352

People and Government: State Nutritionist   326
Skills for Life: Using Small Claims Courts   342
Unit Test   356

Unit 5 Making Decisions in Local Governments

358

★★★

Chapter 17	**Local Governments**	**360**
	1/Kinds of Local Governments	361
	2/How County Governments Provide Services	365
	3/Paying for Local Government	371
	Case Study: Proposition 13—A Homeowners' Revolt	374
Chapter 18	**City Government**	**378**
	1/Plans for City Government	379
	2/City Decision Makers	384
	3/Who Influences City Politics?	389
	Case Study: "Who's Going to Put Out the Fires?"	394
Chapter 19	**Urban Problems**	**398**
	1/How Cities Have Grown	399
	2/City Problems	403
	3/Help from Washington?	411
	Case Study: Worms in the Big Apple	414
Chapter 20	**Taking Part in Community Life**	**418**
	1/Voluntary Groups	419
	2/How Voluntary Groups Are Governed	422
	3/How Volunteers Help Make Democracy Work	424
	Case Study: Teen-agers Volunteer	426

Skills for Life: Reading a Newspaper   **392**
People and Government: Making Plans for a City   **408**
Unit Test   **430**

Unit 6 Our Free Enterprise System   432

★★

Chapter 21	**The Economy**	**434**
	1/Making Economic Decisions	435
	2/Economic Systems	438
	3/Judging an Economy's Performance	442
	Case Study: Competing for Survival	448
Chapter 22	**Production Decisions**	**452**
	1/Organizing and Managing Businesses	453
	2/How Labor Unions Affect Business Decisions	460
	Case Study: Mass Produced Meals	466
Chapter 23	**Consumer Decisions**	**470**
	1/Buying Goods and Services	471
	2/Saving and Borrowing	476
	3/Protecting Consumer Rights	481
	Case Study: Consumer Advocate	486

Skills for Life: Checks	**478**
People and Government: Working to Protect Consumers	**482**
Unit Test	**490**

Unit 7 America and the World

★★★

Chapter 24	**Making Foreign Policy**	**494**
	1/What Is Foreign Policy?	495
	2/Who Makes Foreign Policy in the National Government?	497
	3/From Cold War to Coexistence	503
	Case Study: The Panama Canal Treaties	508
Chapter 25	**Into the Future**	**512**
	1/Our Shrinking World	513
	2/Poor vs. Rich: The New Decisions	519
	3/The United Nations	524
	Case Study: Your Community in the World	529

Skills for Life: Getting Jobs Overseas   **516**
People and Government: Peace Corps Volunteers   **526**
Unit Test   **534**

Resource Section   **536**
Presidents of the United States   537
Facts About the States   538
Names of State Legislative Bodies   539
Flag Etiquette   540
Map of the United States   542
How Many Voted in Your State?   543
Declaration of Independence   544
Glossary   546
Index   554
Acknowledgments   563

Charts, Diagrams, Graphs, and Tables

Decision Tree	31
States Approve the Constitution	50
Three Branches of Government	60
Original Rules About Legislators in Article 1	60
Our System of Checks and Balances	62
First Amendment Rights	96
Steps to Becoming a Naturalized Citizen	103
Responsibilities of Citizenship	107
Who Turned Out to Vote	111
Changes in State Representation After the 1970 Census	120
Standing Committees of Congress	122
Characteristics of the 95th Congress	126
Growth of Congressional Staff	131
How a Bill Becomes a Law	133
Democrats and Republicans in the 95th Congress	141
Sources of National Government Income	143
What Happens to a Paycheck	145
The Cost of National Government	151
How the National Government Spends Its Money	153
1979 National Budget	154
Growth of the National Debt	156
Twentieth-Century Presidents	166
North Carolina Results in Brief	167
Cabinet Departments	177
The Executive Branch	188
Who Works for Washington	196
The Judicial Branch	213
Big Contributors in 1977–1978	239
Political Party Preference	254
Major Political Party Organization	256
Vote by Groups in Presidential Elections Since 1952	260
Interest Groups Rate Members of Congress	282
Results of the Democratic Party Mayoral Primary Election	292
Division of Powers in Our Federal System	300
State Government Organization	301
Standing Committees of the Georgia Senate	305
Occupations of State Lawmakers	306
Organization of State Courts	339
Texas State Expenditures in 1974	357

Local Governments in the United States 362
State Special Service Districts 364
Mayor-Council Plan 379
Council-Manager Plan 380
Commission Plan 381
How American Cities Have Grown 401
How Economic Decisions Get Made 441
Population and GNP in 15 Most Populous Countries 442
GNP from 1947–1977 443
The Percentage of Families in Various Income Groups 444
How Households Spend Their Money 445
How Inflation Gobbles Up Your Paycheck 447
Business in the United States 454
Companies with the Largest Number of Stockholders 455
Today's 10 Biggest Unions 462
Union Membership in the United States 463
Top Ten Corporations in the United States 469
Budget for March, 1979 473
Growth of Consumer Debt 476
OPEC Members 514
Interdependence Is Bringing People Together 515
The United Nations 525
Facts About the World's 10 Most Populous Countries 533
Presidents 537
Facts About the States 538
Map of the United States 542
How Many Voted in Your State? 543

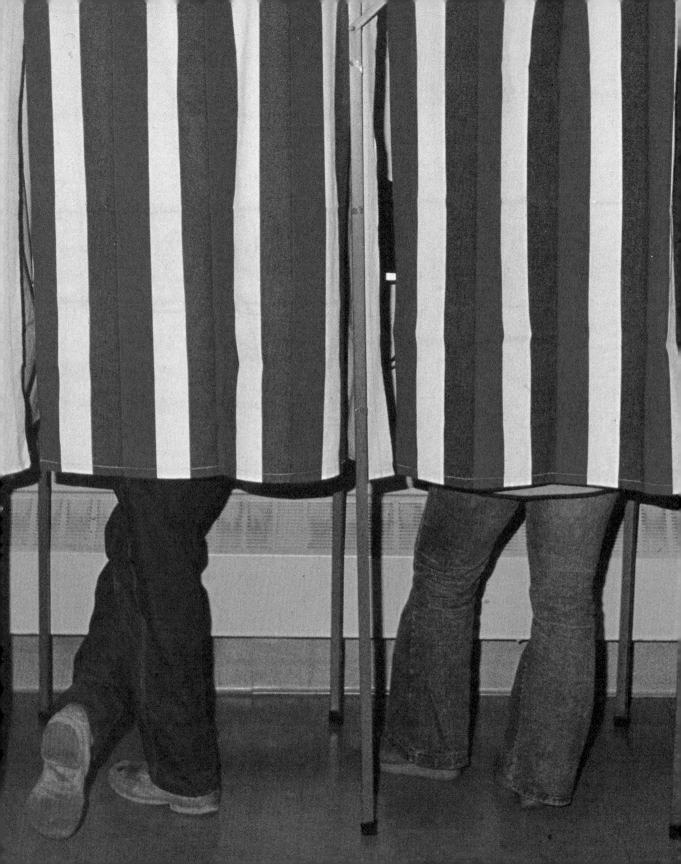

Government and Citizenship

Every country on earth is special in some way to the people who live there. A country may be special because family and friends live there. A person's ancestors may also have lived there. A country's history and a family's history are often tied closely together. In the field of government, however, the United States has been special to people all over the world.

The United States has a plan for government that calls for all citizens to take part in the government. This plan, called the United States Constitution, says that the citizens of the country shall govern themselves. The Constitution has rules that prevent any person or group of persons from taking that power away from the people. The Constitution also states that the citizens of the country have certain other rights and freedoms that shall not be taken away.

The United States Constitution is the oldest written plan for government in the world. (It was written in 1787.) Because it grants great freedom as well as great responsibility to individual citizens, it is admired and respected throughout the world—so much so that some other nations have made constitutions that contain similar rules.

During the course of this book you will find out what it means to be a citizen of the United States and how important the Constitution is to every citizen today.

Perhaps most important, you will find out that as a citizen of the United States, you can help decide what actions the government will take in the future. You will find out that, to a degree, your country's future is up to you to decide.

Voting booths.

Civics in Your Life

★★

The Pilgrim ship *Mayflower* was headed for the Virginia colony. There the 102 passengers planned to settle as citizens of Virginia. But they sailed late in the year and winter winds drove them north. On the morning of November 10, 1620, they spotted land. Men, women, and children shouted, laughed, and wept.

Soon the rejoicing stopped as arguments broke out. Some men said that since they were outside the Virginia territory, no one had the power to command them. These men planned to go off on their own and do as they pleased.

The others pleaded for order and cooperation. "We will need everyone's help just to stay alive," they argued. They pointed out that in this new land there would be no towns like those they knew in England. They would be outnumbered by natives who might not like them.

Discuss: What does it mean to cooperate?

After a long discussion, the men were persuaded that they had to cooperate. The leaders wrote a statement, now known as the **Mayflower Compact,** agreeing to form a government. The Compact was signed by adult male passengers. Every household was represented. The men elected a governor. Then they landed.

Read parts of the May-flower Compact to the class.

Together the citizens cooperated to build houses, gather food, and gain friendly relations with the Indians. They settled their arguments according to law, as they had pledged to do in the Mayflower Compact. Thus the Plymouth Colony survived.

The Mayflower Compact was the first of many agreements made by early colonists and American settlers. It grew out of an experience in civics that remains important today. It shows our continuing need for government, law, and cooperation. In this chapter you will read the following sections:

Discuss: Why do we need government, laws, and cooperation today?

1/How Civics Is Part of Your Life
2/The Kinds of Decisions Governments Make
3/Why We Have Governments
Case Study: Fish Patrol

1/How Civics Is Part of Your Life

Civics is the study of the duties, rights, and responsibilities of citizenship. It comes from the Latin word *civis,* which means "citizen." In ancient Rome, citizens were a small, privileged class of people. They were men who owned land and property. They had the right to go anywhere in the city, and they sat in the councils of government and voted for leaders and laws. With these rights came the responsibility to give the city good laws and good government. Roman citizens took their duty to the city very seriously.

Today nearly 98% of the people living in the United States are citizens. These people have rights and responsibilities of **citizenship** as members of many groups.

Have students look for definitions of "civics" in several sources.

Citizenship in Groups

Civics is part of your life because you belong to many groups. As a citizen of these groups, you have the right to enjoy the benefits of group membership. In return you assume certain responsibilities for the welfare of the groups you are part of.

Tony Martin, age fourteen, takes part in many groups. He lives in a family that includes two sisters, a mother, father, and grandmother. He belongs to St. Francis Church and is a member of the Catholic Youth Organization. He is a ninth-grader at

Discuss: What groups do you belong to?

Discuss: What are some benefits of group membership?

Signing the Mayflower Compact.

5

Discuss: What rights and
responsibilities come with
membership in each group?

Discuss: What rights and
responsibilities do you have
in this class?

Listening to a teacher's explanation
(left) and enjoying good times with
teammates (right).

Hamilton High School, where he is on the junior varsity basketball team. He has friends in the neighborhood with whom he
spends his spare time. As a member of these different groups,
Tony has certain rights and responsibilities. As a family member
he has the right to affection, food, a place to live, and guidance
in growing up. In return he owes his family members consideration and support for the things they try to do. He has certain
chores that help keep the home a good place to live in.

At school, Tony has the right to learn. He has the right to
take part in school activities, like the basketball team. He has the
right to take any courses he is capable of. Through education, he
may prepare himself for any career he wants. In return, Tony
has certain responsibilities. He should follow school rules. He
should cooperate with other students and teachers in helping
make the school a good place to get an education.

Tony Martin has certain civic rights and responsibilities as a
member of a city, a state, and a nation. Tony has the right to
enjoy the services of government. For instance, he has the right
to protection by the local police force. He has the right to play
baseball or to jog in the public park near his home.

In return for these benefits Tony has responsibility for seeing
that the laws in his city, state, and nation are obeyed. First, he
should obey them. After that, he should do all he can to encourage others to obey the laws. He should contribute to the welfare

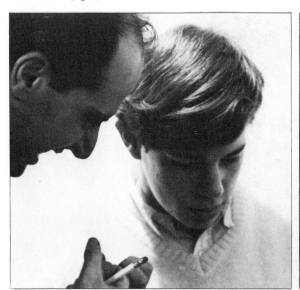

of his community. He owes **loyalty** to his country.

Loyalty usually develops when a person supports, believes in, or identifies with the people and goals of a group. Tony Martin is loyal to the United States because he feels that the people and groups he cares about can get along well here. He also feels free to express beliefs and ideas which are important to him.

Loyalty to a country or nation is called **patriotism.** Singing the national anthem and other patriotic songs and saying the pledge of allegiance are some ways that we show national loyalty. Cooperating with others for the benefit of the nation is an important way to show loyalty. President John F. Kennedy expressed this idea when he said, "Ask not what your country can do for you, but what you can do for your country."

List other examples of patriotism.

Discuss: Why is this still so important today?

Citizens as Decision Makers

As members of groups, citizens take part in decision making. They may decide about rules for the group. They may decide what the group will do.

Discuss: What decisions have you made today?

Deciding is choosing among alternatives. For example, Susan decided to learn Spanish instead of German or French. Taking courses in French or German were alternatives to her **decision** to take Spanish. Sometimes you have many alternatives to choose from. Other times you do not have many choices. If you have no alternatives, you can't make a decision.

Every day people make decisions as group members. At school, for instance, the principal decided that the school open house would be September 24th. The students in each homeroom elected a representative to student council. The teachers decided there would be no smoking in the faculty lounge.

In some groups, many members take part in decisions. Choices are made by majority vote. All members have the right to speak their minds about what the group should do. In other groups, one or a few members make all the important decisions. Most people belong to both kinds of groups. When group members can choose their leaders, decision making is of the first kind. In groups where people do not choose their leaders, decision making is more often in the hands of a few people. At home and work, people are members of this second kind of group. People do not choose their parents; workers do not vote for their boss.

In the United States, all citizens are civic decision makers. As members of a community, a state, and a nation, we choose our leaders and influence the decisions they make.

Friends are loyal.

Section Review

Vocabulary: citizenship, civics, decision, loyalty, Mayflower Compact, patriotism.

Reviewing the Main Ideas

1. Why did the Pilgrims make the Mayflower Compact?
2. What does group membership have to do with civics?
3. How is decision making in groups part of daily life?
4. How is civics part of daily life?

Skill Building

1. Organize the ideas in the section you have just read as they relate to your life. List three groups you belong to. Under each, give three rights you have as a member of the group. Then list three responsibilities you have for the group's welfare.
2. Which of these statements is the main idea of this section of the chapter?
   a. Most people are group members.
   b. In some groups, decisions are made by a few members.
   c. Being a group member gives people rights and responsibilities.

Main Ideas
1. because they needed a government
2. Certain rights and responsibilities come with group membership.
3. p. 7
4. Answers will vary.
Skill Building
1. Answers will vary.
2. c

Supporting the team.

2/The Kinds of Decisions Governments Make

Any group that has power to make and enforce laws acts as a **government.** The United States has a national government that makes and enforces laws for the entire country. The state government of Alabama makes and enforces laws for people living in the state. The city of Birmingham has a government that makes and enforces rules for the city.

Decision making is a main activity of government. People in government make three kinds of decisions. One, they decide what laws, or rules, a group should have. Two, they decide what goals a group should have. Three, they decide how certain benefits may be distributed within a group.

These three kinds of decisions have to do with how groups are governed. They involve rights, responsibilities, and benefits of citizenship. Thus, they are decisions about civics.

Governments Make Decisions About Rules or Laws

A **law** is a rule made by a government. Laws are needed to keep order in a group. Governments decide what laws are needed to settle conflicts, defend the group, and provide services. For example, governments make traffic laws to regulate the use of motor vehicles on streets and highways. Drivers are required to obey speed limits, stop signs, and traffic lights.

Should the speed limit on Main Street be 25 or 30 miles per hour? Should Park Avenue be made into a one-way street? Should stop signs be placed at the corner of Market and Third streets? Your local government makes decisions to answer these kinds of questions about laws. Your government's decisions about laws affect what you and others may or may not do.

Governments decide about how to carry out laws. Drivers who are caught speeding must pay a fine. Government officials decide how much first offenders should pay. They may decide that rule breakers have to attend classes in how to drive safely.

Governments Make Decisions About Goals

Your school's football team might have the **goal** of winning the league championship. A goal is something a person or group tries to reach.

Governments make decisions that set goals for a group. For

Make this comparison for your own area.

Discuss: What other rules must drivers obey?

List school rules and consequences of breaking them.

example, President Nixon decided in the late 1960s to improve relations between the United States and China. The state government in Wisconsin set the goal of attracting more industries to the state. In contrast, the government of Boulder, Colorado. decided to try to slow down the growth of the city.

Governments Make Decisions About Who May Get Certain Benefits

A **benefit** is anything that is for the good of a person. Examples of benefits are money, good health, safety, education, property, skills, respect, and the right of free speech.

Your government's decisions about benefits have important effects on you and others. For example, suppose the government decides to build a recreation center in your neighborhood. This decision would provide benefits of jobs and money to the people hired to build the center. Jobs and money would be given to people hired to manage the center. People in your neighborhood would have the benefit of the programs and facilities of the recreation center.

Sometimes government decisions help some people while hurting others. For example, suppose the government of a community decided to stop the sale of fireworks to the general pub-

Discuss: What goals of the President, your governor, or mayor are you aware of now?

Discuss: Is there anyone else who would benefit? Who?

(Left) the Detroit Food Prescription Center distributes food to needy mothers and children. (Right) a government hospital takes care of veterans wounded in the Vietnam War.

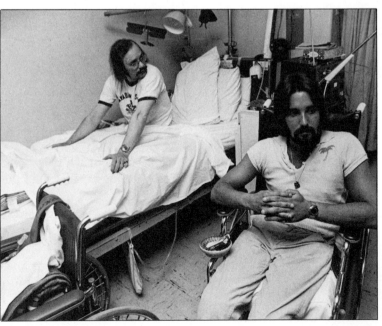

10

lic. Only persons with special permits would be allowed to have a fireworks display.

This decision would take away benefits from the producers and sellers of fireworks. Their sales and profits would drop and jobs and money might be lost.

However, others might gain benefits from the decision. Doctors' groups and parent-teacher groups have argued that the open sale and use of fireworks is a threat to health and safety. They say that fireworks are the cause of many serious burns and accidents. So, passing a law to limit the sale and use of fireworks might bring benefits of greater health and safety to everyone in the community.

Section Review

Vocabulary: benefit, goal, government, law.

Reviewing the Main Ideas
1. What three kinds of decisions do governments make?
2. What do government decisions have to do with civics?
3. How do government decisions affect your life?

Skill Building
1. Which of the two examples is a government decision? Why?
   a. "Based on the latest public opinion polls, I can count on at least 75 percent of the voters in my state to vote for me," the governor said to his election campaign manager.
   b. At his afternoon press conference, the mayor of Smithville announced, "The City Council and I have agreed that we want to help every citizen get a job who can work."
2. For each government decision below, tell whether it is about <u>rules</u> or <u>goals</u> or <u>who</u> <u>will</u> <u>receive</u> <u>benefits</u>.
   a. The President announced that the United States will try to become self-sufficient in supplying its own energy needs by 1990.
   b. The federal government passed a law making the speed limit on national highways 55 miles per hour.
   c. The President of the United States announced today that the federal government will give disaster funds to farmers who had crops killed by the early freeze.

Main Ideas
1. decisions about rules or laws, decisions about goals, decisions about distribution of benefits
2. They involve the rights and responsibilities of citizens.
3. Answers will vary.
Skill Building
1. b. It is a decision about distribution of benefits.
2. a. goals, b. rules, c. who will receive benefits.

3/Why We Have Governments

Whenever a large group of people live together, they form a government to make and enforce laws. Governments help in many ways. Governments in the United States have the power and duty to (1) provide many **public services,** (2) settle conflicts and keep order, and (3) provide security and a common defense against threats from outsiders.

Providing Public Services

Governments make and enforce laws that provide many services we need. Government workers collect garbage, repair the streets, and build parks.

Governments build libraries, schools, hospitals, and recreation centers. Governments keep records of births and deaths and issue licenses to hunters, peddlers, and drivers.

Governments give help to poor and needy people. For example, each of the fifty state governments of the United States pro-

Discuss: What public services are found within walking distance of school? In your community?

Discuss: What public services are being provided in these pictures?

(Top) garbage collection, (bottom) meat inspection, and (right) a teenage summer work program.

12

vides aid to poor families and help to people who are out of work. These governments help crippled and blind people to train for jobs.

Governments make and enforce many laws to keep you and others healthy and safe. For example, members of the fire department inspect your school to detect hazards that could cause damaging fires. Government workers enforce laws to protect the public from being sold spoiled food or dangerous drugs. Government inspectors make restaurant owners and workers obey laws that protect the health of diners. Government officials enforce laws that keep factories safe for workers.

Settling Conflict and Keeping Order

Most people want to live together in groups because when people cooperate to get things done, they can usually accomplish more than those who work alone. However, people who live and work together have **conflict** from time to time. (Conflict is disagreement between people.) Governments have the power and duty to keep order by settling conflicts according to law.

Conflict may happen when people have different beliefs about their rights. For example, two people may disagree about who is the rightful owner of a piece of property. Two groups may have a conflict over who should have the right to use water from a spring or river.

Governments make laws about property rights and about who may use resources like land and water. Government officials make decisions about how to settle conflicts according to these laws. Officials also have the power to enforce their decisions. Thus, conflicts between citizens living under the rules of a government can be settled in an orderly way.

Governments make and enforce laws to keep people from fighting when they don't agree. For example, suppose you believe people have cheated you. They disagree. It is against the law for you to hit them. However, you may bring them into a court of law to have your conflict settled in an orderly manner.

Conflict may happen whenever people disagree about what is best for their group. For example, some might want to use the group's resources to build new and better roads. Others might think that it is more important to spend the money to buy new equipment for schools. Governments make laws about how public resources should be used. Thus, conflicts may be settled in an orderly way.

A Chicago police officer stops to show his horse to a child. Horses make it easier to patrol the parks.

Use a local map. Put markers on all services.

Discuss: What other laws do governments try to enforce?

Discuss: What reason(s) for having government can be found in this picture?

Training new soldiers in how to handle weapons.

Discuss: How is security being provided in the picture above?

Conflict may happen when members of a group are trying to decide who their leaders should be. Governments make and enforce laws that help people to select leaders in an orderly way. Thus, harmony can be kept in the group, so that people can continue to work together for the good of all.

Providing Security and a Common Defense

Whenever a group of people occupies a given territory, one of its major concerns is **security**—how to protect its members and their land from outsiders. Arrangements must be made to fight off possible enemies. This is why governments keep armed forces. The government of our nation has several armed forces: the army, navy, air force, and marine corps are the main ones.

Use a world map to show countries that trade with the U.S.

Even if neighboring groups of people seem friendly, it is useful to have agreed-upon ways of dealing with them. For example, the United States government controls the trading of goods and services with the people of other countries. The need for ways to deal with outsiders is a chief reason for government.

What Would Your Life Be Like Without Government?

What would you do without government? Could you really get along without it?

Families, private businesses, and voluntary groups could take care of almost all needs for goods and services. Schools, libraries, and hospitals could be provided by private groups. Neighbors could pitch in to build and keep up a street or road, and to collect and dispose of garbage. Churches and other private groups could take care of the needy.

But for large groups, most of these things can be done better or more fairly through government. Without government you might not have many services that you now take for granted. Rich people would be able to buy whatever services they needed. Less wealthy people would be unable to afford many services.

Without an orderly way to settle conflicts, there would be much fighting. The best fighters would get what they want. And people and property would get hurt.

When fighting is the way to settle conflicts, most people can not feel safe and secure. They fear that some person or group may seize what they have worked to create and save.

There is chaos and confusion when there is no government. Think about how confusing it would be to try to play basketball without rules. Players would not know what they could or could not do. If players did whatever they wanted, there could be no game.

Discuss: You see the following headline: "Mayor Proposes City Without Government." List the questions you would expect to find answered in the article describing what the mayor means.

People need rules to have a satisfying game of basketball or to play any other kind of game. They also need government to make and enforce rules, if they want to live productively and peacefully in groups.

Section Review

Vocabulary: conflict, public services, security.

Reviewing the Main Ideas

1. Give examples of three public services governments provide.
2. How does government settle conflicts?
3. How does government provide security and a common defense against enemies?
4. Why do people need government?

Skill Building

1. Find evidence or examples to support this statement: Without government you would not have many services that you take for granted.
2. Find evidence or examples to support, or contradict, this statement: People would live freer and more peaceful lives without government.

Main Ideas
1. Answers will vary.
2. pp. 13–14
3. p. 14
4. Answers will vary.
Skill Building
1. Answers will vary.
2. Answers will vary.

Fish Patrol

Discuss: What can you learn about the Coast Guard from these pictures?

Look at a map of the U.S. Point out places where a 200 mile limit would be a problem.

(Left) a Coast Guard officer checks the logs of a Soviet trawler for violations of the Fisheries and Conservation Act. (Right) a Coast Guard ship escorts the trawler into the Boston Coast Guard base.

All nations that border the sea have rules about how far into the water their boundaries extend. They claim the right to enforce their laws within their territorial waters.

When George Washington was President, the United States government claimed control over three miles of ocean extending from the Atlantic shore. Today, the government claims that its territory extends 200 miles into the waters surrounding its coastline. This claim includes all the natural resources within and below the water, such as fish, oil, and minerals. Government leaders hope that the land under the territorial water might someday be a main source of natural resources. The United States Coast Guard patrols these waters day and night. One of its missions is to protect American resources from outsiders.

For instance, one day in 1977 a Coast Guard patrol spotted several boatloads of Russian sailors fishing within American territorial waters. The patrol arrested the Russians, and the United States government notified the government of the Soviet Union. The Soviets had to pay a fine to get their boats back and to have their sailors released.

The Coast Guard also stops citizens of the United States from breaking laws that apply to its waters. For example, it is against the law to catch salmon off the coasts of Oregon and Washington from June 12 to July 1. The purpose of this law is to protect the supply of salmon. If fishermen could catch as many

salmon as they wanted, whenever they wanted, there might be none left for people in the future.

Sometimes the limitation on salmon fishing is extended several weeks, until late August. According to law, government officials may make this decision whenever the numbers of salmon have dropped to a very low level. However, when the government extends the limit, the fishermen are unhappy.

In August, 1978, for example, agents of the Coast Guard stopped fishermen from catching salmon off the coast of Oregon. The fishermen complained they were suffering serious losses of income. They said the decision to limit salmon fishing was a hardship for them and not fair. So they urged the government to change the law. Their problem is not settled yet.

Meanwhile, the Coast Guard continues to patrol the territorial waters to enforce laws of the United States government. They aim to keep out intruders, both citizens of the United States and those of other countries.

Reviewing the Case Study

1. Find an example of a decision about rules.
2. Find an example of a decision that has to do with giving or withholding benefits.
3. Find an example of a decision in this case that involves setting a goal.
4. What kinds of duties is the government carrying out in this case?

CASE STUDY

Discuss: Which side would you be on? Why?

A Coast Guard officer gives instructions to Soviet fishermen 180 miles southeast of Cape Cod.

Chapter One Test and Activities

★★

Vocabulary

Match the following words with their meanings.

1. civics
2. government
3. citizenship
4. law
5. goal
6. loyalty
7. security
8. decision
9. benefit
10. public services
11. Mayflower Compact
12. conflict
13. patriotism

a. a making up of one's mind
b. loyalty to a country or nation
c. a rule made by a government
d. anything that is for the good of a person
e. something a person or group tries to reach
f. the duties, rights, and privileges of citizens
g. the study of the duties, rights, and responsibilities of citizens
h. faithfulness to friends, group, or country
i. the Pilgrims' written agreement to have a government
j. authority that makes and enforces laws in a country or state
k. freedom from danger
l. government work useful or helpful to the people
m. disagreement

Reviewing Chapter Ideas

1. True or false: A law is a rule that members of a group must obey.

2. A citizen has responsibilities to:
   a. obey laws
   b. be loyal to the United States
   c. both
   d. neither

3. True or false: People form governments to make and enforce laws.

4. True or false: Citizenship is only important to teenagers.

5. The Pilgrims signed the Mayflower Compact:
   a. in England
   b. to provide for a government
   c. to name a leader
   d. to name the town of Plymouth

6. Which one of the following is a public service?
   a. a town librarian ordering books
   b. a mother paying a bill
   c. a husband shopping for groceries
   d. all of the above

7. Governments do not usually help to:
   a. repair streets
   b. build schools
   c. manufacture cars
   d. keep order

8. True or false: Loyalty is another word for faithfulness.

9. True or false: Patriotism means loyalty to your country.

10. True or false: "Majority rule" is when at least half the voters decide on a plan.

Using Basic Social Studies Skills

Finding Information

List the subtitles (headings) in this chapter that tell what governments do.

Vocabulary				
1. g	4. c	7. k	10. l	13. b
2. j	5. e	8. a	11. i	
3. f	6. h	9. d	12. m	

18

Ideas			
1. T	4. F	7. c	10. F
2. c	5. b	8. T	
3. T	6. a	9. T	

★★

Comprehending Information

Tell in your own words why people have governments.

Organizing Information

For each government activity listed below, tell if it is (a) a public service, or (b) a way of settling conflicts and keeping order, or (c) to provide security and defense against outsiders.

1. a trial in traffic court
2. job training for handicapped people
3. military training for sailors in the navy
4. garbage collection
5. a curfew law

Evaluating Information

You hear the following:

"Life would be just the same without our government." Do you agree or disagree? Find three statements in this chapter to support your opinion.

Communicating Ideas

Write a paragraph explaining why civics is an important part of a person's life. Use at least five of the words from the Vocabulary. Underline each vocabulary word that you use.

Using Decision-Making Skills

1. Name three kinds of decisions governments make. Give two examples of each.
2. Think about the decisions explained in the Case Study: Fish Patrol.
   a. Give two reasons why people might agree with the decisions the government made.
   b. Give two reasons why people might not agree with the government decisions.
   c. How could the decisions described in Fish Patrol affect your life?

Activities

1. Divide a piece of paper into four parts. In each part draw a picture showing something governments do.
2. Create three newspaper headlines. Have each headline illustrate a main idea from this chapter.
3. Make a list of public services provided by government in your community. Compare your list with other class members' lists. Choose three services from your list or from others' and find out more about them.
4. List at least five ways people can demonstrate they are good citizens.
5. Give two examples of conflicts the government might need to settle. Give two examples of conflicts the government would not need to settle.
6. Name three decisions you have made in the last week. Which was most important to you? Which was least important? Why?
7. Name at least one goal you have. Write a short paragraph telling how you might meet that goal.
8. What three school rules do you feel are the most important? Why?
9. Select a book in which government has an important effect on characters' lives. In discussing the book, tell how this government affects what characters do and what happens to them. Some books of science fiction and fantasy in which government is important to characters and action are *Exiled from Earth,* by Benjamin Bova (E. P. Dutton, 1971), and *The White Mountain,* by John Christopher (Macmillan Publishing Co., Inc., 1967).

Chapter 2

Citizens Make Decisions

★★★

Dolores Santini rubbed her eyes as she shut off the piercing buzz of the alarm. She was starting her day one hour earlier than usual. It was election day, and she wanted to have time to visit the polls before going to school.

Dolores had turned eighteen one month ago. This was her first chance to vote. She had decided to vote for Curtis for mayor and Rossi to represent her district in the city council.

After voting, Dolores caught the bus to school. As she walked into school, George Sawa stopped her.

"Hey, Dolores, you'll sign my petition, won't you?" he asked.

"What's it for?" asked Dolores.

"Well, some of us guys who drive to school want a bigger parking lot," said George. "Maybe the principal and school board will listen if we show that a lot of students agree with us."

"I don't know, George, I'll have to think about it."

During the day, Dolores decided to sign George's petition. She also decided to join the local chapter of the Sierra Club. They were starting an anti-pollution campaign and she wanted to take part in it.

The choices Dolores made are civic decisions. By voting, she was taking part in the selection of people to represent her in government. She was using one of her rights as a citizen when she signed George Sawa's petition. She was using another civil right when she joined the Sierra Club.

To be free, you must have the right to make decisions. But this right is worth much more when you know how to make sensible choices. The main purpose of this chapter is to help you become a better citizen by teaching you a basic citizenship skill—how to make decisions. In this chapter you will read:

1/Making Decisions
2/Judging Decisions
Case Study: The Black Mesa Mine Decision

Discuss: What is a petition? Has anyone signed one? What for?

Note: Some students may be able to bring in examples of petitions.

1/Making Decisions

You must make a decision whenever you face two or more **alternatives.** Even if you do nothing, that is a decision. Alma Kramer had to make a decision one afternoon in school. She looked up during a test and saw Sue Prescott cheating. Alma liked Sue, but she also thought the class rules about no cheating were fair and necessary. Alma realized that she had to decide what to do about Sue's cheating.

When faced with a decision, you should ask yourself three questions: (1) What are my alternatives? (2) What are the likely consequences, or outcomes, of each alternative? (3) Which consequence do I prefer?

What Are the Alternatives?

Alma Kramer did not have much time to decide. Nor did she have the chance to get advice. Alma had to think quickly of alternatives.

One alternative would be to ignore Sue and do nothing at all. A second alternative would be to tell the teacher that Sue had been cheating. There could be other alternatives. Alma had to decide quickly what alternative to pick.

Sometimes when a decision is being made, there is plenty of time to think of alternatives. When there is time, there is often the chance to ask others for advice. You have a better chance of making a good decision when you are aware of all your choices.

Discuss: What other alternatives did Alma have?

Discuss: What decisions are these people trying to make?

Voters face decisions when a poll taker asks their views (below), when asked to sign a petition (bottom), and at election time (left).

21

Joe Reid is a member of the city council. Many citizens in Joe's district want him to sponsor a bill to ban smoking in public places. One influential group, Citizens Against Smoking, has been putting a lot of pressure on Joe.

The mayor, Marvin Thomas, is one of Joe's best friends. He has helped Joe get things done for his district. The mayor is against making any law to ban smoking.

Joe does not want to offend the mayor. However, Joe supports programs to improve public health. He believes that smoking may harm the health of non-smokers as well as smokers.

Joe has been thinking all day about his alternatives. One is to ignore the Citizens Against Smoking and not sponsor a bill. A second choice is to introduce a no-smoking bill. A third alternative is not to sponsor an anti-smoking law but to promote educational activities that teach how smoking is bad for health.

At the moment, Joe Reid is not sure what decision to make. He must do more than think carefully what his alternatives are. He must think through the **consequences** of each alternative.

What Are the Consequences?

Decisions lead to consequences. When you choose one alternative over another, you choose one outcome rather than another. So, an important step in decision making is to predict the good and bad results of each alternative. Your choice of a course of

Discuss: Does Joe have any other alternatives?

Honor is an important tradition to Americans. At no place is that more evident than at the U.S. Military Academy at West Point. Cadets promise not to "lie, cheat, or steal, or tolerate anyone who does." Therefore, when in 1976 a cadet told a visiting congressman that cheating was widespread, people at the academy and across the country were dismayed. The cheating was investigated, about 100 cadets were suspended for the rest of the school year, and the school belief in honor was reaffirmed. (Top) a suspended cadet returns to school, (bottom) cadets in class, and (right) cadets on review.

action will be influenced by what you think are the outcomes of each alternative.

Let's think of the consequences of Alma Kramer's alternatives. If Alma does nothing about Sue Prescott's cheating, a bad outcome is that a cheater gets away with it. A good outcome is that Sue's friendship will stay the same. If Alma picks the alternative of reporting Sue to the teacher, a good outcome would be that the class rule about cheating was upheld. A bad consequence would be that Sue might not be her friend anymore.

When Joe Reid thinks carefully about what he will do, he considers the possible good and bad outcomes of each alternative. For example, a good outcome of supporting an anti-smoking law might be an improvement in public health in the city. A bad outcome for Joe might be loss of support from the mayor.

Discuss: Are there any other consequences Alma or Joe should consider?

Which Consequence Do You Prefer?

Careful decision making is choosing the alternative most likely to lead to the outcome you want. You need to think about your goals in order to make good decisions.

You are thinking about goals when you ask the question, "What do I want?" A goal is something you think is important for you to have. People work to reach their goals.

Sid Grunfeld's goal is to become president of the senior class. Wanda Kucinski is president of Citizens Against Smoking. Her goal is to get a law against smoking in public places. One of Alma Kramer's goals is to maintain classroom rules.

Note: Some students may benefit from working through other decisions, listing alternatives, consequences, and choices.

When you answer the question about what you want, you show your **values.** Values are those things that people think are important or good.

Sid Grunfeld's and Wanda Kucinski's goals show what each values. Sid wants the respect and power that come with being class president. Wanda believes good health is important. She believes that smoke from cigarettes is a hazard to the health of both non-smokers and smokers.

Alma Kramer has several goals. She wants to support honesty and dependability. She wants the respect of her teacher and classmates. She wants Sue to like her.

When people have the same values, it is easy to make some kinds of decisions. For example, most people agree that cheating is wrong and that not punishing cheaters has bad outcomes for the class. We expect teachers to make decisions that prevent cheating in the classroom.

Registering to Vote

As a rule, a person can vote if he or she is over eighteen, a resident of the state where he or she intends to cast a ballot, and a born or naturalized citizen of the United States. But in most communities, people who meet these qualifications must also register to vote before they can take part in an election.

To register, you must complete a voter registration form. This asks your name, address, date of birth, length of residence at your current address, and whether you are a natural-born or a naturalized citizen. If the latter, you must present evidence of naturalization. By registering, you prove that you are qualified to vote. And in most places, a person must register thirty or more days before an election day. People who go to the polls without having registered are not allowed to vote. An exception to registration is found in small communities, where election officials can usually recognize unqualified voters without reference to a registration list.

The Registration Procedure

A person must register in person, at a city or town hall or a county building. In some states, a person must present identification, in others not. In all cases, a person must swear or affirm the validity of stated place of residence, birthdate, and citizenship qualification. Some states require a witness to the registering person's signature.

Usually, if you live in the same locality year after year, and vote in most elections, you need register only once. If you change your address within a city, though, you must notify the proper election authorities. And if you move to another locality, or change your name, or fail to vote for a certain number of years—usually four—you must re-register.

A sample of a voter registration form appears on the opposite page.

Easier Registration

Registering to vote is a simple procedure, and usually, before elections, registration offices are open aside from regular hours to accommodate people. Yet, according to observers, the process can still work a hardship on certain persons. Among these are young people who have not voted before and are uncertain about the procedure, and elderly people who cannot travel easily. Also included in this group are people who find it difficult to get away from work to register, and the handicapped without cars and who have difficulty with public transportation.

Taking these factors into consideration, five states have made registration as easy as it can be. They are Minnesota, Wisconsin, North Dakota, Maine, and Oregon. In these states, people can register on the same day they vote.

In Minnesota and Wisconsin, a person can sign a statement at the polling place saying that he or she is eligible, present some identification—such as a driver's license—and have another person swear to the applicant's residence, and proceed to vote. In North Dakota, a person simply fills out a form at the polling place. No identification is needed. In Oregon and Maine, a person can register on election day at a town or city hall or a county clerk's office, then proceed to a polling place and vote.

The original reasoning behind such procedures is that they would bring more people out to vote. And, following the passage of new laws, voter turnout in those five states did increase.

Over the years, the number of eligible voters going to the polls, even for presidential elections, declined steadily. This was particularly true in local elections. Although voting is one way all citizens can participate in government, fewer and fewer people were taking advantage of the opportunity. In the 1972 and 1976 presidential elections, for example, about 55 percent of all registered voters in America turned out to cast ballots.

In Minnesota in 1976, after the new registration law, the turnout was 72.1 percent, highest of any state in the country. This rep-resented an increase of 4.7 percent over 1972 in Minnesota. Comparing 1972 and 1976, Wisconsin, Maine, and Oregon all increased the percent of voter turnout.

Not everyone favors voting-day registration, however, and despite presidential efforts, Congress in 1977 refused to make it a national law. Opponents of the procedure believe it opens wide the door to fraud. Conceivably, especially under polling-place registration, a person could register and vote more than once, using false identification. Opponents also point out that in the five states with easier procedures voter turnout has always been traditionally high and fraud relatively unimportant. They fear that easier registration laws would increase the chance of fraud in large cities.

VOTER REGISTRATION FORM

PLEASE PRINT OR TYPE

By the time of the next general election, I will be at least 18 years of age, I will be a citizen of the United States, and I will have resided in this State at least 30 days and in the county of _____ at least 30 days. To the best of my knowledge and belief, all the foregoing statements made by me are true and correct. I understand that any false or fraudulent registration or attempted registration may subject me to a fine of up to $1,000.00 or imprisonment of up to 5 years, or both pursuant to R. S. 19:34-1.

Name:

Birth Date:

LAST   FIRST   MIDDLE

MONTH   DAY   YEAR

Residence:

STREET ADDRESS

MUNICIPALITY

I have resided at the above address since:

MONTH   DAY   YEAR

COUNTY

ZIP

Where did you last register to vote?

STREET ADDRESS

MUNICIPALITY

COUNTY   STATE   ZIP

I am a ☐ native born/☐ naturalized (Strike one) citizen.

I was naturalized

MONTH   DAY   YEAR   MUNICIPALITY

SIGNATURE OR MARK

DATE

I, being a registered voter in _____ county in the State of New Jersey, witnessed the above signature or mark.

SIGNATURE

DATE

NAME (Please Print)

STREET ADDRESS   MUNICIPALITY   COUNTY   ZIP

If the voter is unable to sign his or her name, the voter shall make his or her mark, which mark shall be witnessed. The signature, name and residence of the registered voter in the State of New Jersey who filled out this form are:

SIGNATURE

DATE

NAME (Please Print)

STREET ADDRESS   MUNICIPALITY   COUNTY   ZIP

Discuss: What difficult decisions have you had to make?

It is not hard for a mayor to decide to send police to stop a riot. People tend to agree that we must keep public order and protect public safety and property.

Many decisions are difficult to make because they involve conflicts among different goals and values. Careful thought is needed to choose the alternative that will most likely lead to the best outcome.

You might expect Joe to decide easily against public smoking because he values health. However, Joe also believes citizens should have the freedom to decide for themselves whether or not to smoke in public or in private.

In addition, support from voters is important to Joe because he wants to keep his job on the city council. He is not sure how many anti-smoking people there are. Smokers may be in the majority. He must be careful.

Finally, Joe Reid likes having the respect and friendship of Mayor Thomas. He also understands the power that the mayor has to help or hurt him. Joe wants to stay on good terms with Mayor Thomas.

Section Review

Main Ideas
1. p. 21
2. Answers will vary.
Skill Building
1. goal: less street noise; values; answers will vary.
2. goal: win west-side support for his re-election; values: answers will vary.

Vocabulary: alternatives, consequences, values.

Reviewing the Main Ideas

1. What three questions should you ask yourself when faced with a decision?
2. Suppose you are trying to decide what time you should get up on school days. Name two possible alternatives and give two consequences for each.

Skill Building

Following are two examples of goals and values. First, identify the goal in each example. Then link each goal to one or more values that Maria and Homer might have.

1. Maria Johnson thinks her street is too noisy. She has asked the city council to pass a tough law against unnecessary honking, broken car mufflers, and other sources of street noise.
2. Homer Bixby is mayor of Mayville. He wants to win the support of the people in the west side neighborhood in the upcoming election. He has begun plans for the city to build a new recreation center in the west side area.

2/Judging Decisions

The headline of the morning newspaper said: Scenic City Council Bans Swimming in Lake.

Marcia Gordon showed the headline to her brother, Gregg.

"That's a dumb decision!" Gregg moaned. "I planned to do a lot of swimming this summer."

"I did too," said Marcia. "But the paper says the lake is polluted. I think the city council did the right thing."

"I don't agree," replied Gregg. "People should be free to make up their own minds about swimming in polluted water."

Marcia continued to read the newspaper. "Hey, Gregg! Listen to this," she shouted. "A bunch of crazy people are going to demonstrate at city hall against the swimming ban. I don't think they should act that way. Do you?"

"It is OK, Marcia, they have the right to demonstrate, as long as they do it peacefully and obey the law," replied Gregg.

Gregg and Marcia were judging the city government's decision to ban swimming. They were also judging the decisions of certain citizens about how to respond to the no-swimming rule.

What Are Judgments?

Everyone makes **judgments.** You make a judgment when you think a school rule is not fair or is good. You judge a friend's decision when you say, "That is a good idea," or "That's a silly thing to do."

Judging is deciding whether something is good or bad, better or worse, right or wrong. In Marcia's judgment, the city government made a good decision when they banned swimming. Marcia made a negative judgment of certain citizens who decided to demonstrate against the no-swimming rule.

When you judge objects to be good or bad, you are placing a value on them. You are saying what you believe is their worth.

Discuss: What judgments have you made today?

Discuss: What judgments would you make about each sign?

Signs tell of government decisions.

27

Your judgments depend to a great extent upon your beliefs about right and wrong.

Marcia's judgment of the no-swimming decision and the protestors is based on her concern for public health and respect for the authority of the city government. In contrast, Gregg places the freedom of citizens to decide for themselves above public health and safety.

Scenic City is a vacation resort. Many tourists come to swim and boat in the lake. The ban on swimming seemed to threaten the tourist business. Therefore, many owners of businesses and their employees were against the swimming ban. Many workers feared they might lose their jobs if the number of people spending their vacations in Scenic City dropped. Like most people, they place a high value on keeping their jobs. Thus, in their judgment the city government's decision to ban swimming was a mistake.

As a citizen, you make judgments about candidates for government offices such as mayor, governor, or President. You judge the ideas, abilities, and decisions of the different candidates.

As a citizen, you make judgments about the decisions of government officials. These judgments are tied to your beliefs about what is right or wrong.

You judge the decisions of other citizens—friends, teachers, and parents. You may like or dislike how these people decide to use their civil rights or carry out their responsibilities as citizens.

Finally, you judge your own decisions. After choosing an alternative, you may continue to think about the outcome. You may ask yourself, "Did I make the best choice? If I could do it again, would I make the same decision?"

Guidelines for Judging Decisions

Decisions may have good and bad outcomes. Good decisions lead to outcomes that satisfy you and others. These four questions will help you judge choices and the outcomes they lead to:
1. Is the choice practical?
2. How will the choice affect me?
3. How will the choice affect others?
4. Is the choice fair?

Is the Choice Practical? Alternatives are not **practical** if they are tied to outcomes that cannot be reached. Some people can

Note: Some students may find it helpful to identify community problems and the judgments possible.

Discuss: What kinds of judgments have you made about decisions of others?

As the students read, apply each question to the decisions Alma and Gregg made.

move from the city to the country to get away from air pollution. But flying to the moon to escape pollution is not a choice open to anyone. If you cannot really undertake a course of action, it is not a real choice. In a practical decision there is a strong possibility that the choice will really lead to the result that you want.

Make two lists. One should include examples of practical decisions, the other impractical decisions.

How Will the Choice Affect Me? Government decisions may affect your life in many ways. The government's decision to require all new cars to have seat belts could affect your health and safety. A decision to end the sports program at your school could affect the skills you can learn. Laws that prevent unfair treatment because of your race, religion, or sex could affect your ability to earn money. Government decisions about how much income tax you have to pay will affect your budget. To judge these kinds of decisions, you must think about whether the outcomes will give or take away things that you think important.

How Will the Choice Affect Others? Responsible citizens do not think only of themselves. They consider also the welfare of others. When judging a decision you should examine the consequences for all the groups of people affected.

Suppose the government in your area decided to build a super-highway through your neighborhood. At first, you might like this decision, because you and your family could drive more quickly to a nearby town to visit relatives and friends. However, you should also think about how the new highway might affect others.

Will the government have to tear down homes and stores to make room for the new highway? You might check the route of the new road on a map. Or you could read the newspaper. Or you might ask people in the neighborhood. You would be trying to find out what the facts were. Would the new road cause people to move their homes and businesses? Would people who have to move be paid a fair price for their property and the troubles caused by moving? How many people in the community would be helped by the new highway?

As you think about the worth of a decision, realize that different people might be helped or hurt by it. So, they might make very different judgments of the same decision. The owners of stores and homes being destroyed by a new highway might feel differently about the decision to build the highway than a truck driver who wants to use the new road. Do not rush to judge a

(Top) citizens sell T-shirts to raise money to fight highway construction and support mass transit. (Below) the road that went nowhere—government leaders cut off funds to complete this highway because of citizen opposition.

29

decision as good or bad until you think carefully about how it might affect various people.

Is the Decision Fair? Good decisions are **fair.** The fairest decisions help both individuals and their communities. Fair decisions strike a balance between the needs of the individual and the needs of others with whom he or she lives and works.

Whenever possible, decision makers in government should consider the needs of both the majority and minority of citizens in a situation. We often believe that the best decisions are those that serve the needs of the greatest number of people. However, this belief is an acceptable guide to judging decisions only if we remember to protect the rights of minority groups and individuals.

It is true that each person must at times give up some rights and freedom in order to live in harmony with others. A community can not exist when each person does exactly as he or she pleases. However, we should remember that the basic reason for forming communities and governments is to serve individual citizens. A fair decision does not put undue hardship on any individuals.

Using a Decision Tree

Now that you understand what is involved in making and judging decisions, you are ready to use a decision tree. A decision tree can help you think carefully as you make or judge a decision.

The decision tree opposite shows the choices facing Alma Kramer. Notice that there are places on the tree to show the occasion for decision, the alternatives, the good and bad outcomes of each alternative, and the conflicting goals that the decision maker has.

The trunk of the decision tree shows the occasion for decision. When you look at the branches, you find the different alternatives. Notice that Alma might have at least three alternatives.

Look even higher in the tree and you will find the outcomes of each alternative in the leaves. Choosing among alternatives means choosing among their outcomes.

Finally, high above the ground is the goal of the decision, the end to aim at. The tree shows two goals Alma has: (1) "Enforce class rule" or (2) "Cause no trouble for yourself or Sue."

Sometimes it is easy to think first of your goals when you

Discuss: What examples of fair and unfair decisions can you think of?

Discuss: Have you ever given up any rights for others? Why?

need to make a decision. When you use your own decision trees, you may often start at the top by asking, "What do I want?" When you know your goals, the problem is to choose a good alternative to reach them.

Sometimes, however, it will be easy to think of alternatives but hard to think of just what you want. When that happens you will probably start by asking, "What alternatives are there?" Thinking of alternatives will then help you think more clearly about your goals.

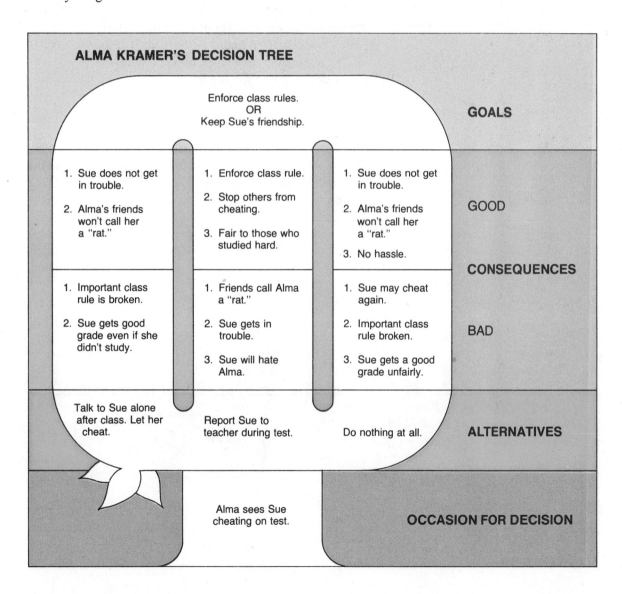

ALMA KRAMER'S DECISION TREE

Enforce class rules.
OR
Keep Sue's friendship.

GOALS

1. Sue does not get in trouble. 2. Alma's friends won't call her a "rat."	1. Enforce class rule. 2. Stop others from cheating. 3. Fair to those who studied hard.	1. Sue does not get in trouble. 2. Alma's friends won't call her a "rat." 3. No hassle.	**GOOD**

CONSEQUENCES

1. Important class rule is broken. 2. Sue gets good grade even if she didn't study.	1. Friends call Alma a "rat." 2. Sue gets in trouble. 3. Sue will hate Alma.	1. Sue may cheat again. 2. Important class rule broken. 3. Sue gets a good grade unfairly.	**BAD**

Talk to Sue alone after class. Let her cheat.

Report Sue to teacher during test.

Do nothing at all.

ALTERNATIVES

Alma sees Sue cheating on test.

OCCASION FOR DECISION

31

Section Review

Vocabulary: decision tree, judgment, fair, practical.

Reviewing the Main Ideas

1. What are four questions you should ask yourself when judging a decision?
2. How can you tell if a decision is fair?

Skill Building

1. Look at Alma's decision tree on page 31.
   a. Which alternative might Alma pick if her goal were to enforce the class rule about cheating? Why?
   b. Which alternatives might Alma pick if her goal were to cause no trouble for herself or Sue? Why?
2. Draw a decision tree for Joe Reid. Write in his alternatives and the good and bad consequences of each. (See pages 22–23 and 26 if you need to review the facts of Joe Reid's occasion for decision.)
3. Suppose Joe Reid decided to oppose a law banning smoking in public places. How would you judge this decision? Use the guidelines for judging decisions (page 28) to explain your answer.

The Black Mesa Mine Decision

The Navajo [nav'ə hō] live in a large reservation in the Southwest. In recent years they have faced a severe conflict about how to use their natural resources.

Until a few years ago, the people of Black Mesa, Arizona, lived as their ancestors had lived—grazing sheep and following ancient Navajo traditions. Then coal was found in the flat-topped hills of the area, and nothing has been the same. Geologists said that Black Mesa covered a very rich, shallow vein of low-sulfur coal. It could become one of the largest coal mines in the world.

Peter MacDonald, Navajo tribal chairman, urged his people to sign a contract with a mining company. In return for the right to take coal from Black Mesa, the mining company would pay a large fee to the Navajo. The mining company also would share profits from the sale of the coal with the Navajo. Finally, more than 300 Navajo would get jobs working at the mine. They would be paid more than $10,000 each year. Most of these people were making less than $3,000 per year.

MacDonald said: "We must use our natural resources to create jobs for our people and put them on the road to economic self-sufficiency."

Many Navajo agreed with MacDonald. They believed that the growing population of over 160,000 could not be supported by farming and herding. Too many people were poor and hungry. They believed that the mine would provide jobs and money. The money could be used to build better schools, hospitals, and other facilities the Navajo needed. With money gained from the Black Mesa mine, everyone would be better off.

Many Navajo disagreed with MacDonald and his supporters. They wanted to keep their old traditions. To these people, the Black Mesa is a sacred place that should not be ravaged in return for money.

They said taking coal from Black Mesa was a sin against nature. A traditional Navajo belief is that all things are sacred— people, animals, plants, earth, stones, water. All natural resources should be used with care and passed on to the next generation unspoiled.

In addition, 78 families living at Black Mesa would have to move if the mining contract were signed. Many Navajo thought this was unfair.

The decision was very difficult and the discussions were bitter. In the end, the tribal leaders agreed to sign a contract that gave a coal company the right to strip-mine coal from Black Mesa for 35 years.

Judgments on the decisions have been mixed. One outcome of the Black Mesa coal mine has been more money and a better standard of living for most of the Navajo.

As one young man said: "I have a steady job at the mine. I've never made so much money in my life."

A young woman said: "We already have been paid millions of dollars for leasing land to coal companies. We'll get lots more from our share of the profits. We can use this money to build the things our people need. We've never had it so good."

However, many are very unhappy about what has happened. Smokestacks, machinery, and power plants stand where sheep used to graze. Railroad tracks, telephone poles, and power lines mark the land instead of trees, shrubs, and grass. Huge machines gouge the earth to extract coal that giant trucks carry away.

Four Corners power plant on the Navajo reservation.

In May, 1976, more than 600 Navajo gathered at Window Rock, Arizona, to protest the decision of their tribal leaders. Their viewpoint was expressed by an old woman: "The Earth is our mother. How much would you ask for if your mother had been harmed? There is no way that we can be repaid for the damages to our mother. No amount of money can repay; money cannot give birth to anything."

Discuss: What would a decision tree look like if Peter MacDonald made one.

Reviewing the Case Study

1. What was the occasion for decision in this case?
2. What were the alternatives?
3. What were the likely consequences of each alternative?
4. What consequence did Peter MacDonald and his followers prefer? Why? What did they hope to gain?
5. How did those who opposed MacDonald judge his decisions? What consequences did they prefer? Why?
6. What is your judgment of the Black Mesa Mine Decision? Explain your thinking.

Chapter Two Test and Activities

★★★

Vocabulary

Match the following words with their meanings.

1. values
2. alternatives
3. consequences
4. judgment
5. practical
6. minority
7. fair

a. less than half
b. useful, leading toward the desired result
c. results or outcomes
d. the limited possibilities you can choose from in making a decision
e. things believed to be good or important
f. an opinion about the worth of something
g. not favoring one more than another

Reviewing Chapter Ideas

1. You are trying to make a decision. You have considered the alternatives. Next you should:
   a. choose the alternative you like best.
   b. consider the consequences.
   c. judge the decision.
   d. none of the above.
2. True or false: When making a decision, it is always necessary to have plenty of time to consider the alternatives and the consequences of each.
3. True or false: Once you have considered the alternatives and consequences you face, it is always easy to make a decision.
4. True or false: You make a decision. It could still result in good and bad outcomes.
5. True or false: A person should never give up individual rights.

6. In the Case Study about the Black Mesa mine, what decision did the tribal leaders make?
7. Why did the leaders make this decision? What were their reasons?
8. Why did many Navajo protest the decision? What were their reasons?

Using Basic Social Studies Skills

Finding Information

1. Use the headings in this chapter to find the guidelines for judging decisions. What page are they on?
2. If you wanted to review the parts of the decision tree, where would you look?

Comprehending Information

Write a paragraph of at least four sentences explaining what makes a decision *fair*.

Organizing Information

Copy the following story. Draw a line under the occasion for decision. Put circles around the alternatives. Put a star next to each consequence.

Wilona and Jim have asked Rose to go to the beach with them. She has a toothache. If she goes to the beach she might have so much fun that she'll forget about her tooth. On the other hand, the toothache might spoil her fun and everyone else's. If she goes to the dentist, she'll get her tooth fixed, but she'll miss out on the fun.

Evaluating Information

Review Joe Reid's problem on pages 22–23 and 26. Does he have enough information to make a good decision? Why do you think that? What, if anything, does he still need to know?

Vocabulary
1. e   4. f   7. g
2. d   5. b
3. c   6. a

Ideas
1. b   4. T   7. pp. 33–35
2. F   5. F   8. pp. 33–35
3. F   6. p. 34

★★

Communicating Ideas

Write a questionnaire Joe Reid might use to get more information. Word the questions carefully to get people's real opinions.

Using Decision-Making Skills

1. Tom hasn't finished his homework. Class is beginning. What are his alternatives? List at least three.

2. Choose one alternative you named for Tom. What are two possible outcomes of this alternative?

3. Which alternative should Tom choose? Why?

4. "Court rules: No Motor Boats Allowed on Lake Patrick." The Axelsons own a motel on the lake. What four questions should they ask in judging the decision?

5. Choose one of those questions. What are three ways the Axelsons might answer it?

6. Draw a decision tree. Fill it in for the Black Mesa Mine Decision.

7. Would you have joined the Navajo protestors at Window Rock or do you think the tribal leaders made the right decision? Explain.

8. You have been asked to sign a petition to ban smoking in public places. Write a brief summary of how you would decide whether to sign or not.

Activities

1. Use an encyclopedia to find out more about the Navajo. Prepare a list of at least five facts about the Navajo not given in this book. Would any of your facts have been useful to Peter MacDonald?

2. Use the *Readers' Guide to Periodical Literature* to see if any articles written in 1976 would give you more information about the Navajo. Write down the name of the magazine, the month, day, year, and page number for each entry that looks as if it is about the Navajo and coal mining.

3. Look up the articles you have located in the *Readers' Guide.* Report to the class any new facts you find about the Navajo and their use of resources. Has any of this information changed your judgment of the Black Mesa Mine Decision? Why or why not?

4. Look at your local paper or listen to the news. Identify an important decision your community is trying to make. List the alternatives your community can choose among. What seem to be the consequences of these alternatives?

5. Select a book in which characters must make serious decisions. After reading the book, answer these questions: (1) What were the occasions for important decisions in the book? (2) What were the alternatives in each case? (3) What goal did the character making the decisions hope to achieve in each case? (4) What is your judgment of the decisions that were made? (One book in which a young person makes a number of important decisions is *Where the Lilies Bloom* by Vera and Bill Cleaver [Lippincott, 1969].)

Chapter 3

Citizens Make a Constitution

★★

Discuss: Why did some people feel the success of the convention depended on Washington?

Early in 1787, George Washington had to decide whether to go to an important meeting in Philadelphia. Several of his friends favored having a convention of representatives from each state to decide how to strengthen the young government. Many had written to Washington urging him to be at the convention. They said its success depended on his being there.

Washington was well aware of the nation's troubles. For several years he had been warning that the young nation might fall apart. The thirteen states had cooperated to win the war against the British. But after the war, the different states quarreled. Many times Washington said that to save the nation each state would have to give up some independence to a more powerful central government. And, too, there were riots around the country. Many citizens were trying to settle their problems by fighting and mob action.

Discuss: What characteristics made Washington a good leader?

So Washington agreed with the goals of the convention in Philadelphia. But he was not certain he should attend. He was fifty-five years old and felt older. Rheumatism racked his body with pain. His brother had just died, and his mother and sister were sick.

In addition to family problems, Washington worried about what the convention could accomplish. Some people viewed it as a meeting of traitors seeking to overthrow the national government. Would people think he was disloyal to the United States?

Have small groups prepare and present radio scripts on George Washington and his life.

When Congress approved the convention, some of Washington's worries were eased. Now no one could think that those who attended were against their national government. So he decided to go and take part in what has become known as the Constitutional Convention. In this chapter you will read:

1/The Background of the Constitutional Convention
2/Decision Making at the Constitutional Convention
3/How the Constitution Was Approved
Case Study: The Whiskey Rebellion

1/The Background of the Constitutional Convention

In 1786, a worried George Washington wrote, "Wisdom and good examples are necessary at this time to rescue the political machine from the impending storm." Why did Washington think of the future of the United States as a "storm"?

In 1781, near the end of the Revolutionary War, the thirteen states had accepted a **constitution** called the Articles of Confederation. A constitution is a basic plan for government. It sets out the powers and duties a government has. It also tells what role citizens can have in the government. The weaknesses of the Articles of Confederation led to the national problem that worried George Washington.

Government Under the Articles of Confederation

Under the Articles of Confederation, the main powers of government were held by the states. Each state was represented in a national Congress. The main job of the Congress was to make laws for the United States. Each state had one vote in the Con-

Examine the Articles of Confederation.

Discuss: What can you tell about the delegates to the convention from examining this picture?

Washington presided over the meetings of the Constitutional Convention.

39

Discuss: What were the strengths and weaknesses of the Articles of Confederation?

Discuss: Why was this national currency an important problem?

The states printed their own money: (top left) Virginia three-pound note, 1775; (center left and bottom) New York bills for one-sixth of a dollar, 1776; (right) South Carolina fifty-pound note, 1776.

gress. The Congress could only pass laws or take action when nine of the thirteen states agreed to do so. The thirteen states were a **confederation,** united only as a "league of friendship" among separate states. The national government was very weak.

Under the Articles, Congress had no power to tax the states. It could not regulate trade between the states. More importantly, Congress had no power to make the thirteen states or their citizens obey its laws or the Articles of Confederation.

The states argued constantly among themselves over boundaries and taxes. The New York legislature, for example, started taxing New Jersey farmers who crossed the Hudson River to sell goods in New York. The states also created their own state armies and navies. Virginia and Pennsylvania fought briefly over conflicting claims to the area around Pittsburgh. An argument between Pennsylvania and Connecticut almost ended in war. The national government lacked power to settle these conflicts.

Another serious problem was money. Without the power to tax, Congress had to beg the states for money. They gave very little. As a result, Congress had little money to pay for services that citizens expect from their government. It could not afford to keep a navy to protect its trading ships from pirates. And it was not able to pay its debts. (Large sums of money had been borrowed to pay for the Revolutionary War.)

There was no national currency such as we have today. Most states printed their own paper money. Often one state's money was not good in another state. Many people did not trust even their own state's money. In North Carolina, people started to use whiskey to pay their bills. In Virginia, many people used tobacco instead of paper money.

All during the 1780s, leaders such as George Washington, John Hancock, Thomas Jefferson, and James Madison argued for a stronger national government. Hancock said that "our very existence as a free nation" depends on strengthening the national government.

Discuss: What did these leaders mean when they said they wanted a stronger national government?

Through the fall of 1786 and winter of 1787, there were disorders and riots in several states. Money problems were so bad that many farmers lost their farms because they could not pay their debts. In Massachusetts, Daniel Shays, a captain in the Revolutionary War, led nearly a thousand farmers in an attempt to keep the state supreme court from meeting. If the court could not meet, it could not sentence poor farmers to jail nor make them give up their farms to pay their debts.

George Washington (top) and Benjamin Franklin (bottom).

Shays's Rebellion was over quickly, but it frightened citizens all over the new nation. By early 1787, it was clear that the national government had to be strengthened. Congress agreed there were problems with the Articles of Confederation. Each state was asked to send delegates to a **convention** in May.

Who Came to the Convention?

Twelve states sent **delegates** to the convention in Philadelphia. Rhode Island's leaders were against having a strong national government and sent no one.

George Washington was one of the first to arrive. He came in a carriage escorted by local soldiers. Bells rang for the general. He was given a hero's welcome.

The fifty-five delegates to the convention in Philadelphia were men of knowledge and public experience. Many had served their country in the American Revolution. Eight had signed the Declaration of Independence. Seven had been governors of their states. Thirty-one had college educations.

At eighty-one, Benjamin Franklin of Pennsylvania was the oldest delegate. He was also world-famous as a diplomat, writer, inventor, and scientist.

Alexander Hamilton came from New York. At age thirty-two, he was one of the youngest delegates. However, he was one of the top lawyers in the country and was highly respected.

James Madison, a great scholar, came from Virginia. He was thirty-six years old. He knew more about history, government,

Alexander Hamilton (top) and
James Madison (bottom).

Main Ideas
1. p. 39
2. pp. 40–41
3. pp. 41–42
Skill Building
1. p. 38
2. Congress approved the
convention.

and public affairs than anyone at the convention. He contributed some of the most important ideas at the convention.

The delegates were a young group. Their average age was only forty-three. Half the delegates were in their mid-thirties. Most of these men had great careers ahead of them. Two, Washington and Madison, later became President of the United States. One, Elbridge Gerry, became Vice-President. Seventeen went on to become senators and eleven to serve in the House of Representatives. Six became judges of the United States Supreme Court.

Two great leaders, Thomas Jefferson and John Adams, were not at the convention. Jefferson was serving his country in Paris as minister to France. Adams was working in London as the minister to Great Britain. Patrick Henry, another leader of the Revolution, was elected as a delegate from Virginia. But he was against the convention and did not go.

It rained heavily the opening week of the convention. Roads from Maine to Georgia were deep in mud, and travel was very difficult. Many delegates were late in arriving. But once all were assembled, they were ready to make some of the most important decisions in American history.

Section Review

Vocabulary: confederation, constitution, convention, delegate.
Reviewing the Main Ideas
1. What were the Articles of Confederation?
2. What were the main weaknesses of government under the Articles of Confederation?
3. Describe the people selected as delegates to the convention in Philadelphia.
Skill Building
1. Make two lists. In one list, put the reasons George Washington thought he should go to the convention in Philadelphia. In the other list put the reasons he did not want to go.
2. What event helped Washington make up his mind?

2/Decision Making at the Constitutional Convention

The delegates met in Independence Hall in Philadelphia. They worked for sixteen and one-half weeks. Usually their sessions started at ten in the morning and ended about three in the afternoon. There was plenty of time to talk over the decisions they were making. During the evening, they often met at the Indian Queen, a hotel where many of them stayed. They also talked informally at dances and parties held for them by leading citizens in Philadelphia.

Decisions About Rules and Goals

The convention started with a **unanimous** decision. With the agreement of everyone, George Washington was chosen to **preside** over the meetings. His job was to recognize speakers, keep order, and prod the group to finish its business.

Note: Some students may need to compare "unanimous" with "majority."

Groups need rules. So, before doing anything else, Washington appointed a committee to write rules for conducting the business of the convention. The committee proposed several rules. After much discussion, the delegates approved them.

One rule was to keep their work secret. The public was not allowed to attend meetings. Each delegate promised not to tell outsiders what was going on in the convention. To keep others away, sentries guarded the doors.

This rule had several good consequences. It made it easy for the delegates to talk freely. They did not worry about pleasing the public with anything they said. It also made it easier for them to change their minds.

Other rules had to do with keeping order during meetings. No one was to talk unless recognized by the presiding officer. While one person spoke, others were expected to listen. Meetings could not be held unless delegates from at least seven states were present. Decisions were to be made by majority vote of the states present. Each state had only one vote. All delegates from a state would decide by majority vote how their state's one ballot would be cast.

After deciding about rules, the delegates discussed goals. The Congress had given them the right to revise the Articles of Confederation. But the delegates agreed that changing the Articles of Confederation was not enough. They decided to have a new

Benjamin Franklin addresses James Madison and George Washington at the Constitutional Convention.

Discuss: How did each rule affect the convention?

43

Discuss: Why did they decide to throw out the Articles?

goal. They would throw out the Articles of Confederation and write a new constitution. At this point, the meeting became the Constitutional Convention.

The delegates were determined to set up a government that all states would accept. Everyone knew that failure to write a new constitution would mean disaster for the young country. Elbridge Gerry of Massachusetts spoke for most when he said, "I would bury my bones in this city rather than [leave] . . . the Convention without anything being done."

Settling a Basic Disagreement

After agreeing about rules and goals, the delegates began to disagree. The most important argument was between delegates of the smaller and bigger states. Big states, such as Virginia and Pennsylvania, wanted to control the new government. Small states, such as New Jersey and Delaware, wanted protection from the big states. Thus, a basic question was: What powers could the different states have in the new government?

Discuss: Why was size such an important issue?

The Virginia Plan. The Virginia delegates were among the first to arrive in Philadelphia. While waiting for the convention to start, they created a plan for a new constitution. On May 29, Edmund Randolph presented their plan to the others.

(Left) Brigadier General and Mrs. Thomas Mifflin, Boston merchants and (right) the commercial district of Boston.

The Virginia Plan called for a government with three branches. A legislative branch would make laws. The executive branch would enforce laws. A judicial branch would decide about the meaning of laws and who should be punished for breaking laws.

The legislative branch would be divided into two parts—a Senate and a House of Representatives. The states were to be represented in the national legislature on the basis of their population or the amount of money they gave to the national government.

Delegates from Massachusetts, Pennsylvania, and Virginia promoted this plan. It gave the big states more influence in the national government than before. Under the Articles of Confederation, each state had one vote, no matter how big or small it was. Delegates from the big states wanted to change that rule.

The New Jersey Plan. Delegates from the small states did not like the Virginia Plan. William Paterson of New Jersey proposed an alternative. It was called the New Jersey Plan. This plan also called for three branches in government. But the legislative branch would have only one house as in the Articles of Confederation. And each state would get one vote.

Delegates from the smallest states—Delaware, New Jersey,

Discuss: What clues can you get about life at this time from the pictures on pp. 44–49?

(Left) New Haven public square, (top) a tollgate on the Baltimore-Reisterstown Road, and (bottom) musicians rehearsing.

and Maryland—liked this plan. It made their states equal in power to the big states.

A decision had to be made. For six long weeks the delegates argued. Each side thought it was right. Neither side wanted to give in. Some delegates even threatened to leave the convention.

Fortunately, all the delegates shared the goal of creating a new constitution. So they kept on working. They knew a **compromise** was needed.

A compromise involves give and take. In a compromise, each side gives up something it wants. But each side also gets something. Compromises are an important part of political life. They can be a way to settle a dispute when no one can agree. The delegates understood this. They looked for a third alternative.

The Great Compromise. Roger Sherman of Connecticut came up with the answer. He proposed Congress have two houses—a Senate and a House of Representatives. The states would be represented equally in the Senate—one state, one vote. This would please the small states. In the House, representation would be based on population. The big states would have more votes than the small states. This pleased the big states.

Sherman's alternative is often called the Great Compromise. After much discussion, the delegates decided to accept this alter-

Discuss: How were the Virginia Plan and New Jersey Plan the same? Different?

Discuss: What other examples of compromise can you name?

(Left) "Night Life in Philadelphia" 1793 and (right) Wall Street, New York City, in the 1790s.

native. Not all were completely happy, but it was a decision that everyone could accept.

The Great Compromise saved the convention. After agreeing to it, the delegates could move on to other important issues and decisions. Often when the delegates could not agree on an alternative, they compromised. As Ben Franklin said, the delegates spent a lot of time "sawing boards to make them fit."

During the ten weeks after the Great Compromise, the delegates created the basic parts of our Constitution. They decided upon the powers and duties of Congress. Their plan also called for a President and a Supreme Court. The Constitution would be the supreme law of the country. Each state would give up some of its powers in the interest of national unity. The national government would be able to enforce its laws throughout the country. (The Constitution is discussed in Chapter 4.)

On September 17, the delegates met for the last time. The finished Constitution was placed on a table to be signed. Benjamin Franklin gave a speech urging the delegates to sign. He said that there were parts of the document that he did not approve. But on the whole, he liked it.

Forty-two of the delegates were present at the final meeting of the convention. Thirty-nine followed Franklin's advice and signed the Constitution.

Discuss: What was the Great Compromise? What parts of each other plan were used?

Discuss: How did the Great Compromise save the convention?

(Left) view of Bethlehem, Pennsylvania, (top) metalworkers, (bottom) The State House in Philadelphia, 1799.

47

Section Review

Vocabulary: compromise, preside, unanimous.

Reviewing the Main Ideas

1. What decisions about rules did the delegates make at the start of the Constitutional Convention?
2. Why were these decisions important to the success of the convention?
3. How did the Virginia Plan differ from the New Jersey Plan?
4. What was the Great Compromise?

Skill Building

Use a decision tree to chart one decision (the Great Compromise) that the delegates made. Fill in the tree by answering these questions.

1. What was the occasion for decision?
2. What alternatives did the delegates have?
3. What was one likely consequence of each alternative?
4. What goals did the delegates have? Which goal did they share?

(Left) Southern plantation owners and (right) Hampton, the seat of General Charles Ridgely, Maryland, 1799.

3/How the Constitution Was Approved

Important decisions had been made at the Constitutional Convention, but new decisions were needed. Citizens of the thirteen states had to judge the new Constitution. Nine states had to **ratify** the Constitution before it could become the law of the land. (Ratify means "approve.") The delegates' work would mean nothing if the Constitution was not ratified.

Taking Sides

Within days of the convention, newspapers all over the country printed the Constitution. Many people were shocked. They had not expected a totally new Constitution. Others were pleased. Citizens' judgments of the Constitution had started.

Each state set up a convention with delegates to vote yes or no on the Constitution. Those for and against the Constitution worked hard to influence the state conventions.

The Federalists. Citizens who supported the Constitution were called Federalists. They were led by people who had been delegates to the Constitutional Convention. James Madison and Alexander Hamilton were the main leaders.

(Left) Indians boating past a newly cleared farm. Note the stumps and log fences. (Top) slaves packing tobacco in barrels for shipping and (bottom) advertisement of a slave sale.

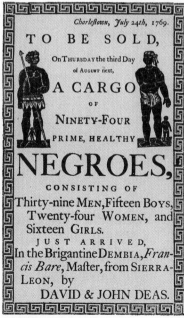

The Federalists talked about the weaknesses of the Articles of Confederation. They warned that the country would face confusion and disorder unless the states united under a strong central government. They were well organized and worked hard.

The Anti-Federalists. Citizens against the new Constitution were called Anti-Federalists. Such men as Patrick Henry, Samuel Adams, and Richard Henry Lee led this group.

The Anti-Federalists feared a strong national government. They feared that citizens would lose their civil rights and liberties. They believed that the new government might not treat all groups of citizens fairly. Finally, they were afraid that the state governments might lose all their powers. Patrick Henry spoke for many of them when he said of the Constitution, "I look upon that paper as the most fatal plan . . . to enslave a free people."

Reaching Agreement

Many citizens agreed with the Anti-Federalists that citizens might lose their rights under the strong central government set up by the Constitution. At this time, most state constitutions included a list of citizens' rights. People wanted the national Constitution to have the same thing. So, it was suggested that a **bill of rights** be added to the Constitution. Thomas Jefferson argued in favor of a bill of rights. He said that "a bill of rights is what the people are entitled to against every government."

This bill of rights would say what rights the government could *not* take away from citizens—the rights of free speech and press, of religious choice, of assembly and association, and certain other liberties. This bill of rights would also protect certain rights and powers of the state governments. (The Bill of Rights is discussed in detail in Chapter 5.)

The Federalists saw that ratifying the Constitution would not be easy. In at least six states, it seemed that the voters might reject it. So to help influence the voting, the Federalists promised to add a bill of rights if the new Constitution was approved.

Some state conventions approved the new Constitution quickly. In other states the struggle went on for eight or nine months. The table on this page shows the date each state approved the Constitution and the vote in each state. Notice how close the vote was in New Hampshire, Virginia, New York, and Rhode Island. The last two states ratified the Constitution after the new government was established.

Discuss: Compare Federalists with Anti Federalists.

STATES APPROVE THE CONSTITUTION

State	Date of ratification	Vote
Delaware	Dec. 7, 1787	30-0*
Pennsylvania	Dec. 12, 1787	46-23
New Jersey	Dec. 18, 1787	38-0*
Georgia	Jan. 2, 1788	26-0*
Connecticut	Jan. 9, 1788	128-40
Massachusetts	Feb. 6, 1788	187-168
Maryland	Apr. 28, 1788	63-11
South Carolina	May 23, 1788	149-73
New Hampshire	June 21, 1788	57-47
Virginia	June 25, 1788	89-79
New York	July 26, 1788	30-27
North Carolina	Nov. 21, 1788	194-77
Rhode Island	May 29, 1790	34-32

*These votes were unanimous

Have students make a map showing how each state felt about the Constitution at the end of the convention. Also include the date when each state ratified the Constitution. Be sure each map has a key.

50

In September of 1788, New York City was chosen as a temporary capital for the government. Members of the new Senate and House of Representatives for each state were elected.

As a member of the first Congress, James Madison proposed twelve **amendments** to the new Constitution. (Changes made in laws are called amendments.) Ten of these amendments became the Bill of Rights. The Federalists had kept their promise. The new government was underway.

Section Review

Vocabulary: amendment, Bill of Rights, Federalist, Anti-Federalist, ratify.

Reviewing the Main Ideas

1. What did the Federalists do to make sure that the Constitution would be ratified?
2. Why did the Federalists support the Constitution?
3. Why were the Anti-Federalists against the Constitution?

Skill Building

In judging the Constitution, people asked themselves: (a) How would it affect me? (b) How would it affect others? (c) Would it be fair?

1. How might a Federalist have answered each of these questions?
2. How might an Anti-Federalist have answered each question?
3. Look at the table on page 50.
   a. In which states was the ratification vote decided by a margin of twenty or less votes?
   b. In which states were there unanimous votes in favor of ratification?

Discuss: Would you have wanted to attend the convention? Would you have been a Federalist or Anti-Federalist? Why?

Main Ideas
1. promised to add a bill of rights
2. They believed the Articles were too weak to provide good government.
3. They feared the power of a strong central government.

Skill Building
1. Answers will vary.
2. Answers will vary.
3. a. Pa., Mass., N. Hamp., Va., N.Y., R.I.
   b. Del., N.J., Ga.

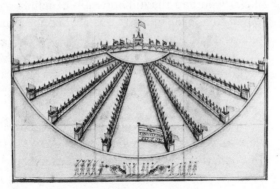

This drawing shows a parade formation of 6,000 New Yorkers celebrating the certainty that their state would ratify the Constitution.

Discuss: Why was
Washington worried? What
did he mean by "an ocean
of difficulties"?

The Whiskey Rebellion

George Washington was sworn in at Federal Hall in New York City on the morning of April 30, 1789. A large crowd was there. Bells rang, and the people shouted, "Long live George Washington, President of the United States!"

The President looked calm and dignified. But he was worried. Washington had said to a friend that he faced "an ocean of difficulties."

Washington had to make decisions unlike those of any other President. He did not inherit an operating government. Rather, he had to create the office of the presidency. He had to guide others as they put the Constitution into practice.

From the start, the President faced challenges to the government's authority. Many citizens were for the new Constitution only so long as it didn't inconvenience them. They defied the new government whenever it asked them to make sacrifices.

A serious challenge came from farmers west of the Appalachian Mountains. They refused to obey the new Excise Law of 1791, which taxed the sale of whiskey.

Western farmers turned much of their corn and rye into whiskey. For many farmers, whiskey was the only cash crop. Whiskey was easier to transport for sale than grain. A pack horse could carry only four bushels of grain. But it could carry twenty-four bushels once the grain was turned into two kegs of whiskey. The tax on whiskey would cut deeply into the farmers' main source of money.

Farmers in western Pennsylvania were furious over the whiskey tax. For many months most refused to pay it. When tax collectors tried to force them to pay, many farmers rebelled. They beat up tax collectors and threatened law officers. One official who had the unhappy job of telling a delinquent farmer he had to appear in court was robbed, beaten, tarred and feathered, and left tied to a tree.

The governor of Pennsylvania, Thomas Mifflin, did nothing to enforce the whiskey tax law. He was popular with the farmers and he did not want to do anything that might cause them to turn against him.

In the summer of 1794, the conflict over the whiskey tax came to a head. There were meetings of angry farmers in western Pennsylvania. They signed agreements pledging never to pay the hated tax. There was even talk of separating from the United

Tarring and feathering a federal tax collector.

States. Local leaders urged resistance to the national government. Finally, on July 17, 1794, several hundred men burned the home of General John Neville, the tax collector in the area.

President Washington had to decide what to do. What were his alternatives? He could send messages to the rebelling farmers that they would be forgiven if they would stop their violence and pay the tax. This he did, but it did not work. He could ignore the situation, but wouldn't that make the government seem as weak as it had been under the Articles of Confederation?

Washington's goal was clear. He wanted to show that the new government was strong. He knew that a government that passes laws but does not enforce them cannot remain in power. Citizens lose respect for such a government. He had to act forcefully to end the Whiskey Rebellion.

President Washington asked the states for a large body of soldiers. Thirteen thousand men responded to the call—a good show of support for the new government. Washington personally led the army into Pennsylvania.

Washington's show of force quickly ended the Whiskey Rebellion. Most rebel leaders fled to Ohio, and their followers paid the tax. Two leaders were captured and convicted of treason, but President Washington pardoned them. It was all right to show mercy now; the authority of the national government was established.

Reviewing the Case Study

1. What was the occasion for decision in this case?
2. What were President Washington's alternatives?
3. What was Washington's decision?
4. What were the consequences of his decision?
5. Was it a good decision? Why?

CASE STUDY

Discuss: How do these illustrations add to your understanding of this case?

Discuss: What is treason?

(Left) Washington at Fort Cumberland reviewing troops before the march to put down the Whiskey Rebellion.

Chapter Three Test and Activities

★★

Vocabulary

Match the following words with their meanings.

1. constitution
2. confederation
3. convention
4. delegate
5. compromise
6. preside
7. chief executive
8. ratify
9. Federalist
10. Anti-Federalist
11. unanimous
12. amendment
13. bill of rights

a. a listing of the rights that government cannot take away from individuals
b. a citizen who supported the Constitution
c. complete agreement
d. a representative at a convention
e. to give formal approval
f. a settlement of a dispute in which both sides give up something
g. a group of independent states joined together for a special purpose
h. law that establishes the framework of government
i. a change offered in a law
j. a meeting for a special purpose
k. the head of one branch of government
l. to have charge of a meeting
m. a citizen who did not want to adopt the Constitution

Reviewing Chapter Ideas

1. Which of the following was a problem that led to the Constitutional Convention?
   a. The states had powers of government.
   b. Congress could not force anyone to obey its laws.
   c. Each state had three votes in Congress.
   d. Congress regulated trade between states.
2. Which of the following was not true of government under the Articles of Confederation?
   a. The states disagreed on boundaries.
   b. George Washington was President.
   c. Congress lacked power to tax the states.
   d. States printed their own money.
3. True or false: Before the Constitutional Convention each state had its own military.
4. Which statement is true of the Constitutional Convention?
   a. Thomas Jefferson led the meeting.
   b. Each state had one vote.
   c. Anyone could attend the meetings.
   d. Delegates from every state had to be there for a meeting to take place.
5. True or false: The Constitution was ratified by all the states at the Constitutional Convention.
6. True or false: The first state to ratify the Constitution was Delaware.
7. Which of the following men favored a strong national government?
   a. Patrick Henry
   b. Samuel Adams
   c. James Madison
   d. all of the above
8. True or false: New York was chosen as the temporary capital.

Vocabulary				
1. h	4. d	7. k	10. m	13. a
2. g	5. f	8. e	11. c	
3. j	6. l	9. b	12. i	

Ideas		
1. b	4. b	7. c
2. b	5. F	8. T
3. T	6. T	

★★★

Using Basic Social Studies Skills

Finding Information

1. Use the index in this book to find all the pages that refer to the Bill of Rights. What are they?
2. Look at those pages until you find the complete Bill of Rights. On what page does it begin?

Comprehending Information

1. Name one way the Virginia Plan and the New Jersey Plan were the same.
2. Name two ways the Virginia Plan and the New Jersey Plan were not the same.
3. Name two ways the Great Compromise differed from the other two plans.

Organizing Information

Make a timeline for 1785–1795. Include at least four events mentioned in this chapter.

Evaluating Information

The news of Shays's Rebellion persuaded many citizens they needed a stronger national government. Why? If people did the same thing today, would you feel your government was too weak? Explain.

Communicating Ideas

If you had been a delegate to a state convention to ratify the Constitution, would you have been a Federalist or an Anti-Federalist? Give your reasons in a short essay.

Using Decision-Making Skills

1. Do you think George Washington made the right choice when he decided to go to the Constitutional Convention? Why?
2. Which do you feel were the two main reasons for needing the Constitutional Convention? Why?

3. What were the most important decisions made at the convention? Explain.

Activities

1. If you want to learn more about Benjamin Franklin, a man who played one of the most important roles at the Constitutional Convention, read the following book: *Benjamin Franklin: A Biography in His Own Words*, edited by Thomas Fleming (Newsweek, distributed by Harper, Row, 1972).
2. Choose one of the men who attended the Constitutional Convention. (If you do item #1, choose someone other than Franklin.) Write a short report about the person you choose. Use an encyclopedia to get your information.
3. Use the card catalog in your library. Are there any books that would give you more information about the man you chose for the question above? Write down the title, author, and publisher for at least three books.
4. Find the three books on the shelves and skim them to see which book looks most interesting to you. Read some of it.

Chapter 4

The Constitution — Our Plan for Government

★★

Our Constitution is almost two hundred years old. It is the oldest written Constitution in the world. Other nations have had to write new constitutions many times. Germany has had four in just over one hundred years.

Discuss: How is life different today?

Life in the United States is very different now from when the Constitution was written. Yet still it serves us. Why has it stood up so well? Here are the opinions of three Presidents of the United States.

Theodore Roosevelt, the twenty-sixth President, saw the Constitution as a flexible plan for government. He said it is "an instrument designed for the life and healthy growth of the nation."

Woodrow Wilson was the twenty-eighth President. He had taught government and history at Princeton University. Wilson said the Constitution was easy to understand and use. "Our Constitution has proved lasting because of its simplicity."

Harry S Truman, the thirty-third President, was a careful student of history. He read about the constitutions and governments of other nations. He studied what other Presidents had said about the United States Constitution. Truman said, "The longer I live, the more I am impressed with our American Constitution. Read it and think about it. It's a plan, but not a strait jacket, flexible and short. Read it one hundred times and you'll always find something new."

Discuss: Do you agree with Truman's suggestion? Why?

Discuss: Did the three Presidents agree? Why?

Every citizen should follow President Truman's advice and read the Constitution. (A copy with notes to help you read it appears on pages 74–93.) It is not necessary to become an expert. That is the job of lawyers, judges, Presidents, and other government leaders. However, all citizens should know the main ideas about government stated in the Constitution. In this chapter you will read:

1/The Purpose of the Constitution
2/Three Branches of Government
3/How State and National Government Are Linked
Case Study: The Constitution Works!

1/The Purpose of the Constitution

The Constitution is the plan for government in the United States. It tells how the government is organized. It says what the government can and cannot do.

The Constitution has three main parts: (1) the Preamble [prē'am'bəl], which gives a statement of goals for our government, (2) the seven articles, which describe our plan for government, and (3) the twenty-five amendments, which have been added to the Constitution.

Locate the page in this book where each section of the Constitution begins.

Citizens and Their Constitution

The Constitution is the highest law in the United States. No citizen is above the law, not even the President. Everyone is expected to obey the law. Thus, the main purpose of a constitution is to help citizens live according to law.

In the United States, government acts according to laws based on the Constitution. Conflicts between citizens, and between citizens and government, may be settled according to law. In this way, the Constitution is the foundation of a peaceful orderly society.

The Constitution tells citizens what they can expect from

(Left to right) Theodore Roosevelt, Woodrow Wilson, and Harry Truman.

57

government. It says what the government may do for citizens. It says what the government may not do to them.

Citizens who know the Constitution have an advantage over others. They know their legal rights. They know how to use the rules to gain services from the government. They know how to protect themselves against any wrong use of government power. Citizens who do not know what is in the Constitution cannot use the rules to help themselves or others. Citizens who do not know their legal rights may lose benefits they deserve. Thus, it is important for citizens, young and old, to know their Constitution.

The Preamble: A Statement of Goals

The **Preamble** is the first part of the Constitution. It is a preface or introduction to the other parts of the Constitution. The Preamble tells why the Constitution was written. It is not law. Rather, the Preamble states purposes, or goals.

The Preamble names six goals that the writers wanted the United States to reach. These goals reflect the beliefs that the makers of the Constitution had about how government should serve citizens. Read the Preamble on page 74.

The first goal stated in the Preamble is "to form a more perfect union." This means that the citizens of the United States wanted a better union of the states than they had under the Articles of Confederation. The central government should be strong in order to unite the state governments as one strong nation.

The second goal is "to establish justice." This means that the United States should have a system of laws. Conflicts between people, or between citizens and their government, should be settled fairly in a court of law.

The third goal is "to insure **domestic tranquility.**" This means that life should be peaceful in all the states. The government should prevent behavior that could threaten health, safety, or property.

The fourth goal is "to provide for common defense." This means that citizens should be able to protect themselves and their country from any enemies. The government should have military forces to defend citizens against attack by outsiders.

Discuss: Why do citizens who know the Constitution have an advantage?

Discuss: Where else do you find a preface?

Examine each goal, reinforcing vocabulary whenever necessary.

The fifth goal is "to promote the **general welfare.**" This means that people should have good living conditions. The government is supposed to help make it possible for citizens to work productively and enjoy the rewards of their work.

The sixth goal is "to secure the blessings of liberty." This means that citizens now and in the future should be free. The government should try to protect civil rights and liberties of all citizens.

As shown by these goals, the makers of the Constitution valued the rights of citizens. They wanted the government to protect citizens' liberties. They also valued security. They expected the government to preserve law and order. Finally, the creators of the Constitution believed that government should be the servant of citizens, not their master.

Section Review

Vocabulary: Preamble, domestic tranquility, general welfare.
Reviewing the Main Ideas
1. Why should citizens of the United States be familiar with their Constitution?
2. What is the Preamble?
3. What six goals for government are stated in the Preamble?
4. In your opinion, which goal is the most important? Why?
Skill Building
1. Rewrite the Preamble, in your own words, so as to include all the goals that are in the original version.
2. What additional goals, if any, would you include in the Preamble if you were writing it today?

Discuss: Have any of the goals been completely met? Are any being worked on today?

Main Ideas
1. p. 58
2. The introduction to the Constitution.
3. pp. 58–59
4. Answers will vary.
Skill Building
1. Answers will vary.
2. Answers will vary.

Enjoying the benefits of life in an orderly society, Americans (left) shop on a summer afternoon and (right) watch a no-hitter.

Discuss: Why are there three branches of government? What is the main role of each?

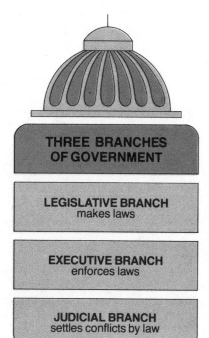

THREE BRANCHES OF GOVERNMENT

LEGISLATIVE BRANCH
makes laws

EXECUTIVE BRANCH
enforces laws

JUDICIAL BRANCH
settles conflicts by law

2/Three Branches of Government

The main body of the Constitution follows the Preamble. (See pages 74–86.) It is divided into seven parts called articles. Each article gives one or more rules or procedures for organizing the government and carrying out its business.

The Constitution separates the powers and duties of government among three branches. The purpose of this separation is to prevent any person or group from having all the power of government. If one person or group had all the power, the rights of citizens might be taken away. The chart on page 62 shows how the branches check and balance each other.

The three branches are (1) the legislative, (2) the executive, and (3) the judicial. The first three articles of the Constitution tell about these three branches of government.

Article 1: Legislative Branch

One main job of government is to make laws. Article 1 says that Congress is the **legislative** (law-making) **branch** of government. Congress is made up of the Senate and the House of Representatives. Article 1 tells who can become members of the Senate and the House of Representatives and how these members are chosen. For examples, see the table on this page.

Article 1 gives the rules Congress must follow in making laws. For example, one rule is that a majority of the members of both the Senate and the House of Representatives must vote in favor of any bill in order for it to become a law.

Article 1 lists the specific kinds of laws that Congress may

ORIGINAL RULES ABOUT LEGISLATORS IN ARTICLE 1		
	REPRESENTATIVES	SENATORS
TERM	2 years	6 years
REQUIREMENTS	• at least 25 years old • a citizen at least 7 years • lives in state represented	• at least 30 years old • a citizen at least 9 years • lives in state represented
HOW MANY	at least 1 per state; the total number is based on the population in the state	2 per state
HOW CHOSEN	by statewide election, each state to decide who is eligible to vote	by the state legislature (Amendment 17 changed this.)
VACANCIES FILLED	by statewide election	by the state legislature; the governor can make temporary appointments (Amendment 17 changed this.)

make. For example, it says that Congress may make laws about collecting taxes, regulating trade and business, coining money, and declaring war.

Article 1 also describes powers that Congress may *not* have. For example, Congress cannot pass a law granting a **title of nobility** to any citizen. This makes titles such as "duke" or "duchess" illegal in the United States. (You will find out more about Congress in Chapter 7.)

Read Article 1 after you examine this section.

Article 2: Executive Branch

The Articles of Confederation did not include an **executive branch.** It did call for a President, but he was just the person who presided over meetings of Congress. His job was to make sure the meetings ran smoothly. He had no special powers. The writers of the Constitution, however, believed the United States needed an executive branch. It would be the job of the executive branch to see to the day-to-day work of the government. In Article 2, they described the executive branch.

Read Article 2 after you examine this section.

The executive branch is the law-enforcing part of government. The President is the chief executive. Thus, the President has the power to carry out laws passed by Congress. The executive branch also includes a Vice-President, who would become the chief executive on the death or incapacity of the President.

The Constitution provides for a new President if one should die in office. Just hours after President Kennedy was killed, Vice-President Lyndon Johnson was on a jet headed for Washington, D.C. A federal judge conducted the swearing-in ceremony on board the plane.

Article 2 tells how the President is elected, who can be President, how to remove a President from office, and gives rules about the President's salary.

Article 2 describes the President's powers and duties. It gives the President the power to command the armed forces, to deal with the heads of other countries, and to appoint officials to help manage the executive branch. (Article 1 gives the President power to **veto** [vē′tō], or reject, bills passed by Congress. The President vetoes bills that he thinks are unwise. But Congress can overturn a veto with a two-thirds vote.)

The President's oath of office is in Article 2. Before becoming President, a person must take this oath: "I do solemnly swear (or affirm) that I will faithfully execute the office of President of the United States, and will to the best of my ability, preserve, pro-

Discuss: What is an oath? When else might you take one?

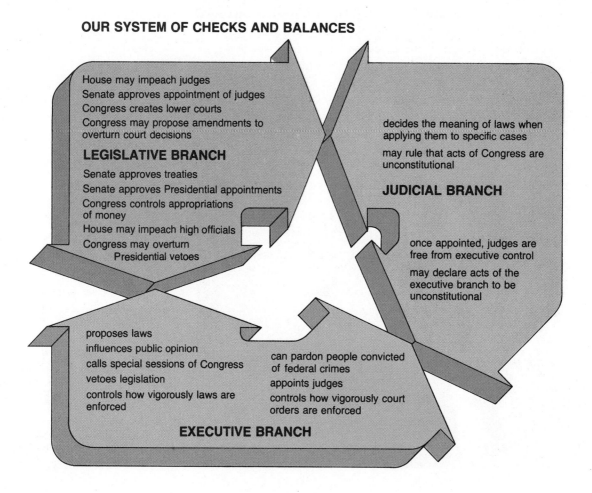

OUR SYSTEM OF CHECKS AND BALANCES

House may impeach judges
Senate approves appointment of judges
Congress creates lower courts
Congress may propose amendments to overturn court decisions

LEGISLATIVE BRANCH

Senate approves treaties
Senate approves Presidential appointments
Congress controls appropriations of money
House may impeach high officials
Congress may overturn Presidential vetoes

decides the meaning of laws when applying them to specific cases

may rule that acts of Congress are unconstitutional

JUDICIAL BRANCH

once appointed, judges are free from executive control

may declare acts of the executive branch to be unconstitutional

proposes laws
influences public opinion
calls special sessions of Congress
vetoes legislation
controls how vigorously laws are enforced

can pardon people convicted of federal crimes
appoints judges
controls how vigorously court orders are enforced

EXECUTIVE BRANCH

tect, and defend the Constitution of the United States." A President may be turned out of office for failing to live up to this oath. For example, a President who breaks the law is not carrying out the oath to "preserve, protect, and defend the Constitution."

Have the class read the oath orally or dramatize someone being sworn in.

You will read more about the executive branch in Chapters 8 and 9.

Discuss: What does the oath mean?

Article 3: Judicial Branch

There are two sets of courts in America, federal courts and state courts. The Constitution describes the federal court system in Article 3. (The states already had their own state court systems at the time the Constitution was written.) Federal courts are the **judicial branch** of our national government.

The Constitution makes the Supreme Court the head of the judicial branch. It gives Congress the power to create lower courts to help in the work of the judicial branch. The Constitution says that federal judges may keep their jobs until they die, so long as they do their work according to the law.

Article 3 says what powers the federal courts have and describes the kinds of cases that should be heard in federal courts. For instance, federal courts hear cases concerning the Constitution. This article also says that people accused of committing crimes against the United States government have the right to a trial by jury.

Federal Judge William Gurock hears an immigration case.

The most serious crime a person can commit against a government is called **treason.** In the history of the world, governments have often got rid of their critics by declaring they were guilty of treason. The writers of the Constitution wanted to protect United States citizens from this misuse of government power. In Article 3, they spelled out exactly what treason is: carrying on war against the United States or helping enemies of the United States. Article 3 says there are only two ways to convict a person of treason. That person must confess in open court or at least two witnesses must testify they saw the accused person commit the same act.

There is more information about the federal courts in Chapter 10.

Section Review

Vocabulary: executive branch, judicial branch, legislative branch, title of nobility, treason, veto.

Reviewing the Main Ideas

1. What are the three branches of government described in the Constitution?
2. Which branch makes laws?
3. Which branch enforces laws?
4. Which branch decides whether laws have been broken?
5. Which branch is headed by the President?
6. Why were powers and duties of government separated into three branches?

Skill Building

1. Read the President's oath of office (page 82). What is the main idea of this oath?
2. Look at Article 1, Section 7, Clause 1 on page 77. What does this passage say about how Congress can raise money?
3. Remember the Revolutionary War was fought over "taxation without representation." Why would the writers of the Constitution make the House of Representatives, and not the Senate, the place for tax laws to begin?
4. Look at Article 2, Section 3 on page 82. What does this passage say about the duties of the President?
5. Look at Article 3, Section 2, Clause 3 on page 83. What does this passage say about trials of people accused of crimes?

3/How State and National Governments Are Linked

How are the state governments linked? How are they tied to the national government? What must the national government do for the states? What do the state governments owe the national government? Answers to these questions can be found in Articles 4 and 6.

Article 4: The States

Article 4 describes how the several state governments are linked to each other and to the national government. It says that only Congress has the power to admit new states to the United States. The national government must make sure that the laws, records, and court decisions of each state are respected in other states.

Article 4 declares that citizens of each state shall enjoy the rights of citizenship in any other state of the union. A citizen of any state may enjoy the rights of citizenship throughout the United States. Also, a citizen accused of a crime cannot escape justice by going to another state. If an accused person does leave, he or she must be returned if the governor of the state where the crime was committed requests it. This process is called **extradition** [ek′strə dish′ən].

The national government must protect the states from invasion and keep law and order in the states. Thus, the national government may send armed forces into a state to put down riots or other acts that threaten the health, safety, and property of citizens.

Chapters 14 through 16 discuss in detail the organization and duties of state governments. They also tell about the rights of citizens in the fifty states.

Article 6: National Supremacy

Article 6 declares that the Constitution, the laws passed by Congress, and treaties made by the national government shall be the highest law in the land. This basic constitutional principle is called **national supremacy.** The state governments must accept that the national government is above them. No state government may act in any way that goes against the Constitution.

Since the Constitution is the highest law, the national government may *not* make a law which goes against the Constitution. Likewise, no state government may make a law which goes

Discuss: How many articles are there? How many related to the branches of government?

Discuss: What does the Constitution say about the role of state government?

The national government helps the states with troops and equipment in times of emergency. (Top) cleaning up after a blizzard in Boston and (bottom) another in Buffalo.

against either the Constitution or a law or **treaty** made by the national government.

A treaty is an agreement between the governments of two or more countries. Two-thirds of the members of the Senate must approve a treaty before it becomes an official agreement of the United States.

Article 5: Amending the Constitution

Note: Some students may find it helpful to summarize each of the articles.

The writers of the Constitution realized that if their work was to last, there needed to be ways to change the Constitution as society changed. They believed that both the national and state governments must take part in amending the Constitution. Article 5 describes how to amend the Constitution.

The most common procedure is for two-thirds of the members of Congress to vote for an amendment. Then three-fourths of the state legislatures have to approve the proposal in order for it to be added to the Constitution. All but one of the amendments to the Constitution have been made this way. The Twenty-First Amendment was approved by special conventions in three-fourths of the states rather than by votes in the state legislatures.

Opponents of the Equal Rights Amendment.

From 1789 to 1980, there have been twenty-six amendments to the Constitution. The first ten amendments, known as the Bill of Rights, were added in 1791. The Bill of Rights is discussed in Chapter 5, along with other amendments having to do with human rights and liberties.

Now, a twenty-seventh amendment is being considered by the states. This amendment, the Equal Rights Amendment (ERA), says: Equality of right under the law shall not be denied or abridged by the United States or by any State on account of sex.

Other amendments to the Constitution have been made to improve the way the government works. Three examples are the Sixteenth, Twenty-Second, and Twenty-Fifth Amendments.

The Sixteenth Amendment was passed in 1913 to allow the government to collect taxes on incomes earned by citizens. Before this law, most taxes were on goods offered for sale. That is, they were sales taxes and tariffs. The income tax was believed to be a fairer tax. It was passed to increase the money available to the government. Thus the government could provide more services that citizens wanted.

The Twenty-Second Amendment was passed in 1951 to keep a President from serving more than two four-year terms of office. It was passed after President Roosevelt was successful in being elected four times. Many people feared that a President could gain too much power by winning election again and again. To avoid this risk, they amended the Constitution.

The Twenty-Fifth Amendment was made in 1967 to spell out clearly how vacancies would be filled in the office of Vice-President. The President picks a Vice-President to fill a vacancy in that office. The President's choice must be approved by a majority vote of both houses of Congress. The Twenty-Fifth Amendment also tells how the Vice-President can take over the duties of the presidency in case the President is too ill to carry on. When the President recovers, he or she can take over again. If recovery does not seem likely, the Vice-President can be approved as the new President by a two-thirds vote of the Congress.

The Twenty-Fifth Amendment allows a President to resign from office. Whenever the office of President becomes vacant, the Vice-President fills it.

The amendments to the Constitution have improved our plan for government. Chapter 5 includes a discussion of amendments that were made to protect citizens' rights and of responsibilities of citizens to preserve and protect the Constitution.

Section Review

Vocabulary: extradition, national supremacy, treaty.

Reviewing the Main Ideas
1. What does the national government do for the states?
2. How may the Constitution be amended?
3. Why was the Sixteenth Amendment made?
4. Why was the Twenty-Second Amendment made?
5. Why was the Twenty-Fifth Amendment made?

Skill Building
1. In which article of the Constitution would you look to find out what rights citizens of one state have in the other states? What does this article say about the rights of citizens?
2. What is the main idea of Article 6?
3. To which of the goals of the Preamble is Article 6 linked? Explain your answer.

Supporters of the Equal Rights Amendment.

The Constitution Works!

During the summer of 1974, the government of the United States faced a crisis. President Richard Nixon had been accused of misusing the powers of his office. Some government officials backed their President. Others wanted to remove him from office. This conflict posed a threat to the orderly conduct of government.

The conflicts about President Nixon stemmed from the "Watergate Affair." On June 17, 1972, Washington city police arrested five men on charges of burglary. These men had broken into the national headquarters of the Democratic Party located in an office building called Watergate. It seemed that the men were trying to get information that could help Nixon and other Republican candidates beat the Democrats in the 1972 presidential elections.

Two reporters for the *Washington Post*, Carl Bernstein and Bob Woodward, turned the "Watergate Affair" into big news. They gathered information and wrote newspaper stories about the break-in. They found evidence that seemed to link the burglars to top government officials, including the President.

From the first, the President and his advisors denied any connection with the Watergate burglars. Yet as time passed, more and more evidence seemed to link the President to the Watergate Affair. In addition, Bernstein, Woodward, and others learned of more illegal acts that seemed to involve the White House staff. Unlawful gifts of money were made to the Committee to Re-elect the President. Illegal wiretaps were found on the phones of Nixon's opponents. Government officials were spying on American citizens that the White House staff said were "enemies." There was a long Enemies List that included many respected citizens—religious leaders, newspaper reporters, entertainers, and professors. The Internal Revenue Service had been told to harass people about their income tax because they had not cooperated with the White House.

The President and his advisors tried to cover up their involvement in illegal actions. They continued to deny any wrongdoing.

The United States Senate formed a special committee to look into the case. The Senate committee found the same evidence. Top White House officials seemed to be guilty of breaking federal laws. Even the President seemed to be involved.

Note: Some students may want to investigate this further. Have them make and explain a Watergate timeline.

(Left to right) Senate Watergate Committee members: Florida Senator Edward Gurney and Massachusetts Senator Lowell Weicker.

Senator Sam Ervin, Chairman of the Senate Watergate Committee, wrote in his official report: "Watergate was a conglomerate of various illegal and unethical activities in which various officers and employees of the Nixon Re-election Committees and Various White House aides of President Nixon participated in varying ways and degrees . . . ." Ervin's report concluded that several high-ranking officials in the executive branch had misused their constitutional powers.

In early August 1974, the Judiciary Committee of the House of Representatives faced a difficult decision. Should they vote to recommend impeaching the President? If so, they would take a big step toward forcing Nixon from office.

Article 1 gives the House of Representatives power to impeach a President. This means that the House publicly considers evidence that the President has committed crimes or otherwise misused his power. The House then decides, by majority vote, that the accused person should stand trial in the Senate.

First, the House Judiciary Committee looks over the evidence to be sure there is enough for it to be worth bringing the impeachment before the full House.

The Judiciary Committee members realized that there was evidence that seemed to indicate Nixon's involvement in questionable activities. Many felt that at least, he seemed to be guilty of foolish and unethical behavior unbecoming to a President. At most, he may have given approval for others to take part in illegal activities.

CASE STUDY

(Left) one of the policemen who arrested the Watergate burglars takes the oath before testifying at the Senate hearings. (Right) members of the Senate investigating committee: Tennessee Senator Howard Baker and Chairman Sam Ervin from North Carolina.

Some members of the Judiciary Committee decided that they should not vote to recommend impeachment. They believed it could cause the public to lose faith in the government. They also felt it might weaken the government so that it could not deal with pressing problems. Finally, they believed that Nixon had not done anything so bad that he should risk impeachment. The consequences of leaving Nixon alone would be better for the country than the consequences of impeaching him would be.

The majority of the committee, however, voted to recommend "the impeachment and trial and removal from office" of the President. The majority believed that Nixon possibly took part in activities that no President should. Thus, he should be impeached and tried publicly for acts of wrongdoing. A consequence of not impeaching him, they believed, might be to cause the public to lose faith in the government. Citizens might believe that government leaders could get away with illegal behavior. They felt it would be bad for the nation if citizens believed that any government official, even the President, is above the law.

It seemed likely that the full House of Representatives would follow the recommendation of the Judiciary Committee and vote to impeach President Nixon. If this happened, the next step would be a trial in the Senate. According to the Constitution, the Senate decides whether or not to remove a President from office. It takes a two-thirds majority to remove a President.

However, before the House of Representatives voted on impeachment, Nixon decided to resign. He spoke on television to the nation on August 8, 1974: ". . . I have concluded that be-

(Left) White House lawyer John Dean listens to his lawyer at the end of his fourth straight day of testifying about White House activities. (Right) President Nixon's televised resignation.

cause of the Watergate matter I might not have the support of Congress that I would consider necessary to back the very difficult decisions and carry out the duties of this office in the way the interests of the nation will require. . . . Therefore, I shall resign the presidency effective at noon tomorrow."

Thus, Vice-President Gerald Ford became President. A short time after taking office, President Ford named Nelson Rockefeller to be the new Vice-President. The Senate and the House of Representatives decided, by majority vote, to approve this appointment. These actions followed rules written in Section 2 of the Twenty-Fifth Amendment: "Whenever there is a vacancy in the office of the Vice-President, the President shall nominate a Vice-President who shall take office upon confirmation by a majority vote of both houses of Congress."

Nixon's dramatic departure from office showed the worth of the Constitution. The President had been forced from office according to the rules of the Constitution. Gerald Ford replaced Nixon according to constitutional law. A new Vice-President took office according to the Constitution.

No riots or other serious disorders marked this change of government power. No soldiers or police were used to put a new leader in the country's highest office. Nixon's opponents followed the law in taking actions to remove him from office. A peaceful, orderly transfer of leadership took place.

After taking office, President Ford remarked: "Our Constitution works; our great Republic is a government of laws and not of men. . . ."

Reviewing the Case Study

1. What were the alternatives facing the House Judiciary Committee in this case?
2. How did the majority of the committee view the likely consequences of the alternatives?
3. Why did Nixon decide to resign?
4. Explain what President Ford meant when he said that "our Constitution works."
5. Why is it important to have clear rules, which everyone accepts, to guide the transfer of government power from one person to another?

Discuss: How did it show the worth of the Constitution?

Discuss: How do the pictures on pp. 68–71 help to explain the case?

Nixon waves good-by before boarding a helicopter on the White House lawn to leave the presidency.

Chapter Four Test and Activities

★★★

Vocabulary

Match the following words with their meanings.

1. Preamble
2. domestic
3. treaty
4. executive branch
5. legislative branch
6. judicial branch
7. veto
8. general welfare
9. treason
10. title of nobility
11. extradition.
12. national supremacy
13. tranquility

a. the introduction to the Constitution
b. to do with one's own country—not foreign
c. the law-enforcing branch of government
d. the federal courts
e. a formal agreement between two or more countries
f. the power to reject a bill
g. the law-making branch of government
h. the most serious crime a person can commit against a government
i. peacefulness
j. return by one state to another of a person accused of a crime
k. the health, prosperity, and happiness of all
l. a name showing rank, such as *duchess*
m. the idea that the nation is above the state

Reviewing Chapter Ideas

1. The President cannot _____ .
   a. veto bills passed by Congress
   b. meet with the leaders of other countries
   c. break the law
   d. command the armed forces
2. Which of the following can Congress make laws about?
   a. taxes
   b. regulating trade and business
   c. coining money
   d. all of the above
3. True or false: Congress is made up of the Senate and House of Representatives.
4. True or false: The main purpose of the Constitution is to help people live according to law.
5. True or false: The main part of the Constitution is divided into ten articles.
6. True or false: The first three articles explain the three branches of government.
7. Where in the Constitution could you find out how state and national governments are related?
   a. Article 2
   b. Article 4
   c. Article 6
   d. b and c
8. The first ten amendments are known as _____ .
9. There are _____ amendments to the Constitution.
10. True or false: In order for a bill to become a law at least half of the members of the Senate and House of Representatives must vote for it.

Using Basic Social Studies Skills

Finding Information

The Preamble to the Constitution states six purposes for the Constitution. Find them and name them.

Vocabulary
1. a   4. c   7. f   10. l   13. i
2. b   5. g   8. k   11. j
3. e   6. d   9. h   12. m

Ideas
1. c   4. T   7. d   10. F
2. d   5. F   8. Bill of Rights
3. T   6. T   9. 26

72

★★★

Comprehending Information

Rewrite the six purposes of the Constitution in your own words.

Organizing Information

1. Name the three branches of government.
2. List three purposes of each of the branches of government.

Evaluating Information

Use the Constitution to answer the questions below. For each case, give the Article, Section, and clause numbers that you would use to support your opinion.

1. Bernard Levin is Jewish. He is 27 years old and works as an insurance salesman. He is an American citizen because he was born in the United States. He wants to be elected to the House of Representatives. Does he meet the qualifications?
2. Marcia Collins, a 35-year-old lawyer, is black. In her work she has sometimes represented people who had problems with the government. She believes she could improve life in the United States if she were a senator. She is a citizen. Does she qualify?
3. The members of both houses of Congress voted themselves a raise in pay. The raise would start on the next Monday. The vote was passed by a two-thirds majority. Will they get their raise?
4. The country needed more money to give the people in the armed services a raise. Because the President is commander in chief of the armed services, he was particularly interested in the problem. So he passed a law raising everyone's income tax by one-half of one percent. Do people have to pay this new tax?
5. A state built a highway that ran across the state. To help pay for it, the state legisla-

ture passed a law calling for tolls at both ends. People going in and out of the state on the highway had to pay the toll. Do citizens of other states have to pay the toll?

Communicating Ideas

Write a paragraph explaining why we have a Constitution. Use at least five of the words from the Vocabulary. Underline each vocabulary word that you use.

Using Decision-Making Skills

Make a decision tree showing the alternatives and consequences President Nixon faced in deciding to resign.

Activities

1. For students who want to learn more about the Constitution or "Watergate," the following books are recommended:

   (a) *The Constitution: A Documentary and Narrative History*, by Page Smith (Morrow, 1978).

   (b) *The Constitution* by Joyce L. Stevos (Scott, Foresman and Company, 1978).

   (c) *Watergate: America in Crisis*, by Jules Archer (Crowell, 1975).

2. Study recent newspapers to find articles that show ways our Constitution works today.

3. Write a constitution for the classroom. Include a preamble that gives goals for classroom government. Include different articles that describe who has power to make what kinds of rules, who has power to enforce rules, who has power to judge whether or not rules have been broken. If there are any powers you feel the classroom government should not have, articles in your constitution should describe them.

The Constitution of the United States

The Constitution is printed in black. The parts that are no longer in force have been crossed out. The spelling and punctuation have been modernized. An explanation of the Constitution is printed in color. The explanation and the headings are not a part of the Constitution.

Preamble

We the people of the United States, in order to form a more perfect Union, establish justice, insure domestic tranquillity, provide for the common defense, promote the general welfare, and secure the blessings of liberty to ourselves and our posterity, do ordain and establish this Constitution for the United States of America.

The writers of the Constitution had six goals: (1) to have a better government than they had under the Articles of Confederation, (2) to have lawful ways of settling conflicts, (3) to have peace in all the states, (4) to be able to protect themselves and the country from enemies, (5) to have good living conditions, and (6) to have freedom for themselves and for future Americans. Most importantly, the Preamble says that "we the people" are the authority for the Constitution.

Article 1/Legislative Branch

Section 1/Congress

All legislative powers herein granted shall be vested in a Congress of the United States, which shall consist of a Senate and House of Representatives.

Legislative power is the power to make laws. All of the power to make laws for the United States is given to a group of people called Congress. Congress is divided into two parts, called houses. One house is the Senate; the other, the House of Representatives.

Section 2/House of Representatives

Clause 1 The House of Representatives shall be composed of members chosen every second year by the people of the several states, and the electors in each state shall have the qualifications requisite for electors of the most numerous branch of the state legislature.

Representatives are chosen every two years by the voters of each state. Citizens who are allowed to vote for state legislators are also qualified to vote for their representative in the national legislature. This clause gives each state the power to decide who is qualified to vote. Several amendments have put limitations on the voting laws states can make. Today, nearly every adult citizen is qualified to be a voter.

Clause 2 No person shall be a representative who shall not have attained to the age of twenty-five years, and been seven years a citizen of the United States, and who shall not, when elected, be an inhabitant of that state in which he shall be chosen.

A representative must be at least twenty-five years old, must have been a United States citizen for at least seven years, and must live in the state from which he or she is chosen.

Clause 3 Representatives and direct taxes shall be apportioned among the several states which may be included within this Union, according to their respective numbers, which shall be determined by adding to the whole number of free persons, including those bound to service for a term of years, and excluding Indians not taxed, three-fifths of all other persons.

The actual enumeration shall be made within three years after the first meeting of the Congress of the United States, and within every subsequent term of ten years, in such manner as they shall by law direct.

The number of representatives shall not exceed one for every thirty thousand, but each state shall have at least one representative; and until such enumeration shall be made, the state of New Hampshire shall be entitled to choose three, Massachusetts eight, Rhode Island and Providence Plantations one, Connecticut five, New York six, New Jersey four, Pennsylvania eight, Delaware one, Maryland six, Virginia ten, North Carolina five, South Carolina five, and Georgia three.

The number of representatives a state has is based on the number of people in the state. A *census,* or count of the people, must be taken every ten years. Congress decides how the count shall be made and uses the census results to decide how many representatives each state shall have. Since 1910, Congress has limited the number of representatives to 435. By 1970, each member of the House served about 465,000 people.

Clause 4 When vacancies happen in the representation from any state, the executive authority thereof shall issue writs of election to fill such vacancies.

If a representative dies or leaves office, the governor of the state he or she represents calls an election to fill the vacancy.

Clause 5 The House of Representatives shall choose their speaker and other officers; and shall have the sole power of impeachment.

The presiding officer of the House of Representatives is called the Speaker. Every two years a new Congress meets. At that time the Speaker of the House and other officers are elected by the representatives.

Only the House of Representatives has the power to *impeach*. This is the power to decide whether or not high executive or judicial officers should go to trial for serious misbehavior in office. When a person is impeached, he or she is formally charged with wrongdoing. Impeachment does not mean guilt. The Senate decides whether or not the impeached person is guilty.

Section 3/Senate

Clause 1 The Senate of the United States shall be composed of two senators from each state, chosen by the legislature thereof, for six years; and each senator shall have one vote.

The Senate is made up of two senators from each state who serve six-year terms. Both get to vote. Amendment 17 has changed the way senators are chosen.

Clause 2 Immediately after they shall be assembled in consequence of the first election, they shall be divided as equally as may be into three classes. The seats of the senators of the first class shall be vacated at the expiration of the second year, of the second class at the expiration of the fourth year, and of the third class at the expiration of the sixth year, so that one-third may be chosen every second year; and if vacancies happen by resignation, or otherwise, during the recess of the legislature of any state, the executive thereof may make temporary appointments until the next meeting of the legislature, which shall then fill such vacancies.

The terms of senators in the first Congress were arranged so that one-third of the senators would change every two years. This is still true. Unlike the House, which can change greatly after one election, the Senate changes slowly.

Clause 3 No person shall be a senator who shall not have attained to the age of thirty years, and been nine years a citizen of the United States, and who shall not, when elected, be an inhabitant of that state for which he shall be chosen.

A senator must be at least thirty years old and a United States citizen for at least nine years. At the time of election, a senator must live in the state that he or she represents.

Clause 4 The Vice-President of the United States shall be president of the Senate, but shall have no vote, unless they be equally divided.

The Vice-President presides at Senate meetings, but votes only if there is a tie.

Clause 5 The Senate shall choose their other officers, and also a president pro tempore, in the absence of the Vice-President, or when he shall exercise the office of President of the United States.

The Senate chooses its other officers, including a person to preside at Senate meetings when the Vice-President is absent. This person is called the President pro tempore, or pro tem for short.

Clause 6 The Senate shall have the sole power to try all impeachments. When sitting for that purpose, they shall be on oath or affirmation. When the President of the United States is tried, the Chief Justice shall preside; and no person shall be convicted without the concurrence of two-thirds of the members present.

Only the Senate has the power to try officials impeached by the House of Representatives. The Senate sits as a jury, and the senators must take an oath to try the case fairly. (The writers of the Constitution knew that some religions do not allow people to take oaths. So they provided that a senator could swear or affirm. *Affirm* means "to declare positively that something is true.") If the President is on trial, the Chief Justice of the United States presides over the trial. In other cases the Vice-President presides. To convict, two-thirds of the senators present must vote guilty.

Impeachment gives Congress a check on both the President and the judicial branch. However, this check is rarely used. In all, the House has impeached only twelve individuals including one President, Andrew Johnson. Only four, all judges, were found guilty by the Senate.

Clause 7 Judgment in cases of impeachment shall not extend further than to removal from office and disqualification to hold and enjoy any office of honor, trust, or profit under the United States; but the party convicted shall nevertheless be liable and subject to indictment, trial, judgment, and punishment, according to law.

The Senate's power to punish a convicted official is limited. All it can do is remove the official from office and keep him or her from ever holding another office in the United States government. However, the official may still be tried in the regular courts for any crimes that caused the loss of office. The official may be punished according to the laws if found guilty.

Section 4/Congressional Elections and Meetings

Clause 1 The times, places, and manner of holding elections for senators and representatives shall be prescribed in each state by the legislature thereof; but the Congress may at any time by law make or alter such regulations, except as to the places of choosing senators.

Each state may decide when, where, and how elections for its senators and representatives are held. However, Congress may pass laws that overrule the state laws.

Clause 2 The Congress shall assemble at least once in every year, and such meeting shall be on the first Monday in December, unless they shall by law appoint a different day.

Congress must meet at least once a year.

Section 5/Congressional Rules

Clause 1 Each house shall be the judge of the elections, returns, and qualifications of its own members, and a majority of each shall constitute a quorum to do business; but a smaller number may adjourn from day to day, and may be authorized to compel the attendance of absent members, in such manner, and under such penalties as each house may provide.

This clause gives Congress the power to decide whether elected members may take office. This power is mainly used when an election is so close that the winner changes each time the ballots are recounted.

Neither the House nor the Senate can hold meetings for business unless it has a *quorum*. That is, more than half the members must be present. The Senate and the House of Representatives also can each make rules and set penalties for not attending meetings.

Clause 2 Each house may determine the rules of its proceedings, punish its members for disorderly behavior, and, with the concurrence of two-thirds, expel a member.

The House and the Senate each make rules for conducting their business. They may punish their members for not following these rules. In either the House or the Senate, two-thirds of the members must agree if they wish to expel a member.

Clause 3 Each house shall keep a journal of its proceedings, and from time to time publish the same, excepting such parts as may in their judgment require secrecy; and the yeas and nays of the members of either house on any question shall, at the desire of one-fifth of those present, be entered on the journal.

The House of Representatives and the Senate must each keep a record of what is done at its meetings. Most of what is said is printed in the *Congressional Record*. When the members decide to keep some matters secret, those things are not printed in the record. If one-fifth of the members present favor it, the record must show how each member voted on any question.

Clause 4 Neither house, during the session of Congress, shall, without the consent of the other, adjourn for more than three days, nor to any other place than that in which the two houses shall be sitting.

During the period that Congress is in session, neither the House nor the Senate shall let three days pass without holding a meeting. Both houses must agree to any recess that lasts more than three days. Both houses must meet in the same city.

Along with other parts of this section, this clause gives Congress power to decide when and where it should meet. Without this power, the Congress could be forced to meet somewhere else without all members present.

Section 6/Congressional Privileges and Restrictions

Clause 1 The senators and representatives shall receive a compensation for their services, to be ascertained by law, and paid out of the treasury of the United States.

They shall in all cases, except treason, felony, and breach of the peace, be privileged from arrest during their attendance at the session of their respective houses, and in going to and returning from the same; and for any speech or debate in either house, they shall not be questioned in any other place.

Senators and representatives are paid out of the

United States Treasury according to the law that sets their salaries.

When members of Congress are attending meetings of Congress, or are going to and from meetings, they cannot be arrested except for treason, serious crime, or breaking the peace. They cannot be sued for anything they say in their meetings, even if it is criminal, except by the house to which they belong.

This clause protects members of Congress from abuses that legislators in other places have faced. Representatives and senators are protected from interference in doing their duty.

Clause 2 No senator or representative shall, during the time for which he was elected, be appointed to any civil office under the authority of the United States which shall have been created, or the emoluments whereof shall have been increased during such time; and no person holding any office under the United States shall be a member of either house during his continuance in office.

Senators and representatives cannot hold other United States government offices while they are members of Congress. During the term for which they have been elected, they cannot resign and take a government position that Congress created during that term. They also cannot take any position for which Congress increased the salary during that term. This provision was included so that no member of Congress would be able to profit personally from laws that he or she helped pass.

Section 7/How Bills Become Laws

Clause 1 All bills for raising revenue shall originate in the House of Representatives; but the Senate may propose or concur with amendments as on other bills.

All bills for raising money must begin in the House of Representatives, which originally was the only group in the United States government that was directly elected by the people. The Senate may amend these bills and usually does. In fact, sometimes it even substitutes an entirely different bill.

Clause 2 Every bill which shall have passed the House of Representatives and the Senate, shall, before it becomes a law, be presented to the President of the United States. If he approves, he shall sign it, but if not he shall return it, with his objections, to that house in which it shall have originated, who shall enter the objections at large on their journal, and proceed to reconsider it. If after such reconsideration two-thirds of that house shall agree to pass

the bill, it shall be sent, together with the objections, to the other house, by which it shall likewise be reconsidered, and if approved by two-thirds of that house, it shall become a law. But in all such cases the votes of both houses shall be determined by yeas and nays, and the names of the persons voting for and against the bill shall be entered on the journal of each house respectively.

If any bill shall not be returned by the President within ten days (Sundays excepted) after it shall have been presented to him, the same shall be a law, in like manner as if he had signed it, unless the Congress by their adjournment prevents its return, in which case it shall not be a law.

For a bill to become a law, it must first pass both houses of Congress. It then becomes a law in one of three ways: (1) the President signs it within ten days (not counting Sundays) of its having been presented, or (2) the President does not sign it, but neither does he or she veto it within the ten-day period, or (3) the President vetoes the bill, but a two-thirds majority of both houses overrides the veto.

Bills passed in the last ten days that Congress is in session must be signed by the President or they do not become law. The President's refusal to sign one of these bills is called a *pocket veto.*

This clause includes checks on both the President and Congress. Congress must pass a bill before the President can sign it or veto it. Thus Congress checks the President. The President's veto is a check on Congress. However, Congress has another check on the President. It can override the veto.

Clause 3 Every order, resolution, or vote to which the concurrence of the Senate and House of Representatives may be necessary (except on a question of adjournment) shall be presented to the President of the United States; and before the same shall take effect, shall be approved by him, or being disapproved by him, shall be repassed by two-thirds of the Senate and House of Representatives, according to the rules and limitations prescribed in the case of a bill.

The President's approval is needed for matters other than laws. If an order, resolution, or vote must be approved by both houses of Congress, it must be approved by the President. As with bills, the President can veto any of these actions, and Congress can override the veto. However, Congress does not need the President's approval to end its meetings for the year.

Section 8/Powers of Congress

Section 8 of Article 1 describes the powers of Congress. It is, therefore, one of the most important parts of the Constitution, for the list of congressional powers is also a list of the major powers of the United States government. The first seventeen clauses list the *expressed* powers of Congress. Clause 18 is the source of the *implied* powers of Congress.

Clause 1 The Congress shall have power to lay and collect taxes, duties, imposts, and excises, to pay the debts and provide for the common defense and general welfare of the United States; but all duties, imposts, and excises shall be uniform throughout the United States;

Congress has the power to raise money by taxing. Taxes can be used (1) to pay the debts of the central government, (2) to defend the country, and (3) to provide services for the good of all the people. All federal taxes, duties, and excise taxes must be the same in all parts of the country.

Clause 2 To borrow money on the credit of the United States;

Congress has power to borrow money for the government to use. The Constitution sets no limit on the amount Congress can borrow.

Clause 3 To regulate commerce with foreign nations, and among the several states, and with the Indian tribes;

Congress can pass laws to control trade with other countries, among the states, and with groups of Indians. The power to regulate commerce has been interpreted loosely. Congress has used this power to set up national banks, regulate radio and television broadcasting, and set speed limits on federal highways.

Clause 4 To establish a uniform rule of naturalization, and uniform laws on the subject of bankruptcies throughout the United States;

Congress can pass laws that say how people born in other countries can become United States citizens. This is the process of *naturalization.* Congress can also pass a bankruptcy law for all the states. *Bankruptcy* is the legal term for "going broke." The federal government was given the power to deal with bankruptcy because it is closely related to commerce.

Clause 5 To coin money, regulate the value thereof, and of foreign coin, and fix the standard of weights and measures;

Congress has power to coin money and to say how much it is worth. It also has the power to say how much foreign money is worth in American money. Congress has the power to define weights and measures so that they will be the same throughout the nation.

Clause 6 To provide for the punishment of counterfeiting the securities and current coin of the United States;

Congress has power to punish persons who make fake government bonds, stamps, or money.

Clause 7 To establish post offices and post roads;

Congress can provide post offices and roads to be used in delivering the mail.

Clause 8 To promote the progress of science and useful arts, by securing for limited times to authors and inventors the exclusive rights to their respective writings and discoveries;

Congress can help science, industry, and the arts by passing patent and copyright laws. Such laws prevent others from profiting from the work of inventors and writers for a certain length of time.

Clause 9 To constitute tribunals inferior to the Supreme Court;

Congress has power to set up courts that are lower in authority than the Supreme Court of the United States.

Clause 10 To define and punish piracies and felonies committed on the high seas, and offenses against the law of nations;

Congress has power to make laws about crimes committed on the seas or oceans. Congress also has power to describe punishments for breaking laws that are recognized by all nations—international law.

Clause 11 To declare war, grant letters of marque and reprisal, and make rules concerning captures on land and water;

Congress has the power to declare war. Congress was originally allowed to give persons permission to capture or destroy ships and goods of enemy nations without being guilty of piracy. This power was given up in 1856 when Congress agreed to follow a rule of international law. Congress can still make rules about seizing enemy property on land or sea.

Clause 12 To raise and support armies, but no appropriation of money to that use shall be for a longer term than two years;

Clause 13 To provide and maintain a navy;

Clause 14 To make rules for the government and regulation of the land and naval forces;

Congress has the power to raise an army and a

navy and to give them supplies. But Congress may not provide money for the army for more than two years at a time. No time limit was put on appropriations for the navy. Congress also has the power to make rules for the organization and control of the armed services.

Clause 15   To provide for calling forth the militia to execute the laws of the Union, suppress insurrections and repel invasions;

The volunteer armed forces of the different states used to be called the *militia.* Since the National Defense Act of 1916, it has been called the National Guard. This clause gives Congress the power to call out the Guard (1) to enforce the national laws, (2) to put down rebellion, and (3) to drive out invading armies.

Clause 16   To provide for organizing, arming, and disciplining the militia, and for governing such part of them as may be employed in the service of the United States, reserving to the states respectively the appointment of the officers and the authority of training the militia according to the discipline prescribed by Congress;

Congress has the power to organize, arm, and discipline the National Guard. Each state has the power to appoint the officers of its Guard and to see that the soldiers are trained according to rules made by Congress.

Clause 17   To exercise exclusive legislation in all cases whatsoever, over such district (not exceeding ten miles square) as may, by cession of particular states, and the acceptance of Congress, become the seat of the government of the United States, and to exercise like authority over all places purchased by the consent of the legislature of the state in which the same shall be, for the erection of forts, magazines, arsenals, dock-yards, and other needful buildings;

This clause gives Congress the power to govern the District of Columbia, the national capital. In 1974, Congress gave the District a charter allowing a mayor and a thirteen-member city council. Still, Congress can overrule city council actions. Congress also governs all places bought from the states for forts, ammunition storage, navy yards, and other uses.

Clause 18   And to make all laws which shall be necessary and proper for carrying into execution the foregoing powers, and all other powers vested by this Constitution in the government of the United States, or in any department or officer thereof.

Congress has the power to make all laws needed to carry out the powers granted in clauses 1–17. Congress also has the power to make all laws needed to carry out powers the Constitution grants to the government or to officials. Clause 18 is called the "elastic clause" because it stretches Congress's powers. It does *not* give Congress power to do whatever it wants. However, this clause has been interpreted generously, and this has increased the power of the United States government.

Section 9/Powers Forbidden to Congress

Clause 1   The migration or importation of such persons as any of the states now existing shall think proper to admit, shall not be prohibited by the Congress prior to the year one thousand eight hundred and eight, but a tax or duty may be imposed on such importation, not exceeding ten dollars for each person.

This clause was part of a compromise between those who favored slavery and those who were opposed to it. It said that Congress could not outlaw slavery before 1808. However, Congress could put a tax as high as $10 on each slave brought into the country. The writers did not use the word *slave* anywhere in the original Constitution. Even the expression "such persons" was part of a compromise.

Clause 2   The privilege of the writ of habeas corpus shall not be suspended, unless when in cases of rebellion or invasion the public safety may require it.

The government cannot arrest and imprison people without showing reason to believe they have broken the law. When a person is arrested, the friends or family can go into court and ask for a *writ of habeas corpus* [hā′bē əs kôr′pəs]. This order directs the jailer to bring the prisoner immediately into court. People can see if the prisoner is all right. The arresting officials must then release the prisoner or give the charges against him or her. Clause 2 says that only when the country is in danger of rebellion or invasion can Congress stop this important guarantee of personal liberty.

Clause 3   No bill of attainder or ex post facto law shall be passed.

Congress cannot pass a bill of attainder—a law convicting or punishing a particular person. This is important to the separation of powers. The legislature must pass general laws. It is up to the courts to decide on the guilt and punishment of specific individuals. Also, Congress cannot pass an ex post facto law—a law that puts penalties on something that was not illegal at the time it was done.

Clause 4 No capitation, or other direct, tax shall be laid, unless in proportion to the census or enumeration herein before directed to be taken.

The only kind of direct taxes on individuals that Congress can levy must be divided among the states in proportion to population. Amendment 16 allowed Congress to pass income taxes.

Clause 5 No tax or duty shall be laid on articles exported from any state.

Congress cannot levy export taxes, that is, it cannot tax goods or products being sent out of any state.

Clause 6 No preference shall be given by any regulation of commerce or revenue to the ports of one state over those of another; nor shall vessels bound to, or from, one state, be obliged to enter, clear, or pay duties in another.

Congress cannot make laws that favor one state over another in matters of trade and commerce. Ships from any state may enter the ports of other states without paying duties.

Clause 7 No money shall be drawn from the treasury, but in consequence of appropriations made by law; and a regular statement and account of the receipts and expenditures of all public money shall be published from time to time.

Government money can be spent only if Congress passes a law for that purpose. An account of how much money is collected and how it is spent must be made public.

Clause 8 No title of nobility shall be granted by the United States; and no person holding any office of profit or trust under them, shall, without the consent of the Congress, accept of any present, emolument, office, or title, of any kind whatever, from any king, prince, or foreign state.

The United States government cannot give a title of nobility (such as count, duchess, earl) to anyone. No one in the service of the United States can accept a title, a present, or a position from another country without permission of Congress. This clause was intended to prevent foreign governments from corrupting United States officials.

Section 10/Powers Forbidden to the States

Clause 1 No state shall enter into any treaty, alliance, or confederation; grant letters of marque and reprisal; coin money; emit bills of credit; make any thing but gold and silver coin a tender in pay-

ment of debts; pass any bill of attainder, ex post facto law, or law impairing the obligation of contracts, or grant any title of nobility.

This clause lists eight things states cannot do. (1) States cannot make treaties with other countries. Nor can they become a part of some other country. (2) States cannot give private citizens permission to fight other countries. (3) States cannot coin their own money or issue paper money. (4) States cannot pass laws that allow anything other than gold and silver to be used as money. (5) States cannot pass laws declaring a particular person guilty of an offense and describing the punishment. (6) States cannot pass laws that would punish a person for something that was not against the law when it was done. (7) States cannot pass laws that excuse people from carrying out lawful agreements. (8) States cannot give titles of nobility.

Clause 2 No state shall, without the consent of the Congress, lay any imposts or duties on imports or exports, except what may be absolutely necessary for executing its inspection laws; and the net produce of all duties and imposts, laid by any state on imports or exports, shall be for the use of the treasury of the United States; and all such laws shall be subject to the revision and control of the Congress.

Clause 3 No state shall, without the consent of Congress, lay any duty of tonnage, keep troops or ships of war in time of peace, enter into any agreement or compact with another state, or with a foreign power, or engage in war, unless actually invaded, or in such imminent danger as will not admit of delay.

These two clauses list actions that states may take only with the approval of Congress. States cannot tax goods entering or leaving a state unless Congress agrees. However, states may charge an inspection fee if necessary. Any profit from state import or export taxes approved by Congress must go into the United States Treasury, and these state tax laws may be changed by Congress. Unless Congress provides otherwise, states may not tax ships, or keep troops (except the National Guard) or warships in time of peace. States cannot make alliances with other states or with foreign countries unless Congress agrees. States cannot go to war unless they have been invaded or are in such great danger that delay would be disastrous.

Article 2/Executive Branch

Section 1/President and Vice-President

Clause 1 The executive power shall be vested in a President of the United States of America. He shall hold his office during the term of four years, and, together with the Vice-President, chosen for the same term, be elected as follows:

Executive power is the power to make sure that laws are put into force. This power is given to the President, who is the chief executive of the United States government. The President serves a four-year term of office. The Vice-President is elected at the same time as the President and serves the same term.

Clause 2 Each state shall appoint, in such manner as the legislature thereof may direct, a number of electors, equal to the whole number of senators and representatives to which the state may be entitled in the Congress; but no senator or representative, or person holding an office of trust or profit under the United States, shall be appointed an elector.

The people do not elect the President directly, although they do have a great deal to say about who will be elected President. A group of electors known as the *electoral college* votes the President into office. Each state legislature decides on the way its electors are chosen. The number of electors from each state is equal to the total number of senators and representatives the state has in Congress. No senators or representatives or anyone holding a position in the national government may be an elector.

Clause 3 The electors shall meet in their respective states, and vote by ballot for two persons, of whom one at least shall not be an inhabitant of the same state with themselves. And they shall make a list of all the persons voted for, and of the number of votes for each; which list they shall sign and certify, and transmit sealed to the seat of the government of the United States, directed to the president of the Senate. The president of the Senate shall, in the presence of the Senate and House of Representatives, open all the certificates, and the votes shall then be counted. The person having the greatest number of votes shall be the President, if such number be a majority of the whole number of electors appointed; and if there be more than one who have such majority, and have an equal number of votes, then the House of Representatives shall immediately choose by ballot one of them for President;

and if no person have a majority, then from the five highest on the list the said House shall in like manner choose the President. But in choosing the President, the votes shall be taken by states, the representation from each state having one vote; a quorum for this purpose shall consist of a member or members from two-thirds of the states, and a majority of all the states shall be necessary to a choice. In every case, after the choice of the President, the person having the greatest number of votes of the electors shall be the Vice-President. But if there should remain two or more who have equal votes, the Senate shall choose from them by ballot the Vice-President.

This clause describes the original way of electing the President and Vice-President. It was changed by Amendment 12.

Clause 4 The Congress may determine the time of choosing the electors, and the day on which they shall give their votes; which day shall be the same throughout the United States.

Congress has power to choose the date electors are chosen and the date they vote. That day must be the same throughout the United States. Congress has set the Tuesday after the first Monday in November in every fourth year as Election Day, the date for choosing electors. The electors cast their votes on the Monday after the second Wednesday in December.

Clause 5 No person except a natural-born citizen, or a citizen of the United States at the time of the adoption of this Constitution, shall be eligible to the office of President; neither shall any person be eligible to that office who shall not have attained to the age of thirty-five years, and been fourteen years a resident within the United States.

To be President, a person must have been born a citizen. The person must be at least thirty-five years old and must have lived in the United States for fourteen years. (Foreign-born persons who were citizens when the Constitution was adopted were also eligible to be President.)

Clause 6 In case of the removal of the President from office, or of his death, resignation, or inability to discharge the powers and duties of the said office, the same shall devolve on the Vice-President, and the Congress may by law provide for the case of removal, death, resignation or inability, both of the President and Vice-President, declaring what officer shall then act as President, and such officer shall act accordingly, until the disability be removed, or a President shall be elected.

This clause describes the original method for the Vice-President to become President. It has been changed by Amendment 25.

Clause 7 The President shall, at stated times, receive for his services, a compensation, which shall neither be increased nor diminished during the period for which he shall have been elected, and he shall not receive within that period any other emolument from the United States, or any of them.

The President's salary cannot be lowered or raised during his or her term of office. While in office the President cannot receive any other salary from the United States government or from any of the state governments.

Clause 8 Before he enter on the execution of his office, he shall take the following oath or affirmation:—"I do solemnly swear (or affirm) that I will faithfully execute the office of President of the United States, and will to the best of my ability, preserve, protect and defend the Constitution of the United States."

Before taking office, the President must take an oath of office, promising to carry out the duties of the job and make sure the Constitution is obeyed.

Section 2/Powers of the President

Clause 1 The President shall be commander in chief of the army and navy of the United States, and of the militia of the several states, when called into the actual service of the United States; he may require the opinion, in writing, of the principal officer in each of the executive departments, upon any subject relating to the duties of their respective offices, and he shall have power to grant reprieves and pardons for offenses against the United States, except in cases of impeachment.

The President commands all of the armed forces in the United States, including the National Guard when it is called into national service.

The President is the chief executive or head of all of the department heads in the executive branch. The department heads report to the President on their work in the day-to-day operation of the government.

The President has power to postpone sentences or pardon those convicted of federal crimes. However, the President cannot interfere with impeachment cases.

Clause 2 He shall have power, by and with the advice and consent of the Senate, to make treaties, provided two-thirds of the senators present concur;

and he shall nominate, and by and with the advice and consent of the Senate, shall appoint ambassadors, other public ministers and consuls, judges of the Supreme Court, and all other officers of the United States, whose appointments are not herein otherwise provided for, and which shall be established by law; but the Congress may by law vest the appointment of such inferior officers, as they think proper, in the President alone, in the courts of law, or in the heads of departments.

The President has power to make treaties with foreign countries. But at a meeting of the Senate, two-thirds of the senators present must approve any treaty.

The President appoints ambassadors, justices of the Supreme Court, and other government officials whose jobs are not described in the Constitution. All must be approved by a majority vote of the Senate. The requirement that the Senate must approve treaties and appointments is a check on the President. The leaders of the executive departments—the *Cabinet*—are among the officials who must be approved by the Senate. However, the President alone has the power to fire them.

Congress may pass laws allowing the President, the courts, or heads of government departments to appoint less important officials.

Clause 3 The President shall have power to fill up all vacancies that may happen during the recess of the Senate, by granting commissions which shall expire at the end of their next session.

The President may temporarily appoint people to fill vacancies that appear while Congress is not in session. These appointments last until the end of the next meeting of the Senate.

Section 3/Other Presidential Powers

He shall from time to time give to the Congress information of the state of the Union, and recommend to their consideration such measures as he shall judge necessary and expedient; he may, on extraordinary occasions, convene both houses, or either of them, and in case of disagreement between them, with respect to the time of adjournment, he may adjourn them to such time as he shall think proper; he shall receive ambassadors and other public ministers; he shall take care that the laws be faithfully executed, and shall commission all the officers of the United States.

This Section is the source of the President's role as chief legislator. It calls for the President to speak regularly to Congress about the nation's condition. This is the State of the Union message the President gives at the beginning of each session of Congress. The President has power to recommend laws and advise Congress about changes in government.

In emergencies, the President may call a meeting of either or both houses of Congress. If the houses of Congress disagree about when to end their meeting, the President may decide when to end it.

The President is the official who meets with representatives of other countries. This power makes the President chief foreign-policy maker because the power to receive ambassadors is the power to recognize foreign governments.

It is the duty of the President to see that the laws of the country are followed. The President must sign the papers that give officers the right to hold their positions.

Section 4/Impeachment

The President, Vice-President and all civil officers of the United States, shall be removed from office on impeachment for, and conviction of, treason, bribery, or other high crimes and misdemeanors.

The President, Vice-President, and other officers of the United States government (except congressmen and military officers) will lose their position in government if they are impeached and convicted of certain crimes.

Article 3/Judicial Branch

Section 1/Federal Courts

The judicial power of the United States, shall be vested in one Supreme Court, and in such inferior courts as the Congress may from time to time ordain and establish. The judges, both of the supreme and inferior courts, shall hold their offices during good behavior, and shall, at stated times, receive for their services, a compensation, which shall not be diminished during their continuance in office.

Judicial power is the power to decide cases in a court of law. This power is given to the Supreme Court and to lower courts set up by Congress. Once appointed, judges hold office for life or until they have been found guilty of wrongful acts. The salary paid to a judge cannot be lowered so long as he or she holds office. The writers of the Constitution wanted judges to be free of political pressures. The provisions about judges' salaries and terms check both Congress and the President.

Section 2/Extent of Judicial Powers

Clause 1 The judicial power shall extend to all cases, in law and equity, arising under this Constitution, the laws of the United States, and treaties made, or which shall be made, under their authority; —to all cases affecting ambassadors, other public ministers and consuls; —to all cases of admiralty and maritime jurisdiction; —to controversies to which the United States shall be a party; —to controversies between two or more states; between a state and citizens of another state; —between citizens of different states; —between citizens of the same state claiming lands under grants of different states, and between a state, or the citizens thereof, and foreign states, citizens or subjects.

Federal courts hear cases that have to do with the Constitution, with laws of the United States, with treaties, and with ships and shipping. They hear any case in which the United States government is one of the two opposing sides. They settle disputes between two or more states. They originally heard cases involving a state and people from another state, but Amendment 11 took away this power. They settle disputes between citizens of different states; disputes about certain claims to grants of land; disputes between a state and a foreign country or its people; and disputes between an American and a foreign country or its people.

Clause 2 In all cases affecting ambassadors, other public ministers and consuls, and those in which a state shall be party, the Supreme Court shall have original jurisdiction. In all the other cases before mentioned, the Supreme Court shall have appellate jurisdiction, both as to law and fact, with such exceptions, and under such regulations as the Congress shall make.

Jurisdiction [jùr'is dik'shən] is the right of a court to hear a particular kind of case. The Supreme Court has *original jurisdiction* in all cases involving a representative from a foreign country or involving a state. This means that it hears the facts of the case and decides which side wins the case. All other cases must be tried in the lower courts first. The decision of the lower courts can then be appealed to the Supreme Court, which has *appellate jurisdiction.* Congress decides which kinds of cases can be appealed.

Clause 3 The trial of all crimes, except in cases of impeachment, shall be by jury; and such trial shall be held in the state where the said crimes shall have been committed; but when not committed within any state, the trial shall be at such place or places as the Congress may by law have directed.

Any person accused of committing a crime against the United States government has the right to a trial by jury. The trial is held in a federal court in the state where the crime was committed. When the crime was committed in a place that is not a state (in a territory, for example), Congress describes by law where the trial is to be held. The only exceptions to these rules are impeachment trials, which are tried by the Senate, as described in Article 2.

Section 3/Treason

Clause 1 Treason against the United States, shall consist only in levying war against them, or in adhering to their enemies, giving them aid and comfort. No person shall be convicted of treason unless on the testimony of two witnesses to the same overt act, or on confession in open court.

Treason is defined as carrying on war against the United States or helping enemies of the United States. Convicting a person of treason is difficult. At least two witnesses must testify in court that the accused person committed the same act of treason. Any confession by the accused must be made in open court. Confessions made elsewhere are not accepted as evidence.

Clause 2 The Congress shall have power to declare the punishment of treason, but no attainder of treason shall work corruption of blood or forfeiture except during the life of the person attainted.

Congress has the power to decide the punishment for treason. The punishment can only apply to the guilty person. No punishment can be set for the heirs or family of the guilty person. No fines can extend beyond the guilty person's lifetime.

Article 4/Among the States

Section 1/Recognition of Each Other's Acts

Full faith and credit shall be given in each state to the public acts, records, and judicial proceedings of every other state. And the Congress may by general laws prescribe the manner states must follow to make their acts, records, and proceedings known.

All states must accept the laws, records, and court decisions of other states as legal and binding. Congress has the power to make laws about how states will know each other's laws, records, and court decisions.

Section 2/Citizens' Rights in Other States

Clause 1 The citizens of each state shall be entitled to all privileges and immunities of citizens in the several states.

A citizen from another state has the same rights as the citizens of the state where he or she happens to be.

Clause 2 A person charged in any state with treason, felony, or other crime, who shall flee from justice, and be found in another state, shall on demand of the executive authority of the state from which he fled, be delivered up, to be removed to the state having jurisdiction of the crime.

People cannot escape justice by running out of state. This clause says that anyone accused of a crime in one state who flees to another state must be returned if the governor of the state where the crime was committed requests it.

Clause 3 No person held to service or labor in one state, under the laws thereof, escaping into another, shall, in consequence of any law or regulation therein, be discharged from such service or labor, but shall be delivered up on claim of the party to whom such service or labor may be due.

Persons held to service or labor were slaves, indentured servants, or apprentices. They could not become free by escaping to another state. They had to be sent back to their owners.

Section 3/New States and Territories

Clause 1 New states may be admitted by the Congress into this Union; but no new state shall be formed or erected within the jurisdiction of any other state; nor any state be formed by the junction of two or more states, or parts of states, without the consent of the legislatures of the states concerned as well as of the Congress.

Congress has power to add new states to the United States. (No way is provided for a state to leave the Union.) No state may be divided to make another state without the consent of the original state and Congress. The consent of Congress and the states involved is also needed for a new state to be made by putting parts of two or more states together.

Clause 2 The Congress shall have power to dispose of and make all needful rules and regulations respecting the territory or other property belonging to the United States; and nothing in this Constitution shall be so construed as to prejudice any claims of the United States, or of any particular state.

Congress can sell or give away government lands and property. It has power to make laws governing lands and other property. This clause is the source of power for Congress to decide how territories are governed before they become states.

Nothing in the Constitution is intended to favor one state over another, or over the United States, in disputes over land claims.

Section 4/Guarantees to the States

The United States shall guarantee to every state in this union a republican form of government, and shall protect each of them against invasion; and on application of the legislature, or of the executive (when the legislature cannot be convened) against domestic violence.

The United States government promises that every state in the Union shall have a government in which representatives are elected by the people. (This is what is meant by a *republican government*.) It promises to protect each state from invasion. It also promises to send help in putting down riots. The help must be requested by the state legislature or, if the state legislature cannot meet soon enough, by the governor.

Article 5/Amending the Constitution

The Congress, whenever two-thirds of both houses shall deem it necessary, shall propose amendments to this Constitution, or, on the application of the legislatures of two-thirds of the several states, shall call a convention for proposing amendments, which, in either case, shall be valid to all intents and purposes, as part of this Constitution, and when ratified by the legislatures of three-fourths of the several states, or by conventions in three-fourths thereof, as the one or the other mode of ratification may be proposed by the Congress; provided that no amendment which may be made prior to the year one thousand eight hundred and eight shall in any manner affect the first and fourth clauses in the ninth Section of the first Article; and that no state, without its consent, shall be deprived of its equal suffrage in the Senate.

There are two ways of proposing amendments to the Constitution. One way is for two-thirds of both the Senate and the House of Representatives to vote for a specific amendment. The other way is for the legislatures of two-thirds of the states to ask Congress to call a special convention to propose amend-ments. All proposed amendments must be ratified by the states. An amendment can be ratified in one of two ways. The legislatures of three-fourths of the states can approve the amendment, or conventions in three-fourths of the states can approve the amendment. Congress chooses the method of ratification at the time an amendment is proposed.

No amendment proposed before 1808 could stop the international slave trade or allow a different method of figuring direct taxes. No amendment can decrease the number of senators a state has unless the affected state agrees to the change.

Article 6/National Supremacy

All debts contracted and engagements entered into, before the adoption of this Constitution, shall be as valid against the United States under this Constitution, as under the Confederation.

All debts and treaties that Congress made under the Articles of Confederation are binding on the United States under the Constitution.

This Constitution, and the laws of the United States which shall be made in pursuance thereof; and all treaties made, or which shall be made, under the authority of the United States, shall be the su-preme law of the land; and the judges in every state shall be bound thereby, anything in the Constitution or laws of any state to the contrary notwithstanding.

The senators and representatives before men-tioned, and the members of the several state legisla-tures, and all executive and judicial officers, both of the United States and of the several states, shall be bound by oath or affirmation, to support this Con-stitution; but no religious test shall ever be required as a qualification to any office or public trust under the United States.

This Constitution, proper laws made by Con-gress, and treaties made by the United States are the highest law of the land. State judges must follow this law, even if state laws or constitutions contra-dict it.

All federal and state officials must promise to support this Constitution. However, no officials or public employees can ever be required to take any kind of religious test in order to hold office.

Article 7/Ratification

The ratification of the conventions of nine states, shall be sufficient for the establishment of this Con-stitution between the states so ratifying the same. Done in convention by the unanimous consent of the states present the seventeenth day of September in the year of our Lord one thousand seven hundred and eighty seven and of the independence of the United States of America the twelfth. In witness whereof we have hereunto subscribed our names.

George Washington— President and deputy from Virginia

Delaware
George Read
Gunning Bedford, Junior
John Dickinson
Richard Bassett
Jacob Broom

Maryland
James McHenry
Daniel of St. Thomas
   Jenifer
Daniel Carroll

Virginia
John Blair
James Madison, Junior

North Carolina
William Blount
Richard Dobbs Spaight
Hugh Williamson

South Carolina
John Rutledge
Charles Cotesworth
   Pinckney
Charles Pinckney
Pierce Butler

Government under this Constitution can begin after nine states have approved it at special conventions. This Constitution was signed on September 17, 1787, in the twelfth year of the country's independence. These were the signers:

Georgia
William Few
Abraham Baldwin

New Hampshire
John Langdon
Nicholas Gilman

Massachusetts
Nathaniel Gorham
Rufus King

Connecticut
William Samuel Johnson
Roger Sherman

New York
Alexander Hamilton

New Jersey
William Livingston
David Brearley
William Paterson
Jonathan Dayton

Pennsylvania
Benjamin Franklin
Thomas Mifflin
Robert Morris
George Clymer
Thomas FitzSimons
Jared Ingersoll
James Wilson
Gouverneur Morris

★★★

Amendments to the Constitution

The date given in parentheses is the date that ratification of the amendment was completed. Most of the amendments were added to meet specific needs as the country grew and changed. The first ten amendments make up the Bill of Rights. They were written by the First Congress at the request of the states. They limit the powers of the national government and protect the rights of individuals. All three branches of government are limited by the Bill of Rights.

Amendment 1 (1791) Religious and Political Freedom

Congress shall make no law respecting an establishment of religion, or prohibiting the free exercise thereof; or abridging the freedom of speech, or of the press; or the right of the people peaceably to assemble, and to petition the government for a redress of grievances.

Congress cannot set up an official religion for the country or pass laws to stop people from following their own religion.

Congress cannot make laws to take away freedom of speech or freedom of the press.

Congress cannot make laws that stop people from holding peaceful meetings or from asking the government to correct a wrong.

Amendment 2 (1791) Right to Bear Arms

A well-regulated militia being necessary to the security of a free state, the right of the people to keep and bear arms shall not be infringed.

The people have the right to protect themselves by serving as armed citizens (militia), and for this reason Congress cannot stop people from keeping and carrying guns.

Amendment 3 (1791) Quartering of Soldiers

No soldier shall, in time of peace be quartered in any house, without the consent of the owner, nor in time of war, but in a manner to be prescribed by law.

In peacetime, citizens cannot be forced to give soldiers a place to sleep or meals in their homes. In wartime, this may be done only in the way Congress describes in a law.

Amendment 4 (1791)
Search and Seizure

The right of the people to be secure in their persons, houses, papers, and effects, against unreasonable searches and seizures, shall not be violated, and no warrants shall issue, but upon probable cause, supported by oath or affirmation, and particularly describing the place to be searched, and the persons or things to be seized.

A person's house cannot be searched and his or her property or papers taken except in ways that follow the law. Courts can issue search warrants, but whoever asks for a search warrant must explain why, exactly where the search is to be made, and who or what is to be taken. (The purpose of a lawful search is to prevent evidence of crime from being destroyed.)

Amendment 5 (1791)
Life, Liberty, and Property

No person shall be held to answer for a capital, or otherwise infamous crime, unless on a presentment or indictment of a grand jury, except in cases arising in the land or naval forces, or in the militia, when in actual service in time of war or public danger; nor shall any person be subject for the same offense to be twice put in jeopardy of life or limb; nor shall be compelled in any criminal case to be a witness against himself, nor be deprived of life, liberty, or property, without due process of law; nor shall private property be taken for public use, without just compensation.

Before anyone can be tried in a federal court for a serious crime, a grand jury must formally accuse that person in an indictment. This rule does not cover members of the armed forces in times of war or public danger.

Once found not guilty of committing a particular crime, a person cannot be tried again for that crime by the federal government. However, if the offense is a crime under state law, the person can be tried as well in a state court.

No one can be forced to say anything in a federal court that would help convict himself or herself of a crime.

The federal government cannot take a person's life, freedom, or property except in the exact ways written in law. Amendment 14 applies this rule to the states, too.

The government cannot take a person's property without paying a fair price for it.

Amendment 6 (1791)
Rights of the Accused

In all criminal prosecutions, the accused shall enjoy the right to a speedy and public trial, by an impartial jury of the state and district wherein the crime shall have been committed, which district shall have been previously ascertained by law, and to be informed of the nature and cause of the accusation; to be confronted with the witnesses against him; to have compulsory process for obtaining witnesses in his favor, and to have the assistance of counsel for his defense.

An accused person has the right to a prompt, public trial by jury. The jury must be chosen from the state and district where the crime was committed, and the district must be one that has already been described in law. The accused must be told of the charges and must be present when witnesses speak in court. The accused has the right to a lawyer and has the power to make witnesses come and speak in court. This amendment applies to federal courts, but Amendment 14 has made parts of it apply to state courts.

Amendment 7 (1791)
Right to Jury Trial

In suits at common law, where the value in controversy shall exceed twenty dollars, the right of trial by jury shall be preserved, and no fact tried by a jury shall be otherwise re-examined in any court of the United States than according to the rules of the common law.

In disputes over property worth more than twenty dollars, either side in the dispute can insist on having a jury trial. Or, both can agree not to have a jury. If the case is appealed to a higher court, that court must follow the rules of law in considering the facts of the case.

Amendment 8 (1791)
Bail and Punishment

Excessive bail shall not be required, nor excessive fines imposed, nor cruel and unusual punishments inflicted.

Bails, fines, and punishments must not be excessive or cruel and unusual. *Bail* is the money or property an accused person gives to a court as a guarantee he or she will show up for the trial.

Amendment 9 (1791)
All Other Rights

The enumeration in the Constitution of certain rights shall not be construed to deny or disparage others retained by the people.

The mention of certain rights in the Constitution does not mean that these are the only rights that people have or does not make other rights less important.

Amendment 10 (1791)
Rights of States and the People

The powers not delegated to the United States by the Constitution, nor prohibited by it to the states, are reserved to the states respectively, or to the people.

The states or the people have all powers that have not been specifically assigned to the central government or specifically prohibited to the states.

Amendment 11 (1798)
Suits Against a State

The judicial power of the United States shall not be construed to extend to any suit in law or equity, commenced or prosecuted against one of the United States by citizens of another state, or by citizens or subjects of any foreign state.

Citizens of other states or of foreign countries cannot sue a state in the federal courts.

Amendment 12 (1804)
Election of Presidents

The electors shall meet in their respective states and vote by ballot for President and Vice-President, one of whom, at least, shall not be an inhabitant of the same state with themselves; they shall name in their ballots the person voted for as President, and in distinct ballots the person voted for as Vice-President, and they shall make distinct lists of all persons voted for as President, and of all persons voted for as Vice-President, and of the number of votes for each, which lists they shall sign and certify, and transmit sealed to the seat of the government of the United States, directed to the president of the Senate;

The president of the Senate shall, in the presence of the Senate and House of Representatives, open all the certificates and the votes shall then be counted;

The person having the greatest number of votes for President, shall be the President, if such number be a majority of the whole number of electors appointed; and if no person have such majority, then from the persons having the highest numbers not exceeding three on the list of those voted for as President, the House of Representatives shall choose immediately, by ballot, the President. But in choosing the President, the votes shall be taken by states, the representation from each state having one vote; a quorum for this purpose shall consist of a member or members from two-thirds of the states, and a majority of all the states shall be necessary to a choice.

And if the House of Representatives shall not choose a President whenever the right of choice shall devolve upon them, before the fourth day of March next following, then the Vice-President shall act as President, as in the case of the death or other constitutional disability of the President.

The person having the greatest number of votes as Vice-President, shall be the Vice-President, if such number be a majority of the whole number of electors appointed, and if no person have a majority, then from the two highest numbers on the list, the Senate shall choose the Vice-President; a quorum for the purpose shall consist of two-thirds of the whole number of senators, and a majority of the whole number shall be necessary to a choice.

But no person constitutionally ineligible to the office of President shall be eligible to that of Vice-President of the United States.

The writers of the Constitution wanted the President and the Vice-President to be the two best qualified persons. For that reason, the original election method provided for the Vice-President to be the person who came in second in the election. But after political parties developed, people wanted a Vice-President who was of the same party as the President, not the person who had lost the election.

The amendment says the electors meet in their

own states, where they cast separate ballots for President and Vice-President. At least one of the candidates they vote for must live in another state. After the vote, the electors make a list of the persons voted for as President and another list of persons voted for as Vice-President. On each list they write the total votes cast for each person. Then they sign their names, seal the lists, and send them to the president of the Senate in Washington, D.C.

In a meeting attended by both houses of Congress, the president of the Senate opens the lists from all the states, and the votes are counted.

The person having the most votes for President is President. However, the number of votes received must be more than half of the total number of all electors (now 270 or more). If no person has this many votes, the House of Representatives selects the President from the three candidates who have the largest number of electoral votes. Each state has one vote, no matter how many representatives it has. Two-thirds of the states must be represented when this vote is cast. The candidate who receives a majority of the votes of the states is President.

If the House of Representatives does not elect a President before the date set for the new President to take office, the Vice-President acts as President. (The date for this was changed by Amendment 25.)

The person who receives the most electoral votes for Vice-President becomes Vice-President. However, he or she must get more than half the electoral votes. If no person has more than half, the Senate chooses a Vice-President from the two candidates with the most votes. Two-thirds of all the senators must be present when the vote is taken. To be elected Vice-President, the candidate must receive the votes of more than half (now 51 or more) of all the senators.

A person who does not have the qualifications for President of the United States cannot be Vice-President.

Amendment 13 (1865)
Abolition of Slavery

Section 1 Neither slavery nor involuntary servitude, except as a punishment for crime whereof the party shall have been duly convicted, shall exist within the United States, or any place subject to their jurisdiction.

Section 2 Congress shall have power to enforce this article by appropriate legislation.

Slavery is not allowed in the United States or in any lands under its control. No one may be forced to work unless a court has set that as punishment for committing a crime.

Congress has the power to make laws that will put this amendment into effect.

Amendment 14 (1868)
Civil Rights in the States

Section 1 All persons born or naturalized in the United States, and subject to the jurisdiction thereof, are citizens of the United States and of the state wherein they reside. No state shall make or enforce any law which shall abridge the privileges or immunities of citizens of the United States; nor shall any state deprive any person of life, liberty, or property, without due process of law; nor deny to any person within its jurisdiction the equal protection of the laws.

Section 2 Representatives shall be apportioned among the several states according to their respective numbers, counting the whole number of persons in each state, excluding Indians not taxed. But when the right to vote at any election for the choice of electors for President and Vice-President of the United States, representatives in Congress, the executive and judicial officers of a state, or the members of the legislature thereof, is denied to any of the male inhabitants of such state, being twenty-one years of age, and citizens of the United States, or in any way abridged, except for participation in rebellion, or other crime, the basis of representation therein shall be reduced in the proportion which the number of such male citizens shall bear to the whole number of male citizens twenty-one years of age in such state.

Section 3 No person shall be a senator or representative in Congress, or elector of President and Vice-President, or hold any office, civil or military, under the United States, or under any state, who, having previously taken an oath, as a member of Congress, or as an officer of the United States, or as a member of any state legislature, or as an executive or judicial officer of any state, to support the Constitution of the United States, shall have engaged in insurrection or rebellion against the same, or given aid or comfort to the enemies thereof. But Congress may by a vote of two-thirds of each house, remove such disability.

Section 4 The validity of the public debt of the United States, authorized by law, including debts incurred for payment of pensions and bounties for services in suppressing insurrection or rebellion shall not be questioned. But neither the United States nor any state shall assume or pay any debt or obligation incurred in aid of insurrection or rebellion against the United States, or any claim for the loss or emancipation of any slave; but all such debts, obligations, and claims shall be held illegal and void.

Section 5   The Congress shall have power to enforce, by appropriate legislation the provisions of this article.

Amendment 14 did several things. It gave citizenship to former slaves, provided ways to protect their rights, canceled the three-fifths clause, punished Confederate officers, and canceled Confederate debts.

A citizen is someone who was born or naturalized in the United States and is subject to the country's laws. Such a person is a citizen of the state in which he or she resides as well as of the United States. States cannot make or enforce laws that prevent any citizen from enjoying rights. States cannot take anyone's life, liberty, or property except in ways that the courts say are legal and proper. Anyone living in any state is entitled to that state's protection and the benefit of its laws. By defining state citizenship, the amendment made it impossible for states to have their own citizenship requirements that keep blacks from being state citizens.

All people, except untaxed Indians, are counted in order to determine how many representatives in Congress each state is to have. This section canceled Article 1, Section 2, clause 3 in which slaves were counted as three-fifths of a free person. A state will lose representatives in proportion to the male citizens over twenty-one who have not committed crimes that it prevents from voting. This provision, intended to force states to allow black men to vote, has never been enforced. However, the due process provision of Section 1 has been used to enforce black voting rights.

Congress worded Section 3 so that Confederate leaders who had previously held national or state office were no longer able to vote or hold office. On June 6, 1898, Congress removed this barrier.

The states or the federal government cannot pay any part of the Confederate debt. The payment of the Union debt cannot be questioned. No payment can be made for slaves who have been emancipated.

Amendment 15 (1870)
Black Suffrage

Section 1   The right of citizens of the United States to vote shall not be denied or abridged by the United States or by any state on account of race, color, or previous condition of servitude.

Section 2   The Congress shall have power to enforce this article by appropriate legislation.

Neither the United States nor any state has the right to keep citizens from voting because of their race or color or because they were once slaves.

Congress has the power to make laws that will put this amendment into effect.

Amendment 16 (1913)
Income Tax

The Congress shall have power to lay and collect taxes on incomes, from whatever source derived, without apportionment among the several states, and without regard to any census or enumeration.

This amendment changes Article 1, Section 9, clause 4 by saying that Congress has the power to put a tax on individual incomes *without* dividing the amount due among the states according to population.

Amendment 17 (1913)
Direct Election of Senators

The Senate of the United States shall be composed of two senators from each state, elected by the people thereof, for six years; and each senator shall have one vote. The electors in each state shall have the qualifications requisite for electors of the most numerous branch of the state legislatures.

When vacancies happen in the representation of any state in the Senate, the executive authority of such state shall issue writs of election to fill such vacancies: *Provided,* That the legislature of any state may empower the executive thereof to make temporary appointments until the people fill the vacancies by election as the legislature may direct.

This amendment shall not be so construed as to affect the election or term of any senator chosen before it becomes valid as part of the Constitution.

This amendment changed the method of selecting senators described in Article 1, Section 3, clause 2 to say that senators would be elected by the people of each state, not by the state legislatures.

Amendment 18 (1919)
National Prohibition

Section 1 After one year from the ratification of this article the manufacture, sale, or transportation of intoxicating liquors within, the importation thereof into, or the exportation thereof from the United States and all territory subject to the jurisdiction thereof for beverage purposes is hereby prohibited.

Section 2 The Congress and the several states shall have concurrent power to enforce this article by appropriate legislation.

Section 3 This article shall be inoperative unless it shall have been ratified as an amendment to the Constitution by the legislatures of the several states, as provided in the Constitution, within seven years from the date of the submission hereof to the states by the Congress.

One year after this amendment was ratified it became illegal in the United States and its territories to make, sell, or carry intoxicating liquors for drinking purposes. It became illegal to send such liquors out of the country and its territories or to bring such liquors into them.

The states and the federal government were to share enforcement duties.

This amendment would not have become a part of the Constitution if it had not been ratified by the legislatures of the states within seven years. The need for ratification within seven years was written into this and later amendments so that the government would not have many partially ratified amendments on the books.

Amendment 19 (1920)
Woman's Suffrage

The right of citizens of the United States to vote shall not be denied or abridged by the United States or by any state on account of sex.

Congress shall have power to enforce this article by appropriate legislation.

Neither the United States nor any state can keep a citizen from voting because she is a woman.

Amendment 20 (1933)
The "Lame-Duck" Amendment

Section 1 The terms of the President and Vice-President shall end at noon on the twentieth day of January, and the terms of senators and representatives at noon on the third day of January, of the years in which such terms would have ended if this article had not been ratified; and the terms of their successors shall then begin.

Section 2 The Congress shall assemble at least once in every year, and such meeting shall begin at noon on the third day of January, unless they shall by law appoint a different day.

Section 3 If, at the time fixed for the beginning of the term of the President, the President-elect shall have died, the Vice-President-elect shall become President. If a President shall not have been chosen before the time fixed for the beginning of his term, or if the President-elect shall have failed to qualify, then the Vice-President-elect shall act as President until a President shall have qualified; and the Congress may by law provide for the case wherein neither a President-elect nor a Vice-President-elect shall have qualified, declaring who shall then act as President, or the manner in which one who is to act shall be selected, and such person shall act accordingly until a President or Vice-President shall have qualified.

Section 4 The Congress may by law provide for the case of the death of any of the persons from whom the House of Representatives may choose a President whenever the right of choice shall have devolved upon them, and for the case of the death of any of the persons from whom the Senate may choose a Vice-President whenever the right of choice shall have devolved upon them.

Section 5 Sections 1 and 2 shall take effect on the fifteenth day of October following the ratification of this article.

Section 6 This article shall be inoperative unless it shall have been ratified as an amendment to the Constitution by the legislatures of three-fourths of the several states within seven years from the date of its submission.

A person who holds office after his or her replacement has been chosen does not have much influence, and so is known as a "lame duck." This amendment shortens the "lame-duck" period. Formerly a President and Vice-President elected in November did not take office until March 4. Now they are sworn in in January. Formerly, new members of Congress waited thirteen months to take their seats. Now they wait only about two. Sections 3 and 4 give procedures for the selection of President and Vice-President in situations not covered by Amendment 20.

Amendment 21 (1933)
Repeal of Prohibition

Section 1 The eighteenth article of amendment to the Constitution of the United States is hereby repealed.

Section 2 The transportation or importation into any state, territory, or possession of the United States for delivery or use therein of intoxicating liquors, in violation of the laws thereof, is hereby prohibited.

Section 3 This article shall be inoperative unless it shall have been ratified as an amendment to the Constitution by conventions in the several states, as provided in the Constitution, within seven years from the date of the submission hereof to the states by the Congress.

This amendment repeals Amendment 18. Prohibition is no longer a national law.

A state can forbid liquor for drinking purposes, and carrying liquor across state boundaries into such a state is a crime against the United States as well as against the state.

Amendment 21 had to be ratified by state conventions chosen specifically for their views on the issue. The conventions had to approve the amendment within seven years; they did so in less than a year.

Amendment 22 (1951)
Presidential Term of Office

Section 1 No person shall be elected to the office of the President more than twice, and no person who has held the office of President, or acted as President, for more than two years of a term to which some other person was elected President shall be elected to the office of the President more than once. But this article shall not apply to any person holding the office of President when this article was proposed by the Congress, and shall not prevent any person who may be holding the office of President, or acting as President, during the term within which this article becomes operative from holding the office of President or acting as President during the remainder of such term.

Section 2 This article shall be inoperative unless it shall have been ratified as an amendment to the Constitution by the legislatures of three-fourths of the several states within seven years from the date of its submission to the states by the Congress.

No person can have more than two terms as President. Holding the office of President, or acting as President, for more than two years will be considered as one full term. This amendment did not apply to Harry Truman, who was President at the time this amendment was both proposed by Congress and ratified by the states.

Amendment 23 (1961)
Voting in the District of Columbia

Section 1 The district constituting the seat of government of the United States shall appoint in such manner as the Congress may direct:

A number of electors of President and Vice-President equal to the whole number of senators and representatives in Congress to which the District would be entitled if it were a state, but in no event more than the least populous state; they shall be in addition to those appointed by the states, but they shall be considered, for the purposes of the election of President and Vice-President, to be electors appointed by a state; and they shall meet in the district and perform such duties as provided by the twelfth article of amendment.

Section 2 The Congress shall have power to enforce this article by appropriate legislation.

This amendment gives people living in Washington, D.C., a voice in choosing the President and Vice-President. It says the District of Columbia may choose electors in the election of the President and Vice-President of the United States. The number of electors is limited to the number of electors from the state with the smallest population. The electors follow the rules for elections described in Amendment 12.

Amendment 24 (1964)
Abolition of Poll Taxes

Section 1 The right of citizens of the United States to vote in any primary or other election for President or Vice-President, for electors for President or Vice-President, or for senator or representative in Congress, shall not be denied or abridged by the United States or any state by reason of failure to pay any poll tax or other tax.

Section 2 The Congress shall have power to enforce this article by appropriate legislation.

Neither the United States nor any state can make the payment of a poll tax or any other tax a requirement for voting in any election for national officers. This rule applies to the election of the President, Vice-President, electors of these, senators, and representatives in Congress. The amendment does not make poll taxes illegal in elections of state officials. However, it makes them unlikely and impractical because to require a poll tax in state elections but not in federal elections, a state would have to keep two different lists of voters and print two different kinds of ballots.

Amendment 25 (1967) Presidential Disability and Succession

Section 1 In case of the removal of the President from office or of his death or resignation, the Vice-President shall become President.

Section 2 Whenever there is a vacancy in the office of the Vice-President, the President shall nominate a Vice-President who shall take office upon confirmation by a majority vote of both houses of Congress.

Section 3 Whenever the President transmits to the president pro tempore of the Senate and the speaker of the House of Representatives his written declaration that he is unable to discharge the powers and duties of his office, and until he transmits to them a written declaration to the contrary, such powers and duties shall be discharged by the Vice-President as Acting President.

Section 4 Whenever the Vice-President and a majority of either the principal officers of the executive departments or of such other body as Congress may by law provide, transmit to the president pro tempore of the Senate and the speaker of the House of Representatives their written declaration that the President is unable to discharge the powers and duties of his office, the Vice-President shall immediately assume the powers and duties of the office as Acting President.

Thereafter, when the President transmits to the president pro tempore of the Senate and the speaker of the House of Representatives his written declaration that no inability exists, he shall resume the powers and duties of his office unless the Vice-President and a majority of either the principal officers of the executive departments or of such other body as Congress may by law provide, transmit within four days to the president pro tempore of the Senate and the speaker of the House of Representatives their written declaration that the President is unable to discharge the powers and duties of his office. Thereupon Congress shall decide the issue, assembling within forty-eight hours for that purpose if not in session. If the Congress, within twenty-one days

after receipt of the latter written declaration, or, if Congress is not in session, within twenty-one days after Congress is required to assemble, determines by two-thirds vote of both houses that the President is unable to discharge the powers and duties of his office, the Vice-President shall continue to discharge the same as Acting President; otherwise, the President shall resume the powers and duties of his office.

This amendment tells how the presidency and vice-presidency are to be filled if either office becomes vacant. It also tells what happens if a President becomes unable to fill his or her duties.

If the President dies or resigns or is removed from office, the Vice-President becomes President.

If the vice-presidency becomes vacant, the President appoints a Vice-President. This appointment must be approved by a majority vote in both houses of Congress.

If the President notifies Congress in writing that he or she is unable to perform official duties, the Vice-President takes over as Acting President until the President notifies Congress in writing that he or she is again able to serve.

If a disabled President is unable or unwilling to notify Congress of his or her disability, the Vice-President may. In such a case, a majority of the Cabinet, or some other group named by Congress in law, must agree. Then the Vice-President becomes Acting President.

The President may notify Congress of a recovery and resume the powers and duties of office. However, if the Vice-President and a majority of the designated group do not agree that the President has recovered, they must notify Congress before four days have passed. Congress must meet within forty-eight hours. They have twenty-one days to discuss the issue. If two-thirds or more of each house votes against the President, the Vice-President continues to serve as Acting President. Otherwise, the President resumes office.

Amendment 26 (1971) Eighteen-Year-Old Vote

Section 1 The right of citizens of the United States, who are eighteen years of age or older, to vote shall not be denied or abridged by the United States or by any state on account of age.

Section 2 The Congress shall have power to enforce this article by appropriate legislation.

Chapter 5

Rights and Responsibilities of Citizenship

★★

Note: Some students may need to examine further the meaning of "ideal." What other examples can they give?

Discuss: What does this mean? How does it try to protect our rights?

Discuss: Do we all have equal rights? Explain.

The United States of America was born with a declaration of ideals about the rights of citizens. An **ideal** is a belief about the way something should be. Those who signed the Declaration of Independence in 1776 believed that government should protect the rights of citizens. They declared:

> We hold these truths to be self-evident: That all men are created equal; that they are endowed by their Creator with certain unalienable rights; that among these are life, liberty, and the pursuit of happiness.
>
> That to secure these rights, governments are instituted among men, deriving their just powers from the consent of the governed.

This then is the ideal: everyone should have an equal opportunity to enjoy certain rights. We know that people are not born with the same abilities. However, we might hope that all could have equal chances to develop their abilities. Laws and courts should treat everyone the same. People should each have an equal voice in the election of representatives in government.

Equality of opportunity and liberty did not exist for many Americans when the Declaration of Independence was written. Yet these ideals have influenced the thoughts and actions of Americans from 1776 until the present. The history of the United States has been marked by steady progress in the achievement of citizens' rights under the Constitution.

One purpose of this chapter is to show how the Constitution has been changed, or amended, to extend the rights of citizens. A second purpose is to teach about the responsibilities citizens must have if they are to preserve their rights under the Constitution. You will read:

1/Extending Citizens' Rights and Liberties
2/Gaining and Losing Citizenship
3/Citizens' Responsibilities
Case Study: Deciding to Lower the Voting Age

1/Extending Citizens' Rights and Liberties

Citizens have amended the Constitution to gain legal protection of their civil rights and liberties. The first ten amendments were added in 1791, only three years after the Constitution was ratified. These are called the **Bill of Rights.** They have been a symbol of human freedom to Americans and others around the world.

The Bill of Rights

The Bill of Rights put limits on the power of the national government. Its purpose is to protect the rights and liberties of citizens. Of the ten amendments that make up the Bill of Rights, the First Amendment has to do with important citizen freedoms.

The First Amendment. The First Amendment protects freedom of speech. It says the government cannot make laws that stop people from speaking and writing their ideas. People have the right to criticize government decisions. If they believe that the President is doing a poor job, they are free to say so in speeches and in newspapers, books, and magazines. If citizens

Discuss: Why do we have a Bill of Rights?

Examine each amendment in the Constitution as you read this section.

Discuss: How do the pictures on pages 95–96 help to explain the First Amendment?

The freedom to express one's beliefs is a basic American right.

Discuss: How does this chart help to explain the First Amendment?

FIRST AMENDMENT RIGHTS

Freedom of Religion

Freedom of Speech

Right of Peaceable Assembly

Freedom of the Press

Right to Petition Government

Exercising the right of free speech on Boston Common.

have ideas about how to improve their government, they may tell their opinion to others, including government officials.

Freedom of speech and the press does *not* mean that people can say absolutely anything they want to anywhere they want to. Courts have decided that if you print lies that damage a person's business or reputation, you can be sued for libel and made to pay. Also, people cannot make speeches or print papers that urge the *violent* overthrow of government. You do not have the right to shout "Fire!" in a crowded theater just to see what happens. People cannot abuse freedom of speech. Freedoms must be used responsibly.

Freedom of speech and the press means that citizens have the right to read and listen to the opinions of others. They may read and hear unpopular opinions as well as ideas that the majority of people believe.

According to the First Amendment, citizens are free to join groups and to hold meetings. These groups may use their rights of free speech and press to discuss and spread their ideas.

Groups of citizens may organize marches or parades to draw attention to their ideas. They may have meetings in parks or other public places. They may stand on street corners and pass out handbills to spread their beliefs. For protection and for the convenience of others, a government may require groups to get a permit before using public places or streets to have meetings or parades.

The First Amendment also protects freedom of religious choice. Americans are free to practice any religion they choose. They may decide to have no religion. The national government may not establish an official religion for the United States. The states may not pass laws that favor any religion.

The Second Amendment. The Second Amendment gives citizens the right to bear arms. The government cannot pass a law that stops people from having weapons. It can restrict the possession of particular weapons. For example, it is against the law to own sawed-off shotguns.

The Third Amendment. This amendment says that the government cannot force citizens to let soldiers live in their homes unless the country is at war. Even then, Congress must make a special law telling exactly how soldiers may or may not use the homes of citizens.

The Fourth Amendment. Amendment Four gives citizens the right to privacy. A person's property cannot be seized. His or her house cannot be searched. However, courts of law can issue **search warrants** that allow police officers to enter a home when there is good reason to believe they will find evidence about a crime. The purpose of this legal kind of search is to prevent evidence of a crime from being moved or destroyed.

Discuss: What is privacy? Give examples of privacy.

The Fifth Amendment. This amendment gives protection to people accused of crimes. First, a grand jury must decide that there is enough evidence against a person before he or she can be tried for a serious crime in a federal court. (This right does not apply to members of the armed forces during wars or public danger.) Also, the Fifth Amendment says a person found *not guilty* of a certain crime cannot be tried again for the same crime. Further, people can refuse to give evidence in court that could be used against them. Finally, the government cannot take away someone's life, freedom, or property without **due process** of law. This means government officials must deal with people according to law. The people have the right to equal treatment under the law.

Discuss: What does "due process" mean?

The Sixth Amendment. Amendment Six gives people accused of crimes the right to a prompt, public trial by jury. Accused persons have the right to be defended by a lawyer. They also must be present when accused of a crime and when evidence is given against them.

Discuss: Which Amendment(s) does this picture relate to?

As cameras are not permitted in most courtrooms, artists work for newspapers and television news programs. Drawings like this are used to illustrate events in a trial.

Reporting the News

A free press, as guaranteed by the First Amendment, is important to all United States citizens. It helps keep our form of government working as it's supposed to work. With a free press, people who disagree with those in power can print what they think. Citizens are given the chance to know all sides of a question before they vote or take other political action.

People who gather the news are reporters. People who decide which news stories will be printed in papers, read on the radio, or read on television newscasts are called editors.

Barbara Lamont is a reporter for both a radio station and a television station in New York. She gathers information and writes stories about local events and local people.

Before Barbara begins work on a story for the radio station, she discusses her plans with the station's news editor.

On this particular day Barbara goes to a workshop where older people do work for large companies. She interviews men and women to find out what they think of the workshop program.

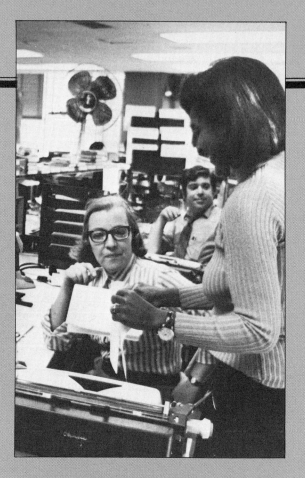

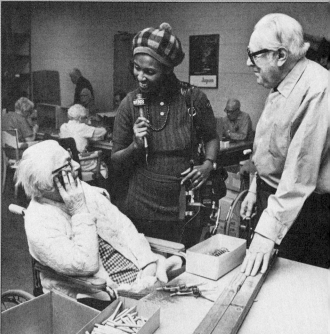

People and Government

1. Later, Barbara talks to political leaders about the poor condition of streets and sidewalks in one of the city's shopping areas.

2. After Barbara has taped an interview, she returns to the station. She listens to the recording and writes a narrative that describes what she has seen and heard. She will include the most interesting and important parts of the taped interview in the story.

3. Once a narrative is written, Barbara records it in a soundproof room.

4. A sound engineer helps prepare the tape. It will be used in one or more upcoming broadcasts.

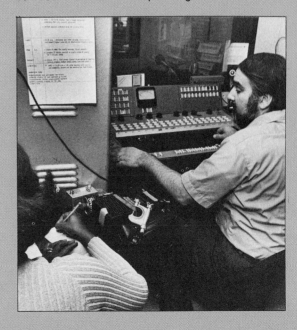

The Seventh Amendment. This amendment gives people the right to a trial by jury to settle conflicts over property rights. However, if both parties to the conflict agree, a judge may decide the case without a jury.

The Eighth Amendment. Amendment Eight says that courts cannot require an unusually high **bail.** Bail is the money or property that an accused person gives the court so that he or she may stay out of jail until the trial. The bail is a guarantee that the person will appear at the trial. After the trial, the money or property is returned. Fines and punishments, too, cannot be cruel or unusual.

Note: Some students may want to discuss bail and how it is raised.

The Ninth Amendment. According to this amendment, the civil rights stated in the Constitution are not the only rights that people have. And they are not necessarily the most important rights. This amendment recognizes the many other civil rights and liberties in state constitutions and in state and local laws.

The Tenth Amendment. The last amendment in the Bill of Rights says that if the Constitution does not give a certain power to the national government, then that power belongs to the states. For example, the Constitution does not give the power to make rules about marriage and divorce to the national government. The Constitution also does not say the states cannot have this power. Thus, according to the Tenth Amendment, the state governments may have it. Other examples of powers "reserved to the states" are making rules about the establishment of schools, holding public elections for state and local offices, granting hunting and driving licenses, and many others.

Increasing the Peoples' Rights

Many of the amendments that have been made since 1791 have increased the rights or freedoms of citizens in one way or another. These amendments may be thought of as additions to the Bill of Rights.

The Thirteenth, Fourteenth, and Fifteenth amendments were made at the end of the Civil War to extend rights and liberties to black people.

The Thirteenth Amendment passed in 1865. It ended slavery in the United States and lands controlled by the United States.

The Fourteenth Amendment, passed in 1868, protects the rights of citizenship. A person is both a citizen of the state in which he or she lives and of the United States. No state government can take away any civil rights or liberties that belong to a citizen of the United States. All citizens have the right to equal protection of the law in all states.

The Fifteenth Amendment, passed in 1870, protects the right of black people to vote. It says that no state may take away a person's right to vote on the basis of race or color.

The Seventeenth Amendment, passed in 1913, says that senators shall be elected from each state by eligible voters from that state. Before this amendment, members of state legislatures, rather than eligible voters, picked the senators.

Four amendments passed in this century give more people the right to vote.

Discuss: How are Amendments 13–15 related?

Discuss: What amendments do each of the pictures on pp. 101–102 refer to?

(Top) registering to vote, (bottom) instruction in using a voting machine, (left) waiting to vote.

Discuss: How did these amendments give more people the right to vote?

(Top and center) National Woman's Conference, 1977. (Bottom) National Organization for Women rally.

The Nineteenth Amendment (1920) says that women shall have the right to vote.

The Twenty-Third Amendment (1961) says that residents of the District of Columbia may take part in the election of the President and Vice-President.

The Twenty-Fourth Amendment (1964) says that payment of a poll tax may not be a requirement for voting. Thus, poor people could not be kept from voting by making them pay a tax in order to vote.

The Twenty-Sixth Amendment (1971) lowered the voting age to eighteen.

Section Review

Vocabulary: bail, Bill of Rights, due process, ideal, search warrant.

Reviewing the Main Ideas
1. Which amendments are part of the Bill of Rights?
2. Give at least five examples of civil rights or liberties protected by the Bill of Rights.
3. What rights are extended to citizens in the Fourteenth, Fifteenth, and Seventeenth amendments?

Skill Building
1. What specific rights or freedoms are violated in the three examples below?
   a. Martha Owens had to pay a twenty-dollar fine to the city government. She was punished for criticizing the mayor at a public meeting. She had called the mayor "lazy and not smart enough to do his job right."
   b. Mickey Jones was arrested for standing on a streetcorner and passing out pamphlets to anyone who would take them. The pamphlets said that the people should oppose the governor's plans to raise taxes.
   c. Margaret Johnson does not belong to any church, and she practices no religion. So, she was not allowed to be a candidate for mayor of her city.
2. Read the Nineteenth Amendment. What is the main idea of this amendment?

Main Ideas
1. the first ten
2. Answers will vary.
3. p. 101

Skill Building
1. a. freedom of speech and assembly   b. freedom of press   c. freedom of religion
2. women have the right to vote

2/Gaining and Losing Citizenship

Every country has rules about how to gain the rights of citizenship. In the United States, the Fourteenth Amendment says there are two ways to become a citizen: (1) by birth, and (2) by **naturalization.**

Note: If necessary, reread the Fourteenth Amendment.

Citizenship by Birth

Most people in the United States gain their citizenship by being born in this country. Sylvia Lazar was born in Cleveland, Ohio. Sylvia became a citizen of the United States because of the place of her birth. Anyone born in one of the fifty states, the District of Columbia, or the Territories of Guam, Puerto Rico, or the Virgin Islands is a citizen at birth.

Sarah Kaplan, Sylvia's best friend, also gained United States citizenship at birth, even though she was born in Paris, France. Sarah's mother and father are citizens of the United States. They were living in Paris when Sarah was born. The law says that persons can claim to be citizens at birth, no matter where they are born, if both parents are United States citizens or if one parent is a citizen who has lived in the United States at least ten years.

Citizenship by Naturalization

Several million **aliens** live in the United States. Aliens are citizens of other countries.

Some aliens are not **immigrants.** They come with the permission of our government to study in our colleges and universities, or to work for a while. Others are permitted to visit relatives or friends. These aliens intend to remain citizens of their own countries.

However, most aliens in the United States are immigrants. They enter the country to stay. They want to become naturalized citizens. So, they intend to take certain steps, required by law, to gain citizenship in the United States.

The first step is to sign a statement that says they want United States citizenship. This statement is filed with the Immigration and Naturalization Service of the United States government.

For most people, the second step comes after living in the United States at least five years. (Any alien who is married to a citizen waits only three years.) At this time, they file a petition

**STEPS TO BECOMING
A NATURALIZED CITIZEN**

1. File a Declaration of Intention with the Immigration and Naturalization Service. (This step is optional.)

2. After 5 years residence in the United States (3 years if married to an American citizen), file a Petition for Citizenship.

3. Have two citizens testify that you have met the residence requirement, have a good moral character, and believe in the Constitution.

4. Take an examination to prove you can read and write English and know American history and government.

5. Pledge an oath of allegiance to the Constitution and laws of the United States and sign a certificate of naturalization.

Discuss: What is the artist trying to say about immigrants?

"Albert Einstein with other Immigrants" by Ben Shahn.

Discuss: How can a person become a citizen?

Claire Schwaller waves one of the American flags given to newly naturalized U.S. citizens.

asking for citizenship. Applicants must be at least eighteen years old. In the third step, the alien comes before a judge. Two citizens must testify that the alien has lived in the United States for the required period of time and that he or she would be a good citizen.

The fourth step is a citizenship exam that determines whether the alien can read and write English and knows basic facts about the history and government of the United States.

After a person passes the citizenship examination, he or she must wait thirty days. During this time, officials of the Immigration and Naturalization Service take a final look into the alien's background. They want to be sure that everyone applying for citizenship deserves this privilege.

The final step in naturalization is to pledge an oath of allegiance. The alien swears to obey and defend the Constitution and other laws of the United States and to be loyal to this country above all others. Then the alien signs a certificate of naturalization and becomes a citizen of the United States of America.

Naturalized citizens have the same rights and duties as those who gained citizenship by birth except for one right. They are not eligible to become President or Vice-President of the United States.

How to Lose Citizenship

Citizenship in the United States may be lost in one of three ways: (1) treason, (2) expatriation, (3) **denaturalization.**

Citizenship may be taken from a person as punishment for treason. Treason is defined in Article 3, Section 3 of the Constitution. Anyone trying to overthrow the government by force commits the crime of treason. Trial and conviction for such crimes have been very rare.

People who withdraw allegiance from their country are **expatriates.** Thus, a person who takes an oath of loyalty to another country loses the rights of citizenship in the United States. Children may be expatriated if their parents become citizens of another country.

Discuss: How can you lose your citizenship?

Denaturalization happens when it is proved that a naturalized citizen got citizenship by fraud or that the oath of allegiance was not taken in good faith.

Discuss: What does "good faith" mean?

Section Review

Vocabulary: alien, denaturalization, expatriate, immigrant, naturalization.

Reviewing the Main Ideas

1. What are the two main ways to become a citizen of the United States?
2. What are the steps a person must take to become a naturalized citizen?
3. How might a person lose United States citizenship?

Skill Building

Tell whether the following statements are true or false. Give the page number in this book that backs up your answer.

1. It is possible for a person born outside the United States to have citizenship in this country by birth.
2. All aliens in the United States are immigrants.
3. Most immigrants must wait at least five years after entering the United States before they can become naturalized citizens.
4. Immigrants must show they can read and write and know basic facts about United States history and government in order to become naturalized citizens.
5. Naturalized citizens have every right under law that natural-born citizens have.
6. Citizenship cannot be taken away from a natural-born citizen.

Main Ideas
1. by birth and by naturalization
2. p. 103
3. treason, expatriation, or denaturalization
Skill Building
1. T, p. 103
2. F, p. 103
3. T, p. 103
4. T, p. 104
5. T, p. 104
6. F, p. 105

3/Citizens' Responsibilities

Discuss: What responsibilities do you have at home? In class?

Citizens who want to keep their rights must assume **responsibility** for preserving, protecting, and defending them. They must act to preserve the Constitution, which is the legal source of citizens' rights.

Responsibilities of Knowing and Respecting the Law. The first duty of citizens is to respect and obey their laws. There can be no peace, cooperation, or progress where there is no **respect** for law.

Three chief duties of citizenship are (1) to pay taxes for the services of government, (2) to serve, if called, as a member of a jury, and (3) to testify in a court of law if called as a witness.

Knowing About Rights. Another duty of citizens is to be informed. People who are ignorant of their legal rights are in a poor position to use or defend these rights. Part of being a good citizen is learning about the freedoms and opportunities provided by our federal, state, and local laws.

Citizens should know how their government works and how public officials make decisions that affect them. You need to know how to use government and laws so as not to lose benefits you deserve to have. News items about laws under discussion or about Supreme Court decisions are your business.

Respecting the Civic Rights of Others. To enjoy your own rights fully, you must respect the rights of others. By treating others with respect, you help create a climate of good feeling and cooperation among people. You may encourage others to treat you with respect.

To respect the rights of others, you should remember this rule: Your freedom ends where the other person's freedom begins. By remembering this rule, people keep from stepping on each other's rights. For instance, your neighbor has the right to keep a dog as a pet. But she also has the duty of making sure her dog does not damage other people's property. Suppose her dog digs holes in your garden and barks all afternoon. Her right to a pet stops where your property rights begin. It is her duty to stop her dog from damaging your yard. Her right to a pet stops where your rights to peace and quiet begin. She has the duty to keep her dog from barking.

Our government has many laws that reduce areas of conflict.

Getting a ticket.

For example, many cities have a law that dogs must be leashed when outside. This is partly a health and safety measure. But it is also aimed at reducing conflict when a pet becomes a nuisance to others. In the case of dog ownership, respecting the rights of others involves obeying the laws on dog ownership.

Respecting the rights of others means obeying the traffic laws that were passed to safeguard the rights of all highway users. It means obeying a no-talking rule in study hall so that the rights of those who want to study are respected.

Acting to Defend Civil Rights and Liberties. To be a responsible citizen in some countries, one must only be obedient. The rulers expect passive followers who do not question their decisions.

Much more is expected of a responsible citizen in the United States. Of course, citizens are expected to obey laws and to respect leaders. They also are expected to think for themselves and to question what their leaders tell them.

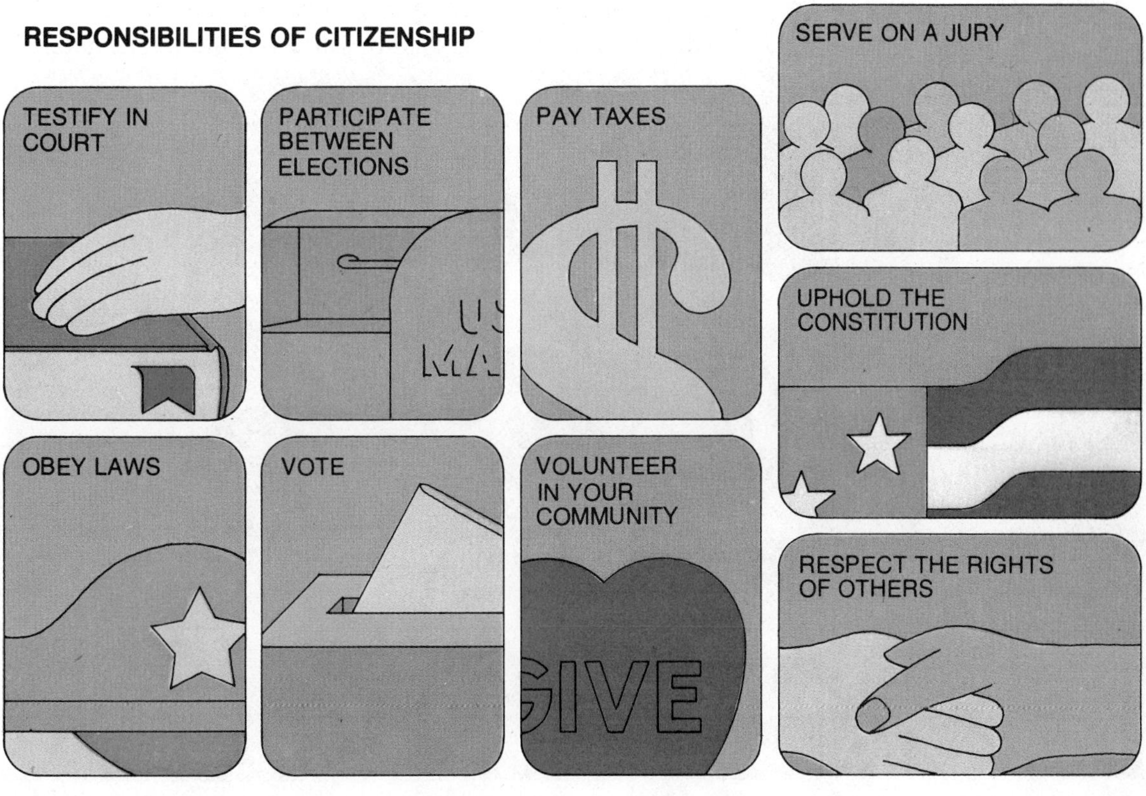

Discuss: What other examples can you give to explain "Your freedom ends where the other person's begins"?

RESPONSIBILITIES OF CITIZENSHIP

TESTIFY IN COURT

PARTICIPATE BETWEEN ELECTIONS

PAY TAXES

SERVE ON A JURY

UPHOLD THE CONSTITUTION

OBEY LAWS

VOTE

VOLUNTEER IN YOUR COMMUNITY

GIVE

RESPECT THE RIGHTS OF OTHERS

In his Gettysburg Address, Abraham Lincoln said that we should preserve "government of the people, by the people, for the people." Citizens who would rule themselves must be able to make their own decisions. Also they must know how to form their own opinions about the decisions of others, especially their representatives in government.

In the United States, citizens have the right to speak freely against government actions they think wrong or unwise. They also can defend the civil rights and liberties of citizens against government officials or others who might try to abuse them.

If citizens fail to use their legal rights, they risk losing them. Thus, citizens of the United States should be ready and willing to preserve, protect, and defend the Constitution—the legal source of citizens' rights.

Responsibilities to Participate in Civic Life. Choosing the leaders of government by voting is a basic right of citizens. Citizens who take the trouble to vote for good leaders may be rewarded with good government. A position in government carries much power. It is important to give this power wisely. Citizens should try to elect people who will serve the public interest.

Discuss: Which duties or rights of citizens are represented in the pictures on pp. 106, 108 and 109?

Speaking out at a candidates' meeting, San Francisco, 1975.

Bad government often results when citizens do not bother to vote or when they vote without first finding out the strengths and weaknesses of the candidates. Thus, citizens of the United States should be thoughtful voters in public elections.

Participating Between Elections. Citizens should try to influence government between elections as well as during elections. Leaders are more likely to respond to public needs if people are checking on their work between elections. And law makers need to know the views of the people they represent. Thus, citizens of the United States should be as involved as possible in the affairs of government.

Acting for the Good of the Community. Responsible citizens think about others as well as themselves. They are willing to give time, effort, and money to help others and to improve their own communities. They may volunteer their spare time to help needy people or to remove litter from public places. They may donate money to various charities that aid poor or sick people.

The Citizens Committee for New York City is just one example among many groups of **volunteers** who work to help handicapped people, to improve services in schools, libraries, and hospitals, and to clean up public parks.

Students volunteer to tutor a handicapped child.

Section Review

Vocabulary: respect, responsibility, volunteer.

Reviewing the Main Ideas
1. Why is it important for citizens to know about their rights?
2. What rule helps you balance your own rights with the rights of others?
3. Why should citizens take part in elections?
4. Why should citizens be involved in civic activities between elections?

Skill Building

What does responsible citizenship mean to different people? You can find out by asking them. Interview at least five people to find out what is their ideal of a good citizen. Ask each person: What is your definition of responsible citizenship? Then write a report telling (1) what the people you interviewed said, and (2) your opinions of what they said.

Main Ideas
1. p. 106
2. Your freedom ends where the other person's freedom begins.
3. pp. 108–109
4. p. 109
Skill Building
Answers will vary.

Deciding to Lower the Voting Age

At what age does a youngster become an adult? Age twenty-one has been the usual answer to this question. From the earliest days of our country, it was a tradition that people become an adult on their twenty-first birthday.

According to the Tenth Amendment, the power to make voter eligibility laws is reserved to the states. And in line with tradition, twenty-one became the minimum voting age in every state in the country.

Then, in 1943, Georgia lowered the voting age to eighteen. In 1955, Kentucky followed Georgia's example. In 1959, Alaska set the voting age at nineteen and Hawaii at twenty. Still, the other forty-six states kept twenty-one as the minimum voting age.

During the 1960s there was much debate about whether to lower the voting age to eighteen throughout the country. It seemed necessary to amend the Constitution in order to change the voting age all at once in every state.

Those who favored giving the right to vote to eighteen-year-olds used the following arguments:

1. Males were at that time drafted into the armed forces at age eighteen. They were fighting and dying in Viet Nam but they could not vote. Somehow this seemed wrong.
2. Young people, at age eighteen, seemed to be more educated and mature than they were in previous times. They seemed as qualified to vote as older people.
3. Younger people would be more responsible citizens if they had the right to vote. It is easier to learn how to be a responsible citizen by taking part in government than merely by reading about it.

4. Eighteen-year-olds seemed motivated to contribute to society. They seemed to want to take part in elections.

Those who were against giving eighteen-year-olds the right to vote used these arguments:

1. What had been good in the past was still good. Why change when the old law has worked?
2. Eighteen-year-olds do not know enough to vote wisely. They seemed too immature to make sound judgments.
3. Citizens who were settled and who had steady jobs were more responsible. Most eighteen-year-olds did not seem to be settled yet. They did not have enough of a stake in society to make wise judgments about voting.

Discuss: Did your state lower the voting age before the Twenty-Sixth Amendment was passed? If so, when? To what age?

4. Eighteen-year-olds did not seem to care enough to take part. Why give them the right to vote? Most would not bother to use the right.

These arguments reached a peak in 1970. Early in 1971, an amendment was put before the Congress: "The right of citizens of the United States, who are eighteen years of age or older, to vote shall not be denied or abridged by the United States or by any state on account of age."

More than two-thirds of the members of Congress voted for this amendment. At least three-fourths of the fifty states had to approve the amendment in order to make it part of the Constitution. At the end of June 1971, Ohio's legislature became the thirty-eighth to ratify the proposal. So, it became the Twenty-Sixth Amendment to the Constitution.

More than 11 million new citizens, from ages eighteen to twenty-one, were added to the lists of eligible voters. However, their impact on most elections has been slight. As the graph shows, in 1976, the youngest voters were the least likely to take part in elections. The general turnout of young voters during the 1970s was a disappointment to those who had worked to extend them the right to vote.

Some groups of young voters have been active in a few local elections around the country. These small groups of younger citizens have shown that they can have an impact on election outcomes. Will you accept the responsibility of voting? If so, you might be part of a movement to increase the turnout of young voters in the elections of the 1980s.

Reviewing the Case Study

1. What were the arguments in favor of lowering the voting age?
2. What were the arguments against lowering the voting age?
3. Why was it necessary to amend the Constitution in order to make a decision in this case?
4. Describe the amendment process used in this case.
5. What has been the main consequence of this decision to lower the voting age?
6. What in your opinion are the reasons younger Americans do not vote in large numbers?
7. What could be done to improve the voting record of this group?

WHO TURNED OUT TO VOTE
(1976 Presidential Election)

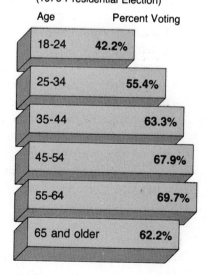

Age	Percent Voting
18-24	42.2%
25-34	55.4%
35-44	63.3%
45-54	67.9%
55-64	69.7%
65 and older	62.2%

111

Chapter Five Test and Activities

★★★

Vocabulary

Match the following words with their meanings.

1. search warrant
2. ideal
3. aliens
4. naturalization
5. Bill of Rights
6. expatriate
7. immigrant
8. respect
9. volunteer
10. responsibility
11. bail
12. due process

a. the first ten amendments to the Constitution
b. becoming a citizen
c. honor
d. a person who gives up his or her citizenship
e. a belief about the way something should be
f. duty
g. citizens of other countries living in the United States
h. a person who serves without pay
i. a person who moves permanently into another country
j. the protection of the laws, lawful treatment
k. money left with a court as a guarantee a person will appear for trial
l. a court order permitting law officers to search a place for evidence of a crime

Reviewing Chapter Ideas

1. True or false: A main purpose of the Bill of Rights is to protect your rights and liberties.
2. Each of the following is a guarantee of the First Amendment except

a. to be able to organize parades
b. to be able to establish schools
c. to be able to speak and write ideas
d. to be able to choose any religion

3. True or false: The Second Amendment gives a person the right to have a gun.
4. True or false: The Ninth Amendment guarantees that once found innocent you cannot be tried again for the same crime.
5. True or false: The Fourth Amendment says that your house cannot be searched without a warrant.
6. All of the following are citizens of the United States except:

a. Helen was born in Spain. Her parents are United States citizens.
b. Ned was born in Puerto Rico. His parents were born in Spain.
c. Daisy was born in England. Her mother, a naturalized United States citizen, was born there too. Her father was born in New York and lived there until two years ago.
d. Leon has lived in Chicago for two years. His father and mother are citizens of Norway. He was born in Norway.

7. Citizenship may be lost by which of the following:

a. treason
b. denaturalization
c. taking an oath of loyalty to another country
d. all of the above

8. True or false: To be a responsible citizen you must not question the decisions of leaders.
9. True or false: An important duty of citizenship is to respect and obey the laws.
10. True or false: A larger percentage of people

Vocabulary			
1. l	4. b	7. i	10. f
2. e	5. a	8. c	11. k
3. g	6. d	9. h	12. j

Ideas			
1. T	4. F	7. d	10. F
2. b	5. T	8. F	
3. T	6. d	9. T	

★★★

between the ages of eighteen and twenty-four vote than any other age group.

Using Basic Social Studies Skills

Finding Information
1. Find the Declaration of Independence in this book. On what page does it begin?
2. Find the Bill of Rights in this book. On what page does it begin?

Comprehending Information
Which document, the Declaration of Independence or the Bill of Rights, gives the basic freedoms the United States government guarantees to its citizens?

Organizing Information
Put the items below into two lists. Head one Rights of United States Citizens. Head the other Rights United States Citizens Do *Not* Have.
1. to have news reports about wrongdoing in government
2. to picket in front of the White House
3. to write about government wrongdoing on the walls of public buildings
4. to have a lawyer if you're accused of a crime
5. to have equal pay for equal work
6. to vote in elections if you're eighteen or older
7. to have any kind of weapons you want
8. to make speeches urging people to beat up government officials
9. to force witnesses to testify for you in court
10. to keep police out of your house unless they have a search warrant

Evaluating Information
Tom Jones was convicted of first-degree murder and was sentenced to life imprisonment. Later, his lawyer discovered new evidence that proved Jones was nowhere near the scene of the crime when it occurred. Jones's lawyer asked for a new trial. Read the Fifth Amendment carefully. Is there anything in it that would prevent Jones from having another trial?

Communicating Ideas
Write a paragraph explaining the main ideas of this chapter. Use at least five of the words from the Vocabulary. Underline each vocabulary word that you use.

Using Decision-Making Skills

Will you vote in the first election after you are of age? Explain.

Activities

1. Use current newspapers and magazines to find examples of what people can do because of the First Amendment. This kind of headline would be an example: "Group Passes Out Handbills on Main Street."
2. Invite a naturalized citizen to class to tell about his or her experiences in becoming a citizen.
3. For students who want to learn more about constitutional amendments and citizen rights, the following books are recommended:

   (a) *The Rights of Young People: The Basic ACLU Guide to a Young Person's Rights*, by Alan Sussman (Avon, 1977).

   (b) *The Law in Your Everyday Life*, by Elinor Porter Swiger (Prentice-Hall, 1978).

   (c) *The Bill of Rights*, by Ernest Barksdale Fincher (Watts, 1978).

   (d) *Your Legal Rights As a Minor*, revised edition, by Robert H. Loeb and John P. Maloney (Watts, 1978).

Finding	Comprehending	Organizing
1. p. 544	Bill of Rights	Rights: 1, 2, 4, 6, 9, 10
2. p. 86		Not Rights: 3, 5, 7, 8

Unit One Test

★★

Vocabulary

Write *true* if the underlined word or phrase is used correctly. Write *false* if it is not used correctly.

1. <u>Civics</u> is the study of the rights and responsibilities of citizens.
2. Delegates from the different states voted to approve the <u>Mayflower Compact</u>.
3. A government passes <u>goals</u> for all the people to follow.
4. It takes a <u>minority</u> of the people voting for a bill to become a law.
5. A <u>practical</u> decision is one that is possible and would lead toward desired outcomes.
6. When someone says, "That's a rotten idea!" that person is making a <u>judgment</u>.
7. The <u>Federalists</u> wanted a strong central government, so they supported the Constitution.
8. The <u>Anti-Federalists</u> wanted a strong central government, so they supported the Constitution.
9. Changes made in laws are called <u>amendments</u>.
10. The first ten amendments to the Constitution are called the <u>Preamble</u>.
11. The branch of government that makes laws is the <u>judicial branch</u>.
12. The branch of government that includes the federal courts is the <u>legislative branch</u>.
13. The branch of government that includes the President is the <u>executive branch</u>.
14. <u>Aliens</u> are citizens of other countries who live in the United States.
15. Immigrants can try for <u>citizenship</u> in the United States.

Recalling Information

1. True or false: Being a group member gives people both rights and responsibilities.
2. What rights can citizens of the United States expect their government to protect?
   a. the right to help choose leaders
   b. the right to live wherever they want
   c. the right to be treated according to the laws
   d. *a* and *c*
3. What responsibilities do citizens have toward the United States?
   a. to be loyal
   b. to uphold the laws
   c. to vote wisely
   d. all of the above
4. True or false: People making decisions should consider the consequences of the different alternatives they face.
5. In 1787, leaders in the states wanted a convention to improve the Articles of Confederation because
   a. the national government did not have the power to settle conflicts between states
   b. the country had severe money problems and the national government did not have the power to solve them
   c. there were disorders and riots in several states
   d. all of the above
6. At the Constitutional Convention, the delegates decided to _____ the Articles of Confederation.
   a. revise
   b. throw out
   c. ratify
   d. approve

Vocabulary				
1. T	4. F	7. T	10. F	13. T
2. F	5. T	8. F	11. F	14. T
3. F	6. T	9. T	12. F	15. T

Recalling		
1. T	4. T	7. c
2. d	5. d	8. a
3. d	6. b	9. T

114

7. The Great Compromise settled an argument about
   a. how much power the President should have
   b. how many district courts there should be
   c. how many legislators each state would have
   d. what to do about a bill of rights

8. President Washington decided to put down the Whiskey Rebellion with force because
   a. he wanted to show that the new government could enforce its laws
   b. he wanted western Pennsylvania to separate from the United States
   c. he was an Anti-Federalist
   d. all of the above

9. True or false: The words "We the People" in the Preamble to the Constitution are important because they show that the government's authority comes from the people.

Skill Building

Below are some rights guaranteed by the Constitution. Following is a list of cases involving these rights. For each case, give the letter or letters of the rights involved.

a. freedom of speech
b. freedom of religion
c. freedom of the press
d. right of assembly and to petition government
e. right to keep and bear arms
f. protection from illegal searches and seizures
g. right to a grand jury hearing before being charged with a serious federal crime
h. once found innocent of a charge, protection from being tried again
i. protection from being required to witness against oneself
j. right to due process of the laws
k. right to know charges against oneself and to question the witnesses in court
l. right to a lawyer
m. protection from excessive bail
n. protection from cruel and unusual punishments

1. George Chow is tried and found innocent of the murder of his uncle. A year later, an eye witness is found who agrees, finally, to swear in court that he saw George shoot the uncle. Can George be tried again?

2. Nancy Washington read in the paper that a man being questioned by a Senate investigating committee refused to answer when asked if he was connected with organized crime. Can he get away with this?

3. The leader of a gang suspected of bombing an airport was arrested. For three days she was questioned by the police. They did not let her call a lawyer because they said they weren't formally charging her, they were just questioning her. At the end of three days, she confessed. Then she was charged with a federal offense and bail was set at $3 million.

4. A certain state senator voted to spend government money because he had been bribed by a manufacturer who was sure to get much business from the vote. A group of citizens learned of the bribe and called a meeting to decide what to do. The senator phoned his friend the governor to call out the National Guard. The Guard broke up the meeting and arrested the leaders.

Skill Building
1. h   4. a, d
2. yes, i
3. g, j, k, l, m

115

Making Decisions in the National Government

In 1787, when the Constitution was written, there were fewer than 4 million people in the United States. The government that was set up after the Constitution had been ratified was small as compared with government today. President George Washington had only 780 people working for him in the executive branch by 1792. There were only twenty-six senators and sixty-four representatives.

In addition to being small in size, the national government was "small" in power during its first years. Problems that had to be dealt with by government were most often handled by state and local governments.

Today the national picture has changed. There are now more than 220 million people in the United States. They live very differently from the way people lived in the late 1700s. The problems people are having in one part of the country are often tied to the problems people are having in other parts of the country. Thus, the national government has taken a larger role.

The rules laid down in the Constitution have allowed the national government to change as the nation as a whole has changed. Most noticeably, the national government has grown. There are many more people working in the national government. In addition, rules and programs created by the national government touch many more areas of life than they once did.

You'll learn the details of how the national government is organized and you'll learn more about the work it does today in this unit.

Discuss: How might these individuals influence us?

House Judiciary Committee

Chapter **6**

Decision Making in Congress

★★★

On a hot day in June, Representative Harold Jackson arrives at his office on Capitol Hill at 8:00 A.M. After a quick look at the newspaper, he meets with three members of his staff. They talk about bills ready for action in the House of Representatives and about bills coming before the four committees on which Jackson serves. At 9:00 Jackson goes to a meeting of the Post Office and Civil Service Committee. The Postmaster General wants to raise the cost of first-class mail. Back at his office by 11:00, Jackson takes a phone call from a lobbyist representing the nation's steel-workers. The lobbyist wants Jackson to vote for an industrial-safety bill. Then an aide to the President calls. He and Jackson talk about an education bill the President wants Jackson to introduce in the House. At 11:45 Jackson has lunch with an editor from his hometown newspaper.

By 2:00 P.M. Jackson is back in his office reading and signing outgoing mail. At 2:30 Jackson goes to the House floor. During the debate on a farm bill, he tells House members that farmers in his district want the bill put into law. At 4:00 Jackson meets with people from the Department of Defense. He tells them why his district would be a good place to build an army supply warehouse. At 5:00 Jackson rushes back to his office to have his picture taken with a group of mayors from his state. He promises to look into some problems they are having with the Department of Housing and Urban Development. Jackson then drives to a hotel for dinner with several members of Congress from his state. They discuss their plans for re-election. Arriving home about 8:30, Jackson settles down to read several committee reports.

Such is a day in the life of a typical—but imaginary—member of Congress. In this chapter you will learn more about Congress. You will read:

1/How Congress Is Organized
2/The Job in Congress Today
3/Making Laws
Case Study: To Cut or Not to Cut?

1/How Congress Is Organized

Congress, as you know, is the national legislature of the United States. Its basic job is to make laws. According to the Constitution, Congress has the power to tax and spend to promote the general welfare. It also has the power to regulate trade and to coin and borrow money. Congress can build post offices and highways. It can set up federal courts under the Supreme Court. It can declare war and raise and maintain an army and navy, and it can call on armed forces to put down rebellions or stop invasions. Finally, Congress can make all laws necessary to carry out its other stated powers.

In part because they gave Congress so much power, the men who wrote the Constitution decided to make Congress a **bicameral** legislature—a legislature made up of two houses. Instead of giving all legislative power to one group of people, they divided legislative power between two groups. The two houses have to agree on a bill before it becomes a law. Each house can "check and balance" the work of the other.

The House of Representatives

The House of Representatives has 435 voting members. After each ten-year census, Congress decides how the 435 representa-

Discuss: What does it mean when it says "Congress is the national legislature of the United States"?

New York Senator Daniel Moynihan holds a press conference to describe his new tax proposal.

Discuss: How is the number of congressional districts in a state decided? Does the number change? Has it changed since 1970? When will it change again?

tives are to be divided among the states. Look at the map to see how the representatives changed after the 1970 census.

Representatives are elected for two-year terms from **congressional districts** in their states. There is one representative for each congressional district. It is up to each state legislature to decide where the boundaries of the congressional districts are. However, state legislatures must draw the boundaries so that the districts are equal in population.

Most powers granted to Congress in the Constitution are shared by the Senate and the House of Representatives. However, each of the two houses has some powers that are not shared. The House of Representatives has these special powers:
1. The House has the power to start all bills, or proposed laws, that raise money.

The men who wrote the Constitution believed that the members of Congress closest to the people should be the ones to tax the people. They designed Congress so that members of the House would be closer to the people than would members of the Senate. Representatives face election every two years, and they represent a smaller number of people than members of the Senate do. As a result, they are usually more concerned about local problems than are members of the Senate.
2. The House also has the power to start the impeachment pro-

CHANGES IN STATE REPRESENTATION AFTER THE 1970 CENSUS

Every ten years the government takes a census to find out how many people live in the United States and where they live. Then it changes the number of representatives a state may have in Congress. States that have gained population in relation to the other states get more representatives than they had before. States that have lost population lose representatives.

☐ GAINED REPRESENTATION
☐ LOST REPRESENTATION
☐ NO CHANGE

Large numbers indicate number of representatives in the House.
Small numbers indicate seats gained or lost.

120

cess to dismiss the President and certain other high officials. It was the House Judiciary Committee that drew up articles of impeachment against President Nixon in 1974.

3. If no candidate for President wins a majority of votes, the House of Representatives picks the President. This happened with Thomas Jefferson in 1800 and with John Q. Adams in 1824.

The Senate

The Senate is made up of two members from each state. The members, called senators, are elected for a term of six years. Each one represents his or her entire state.

Discuss: What special roles does the Senate have?

Like the House of Representatives, the Senate has a number of powers that are its very own:

1. The Senate has the power to approve presidential appointments of Supreme Court justices, federal judges, cabinet members, ambassadors, and other high executive officials.

2. The Senate holds trials for public officials impeached by the House. This has happened twelve times in the nation's history.

3. The Senate has the power to approve all treaties made by the United States.

4. If no candidate for Vice-President gets a majority vote, the Senate chooses the Vice-President.

Most senators are better known in Washington, D.C., and at home than are most representatives. This is partly because there are fewer senators. Also, a senator's term of office is three times longer than a representative's is.

Congressional Leaders

Within each house of Congress individuals and small groups take on special jobs. Congressional leaders have jobs that are especially important. They direct the activities of Congress.

House Leaders. The most powerful leader in the House of Representatives is the **speaker of the House.** The speaker directs business on the floor of the House and is the leader of lawmaking. In addition, the speaker influences who gets other House leadership jobs. If anything happens to the President and Vice-President, the speaker becomes President. The job of speaker has always gone to a member of the House **majority party,** the political party with most members. Like other leaders in the House and the Senate, the speaker is usually a long-time member of Congress.

The Speaker's platform in the House of Representatives. The Speaker is Massachusetts Representative Thomas (Tip) O'Neill, on the left. House minority leader John Rhodes is standing next to him.

121

Both the House majority party and the House **minority party** elect a **floor leader** and a **party whip.** The floor leaders try to influence party members to vote the way the party wants. Working with other House leaders, the floor leaders also decide when bills will be introduced. The whips help the floor leaders. They see that representatives are present for important votes. They keep track of how party members plan to vote on key issues.

Senate Leaders. The Constitution states that the Vice-President of the United States will serve as president of the Senate. The Vice-President acts as a chairperson of the Senate but votes only in case of a tie. The Vice-President does not have much influence on Senate decisions, and today Vice-Presidents do not usually spend much time on this job.

The person who acts as chairperson of the Senate most of the time is an officer elected by the Senate called the **president pro tempore** ([prō tem′pər ē] or pro tem for short). This officer is usually a member of the majority party. As is true of the Vice-President, the president pro tempore has little influence over the Senate.

The real leaders in the Senate are the majority party leader and the minority party leader. These leaders are chosen by members of their parties. They steer bills through the Senate. They also set up the Senate's work **agenda.** When the majority leader is in the same political party as the President, he or she usually tries to push the President's program through the Senate. The two Senate leaders are assisted by whips, as in the House.

Committees: Little Legislatures

The real action in Congress is in the many House and Senate committees. Committees are small groups of senators and representatives who work in special areas like foreign policy or farm problems.

Ninety percent of all lawmaking work is done in committee rather than on the floor of the Senate or House. So many bills are introduced in Congress each year that few of them would be considered if the work weren't divided among many committees. Committee members and the staff hired to assist them work on the bills that will be voted on by the full House and Senate. They make the decisions about what is put in the bill and what is not. Bills are rarely changed after they leave a committee.

When senators and representatives first come to Congress,

STANDING COMMITTEES OF CONGRESS

House Committees

Agriculture
Appropriations
Armed Services
Banking, Finance and Urban Affairs
Budget
District of Columbia
Education and Labor
Government Operations
House Administration
Interior and Insular Affairs
International Relations
Interstate and Foreign Commerce
Judiciary
Merchant Marine and Fisheries
Post Office and Civil Service
Public Works and Transportation
Rules
Science and Technology
Small Business
Standards of Official Conduct
Veterans' Affairs
Ways and Means

Senate Committee

Agriculture, Nutrition, and Forestry
Appropriations
Armed Services
Banking, Housing, and Urban Affairs
Budget
Commerce, Science, and Transportation
Energy and Natural Resources
Environment and Public Works
Finance
Foreign Relations
Governmental Affairs
Human Resources
Judiciary
Rules and Administration
Veterans' Affairs

they try to get on important committees that are of interest to them. Members of Congress from farm areas might want to serve on agriculture committees. Those with many factories in their districts might be interested in labor committees.

Representatives usually serve on four or five committees and subcommittees. A senator may serve on ten committees and subcommittees, and most chair at least one subcommittee.

Discuss: Why are committees so important?

More Than 300 Committees. There are several different kinds of committees in Congress. There are standing committees and their subcommittees, special committees, and joint committees. **Standing committees** are permanent committees that continue their work from session to session. Each standing committee covers a special area like education, veterans affairs, or banking. The Senate has 15 standing committees. The House has 22 standing committees.

Each standing committee is divided into **subcommittees.** Subcommittees deal with particular problems and issues in the area handled by the "parent" committee. For example, the Senate Veterans Affairs Committee has subcommittees on health and hospitals, education and housing, and insurance. Some subcommittees are very powerful. Others are not.

Discuss: What kinds of committees are there? What are their special roles?

Hawaii's Congressman Daniel Akaka and Senator Spark Matsunaga outside the Capitol.

Note: Some students may
be able to find articles on
current committee work to
share with the class.

Both the Senate and House also have **special committees.**
These committees are set up to do a special job. In 1976, for
example, the House Select Committee on Assassinations was
formed. The committee's main job was to investigate the facts
surrounding the assassinations of President John F. Kennedy
and Dr. Martin Luther King, Jr. Like all special committees, the
House Assassinations Committee disbanded when it finished its
work.

Congress also has seven joint House-Senate committees.
These **joint committees** are made up of both senators and representatives. The Joint Committee on Atomic Energy, for example, is a group of members of both houses of Congress who
considers problems and bills related to nuclear energy and fuel.

Committee Chairpersons. Every committee has a leader who
acts as the chairperson. The chairperson controls the work of his
or her committee. The chairperson normally decides when and if
a committee will meet. He or she also decides what bills will be
studied by a committee.

Because standing committees are important, the chairpersons
of standing committees are important congressional leaders.
They can have great influence on the lawmaking work of Con-

Discuss: What did the
committee accomplish?

Evidence presented to the House
committee investigating the assassination of Martin Luther King, Jr

124

gress. The knowledge they have on the subject of their committees adds to their influence.

Committee chairpersons are almost always chosen by **seniority rule,** which is not really a rule but a custom. Seniority rule means that the majority party member with most years on a committee gets to be chairperson.

Some people think seniority rule is a good idea. They say it prevents fights over committee jobs. It makes sure that those chosen to be chairpersons will have experience. It also allows members of Congress from small states to gain important jobs in Congress. Other people think seniority rule is a bad idea. They say that all a person has to do to become a leader is stay alive and be re-elected. In fact, there has been so much criticism of seniority rule over the years that both political parties have moved slightly away from it. The senior majority party member on a committee still usually wins the role of chairperson, but it is no longer guaranteed.

Discuss: What is the seniority system? What is the role of the seniority system today?

Section Review

Vocabulary: agenda, bicameral, congressional district, floor leader, majority party, minority party, joint committee, president pro tem, seniority rule, speaker of the House, standing committee, subcommittee, party whip.

Reviewing the Main Ideas

1. What are three special powers that the House has which the Senate does not have?
2. What are three special powers the Senate has that the House does not?
3. Who elects the floor leaders and whips in the House of Representatives?
4. Why are committees important?

Skill Building

1. According to the map on page 120, how many states lost seats in the House after the 1970 census?
2. List these three House jobs in the order of their importance (most important first) and briefly describe the work of each: majority party floor leader, majority party whip, speaker of the House.
3. How does the work of a standing committee differ from that of a special committee?

Main Ideas
1. pp. 120–121
2. p. 121
3. representatives of each party
4. They do 90% of the lawmaking work.
Skill Building
1. Nine
2. speaker, floor leader, whip pp. 121–122
3. pp. 123–124

125

2/The Job in Congress Today

Congress is more than formal rules and powers. It is people. More than 19,000 people work full time in the Congress. This number includes senators and representatives and their assistants, secretaries, clerks, and many other workers. The most important people, of course, are senators and representatives.

Members of Congress

The legal qualifications for members of Congress are simple. They deal only with age, citizenship, and residence. (See page 60.) However, as the chart on this page shows, members of Congress have more in common than legal qualifications. Note that most members are white, male, and belong to one of the two major political parties. What does the chart show you about the educational level and occupational background of Congress members?

Discuss: Will this change in the next election?

As you can see, some groups are not well represented in Congress. About eleven percent of the population of the United States is black. Only one percent of the Senate and four percent of the House is black, however. Can you think of other groups who are underrepresented in Congress?

People who are active in community organizations gain experiences and make contacts that help them get elected to Con-

---

CHARACTERISTICS OF THE 95th* CONGRESS

HOUSE		SENATE
PARTY		
292	Democrats	61
143	Republicans	38
0	Independent	1
SEX		
418	Men	100
17	Women	0
AGE		
27	Youngest	34
77	Oldest	80
49	Average	54
RELIGION		
255	Protestants	69
107	Catholics	12
18	Jewish	5
4	Mormons	3
51	Others	11

HOUSE		SENATE
PROFESSION		
215	Lawyers	65
81	Business leaders and bankers	13
45	Educators	6
14	Farmers and ranchers	6
22	Career government officials	0
24	Journalists, communications executives	4
2	Physicians	0
1	Veterinarians	1
1	Geologists	2
6	Workers and skilled tradespeople	0
25	Others	3
ETHNIC MINORITIES		
17	Blacks	1
2	Orientals	3
4	Spanish	0

*Each Congress is numbered. The First Congress met after the Constitution was ratified. It was elected in 1788 and met from 1789-1790. Each Congress lasts for two years. The 95th Congress met from 1977-1978.

gress. Members of Congress tend to be "joiners." They are more likely than the average citizen to belong to such groups as the Masons, Knights of Columbus, or Rotary Club.

In addition, many Congress people have had previous political experience. One study of senators showed that the average senator had held three public offices and spent ten years in government service before being elected to the Senate.

Representing the People

What do people do once they are elected to Congress? The basic job of senators and representatives is to represent the people. In carrying out that responsibility, members of Congress do four different kinds of jobs.

Discuss: What are the key roles of members of Congress once they are elected? Why are they important?

Making Laws. The job of making laws is given to members of Congress by the Constitution. Members do this by writing and introducing bills, by taking part in committee work, by listening to the information and ideas of people for and against a bill, and by voting on the floor of the House or Senate.

Troubleshooting. Though lawmaking is important, most members of Congress are lucky if they can spend half their time doing that work. Much of their time is spent acting as troubleshooters for people from their home district or state who need

Senior citizens from Michigan tell their Senator, Don Riegle, that they want him to vote for a National Health Insurance bill.

127

Discuss: Why is troubleshooting such an important role?

help in dealing with the federal government.

Most requests for help reach members of Congress through the mail. A busy congressional office may get 6,000 letters every week. About 25 percent of this mail asks the senator or representative to vote a certain way on bills before Congress. The rest ask for help of one kind or another.

With what problems do people need help? One congressional aide put it this way. "Usually, it's a problem of some sort with the bureaucracy. A social security check doesn't come. Or a veteran's claim is held up. Maybe it's a slipup by a computer . . . but getting action . . . is tough for the average person."

Some more examples follow:

• A woman in the Navy asks for a special transfer so that she can be near her sick father.

• A young man asks how and where to apply for a government job.

• The owner of a small business asks for information on how to sell his company's products to the government.

• A high-school student asks for information from the Library of Congress.

• A retired woman writes because the Social Security Administration has stopped sending her monthly check.

Kansas Senator Nancy Kassenbaum talks with constituents.

128

Most requests for help are handled by the congressperson's office staff. Staff members contact federal agencies, such as the Veterans Administration, to gather information and make requests. Then they report back to the person they are trying to help. Often a question from a staff person is all that is needed to get things moving again. When a staff person cannot get action, the senator or representative usually steps in to help. Senator Jacob Javits of New York once said, "My staff handles problems until the moment of truth. Then I'm called in to push a button, so to speak, to make a phone call at a crucial moment."

Most members of Congress accept this troubleshooting job. They know it will help them be re-elected. People they help are a source of support election after election.

Helping the District or State. Another part of a representative or senator's job is to try to influence government decisions that will benefit his or her own district or state. Every year the national government spends more than $400 billion. Business leaders, labor leaders, farmers, and other groups with special interests expect their representatives in Congress to help direct some of that money into their state or district.

Business owners, for example, want federal contracts. One contract to make shoes for the army can bring a small business a lot of work. Labor leaders want their members to benefit from government actions. For example, the decision to build a dam in a district could create many jobs for workers in the area. Governors, state lawmakers, and local mayors want federal programs they can take credit for.

The late Senator Kerr once said, "I am a senator of the United States, but I want it fully understood that I represent the state of Oklahoma." Senator Kerr was very skillful at bringing federal money and projects into his state.

Keeping an Eye on the Executive Branch. Yet another job that members of Congress do is to watch over the executive branch. They make sure that executive branch departments carry out programs in a way that was intended by Congress.

Over the years, Congress has created many federal programs. The executive branch under the President is supposed to carry out these programs. Naturally, members of Congress have an interest in watching how these programs work. When laws are carried out poorly, members of Congress get complaints from

Note: Look for examples of current local activities of members of Congress.

One way Congress checks the executive branch is through the Senate Government Affairs Committee. In 1977, this committee looked into charges against Bert Lance, director of the Office of Management and Budget. Eventually, Lance resigned. (Top) Lance consults his lawyer during the hearings. (Bottom) Lance testifying.

voters and from interested groups. Factory owners in a state, for instance, may complain if they think the Environmental Protection Agency is unfair to them. Farmers will be angry if they think the Department of Agriculture is not carrying out a farm program in the way Congress intended.

Congress can do several things in carrying out its "watchdog" duties. Members of Congress can hold committee **hearings** to investigate special problems in an agency. They can also create or abolish federal agencies. In addition, senators can investigate federal agency leaders appointed by the President.

Congressional Staff—The Silent Helpers

In 1893, members of Congress got $100 each to hire staff help. Today, each representative can spend $255,144 a year for staff help, and senators from large states can spend $902,301 a year. What has happened since 1893?

During the early years of our history Congress met only a few months each year. Today, serving in Congress is a full-time job. The duties are far too many for one person to handle. Every year more than 25,000 bills are introduced. Members of Congress get millions of requests for help. There are thousands of committee hearings. And, of course, members of Congress must run for re-election every few years. In 1977, Senator Hubert

Discuss: How is this congressional role supporting the "check and balance" plan proposed in the Constitution?

Discuss: Who are the "silent helpers"? Why are they so important?

A farmers' protest in front of the U.S. Capitol, January, 1979.

Humphrey summed up the change that had occurred in Congress during the previous twenty-eight years when he said, "This is another world from the time I came here. Then it was a picnic; now it's a treadmill."

To get help with their work, members of Congress hire a **staff** of clerks, secretaries, and special assistants. You may not hear much about these people in the news, but they are important. Staff members run their boss's congressional office in Washington as well as one or more in the home state or district. They gather information on new bills and issues that are before Congress. They arrange for meetings and speeches. And they work for their boss's re-election.

Section Review

Vocabulary: hearings, staff.

Reviewing the Main Ideas
1. List four jobs that members of Congress do.
2. List three duties of congressional staff people.
3. Why is it necessary for members of Congress to watch the activities of the executive branch?

Skill Building
1. Look at the story of Representative Jackson in the chapter introduction on page 118. Find examples in his day of the four kinds of congressional jobs described on pages 127–130.
2. Look at the table that shows characteristics of the 95th Congress on page 126. There are many more workers and skilled tradespeople in the United States than there are lawyers. Which are there more of in Congress?
3. Do you think this means that workers and skilled tradespeople are poorly represented in our national government? Explain your thinking.

Main Ideas
1. making laws, trouble-
shooting, helping state or
district, and keeping an eye
on the executive branch.
2. pp. 129–130
Skill Building
1. p. 118
2. lawyers
3. Answers will vary.

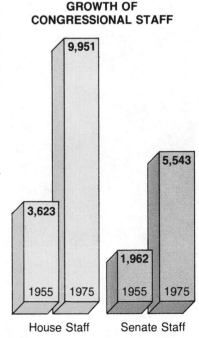

GROWTH OF CONGRESSIONAL STAFF

House Staff: 1955 — 3,623; 1975 — 9,951
Senate Staff: 1955 — 1,962; 1975 — 5,543

3/Making Laws

Congressional leaders, members, and staff work together to pass new laws. Sometimes an individual member of Congress will introduce a bill. However, most ideas for new laws start outside Congress. Eighty percent of all bills that become law begin in the White House. Other new bills are started by **special interest groups** working with one or more members of Congress. (Special interest groups are organizations of people who have some common interest and who try to influence the decisions of government officials.)

How a Bill Becomes a Law

Discuss: How does a bill become a law? Why is each step important?

Just how do senators and representatives turn ideas into the law of the land? With 535 members of Congress, many rules are needed to keep the lawmaking job fair and orderly. These rules make it hard for a bill to become a law. More than 20,000 bills are started in Congress each year. Only about 500 to 600 ever become law.

The numbered items below show the steps a bill must follow to become a law.

1. Introduction. Any senator or representative can introduce a bill. However, many bills must start in the House because they involve money. Every bill is given a number when it is submitted. Then it is sent to the standing committee that seems most qualified to handle it.

2. Hearings. In considering a bill, a committee may hold public hearings. Private individuals and people from different interest groups **testify** before the committee. They state their opinions about the bill and give facts to support their opinions. They may argue for or against the bill. People may also send written statements. Sometimes committee members ask experts to present evidence for or against the bill.

3. Committee Decisions. Standing committees have life and death power over bills. After public hearings, committee members make one of several decisions. (The decisions are almost always made in secret.) The committee can (1) suggest that the bill be adopted with few changes, (2) change the bill almost completely, (3) ignore the bill and stop it by not acting on it, or

Texas Congresswoman Barbara Jordan.

132

HOW A BILL BECOMES A LAW

Except for money bills, a bill can be started in either house. This diagram shows a bill starting in the House of Representatives, but the same process would be followed for a bill started in the Senate. In practice, many bills are started in both houses at the same time.

A representative has an idea for a law.

His or her staff writes up the bill.

The representative introduces the bill in the House. The bill is sent to a committee.

House committee collects evidence, holds hearings, suggests amendments, votes.

If the committee approves it, the amended bill is sent to the Rules Committee.

Rules committee decides the rules for debate in the House. The rules committee decides to send the bill to the whole House.

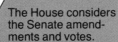

The House debates and votes.

If a majority favor it, the bill goes to the Senate. The bill is sent to a committee.

The Senate committee holds hearings, collects evidence, amends bill, votes.

A favorable vote sends the bill to the whole Senate.

The Senate votes. If a majority favor it, the bill is returned to the House.

The House considers the Senate amendments and votes.

A conference committee from both houses rewrites any unacceptable amendments.

Both houses vote on the amended bill.

A favorable vote sends the bill to the President.

If the President signs it, the bill becomes law.

(4) kill the bill by majority vote. The full House or Senate can overrule the decision of its committees, but this hardly ever happens. When a committee is against a bill, the bill almost never becomes a law.

4. Introduction to Full House or Senate. Bills that are approved in committee are ready for floor action in the House or Senate. In the House they go to the **Rules Committee** first. This group is the House "traffic cop." It decides the rules of debate when the bill goes to the floor of the House. The Rules Committee can kill a bill by not letting it get to the floor.

5. General Debate, Amendments, Vote. On the floor of the House or Senate, the bill is debated—reasons for and against the bill are stated. Amendments may be added at this time. After amendments have been voted on, debate continues. Eventually,

A citizen discusses her support for House bill 10738—an amendment to improve home-care benefits in the Medicare program.

the bill is voted on as a whole. A simple majority is needed to pass a bill. If either the Senate or the House rejects a bill, it is dead. If a bill passes in one house, it is sent to the other.

6. Conference Committee. If either house of Congress makes changes in a bill after receiving it from the other house, the bill is sent to a **conference committee.** Five members from each house meet privately and work out differences between House and Senate versions of the bill. Only about ten percent of all bills go to a conference committee, but they are usually the most important bills.

7. Vote on Conference Report. Once a bill is released from the conference committee, the House and Senate must vote on the final version of the bill.

8. Presidential Action. When a bill is approved by both houses of Congress, it goes to the President. Then one of three things happens. The President may sign the bill and declare it a new law. The President may veto the bill—refuse to sign it and send it back to Congress. Or the President may keep the bill for ten days without signing it. If the President does the latter while Congress is in session, the bill becomes law. If Congress is not in session, the bill does not become law. This is called a **pocket veto.**

Discuss: Why is a "pocket veto" such an important tool?

Section Review

Vocabulary: conference committee, special interest group, House Rules Committee, pocket veto, testify.

Reviewing the Main Ideas
1. Where do eighty percent of all bills that become law begin?
2. About how many bills are introduced in Congress each year?
3. What four things can happen to a bill after it is sent to committee?

Skill Building
1. List the steps an imaginary farm bill would have to go through before it could become law. (Make this a bill that goes to a conference committee and one that is signed by the President as soon as he receives it.)
2. Why would a committee hold hearings on a proposed law?

Main Ideas
1. in the White House
2. more than 20,000
3. pp. 132–134
Skill Building
1. pp. 132–134
2. to get information to help committee members decide

To Cut or Not to Cut?

In late 1968, the building industry began to run short of wood. A dry summer in 1967 had caused logging to stop because of the danger of fire, and a boxcar shortage and dock strike slowed the delivery of what timber there was. Furthermore, much of the available timber was being sold out of the country.

Because wood is an important building material, the shortage slowed the building of houses. Home builders begged the timber industry for more wood. Naturally, the timber industry wished it had more wood to sell builders.

In 1969, leaders from the National Forest Products Association, representing 1500 forest product companies, and the National Association of Home Builders met in Houston, Texas. The two groups decided to work together to get Congress to pass a law allowing more trees in the national forests to be cut for timber. Other groups who thought a timber-cutting bill was in their interest gave support to the effort.

The timber-cutting bill was first introduced in Congress by Senator John Sparkman of Alabama. On April 18, 1969, the bill

Clear cutting logs in Washington State.

was sent to Senator Allan Ellender's Agriculture Committee. Ellender decided to do nothing with the bill until the House of Representatives acted on its own version.

Shortly after the timber-cutting bill was introduced in Congress, several different groups who were against the bill came together. They called themselves the Conservation Coalition. Members of the Coalition objected to the bill for several reasons. They reminded people that the national forests were used for many things. Timber was only one use. If more trees were cut for timber, wildlife habitats, recreation areas, and watershed management would all suffer. They feared the legislation would bring protection of wilderness areas and scenic lands to a halt. Further, the Coalition believed that increased logging would not solve the housing shortage. They said the housing problem was caused by high interest rates, high labor prices, and high land prices.

Action in the House began on May 21-23, 1969. Representative John McMillan's Subcommittee on Forests held hearings on a House version of the bill. People from both the Conservation Coalition and the pro-timber group testified at the hearings.

(Left) logging in Flat Head National Forest, Montana, and (right) loading pulp at Wilmington Harbor, North Carolina.

CASE STUDY

Each group presented information for its side. As a result, a revised House bill (called HR 12025) came out of the subcommittee. By February, 1970, the bill had reached the floor of the House, where it would be debated and voted on by all members.

During 1969 HR 12025 had become the target of support or attack, depending on which side a person was on. There was a good chance the Senate would act favorably on its own timber bill if the House passed HR 12025. So both sides worked hard for their cause.

On December 21, volunteers from the Conservation Coalition delivered information kits to members of Congress. The kits gave facts that supported the conservation view of the effects of HR 12025 on the national forests and the housing industry. The Coalition also sent telegrams to all members of Congress, and they sent a representative to speak directly to members of Congress or their staff members. In addition, four groups in the Coalition asked their members to write or telegraph their senators and representatives in support of the Coalition view.

The pro-timber group was also hard at work. In January, the group prepared a 36-page booklet arguing in favor of HR 12025. The booklet was sent to all members of Congress and to five

(Left) logs at a paper processing plant and (right) waiting processing at Plum Creek, Montana.

thousand journalists across the country. Supporters of HR 12025 also talked directly with congressional staff and members. And pro-timber leaders sought the support of city groups concerned about housing and jobs. One response, a letter from the president of the National Urban League, was given to all members of Congress.

The showdown came on the floor of the House of Representatives, February 26, 1970. The House voted on whether to consider HR 12025 for passage or to send it back to committee. The House voted 228 to 150 not to consider the bill. HR 12025 was dead.

Reviewing the Case Study

1. What decision did House members face on February 26, 1970?
2. What did the Conservation Coalition see as consequences of passage of HR 12025?
3. What did the pro-timber group believe to be the consequences of passing this bill?
4. What is your judgment of the House decision? Give your reasons.

Housing constructed from timber, Berkeley, California.

Chapter Six Test and Activities

★★★

Vocabulary

Match the following words with their meanings.

1. bicameral
2. agenda
3. congressional district
4. hearing
5. testify
6. party whip
7. seniority rule
8. joint committee
9. special interest group

a. a committee of members of both houses of Congress
b. an opportunity for members of Congress to learn the possible consequences of a bill before voting it into law
c. a customary way of picking committee chairpersons in Congress
d. made up of two houses
e. the list of bills and other items a committee or house will work on
f. give evidence, information, and opinions formally at a hearing
g. an organization of people with a common goal who try to influence government
h. an area within a state that is represented by one member of the House of Representatives
i. a leader who makes sure party members are present for important votes

Reviewing Chapter Ideas

1. True or false: Congress is the national legislature of the United States.
2. True or false: The most important job of Congress is to make laws.

3. Which of the following does Congress have the power to do?
   a. establish local voting rules
   b. coin money
   c. build churches
   d. all of the above
4. The number of representatives from each state _____ .
   a. never changes
   b. is equal for all states
   c. is larger for the original thirteen colonies
   d. varies according to the population
5. The House of Representatives does not have the power to _____ .
   a. approve presidential appointments
   b. start a bill to raise money
   c. start the impeachment process
   d. pick the President if no candidate receives a majority of the votes
6. What is the number of senators from each state?
   a. one
   b. two
   c. three
   d. It varies according to population.
7. True or false: The most powerful person in the Senate is the president pro tempore.
8. True or false: Most work on bills is done on the floor of the House and Senate.

Using Basic Social Studies Skills

Finding Information

Read the graph below to answer these questions.

1. What was the majority party in the Senate?
2. What was the minority party in the House?

Vocabulary
1. d   4. b   7. c
2. e   5. f   8. a
3. h   6. i   9. g

Ideas
1. T   4. d   7. F
2. T   5. a   8. F
3. b   6. b

140

★★★

3. Which party had the most members in Congress?
4. How many did it have?

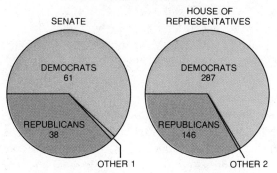

DEMOCRATS AND REPUBLICANS IN THE 95TH CONGRESS

SENATE

HOUSE OF REPRESENTATIVES

DEMOCRATS 61

DEMOCRATS 287

REPUBLICANS 38

REPUBLICANS 146

OTHER 1

OTHER 2

Comprehending Information
1. Why are senators generally better known than representatives?
2. What is the difference between a standing committee and a special committee?

Organizing Information
Draw a diagram to show how a bill about energy conservation might become a law.

Evaluating Information
Do you think members of Congress are concerned about which committees they serve on? Why or why not?

Communicating Ideas
Write a paragraph telling how members of Congress make decisions.

Using Decision-Making Skills

1. What alternatives did members of Congress have in the case of the timber-cutting bill?
2. What would have been the consequences of each alternative?

3. What personal values may have influenced those who voted for the timber-cutting bill? What values may have influenced those who voted against the bill?
4. Do you think the vote to kill the bill was wise? Why or why not?

Activities

1. Find out who the representative is from your congressional district. Learn what you can about him or her. Tell whether or not you would work for him or her during the next election campaign in light of what you have learned.
2. Learn who your senators are. Write a letter to one. Ask for a list of the committees on which he or she is working.
3. Use the current *United States Government Manual* or another appropriate source to find out who presently fills each of the following positions:
   - speaker of the house
   - president of the Senate pro tempore
   - Senate majority leader
   - Senate minority leader
4. The following books are recommended for those students who want to learn more about the work of Congress:
   (a) *Lobbying,* by Karen Sagstetter (Watts, 1978).
   (b) *The American Congress,* by Ann E. Weiss (Messner, 1977).
   (c) *I Want to Know About the United States Senate,* by Senator Charles Percy (Doubleday, 1976).
   (d) *There Ought to Be a Law! How Laws Are Made and Work,* by Ellen Switzer (Atheneum, 1972).

Chapter 7

Paying for National Government

★★

Discuss: How is the national government influencing us in this situation?

"Can't we move a little faster?" Bill asked. "Uncle Ted said we could go to the lake if we get to his house early enough."

Sally Ramsey looked in the rear-view mirror at her brother, who was sprawled across the back seat. "I can't go more than 55, Bill. It's the law."

"Why 55?" Bill asked.

"Because it uses less gas to go 55 than 70 or 75," Sally explained. "The speed limit used to be higher, but there were gas shortages in the early '70s all over the nation, and lots of people said that things were going to get worse. To help save gas, the national government passed a law that says we can't drive over 55 anywhere in the country."

"But how can the national government tell people how fast they should drive?" Bill complained.

"There are several reasons," answered Sally. "But one important reason is that the national government pays most of the cost of building and repairing the country's interstate highways. If a state doesn't go along with the new speed limit, the national government won't give it the highway money it needs."

"Besides," Sally said with a smile, "55 is safer than 70, so relax and enjoy the ride!"

Speed limits are only one example of national government decisions that affect the daily lives of citizens. The national government spends millions of dollars each year to make and enforce rules and to provide services and benefits. These rules, services, and benefits touch almost every part of American life. Where does the money come from to pay the cost of government? How is the money spent? Who decides what the cost of government should be? In this chapter you will read:

1/Where the Money Comes From
2/How the Money Is Spent
3/Making the Federal Budget
Case Study: Housing in Saul Hollow

1/Where the Money Comes From

In 1792, when George Washington was President, 780 people worked under him in the executive branch of government. This small government served a nation of fewer than 4 million Americans. In Washington's day, the national government spent less than $10 million a year. Today the yearly cost of government is more than $490 billion. This big government serves a nation of more than 220 million people.

Discuss: Where does the government get the money it needs?

Taxes

The national government gets most of the money it needs from **taxes.** Taxes are fees that people must pay to support the government. The government borrows most of the rest of the money it needs. The graph on this page shows the proportions of government income that come from various sources.

Income Tax. The tax that brings in most money to the national government is the **personal income tax.** This tax is charged on the income each person earns in a year. Personal income

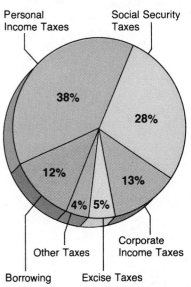

SOURCES OF NATIONAL GOVERNMENT INCOME*

Personal Income Taxes — 38%

Social Security Taxes — 28%

12%

4% 5%

13%

Other Taxes

Borrowing

Excise Taxes

Corporate Income Taxes

*Based on actual income in fiscal 1977.

A sign on the Baltimore-Washington Parkway warns drivers to reduce speed during the 1973 energy crisis.

143

taxes amount to nearly 40 percent of the money taken in by the government—more than $150 billion.

Discuss: Why don't we pay taxes on all the money we earn? How does the chart on p. 145 help to answer this question?

Not every dollar that a person earns is taxed. The tax laws passed by Congress allow people to deduct certain expenses from their income before figuring the tax. These amounts are called **deductions.** For example, if a person has children, he or she does not have to pay taxes on some of the money used to care for the children. People do not have to pay taxes on income given to charities. People can deduct part of the money they spend on medicines and on doctor and hospital bills.

People do not all agree that the tax laws are fair. Deductions seem to favor some groups over others. Renters, for example, pay higher taxes than homeowners. So tax reform is something that people want. Candidates running for office often promise to try to make the tax laws fairer. But they have a very hard time doing so because people cannot agree about what is fair. Is it fair to make the people who get the most benefits from government pay the highest taxes? Or should people who have the most income pay the most in taxes?

Our tax laws accept the second line of reasoning. After people have taken their deductions, the amount that is left is called **taxable income.** The tax rate on taxable income varies. People with more income pay a higher percentage of their income in personal income tax than others with less income. For example, in 1977 Janice Benson had a taxable income of $20,000. In that year, people who made as much as she were taxed at a rate of 18 percent. Her tax was $3,678. Her neighbor Robert Green had a taxable income of $10,000. His tax rate was 11 percent; his tax was $1,135. While his taxable income was exactly half of hers, his tax was much less than half.

Discuss: Why is social security so important?

Social Security Tax. The social security tax is another kind of income tax. Most of the money collected by this tax is used to give income to retired people. All people pay social security tax at the same rate up to a certain limit. Through 1980, the limit was $25,900. This means that people did not pay social security tax on any money over $25,900.

Note: Have a social security card available to examine.

Each worker covered by the social security system has an account with the federal government. This account is identified by a number. Your social security number identifies your account. As you earn money, social security taxes are held out of your paycheck and paid into your social security account. On your paycheck, this amount is often labeled FICA for Federal Insurance Contribution Act—the law that set up the social security taxes. Your employer also pays into your account, matching every dollar you pay with another. Then, when you retire or become unable to work, you will receive money every month. Social security also pays benefits to the minor children and husband or wife of a worker who dies.

Corporate Income Tax. Taxes on businesses rank second as a source of money for the national government. Businesses pay more or less tax according to their profits. (**Profit** is the money left over after the cost of doing business has been subtracted from a company's income.)

Like individuals, corporations may deduct certain expenses to lower their taxable incomes. For example, they may subtract money paid to buy new machinery or to build a new office building. And like individuals, the tax rate on businesses varies with

Discuss: Who would be most affected without social security?

WHAT HAPPENS TO A PAYCHECK

When workers get a paycheck, they also get a perforated stub that explains what has happened to the money they have earned. No one takes the whole amount home. Money is held out to pay for taxes. This money is sent directly to the federal government. Also, money is often held out to pay for health insurance and retirement benefits. Often workers ask to have money held out and paid directly to their own credit union accounts, or to buy bonds, or to charities such as the Community Chest. Look at Harley Johnson's paycheck stub. Where did his money go?

amount earned — amount withheld for income tax

RETAIN PERMANENTLY FOR YOUR RECORDS

0249 39

amount withheld for social security tax

amount the worker receives

SOCIAL SECURITY NUMBER	PAY PERIOD ENDING MO	DAY	YR	HOURS REG.	PREM.	EARNINGS REGULAR	PREM.	*	OTHER AMOUNT	GROSS	FEDERAL	TAXES WITHHELD STATE MISC.	F.I.C.A.
333 30 1013	01	10	79	3620	610	12670	1068		14140	27878	4153	6971	709

RETIREMENT PLAN	SAVINGS PLAN	SAVINGS BONDS	GRP INS LTD INS	DONATIONS	UNION DUES INIT	** AMOUNT OTHER	** AMOUNT OTHER	** AMOUNT OTHER	** AMOUNT OTHER	NET PAY
		229 251	107	X 300						20432

DEDUCTIONS

* OTHER EARNINGS CODES	H — TIPS REPORTED	A — POLICY	D — BONUS	MISC TAXES	DI — STATE AND
4 — SICK PAY	M — MEALS	B — COMMISSION	E — INCENTIVE	LOCAL	VOLUNTARY
5 — OTHER COMP	Y — MDSE PAYMENTS	C — P M PAYMENTS	V — VACATION	STATE UNEMP	WORKMANS COMP
** OTHER DEDUCTION CODES	G — CREDIT UNION	X — LIFE INSURANCE	8 — MEALS		
E — WAGE ASSIGNMENTS	J — GARNISHMENTS	Z — MISCELLANEOUS	9 — MDSE PAYMENTS		
C — COMPANY LOANS	T — AUTO INSURANCE	6 — TIPS REPORTED	* — COMBINATION OF 6, 8, 9		

Filing an Income Tax Return

Many single people who have only one source of income and who do not itemize such tax deductions as interest payments on a home mortgage and medical bills file federal income tax form 1040A. This is called the "short form." A filled-out Form 1040A appears on the opposite page and the following discussion refers to it.

John R. Brown is a high-school student. Working after school, on weekends, and during the summer, in 1978 he earned a total of $3,552.00. In March 1979 John filled out and filed a Form 1040A to meet the April 16 filing deadline that year.

At the top of the form, John printed his first name, middle initial, and last name on the appropriate lines. He next filled in his street address, and his city, state, and zip code. Then he placed his social security number on the form at the right top and gave his occupation as "student." He decided that he wanted a dollar of his tax to go to the Presidential Election Campaign Fund, so he checked the "yes" box for that.

Being single, John checked box 1 after "filing status." He then went to box 5a, checking that. Each person is entitled to a $750 exemption for him- or herself and an equal amount for each of any dependents. This exemption, subtracted from income, is figured in the tax tables. John then entered "1" in the box to the right, and the same in the box to the right of line 6.

John then went to line 7. Here he entered his 1978 income, $3,552.00. He had received from his employer a W-2 form which showed his income and the amount of taxes his employer had withheld from his wages and sent to the government. John would attach a copy of his W-2 to his return. The amount withheld was $64.20. He skipped lines 8 and 9, and at 10 entered his income again, $3,552.00. Line 11a did not apply, so John went to 11b, where he entered $64.20—the tax withheld—from his W-2. He placed the same figure on line 12.

Now John looked at the appropriate tax table included in the set of Internal Revenue Service instructions he had obtained at a bank—"Tax Table A—Single." Reading the first two columns on the left, John found that his income fell between $3,550 and $3,600. He claimed one exemption, so he then read the third column (under number 1) to find his tax. He discovered it to be $54, which he entered on line 13.

More than enough tax had been withheld from John's wages, so he was due a refund from the government. He subtracted line 13 from line 12, and placed $10.20, the amount to be refunded, on line 14. John then signed the return and dated it. In about six weeks he would receive his refund from the government.

1978 Tax Table A—SINGLE (Filing Status Box 1) (For 1040.

To find your tax: Read down the income column until you find your income as umn headed by the total number of exemptions claimed on Form 104(is your tax. Enter on Form 1040A, line 13.

The $2,200 zero bracket amount, your deduction for exemptions, and the ger the tax shown in this table. Do not take a separate deduction for them.

Caution: *If you can be claimed as a dependent on your parent's return AND you more AND your earned income is less than $2,200, you must use Form*

If Form 1040A, line 10, is—		And the total number of exemptions claimed on line 6 is—			If Form 1040A, line 10, is—		And the tota of exemptior on line (	
Over	But not over	1	2	3	Over	But not over	1	2
		Your tax is—					Your ta	
If $3,200 or less your tax is 0					5,800	5,850	419	264
					5,850	5,900	427	273
3,200	3,250	4	0	0	5,900	5,950	436	283
3,250	3,300	11	0	0	5,950	6,000	444	292
3,300	3,350	18	0	0				
3,350	3,400	25	0	0	6,000	6,050	453	302
					6,050	6,100	461	311
3,400	3,450	32	0	0	6,100	6,150	470	321
3,450	3,500	39	0	0	6,150	6,200	478	330
3,500	3,550	46	0	0				
3,550	3,600	54	0	0	6,200	6,250	487	340

Form **1040A**

Department of the Treasury—Internal Revenue Service
U.S. Individual Income Tax Return **1978**

Your first name and initial (if joint return, also give spouse's name and initial)	Last name	Your social security number
John R.	Brown	123 45 6789

Present home address (Number and street, including apartment number, or rural route)
123 First Street

City, town or post office, State and ZIP code
Atlas, Ohio 10215

Spouse's social security no.

Your occupation **Student**

Spouse's occupation

Do you want $1 to go to the Presidential Election Campaign Fund? **X** Yes ☐ No
If joint return, does your spouse want $1 to go to this fund? . . ☐ Yes ☐ No

Note: Checking Yes will not increase your tax or reduce your refund.

Filing Status

Check Only One Box

1 **X** Single
2 ☐ Married filing joint return (even if only one had income)
3 ☐ Married filing separate return. If spouse is also filing, give spouse's social security number in the space above and enter full name here ▶
4 ☐ Unmarried head of household. Enter qualifying name ▶ See page 11 of Instructions.

For Privacy Act Notice, see page 5 of Instructions

Exemptions

Always check the box labeled Yourself. Check other boxes if they apply.

5a **X** Yourself ☐ 65 or over ☐ Blind
b ☐ Spouse ☐ 65 or over ☐ Blind

Enter number of boxes checked on 5a and b ▶ **1**

c First names of your dependent children who lived with you ▶ ....

Enter number of children listed ▶

d Other dependents: (1) Name	(2) Relationship	(3) Number of months lived in your home.	(4) Did dependent have income of $750 or more?	(5) Did you provide more than one-half of dependent's support?

Enter number of other dependents ▶

6 Total number of exemptions claimed . . . .

Add numbers entered in boxes above ▶ **1**

7 Wages, salaries, tips, and other employee compensation. (*Attach Forms W-2. If you do not have a W-2, see page 7 of Instructions*) . . . . | 7 | 3,552 | 00

8 Interest income (*see page 4 of Instructions*) . . . . | 8 |

9a Dividends .... 9b Exclusion .... Subtract line 9b from 9a ▶ | 9c |
(See pages 4 and 8 of Instructions)

10 Adjusted gross income (*add lines 7, 8, and 9c*). If under $8,000, see page 2 of Instructions on "*Earned Income Credit.*" If eligible, enter child's name ▶ | 10 | 3,552 | 00

11a Credit for contributions to candidates for public office. *Enter one-half of amount paid but do not enter more than $25 ($50 if joint return). (See page 8 of Instructions).* | 11a |
IF YOU WANT IRS TO FIGURE YOUR TAX, PLEASE STOP HERE AND SIGN BELOW.

b Total Federal income tax withheld (*if line 7 is larger than $17,700, see page 8 of Instructions*) . . . . | 11b | 64 | 20

c Earned income credit (*from page 2 of Instructions*) . . . . . | 11c |

12 Total (*add lines 11a, b, and c*) . . . . | 12 | 64 | 20

13 Tax on the amount on line 10. (*See Instructions for line 13 on page 9, then find your tax in the Tax Tables on pages 14–25.*) . . . . | 13 | 54 | 00

14 If line 12 is larger than line 13, enter amount to be **REFUNDED TO YOU** . . . . ▶ | 14 | 10 | 20

15 If line 13 is larger than line 12, enter **BALANCE DUE**. Attach check or money order for full amount payable to "*Internal Revenue Service.*" Write social security number on check or money order ▶ | 15 |

Under penalties of perjury, I declare that I have examined this return, including accompanying schedules and statements, and to the best of my knowledge and belief, it is true, correct, and complete. Declaration of preparer (other than taxpayer) is based on all information of which preparer has any knowledge.

Your signature *John R. Brown* Date 3/15/79

Spouse's signature (if filing jointly, BOTH must sign even if only one had income)

Please Attach Copy B of Forms W-2 Here

Please Attach Check or Money Order Here

Please Sign Here

Paid Preparer's Information

Preparer's signature ▶

Preparer's social security no.

Check if self-employed ▶ ☐

Firm's name (or yours, if self-employed), address and ZIP code ▶

E.I. No. ▶

Date ▶

☆ U.S. GOVERNMENT PRINTING OFFICE : 1978-O-263-291 04-1213190

Form **1040A** (1978)

their taxable income. Businesses with higher profits pay a tax at a higher rate.

The law allows some organizations to pay no income taxes. These are nonprofit corporations or groups such as churches, universities, labor unions, and hospitals.

Excise Taxes. Excise taxes are collected on certain goods made and sold in the United States. When people buy gasoline, liquor, and cigarettes, they must pay a small tax. There is also an excise tax on the purchase of certain services. People pay a small tax when they buy a ticket to travel on an airplane.

Excise taxes are placed on luxury goods or services. Excise taxes are not put on items that people need to live adequately, such as food or clothing.

Customs Duties. People must pay customs duty on certain products brought into the United States. For example, suppose you visit Germany. You buy a German camera, wrist watch, and radio to give to friends in the United States. When you return to the United States, you must pay a customs tax on the German products.

A **protective tariff** is a special kind of customs tax. Products from a foreign country that are made at a lower cost than similar goods in the United States are taxed with a protective tariff. This

Discuss: Why is a protective tariff especially important today?

Discuss: Which tax does this picture help to explain?

Foreign made cars arriving at Boston Harbor.

tax protects American companies against competition from low-cost foreign products. For example, auto makers in Japan produce their cars at a much lower cost than American companies do. To protect American auto makers, the United States government puts a protective tariff on the Japanese cars. This tax raises the price of Japanese cars in the United States. As a result, Americans are less likely to buy Japanese cars and more likely to buy American cars.

Estate and Gift Taxes. Every year the national government takes in a few billion dollars from estate and gift taxes. An **estate tax** is paid on money, property, and other valuables left by a person who has died. (There is no tax on an estate that has a value below a certain sum fixed by law.) A **gift tax** is money collected on any gift, including cash, that is worth more than a certain amount set by law. These taxes prevent people from avoiding personal income taxes by giving money to family members or friends.

Discuss: Why are estate and gift taxes important?

National Borrowing

When the government spends more money than it collects in taxes, it borrows money to make up the difference. In 1977, about 11¢ out of each dollar the government took in was borrowed money. The national government has had to borrow mon-

A sign at a credit union urges members to buy United States savings bonds.

Discuss: Why is it also necessary to borrow money?

Note: Have a bond available for students to examine.

Main Ideas
1. taxes
2. borrowing
3. pp. 144–145
Skill Building
1. 38%
2. 13%
3. 5%
4. $0.00

ey every year since 1960 in order to pay its bills. The amount of money the government owes is known as the national public debt.

The government borrows money by selling government **securities** to citizens, banks, and businesses. These securities are treasury bonds, savings bonds, and treasury notes and bills. When you buy a United States savings bond, you are loaning money to the government. Let us say you go to buy a $50 bond. You pay $37.50. Then you hold the bond for 10 years in a safe place. At the end of this time we say the bond has reached **maturity.** At maturity, you turn it in for $50. The difference between what you paid for it and what you get at maturity is **interest.** Interest is the payment a borrower makes to a lender for the use of the money. At the time the government issues the security, it says how much it will pay in interest and over how long a period of time.

Section Review

Vocabulary: corporate income tax, customs duty, deductions, excise tax, estate tax, FICA, gift tax, interest, maturity, personal income tax, profit, protective tariff, securities, social security tax, taxable income, taxes.

Reviewing Main Ideas
1. Where does most of the money for running the government come from?
2. Taxes do not pay all the costs of government. How else does the government get money?
3. Explain how social security works.

Skill Building
1. According to the graph on page 143, what percent of federal government income is raised through personal income taxes?
2. What percent comes from taxes on businesses?
3. What percent comes from excise taxes?
4. Suppose you earned $1500 one year working in the summer and on weekends. Use the information on the Skills for Life page (page 146) to figure how much income tax you should pay.

2/How the Money Is Spent

The cost of national government is skyrocketing. Twenty years ago, government cost less than $100 billion per year. Today it costs over $500 billion. And the cost has not risen at an even rate. The graph on this page shows the increase in recent years.

Who gets the billions of dollars collected and spent by the national government each year? The greatest share of government expenses involves services and cash payments given directly to individuals who have some special need or special right to collect it. In 1977, 37¢ of every dollar, $150 billion, was spent for benefits to these people. Those who receive these funds include the following: (1) Thirty-five million people got social security cash benefits. Retired citizens, widows, orphans, and those physically unable to work are included in this group. (2) Nearly five million veterans got cash payments related to their past service in the military. Three million of these received money because they were disabled in some way. The other two million got retirement income. (3) Fourteen million people got money in the form of food stamps. These stamps let people buy food at much lower costs than is normal, with the national government picking up the difference. (4) Fourteen million older citizens received

Discuss: Who gets the biggest share of government money? Who else receives money from the government?

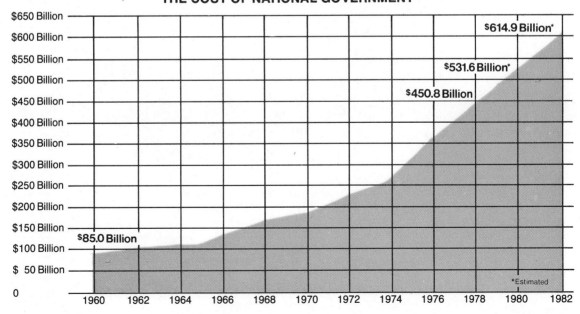

THE COST OF NATIONAL GOVERNMENT

$85.0 Billion

$450.8 Billion

$531.6 Billion*

$614.9 Billion*

*Estimated

funds to help pay their medical care costs through Medicare, a government health insurance plan. (5) About twenty-four million poorer citizens who did not qualify for Medicare got help with their medical-care costs through Medicaid.

The money that government spends on the military each year is also a very large sum. As you can see on the graph on page 153, 24¢ of every dollar was spent on national defense in 1977. This amounted to more than $97 billion. More than half of this money went into salaries for members of the armed forces. Most of the rest was spent on weapons.

Seventeen cents of every dollar spent by the national government in 1977 was spent in **revenue sharing** or **grants-in-aid** to the states and local governments. Revenue sharing is a plan in which the national government regularly turns over a certain amount of the taxes it collects to state and local governments. There are few strings attached. State and city governments spend the money for a variety of needs or programs. Grants-in-aid are contributions to state or local governments for specific programs. For example, the federal government pays part of the costs of school lunch programs, with the state or local school districts paying the balance. Other grants-in-aid go for helping the needy, the blind, farmers, airlines, and shipbuilders, among countless oth-

Discuss: How do these pictures help explain how the government spends its money? Find other examples to share with the class.

(Above) military training. (Right) a government official explains the advantages of Medicare to Pennsylvania's oldest resident, Emma J. Thompson, age 108.

152

ers. Such grants usually set rules for how the money is to be used. Usually the state or local government must make a matching amount available, although the national government often pays the larger part of the costs.

Fourteen percent of the 1977 budget was spent on operating the federal government. This amount includes the salaries and benefits paid to government workers. About one out of every twenty Americans has a job in the national government. These workers carry the mail, build highways and dams, deal with foreign nations, conserve natural resources, and do many other jobs.

Another part of the yearly cost of government is payment of interest on money that has been borrowed by the government in the past. In 1977, 8¢ of every dollar the government spent went for this purpose. This amounted to more than $38 billion.

Through taxing, the government collects different sums of money from different people. Through spending for various services and programs, the government spreads this money among citizens with different needs. Through taxing and spending, the national government transfers billions of dollars each year from the pockets of some citizens to the pockets of others.

Section Review

Vocabulary: grants-in-aid, revenue sharing.

Reviewing Main Ideas

1. What is the biggest area of government expenses?
2. Name five different reasons an individual might get payments from the national government.
3. Is national defense a large part of government costs? Explain your answer.
4. Is interest on the national debt a large part of government costs? Explain your answer.

Skill Building

Use the information presented in the graph on page 151, "The Cost of National Government," to support or deny this statement: The cost of running the national government has not changed much in twenty years.

HOW THE NATIONAL GOVERNMENT SPENDS ITS MONEY*

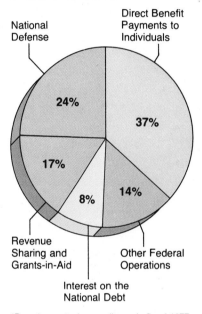

National Defense

Direct Benefit Payments to Individuals

24%

37%

17%

8%

14%

Revenue Sharing and Grants-in-Aid

Interest on the National Debt

Other Federal Operations

*Based on actual expenditures in fiscal 1977.

Main Ideas
1. service and payment to individuals
2. pp. 151–152
3. yes, it is the second largest item
4. p. 153, answers will vary.
Skill Building
Not true. The cost has increased.

3/Making the Federal Budget

Discuss: Why is it important to have a federal budget?

The federal **budget** is the national government's plan for gathering and spending money. It covers a twelve-month period from October 1 of one year to September 30 of the next year. Any year-long period set up for budget purposes is called a **fiscal year.** Thus we say that the government's fiscal year begins October 1.

The budget shows the amount of money the government has to spend. It lists both the sources of these funds and the expenses of government. It lists each kind of cost that is to be paid. See the chart below for a summary of the receipts and expenses listed in President Carter's 1979 budget.

Discuss: Why is it necessary to identify national priorities?

National Priorities. The government's budget reveals national priorities. **Priority** refers to what comes first. We give high priority to activities that we believe to be very important. We decide to do them before we do other things. If, for instance, you put a high priority on your education, you would complete your homework before making long phone calls or watching TV. Budget makers allow most money for things that seem most important. They allow least money for those things that seem

1979 NATIONAL BUDGET

INCOME

Taxes on individual incomes	$227.3 bil.
Social Security taxes	$136.6 bil.
Taxes on corporate profits	$ 71.0 bil.
Excise taxes	$ 18.5 bil.
Unemployment-insurance taxes	$ 15.9 bil.
Estate and gift taxes	$ 6.0 bil.
All other revenue	$ 27.3 bil.
Total income	**$502.6 bil.**

OUTGO

National defense	$125.8 bil.
Social Security benefits	$115.2 bil.
Interest on public debt	$ 65.7 bil.
Medicare, other health programs	$ 53.4 bil.
Public assistance, food stamps, other aid	$ 31.4 bil.
Education, manpower, social services	$ 30.2 bil.
Aid to veterans	$ 20.5 bil.
Aid to transportation, business	$ 19.3 bil.
Civil-service retirement	$ 13.8 bil.
Unemployment compensation	$ 12.4 bil.
International affairs, economic and military aid	$ 8.2 bil.
Energy	$ 7.9 bil.
Aid to community, regional development	$ 7.3 bil.
General-revenue sharing	$ 6.9 bil.
Rivers, dams, natural resources	$ 6.8 bil.
Science, space, technology	$ 5.5 bil.
Pollution control	$ 4.7 bil.
Aid to agriculture	$ 4.3 bil.
Payment to the Postal Service	$ 1.7 bil.
All other spending	$ 9.6 bil.
Rents and royalties on outer continental shelf	–$ 2.6 bil.
Deductions of interagency transactions that appear as spending above	–$ 16.4 bil.
Total outgo	**$531.6 bil.**
DEFICIT	**–$ 29.0 bil.**

least important. So the budget shows us what leaders in government believe to be the relative importance of their programs.

Having a large and strong army, navy, and air force has been a very high national priority since 1940. During this time, more money has been spent on national defense than on any other budget item.

When John Kennedy was President, the space program was given a high priority. The President had the goal of putting a man on the moon before the end of the 1960s. The government spent large sums of money for several years to reach this goal.

In 1978, President Carter's budget planning showed great concern for programs in education, health care, and public works to create new jobs. National defense remained a high priority. However, he planned to cut down on the money set aside for the armed forces.

A Balanced Budget. When income is equal to expenses, we say a budget is balanced. Look at the budget on page 155. Is it a **balanced budget?**

Discuss: Should the budget be balanced? Why?

When income is less than expenses, the difference is called a **deficit** [def′ə sit]. The government borrows money to make up the deficit, and interest on this borrowed money becomes an item in the budget. It has become very common for the govern-

On July 20, 1969, an American astronaut became the first human to walk on the moon.

155

ment to run on an unbalanced budget. As a result, the national debt is climbing. It is well over $750 billion.

Most of the national debt was caused by the wars in this century. The government borrowed money to buy the weapons and pay the troops needed to fight World War I, World War II, the Korean War, and the Vietnamese War. Budget deficits have added to this already enormous debt. The chart on this page shows this growth.

Recently, many people have been concerned about the growth of the national debt. When Jimmy Carter ran for President in 1976, he promised to balance the budget by 1980. This promise attracted many votes. A balanced budget would not get rid of the national debt, but it would keep it from growing.

Discuss: How is a national budget made?

Steps in the Budget-making Process. The first draft of the budget is created by the executive branch of government. The President, who has the overall responsibility for creating this first copy, sets the goals and general direction. The Office of Management and Budget, (OMB), works out the details.

Making the first draft of the budget requires many months of hard work. All government agencies and bureaus present yearly requests to the budget makers. The agencies try to get as much

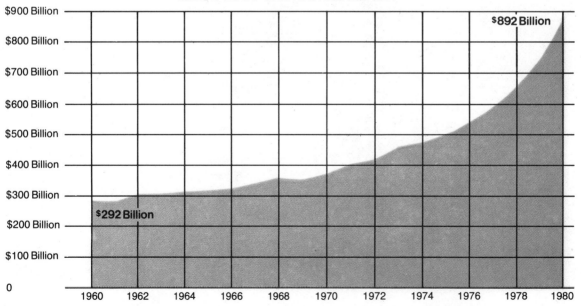

GROWTH OF THE NATIONAL DEBT

funding as possible so that they can carry out or expand their programs. Before making final decisions about the budget, the OMB and the President spend months studying and discussing the many requests. The end result is a compromise between what the various groups want and what decision makers think they ought to get.

Once the executive branch has completed its work on the budget, the President sends a budget message to Congress. This message tells the President's budget proposal and urges Congress to pass it. Traditionally, the budget message has been delivered in January of each year.

Note: Have copies of recent budget messages available to examine.

After receiving the budget proposal, members of the House of Representatives and Senate set to work on it. According to the Constitution, all proposals approving government use of money must be passed first by a majority of the House of Representatives. Next, a majority of the Senate must give approval. In this manner, a majority of the members of Congress must approve the budget before any money can be spent.

In the course of the work they do, Congress almost always makes changes in the budget, adding to or subtracting from the President's proposal. The final budget is a compromise between what the President wants and what Congress wants.

Funds provided by the Comprehensive Employment and Training Act paid for these students to learn auto repairs.

Once the budget is approved, the President and other top officials of the executive branch are responsible for spending the money. They are expected to follow the budget approved by Congress.

The judicial branch also has a role to play in these money matters. It has power to settle arguments about collecting and spending government money. Suppose there is evidence that officials of the executive branch have not followed the approved budget. If these officials are taken to court, federal judges would decide whether or not they had broken the law.

Making the budget involves important decisions about giving and withholding benefits from different citizens. A decision to cut back on defense spending would mean a loss of profits for companies that make weapons. It would also result in a loss of jobs and incomes for workers in these companies. A decision to spend more for health care for older people would not only aid senior citizens; it also would give more money to doctors, nurses, hospitals, and druggists. A decision to raise or lower income taxes for certain groups leads to more or less money in the pockets of different citizens. Thus, citizens should pay attention to important budget decisions in the national government.

Section Review

Vocabulary: balanced budget, budget, deficit, fiscal year, OMB, priority.

Reviewing the Main Ideas

1. Which branch of government prepares the budget?
2. Which branch of government approves the budget?
3. How does a budget show national priorities?

Skill Building

1. According to President Carter's budget for fiscal 1979, what three items have the highest priority for the national government?
2. How would you assign priorities to your own activities? What three things would you give most attention to?

Housing in Saul Hollow

The national government today needs much more money than even twenty years ago. The national government also provides more services and it makes more rules that affect daily lives. Decisions made in the national government affect the food people eat, the cars they drive, the clothes they wear, the water they drink, the air they breathe, and the houses they live in.

What happened to Charlie and Betty Johnston is a good example of how national government decisions affect individuals. The Johnstons are not experts on the national government. But they could tell you that national government programs combined with action by private citizens have recently made a big difference in their lives.

The Johnstons and their seven children live in Saul Hollow, Kentucky. For more than twenty-eight years the Johnstons had lived in a crowded, four-room wooden shack. Like most of their neighbors, they could not afford to move.

Private citizens worked with government programs to help families move out of houses like this one.

Reverend Yost, in the hat, admires local livestock.

Charlie worked hard as a janitor at the local school, but in 1975 he was making only $4,000 a year. Like more than 50 percent of their neighbors in Clay County, the Johnstons' family income was well below the poverty level set by the national government. The Johnstons were too poor to buy a new home. They were too poor to qualify for a home loan from the national government.

Although they were not aware of it at the time, things were starting to change for the Johnstons and many other families in 1973. That's when the Reverend M. Dwayne Yost decided to try to change things in the area. A minister at a local church, Yost took a six-month leave from his church to work for better housing in Clay County. Yost talked with other church leaders and with local business people. Church leaders and others provided the money and volunteers to help Yost form an organization called the Kentucky Mountain Housing Development Corporation.

Once it had been formed, Kentucky Mountain Housing went to the national government to ask for money to start building new homes and fixing up old ones. They succeeded in getting a grant and started their program.

Today the Johnstons live in a new, three-bedroom, white frame house. Their new home has indoor plumbing, a new stove and refrigerator, a vegetable garden, and even a nice lawn. Here's how the government program worked in the Johnstons' case: Kentucky Mountain helped Charlie and Betty get a special $13,200 home loan from the Farmers Home Administration of the Department of Agriculture. At the same time, another federal government program—the Comprehensive Employment and Training Act (CETA)—provided the money to pay local workers to build the Johnston home for Kentucky Mountain. A third federal government agency—the Community Services Administration (CSA)—provided part of the money to run Kentucky Mountain Housing.

In addition to the federal government, private individuals and groups helped. A local coal company donated the use of its bulldozer. By 1978 Kentucky Mountain Housing had built 60 new homes. In addition, they had repaired another 400 homes in Clay and Jackson counties.

Many of the people who moved into these homes were even poorer than the Johnstons. One family had an income of just $1,100 per year. Yet by 1978 not one family had failed to make regular payments on its loan. The program started by Reverend Yost and other citizens in Clay County was a success.

The homes now owned by the Johnstons and other families in Eastern Kentucky could not have been built without federal money. However, the actions of private citizens were equally important. New homes were built because private citizens used government programs to help them reach their own goals. They were built because citizens like Reverend Yost and other community leaders worked together.

Reviewing the Case Study

1. Why were the Johnstons unable to qualify for federal home loans?
2. How did the Kentucky Mountain Housing Corporation and the national government change the housing alternatives facing the Johnstons?
3. Explain why this case study is an example of how the national government affects citizens' everyday lives.

The new house completed, a delighted home owner takes the title from an officer of Kentucky Mountain Housing as Reverend Yost looks on.

Chapter Seven Test and Activities

★★

Vocabulary

Match the following words with their meanings.

1. interest
2. securities
3. tax
4. protective tariff
5. personal income tax
6. social security tax
7. grants-in-aid
8. OMB
9. FICA
10. budget

a. a tax charged on the income each individual earns each year
b. any money paid by people for the support of their government
c. a fee paid by a borrower to a lender for the use of the money borrowed
d. a plan to get and spend money
e. a tax used to provide income for retired people
f. the law that set up social security taxes
g. treasury bonds and United States savings bonds
h. a department that helps make the budget
i. a tax on foreign-made goods
j. money the federal government gives state and local governments for certain projects

Reviewing Chapter Ideas

1. Which of the following is a source of federal income?
   a. customs duty
   b. protective tariff
   c. personal income tax
   d. all of the above

2. Taxable income is:
   a. all the money an individual earns in a year
   b. money paid to children of a worker who has died
   c. earnings minus deductions
   d. earnings minus profits

3. Excise taxes are collected on:
   a. gasoline
   b. food
   c. clothing
   d. all of the above

4. Securities are:
   a. bonds the government sells to borrow money
   b. taxes on foreign-made goods
   c. fees paid to assure an accused person will appear in court
   d. none of the above

5. True or false: The President has chief responsibility for proposing the federal budget.

6. True or false: In order to raise money, the government collects taxes.

7. The executive branch _____ .
   a. has nothing to do with the budget
   b. approves the budget
   c. makes up the budget
   d. none of the above

8. True or false: Every dollar that a person earns during a year is taxed.

9. True or false: A cut in defense spending could put people out of work.

10. True or false: The largest expense in the federal budget is social security benefits.

Vocabulary
1. c   4. i   7. j   10. d
2. g   5. a   8. h
3. b   6. e   9. f

Ideas
1. d   4. a   7. c   10. F
2. c   5. T   8. F
3. a   6. T   9. T

★★

Using Basic Social Studies Skills

Finding Information

Use the index of your book to find out where taxes are discussed other than in this chapter. List the pages. Circle one of the pages, read what it says about taxes, and then summarize what you learned.

Comprehending Information

1. What is the current federal fiscal year?
2. The maximum speed on highways is 55 miles per hour. Why is that so?
3. Give a reason citizens should take an interest in the federal budget.

Organizing Information

List the sources of national government income from largest to smallest. Then list five of the national government's expenses from greatest to smallest.

Evaluating Information

If the national budget were a balanced budget, what effect would it have on the national debt?

a. It would make the national debt grow larger.
b. It would make the national debt smaller.
c. The national debt would stay the same.

Communicating Ideas

Suppose someone asked you why the United States government spends close to $500 billion a year. Describe three or four of the most expensive items in the national budget.

Using Decision-Making Skills

Pretend that you can make changes in the national budget. List the sorts of programs that you would like to see the country give more money to. List the programs that you would like to see the country give less money to. Make a list of reasons that have influenced you to make these choices. Compare your list with others in the class to see whether it would take great or little effort for the class to agree on a budget.

Activities

1. Look up the current national budget in a recent almanac. Compare it to the one for 1979 on page 154.
   a. Is the budget balanced or is there a deficit? (If there is a deficit, how much is it?)
   b. What is the total cost of expenses in the current budget? Is this a larger or smaller amount than in 1979?
   c. What percent of the expenses is the amount for national defense? Is this more or less than the 24% spent in 1977?
   d. What amount is going to be spent for social security benefits? Is this amount larger or smaller than the amount spent in the 1979 budget?
2. Those students who are interested in learning more about taxation might read *Who Shall Pay? Taxes and Tax Reform in America,* revised edition, by Robert A. Liston (Messner, 1976).

Chapter 8   The Presidency

★★

Discuss: Would you like to be President?

It is early morning in Washington, D.C. A telephone rings in one of the city's bedrooms. "Good morning, Mr. President," a voice says at the end of the line. "It is six o'clock, sir." The man who has thus been awakened gets up and begins another day as President of the United States.

What is it like to be President of one of the most powerful nations in the world? What goes along with the office?

The President lives and works in the White House. The President and his family do not have to bother with many things that take an average family's time. Grocery shopping, cooking, house cleaning, cutting the lawn, and other chores are done for them by the White House domestic staff of over eighty people.

There are plenty of ways to relax at the White House. A private movie theater is available. For exercise, there are tennis courts, a small gym, a one-lane bowling alley, and a heated, outdoor swimming pool. For reading, there is a private library.

When the President needs to travel, he commands a fleet of special cars, helicopters, and airplanes. For long trips the President uses a Boeing 707 jet called Air Force One.

The presidency can be a life-threatening job. Three Presidents have been assassinated. Wherever the President and his family go, they are guarded by Secret Service agents.

The presidency can be a life-threatening job in another way. Most Presidents work long hours. They must make very important decisions. It is believed that the hard work and responsibility can shorten a person's life by several years. To help him stay healthy, the President has his own doctor. There is also a medical staff and small clinic inside the White House.

Discuss: What does it mean to "live like an average citizen"?

As you can see, the President does not live like an average citizen. In this chapter you will learn about the person who leads such a special life. You will read about:

1/Getting Elected
2/The President's Job
3/Presidential Advisers
4/How Presidential Decisions Get Made
Case Study: The B-1 Bomber

1/Getting Elected

The presidency is the top political job in the United States. The person who holds the job has the power to make decisions that affect people in all parts of the world. For these and other reasons, many people have tried for the office. Only thirty-nine have made it.

Requirements

People who have been elected President in the past have had many things in common. Naturally, all of them have met requirements stated in Article 2, Section 1 of the Constitution. Each has been (1) at least 35 years old, (2) a natural-born citizen, and (3) a resident of the United States for at least 14 years.

Discuss: Who can be President?

Former Presidents have also had traits in common that are not formally required. For example, all have been white, and all have been men. All have been of European descent. Most have had previous political jobs. Most have had a college education. Many have been lawyers. Most have been from states that have large populations. And, for as long as national political parties have existed, all have been members of major political parties.

Discuss: What have most Presidents had in common?

On the White House Lawn, President Carter congratulates Egypt's President Anwar Sadat and Israel's Premier Menahem Begin on signing a peace treaty between their two countries. Carter had helped negotiate the treaty.

165

Discuss: Are there general statements you could make about the personal appearance of the President? Are looks important?

Look at the chart below.

At recent nominating conventions, women and nonwhites have challenged the idea that only white males can be President. To date, however, the major political parties have not been persuaded that a woman or a nonwhite could win a presidential election.

Election of the President

To many people, a presidential election is one of the most exciting political events in the United States. The election process includes three major steps: (1) the nomination of candidates, (2) the campaign, and (3) the vote.

Nomination. Presidential hopefuls start early in the year. They meet commuters on railroad platforms, shake hands in shopping centers, make speeches and radio and television commercials. They fly from state to state trying to persuade voters to

TWENTIETH-CENTURY PRESIDENTS

Name	Sex	College Education	Age Elected	Religion	Ethnic Background	State	Political Party	Early Career
Theodore Roosevelt (1901-1909)	Male	Yes	42	Protestant	Dutch & French	Large (New York)	Republican	Author & politician
William Howard Taft (1909-1913)	Male	Yes	51	Protestant	British	Large (Ohio)	Republican	Lawyer
Woodrow Wilson (1913-1921)	Male	Yes	56	Protestant	British	Medium (New Jersey)	Democrat	Teacher
Warren Harding (1921-1923)	Male	Yes	55	Protestant	British & Dutch	Large (Ohio)	Republican	Newspaperman & politician
Calvin Coolidge (1923-1929)	Male	Yes	51	Protestant	British	Medium (Massachusetts)	Republican	Lawyer & politician
Herbert Hoover (1929-1933)	Male	Yes	54	Protestant	Swiss-German	Large (California)	Republican	Engineer & businessman
Franklin D. Roosevelt (1933-1945)	Male	Yes	51	Protestant	Dutch & French	Large (New York)	Democrat	Lawyer & politician
Harry S Truman (1945-1953)	Male	No	60	Protestant	British	Medium (Missouri)	Democrat	Storekeeper & politician
Dwight D. Eisenhower (1953-1961)	Male	Yes	62	Protestant	Swiss-German	Large (Pennsylvania)	Republican	Military leader
John F. Kennedy (1961-1963)	Male	Yes	43	Roman Catholic	Irish	Medium (Massachusetts)	Democrat	Author & politician
Lyndon B. Johnson (1963-1969)	Male	Yes	55	Protestant	British	Large (Texas)	Democrat	Teacher & politician
Richard M. Nixon (1969-1974)	Male	Yes	56	Protestant	British	Large (California)	Republican	Lawyer & politician
Gerald R. Ford (1974-1977)	Male	Yes	61	Protestant	British	Medium (Michigan)	Republican	Lawyer & politician
Jimmy Carter (1977-)	Male	Yes	52	Protestant	British	Small (Georgia)	Democrat	Businessman & Politician.

elect delegates favorable to them to the national nominating conventions.

In summer, both major parties hold national conventions to nominate, or to name, their candidate for President. To this convention come delegates from each state, the District of Columbia, and the territories of the United States. In some states, delegates are chosen at state conventions. In other states, delegates are elected by the voters. The size of a state's delegation depends chiefly on its population. Large states have many delegates. Small states have fewer delegates.

In the 1976 selection of a President, there were elections for delegates in 31 states. No presidential hopeful ran in all the states. It takes a great deal of money and energy to run a successful campaign. The hopefuls chose the states where they felt they could be most effective.

The earliest election was in New Hampshire on February 24. The last ones were in Ohio, California, and New Jersey on June 8. As the elections rolled by, the hopefuls picked up convention delegates. After each state election, "score cards" like the one shown here were printed in newspapers and magazines and shown on the evening television news shows.

The rules about how delegates must vote at the convention vary from state to state. Some delegates represent certain hopefuls. By law they must honor a **binding commitment** to vote for their person on the first ballot taken at the convention. Other delegates have stated a preference for certain people, but they are free to change their minds. Still others are **uncommitted.** They will make their decision on the convention floor.

Some delegates are pledged to a **favorite son.** This is a person from the home state who does not have a real chance to be the presidential candidate. However, the group pledged to the favorite son votes as a block. For instance, in 1976, the Illinois delegation with its 86 votes was pledged to Illinois senator Adlai Stevenson. The Illinois delegation became important at the convention. When Senator Stevenson released his delegates, he gave 86 more votes to Jimmy Carter.

The conventions are very big affairs. The delegates wear buttons and carry signs. There are many speeches. Bands play. Balloons are released from the ceilings in large numbers. And, unless one person wins on the first vote, there is a great deal of bargaining and vote trading on the convention floor. In the end, a candidate emerges. The candidate picks the person to run for

Note: Have students find out how delegates are chosen in their state.

NORTH CAROLINA RESULTS IN BRIEF

In Republican Primary

Reagan	101,448, or 52%
Ford	88,924, or 46%
No preference	3,345, or 2%

Reagan won 28 of the State's 54 delegates to the Republican National Convention, Ford 25. One delegate was uncommitted.

In Democratic Primary

Carter	321,059, or 54%
Wallace	209,807, or 35%
Jackson	25,698, or 4%
Udall	14,122, or 2%
Harris	6,136, or 1%
No preference	22,585, or 4%

Carter won 36 of North Carolina's delegates to the Democratic National Convention. Wallace the other 25.

BOX SCORE ON DELEGATES

Votes based on binding requirements or stated preferences of delegates selected to date.

Republicans		Democrats	
Ford	206	Carter	187
Reagan	81	Wallace	86
Uncommitted	62	Stevenson	85
Needed to		Jackson	55
nominate	1,130	Udall	23
		Others	24
		Uncommitted	53
	Needed to nominate		1,505

Vice-President and the delegates approve the choice by a unanimous vote. This is possible because all the bargaining has gone on before the choice is announced.

Campaign. Once the party conventions are over, the candidates campaign to attract voter support. Presidential campaigns are usually in full swing by October. They go on until election day in November.

During the campaign, candidates travel across the country. They give speeches to many different groups. They appear on television and hold press conferences. They meet state and local political leaders, and they urge members of their party to work for them. Party workers and other volunteers work for their candidate by passing out literature, ringing doorbells, collecting money, making phone calls, and holding rallies.

The Vote. Presidential elections are held every four years (1976, 1980, 1984, etc.) on the Tuesday after the first Monday in November. This election is called the **popular vote.** On this day, every citizen who has registered may vote.

People who take part in a presidential election are not selecting the President directly. Instead, they are actually voting for a group of presidential electors from their state. The electors meet in their state capitals in December to cast the electoral votes for President and Vice-President. The electors, known as the **electoral college,** send their votes to Congress. There, they are

Note: Have someone check the calendar to determine the exact date of the next presidential election.

(Left) Jimmy Carter and (right) Gerald Ford campaigning for President in 1976.

counted. The winner is declared the President of the United States.

Each state has as many presidential electors as its total of representatives and senators in Congress. California has forty-three representatives and two senators. Thus, California has forty-five electoral votes.

If the majority of the popular votes in a state go to the candidate of one party, then that person is supposed to get all of that state's electoral votes. This custom is called **winner-take-all.** It does not happen every time, however. In 1976, one elector from Washington broke with custom. The elector voted for Ronald Reagan, even though most of the popular votes in that state were cast for Gerald Ford. Nonetheless, the winner-take-all custom usually means that the winner's margin of victory, as indicated by electoral votes, is larger than his popular vote margin.

Section Review

Vocabulary: binding commitment, electoral college, favorite son, nominate, popular vote, uncommitted, winner-take-all.

Reviewing the Main Ideas

1. What three requirements must a person meet before he or she can be elected President?
2. What two traits that are not required have most Presidents had in common?
3. What is the purpose of the nominating conventions?
4. What sorts of activities go on during a presidential campaign?
5. How often are presidential elections held?

Skill Building

1. Why can the electoral college system be called a winner-take-all system?
2. According to the chart on page 166, who are the two youngest Presidents to be elected in the twentieth century?
3. Read the "score card" on page 167 to answer these questions.
   a. Which Republican won the most delegates in North Carolina's elections?
   b. Which Democrat won the most delegates?
   c. In which party were there more uncommitted delegates?

Discuss: Why is the role of the electoral college important?

Note: Have students figure how many electors their state has.

Note: Some groups favor eliminating the electoral college. How would this change the election process? Would it be a good idea?

Main Ideas
1. p. 165
2. p. 165
3. to choose the party's candidate
4. p. 168
5. every 4 years
Skill Building
1. p. 169
2. Theodore Roosevelt and John Kennedy
3. a. Reagan, b. Carter, c. Republican

2/The President's Job

Discuss: Why is the President the most powerful public official in the United States? What roles does a President have?

The President is the most powerful public official in the United States. Where does the President's power come from? What is the President's job today?

Constitutional Powers

The Constitution is the basis of the President's power. Article 2 of the Constitution says that the executive power shall be given to a President of the United States. Thus, the President's main job is to execute, or carry out, the laws passed by Congress.

The Constitution also gives the President the power to do the following:

- veto laws proposed by Congress
- call Congress into special session
- serve as commander in chief of the armed forces
- receive leaders and other officials of foreign countries
- make treaties with other countries (These treaties must have Senate approval.)
- appoint heads of executive agencies, federal court judges, ambassadors, and other top government officials (These also must have Senate approval.)
- pardon people convicted of federal crimes, lower the amount of time a person has to spend in jail, or lower the fine a person has to pay

Because the Constitution requires the President to give Congress information about the "state of the union," the President gives several speeches to Congress each year. The most important is the "State of the Union" speech. In this message the President describes the new programs he or she would like Congress to start.

Note: Have students read the statements in the Constitution that state the term of office.

The President's term of office, also stated in the Constitution, is four years. The Twenty-second Amendment limits the President to two elected terms in office.

The Job Today

The President fills a number of different **roles.** Four of these roles come directly from constitutional grants of power. These roles are foreign-policy leader, commander in chief, chief executive, and chief legislator. Three other roles that have developed over the years are not established in the Constitution. These roles are head of state, economic leader, and party chief.

Foreign-Policy Leader. As foreign-policy leader, the President directs the foreign policy of the United States. It is the President who makes the key decisions about how the United States acts toward other countries in the world. Most Presidents spend a lot of time working on foreign-policy problems.

Discuss: What are the key roles given the President in the Constitution? Explain each.

Commander in Chief. The President's role as commander in chief is related to his or her foreign-policy role. The President is in charge of the Army, Navy, Air Force, Marines, and Coast Guard. All military officers take their orders from the President. The President also has the right to decide how weapons and troops will be used.

Discuss: Which of these roles is most important? Why?

The power to make war is divided between the Congress and President. The Constitution gives Congress the power to declare war, but it is the President who really decides if there will be war or peace. Congress has declared war only five times: the War of 1812, the Mexican War, the Spanish-American War, World War I, and World War II. Presidents have sent troops into action overseas more than 150 times since 1789. The entire Vietnam War was fought without a declaration of war from Congress.

As foreign policy leader, President Richard Nixon made a historic trip to China in 1972 to improve U.S.-China relations.

Chief Executive. As chief executive, the President is responsible for carrying out the laws passed by Congress. To do this, the President is in charge of the nearly three million people who work for the government. The President does not supervise all these people personally, but the President does appoint the top leaders of these workers. By appointing these leaders the President can influence the many parts of the executive branch. To keep their jobs, these leaders must follow the President's policies and ideas.

Chief Legislator. The President can be considered chief legislator of the United States because most of the bills Congress considers each year are sent to Congress by the President's staff or by agencies in the executive branch. Congress has the power to pass laws, but the President largely determines what the business of Congress will be.

Every President has a **legislative program.** These are new laws that he or she wants Congress to pass. The President makes speeches to build support for this program. The President often meets with senators and representatives to try to convince them to support the proposed laws. In addition, the President appoints several staff members to work closely with members of Congress on new laws.

President Carter's legislative program encouraged people to cut down their use of oil. (Left) insulating a new factory to reduce the amount of oil burned for heat, and (right) solar collectors on an apartment building roof use sunlight to help heat the building. The windmill uses wind to generate electricity.

All through United States history, there has been tension between the President and Congress over what new laws should be passed. One source of tension is that Presidents represent people all over the United States while members of Congress represent only the people of their states or districts. To be elected or re-elected, the President must try to appeal to the entire country. No one group controls the President's attention. Individual members of Congress are not as free as the President to be concerned about nationwide problems.

Discuss: When do tensions develop between the President and Congress? Look for news items of current tensions.

Another source of tension is the difference in the length of time that Presidents and members of Congress can serve. Presidents can serve no more than two elected terms, while members of Congress can serve an unlimited number of terms. Therefore, many members of Congress do not want to move as quickly on programs as the President does. Presidents often complain that Congress is "dragging its heels" on new programs.

Head of State. As head of state, the President is the living symbol of the country. In this role, the President greets visiting kings and queens, prime ministers, and other leaders. The President meets with boy scouts and girl scouts, lights the nation's Christmas tree, and gives medals to the country's heroes. The President is expected to represent all United States citizens.

Discuss: What is the importance of each of the roles not identified in the Constitution?

Economic Leader. As economic leader, the President tries to help the country's economy work well. Citizens want the President to take the lead in dealing with such problems as unemployment or high prices or high taxes. Business leaders, for example, may want the President to protect their industry from foreign competition. Labor leaders may want the President to start new job-training programs for people who are out of work. One job that the President must do each year as economic leader is to plan the national budget.

Party Chief. As party chief, the President is regarded as leader of one of the major political parties. Members of the President's party work hard to elect the President. In turn, the President gives speeches to help party members who are running for office as mayors, governors, and members of Congress. The President helps the party raise money for its candidates, and the President works with other leaders to plan party activities.

The White House.

Section Review

Vocabulary: chief executive, chief legislator, commander in chief, economic leader, foreign-policy leader, head of state, legislative program, party chief, role.

Reviewing the Main Ideas

1. List three powers given to the President in the Constitution.
2. Name two presidential roles that are based on powers granted by the Constitution. Name one role that is not based on constitutional powers.
3. What does the President do that makes it appropriate to call him chief legislator?

Skill Building

Here are three presidential actions. Using what you have read, tell which constitutional power the President was basing his actions on in each case.

a. During the Korean War, President Truman fired General Douglas MacArthur. Truman later said, "I fired him because he wouldn't respect the authority of the President."
b. President Jimmy Carter named Mr. Cyrus Vance to be his new Secretary of State.
c. In a major speech to Congress, President Johnson called for a new government program to help poor people.

Main Ideas
1. p. 170
2. p. 170
3. p. 172
Skill Building
a. commander in chief
b. chief executive
c. chief legislator

3/Presidential Advisers

In 1801, President Thomas Jefferson could do his job with the help of a few **advisers,** one messenger, and a part-time secretary. Today more than 5,000 people assist the President.

Discuss: Who are the key advisors of the President? What is the role of each?

The Executive Office of the President

Many of the President's advisers are part of the Executive Office of the President. The Executive Office was created by Franklin D. Roosevelt in 1939 to help him do his job. It has been growing ever since. The costs for the Executive Office today are about $150 million a year.

The men and women who work in the Executive Office look into many different issues and problems. They give the President advice. They help write new bills for the President to send to Congress. They help coordinate what is going on in the many different parts of the executive branch.

One advisory group that is part of the Executive Office is the **Domestic Council.** This group was created in 1970 by President Nixon. Its job is to come up with ideas for the President on domestic issues such as health care for the poor or job programs for teenagers.

The President's closest personal advisers work in the **White House Office,** which is another part of the Executive Office of

President Carter's cabinet.

175

the President. These advisers are often people who have known the President for years and have worked for his election.

People in the White House Office advise the President in all areas of decision making. Will Congress accept a tax increase? Will business leaders support a new energy-saving program? How can the President lower unemployment? What should our foreign policy toward Cuba be?

People in the White House Office also act for the President. They write speeches for the President. They plan the President's trips. They arrange official dinners and White House parties. They work with local and state political leaders.

The Cabinet

Discuss: Who are some of the other Cabinet members?

The Cabinet is another important presidential advisory group. Each Cabinet member heads one of the government departments shown in the margin. Most are called Secretary. Thus, the Secretary of Labor, the Secretary of Defense, and so on are members of the Cabinet. The head of the Justice Department is called the Attorney General. Every President from George Washington's time to the present has had a Cabinet to help make executive branch decisions. In 1789 there were only four Cabinet members. Today there are twelve. The President appoints these people with the approval of the Senate.

The Vice-President

Have you ever heard of Daniel Tompkins, George M. Dallas, William R. King, Levi P. Morton, or Garret A. Hobart?

Vice-President Hubert Humphrey in his White House office.

Chances are you have not. However, each of these men was at one time a "heartbeat away from the presidency." They were all Vice-Presidents of the United States.

Vice-Presidents are usually invisible figures. Yet, if the President dies, is removed from office, or resigns, the Vice-President becomes President. Thirteen Vice-Presidents have become President. Eight of these thirteen became President upon the death of the President.

The Constitution gives little authority to the Vice-President. It states only that Vice-Presidents preside over the Senate. Beyond this, what the Vice-President does is up to the President.

Throughout the country's history, most Presidents have ignored their Vice-Presidents. Recent Presidents have made some efforts to give their Vice-Presidents more responsibility. Recent Vice-Presidents have been appointed to serve as members of special presidential advisory groups. They have often been sent on visits to foreign nations as representatives for the President. In these and other ways they have sometimes served as advisers. However, no Vice-President has ever really become an important decision maker in any President's administration.

Discuss: What does it mean when the Vice-President is said to be invisible?

Note: Have students find out who the last 5 Vice-Presidents were. How many have they heard of? Look for articles on roles of the current Vice-President.

Section Review

Vocabulary: advisers, Cabinet, Domestic Council, Executive Office of the President, White House Office.

Reviewing the Main Ideas
1. Who was the first President to have a Cabinet?
2. List the departments that Cabinet members head.
3. Would the Domestic Council concern itself with an issue like oil imports from Iraq? Why or why not?
4. Why do the Vice-President's duties change from President to President?

Skill Building
1. Would you say that people who work in the Executive Office of the President deal with many kinds of problems and many tasks or only a few? Explain your answer.
2. What do all the jobs described in this section have in common? Does the section heading show that connection? Explain your answer.

CABINET DEPARTMENTS

Department of State
Department of Defense
Department of Health, Education, and Welfare
Department of the Treasury
Department of Justice
Department of Labor
Department of Housing and Urban Development
Department of the Interior
Department of Agriculture
Department of Commerce
Department of Transportation
Department of Energy

Main Ideas
1. George Washington
2. p. 177
3. No; it deals only with concerns inside the United States.
4. What the Vice-President does is up to the President.
Skill Building
1. many, p. 175
2. They are all advisers to the President. Yes.

177

4/How Presidential Decisions Get Made

Discuss: Who makes the important decisions?

Presidents have many assistants to help them, but in the end, the President must make the important decisions. Andrew Jackson once said, "I have accustomed myself to receive . . . the opinions of others but always take the responsibility of deciding for myself."

The decisions Presidents have to make are often difficult. President Eisenhower put it this way, "There are no easy matters that will come to you as President. If they are easy, they will be settled at a lower level."

Problems for Decision

Discuss: What kinds of decisions must a President make?

Every President has to make many different kinds of decisions. Some decisions are not expected. They have to be made in a hurry. At other times, a President may have time to prepare for a decision. Sometimes a President decides after weeks, months, or even years of study. Here are examples of the kinds of decisions Presidents face as they do their job.

Note: Have students find examples of decisions the President is currently facing.

- whether to add money to the national budget for schools or for the space program
- who a new director for the FBI will be
- whether lowering taxes will help the economy grow stronger
- whether to go to New York or Florida to help the party's candidates for governor when there is not time for both
- whether or not to veto a new law that will cost more than was in the budget

Influences on a President's Decisions

Many factors can influence a President's decisions. Four of the most important are (1) the President's personal beliefs, (2) public opinion, (3) Congress, and (4) laws.

Personal Beliefs. A President's personal beliefs about government, about people, and about other countries often help shape presidential decisions. President Franklin D. Roosevelt believed the national government should actively try to solve social problems like poverty. President Nixon felt many social programs should be left to the states, not to the national government. Each man worked for programs that would help achieve the kinds of goals he believed in.

Public Opinion. Presidents know they need the support of the public to carry out their programs. As a result, their decisions are affected by what they learn from public opinion polls, newspapers, and magazines. These are sources of information about citizens' views. On the other hand, Presidents try to shape public opinion through televised speeches and news conferences.

Discuss: How is a President influenced?

Congress. Presidents care about what members of Congress think, too. Presidents depend on Congress to pass laws they want and to approve their appointment of top officials. As a result, Presidents sometimes shape decisions to fit what Congress will accept. In 1977, for example, President Carter learned that many members of Congress opposed his choice for Director of the Central Intelligence Agency (the **CIA**). Instead of fighting the issue, the President changed his decision. He picked a new person more acceptable to Congress.

Laws. The Constitution and laws passed by Congress also limit or shape the President's decisions. In 1973, for example, Congress passed the War Powers Act. This law limits the President's power to send troops into combat without a declaration of

Public opinion influences a President's decisions.

179

war by Congress. As a result, Presidents will not be able to make some of the same decisions they have made in the past.

Section Review

Vocabulary: CIA, public opinion.

Reviewing the Main Ideas
1. Who must take responsibility for the most important executive branch decisions?
2. List four important factors that can influence a President's decisions.

Skill Building
1. Which of the roles described on pages 171–174 would the President be taking as he or she made each of the decisions listed on page 178?
2. Rank the four factors discussed on pages 178–180 to show which you think is most important and which is least. Explain your ranking.

The B-1 Bomber

During the summer of 1977, Jimmy Carter had to decide whether or not the government should build a new fleet of bombers. The decision involved billions of dollars, thousands of jobs, and the national security of the United States.

In the 1970s, the Defense Department had been planning a new bomber—the B-1. By 1977, the Department was ready to start building 244 B-1 bombers. Each new B-1 would cost about $100 million.

The Air Force wanted the B-1 to replace the older B-52 bombers. They said the B-52s were no longer useful. They also warned that Russia was building new bombers. Many citizens, military planners, and members of Congress said the B-1 was needed for national defense.

Some companies wanted the B-1. General Electric had a 744 million-dollar government job to make parts for the B-1. Rockwell International had a 1.37 billion-dollar job to build the airframes for the B-1.

Many citizens, labor unions, religious groups, newspaper editors, and members of Congress were against the B-1. They argued that the plane was too costly. They said the new bomber had not been properly tested. And they said Russia's new bombers were no real threat to the United States.

The B-1 bomber.

During the 1976 presidential campaign, President Ford supported the B-1. His opponent, Jimmy Carter, was against the B-1. Carter said the B-1 "would be wasteful to taxpayers' dollars." Carter won the election. As President, it was his decision: build the B-1 or not?

After the election, Carter gave himself time to make a decision. He collected information about his two alternatives. He talked often with the Secretary of Defense. He sought advice from White House staff members. He met with members of Congress. He received reports from the Air Force and other military advisers.

On the weekend before his decision, the President went to Camp David, a mountain resort for Presidents. There he reviewed the question. He asked the Vice-President, the Secretary of State, and several other top aides for written opinions. To help him decide, Carter made a list of the pros and cons of the B-1.

It was clear that building the B-1 would be a popular alternative with the Air Force and with many Republican members of Congress. These people thought the B-1 was necessary for the defense of the country. Continued support was coming from business leaders who would make money from building the B-1 and from people who would work on the B-1. In addition, Japanese leaders said they hoped the B-1 would be built. Japan is close to Russia and the Japanese were afraid a "no" decision would encourage the Russians to become more aggressive.

People against the B-1, many of whom had voted for Carter, continued to say that the B-1 was not necessary to the national defense. They said building it would waste taxpayers' money. Some said that B-52s could be fitted with a weapon called the cruise missile, which would make B-52s as effective as the B-1. The cost of adding cruise missiles to the B-52s would be much less than the cost of building B-1s. Leaders of Western European nations were among those who were hoping Carter would say "no" to the B-1. They thought that cruise missiles could protect their countries better than the B-1 bomber.

On June 30, President Carter announced, "My decision is that we should not continue with . . . the B-1, and I am directing that we discontinue plans for production of this weapon system." The President allowed some research on the B-1 to continue, and directed that B-52s be fitted with cruise missiles.

Reaction to the decision came quickly. One newspaper said:

Wisconsin Senator William Proxmire expresses his opposition to the B-1 at a news-conference.

"We are disappointed by President Carter's action . . . He is taking a great gamble." But another paper said, "It took a lot of [courage] . . . Carter's move makes sense." Some people called the decision a "tragic error." However, others called the decision "wise."

Rockwell International announced that 8,000 workers might have to be laid off within weeks of the decision. General Electric said 300 workers at an Ohio plant that made B-1 engines would probably be laid off. Many engineers started looking for new jobs.

Other companies were happy, for they would be building cruise missiles. Williams Research Corporation began building a new factory to make parts for cruise missile engines. Boeing workers would have plenty of work fixing the old B-52 bombers to carry the cruise missiles.

The President was glad to have the decision over with. Like all Presidents, he had new issues to deal with and many other decisions to make.

Reviewing the Case Study

1. What role was President Carter acting in when he made the B-1 decision? Give evidence to support your answer.
2. What personal beliefs about the B-1 did the President have when he started making the decision?
3. Do you agree with the decision that President Carter made? Why or why not?

Boeing Company employees learn that the B-1 will be discontinued.

Chapter Eight Test and Activities

★★

Vocabulary

Match the following words with their meanings.

1. candidate
2. campaign
3. nominate
4. electoral college
5. commander in chief
6. Cabinet
7. adviser

a. group of people the President chooses to help him or her run the executive branch of government
b. a person running for an office
c. activities to get someone elected
d. person who gives advice
e. person in charge of the armed forces of the United States
f. name a candidate for office
g. group of people chosen by the voters to elect the President

Reviewing Chapter Ideas

1. True or false: A presidential nominating convention is a meeting to choose the party's candidate for President.
2. True or false: A candidate for Vice-President is also chosen at the presidential nominating convention.
3. The President has the power to _____ .
   a. call Congress into special session
   b. appoint federal court judges
   c. serve as commander in chief of the armed forces
   d. all of the above
4. The President's main job is to _____ .
   a. veto bills
   b. entertain leaders from foreign countries

c. carry out laws passed by Congress
d. make treaties with other countries

5. True or false: The President is able to pardon some criminals.
6. True or false: The Twenty-second Amendment says that the President can be in office for only four years.
7. The President's closest personal advisers work in the White House Office, which is part of _____ .
   a. the Executive Office of the President
   b. the Cabinet
   c. the Justice Department
   d. the Congress
8. When the President sends bills to Congress, he is taking the role of _____ .
   a. chief executive
   b. chief legislator
   c. head of state
   d. economic leader
9. True or false: United States citizens vote for President once every four years in the month of November.
10. True or false: The President's Cabinet has eight members.
11. Which of the following can influence a President's decisions?
    a. personal beliefs
    b. public opinion
    c. Congress
    d. all of the above
12. To be legally qualified to be President, a person _____ .
    a. must be thirty-five years old
    b. must have been a citizen of the United States for twenty years
    c. must have been Vice-President
    d. all of the above

Vocabulary
1. b   4. g   7. d
184   2. c   5. e
3. f   6. a

Ideas
1. T   4. c   7. a   10. F
2. T   5. T   8. b   11. d
3. d   6. F   9. T   12. a

★★

Using Basic Social Studies Skills

Finding Information

Skim the heads and subheads in this chapter to find out how many people are in the Cabinet. What is the number? How did the heads and subheads help you find it quickly?

Comprehending Information

1. Would you say that Vice-Presidents are people with great power or little power? Explain your answer.
2. Minnesota has ten electoral votes. Explain what that means.
3. Why might the President be influenced by the views of Congress?

Organizing Information

Outline the information in Section 1 of this chapter. The section heads and subheads should be used in the outline. Your outline should show three of the main steps in getting elected President.

Evaluating Information

1. If you were to hear the following statement, would you agree or disagree? (Explain your answer.) Electing a President for four years is not a good idea.
2. What would you like best about being part of the "First Family"?
3. If you were President, which part of the job would you like best? Why?

Communicating Ideas

1. Imagine that you have a chance to influence a presidential decision. Write the President a letter, saying what you would like him to do.
2. Write a paragraph explaining the importance of decisions the President must make.

Using Decision-Making Skills

Fill out a decision tree that describes President Carter's B-1 decision. Show the alternatives considered by the President and what the consequences of those alternatives appeared to be. One goal in the decision was national security. Can you think of other goals that were involved?

Activities

1. List the names of people in the President's Cabinet. (Use the current *United States Government Manual,* a current almanac, or another appropriate source.)
2. Cooperate with others in a small group in finding articles about the President in recent newspapers and magazines. Create a bulletin-board display in which you use the articles to show that the President fills many roles.
3. For those students who want to learn more about the presidency, the following books are recommended:
   (a) *The Presidency: An American Invention,* revised edition, by Ernest B. Fincher (Abelard-Schuman, 1977).
   (b) *The American Presidency,* by Ann E. Weiss (Messner, 1976).
4. For those students who want to find out more about how a President is elected, these books are recommended:
   (a) *How We Choose a President; the Election Year,* fourth edition, by Lee Learner Gray (St. Martins, 1976).
   (b) *We Elect a President,* revised edition, by David E. Weingast (Messner, 1977).

Chapter 9   Decision Making in the Federal Agencies

★★

More than three million people work for agencies in the executive branch of the national government. They work in offices throughout the United States as well as in other parts of the world. Many of the three million are secretaries and clerks. Others are doctors, lawyers, scientists, and engineers. They are part of what is often called the **bureaucracy** [byú rok′rə sē]. They are grouped into departments, divisions, bureaus, and commissions to do the day-to-day work of the executive branch. Here are some examples of the decisions they make:

Washington, D.C.—The Civil Aeronautics Board rules that an airline that loses your luggage may have to pay you up to $750.

Cheyenne, Wyo.—The Federal Fish and Wildlife Service in the Department of the Interior wants to make 13 million acres in Wyoming, Montana, Idaho, and Washington a special area for grizzly bears.

New York, N.Y.—The U.S. Food and Drug Administration in the Department of Agriculture is recalling more than 19,000 jars of peanut butter from stores here. The peanut butter has higher levels of aflatonium (a chemical) than government rules allow.

Jackson, Miss.—The Justice Department rejects Mississippi's "open primary" law, saying the 1970 law might discriminate against blacks.

Washington, D.C.—The National Labor Relations Board has entered the dispute between striking workers and several steel companies.

Washington, D.C.—The Department of Health, Education, and Welfare is starting a new anti-smoking program.

In this chapter you will find out more about the federal agencies and how decisions get made there. You will read about:

1/The Work and Organization of the Federal Agencies
2/Decision Makers in Federal Agencies
3/Those Who Influence the Decision Makers
Case Study: The Fight over Concorde

1/The Work and Organization of the Federal Agencies

As part of the executive branch of government, **federal agencies** are set up to carry out laws passed by Congress. This means they are to enforce laws and to actually run government programs called for in new laws.

Discuss: What are the key roles of federal agencies?

To carry out laws, federal agencies must often make decisions about rules. For example, the Environmental Protection Agency (EPA) is supposed to carry out the many laws dealing with the pollution of land, air, and water. To do this the EPA makes rules about air and water pollution standards that cities and businesses must follow.

In doing their job, federal agencies may also act like courts. They sometimes settle conflicts about a law. For example, Congress has passed laws that control how much trucking companies can charge to carry certain kinds of freight. If one company thinks another company is not charging the right prices, it can file a complaint with the Interstate Commerce Commission (ICC). The ICC will settle the conflict.

As the chart on page 188 shows, the executive branch includes many federal agencies and they handle many programs. At last count there were 12 Cabinet departments, 55 major in-

NASA, the National Aeronautics and Space Administration, is a federal agency. It runs our space program and trains astronauts.

dependent agencies, and over 2,000 other committees, boards, and advisory groups. These federal agencies administered 1,026 aid programs, 400 education programs, 228 health programs, 158 income-security programs, and 83 housing programs.

Cabinet Departments

The major executive agencies in the federal government are the twelve Cabinet departments. Each department is responsible for a special area such as national defense, labor, or agriculture. The special work of each Cabinet department is described briefly on pages 189 and 192.

Discuss: How does this chart help you to better understand the roles of federal agencies?

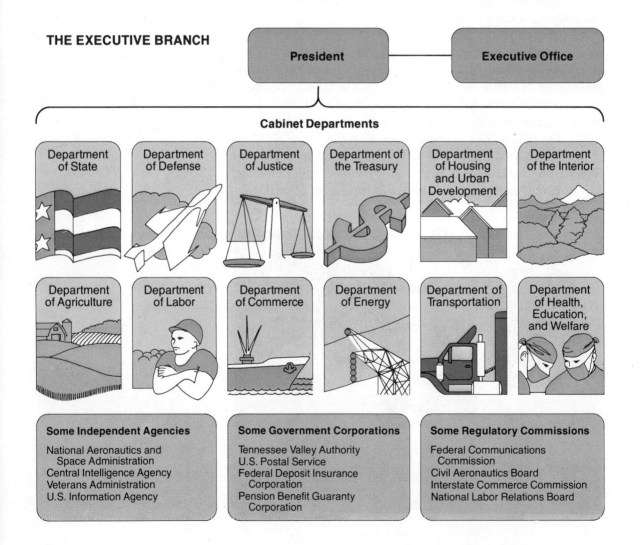

THE EXECUTIVE BRANCH

President — Executive Office

Cabinet Departments

Department of State

Department of Defense

Department of Justice

Department of the Treasury

Department of Housing and Urban Development

Department of the Interior

Department of Agriculture

Department of Labor

Department of Commerce

Department of Energy

Department of Transportation

Department of Health, Education, and Welfare

Some Independent Agencies

National Aeronautics and Space Administration
Central Intelligence Agency
Veterans Administration
U.S. Information Agency

Some Government Corporations

Tennessee Valley Authority
U.S. Postal Service
Federal Deposit Insurance Corporation
Pension Benefit Guaranty Corporation

Some Regulatory Commissions

Federal Communications Commission
Civil Aeronautics Board
Interstate Commerce Commission
National Labor Relations Board

Department of State. Arranges treaties and other agreements with foreign governments. Represents the United States in the United Nations. Arranges economic, educational, and cultural programs with other countries.

Department of Defense. Directs the military forces of the United States. Conducts research on weapons. Collects information about other military forces in the world. Provides military aid and sells weapons to other countries.

Department of Health, Education, and Welfare (HEW). Administers social security, medical assistance, and welfare programs. Operates many services for the poor and for the physically and mentally handicapped. Sets up guidelines for granting financial aid to schools and colleges and then gives out that money.

Department of the Treasury. Collects taxes, manufactures paper money and coins, and carries out laws about banking. Controls taxes on alcohol, tobacco, and firearms. Directs the Secret Service, which guards the President and other top leaders.

Department of Justice. Deals with law enforcement and crime prevention. Operates the Federal Bureau of Investigation (FBI) and federal prisons. Carries out the nation's civil rights, drug, and immigration laws. Also responsible for laws aimed at promoting fair competition among private businesses.

Note: It has been suggested that the President should increase the size of his Cabinet. How does the President feel about this? What new department could be created?

The Department of the Treasury oversees the printing of money.

At Work for the Forest Service

People who work for national government agencies live in all parts of the country and do many types of jobs. For people whose first love is the forest—best of all, forests that have been largely untouched by humans—Penny and Emil Keck have an ideal government job.

The Kecks work for the United States Forest Service, which is part of the Department of Agriculture. They work in the Moose Creek District of the Nez Percé National Forest in the Selway-Betterroot Wilderness of Northern Idaho. The Kecks are in charge of fire control for the area. During the summer, the Kecks spend time every day watching for signs of fire from this tower.

The area in which the Kecks work has been set aside as wilderness. The mountains, forests, streams, and wildlife receive special protection from the government. Human activity is limited. Cars and other vehicles are not allowed into the area at all. People who want to go there must enter on foot or by horseback, canoe, raft, or airplane. The hikers below have come in on foot.

Penny and Emil often set up camp in remote parts of the forest so that they can be close to winter work.

When winter arrives, fire control duties end. The Kecks spend many winter days repairing trails and foot bridges. They build them as well.

Department of Labor. Carries out laws related to safe working conditions, a minimum wage, unemployment insurance, and pay for injured workers. Operates job-training programs. Studies changes in employment and prices.

Department of Housing and Urban Development (HUD). Operates programs to help families buy houses. Provides money to build housing for the elderly and for low-income families. Grants money to communities to improve streets, sewers, and parks. Studies city problems.

Department of the Interior. Carries out laws on the use of public lands. Operates the national parks and historical places. Is responsible for mine safety and some dams. Operates programs for American Indians.

Department of Agriculture. Works to improve farm income and support American farm products. Operates food-stamp and national school-lunch programs. Inspects foods and controls crop and animal diseases.

Department of Commerce. Provides economic information to business and government planners. Makes loans to small businesses. Directs the United States Merchant Marine. Promotes American business opportunities in other countries.

Department of Transportation. Administers programs for building and maintaining interstate highways, railroads, airports, and some waterways. Directs the Coast Guard during peacetime. Studies traffic problems and auto safety.

Department of Energy. Created in 1977 to deal with the nation's growing energy problems. Explores new ways to use oil, gas, and coal resources. Develops new energy sources such as solar energy. Promotes energy conservation. Enforces governmental regulations affecting oil and gas companies.

Independent Agencies

The executive branch also includes more than fifty independent agencies. They are called **independent** because they are independent of the Cabinet.

Most independent agencies are smaller than Cabinet depart-

Discuss: What are the roles of independent agencies?

ments. They are set up to do special jobs. The National Aeronautics and Space Administration (NASA) is an example. Congress created NASA in 1958. It runs the United States space program. The Central Intelligence Agency (CIA) is another example. The CIA was set up to gather and study information about other countries.

Some independent agencies are **government corporations.** In other words, they are businesses run by the government. The United States Postal Service, for example, is a government corporation. The Postal Service tries to make money by delivering the mail. The Postal Service also gets money to operate from the Congress.

Regulatory Commissions

Regulatory [reg′yə lə tôr′ē] commissions are also independent agencies. They are different from other independent agencies, however, in that they do not have to report to the President. Commission members are named by the President, but they cannot be fired by the President. They can only be removed from office by congressional impeachment.

Regulatory commissions regulate: that is, they make rules for certain industries. For instance, the Federal Communications Commission makes broadcasting rules for the nation's television stations.

Sometimes the regulatory commissions act like courts. For example, the people who run a commission may bring charges

Note: Some students could report on these agencies.

Discuss: Why are regulatory commissions important?

The National Bureau of Standards is an agency in the Department of Commerce. It was set up to provide a national basis for measurement standards. It gets involved with energy conservation, fire protection, and product safety projects. Here material is being tested to determine its resistance to flame.

against a business for breaking one of the commission's rules. The commissioners will then hold hearings and collect evidence. Lawyers for the company and the commission often testify about the problem under study. If the charge is supported by evidence, the commission may set a penalty.

Section Review

Vocabulary: bureaucracy, Cabinet departments, federal agencies, government corporations, independent agencies, regulatory commissions.

Reviewing the Main Ideas

1. What is the main job of the federal agencies?
2. How many Cabinet departments are there? Name six of them.
3. Name one type of agency other than the Cabinet departments that is part of the executive branch.
4. Use the information in this section to tell whether these statements are true or false.
   a. The job of government corporations is to make rules for certain industries.
   b. The federal agencies are part of the executive branch of government.
   c. Independent agencies are part of the Department of Defense.
   d. All federal workers are in Washington, D.C.

Skill Building

1. The federal agencies are often called the federal bureaucracy. Look up the meaning of *bureaucracy* in the glossary. Tell why the word *bureaucracy* describes the workings of the federal agencies.
2. Which Cabinet department do you think would be responsible for the following:
   a. the use of national forests
   b. farm problems
   c. enforcing civil rights laws
   d. operation of passenger railroads
   e. city housing problems
   f. solar energy

Main Ideas
1. p. 187
2. 12, p. 188
3. independent agencies or government corporations or regulatory commissions
4. a. F, b. T, c. F
Skill Building
1. Answers will vary.
2. a. Interior, b. Agriculture, c. Justice, d. Transportation, e. HUD, f. Energy

2/Decision Makers in Federal Agencies

Decisions must be made at many levels in federal agencies. The decisions that get most public attention are made by agency leaders. However, many other agency workers make important decisions too.

Political Appointees

The top leaders in federal agencies are named by the President. These are the Cabinet **secretaries,** agency directors, deputy directors, and their assistants. These politically appointed leaders are expected to set the overall policy for the agency. They also make the key political decisions for the agency.

Political decisions are those that interest Congress, news reporters, and strong interest groups. The Secretary of Defense, for example, may have to make important decisions about new weapons. The Secretary of Commerce may make decisions about creating business opportunities for minority groups and for women. The Secretary of the Interior makes key decisions about oil and gas pipelines, new dams, strip mining, national parks, and offshore oil drilling.

Top agency leaders do not make key decisions alone. The alternatives from which they choose are often set by people

Discuss: Who are the key decision makers in federal agencies? How do they get their jobs? What are their roles?

Discuss: How has this decision affected your state?

The Alaska pipeline.

working far below them in the agency. When considering the alternatives, leaders will usually talk with some of these people. They may also talk with the President or members of Congress interested in the decision. They may study facts collected by staff people and interest groups affected by the decision.

Presidents, of course, want the decisions of agency leaders to reflect their own ideas. As a result, Presidents try to appoint leaders with whom they share political views. Presidents need to do this to get some control over the huge federal bureaucracy.

Where do the top leaders come from? Who are they? Most top leaders are successful people in business or the professions. Almost all have a college education. Some may be Ph.D.'s. They are usually not experts in the work of the agency they head, but they often have some experience in the same area. Many have served in government before. Some have been elected officials.

Career Workers

Most people who work in federal agencies are career workers. Unlike the political appointee, whose job usually ends when a new President is elected, the career worker's job is permanent. Career workers get their jobs through the **civil service system.**

The **Office of Personnel Management** directs the civil service system. The Office sets standards for federal jobs, and it gives

---

WHO WORKS FOR WASHINGTON

WHITE-COLLAR WORKERS

Number of Federal Workers

Secretaries and clerks	211,068
Mail Carriers	202,262
Engineers (all types)	146,940
Scientists (all types)	85,501
Nurses and nurses' aides	67,904
Personnel administrators	35,331
Accountants	31,780
Teachers	26,284
Air-traffic controllers	26,005
Internal Revenue Service agents	21,155
Investigators	21,133
Inspectors	17,427
Forestry workers	14,624
Mathematicians and statisticians	13,550
Guards	13,477
Attorneys	12,761
Fire fighters	11,875
Computer operators	11,602
Key punchers	10,932
Doctors	8,033
Librarians	6,643
Telephone operators	5,059
Economists	4,798
Payroll clerks	4,553
Customs agents	4,301
Purchasing agents	3,959
Writers and editors	3,577
Psychologists	3,099
Photographers	3,061
Veterinarians	2,284
Pharmacists	1,439
Dentists	925
Chaplains	461

BLUE-COLLAR WORKERS

Mobile-industrial-equipment workers	72,841
Manual laborers	57,383
Fixed-industrial-equipment workers	44,777
Service employes (all types)	43,706
Warehouse workers	42,344
Aircraft service people	32,074
Metal workers	29,765
Electronic-equipment workers	29,576
Machine-tool workers	19,547
Boat operators and service people	17,980
Ammunition and armament workers	16,213
Woodworkers	15,545
Plumbers and pipefitters	15,279
Printers	12,137
Painters and paperhangers	10,627

Note: Civilian workers. Latest total's available— white collar, October 1974; blue collar, October 1972.

tests to people who want those jobs. People who are hired are chosen from lists of those who have passed the tests or otherwise met civil service standards. The civil service system is a merit system. It is not "who you know" but "what you know" that is supposed to count in getting a civil service job.

Those career workers who make important decisions about day-to-day agency business are managers and specialists. Most civil service managers have worked for the government fifteen years or more. They have usually worked their way up from low-level jobs to the top career jobs. Many have never worked in Washington. Instead, they work in one of their agency's local offices around the country.

In carrying out their agency's program, career managers wrestle with decisions like these: What kind of cancer research project should we give money to? How should we set up the new school lunch program passed by Congress? Most of these decisions do not make headlines, but the decisions are important nonetheless. In many ways, the policy of the national government is formed by these decisions.

Discuss: What are the advantages of a "merit system"?

Section Review

Vocabulary: career workers, Office of Personnel Management, civil service system, secretaries, political appointees.

Reviewing the Main Ideas

1. What sorts of positions do presidential appointees hold in the federal agencies?
2. Who usually make the federal agency decisions that get most public attention—political appointees or career workers?
3. What is the civil service system?

Skill Building

1. Write a description of a fictional top political appointee to a federal agency. Your appointee should fit at least some of the characteristics described in this section.
2. Name one type of career worker who would be responsible for making important agency decisions. (Describe the type of job and the type of experience the person would probably have.)
3. From the table on page 196, pick out three jobs that you might like to do. Name each job and tell how many federal workers presently do that job.

Main Ideas
1. top leaders
2. political appointees
3. p. 197
Skill Building
1. Answers will vary.
2. Answers will vary.
3. Answers will vary.

3/Those Who Influence the Decision Makers

Federal agency workers face many pressures when making decisions. The Congress, the President, the clients whom federal agencies serve or regulate, and other agencies all have an influence on the decisions they make.

Congress

Discuss: How does Congress influence the decision makers?

Congress can influence agency decision makers in several ways. First, Congress has the power to set up or end agency programs. The House or Senate Armed Services Committee, for instance, can start or stop programs in the Department of Defense.

Second, Congress has the power to pass or not pass laws an agency wants. The Environmental Protection Agency may study pollution in rivers and draft a new bill to deal with it, but only Congress can turn that bill into law.

Third, each agency depends on Congress for money. Without money from Congress, agencies would have to go out of business. Every year when it passes the federal budget, Congress decides whether or not to approve the money for each agency.

Pollution on the Blackstone River.

The President

As head of the executive branch, the President has several ways of influencing agency decisions. First of all, the President names the top leaders in most agencies. These leaders will try to influence others in their agency to carry out the President's policies.

Second, the President can use the budget to get some control over federal agencies. Congress approves each agency's budget, but it is the President who decides how much money to request for each agency.

Third, the President may set up new agencies to work on programs that deserve special attention. Sometimes this is done by moving people from existing agencies into a new one.

There are also many limitations on the President's influence. The President can appoint and fire top agency leaders, but the jobs of civil service workers are protected by complex rules. It is difficult to fire them. Since Presidents cannot appoint and cannot fire civil service workers, it is hard for Presidents to influence those people.

Another limitation on presidential influence is the fact that Presidents come and go, while many civil service workers hold their jobs for twenty years or more. The decision makers among this group have their own ideas about how things should be run. They are often more interested in their agency's programs than in any new ideas the President may have.

Discuss: What is the role of the President in influencing decision makers?

Client Groups

Clients are those citizens who work with and are most affected by the decisions of federal agencies. Every agency has its own set of clients. The Department of Agriculture, for example, works with farmers and others in the farming business. The Federal Communications Commission makes decisions that involve telephone and telegraph companies and radio and television stations. These client groups are a third source of influence on agency decisions. The groups are often represented by lobbyists. The lobbyists write letters, testify at agency hearings, and do other things to get their group's ideas across to an agency. Sometimes a client group does not get the results it wants. Then its members may try to get help from a member of Congress or even from the President.

For agency officials and clients to work together is normal. Indeed, agency officials must often work closely with client groups if they are to get anything done. Working closely with a

Discuss: Why are client groups important?

Discuss: What roles do watchdog agencies have?

client group, however, may cause special problems for the regulatory commission. Regulatory commissions are often called **watchdog agencies.** They are supposed to regulate industries for the public good. They set and enforce safety standards for products and enforce laws against unfair business practices.

Over the years these watchdog agencies have developed close associations with the industries they regulate. Commissioners often come to their government jobs from these industries. And after they work for the government, they often go back to the same industries again. Some observers say these close ties are quite natural. They say that if watchdog agencies are to make fair rules, they must know a lot about the industries they regulate. Many other critics say that such close ties make it hard for the regulatory commissions to do their job. They charge that the watchdog agencies protect the industries they are supposed to regulate rather than the public interest, as they should.

Other Federal Agencies

Discuss: How do other agencies influence decision makers?

A fourth source of influence on federal agencies is other agencies. Sometimes programs or rules in different agencies conflict with each other. For example, rules about hiring members of minority groups made by the Department of Justice may conflict with policies set by the Office of Civil Rights in the Department

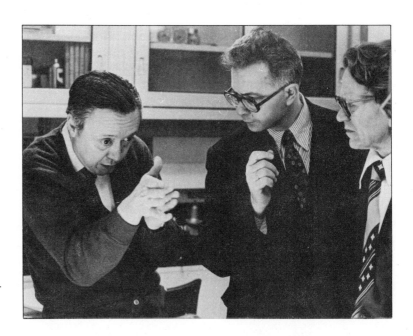

A physicist from the National Bureau of Standards discusses x-ray uses with a soviet delegate from the U.S.-U.S.S.R. Joint Working Group on Cooperation in the Field of Meteorology.

of Health, Education, and Welfare. Decision makers in each agency may try to influence the others to accept their program or rules.

Section Review

Vocabulary: client groups, watchdog agencies.

Reviewing the Main Ideas

1. List four individuals or groups that have influence on federal agency decisions.
2. Describe how client groups may try to influence agency decisions.

Skill Building

1. List three ways that Congress has of influencing agency decisions.
2. Page 199 gives ways that a President can influence agency decisions. Which kind is being used in these examples?
   a. The President appointed JoAnn Smith to be Secretary of Agriculture today. Ms. Smith is a long-time supporter of the President.
   b. The White House said the President will ask Congress to create an agency to deal with the nation's energy problems.
   c. The President said she will cut $4 million from the Defense Department budget next year.

Main Ideas
1. pp. 198–201
2. pp. 199–200
Skill Building
1. p. 198
2. a. names top leaders, b. sets up new agencies, c. uses the budget

The Fight over Concorde

In the winter of 1976, Secretary of Transportation Bill Coleman faced a tough choice. He had to decide whether or not to let Concorde jetliners land at Dulles Airport near Washington, D.C., and at Kennedy Airport near New York City. The Secretary of Transportation has the power to grant or deny landing rights at United States airports to new kinds of aircraft. Usually this is a routine decision. Concorde, however, was no ordinary plane. Concorde was a supersonic transport, an SST, a jet that could fly at twice the speed of sound. It had been built by Britain and France at a cost of $3 billion over 13 years.

In January of 1976, Coleman held hearings. Many different groups tried to influence Coleman's decision.

The British and French testified that the Concorde would cut flying time between the capitals of Europe and New York City or Washington, D.C., in half. They said the Concorde was safe and not much louder than regular jets. Further, they argued that the decision was important to their governments. Billions of dollars and the jobs of thousands of British and French workers

Brian Lovison, president of an anti-SST group called Concorde Alert, testifies at the New York Port Authority hearings.

were involved. If the United States did not cooperate, the French and British might strike back. They could, after all, restrict the operation of American planes in England and France. They might refuse to buy American planes or refuse to let new kinds of American planes land in their countries.

Major opposition to the Concorde came from the Environmental Protection Agency. Roger Strelow of the EPA testified that jet exhaust from many Concordes could put a layer of gases, dust, and water vapor in the upper air. This could ruin the weather on earth by heating or cooling the planet. Further, some studies had shown that exhaust from the Concorde might damage the ozone layer. Ozone gas in the atmosphere protects the earth from the sun's deadly rays. Damage to the ozone layer might cause 200 or more cases of skin cancer in the United States each year. Finally, Strelow was worried that the Concorde would be much louder than other jet planes. He said it did not fit with government programs aimed at lowering noise levels.

The National Aeronautics and Space Administration disagreed with EPA's position. NASA officials agreed that the new plane might be a little noisier than others, but they said that it

The SST *Concorde.*

would not seriously damage the ozone layer nor change the world's weather. They noted that fighter planes had flown higher and faster than the Concorde for years. They said these planes had not hurt the ozone layer.

Finally, Secretary of State Henry Kissinger expressed the State Department's concern about how the decision would affect foreign policy. He urged Coleman to decide "yes." He argued this would show friendship for France and Britain.

In addition to the agencies of the government, others were interested in the problem. Environmental groups were against the Concorde. In addition to the reasons given by the EPA, these groups argued that the Concorde was a gas guzzler. It would use two or three times more fuel than other jets.

The New York Port Authority was against letting the Concorde land. The Port Authority runs Kennedy Airport in New York. New Yorkers living near the airport had been fighting jet traffic at Kennedy Airport since the 1960s. They did not like the noise jets made. They were very much against the Concorde.

After the Department of Transportation hearings, Secretary Coleman studied the evidence. He talked with staff members and

United States Secretary of State Henry Kissinger (on the left) with British Prime Minister James Callaghan.

others. On February 4, 1976, he announced his decision to let the Concorde land on a limited basis. His permission was for one year only, after which the decision would be reviewed. Only two flights a day could land at Kennedy Airport; only one a day at Dulles. All flights could be cancelled at any time.

The New York Port Authority refused to let the Concorde land, in spite of Coleman's ruling. A year after the decision, Concordes were flying from Paris and London to Washington. They still were not going to New York.

Reviewing the Case Study

Make a decision tree to study Coleman's decision. Use the tree to answer these questions:
1. What was the occasion for decision?
2. What alternatives did the Secretary have?
3. What were the likely consequences of each alternative?
4. What governmental goals could affect the decision?
5. Do you think the decision Coleman made was a good one? Explain your thinking.

Anti-SST demonstration at Kennedy Airport.

Chapter Nine Test and Activities

★★

Vocabulary

Match the following phrases with their meanings.

1. regulatory commissions
2. client groups
3. government corporations
4. independent agencies
5. Cabinet departments
6. civil service system

a. the twelve major agencies of the executive branch, each responsible for an area such as defense or labor
b. executive agencies that are independent of the Cabinet but not independent of the President
c. businesses run by the government
d. agencies that are independent of the President and whose job it is to make rules for certain industries
e. a system for hiring government workers
f. people most affected by federal agency decisions

Reviewing Chapter Ideas

1. Match the Cabinet departments and the work they do by writing the name of the department after the appropriate letter. (Department of State; Department of Defense; Department of Health, Education, and Welfare; Department of Labor; Department of the Treasury; Department of Housing and Urban Development; Department of the Interior; Department of Agriculture; Department of Commerce; Department of Justice; Department of Energy; Department of Transportation)
   a. collects taxes
   b. operates job-training programs
   c. helps farmers

d. directs the armed forces
e. gives information to businesses
f. arranges treaties with other governments
g. operates programs for the poor, elderly, and handicapped
h. examines problems of cities
i. operates the FBI
j. studies problems of auto safety
k. promotes energy conservation
l. operates the national parks

2. True or false: There are many federal agencies other than Cabinet departments.
3. Over _____ people now work for federal agencies.
   a. 200,000
   b. 500,000
   c. 1,000,000
   d. 3,000,000
4. Federal agencies are part of the _____ branch(es) of government.
   a. executive
   b. legislative
   c. judicial
   d. three national
5. Congress does <u>not</u> have the power to _____ .
   a. create a federal agency program
   b. select federal agency leaders
   c. approve the money an agency asks for
   d. pass the laws an agency wants
6. True or false: All workers in federal agencies are replaced with new employees when a new President is elected.

Ideas
1. a. Treasury
   b. Labor
   c. Agriculture
   d. Defense
   e. Commerce
   f. State
   g. HEW
   h. HUD
   i. Justice
   j. Transportation
   k. Energy
   l. Interior

★★★

Using Basic Social Studies Skills

Finding Information

Under which section head (the numbered heads in this book) would you look if you wanted to find out what job regulatory commissions are supposed to do? Which words in the head indicate that you are looking in the right section? How do they indicate that?

Comprehending Information

How do regulatory agencies differ from other independent agencies in their relationship to the President.

Organizing Information

Outline Section 3 of this chapter. Use the section heads and subheads as the heads on your outline.

Evaluating Information

Do you think the civil service system is a good system for hiring government employees? Why or why not?

Communicating Ideas

Imagine that you have a chance to suggest a new Cabinet department to the President. Write a paragraph stating what the department will be, what its main jobs would be, and why you think it is needed.

Using Decision-Making Skills

The Secretary of Transportation and the New York Port Authority disagreed in their response to the Concorde jetliner case. Why do you think they made decisions that differed from one another?

Ideas

2. T   5. b
3. d   6. F
4. a

Activities

1. Use the *Readers' Guide to Periodical Literature* to locate articles that were written about one of the twelve Cabinet departments in the past year. Write the titles of five of the articles and tell where each one can be found.

2. Pick one of the articles referred to above. Read it and write a summary.

3. Cooperate with other students in your class in preparing a large chart that shows the work of the major independent agencies in the executive branch.

4. Use telephone books in your public library to find out which large cities in your state have federal agency offices. Contact one of those offices by mail to find out what work it does in your region.

5. For students who want to learn more about federal agencies, the following books are recommended:

   (a) *The FDA,* by Scott Lucas (Celestial Arts, 1978).

   (b) *The FBI and the CIA; Secret Agents and American Democracy,* by James Munves (Harcourt, 1975).

   (c) *Warning! Your Health Is at Stake: The Story of the Fight for Pure Food and Drug Standards,* by Charles Paul May (Hawthorn, 1975).

Chapter 10

Decision Making in the Federal Courts

★★★

A bailiff looks through the rear door of a courtroom. Suddenly he calls loudly, "All rise and remain silent!"

A judge in a long, black robe enters the room. The judge pauses and the bailiff chants, "Hear ye, hear ye, hear ye, the United States District Court is now in session. Draw near that you may be heard. God save the United States and this honorable court. Please take your seats." The judge sits down and the court is in session.

Nearly five hundred federal judges start each court day this way. These judges are part of the federal court system. They are powerful decision makers, as the examples below show.

In Boston, the district court ordered the busing of 24,000 students to get more mixing of blacks and whites in the city's schools. The court also ordered the spending of $235,000 for repairs at South Boston High School.

In Texas, Judge Carole O. Bue, Jr., ruled that overcrowding existed in Harris County jails. The judge ordered many changes. He said that prisoners must have clean clothes daily instead of weekly. He said that inmates must be allowed at least three hours of exercise per week.

In Oklahoma City, a federal court made a $259 million antitrust judgment against IBM, a giant corporation. The court's decision led to a big drop in the price of IBM stock at the New York Stock Exchange.

In Detroit, Judge Damon Keith ordered the city of Hamtramck and the Department of Housing and Urban Development to build low-cost housing for blacks displaced by urban-renewal projects.

This chapter describes the federal court system. You will learn:

1/How Laws and Courts Serve the People
2/How the Federal Courts Are Organized
3/What the Supreme Court Does
Case Study: *Brown* v. *Board of Education*

Discuss: Would any of these decisions affect your community? How?

1/How Laws and Courts Serve the People

There are four different kinds of laws in the United States. Laws made by lawmaking bodies such as Congress, state legislatures, or city councils are **statutory laws.** For example, a state law that says a driver must signal before making a left turn is a statutory law.

Discuss: What kinds of laws do we have in the United States? What is the role of each?

Another type of law, called **common law,** has developed from common practice and customary ways of dealing with problems. For example, having twelve people on a jury is part of common law. It is traditional. The decisions of judges also make up common law. When a judge is deciding a case, he or she looks at the ways other judges have decided similar cases.

Administrative laws are those laws made by government agencies. The Department of Transportation ruling that all passenger cars must have seat belts is an example of an administrative law. As federal and state governments have grown, the number of administrative laws has grown too.

Finally, there is **constitutional law.** Constitutional law is based on the Constitution and the interpretations of the Constitution described in Supreme Court decisions.

Lawyers argue whether or not a piece of evidence is admissible. The court reporter on the left keeps a record of all proceedings. The judge will decide the matter.

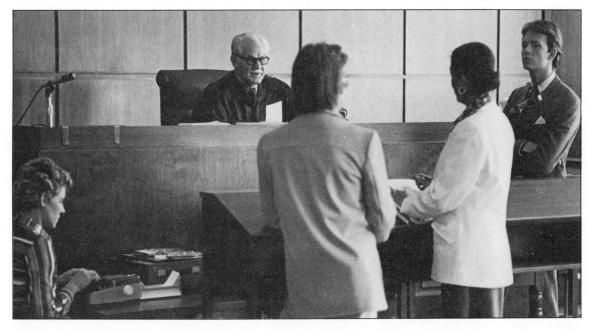

Courts use these different kinds of law to settle disputes. Whether the dispute is between people or between a person and the government, the parties to the dispute come before a court. Each argues for its side. The court then applies the law to the facts that have been presented, and a decision is made in favor of one or the other.

Equal Justice for All

Our legal system is based on an important ideal—**equal justice** for all under the law. The goal of the legal system is to treat every person the same. Under the Constitution, every person accused of breaking the law has the right to a public trial. Every accused person has the right to a lawyer. If an accused person cannot afford a lawyer, the courts will appoint one and will pay the lawyer's fee. Every person is considered innocent until proven guilty. And a person has the right to ask for a review of his or her case if, in that person's view, the courts have made a mistake.

The ideal of equal justice is a difficult goal to reach. Judges and juries are not free from the prejudices of their communities. Poor people do not have the money to spend on legal help that wealthy citizens or large companies do. Nonetheless, Americans believe in the ideal. There are some countries in the world where prejudice is legal and where there are different laws for different groups of people. In the United States, all people are equal be-

Judge James McCrystal reviews videotaped evidence. In his court, he allows lawyers to present taped interviews and cross-examinations of witnesses. This lets witnesses give evidence at their convenience. The jurors look at the videotapes—they never see these witnesses in person.

fore the law. If injustice occurs, citizens have the right to speak out and correct it.

The Cases Heard in Federal Courts

The federal courts are the third branch of the national government. They have authority to hear certain kinds of cases.

Cases Involving the Constitution. Federal courts have **jurisdiction** over cases involving the Constitution. Jurisdiction is the authority to judge and administer the law. If the law in question is the Constitution, including the amendments, the case must be heard in a federal court.

Discuss: What kinds of cases are handled in federal courts?

Cases Involving Federal Laws. If a person is accused of breaking a federal law, such as kidnaping, tax evasion, or counterfeiting, the case is heard in a federal court. Disputes that involve issues over which the national government has constitutionally granted control—such as patent rights or bankruptcy—are also heard in federal courts.

Disputes Between States or People from Different States. Any disagreement between state governments is brought to trial in a federal court. Lawsuits between citizens of different states also come under the federal courts. For example, Mrs. Armand of Nebraska may bring suit in a federal court against Mr. Duvall of New York for not fulfilling his part of a business agreement. Such suits must involve a sum of at least $10,000 to be handled in federal court.

Disputes Involving the Federal Government. The United States government may sue someone. For example, the Defense Department might sue a company that had contracted to build missile parts if the job was not completed on time. The suit would be heard in a federal court. Also, the government can be sued. For instance, if you were hit by a Postal Service truck, you could sue the United States Postal Service to pay for your medical expenses.

Disputes Involving Treaties or Admiralty or Maritime Law. Disputes between the United States and other governments are heard in federal courts. A treaty case might involve a dispute over the way the State Department interpreted a trade agreement. Admiralty and maritime laws have to do with rules on the high seas. Disputes involving shipping commerce, collisions, or crimes committed at sea are all heard in federal courts.

Section Review

Vocabulary: administrative laws, common law, constitutional law, equal justice, jurisdiction, statutory laws.

Reviewing the Main Ideas

1. Name and describe the four major types of law in the United States.
2. Describe the job of the courts in our legal system.
3. Explain in your own words what is meant by "equal justice for all."

Skill Building

Read Article 3, Section 2, clause 1 of the Constitution and Amendment 11 to answer these questions:

1. Can a citizen of Ohio sue the state of Alabama in a federal court?
2. If a citizen of France sues the state of New York, will the case be heard in a federal court or in a New York state court?
3. If a ship owned by a woman from Delaware collides with a ship owned by a man from South Carolina, what kind of court will decide who was at fault?

A law student argues her case before real judges in "moot court." This kind of practice comes near the end of a lawyer's schooling

212

2/How the Federal Courts Are Organized

There are three main levels of federal courts: district courts, courts of appeal, and the Supreme Court. In addition, there are several special courts. The chart below shows the relationships among courts in the federal court system.

Discuss: How are federal courts organized? What are the key roles of each type of court?

United States District Courts. Most federal cases are handled in the ninety-one United States district courts. Every state has at least one district court. Some states have two, three, or four such courts. In all, there are eighty-nine district courts in the fifty states, one in the District of Columbia, and one in Puerto Rico. Each has from one to twenty-seven judges, depending on need.

Almost all federal court cases begin with a trial in a district court. District courts are the only federal courts where juries are used and witnesses are called. Many cases do not end in the

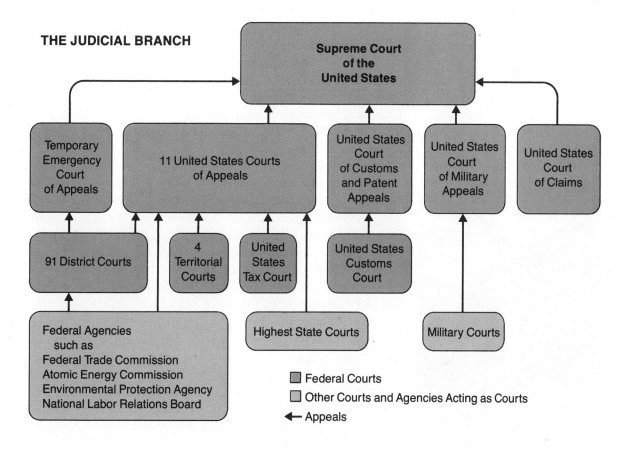

THE JUDICIAL BRANCH

Supreme Court of the United States

Temporary Emergency Court of Appeals

11 United States Courts of Appeals

United States Court of Customs and Patent Appeals

United States Court of Military Appeals

United States Court of Claims

91 District Courts

4 Territorial Courts

United States Tax Court

United States Customs Court

Federal Agencies such as Federal Trade Commission Atomic Energy Commission Environmental Protection Agency National Labor Relations Board

Highest State Courts

Military Courts

■ Federal Courts
□ Other Courts and Agencies Acting as Courts
← Appeals

district courts. Cases may go on to the next level of the court system—the appeals courts.

United States Courts of Appeals. The job of the appeals courts is to review decisions made in the district courts. There are eleven federal appellate courts. Each one covers an area called a **circuit.** There are ten circuits in the fifty states. The eleventh circuit is in the District of Columbia.

Note: Have a map of ten circuits available.

Sometimes mistakes are made in district courts. Thus, every person has the right to ask for a review of his or her case in a United States court of appeals. Appeals are usually made when lawyers think the law was not correctly applied in a case or wrong procedures were used. An appeal can also be made if new evidence turns up.

There are no trials in a court of appeals. Instead, a panel of three or more judges reviews the record of the case being appealed from the district court. The judges also listen to arguments from lawyers for each side. The judges then meet privately and make a decision by majority vote.

When an appeals court decision is made, one judge writes an **opinion** for the court. The opinion explains the reasons for the decision. If the appeals court finds a mistake, it sends the case back to the district court for a new trial. If the appeals court finds that justice was done, the decision made in the district court is upheld. In the vast majority of cases, the decision of the appeals court is final.

A Justice explains the role of the Court in one of two public conference rooms.

The United States Supreme Court. The Supreme Court stands above all other courts in the land. The main job of the Supreme Court is to decide whether or not laws are in agreement with the Constitution. Although many people do not know it, citizens do not have the right to have their cases heard in the Supreme Court. The Constitution gives Congress the power to decide which kinds of cases may be appealed to the Supreme Court. Except for certain kinds of cases involving the Constitution, the Supreme Court decides which cases it will hear. When the Court refuses to review a case, the decision of the lower court remains unchanged.

Other Federal Courts. From time to time, Congress has created special courts. The chart on page 213 shows these special courts. They are the Temporary Emergency Court of Appeals, the Court of Claims, the Court of Customs and Patent Appeals, the Customs Court, the Territorial Courts, the Court of Military Appeals, and the Tax Court.

The Temporary Emergency Court of Appeals has been in operation since 1972. In 1971, Congress passed certain laws aimed at keeping the country's economy stable. It set up this special court to handle appeals from the district courts in cases having to do with these laws.

Discuss: What are the roles of each of these courts?

The Court of Claims handles cases involving suits against the national government. If the court rules against the government, the person suing the government is usually granted a sum of money.

As you can tell from its name, the Court of Customs and Patent Appeals is an appeals court. It reviews cases decided in the Customs Court. It also settles disputes between inventors and the national government Patent Office. The Customs Court settles disputes between merchants from other countries and the United States officials who tax their goods.

The Territorial Courts are like district courts for the territories of the United States. There is one each in Guam, the Virgin Islands, the Canal Zone, and the Northern Mariana Islands. These courts handle both the kinds of cases federal courts hear and the kinds state courts hear. (The territory of Puerto Rico also has a federal court, but it is classified as a district court.)

The Court of Military Appeals is the appeals court for the armed services. It reviews court-martial decisions. The judges on this court also have responsibility for recommending improvements in the country's system of military justice.

Tax Court is the final decision maker for disputes about federal taxes. Citizens who believe that the government has not figured their taxes correctly may argue their case before this court.

Decision Makers in the Judicial Branch

The chief decision makers in the judicial branch are the **federal judges.** They are appointed to their jobs by the President. The Senate must agree to the appointment for a person to become a federal judge. Usually, the President asks the senators for their recommendations.

Discuss: Who are the key decision makers in the judicial branch? How do they get their jobs?

In 1978, 117 new district court judgeships were set up. Four of these were in Virginia. President Jimmy Carter had issued an executive order that said senators should set up nominating commissions made up of lawyers and non lawyers, men and women, members of minority groups, and people with differing political opinions. These commissions would make recommendations to the senators, and the senators should pass along their choices from the commission's list. Senator Harry Byrd of Virginia ignored the President's order and submitted a list of ten names he had chosen; all ten were white males. The Justice Department told him his list was unacceptable, and that he must send in a list that included the names of minorities and women. "There is no way Carter will appoint four more white males to the bench in Virginia," said a Justice Department official.

Of course, if the President makes enough senators angry, he will not be able to get Senate approval for his appointments. Thus there is give and take between the executive and legislative branches in making appointments to the judicial branch.

Once appointed, a federal judge has a job for life if he or she wants it. A judge can be removed from office only through impeachment. The writers of the Constitution gave federal judges this sort of job security because they wanted judges to be able to decide cases without interference from others.

Judges do not work alone. They have help from many others. Judges appoint clerks, secretaries, court reporters, probation officers, and United States **magistrates.** Magistrates take care of much of a judge's routine work. They issue search and arrest warrants in federal cases. They also decide whether people who have been arrested should be held in jail or released on bail.

The Executive Branch in the Courts

Each district court has a **United States attorney** and one or more deputies. United States attorneys are government lawyers who prosecute people accused of breaking federal laws. They look into complaints of crime, prepare formal charges, and then present evidence in court. United States attorneys are appointed to a four-year term by the President with consent of the Senate. They are members of the executive branch. Their boss is the Attorney General of the United States, the head of the Justice Department.

Each district court has a United States **marshal** too. Marshals and their staffs make arrests, collect fines, and take convicted persons to prison. They protect jurors, serve legal papers, and keep order in federal courts. Like the United States attorneys, the marshals are members of the Department of Justice.

Discuss: Has this proved to be a good idea?

Discuss: What is the role of the executive branch in the courts?

216

Section Review

Vocabulary: circuit, court of appeals, district court, federal judge, marshal, opinion, United States attorney.

Reviewing the Main Ideas

1. What are the three main types of federal courts?
2. What is the job of a United States court of appeals?
3. Name two of the special federal courts that Congress has created and tell what kinds of cases each hears.

Skill Building

Read the chart on page 213 to answer these questions.

1. If you do not agree with the Internal Revenue Service about how much tax you have to pay, which court would hear the case and make the final decision?
2. Suppose you were in the army and were mistakenly accused of helping the enemy. In your court-martial a witness lies, and you are convicted and jailed. Then evidence is finally found that proves you could not have done the crime. To what court would you appeal your case?
3. Suppose you own a business regulated by the Federal Trade Commission and you don't agree with a ruling the Commission makes against you. To what court could you appeal their decision?

Main Ideas
1. district courts, courts of appeals, the Supreme Court
2. p. 214
3. pp. 214–215
Skill Building
1. Tax Court
2. Court of Military Appeals
3. Court of Appeals

The Supreme Court building.

3/What the Supreme Court Does

The Supreme Court is in Washington, D.C., but the Court's influence is felt all across the United States. Supreme Court justices are important political decision makers. Their decisions often affect citizens as much as do the decisions made by Congress or the President.

Justices of the Supreme Court

Discuss: What are the roles of the Supreme Court justices? What qualifications must they have?

The Supreme Court is made up of eight associate justices and one chief justice. The justices work in Washington from October through June. Each month during this time, they spend two weeks listening to oral arguments on cases and then two weeks in recess. During recess the justices write opinions and study new cases. During the summer they take their "homework" with them. They study applications for review, write opinions, and catch up on other legal work.

The President appoints Supreme Court justices with the consent of the majority of the Senate. By 1976 the Senate had approved all but 28 of the 130 Supreme Court nominations sent to it. Senators have usually felt that the President should have a fairly free hand in picking new Supreme Court justices.

Supreme Court justices are always lawyers. They have had successful careers practicing or teaching law, serving in lower courts, or holding other public positions.

Political support and agreement with the President's ideas are important factors in who gets appointed. Presidents want to nominate a person who agrees with their own political ideas. Of course, once appointed, a justice may make decisions that the President does not like.

Judicial Review

The main job of the Supreme Court is to decide whether laws or actions by government officials are allowed by the Constitution or are **unconstitutional.** It does this by using a power called **judicial review.** This is the power to say that a law or action of the executive branch goes against the Constitution. The Constitution does not say that the Supreme Court has the power of judicial review. However, Americans agree that if the Constitution is to be upheld as the highest law in the land, then the highest court in the land must have the power to decide if governmental laws and actions go against it. If the Court decides a law is unconstitutional, then it is no longer in force.

Discuss: What is the importance of judicial review?

John Marshall, who served as chief justice from 1801 to 1835, wrote the first opinion about the constitutionality of a law in 1803. The case was between William Marbury, who had been promised a justice-of-the-peace appointment, and Secretary of State James Madison. All cases are called by the names of the parties to the dispute; this one is called *Marbury* v. *Madison.* (The *v* stands for the Latin word *versus,* which means "against.")

Note: Have students look for other examples of its use.

Marbury that said the Judiciary Act passed by Congress in 1789 allowed the Supreme Court to write a special kind of court order that would force the Secretary of State to give him his appointment. In the Supreme Court's now-famous opinion, Marshall wrote that the Judiciary Act of 1789 went against the Constitution. The Act gave the Supreme Court powers it should not have.

Opinions of any court set **precedents.** A precedent does not have the power of law, but it is a very powerful argument in court. Ever since 1803, *Marbury* v. *Madison* has been the precedent for the Supreme Court's power of judicial review.

Discuss: Where do cases begin?

How Cases Reach the Supreme Court

The Supreme Court is both a trial court and an appeals court. Three types of disputes have their original trials in the Supreme Court: (1) cases involving the official representatives of other nations, (2) suits between states, such as an argument between California and Arizona over water from the Colorado River, and (3) cases involving a state and the national government. Most cases, however, are appealed from a lower court.

No matter where they start, all cases submitted to the Supreme Court are real legal disputes. To test whether or not a law is constitutional in the Supreme Court, someone must actually break the law, or someone must show that he or she was directly affected by the law. A person cannot simply ask the Supreme Court to decide whether or not a law is constitutional. This way of determining what the Supreme Court can and cannot review is sometimes called the **real case rule.**

Discuss: Why is the "real case rule" important?

Discuss: How do the pictures in this section help you to better understand the Supreme Court?

A mailbag holding one day's worth of business waits for a Justice in his office.

The Court at Work

Every case reviewed by the Supreme Court goes through a series of steps. These steps are (1) acceptance, (2) written arguments, (3) oral arguments, (4) conference, (5) opinion writing, and (6) announcement. Let's look at each step.

Acceptance. The thousands of cases sent to the Court each year go first to the Office of the Clerk of the Court. Staff members summarize each case and send copies to each of the nine justices. From the many cases submitted to them, the justices make a list of cases they want to discuss more carefully. Once a week the justices meet to pick from this list the cases the court will actually review. The Court can accept for review just about any case it wants to accept, and it can and does turn down those cases it does not want to hear.

Written Arguments. Once a case is accepted, the lawyers for each side are asked to prepare a **brief.** A brief is a written document that explains one side's position on the case. The justices study the briefs given them by the lawyers.

Oral Arguments. The next step is for lawyers for each side to present oral arguments to the Court. The lawyers stand facing the nine justices to make their arguments. The justices often question the lawyers about the case.

Conference. On Fridays the justices meet in a large conference room to make their first decisions about the cases they have been studying. Each justice has one vote. If, as usually happens, all nine justices vote on a case, five votes are required to decide a case.

Opinion Writing. Once a decision is made, one justice is given the job of writing a majority opinion for the five or more justices who voted the same way on the case. This is an important step, for there is still time for justices to change their minds about a case. A well-written opinion may influence a justice to change his or her vote.

(Above) the courtroom where the Justices hear arguments and issue opinions, (left) in conference, and (below) the nine Justices in the Court's east conference room.

Discuss: What steps does a case go through in the Supreme Court?

A member who disagrees with the majority's decision may write a **dissenting opinion.** Sometimes two, three, or even four members write dissenting opinions. A justice who agrees with the majority, but for different reasons, may write a **concurring opinion.**

Announcement. When the opinion writing is finally completed, the Court makes a public announcement of its decision. Printed copies of the opinion are given to waiting news reporters. The written opinions are used by the Supreme Court and other courts around the country to guide decisions in new cases.

What Influences Supreme Court Decisions?

Discuss: How are Supreme Court decisions influenced?

In the United States, the law is supposed to be the most important influence on a justice's decisions. Justices look at the Constitution when making decisions. The Bill of Rights has been the focus of many important Supreme Court decisions.

Note: Make a decision tree for this case.

The Law. Here is one example of how the Supreme Court interprets the law: In early December of 1965 Chris Eckhardt and John and Mary Beth Tinker decided to wear black armbands to school to protest American involvement in the Vietnam War.

On December 14, officials of the school system found out about the students' plan. They feared the protest would cause disruptions in the schools, so they made a special rule. Any student wearing an armband to school would be asked to remove it. Students who refused would be suspended until they came to school without an armband. A few days later Mary Beth, Chris, and John wore black armbands to school and were suspended.

The students' parents sued the school officials in a United States district court. Their lawyers argued that the school's armband rule violated a student's constitutional right of free expression of ideas. The First Amendment says: *"Congress shall make no law . . . abridging the freedom of speech."*

The First Amendment applies not just to Congress but also to state officials such as school principals because of the Fourteenth Amendment. That Amendment says: *"No state shall make or enforce any law which shall abridge the privileges . . . of citizens of the United States; nor shall any state deprive any person of . . . liberty . . . without due process of law . . . ."*

School officials argued that the armband rule was necessary

because wearing armbands might cause disturbances in school. They said it was their duty to stop any behavior that could interrupt schoolwork.

The district court agreed that the school officials' action was reasonable in order to prevent disturbance of school discipline. The Tinkers appealed to a United States Court of Appeals. In 1967 the appeals court upheld the decision of the district court. The Tinkers then appealed their case to the Supreme Court. In 1968 the Supreme Court agreed to hear the case.

It was now up to the Supreme Court to interpret the Constitution. Did the Constitution give students the right to free speech while in school? Under what conditions, if any, could students express their opinions?

The Supreme Court made its decision on February 24, 1969. The Court supported the students. It declared the action of the school officials to be unconstitutional. The Court decided that the "armband rule" violated the First Amendment and was, therefore, illegal. In stating the Court's opinion, Justice Abe Fortas wrote:

> First Amendment rights . . . are available to teachers and students. Students in schools as well as out of school are 'persons' under our Constitution. They are possessed of fundamental rights which the state must respect, just as they themselves must respect their obligations to the state . . . In the absence of a specific showing of constitutionally valid reasons to regulate their speech, students are entitled to freedom of expression of their views.

However, the Supreme Court also said that students' free-speech rights had certain limits. The Court said schools could stop students from expressing their views if their speech would seriously disrupt the work and discipline of the school. The Supreme Court decision applied to all schools in the country.

Precedents. Justices also look at earlier court decisions when settling a case. The Court's decision in the Tinker case was based on the idea that students have constitutional rights like adults. One precedent the Court used to support the majority opinion in the Tinker case was in the case of *West Virginia State Board of Education* v. *Barnette*. In that case the board of education required students to salute and pledge allegiance to the flag each day or be expelled. The Court said this rule violated students' rights under the First and Fourteenth Amendments.

Discuss: How do precedents influence the decisions of the Supreme Court?

In the 1960s, many Supreme Court decisions meant that arresting officers had to safeguard the rights of people they accused of crimes. The two cartoons below show opposite opinions of these Court decisions. Which cartoonist agreed with the Court? Which disagreed?

"Tell it to the Judge, Bud."

"What Do They Think People Are—Innocent Until Proved Guilty?"

Sometimes there are precedents that support opposite sides in a case. In the Tinker case, for example, Justice Black dissented from the majority. To support his argument that students' constitutional rights to free speech could be limited in school, he referred to the case of *Cox* v. *Louisiana.* In it the Supreme Court had ruled that the rights of free speech "do not mean everyone with opinions or beliefs to express may address a group at any public place and at any time."

Social Conditions. The social situation in the country can also influence Supreme Court decisions. When social conditions change, the Court may make new interpretations of the law. Justices, like all citizens, are affected by what other people around the country believe about important social issues. Further, their thinking on legal problems can be influenced by social science research and by the writings of legal scholars.

Personal Beliefs. Finally, the personal beliefs of the justices influence Supreme Court decisions. Some members, for example, believe that the Court should be very active and hear many different kinds of cases. Others believe that the Court should be careful not to involve the Court in issues the public disagrees about.

Section Review

Vocabulary: brief, concurring opinion, dissenting opinion, judicial review, precedent, real case rule, unconstitutional.

Reviewing the Main Ideas
1. Why is *Marbury* v. *Madison* an important case?
2. List and briefly describe the steps a case goes through after it is appealed to the Supreme Court.
3. List the factors that can influence Supreme Court decisions.

Skill Building
1. What qualifications do you think a Supreme Court justice should have? Explain your reasons.
2. Why would a President want to appoint justices who agreed with his or her political ideas?
3. Explain what it means for the Supreme Court to interpret the law. Use the Tinker case as an example.

Main Ideas
1. It established judicial review as a function of the Supreme Court.
2. pp. 220–222
3. law, precedents, social conditions, and justices' personal beliefs.

Skill Building
1. Answers will vary.
2. to influence the decisions of the Court
3. pp. 222–223

Brown v. *Board of Education*

Brown v. *Board of Education of Topeka, Kansas,* is one of the most important Supreme Court decisions in this century. It overturned an earlier Supreme Court ruling and was a victory for black Americans. This is the story of that case.

Back in the late 1800s, about half the states passed laws that kept nonwhite people separate from white people in such public places as trains and theaters. Angered, a group of blacks formed a committee to test the constitutionality of these laws in the courts. In 1892, a member, Homer Plessy, got himself arrested for refusing to move to a railroad car for blacks only. He was convicted and eventually his case reached the Supreme Court.

In 1896, the Court announced its decision in *Plessy* v. *Ferguson.* It said that as long as the separate facilities for blacks were equal to the ones for whites, the Fourteenth Amendment was not violated; the segregation laws were not unconstitutional.

After that, more segregation laws were passed. Blacks could not use the same schools, restaurants, telephone booths, even drinking fountains as whites. In one state, courtrooms had separate Bibles for black witnesses. These laws also kept American Indians and people of Mexican, Japanese, and Chinese descent from using facilities for white people.

Black children had to attend separate schools from whites.

There was no real challenge to the *Plessy* decision for forty years, even though in most cases the separate facilities for non-whites were clearly not equal to those for whites.

In the late 1930s and early 1940s, the Court made some rulings requiring the separate facilities to be equal. Several states spent large amounts of money to improve the schools and universities for blacks. In 1954, Georgia spent $27.4 million of its $102 million school budget on its black schools. Some black schools became excellent places to get an education. However, very few Americans would have said that most black schools were anywhere near as good as those for whites.

By 1950, seventeen states still had segregation laws. The National Association for the Advancement of Colored People (NAACP) went to work raising money and providing lawyers to fight these laws in court. Late in 1952, the Supreme Court agreed to hear five cases together. In each, black parents had sued a school district to let their children attend the white schools. The cases came from district courts in Delaware, Kansas, South Carolina, Virginia, and Washington, D.C. Because Oliver Brown, father of eight-year-old Linda Brown, had the first name in the alphabetical listing, the famous case now bears his name.

The lawyers who argued the case were highly respected men. The main lawyer for the NAACP was Thurgood Marshall, who later became a Supreme Court justice. He argued that separate schools never could be equal. There were many experts whose testimony was part of the brief he had given the Court. All of it showed that it hurt black children to keep them apart from whites.

On the other side was John W. Davis. He had been United States ambassador to Great Britain and the Democratic candidate for President in 1924. He said that the Court would be stepping into an area that should be decided by Congress or the state legislatures if it changed the segregation laws. The Court should not be in the business of drastically altering society, he argued.

The arguments ended on December 11, 1952. However, by June, when the Court recessed, no decision had been made. The Court said it would hear more testimony in the fall.

All summer, the two sides prepared their new arguments. In addition, the Court invited the Department of Justice to give an opinion. The last testimony was heard on December 9, 1953.

Conference was prompt. But the opinion writing took another five months. On May 17, 1954, the Court handed down its unanimous opinion in the case of *Brown* v. *Board of Education of Topeka, Kansas.* It said in part:

> Does segregation of children in public schools solely on the basis of race, even though the physical facilities . . . may be equal, deprive the children of the minority group of equal educational opportunities? We believe that it does. . . . To separate them from others . . . solely because of their race generates a feeling of inferiority as to their status in the community that may affect their hearts and minds in a way unlikely ever to be undone. . . . We conclude that in the field of public education, the doctrine of "separate but equal" has no place. Separate educational facilities are inherently unequal.

Reviewing the Case Study

1. What was the occasion for decision in this case?
2. What alternatives did the Court have?
3. What was Marshall's main argument? Davis's argument?
4. Do you agree with the Court's decision? Give your reasons.

(Left) a crowd lines up for seats to hear closing arguments in the *Brown* case. (Above) Thurgood Marshall, between two colleagues, is happy after hearing the Court's decision.

Chapter Ten Test and Activities

★★★

Vocabulary

Match the following words with their meanings.

1. precedent
2. brief
3. statutory laws
4. unconstitutional
5. common law
6. judicial review
7. administrative law
8. constitutional law
9. court
10. circuit

a. illegal according to the Constitution
b. the area covered by a United States court of appeals
c. laws made by lawmaking bodies
d. laws given in the Constitution
e. rules made by government agencies
f. a place to settle legal disputes
g. a legal decision that may serve as an example for later legal cases
h. unwritten laws—legal customs, traditions, and judges' decisions
i. a written document that explains one side's position in a legal case
j. the power to declare laws and the actions of government officials to be unconstitutional

Reviewing Chapter Ideas

1. The case that set the precedent for the Supreme Court's power of judicial review is:
   a. *Marbury* v. *Madison.*
   b. *Plessy* v. *Ferguson.*
   c. *Brown* v. *Board of Education.*
   d. none of the above.
2. True or false: A United States marshal has the power to make arrests.
3. True or false: One justice wrote a dissenting opinion in the school desegregation case, *Brown* v. *Board of Education.*
4. Federal courts settle disputes that involve which of the following?
   a. the Constitution
   b. federal laws
   c. treaties
   d. all of the above
5. True or false: Most federal cases are handled in the Supreme Court.
6. True or false: The Supreme Court is made up of eight associate justices and one chief justice.
7. Federal judges are appointed by _____ .
   a. the Senate
   b. the House of Representatives
   c. the President
   d. the attorney general
8. In which of these federal courts would you see a jury?
   a. a district court
   b. the Supreme Court
   c. an appeals court
   d. all of the above
9. Which of these is not one of the special courts that have been created by Congress?
   a. the Court of Claims
   b. the Customs Court
   c. the Tax Court
   d. the Supreme Court
10. The most important influence on a Supreme Court justice's decisions should be _____ .
    a. personal beliefs
    b. the law
    c. the social situation in the country
    d. the views of private citizens

228

Vocabulary			
1. g	4. a	7. e	10. b
2. i	5. h	8. d	
3. c	6. j	9. f	

Ideas			
1. a	4. d	7. c	10. b
2. T	5. F	8. a	
3. F	6. T	9. d	

★★

Using Basic Social Studies Skills

Finding Information

1. Use the subheads in the chapter to find out how many United States district courts there are. What is the number? How did the subheads help you find the answer quickly?
2. Use the index in the back of your book to find out if there are pages in your book outside of this chapter that tell about courts. List the page numbers if you find some. Circle one of the page numbers, skim the page to find out what sort of court is being discussed. What type of court is it?

Comprehending Information

1. How are Supreme Court opinions used?
2. What is the "real case rule"?
3. Explain what "equal justice under the law" means.
4. What is the Supreme Court's most important job?

Organizing Information

1. Make a diagram that shows how the federal court system works.
2. Explain how a case is handled in the Supreme Court by listing and explaining the steps each case goes through.

Evaluating Information

1. Is it important that the Supreme Court has the power of judicial review? Why or why not?
2. Federal judges can have their jobs for life unless they are impeached. Do you feel this is a good idea? Why or why not?

Communicating Ideas

Write a description of what you think the ideal federal judge would be like.

Using Decision-Making Skills

1. What alternatives did the Supreme Court have in the Tinker case?
2. What were the possible consequences of each alternative?
3. Do you agree with the majority opinion? Why or why not?
4. Why do you think the lower courts ruled against the Tinkers?

Activities

1. Use an encyclopedia to write a report on some person who has served as chief justice of the Supreme Court.
2. Use the *Readers' Guide to Periodical Literature* to find articles on recent Supreme Court cases. List the titles of three articles as well as their sources. Read one of the articles and summarize it.
3. For students interested in learning more about the Supreme Court, the following books are recommended:
   (a) *The Supreme Court, Justice, and the Law,* second edition, Congressional Quarterly Staff (Congressional Quarterly, Inc., 1977).
   (b) *Changing America and the Supreme Court,* revised edition, by Barbara Habenstreit (Messner, 1974).

Unit Two Test

★★

Vocabulary

Write *true* if the underlined word or phrase is used correctly. Write *false* if it is not used correctly.

1. A <u>tax</u> is a fee that a person pays to support his or her government.
2. <u>Congressional district</u> is a term that refers to the place where Congress meets in Washington, D.C.
3. <u>Seniority rule</u> is the tradition of selecting the majority party member with fewest years on a congressional committee to head the committee.
4. A <u>congressional hearing</u> gives people the chance to give their opinions on an issue being studied by a congressional committee.
5. A <u>lobbyist</u> is a person who tries to influence decisions in government.
6. To be <u>nominated</u> at a presidential nominating convention means that someone has been elected President.
7. The <u>electoral college</u> are those people who vote directly for the President.
8. The <u>Cabinet</u> is a group of Congress members who advise the President.
9. The <u>civil service system</u> is a system for hiring government workers.
10. A federal agency's <u>clients</u> are those people who work for the agency.
11. A law is <u>unconstitutional</u> if it does not agree with the Constitution.
12. The power of <u>judicial review</u> is the power to decide whether or not laws are unconstitutional.
13. A <u>precedent</u> is any court decision that serves as a guide in later decisions.

Recalling Information

1. True or false: The Congress is made up of two houses—the Senate and the House of Representatives.
2. True or false: The President heads the legislative branch of government.
3. True or false: The personal income tax is used to provide income for retired people.
4. Each state has _____ senators.
   a. 2
   b. 4
   c. 6
   d. 8
5. The number of House members that each state has is determined by _____ .
   a. the amount of taxes a state pays
   b. the number of square miles in the state
   c. the number of people in the state
   d. the year in which the state entered the union
6. Which of these is a power of the Senate but not of the House?
   a. the power to start the impeachment process
   b. the power to approve presidential appointments of Supreme Court justices
   c. the power to start all tax bills
   d. the power to choose a President if no candidate receives a majority of votes
7. True or false: The party whips in the House assist the floor leaders.
8. True or false: The most powerful leader in the Senate is the president pro tempore.
9. A standing committee _____ .
   a. chooses the leaders of all the other committees in Congress
   b. is a committee that handles a particular problem and disbands when the problem is solved

c. meets to settle differences of opinion when the Senate and the House cannot agree on a particular bill

d. is a permanent committee that deals with one particular kind of legislation

10. According to the Constitution, the President has power to _____ .
    a. create federal courts
    b. make treaties with other countries
    c. impeach the Chief Justice of the Supreme Court
    d. all of the above

11. The Constitution requires that in order to be elected President a person must _____ .
    a. be a lawyer
    b. be fifty-five years old
    c. be a natural-born citizen
    d. be a member of a major political party

12. The President's term of office is _____ years.
    a. 2
    b. 4
    c. 6
    d. 8

13. Most of a Vice-President's duties are created by _____ .
    a. the Congress
    b. the Constitution
    c. the President
    d. none of the above

14. Which Cabinet department is in charge of collecting taxes?
    a. the Department of Defense
    b. the Department of Housing and Urban Development
    c. the Department of the Treasury
    d. the Department of Transportation

15. Federal agency decisions are influenced by _____ .
    a. the President
    b. Congress
    c. client groups
    d. all of the above

16. A law made by a government agency is called _____ .
    a. a common law
    b. a statutory law
    c. a constitutional law
    d. an administrative law

17. The federal court in which you would have a jury trial is _____ .
    a. a district court
    b. an appellate court
    c. the Supreme Court
    d. none of these courts

18. What is a federal judge's term of office?
    a. two years
    b. ten years
    c. twenty years
    d. life

Building Skills

Pretend that you are a member of Congress and are asked to vote on a bill that would provide more money for space exploration. Tell how you would vote. If you were to vote for the bill, where would you plan to get the money to pay for it? Who do you think would support your decision? Who would oppose it? What information might the opposition be able to provide that would convince you to change your mind? What goals or values do you have that would explain your final decision?

How Citizens Influence Government

During the first week of November, 1978, four people campaigned for the job of United States senator from Iowa. The two major candidates were Senator Dick Clark and Roger Jepsen.

Clark and Jepsen had different views on many issues. They had different ideas on women's rights, on gun control, on what United States relations should be with some other countries, on how much help the national government should give to poor people, and on whether or not parents with children in private schools should be given tax relief.

On November 7, 1978, about 850,000 Iowans went to the polls. Another 700,000 or so could have voted but didn't.

On November 8, the final vote was in. Jepsen had received 421,598 votes. Clark had received 395,066 votes. Only 27,000 votes had made the difference.

The people who voted for the winning candidate had to feel good. They knew that their votes had made the difference. During the next two years the candidate of their choice would represent them in Congress. Even the losing voters knew that they had done what they could. They had shown that their candidate, too, had strong support. On the other hand, people who could have voted but didn't had missed a good chance to exercise influence as citizens.

Not every election is as close as the election just described, but every vote is important. Voting is the one constitutionally granted method that every citizen has for influencing government decisions. Without it, voters would have no guaranteed say in the way that government is run.

Citizens can also influence government decisions through participation in interest groups and participation in political parties. Both of these ways of participating grew up after the Constitution was written. All three methods—voting, interest groups, and political parties will be discussed in this unit.

Citizens demonstrate against high food prices.

Discuss: How are these citizens influencing the government?

233

Taking Part in Interest Groups

★★

Should senior citizens have the right to work until they are seventy years old? In 1977 and 1978 members of Congress examined the possible consequences of extending the retirement age from sixty-five to seventy.

Leaders of the National Urban League and of some women's groups were opposed to the idea. They believed that the law could delay job opportunities for members of minority groups and for women. Some business leaders opposed the idea too. One concern was that keeping older workers would slow up promotions for younger employees.

Other organizations, including the Gray Panthers and the American Association of Retired Persons, supported the change. Maggie Kuhn, a leader of the Gray Panthers, argued that older people should have the choice of retiring later. Kuhn said that many older people continue to be fit and alert. They have much to offer. Kuhn also pointed out that the cost of living continues to increase, and that many senior citizens cannot afford living expenses when they have only fixed pension incomes.

Senior-citizen leaders campaigned to win public opinion to their side. Maggie Kuhn appeared on television. She made speeches. She testified before congressional committees.

Members of Congress were impressed by the political activism of senior citizens. They also were influenced by public opinion polls that showed more than eighty-five percent of the nation's citizens favoring a new retirement law. As a result, Congress voted to extend the retirement age to seventy. On April 6, 1978, President Carter signed the new law.

The different organizations that had clashing opinions about extending the retirement age are called interest groups. The main purposes of this chapter are to help you learn:

1/Why Citizens Join Interest Groups
2/How Interest Groups Influence Government
3/How Citizens Can Take Part in Interest Groups
Case Study: Conflict over Bottles

Discuss: What are the pros and cons of extending the retirement age? Could it be extended further?

Note: If interest is sufficient, a panel of citizens seventy or older might be invited to class to discuss the issue.

1/Why Citizens Join Interest Groups

Interest groups are organizations of people who share common beliefs and interests and who try to influence government decisions. Citizens join interest groups because they believe that by pooling their resources (time, money, knowledge, and energy), they will increase their chances of influencing decision makers.

Different Interest Groups

There are hundreds of interest groups in the United States. Here are some examples. The National Association of Manufacturers (NAM) is an interest group of business owners and managers. It works on behalf of its members' interests. The AFL-CIO is an alliance of labor unions. It works to support the interests of workers. The American Farm Bureau Federation represents the interests of farmers. The American Legion works on behalf of veterans. The National Education Association promotes the interests of teachers. The American Medical Association supports the interests of medical doctors.

Interest groups with different values may clash. One group may have goals that conflict with the goals of another group.

Discuss: What reasons do people have for joining interest groups?

Senior citizens give their candidate, Idaho Senator Frank Church, a show of support during his re-election campaign.

Discuss: How do interest groups influence government decision making?

Members of each group try to influence government officials to support their point of view. For example, there has often been conflict between groups about how much money government should spend on public education. In one state, the teachers' association tried to influence lawmakers to pass a larger school funding bill. "If the state doesn't spend more, it will end up providing poor education," the president of the association said. "Our state ranks very low in the amount of public funds spent on each pupil," he reminded the lawmakers.

However, some other groups in this state opposed spending more money to improve public schools. One wanted any available funds to be used to improve public transportation. Another wanted more money for welfare programs. Still another wanted the government to cut back all spending and lower taxes. Each group tried to influence decision makers in government to support its interests.

Discuss: What interest groups are active in your community? Are there some groups needed that aren't there now?

Many interest groups, such as business, labor, and professional groups, are concerned with the economic interests of their members. There are other organizations, however, whose inter-

A group of unions work together for Proposition 14—a referendum on the California ballot that would allow unions to go on farms to recruit new members.

236

ests are not economic. These groups support a variety of causes and issues. Consumer protection, protection of the environment, protection of civil rights, and concern with the welfare of people who have special problems are some of their concerns. When they take stands that are seen as promoting the interests of most citizens, they are sometimes called **public interest groups.**

Common Cause is one example of a public interest group. It was founded by John Gardner in 1970 to help ordinary citizens get a better deal from government decision makers. Gardner argued that citizens with many resources (for example, those with great wealth) have a better chance than others to influence government officials. However, he believed that government officials should serve the common needs of all citizens rather than the interests of a few.

Since 1970, Common Cause has become a big organization with more than 325 thousand members. It has a budget of more than $6 million a year. It has influenced the passage of laws to control pollution, to reform election campaign practices, and to protect the rights of consumers.

The League of Women Voters is another example of a public interest group. The League aims to educate voters about candidates, public issues, and participation in elections. League members study problems at the local, state, and national level. After the members agree on how a problem should be solved, they work to influence legislation. The League does not endorse candidates or back one political party over another.

As part of its work to educate voters, the League of Women Voters paid for a series of TV debates between Jimmy Carter and Gerald Ford, the leading candidates for President in 1976.

Deciding Which Groups to Support

If at some time you join an interest group, you will want the decision to be a good one. The following five questions may help you decide whether or not a group deserves your support:

1. Does the group support programs, goals, and values with which you agree?
2. Do people that you respect belong to the group?
3. Does the group try to accomplish its goals in a legal and honest way?
4. Does the group set goals that it can achieve or does it try to achieve impossible goals?
5. Is decision making within the group in the hands of a few leaders or is decision making shared by all members?

If the answers to these questions meet with your approval, then giving support is probably a good idea.

Discuss: Why are these five questions important?

Section Review

Vocabulary: interest group, public interest group.

Reviewing the Main Ideas

1. Why do people join interest groups?
2. What ideas should guide your thinking when you are trying to decide whether or not to join a particular interest group?
3. Name one public interest group.

Skill Building

1. Look at these examples of citizens' decisions about interest groups. Tell whether each citizen made a good or a bad decision. Explain your answer. Use the five questions on page 237 to judge each example.

   a. Marty joined a local environmental group because his two best friends joined. He did not know much about the group, but he decided to do what his friends did.

   b. Janet joined a local citizen-action group because she liked its ideas about how to bring better government to the community. However, the group had few resources and no outstanding leaders.

   c. Mark decided to drop out of an interest group that he had joined a few weeks ago. He left after finding out that some leaders were found to be involved in illegal activity.

2. Find one of the interest groups described in this section that has an office in your city or in the nearest large city. Use the telephone books at your public library to get this information. Write the office and ask for information about the organization.

2/How Interest Groups Influence Government

In order to be able to influence political decisions, interest groups must have **political resources**—the time, money, skills, or information needed to help achieve their goals. Groups with the most resources tend to have the most influence.

Discuss: What resources are necessary to influence government decision making? How do they help?

Political Resources

Time can be a valuable political resource because it takes time to do political work. People who must work seven or eight hours a day may be able to give some time to political activities at night. There are others, however, who can give time during the day as well. College students and people who can arrange their own work schedules are part of this group.

Money is a political resource that can be used in many different ways. Some groups use money to contribute to the election

---

BIG CONTRIBUTORS IN '77-'78

Corporations and labor unions were two big contributors to congressional election campaigns in 1977-1978. Corporations gave about $9 million. Labor unions gave about $9.5 million. There were big contributors in other fields too. Some individual contributors are listed below.

AFL-CIO	$ 830,150
American Conservative Union	238,654
American Medical Association	1,562,545
Associated Milk Producers, Inc.	404,761
International Paper Company	164,818
National Association of Realtors	1,168,378
National Automobile Dealers Association	968,775
National Rifle Association of America	317,736
Standard Oil of Indiana	144,600
United Auto Workers	897,475

campaigns of people who support their views. (See the table on page 239.) Groups also use money to hire lawyers, lobbyists, and other workers, and to pay for advertising campaigns.

Information and ideas are political resources too. Both voters and elected officials need accurate and complete information on which to base decisions. When interest groups are able to provide that kind of information, they can be very influential. For example, Ruth Sander, a member of an interest group that is fighting water pollution in her local area, made a study of Clear Creek and found that a nearby factory was dumping chemical wastes into the creek. She wrote a report and gave it to members of the city council. As a result, the council passed a law to prevent the factory from dumping chemical wastes into the creek. Ruth used her knowledge to influence the decisions of government officials.

Discuss: Do groups with the most resources tend to have the most influence?

Skill in presenting facts and opinions and skill in getting along with others are also political resources. A skillfully prepared and presented report can stir people to action, whereas a carelessly done report can have the opposite effect. In a similar manner, a person who can get along with others, who is liked and respected, will have more influence with decision makers than will someone who is not liked and respected.

Using Resources to Influence Voters

As you have already learned, some groups use political resources to try to promote certain candidates at election time. The National Rifle Association (NRA) is against laws that would ban or severely limit the use of guns by citizens. In 1976, Richard Lugar was the Republican candidate for United States senator from Indiana. Lugar opposed gun control laws strongly. In contrast, Lugar's Democratic party opponent, Vance Hartke, was in favor of gun control laws. The NRA donated money to Lugar's campaign, and they mailed letters to voters telling them to back Lugar. Lugar won, and NRA support was an important factor in his victory.

The Illinois Education Association (IEA) is an interest group representing more than 65,000 teachers. The IEA tries to win better working conditions and higher pay for teachers. In October, 1976, leaders of the IEA invited the Republican and Democratic party candidates for governor of Illinois to talk with them.

After the meeting they decided to endorse Republican James Thompson rather than his Democratic opponent, Michael Howlett. The IEA leaders said that Thompson seemed to be in agreement with their ideas more often than Howlett was. As a result, they tried to convince their members to vote for Thompson, and they donated money, time, ideas, and skills to his campaign. In return, the IEA expected Thompson to honor his promise to support their interests if he was elected.

Interest groups also take sides in another type of election—elections in which citizens make decisions about laws. An example was the California election of November, 1978. The issue that voters had to decide was whether or not smoking should be restricted in some public places. The smoking restriction was listed on the ballot as Proposition 5.

The interest group that organized support for Proposition 5 was a California citizens' group called the Campaign for Clean Indoor Air. They collected the 600,000 signatures needed to get the issue on the ballot. They also collected about $625,000 to run the campaign. Groups giving support included the California Medical Association, the California PTA, the California division of the American Cancer Society, the American Association of Retired Persons, and the California Lung Association. The Campaign for Clean Indoor Air argued that the health of nonsmokers was endangered when they were forced to breathe the smoke of other people's cigarettes.

The main opposition to Proposition 5 came from the American Tobacco Institute and some of the nation's largest cigarette makers. The opposition campaign was paid for almost wholly by the cigarette makers. They had great amounts of money to spend (well over $5 million was spent by the end of the campaign) and were willing to do so in an attempt to keep Proposition 5 from passing. They argued that the law would be hard to enforce and would greatly limit the freedom of smokers.

The difference in resources available to the two sides seems to have had a clear effect on voter attitudes. In August, about two and a half months before the election, a survey of voters showed that Proposition 5 was supported by fifty-eight percent of the California population and opposed by thirty-eight percent. At that point the cigarette companies had spent about $1 million to fight the measure. During the next two months the cigarette companies spent over $4 million more—much of it on television and radio advertising. By election day, the cigarette

Discuss: How can political resources be used to influence voters?

Proposition 5 supporters distribute information in an effort to persuade voters.

makers' advertising campaign had apparently influenced many voters Proposition 5 was defeated, fifty-four percent to forty-six percent.

Using Resources to Influence Government Decision Makers

Interest groups often use political resources to influence government decision makers. They try to convince lawmakers to pass or reject certain laws. They also try to influence the government officials who carry out or enforce laws.

Discuss: How are lobbyists important in government decision making?

To help get what they want, special interest groups hire **lobbyists.** Lobbyists serve as a link between special interests and government decision makers. Lobbyists give information about their group's position. They sometimes write bills for members of Congress to consider. They suggest solutions to problems and issues.

Lobbyists get their name from a practice that they once used. They would stand in the lobby outside legislative meeting rooms waiting for lawmakers to come out. Then they would try to influence the lawmakers' opinions.

Today, lobbyists usually phone government officials to make appointments. They talk with officials or their staff members in government offices. They also may discuss business over lunch or dinner in a restaurant or private club.

Lobbyists try to get help in their attempts to influence. They get such people as mayors and business leaders to visit or call members of Congress in support of a position. They also try to get the general public to pressure members of Congress.

Information is one of the lobbyist's most important resources. Lawmakers need up-to-date information about public issues. The most effective lobbyists are able to supply useful information to lawmakers that helps their own case. For example, leaders of the Committee on Political Education (COPE) of the AFL-CIO regularly give facts to government officials about working conditions in factories, mines, and offices. These facts help influence official thinking and win support for the labor point of view.

The top lobbyists in Washington, D.C., are well educated. They have great skill in presenting information. But most of all, the top lobbyists represent important interest groups with many resources. Those with the most resources have the best chance to be effective.

Using Resources in the Courts

Interest groups also use political resources in state and federal courts. When a law is on the books, but is—in the opinion of an interest group—not being properly enforced, the group may sue the party who is breaking the law. A group may also use the courts to show that an existing law is unconstitutional. Before going to court, the interest group must have knowledge of the problem, the time and skills to investigate the problem, and the money to pay for legal help. The National Association for the Advancement of Colored People (NAACP) is one group that has often used its resources in this way. By so doing, it has improved the legal rights of blacks.

Discuss: How do interest groups influence the courts?

Section Review

Vocabulary: lobbyist, political resources.

Reviewing the Main Ideas

1. What are four different kinds of political resources?
2. How can political resources be used to influence elections?
3. How do interest groups try to influence members of Congress?
4. What is a lobbyist's job?
5. How can interest groups use the courts to achieve their goals?
6. Why are some interest groups more likely than others to be effective?

Skill Building

1. Find an example of interest-group activity in the newspaper. Describe the activity in a one-paragraph report. Tell whether or not you think this interest group can be effective. Give your reasons.
2. Find a newspaper article that includes an example of people using political resources. Write a paragraph that describes how the resources were used to influence government.

Main Ideas
1. pp. 239–241
2. pp. 240–241
3. p. 242
4. p. 242
5. p. 243
6. Answers will vary.
Skill Building
1. Answers will vary.
2. Answers will vary.

3/How Citizens Can Take Part in Interest Groups

Why are some citizens and groups more effective than others when they take part in political activities? As you have seen, one answer is that some have many more resources than others. But there is a second answer too. Citizens who know how to make the best use of their resources, whatever those resources may be, are more effective than citizens who do not.

Guidelines for Effective Group Action

Discuss: How can a citizen be most effective in an interest group? How is each guideline helpful?

The guidelines that follow should help citizens make better use of group resources. Those who follow the guidelines are more likely to have influence than those who ignore them.

Guideline 1: Use Resources Wisely. Some people with many resources fail to have much influence because they waste their resources or use them foolishly. In contrast, some people with few resources achieve their political goals because they use their resources wisely. They do not try to achieve impossible goals.

To use resources wisely, a group should find out what it has. Who are the good speakers? The good writers? The organizers? The poster-makers? Who might be able to donate money? How many people will take part in a demonstration? It is wise to use people's talents. The group's spokesperson should be a good speaker, not necessarily its most well-known member.

Knowing what it has to use can help a group decide which political activities to take part in. A group that has plenty of money can donate to an election campaign. It can buy ads and hire skilled publicity people. A group that has little money and few other political resources will need to use a different approach. Often such groups find that they can be effective by organizing marches or other public meetings to draw attention to their cause.

Guideline 2: Pool Your Resources. Citizens form groups because they realize that groups are usually more effective than people working alone. Groups, too, can be more effective by joining and pooling resources. When interest groups join together to reach a goal, they are said to have formed a **coalition** [kō′ə lish′ən]. By forming coalitions, groups increase their chances of reaching their common goal.

Note: Have students look for examples of coalitions.

244

Guideline 3: Do Not Try to Do Too Much. Some groups try to do too much at one time. They usually achieve little or nothing. They spread their resources too thinly across too many different political activities and goals. People who stress one or two goals at a time increase their chances of success.

Discuss: How is time a factor in effective group action?

Guideline 4: Do Not Give Up Easily. Some persons and groups get excited about a cause. They put on a whirlwind campaign to reach their goal. But when they do not see progress right away, they quit. They do not realize that reaching goals is almost always a slow and hard process. The cost of victory is a large pay-out of time and energy. Some groups work for years to reach their goals. It took the National American Woman Suffrage Association decades to win what they wanted—women's right to vote. Those who stick with a cause raise their chances for success.

Communicating with Government Decision Makers

Discuss: How is it possible to communicate with government officials?

One skill that all interest-group members need is the ability to communicate their ideas in writing. Government officials pay attention to letters they get from voters—especially when many voters begin to express the same view. Congressman Jim Wright of Texas once said that "every member of Congress who has served as much as one term in the national lawmaking body has developed respect for the opinions of certain people through the letters they write."

Women United for Action picket during a 1973 meat boycott. This group was part of a coalition of consumer groups that was so effective that meat sales dropped 50%–80% across the country.

Most often, interest-group members write to government officials in order to state opinions about laws. Usually citizens write when a bill in which they are interested is being studied and discussed. They hope to influence the way a state legislator or member of Congress will vote.

Just as you can do a good or bad job of painting a fence or baking a cake, you can write a good or bad letter. A carefully written letter is more likely to influence a lawmaker than a poorly written letter. Read the tips for effective letter writing that Senator Howard Baker provides on the following page.

Section Review

Vocabulary: coalition, communicate.

245

Senator Baker's Tips for Effective Letter Writing

1. Address the official properly. For example, when writing a member of the Senate or House, write: "The Honorable (name) , Senate (or House) Office Building, Washington, D.C. 20510." When addressing the official in the letter itself, say "Dear Senator (or Representative) (name) ."

2. Make sure that your handwriting is neat so that your letter is readable.

3. Include your name and address. This will enable your representative to write back to you.

4. Be as brief as possible.

5. Try to explain why you feel as you do about an issue. A flat statement of support or opposition to a bill is OK as far as it goes, but it means more if there is some reasoning behind it.

6. Talk about only one issue in a letter. If you can, give the name or number of the bill you are interested in.

7. Be courteous and reasonable. Even if you are angry, do not be rude.

8. Use your own words and stationery. This shows you are interested enough in a problem to make an effort to write a personal letter.

9. Don't apologize for writing or taking the lawmaker's time. Your lawmaker will be glad to hear from you.

Reviewing the Main Ideas

1. What are four guidelines to effective political participation?
2. Why do citizens write letters to members of Congress?

Skill Building

The letter below is *not* a good example of how to influence a representative in government. Study the letter and tell what is wrong with it. Use Senator Baker's tips to rewrite the letter so that it is a good example of how to get in touch with a representative in government.

John Jones
Senate Office Building
Washington, D.C. 20510

Dear John Jones:

As a citizen and taxpayer I demand you do not lower the truck speed limit to fifty miles per hour. If you lower the speed limit, I will not vote for you again. The legislature should also give more money to repair the roads in our state. Lowering the speed limit would mean it would take much longer for my trucking company to make deliveries. This would cost my company money. In our country today truck drivers need more support from lawmakers. Our schools also need your support. We also need better gun control laws in this country. You should vote for them.

I hope you will excuse my writing to you. I am sorry to bother you.

Albert Smith

Main Ideas
1. pp. 244–245
2. to communicate ideas and information and to influence their decisions
Skill Building
Answers will vary.

Conflict over Bottles

CASE STUDY

For Purple Mountain Majesties

Each year Americans throw away 40 billion bottles and cans, 4 million tons of plastics, 100 million tires, 30 million tons of paper, and millions of worn-out gadgets. Much of this waste clutters our landscape.

Ellis Yochelson, a scientist living in Bowie, Maryland, had researched this problem. He could show how waste products damage surroundings and make lives less pleasant.

In the spring of 1970, the principal of a high school in Bowie asked Yochelson to be the main speaker at an "Earth Day" program the school was holding. When the day arrived, Yochelson gave a stirring talk. He showed how throwaway cans and bottles littered the community and how they could scar the landscape of the Bowie area in the future.

Yochelson ended his talk with a rousing call to action. He passed out petition forms to the students. The forms asked that the Bowie City Council pass a law banning the sale of throwaway bottles. He asked the students to sign the petitions and to influence their parents and their friends to sign. He wanted to present the signed petitions to city council members to show them that the people of Bowie wanted a law banning throwaways.

The students responded enthusiastically. In a short time they had more than 2,000 names on the petitions, and they presented them to the city council. They also took a poll of city residents about the ban-the-throwaways issue. They found that seventy-six percent favored a law against throwaways. This finding appeared in local newspapers and on radio and television broadcasts.

Bowie's mayor saw the petitions and read about the students' poll. He sent the students a note to say that he supported their work.

Several local groups backed Yochelson and his student followers. The groups included the Jaycees and the Parent-Teacher Association. A national group also gave support. It was the National Resources Defense Council, a group of lawyers who support environmental causes.

Opposition to the ban-the-throwaways proposal came from various business and industrial groups—the nearby Bethlehem Steel Company, the United Brewers Association, liquor dealers, the local merchants' association, container manufacturers, and a soft-drink producers group. These groups warned that a ban on throwaway bottles would be costly. The price of soft drinks would go up. Many jobs in the container industry would be lost. Anyway, it was cheaper, they said, to produce throwaways than to handle returnable bottles.

The opponents talked to the mayor and to members of the city council to persuade them to vote *no* on the proposal. They bought ads in local papers to try to influence public opinion.

Ellis Yochelson and his backers responded with letters to local papers in support of the ban. Yochelson and the leaders of interest groups who supported him talked to members of the city council. They tried to persuade council members to vote *yes* on the proposal.

In July, 1970, the city council voted unanimously to pass a law banning nonreturnable bottles. In the following months the city council continued to study the issue. In 1971, the council passed a new law which required a deposit on all beverages sold in bottles and cans. The deposit was meant to motivate citizens to return the bottles.

However, the throwaway-bottles conflict continued in Bowie. The Washington, D.C., Soft Drink Association and the local liquor dealers' association sued the city of Bowie for passing the bottle law. The Natural Resources Defense Council helped the city of Bowie prepare its defense. In March, 1974, the suit came to trial in the County Circuit Court. The court ruled in favor of the Bowie law.

The Bowie law got nationwide publicity. City officials got more than 6,000 letters asking for copies of the law and details about how it was passed. Officials from all over the United States and Canada asked Yochelson to help them prepare similar laws. The interest group that had formed in Bowie to push for a ban on throwaways influenced government decisions not only in its own community but in other places as well.

Reviewing the Case Study

1. What was the occasion for decision in this case?
2. What were the alternatives?
3. Which individuals and groups supported each alternative?
4. How did the different individuals and groups try to influence government decision makers in this case?

Chapter Eleven Test and Activities

★★★

Vocabulary

Match the following words with their meanings.

1. interest group
2. public interest group
3. political resources
4. lobbyists
5. communicate
6. coalition

a. an organization that tries to influence government decisions and that is made up of people who share interests and beliefs
b. people hired by interest groups to try to influence government decision makers
c. the time, money, skills, or information needed to help achieve political goals
d. a number of groups that have joined together to work for some cause
e. give information by writing or speaking
f. a group that tries to influence the government to make decisions that will benefit the majority of the people

Reviewing Chapter Ideas

1. True or false: Citizens join interest groups to pool resources and thus increase their chances of influencing decision makers.
2. Which of the following is a guideline for political participation by interest groups?
   a. Try to accomplish many things at one time.
   b. If you do not reach your goal quickly, give up.
   c. Always work alone.
   d. Make the best of the resources you have.
3. True or false: The AFL-CIO represents the interests of manufacturers.

4. Common Cause has been involved in all but which of the following?
   a. controlling pollution
   b. collecting taxes
   c. changing election campaign practices
   d. protecting the rights of consumers
5. True or false: People join interest groups to support things that they value.
6. The League of Women Voters would not _____ .
   a. try to educate voters
   b. try to improve local government
   c. endorse a political party
   d. do any of the above
7. Which of the following is a point that the authors say should be considered before you join an interest group?
   a. the group's programs and goals
   b. how decisions get made in the group
   c. the type of people who are members
   d. all of the above
8. Which of the following should you do when writing your senator?
   a. talk about as many issues as you know about
   b. include your name and address
   c. write a very long letter
   d. apologize for writing

Using Basic Social Studies Skills

Finding Information
Find the "Guidelines for Effective Group Action." List them.

Comprehending Information
1. Lisa and her friends have decided to pool their resources. What does that mean?
2. Explain when an interest group is likely to support a candidate in an election.

Vocabulary
1. a or f   4. b
2. f or a   5. e
3. c   6. d

Ideas
1. T   4. b   7. d
2. d   5. T   8. b
3. F   6. c

250

★★★

Organizing Information

List four political resources. Under each write a statement telling why the resource can be useful in achieving political goals.

Evaluating Information

1. Do you think that citizens with limited resources can influence government decisions? Why or why not?

2. Do you think groups are usually more effective than individuals? Why or why not?

3. What do you think is the cartoonist's attitude toward throwaway containers?

Communicating Ideas

Pretend that you are an interest-group leader who wants to hire a lobbyist. Describe the kind of person you would want to hire and list the duties you would expect the person to perform.

Using Decision-Making Skills

1. What decision did members of Congress have to make in the retirement-age issue of 1978?

2. What were the possible consequences of each decision?

3. Do you agree with the decision that was made? Why or why not?

Activities

1. Pretend that you are interested in a bill that would provide federal money for schools. Write a letter to your senator telling whether or not you think the bill should pass and why you think so.

2. Use the *Readers' Guide to Periodical Literature* to find an article on lobbying. Read and summarize the article.

3. Students who want to learn more about interest groups may want to read *Lobbying* by Karen Sagstetter (Franklin Watts, 1978).

4. Students who want to learn more about how to contact government officials may want to read *Getting in Touch with Your Government* by Robert A. Liston (Messner, 1975).

5. Students who want to learn how public opinion is checked through polling should read *Public Opinion Polls,* by Michael Edison and Susan Heiman (Franklin Watts, 1972).

6. Pick an issue that was debated and voted on in Congress during the past few years—a debate in which interest groups took part and lobbyists were active. (The energy legislation passed in 1978 is one example.) Work with others in your class to do the following: Role play the parts of lobbyists talking to members of Congress and role play members of Congress engaged in the decision-making process (perhaps a committee hearing). "Members of Congress" should vote on the issue and explain their votes.

Chapter 12

Taking Part in Political Parties

★★★

Joe Molina is the owner of a small insurance agency. His job keeps him very busy. However, because he is a loyal supporter of the Republican party, Joe makes time for political party work. Here is what Joe said about his activities during an interview with Janice Karlson, a local reporter:

Karlson: Why do you give so much of your time and energy to political party work?

Molina: I have beliefs that are important to me. Working in politics gives me a chance to do something about them.

Karlson: What are your most important party contributions?

Molina: Winning elections is the name of the game in politics. So, I do my bit to turn out Republican voters.

Karlson: What do you do to win voters to your side?

Molina: First of all, I keep tabs on who the loyal Republicans are around here. I try to persuade as many as possible to take an active part in election campaigns. Another thing I do is to talk to voters who might want to switch to my party.

Karlson: How does your political party work contribute to good government in this town?

Molina: I've tried to help good people get elected—not only people who have ideas like mine, but also leaders who'll be honest and fair. I feel that we get the government we deserve. If we want better government, we have to work for it.

Karlson: Does your party work give you influence with candidates you've helped to elect?

Molina: When I've done a good job for them, yes, they help me out. When I ask them to help people in my neighborhood, they often listen to me.

This chapter tells you more about political parties and citizens who take part in them. You will learn about the following:

1/Political Parties in the United States
2/Deciding Whether or Not to Give Support
3/The Role of Political Parties
Case Study: California Frontlash

Discuss: What is politics?

1/Political Parties in the United States

A **political party** is an association of voters who wish to influence and control decision making in government by electing members to public office. Party members usually share many ideas about government. They pick candidates who support their ideas to represent the party in public elections. They try to persuade a majority of voters to back the party's candidates.

A Two-Party System

During most of the nation's history, there have been two major parties competing at election time. Other parties have sometimes competed too, but they have seldom won elections. For these reasons, the United States is said to have a **two-party system.**

Discuss: How has a two-party system developed in the U.S.?

Major Parties. The Republicans and the Democrats have been the two major parties for many years. The Republican party was formed in 1854. The Democrats can trace their roots to Thomas Jefferson, who was President from 1800 to 1808.

Although the Democratic party is the larger of the two major parties (see the table on page 254), both the Republicans and the

Delegates at a national nominating convention.

Democrats have many supporters in all parts of the country. In fact, they have so much strength that since the 1860s one or the other has always held the presidency. They have held most seats in Congress as well.

Minor Parties. The Socialists, Populists, Progressives, and Prohibitionists are examples of the many minor parties in United States history. Minor parties sometimes last a long time. The Prohibitionist party was started in 1869; the Socialists in 1901. However, minor parties have few supporters compared to the major parties. Thus, they win few elections. Some have won seats in Congress. Others have held local office, such as mayor or county commissioner.

Some minor parties hope to grow into major parties someday, but most want only to gain acceptance for certain ideas. The Prohibition party, for example, wants to ban the sale of alcoholic drinks. The party's candidates don't expect to win elections; they use election campaigns to try to influence citizens to accept the party's ideas about drinking. They hope to influence government officials to make laws against the sale of alcoholic beverages. They have achieved this goal in some parts of the United States.

Third Parties. Some minor parties become temporary challengers to the two major parties. Thus, they are called "third

Discuss: What roles do minor parties play in a two-party system?

POLITICAL PARTY PREFERENCES By percent

	1971	1975	1976	1978
Republican	30	19	25	22
Democrat	47	49	49	43
Independent	19	27	22	29
Other	1	1	2	2
Not Sure	3	4	2	4

Union organizer and one-time Indiana legislator Eugene Debs campaigning for President. He was the Socialist party's candidate four times between 1900 and 1920.

parties." Third parties appear to have growing support for a short period of time. A third party may win many votes and even influence the outcome of a national election. One third party that did exactly that was the Progressive party.

The Progressive party was formed in 1912 to challenge the Democrats and Republicans in the presidential election of that year. The Progressives ran Theodore Roosevelt, who had already served as President from 1901–1909. When the election was over, Roosevelt had received more votes than the Republican candidate, William Taft, but fewer votes than the Democratic candidate, Woodrow Wilson. Although Roosevelt lost, his candidacy had an important effect on the election. Roosevelt had many supporters who might otherwise have voted for Taft. Thus, Roosevelt and his Progressive party helped Wilson to win the presidency.

Roots of the Two-Party System. The Constitution says nothing about political parties. Many delegates to the Constitutional Convention were against them. George Washington warned that parties would be the source of conflicts that could disrupt the nation.

In spite of Washington's warning, rival political groups did form a short time after Washington became President. Thomas Jefferson and Alexander Hamilton became leaders of the two groups. Jefferson was the Secretary of State and Hamilton the

Discuss: How have George Washington and other leaders influenced the development of political parties?

A campaign car sponsored by the Women's Bureau of the Democratic National Committee and used in Woodrow Wilson's successful re-election campaign in 1916.

Secretary of the Treasury under President Washington. They disagreed strongly about what the government should do.

Hamilton wanted to make the national government stronger. He especially wanted the President to have stronger powers. His group was called the Federalist party.

Jefferson wanted to limit the power of the national government. He argued for stronger protection of civil rights and liberties. He favored more power for the state governments, because they were closer to the citizens. As first, Jefferson's group was called the Anti-Federalists. Later, it was called the Democratic-Republican party. In 1828, under the leadership of Andrew Jackson, the name was shortened to the Democratic party.

From 1800 to 1816 the party of Jefferson grew stronger as the party of Hamilton (the Federalists) grew weaker. In fact the Federalists lost so much support during those years that from 1816 to 1828 the party of Jefferson faced no serious challenges. In 1830 the Whig party rose up to challenge the Democrats. The Whigs and the Democrats remained rivals until 1850.

In 1854, the Republican party was formed; it soon replaced the Whigs. In 1860, the first Republican President, Abraham Lincoln, was elected. Since the 1860s, Republicans and Democrats have competed as the major parties in our system.

Party Organization

Political parties are organized at the local, state, and national levels. The diagram on page 256 shows the main features of both Republican and Democratic party organization.

The national committee includes one man and one woman from each state and territory. One of its jobs is to raise money for the party. Its other main jobs are to conduct the party's national convention and to help direct the presidential election campaign every fourth year.

The second level in the diagram shows the congressional campaign committees. Both major parties have a campaign committee in each house of Congress. The committee's main job is to help members of Congress get re-elected.

Each party also has state committees made up of leaders who represent lower level organizations. State committees oversee and regulate party activities throughout the state.

Counties and cities have party committees too. Each county and city committee is headed by a chairperson, who usually is a very important party leader. The main job of these committees is

Note: Some students may need to review the views of the Federalists and Anti-Federalists.

Discuss: How are political parties organized?

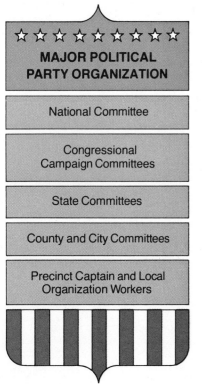

★ ★ ★ ★ ★ ★ ★ ★ ★

MAJOR POLITICAL PARTY ORGANIZATION

National Committee

Congressional Campaign Committees

State Committees

County and City Committees

Precinct Captain and Local Organization Workers

to see that party candidates for local offices win elections.

Cities and counties are divided into **precincts,** or neighborhood election districts. Each precinct has from 200 to 1000 voters who cast their ballots at the same polling place. A precinct leader is elected or appointed by each party.

Note: A precinct map of your local area would be helpful, if available.

Higher level party leaders depend on precinct leaders to build the party at the **"grass roots,"** or neighborhood level. Where the precinct organization is strong, precinct leaders work throughout the year to win converts to the party, to register voters, and to bring the party's supporters to the polls on election day. The precinct organization often is the key to the party's success on election day.

Discuss: "ELECTION WON AT GRASS ROOTS LEVEL!" What does this recent headline mean?

There is no chain of command that enables the national committee to control the state and county committees. The head of the national committee, the national chairperson, does not direct the activities of the various state and local party leaders. Rather the national, state, and local party committees are only loosely tied together. One common bond is a loyalty to similar political beliefs. The committees are also held together by the desire to win public office for the party's candidates.

Section Review

Vocabulary: "grass roots," major party, minor party, political party, precinct, third party, two-party system.

Reviewing the Main Ideas
1. Why are political parties formed?
2. Describe our two-party political system.
3. What are the aims of a minor party in a two-party system?

Skill Building
1. What level of political party organization do you think is most important? Why?
2. Use an encyclopedia to find information about one of the minor political parties in American politics. Write a brief report on the purposes of the party and its contributions to American politics and government.

Grass roots politicking—San Francisco Supervisor Bob Gonzales rides in an open car at a parade. Such appearances help keep a politician's face before the public.

Main Ideas
1. to influence and control decision making in government
2. pp. 253–254

3. p. 254
Skill Building
1. Answers will vary.
2. Answers will vary.

2/Deciding Whether or Not to Give Support

Discuss: How does a citizen decide to support a political party?

Which party should you support? Should the Democrats have your loyalties? Should you back the Republicans? Should you belong to some minor party? Or should you be an **independent voter,** supporting no party all of the time, or even most of the time. How should you decide about party loyalties?

What's the Difference?

The first step in making your decision is to know what the two major parties stand for. What's the difference between Democrats and Republicans? "Not much," say some people.

Both major parties have tried to appeal to as many voters as possible. To ignore large numbers of voters may mean defeat at election time. Thus, the leaders of both parties often seem to be saying the same things. Leaders of both the Democrats and Republicans declare the need to keep our military forces strong, to spend money to help handicapped people, to support the United Nations, to promote full employment of workers, and so on. However, there are many differences between Democrats and Republicans.

Different Beliefs. One important difference has to do with the duties of government. Over the years Democrats have been more likely than Republicans to want the national government to deal with various kinds of social problems. For example, Democrats have tended to favor national government programs that give aid to poor people. They have also been more likely than Republicans to support the taxes needed to pay the costs of these services. Republican leaders, on the other hand, have tended to urge less responsibility for the national government in dealing with various social problems. They have urged that private groups do more to help needy people. They have also stressed the role of state and local governments in dealing with the needs of citizens.

Both parties support the interests of labor unions and business organizations. However, the Democrats more often seem to be a closer ally of labor. The Republicans are more often viewed as boosters of business goals. (The use of words such as *tend to* and *often* in discussing differences between Democrats and Republicans reminds us that various points of view can be found in the ranks of both parties. These words also should alert us to changes in opinions of party leaders from time to time.)

One easy way to find out how the parties differ at a particular time is to read the **party platforms.** The platforms are written at the presidential nominating conventions that are held every four years. Each platform is a series of statements on election issues. Each important statement is called a **"plank."** The Democratic platform tells what the Democrats think about the issues. The Republican platform tells what the Republicans think about the issues.

During their national party convention in 1976, the Democrats created a platform that included these ideas: (1) control the making and owning of handguns, (2) cut spending on weapons and on programs that expand our military forces, (3) start government programs that help people without jobs find work, (4) support government programs that aid poor people.

The Republicans included these planks in their 1976 platform: (1) oppose strict regulation on the ownership of guns, (2) increase spending on military forces, (3) support programs of private groups that help poor people, (4) oppose the spread of government programs that help poor people.

Different Kinds of Supporters. There is another way to look at differences between Democrats and Republicans. We can look at the tendencies of various social and economic groups to sup-

Discuss: Why is it important to examine the party platform?

Discuss: How does each current party platform compare with the 1976 platform?

Former California Governor Ronald Reagan receives an ovation at a Republican gathering. A candidate for the Republican nomination for President, his views were reflected in several planks in the party's 1976 platform.

Discuss: What must you consider when choosing a political party?

port one party or the other. The table below gives some facts.

Keep in mind that what is true of the past may not be true in the future. Political conditions may change greatly from one time to another. What is true about voter preferences today may not be true tomorrow.

Should I Work for a Major Party?

Knowing how the Republican and Democratic parties differ is a first step in deciding where to give your political support. But there are other points to consider too.

Will your efforts be put to best use inside one of the major parties or outside? Many people would answer "inside." They would say that since most public officials are either Democrats or Republicans, it is easier to influence the government by being a supporter of one of the two major parties. They would advise you to think carefully about the disadvantages of being an in-

VOTE BY GROUPS IN PRESIDENTIAL ELECTIONS SINCE 1960
(Based on Gallup Poll Survey Data)

	1960 Dem. percent	1960 Rep. percent	1964 Dem. percent	1964 Rep. percent	1968 Dem. percent	1968 Rep. percent	1968 3rd Party percent	1972 Dem. percent	1972 Rep. percent	1976 Dem. percent	1976 Rep. percent	1976 3rd Party percent
TOTAL	50.1	49.9	61.3	38.7	43.0	43.4	13.6	38	62	50	48	1
RACE												
White	49	51	59	41	38	47	15	32	68	46	52	1
Nonwhite	68	32	94	6	85	12	3	87	13	85	15	*
EDUCATION												
College	39	61	52	48	37	54	9	37	63	42	55	2
High School	52	48	62	38	42	43	15	34	66	54	46	*
Grade School	55	45	66	34	52	33	15	49	51	58	41	1
OCCUPATION												
Prof. & Bus.	42	58	54	46	34	56	10	31	69	42	56	1
White Collar	48	52	57	43	41	47	12	36	64	50	48	2
Manual	60	40	71	29	50	35	15	43	57	58	41	1
AGE												
Under 30 yrs.	54	46	64	36	47	38	15	48	52	53	45	1
30-49 yrs.	54	46	63	37	44	41	15	33	67	48	49	2
Over 50 yrs.	46	54	59	41	41	47	12	36	64	52	48	*
REGION												
East	53	47	68	32	50	43	7	42	58	51	47	1
Midwest	48	52	61	39	44	47	9	40	60	48	50	1
South	51	49	52	48	31	36	33	29	71	54	45	*
West	49	51	60	40	44	49	7	41	59	46	51	1

*Less than one percent. Note: 1976 results do not include vote for minority party candidates.

dependent or minor party member. Here are some of their arguments:

(1) The rules of public elections make it very hard for an independent or a minor party candidate to get on the ballot. Thus, it is very hard for someone who is not a major party member to run for public office.

(2) Independents and minor party candidates get little notice in the papers or on radio and television. Thus, it is hard for them to tell others about their ideas.

(3) Groups that support independent or minor party candidates usually have few resources.

(4) The rules of government hinder independents or minor party candidates who may be elected to public office. For instance, Congress picks its leaders and assigns members to committees on the basis of membership in one of the two major parties.

Citizens who prefer to be independents or minor party members also have arguments that support their position. They might say the following:

(1) Independent or minor party candidates can criticize both parties. Thus, they might influence many citizens to favor needed reforms. Even if they do not win election to office, they can educate the public and influence the government.

(2) Independents or minor party voters can bargain with candidates of both major parties. The candidate who responds best to their demands will get their votes. In a close election, this support might be the difference between victory or defeat.

(3) Citizens should not permit the two major parties to take any group for granted. If either party can always count on your vote, why should it try to do favors for you? It may be easier to have influence by bargaining with both major parties instead of joining either one.

Making a Choice

Deciding where to give your political support can be difficult. The guidelines that follow may help.

Guideline 1. Choose the party that tends to stand for political beliefs with which you agree. If no one party seems to represent your ideas, you might prefer to be an independent.

Guideline 2. Choose the party that tends to nominate candidates who appeal to you. Think about the people that each party nominates. Do you agree with their ideas? Do they have the ability to be good leaders and decision makers? Would you be proud to be represented by them? If neither major party tends to nominate appealing candidates, then you might want to be an independent or a minor party member.

Guideline 3. Choose the party that seems most open to changes that you, and those like you, might suggest. Good citizens are constructive critics; they offer ideas for changes that seem likely to improve their society. Once again, if neither major party is open to reforms that you support, then maybe you should be a political independent or a minor party supporter.

Discuss: How do these guidelines help? Should there be others?

Section Review

Vocabulary: independent voter, party platform, plank.

Reviewing the Main Ideas

Main Ideas
1. pp. 258–259
2. p. 261
3. p. 261
Skill Building
1. p. 260
2. Democrats

1. What are two differences between the Democratic and Republican parties?
2. What are two arguments for being a loyal supporter of a major party?
3. What are two arguments for being an independent?

Skill Building

1. Look at the table on page 260. Which groups or individuals have been more or less likely to support Democratic or Republican candidates in presidential elections?
2. Look at the table on page 254. Did more people prefer the Democrats or Republicans during the 1970s?

3/The Role of Political Parties

Political parties play an important role in our system of government. They select candidates for public office. They keep people informed and interested in the issues and the candidates. They try to see that those party members who are elected to office do a good job. They keep an eye on the opposition, calling the public's attention to actions that they don't approve. They also act as a kind of link between different branches and levels of government.

The parties carry out these activities during every month of every year. Their activities are most obvious, however, at election time.

Parties Nominate Candidates

Political parties are the only organizations that select and offer candidates for public office. They do this through the **nomination** process. In the United States, candidates are nominated in one of four ways: (1) direct primary, (2) party convention, (3) self-nomination, (4) petition.

Discuss: What role do political parties play?

No one expected Jane Byrne to win the Democratic party's nomination for mayor of Chicago. The mayor running for re-election was a Democrat; he had most of his party's support. Byrne's campaign had a small staff and scarce funds. However, winning the primary meant the party would work for her election as mayor. Shown here, she is nursing a sore throat the day after the primary election.

Direct Primaries. Most nominees at all levels of government are chosen in **direct primaries.** The direct primary is a preliminary election in which voters choose candidates to represent each party in a general, or final, election to public office.

There are two main forms of the direct primary: the closed and the open primary.

The **closed primary,** used in most states, is an election in which only the declared members of a party are allowed to choose the party's nominees. In many closed primary states the voters go to the **polling place** on primary election day. They tell their party choice to a polling place clerk. Then they choose among candidates of this party to represent them on the general election day. (Candidates usually get their names placed on the primary ballot simply by announcing the desire to run and by paying a filing fee.) If a voting machine is used, the machine will be set so that the voter can vote only for candidates of the chosen party. If a paper ballot is used, voters receive a ballot with candidates of their party only.

In some states voters must be registered in advance as Republican or Democrat in order to vote in the closed primary. There are also states in which voters who switch their choice of parties from the last primary may be asked to take an oath saying that they supported their new party in the previous general election or intend to do so in the coming election.

The **open primary,** used in a few states, is a nominating election in which qualified voters may take part without telling their party preference. In most open-primary states, the voter chooses a party in the privacy of the voting booth. Where written ballots are used, a polling-place clerk gives the voter the ballots of all political parties involved. The voter marks one ballot and discards the others. Where voting machines are used, the voter moves the levers of only one party and the other ballot is locked automatically.

In two states—Alaska and Washington—the voter may vote for anyone on the ballot regardless of party. For example, voters who think of themselves mainly as Democrats can still vote to nominate some Republican candidates in these wide-open primary elections.

People who favor the closed primary say that it helps keep the members of one party from crossing over into the other party's primary to try to name weak candidates. (Weak candidates are desirable from the opposition's point of view, because they are easy to defeat.) An argument against the closed primary, on the other hand, is that it doesn't permit a truly secret ballot, since voters must declare a party preference. It also discourages independent voters from taking part in the primary election.

Other Methods of Nomination. In a few states **party conventions** are used to nominate candidates for elective state offices. Members of the party from all parts of the state pick delegates to represent them. These delegates then meet as a convention to nominate the party's candidates through majority vote.

Another way of getting nominated is **self-nomination.** It is used by write-in candidates as a way of putting themselves before the public in a general election. The candidate simply announces that he or she is running and then encourages voters to write his or her name in the appropriate place on the ballot. In some states a write-in candidate may distribute stickers that show his or her name. The voters can then paste the name on the ballot instead of writing it.

Independents and minor party candidates are nominated in most states by **petition.** This means that a certain number of qualified voters must sign papers declaring support in order for a candidate to get his or her name on the ballot. For example, in 1972 several thousand voters in Maine signed petitions to put James Longley's name on the ballot as an independent candidate for governor. He then upset the major party candidates in the general election.

Discuss: How are candidates nominated? Is one method better than the others? Why?

Parties Campaign for Their Candidates

Once a party has nominated its candidates for office, it begins to campaign for them. The party's goal during the campaign is to gather support for its candidates, but it also helps inform the voters about public issues and about the way government works.

Discuss: How do parties campaign for their candidates? Would it be better to have a time limit for campaigning?

The types of activities that party workers and other interested people engage in at election time vary greatly, but most have to do with gathering information or getting information out to the voters. Party workers and volunteers **canvass** neighborhoods, visiting homes to give out information and to find out who is and who is not supporting their candidates. Many also work at party headquarters. They stuff envelopes with information about the candidates and send the material out to voters. They answer telephones and type letters. They arrange for rallies and dinners that will help raise the money needed to pay for

Campaign Workers

Working in an election campaign is one good way to influence government. There are indoor jobs and outdoor jobs in every campaign. There are jobs that require much experience and others that require no experience at all.

The campaign manager oversees all the work of the campaign. Since winning is the goal of the campaign, the campaign manager must come up with a plan that will help reach that goal.

Under the direction of the campaign manager are other jobs that require skill and experience. Most campaigns have a publicity chairperson. This person is responsible for creating posters and ads, for writing information that will appear in letters and leaflets, and for getting information out to the press.

The campaign treasurer keeps track of money that comes in (donations) and money that goes out. Usually campaigners must pay for office space, telephones, the printing of posters and campaign literature, and sometimes advertising time on radio and television.

A coffee coordinator is in charge of "coffees" held in the homes of supporters. In a local election people who attend coffees may get to meet the candidate. One goal of the coffees is to find additional campaign workers.

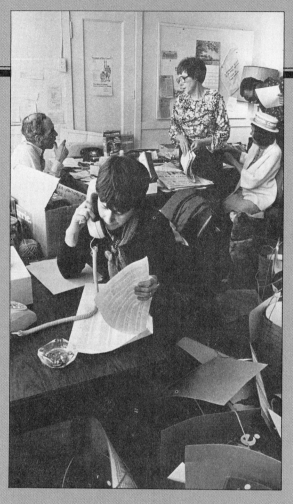

People and Government

Many neighborhood workers go out weeks in advance of election day. Some pass out campaign literature to people they meet on the street. Others go to the homes of voters. They encourage people to register and they try to find out who is supporting their candidate.

Closer to election day, workers stuff mailboxes with information about the candidate. They put up posters that support the candidate.

When election day arrives, some campaign workers become "poll watchers." They work at the polls to see who has and who has not voted. Other workers called "runners" go to the homes of people who have not voted to remind them that there is still time. Some runners help voters get to the polls by offering rides or by sitting with children.

Within the office there are other jobs to do as well. Every campaign needs people to handle telephone calls. Workers use phones to ask for donations, to contact people about coffees, and to line up workers. Envelope addressers and stuffers are a must as well. These people send out fund-raising appeals and information about the candidate. Still other people put together poll lists, leaflets, and other materials for workers to use when they go into the neighborhoods to contact voters. The person who is in charge of these indoor activities is the office manager.

The jobs that need to be done "on the streets" are just as important as those done in the office. The people in charge of neighborhood workers are the area chairpersons. Each area chairperson is responsible for a particular area within the candidate's district. An area chairperson sees that the neighborhood workers are organized and informed so that they can work effectively.

advertising and other campaign costs. Supporters hold meetings in their homes so that candidates or their representatives can meet the voters and try to persuade them to help the campaign.

Parties Help to Manage Government

Discuss: What is the role of a political party once an election is over?

Party activities are less noticeable once an election is over, but they are important nonetheless. In fact, parties are involved in one of the first tasks that come up after an election—the appointment of people to government jobs.

Many government jobs are filled according to civil service rules. However, chief executives in national, state, and local government have the power to appoint their trusted supporters to many jobs. These supporters will usually be party members. In addition, when the chief executive has jobs to fill and no names in mind, he or she often seeks advice from party leaders. The head of a Republican city committee, for instance, may give a newly elected Republican mayor the names of interested loyal Republicans. A county chairperson of the Democratic party may similarly influence appointments if a mayor or governor happens to be a person he or she helped elect.

Party members distribute literature for their candidates.

Party ties are also important in forming links between different levels of government (state, national, and local) and between different branches of government (executive and legislative). For example, a Democratic President may have more influence with a Democratic governor than with a Republican governor. Likewise, when a majority of legislators are of the same party as the chief executive, cooperation between the two branches is likely to be better than if they are not of the same party.

Finally, the parties play an important "watchdog" role after an election. The party that is out of power (the party not in control of the presidency, the governor's office, the Congress) watches for any mistakes or misuse of power by those who are in power. The party out of power tries to find issues that can help its candidates win control of the government in the next election. In this way, competition between political parties can serve the cause of good government.

Discuss: Is the general role of political parties increasing? Why?

Section Review

Vocabulary: canvass, closed primary, direct primary, nomination, open primary, party convention, petition, polling place, self-nomination.

Reviewing the Main Ideas

1. How do the open and closed primaries differ?
2. What is the chief reason for having a closed primary?
3. What is one advantage of the open primary?
4. Describe three nomination methods other than primaries.
5. What is the most widely used method for nominating candidates in the United States?
6. What role do political parties fill at election time? Between elections?

Skill Building

Team up with one other person and conduct a canvass of one block in your neighborhood. Try to find out (1) if the people voted in the last election, (2) which party they backed, and (3) whom they intend to vote for in the next election. Tell people you are students conducting a canvass for your civics class. If people don't want to answer your questions, that's their right. Thank them for their time and go on to the next door. Summarize your findings in a brief report.

Main Ideas
1. pp. 264–265
2. It prevents cross-overs.
3. It protects the secrecy of the ballot.
4. p. 265
5. direct primaries
6. pp. 263, 268–269
Skill Building
Answers will vary.

California Frontlash

Democratic party leaders in California faced a tough decision at the start of the 1970 election campaign. Should they accept the offer of youth groups who wanted to work for Democratic candidates?

One group, the California Frontlash, seemed as if it might be helpful. The group included hundreds of teenagers and young adults. Some were students in college and high school. Others were factory workers. California labor unions supplied much of the group's leadership and financial support. The California Frontlash had local organizations in the big cities of California, such as Los Angeles, San Francisco, and San Jose.

The Frontlash leaders proposed that group members work as canvassers and voter-registration workers (helping people qualify to vote by filling out the proper forms). They would promote the cause of Democratic party candidates for the state legislature. They would help John V. Tunney in his bid to unseat George Murphy, California's Republican member of the United States Senate.

Some Democratic party leaders were unsure about whether to use Frontlash campaign workers. They feared that many voters might be "put off" by young canvassers. Some older voters at this time believed that many young activists had radical, or extreme, political beliefs. Democratic party leaders worried whether older voters would take younger citizens' advice seriously. Might they even decide to vote against people that the youths promoted? Should they take the risk of using Frontlash workers?

Finally, the party leaders decided to take a chance on using the young people as canvassers and voter-registration workers. They would use them in neighborhoods of traditional Democratic strength.

More than 2,000 Frontlash volunteers went into action in California cities. Most citizens responded positively to them. Many said they were pleased to see teenagers using their time this way. Most citizens seemed willing to talk politics with the Frontlash canvassers.

During the summer and autumn of 1970, the Frontlash volunteers registered more than 100,000 new voters who seemed likely to back the Democratic party candidates. They gathered information about voter preferences and found out who needed

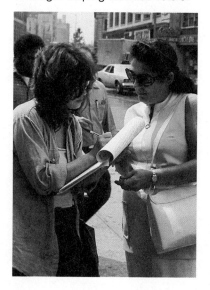

Teenager helping canvass voters.

transportation or baby-sitting services in order to get to the polls on election day.

When election day arrived, more than 3,000 Frontlash volunteers worked to help Democratic voters get to the polls. The outcome was a smashing victory for the Democratic party. A majority of Democratic candidates were elected to the California legislature. And John V. Tunney won election to the United States Senate.

Certainly, many individuals and groups contributed significantly to the Democrats' success. However, the Frontlash workers were an important part of the victory. They showed that young citizens can participate effectively in an election campaign.

Reviewing the Case Study

1. What was the occasion for decision in this case?
2. What alternatives did the Democratic party leaders consider? What seemed to be the possible positive and negative consequences of each alternative?
3. What decision did they make? Why?
4. What is your judgment of the decision?
5. What does this case show about how young citizens can contribute to the work of political parties?

Senator Tunney gives his autograph to a supporter.

Chapter Twelve Test and Activities

★★★

Vocabulary

Match the following words with their meanings.

1. political party
2. major party
3. minor party
4. two-party system
5. third party
6. canvass
7. petition
8. direct primary
9. independent voter
10. plank
11. closed primary
12. open primary
13. party convention
14. precinct

a. neighborhood election district
b. a voter who supports no one party all of the time or even part of the time
c. a minor party that, at least for a time, challenges the control of the major parties
d. a party that has a long history of winning many important elections
e. a party that seldom wins elections and whose main goal may be to draw attention to certain ideas
f. any group formed to nominate and support candidates for election to public office
g. a system of government in which public officials usually come from one of two major political parties
h. an important statement in a party platform
i. to gather information about voter attitudes and gather support for candidates
j. a preliminary election in which voters choose candidates to represent a political party in a final, or general, election
k. an election to nominate candidates in which only party members can vote
l. an election to nominate candidates in which anyone can take part
m. a meeting of political party delegates to nominate candidates to public office
n. papers making a request of some sort that have been signed by a certain number of citizens to show support for the request

Reviewing Chapter Ideas

1. The first political parties formed because _____ .
   a. Hamilton and Jefferson differed in their ideas about government
   b. Washington directed Hamilton and Jefferson to form them
   c. the Constitution required them
   d. Washington and his opponent needed parties to help them campaign
2. True or false: The Republican party is the older of the two major political parties.
3. True or false: The Constitution tells how to organize and run political parties.
4. Which of the following is not a way that political parties get involved in government?
   a. Government officials appoint party supporters to government jobs.
   b. The party out of power plays a "watchdog" role.
   c. The party out of power runs the Justice Department.
   d. Party ties link levels of government.
5. What percent of the population were "independents" in 1978?
   a. four percent
   b. twenty-nine percent
   c. nineteen percent
   d. forty-three percent

Vocabulary
1. f 4. g 7. n 10. h 13. m
2. d 5. c 8. j 11. k 14. a
3. e 6. i 9. b 12. l

Ideas
1. a 4. c 7. T
2. F 5. b
3. F 6. a

6. Mary F. is working to raise money for her political party, helping to direct its national convention, and helping to organize the presidential election campaign. She is most likely on her party's _____ .
   a. national committee
   b. congressional campaign committee
   c. state committee
   d. precinct committee
7. True or false: Most candidates for office are nominated in direct primaries.

Using Basic Social Studies Skills

Finding Information

Use your book index to help you locate "guidelines for choosing a political party." Under what entry word did you find the page(s) listed? What are the guidelines?

Comprehending Information

1. Skim the discussion of party platforms on page 259. Summarize the most important differences between Republicans and Democrats in 1976.
2. How might reading the party platforms help you decide which political party to join?

Organizing Information

List the various ways that people are nominated for public office. Write a short description next to each method.

Evaluating Information

Which do you think is the better method of nominating candidates—the *closed primary* or the *open primary?* Explain your answer.

Communicating Ideas

The authors give arguments for and against being an independent. Write a paragraph telling which arguments you found most convincing and why.

Using Decision-Making Skills

People often join a political party because they think that it stands for goals or values that they share. What values or goals do you have that you would look for in a political party?

Activities

1. Attend a local meeting of a major political party and report your observations to the class.
2. The authors suggest a number of jobs that citizens can do for a political party. List three jobs you might consider doing. Then contact the local branch of a major political party. Find out if they could use the kind of help you would like to give. Report your findings to your class.
3. Cooperate with others in your class to create a bulletin-board display of pictures and news articles that show current political-party activities.
4. Students who want to learn more about political parties and their activities may want to read one of the following:
   (a) *Where Have All the Voters Gone? The Fracturing of America's Political Parties,* by Everett Ladd (Norton, 1978).
   (b) *Primaries and Conventions,* by Roy Hoopes (Franklin Watts, 1978).
   (c) *Careers in Politics for the New Woman,* by Alice Lynn Booth (Franklin Watts, 1978).

Chapter 13   Voting

★★★

At 4:45 A.M. Susan Sertich walked into the large room at the front of Markham Elementary School. She was bursting with pride. It was election day and she was to be in charge of the polling place in her neighborhood. Within minutes, other poll workers began to arrive. The polls were to open in little more than an hour and there was work to be done first.

At five o'clock Susan called the workers together and reminded them of their duties for the day. Then she added, "Don't forget, only election officials and voters are allowed in the polling place. No one can try to influence voters within fifty feet of the polling place."

The workers checked the two voting machines to make sure they were ready. Then they marked the entry way to the polling place and posted voting instructions.

When the preparations had been completed, Susan called the group together and asked them to take an oath to carry out the election laws faithfully. Then—promptly at 6:00 A.M.—Susan let the first voters inside.

By late afternoon over four hundred people had voted. The day had passed without a serious problem. At 6:00 P.M. Susan closed the polling place.

When the last voter was finished, Susan and two helpers read and recorded the vote totals from the counters on the back of the machines. Susan locked the machines and then opened a package of absentee ballots. They had been marked prior to election day by voters who knew they would be out of town on that day. Susan added these votes to the totals.

After finishing the tally of the precinct votes, Susan thanked the other workers. As she prepared to leave, she was still feeling excited about her part in the election. Now she was anxious to hear the results from other parts of the city and state.

In this chapter you will learn about the rules that govern voting and about voter decisions. You will read:

1/Rules for Voting
2/Deciding How to Vote
Case Study: The Winner

Discuss: Why is Susan's role important?

274

1/Rules for Voting

During our nation's early years, the only people who had the right to vote were white male property owners. The many people who were not eligible to vote included all women, black males, Indian males, persons under age twenty-one, and white adult males who did not own property.

In a democracy, all—or nearly all—adults should be eligible to vote. Today the rules are quite different from what they were in 1790.

Discuss: Who can vote?

Qualifying to Vote

The Constitution grants states the right to decide who is qualified to vote. However, the Constitution also says that no state can deny the right to vote because of race, color, or sex. As a result of these statements and Amendments 15, 19, and 26, most

An election board tallies the vote from poll sheets turned in from the precincts.

275

states today have similar voting qualifications. With only a few exceptions, a person may vote if he or she is (1) at least eighteen years old, (2) a resident of the state in which he or she wants to vote, and (3) a citizen of the United States. People who have been convicted of serious crimes are the most common exception to the general rules. Most states deny them the right to vote—at least until they have served their sentences.

In most large communities, people who meet the personal qualifications for voting must also register before they can take part in an election. Rules that require people to register in person in a government office can make it hard for some people to qualify to vote. Many people may find it difficult to get to the office during the hours when it is open. To help solve this problem some states permit registration at more convenient times and places.

Discuss: How does this compare to your community? Are the voting requirements fair? Should any be changed?

Like other rules covering registration, registration deadlines affect the number of people who qualify to vote. In over half the states it is too late for people to register if they wait until the last few weeks before an election. In these states the deadline for registration is thirty or more days before election day. In a few states, the deadline is much later—ten or fewer days before the election. In states where the deadline is near election day and where voters can register in convenient places, both registration and voter turnout tend to be higher than in other states.

Casting a Vote

Discuss: What is the voting procedure in your area?

On election day, voters go to the polling place in their neighborhood. Once inside, they follow rules passed by the state government. The rules are very similar from one state to another.

The following example tells what happens at one precinct polling place. This polling place may not have the same rules as polling places in your state. However, the example will give you a general idea of what goes on when people vote.

When voters first arrive at the polling place, some study the sample **ballot** posted on the wall of the entry way. Once inside, voters go to the clerk's table. Here, each voter writes his or her name and address on an application form. The clerk reads the name aloud and passes the form to a challenger's table.

The challenger (there are challengers representing each party) locates the voter's registration form and compares the signature on it with the signature on the application form. If the two do not appear to match, the challenger may require further identification. A voter whose registration form is not on file will be required to get proof of registration.

When the challenger is convinced that the voter is eligible to vote, she initials the application form and returns it to the voter.

A voter's last stop is the voting machine. The voter hands the application form to a judge and the judge provides whatever further help is needed.

The judges do a number of different jobs on election day. Judges make sure that everyone can vote in secret. They watch to see that no one tries to tell anyone else how to vote inside the polling place. They help voters who are crippled, blind, elderly, or who can't read. They also make certain that the vote totals are recorded accurately at the end of the day. When people finish voting, judges make sure that the voting machines are ready for the next person.

When a new voter enters the machine, the first thing he or she does is to close the curtain. This ensures privacy and prepares the machine to record a new vote. In a general election, the voter chooses among major party candidates, minor party candidates, and independents. The voter picks one person for each office. If the voter chooses some candidates from one party and some from another, he or she is said to be voting a **split ticket.** Of course, the voter may decide to vote a **straight ticket,** voting for all the candidates in one party. He or she may also vote for someone who is not on the ballot. In that case the voter fills in the **write-in** spot.

When finished, the voter opens the curtains and steps away from the machine. When the curtains open, the vote is recorded.

Discuss: What are the cartoonist's views on voting?

the small society   **by Brickman**

Washington Star Syndicate, Inc.

Casting a Ballot

There are three ways to cast a vote in the United States. One is by marking a paper ballot; a second is by using a voting machine; a third is by using an electronic punch-card device.

Paper ballots are used in many local elections. In some places they are used in state and national elections too. (See the sample ballot **A** at right.)

To vote for a specific candidate on a paper ballot, the voter marks an *X* in the appropriate place following the candidate's name. To vote a "straight ticket," the voter places an *X* after a party name. If a person wants to write in a name not on the ballot, there is space for that too.

Voting machines are a familiar sight to most adults. More than half of all votes cast in national elections are cast on voting machines.

The first thing that a person does when using a voting machine is to pull the large lever that closes the voting machine's curtain. Once inside, the voter faces a panel that looks like panel **B** opposite.

Listed on the panel are the names of candidates running for office. Political questions may also be listed, just as they are on paper ballots. These questions sometimes propose changes in a state constitution. Question 1 at right asks if the voter approves of the proposed amendment that is summarized below. The voter is expected to vote "yes" or "no."

The person casts his or her votes by moving small levers. There is a lever next to each candidate's name and there are levers next to each question. There are also levers next to party names for straight-ticket voters. To vote for a "write-in" candidate, the person moves a lever that opens a slot which exposes paper where a name can be added. As long as the curtain is closed, the person can change a vote. When the curtain is opened, the vote is recorded.

Electronic punch-card voting is relatively new. When this method is used, the voter receives a card in an envelope. The voter puts the card under a book that contains candidates' names, party names, and dots to be punched. The voter reads the names and then uses a punch to press through the appropriate dots. (**C** below) Space for write-ins appears on the punch-card envelope.

When the voter has finished using a punch-card device, he or she puts the card into its envelope and then into a special box. Votes cast the punch-card way are counted by computer. The machine "reads" the card by noting where the holes have been punched.

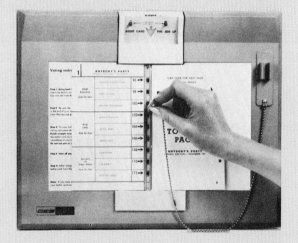

GENERAL ELECTION
(ELECCION GENERAL)

(Condado de) _____ County, Texas

November 7, 1978 (7 de noviembre de 1978)

INSTRUCTION NOTE: (NOTA DE INSTRUCCION:)
Vote for the candidate of your choice in each race by placing an "X" in the square beside the candidate's name. You may vote a ~~by~~ placing an "X" in the square beside the name of the party of your choice at the head of the party column. (Vote por el candidato para cada candidatura marcando con una "X" el cuadro al lado del nombre del candidato. Usted puede votar por todos los candi~~...~~ partido marcando con una "X" el cuadro al lado del partido de su preferencia a la cabeza de la columna para partidos.)

Candidates for: (Candidatos para:)	Democratic Party (Partido Democratico)	Republican Party (Partido Republicano)	Raza Unida Party (Partido Raza Unida)	Socialist Workers (Partido de Traba~~...~~ dores Socialistas)
United States Senator (Senador de los Estados Unidos)	Robert (Bob) Krueger	John Tower	Luis A. Diaz DeLeon	Miguel Pendas
United States Representative, ___ District (Representante de los Estados Unidos, Distrito Núm. ___)				
Governor (Gobernador)	John Hill	Bill Clements	Mario C. Compean	Sara Jean Johnston
Lieutenant Governor (Gobernador Teniente)	Bill Hobby	Gaylord Marshall		Andrea Doorack
Attorney General (Procurador General)	Mark White	Jim Baker		Agnes Chapa
Comptroller of Public Accounts (Contralor de Cuentas Públicas)	Bob Bullock			

WARNING
Do not open any slots unless you are going to cast a write-in vote. To vote for a person not listed for an office, open appropriate slot and write in person's name and address, or affix a preprinted sticker.

QUESTIONS ☞

QUESTION 1
PROPOSED AMENDMENT TO THE CONSTITUTION

Do you approve of the adoption of an amendment to the Constitution summarized below, which was approved by the General Court in joint sessions of the House of Representatives and Senate on May 28, 1975, by a vote of 220-53, and on September 7, 1977, by a vote of 243-20?

SUMMARY
The proposed constitutional amendment would permit the legislature to establish as many as four different classes of real property for tax purposes. Property in any one class would be required to be assessed, rated and taxed proportionately but property in different classes could be assessed, rated and taxed differently. The legislature could grant reasonable exemptions. The constitution presently requires all property (other than wild lands, forest lands, and certain agricultural and horticultural lands) to be assessed and rated equally at full value for tax purposes.

QUESTION 2
PROPOSED AMENDMENT TO THE CONSTITUTION

Do you approve of the adoption of an amendment to the Constitution summarized below, which was approved by the General Court in joint sessions of the House of Representatives and Senate on May 28, 1975, by a vote of 267-3, and on August 10, 1977, by a vote of 250-1?

SUMMARY
The proposed constitutional amendment would allow a governor who had not served in the preceding year as governor to submit a proposed budget to the legislature within eight weeks of the beginning of the legislative session. A governor who had served in the preceding year would still be required to submit a proposed budget within three weeks of the beginning of a legislative session.

QUESTION 3
PROPOSED AMENDMENT TO THE CONSTITU~~...~~

Do you approve of the adoption of an amend~~...~~ the Constitution summarized below, which approved by the General Court in joint sessions House of Representatives and Senate on Jun~~...~~ 1976, by a vote of 244-6, and on August 10, ~~...~~ by a vote of 253-1?

SUMMARY
The proposed constitutional amendment w~~...~~ require the Secretary of the Commonwealth send information about questions that appear on the state election ballot to each son eligible to vote in the Commonwealth, every residence in the Commonwealth wher~~...~~ or more eligible voters live. Presently, the C~~...~~ tution requires the Secretary to send this mation to each registered voter in the Com~~...~~ wealth.

YES NO   YES NO   YES N~~...~~

OFFICES ☞

MODEL 105

1	2	3	4	5	6	7	8	9	10	11	12
SENATOR IN CONGRESS Vote for ONE			GOVERNOR LIEUTENANT GOVERNOR Vote for ONE		ATTORNEY GENERAL Vote for ONE		SECRETARY Vote for ONE		TREASURER Vote for ONE		

CANDIDATES ☞

| 1 A EDWARD W. BROOKE 535 Beacon Street Newton REPUBLICAN Candidate for Re-election | 2 A PAUL E. TSONGAS 88 Mansur Street Lowell DEMOCRATIC | 3 A | 4 A HATCH and COWIN REPUBLICAN | 5 A KING and O'NEILL DEMOCRATIC | 6 A FRANCIS X. BELLOTTI 120 Hillside Avenue Quincy DEMOCRATIC Candidate for Re-election | 7 A WILLIAM F. WELD 28 Fayerweather Street Cambridge REPUBLICAN | 8 A MICHAEL JOSEPH CONNOLLY 127 Montclair Avenue Boston DEMOCRATIC | 9 A JOHN W. SEARS 3 Brewster Street Boston REPUBLICAN | 10 A ROBERT Q. CRANE 1 Bradford Street Wellesley DEMOCRATIC Candidate for Re-election | 11 A LEWIS S.W. CRAMPTON 15 Bradford Street Boston REPUBLICAN | 12 A THA~~...~~ BU~~...~~ 4? Be~~...~~ ~~...~~ |

Section Review

Vocabulary: ballot, split ticket, straight ticket, voter registration, write-in.

Reviewing the Main Ideas

1. What are the main qualifications for voting?
2. Why is voter registration usually required?
3. How can rules about where and when to register make it easier or harder for a person to qualify to vote?
4. Who are the officials at a polling place and what jobs does each do?

Skill Building

Find and read the voter registration laws for your state. Then answer these questions for the people described below: (a) Which of these people would be allowed to vote, according to your state laws? (b) Which persons must update their registration forms or fill out new forms to be able to vote? (c) In your opinion, should rules be changed to permit any of the unqualified people to vote?

1. Larry is nineteen and out of work. He is a school dropout and can barely read. He has never held a job longer than six weeks. He was born and raised in your community and lives with his parents.
2. Janet, age thirty, is a skilled secretary. At age nineteen she went to prison for a serious crime, but everyone who knows Janet today sees her as a model citizen.
3. Mirko, age twenty-two, moved from Yugoslavia to your town two years ago. He wants to become a citizen of the United States soon. Mirko speaks English very well. He is well educated and seems bright. He also has a good job. He likes politics and wants to vote in the next election.
4. Paul and Margie are married and have lived in your town for the past twenty years. They enjoy politics and have voted in every election. Last month they bought a new home about two miles from their old one.
5. Anne has been a registered voter. She was married last month.
6. Judy was a registered voter in 1970. However, she has not voted since 1972.
7. Martha, a nineteen-year-old high-school senior, has not registered. The next election takes place in five days.

2/Deciding How to Vote

People have different reasons for choosing one candidate over another. Many people vote a straight party ticket. The party a candidate belongs to has more influence on these voters than anything else about the person. Other voters are interested mostly in the issues. They tend to vote for candidates who have opinions similar to their own. Still other voters are most influenced by the candidate's personality and appearance. They tend to be attracted, or put off, by the way a candidate looks or the way he or she speaks.

How about you? Do party labels mean more to you than the issues or the personalities of the candidates? If you are more interested in the person than the party, are you always able to judge what the candidates are really like and where they really stand on the issues? This chapter will provide some help in judging candidates and their campaign appeals.

Discuss: What is the best way to decide how to vote?

Choosing the Best Candidate

Why would you vote for one candidate over another? Thoughtful voters consider a number of points when making that decision. Knowing what others look for may be helpful to you.

California Congressman Ronald Dellums.

Goals and Values. Many experienced voters look for candidates who tend to support programs, goals, and values with which they agree. They do so in hopes that these candidates will make political decisions of which they approve.

How does a person learn about a candidate's goals and values? The most common sources of information are newspapers, news magazines, TV, radio, and such publications as the *Congressional Quarterly Reports* and *The Congressional Record.* All these sources report on the decisions and beliefs of candidates.

Many interest groups also provide information. Some give out regular reports that rate members of Congress on their support of the group's programs and values. Six of those groups are (1) Americans for Democratic Action (ADA), (2) AFL-CIO Committee on Political Education (COPE), (3) National Farmer's Union (NFU), (4) Americans for Constitutional Action (ACA), (5) United States Chamber of Commerce (USCC), and (6) American Conservative Union (ACU). If you agree strongly with one of these groups, you might use the group's ratings of your representatives in Congress to help you decide whether or not to support them. The table below shows how the six interest groups rated six senators and representatives from Indiana and Kentucky in 1976.

Reliability and Honesty. Many voters also look for candidates who are reliable and honest. Does the candidate tend to live up to campaign pledges and other public statements? Can the candidate be trusted to do a good job? Some voters look at a candidate's record of public promises and compare these against

INTEREST GROUPS RATE MEMBERS OF CONGRESS

Indiana	ADA	COPE	NFU	USCC	ACA	ACU
Senator Bayh	72	73	70	0	0	4
Senator Hartke	72	73	90	6	5	9
Rep. Myers	0	26	36	88	93	89
Kentucky						
Senator Huddleston	50	55	90	25	17	27
Senator Ford	56	73	90	31	26	26
Rep. Snyder	5	13	54	64	86	83

A rating of 100 means that the person always voted in agreement with the values of the interest group. A rating of 0 means that the person never voted in agreement with the values of the interest group.

the candidate's actions. When the candidate fails to live up to pledges, the voters expect a good explanation. Voters also look for willingness to answer questions openly. For example, public officials should be willing to reveal their income and financial assets.

Effectiveness. Experienced voters also try to judge how effective a candidate will be. If two candidates are acceptable in other respects, many voters ask themselves who would better be able to get the most done. One way to answer this question is to make a rough account of the person's resources. How much experience does the candidate have? What are the candidate's political connections? Is the candidate respected by other political leaders?

Chances for Election. Many voters think carefully before voting for candidates who have no real chance to be elected. Voters are faced with a difficult problem when their favorite candidate seems to be a sure loser. Should they be loyal to the person they believe to be the best candidate even if the person cannot win?

When faced with this problem, many people vote for the person having the best chance of beating the candidate they like the least. Other people, however, may be willing to support a sure loser just to register a protest vote. For example, suppose that candidate Smith calls for the development of three new city swimming pools, an idea that you support. You might hope that a large minority will vote for Smith with you. Even though

1972 Presidential candidate George McGovern (arm raised) lost the election in part because voters did not believe he could be as effective as his opponent Richard Nixon. As it became obvious that McGovern's chances of winning were slim, even more people decided not to vote for him.

Discuss: Are there any other areas that should be considered?

Smith loses, the winner may take notice of the strong support for the new pools. This showing might convince the winner to support the pools too.

Detecting Propaganda in Campaign Appeals

The goal of an election campaign is to influence as many voters as possible to vote for a certain candidate. Various methods are used to persuade the voters. Billboards, bumper stickers, posters, leaflets, speeches, and newspaper ads have all been used for a long time. In recent years, however, candidates have relied more and more on television and radio to "sell" themselves to voters.

The spot commercial is the most common method for advertising candidates on television or radio. These are sixty-second commercials aimed at increasing the candidate's appeal to voters. Spot commercials are usually designed to appeal to voters' emotions. Campaigners also create filmed documentaries to be shown on television. These films highlight the candidate's best qualities.

An important purpose of any election campaign is to educate voters about public issues, candidates, political parties, and government. Unfortunately, not all campaigns are as straightforward as they should be. Appeals to emotions may be used more often than appeals to reason. Clever **propaganda techniques** may be used to influence voters.

Discuss: How can propaganda affect voters? Are there any ways to avoid being influenced?

In order to vote wisely, you should avoid being swayed by propaganda. To do that, you must know how to spot propaganda techniques when you see them. They include the following: name-calling, glittering generality, transfer, testimonial, plain folks, card-stacking, and bandwagon.

Name-calling. To name-call is to give a candidate a bad label. The aim is to influence voters to reject the candidate without looking at the evidence. Suppose Jones and Smith are running for mayor. Jones makes speeches in which he calls Smith "un-American." However, Jones does not give evidence to convince voters that Smith is not a good American. Rather, he tries to bias voters against Smith by calling him a bad name.

A particular danger of name-calling is that it can damage the reputation of the person accused. The mere accusation is enough to get many people to believe the worst. Whenever name-calling is used to influence our opinions, we should look for evidence to support the accusation.

Glittering Generality. Candidates who use broad, vague words are trying to influence you to accept them and their ideas without looking at the evidence. They are using glittering generalities to make it difficult for you to know exactly what they mean. For example, in making a campaign speech, Senator Blue said, "I'm for peace, prosperity, and the pursuit of happiness." However, Senator Blue didn't explain what she meant by these words and gave no evidence to back up her words. She was using a glittering generality to sway voters' minds. The glittering generality is used to give a person, an idea, or a cause a good name.

Transfer. The technique of transfer is to associate something everyone thinks is good with a candidate. The purpose is to influence voters to transfer their good feelings for that thing (such as the American flag) to the candidate. This is why some candidates use patriotic slogans or songs at their campaign rallies. For example, when Senator Stone ran for President, he used the slogan, "A Vote for Stone Is a Vote for America." He was trying to get voters to transfer their feelings of patriotism to him.

Testimonial. A candidate who gets a famous, well-liked person to say good things about him or her is receiving a testimonial. The purpose is to suggest that if this person supports the candidate, other voters should support the candidate too. For example, Governor Green may get a famous movie star to say, "I'm for Green. He's the best candidate for governor." Governor Green hopes that this testimonial will influence voters to support him.

The person who hears or sees a testimonial should ask these questions: Is this well-known person really qualified to express such an opinion? Was the testimony purchased? Was the well-known person quoted correctly and fully?

Plain Folks. When the "plain folks" technique is used, a candidate tries to convince voters that he or she is just like them—just an ordinary person. The candidate hopes to get support in this way. For instance, candidate Mike Murphy may say that he is the workingman's friend. He may appear on a speaker's platform wearing a "hard hat" to show that he identifies with construction workers. Another candidate may have her picture taken while mowing the lawn, milking a cow, or eating pizza at the corner restaurant. She is just "plain folks" like the rest of the people. The important thing to remember is that these pictures are meant to create images in your mind. Ask yourself, what is the candidate really like?

Card-stacking. When candidates present only the facts that are favorable to them, they are using the propaganda technique of card-stacking. They are presenting only one side of an issue—their side. For example, a state senator may say that he helped defeat tax increases. Thus, the voters should support him. However, he does not report that several programs to help handicapped people train for jobs had to be ended because of lack of money that would have been provided by new taxes.

Bandwagon. When a candidate says, "Most people in your group are voting for me; you should too," he is using the bandwagon propaganda technique. He is trying to create the impression that the majority of people you care about are for him. Thus, you should go along with the others and be for the candidate too. When a candidate "leaks" a private poll to the press

PEANUTS ®   **By Charles M. Schulz**

Discuss: Is this a good reason for voting for a candidate?

286

reporting that she is favored by a large majority of the voters, she is trying to create the impression of a "bandwagon." She is suggesting that others ought to be with the majority and vote for her too.

How Voters Learn the Facts. To avoid being taken in by the exaggerated claims of the propagandist we must try to get all the facts. There are a number of solutions. For one, public debates can be held during a campaign. Candidates who present their cases can be questioned by the audience. For another, people can get information about candidates from both parties and from newspapers. When the candidates disagree on an issue, facts and opinions are usually available from interest groups who are affected by the issue. The more we insist on hearing all sides, the less we will be influenced by the exaggerations of the persuader.

Discuss: Have you ever been influenced by any of these techniques?

Candidates who depend on propaganda tend to rely on controlled communications with voters. They present themselves through radio and television commercials, documentaries, and set speeches rather than through spontaneous interactions with voters or other candidates. The kind of communication they use is controlled because the candidate has complete command over what is said or done. In contrast, when a candidate faces unrehearsed questions and criticisms of voters or other candidates, he or she is not completely in control of the situation.

It is easier to use propaganda techniques during controlled communications. It is easier to "smoke out" the real beliefs and behaviors of candidates when they cannot control the questions they are asked. Voters should be suspicious of any candidate who usually appears in situations where communication with voters is totally under his or her control.

Section Review

Vocabulary: bandwagon, card-stacking, glittering generality, name-calling, plain folks, propaganda techniques, transfer, testimonial.

Reviewing the Main Ideas
1. Explain why many voters believe that each of the following points should be considered before voting: (1) a candidate's goals and values, (2) a candidate's honesty and reliability, (3) a candidate's potential effectiveness, (4) a candidate's

Main Ideas
1. pp. 282–283

chance of being elected.

2. How can a voter get the information he or she needs to judge each of the first three points mentioned in question 1?

3. What is *controlled communication?* Why do some candidates use it?

Skill Building

Can you spot the examples of propaganda in the list below? Identify the method that is being used in each example.

1. "My opponent has taken part in public protest demonstrations. He is a dangerous radical and agitator who probably is in sympathy with communist causes."

2. "A majority of the people in the community are supporting Stonewall Smith for governor. Where do you stand?"

3. "The President says that Stonewall Smith should be re-elected as governor of our state. Will you go along with the President and vote for Smith?"

4. Stonewall Smith makes a campaign appearance in a small town. He begins his talk by telling the audience that he was born in a small town and thinks of himself as a "small-town boy."

5. "If you believe in freedom, justice, and equality of opportunity, then you should vote for Stonewall Smith."

6. Stonewall Smith travels around the state in a bus decorated with American flags and pictures of bald eagles. A sign painted on both sides of the bus says, "Stonewall Smith believes in America."

7. A newspaper ad tells how Stonewall Smith saved thousands of tax dollars during his first term as governor. But the ad says nothing about the enormous cutback in services to the poor, sick, and elderly that resulted from his budget cuts.

Main Ideas
2. p. 287
3. p. 287
Skill Building
1. name-calling
2. bandwagon
3. testimonial
4. plain folks
5. glittering generality
6. transfer
7. card-stacking

288

The Winner

Richard Daley was a big winner in politics for many years. He was first elected to public office in 1936 as a member of the Illinois House of Representatives. He went on to become mayor of Chicago in 1955 and was re-elected as mayor six times. He was never defeated. He died in office in 1976.

Political observers talked often about what it was that made Daley a winner. They gave a number of reasons. A look at Daley's last important political campaign will help make some of those reasons clear.

In February, 1975, the Democratic party held its primary election. From among those listed on the ballot, party members were to nominate one person to be their candidate for mayor in April's general election. Daley was on the primary ballot. Wil-

Victory celebration for Daley after the 1975 primary election.

liam Singer, Richard Newhouse, and Edward Hanrahan were on the ballot as well.

The winner of the Democratic primary was almost certain to be elected mayor. The Republican party in Chicago had little power. The Republican candidate stood little chance of winning.

Daley's main opponent in the primary was William Singer. Ever since 1971, when Singer had first been elected to the Chicago City Council, he had been a critic of Daley. By 1975, Singer had over 2,800 volunteers ready to campaign for him. He had raised $240,000 to finance his bid for mayor.

Singer's main criticisms of Daley were directed at the way Daley used and maintained power. Singer and his supporters believed that Daley had too much power. They said that Daley's power to reward political friends with jobs and other favors was bad for the city. They wanted to change the city government so that the mayor would not be so powerful.

Singer's supporters also were disturbed by the fact that several of Daley's closest political friends had been accused or convicted of such crimes as vote fraud, mail fraud, and bribery. No one accused Daley of breaking laws, but Singer said that Daley was at fault for having chosen to work with people who were corrupt.

Singer's criticisms came at a time when a growing number of independent voters were ready for change in Chicago. Singer's support was sizeable because many people agreed with Singer's ideas and the goals he had for government.

Daley, however, was a powerful figure to oppose. He had many sources of support. First, as mayor and the county chairman of the Democratic party, Daley controlled a great many rewards. Public works contractors, city employees, and public officials were three groups that stood to receive these rewards if Daley won. Public works contractors hoped to get contracts from the city to build roads, offices, schools, and bridges. City workers wanted to keep their jobs or get better jobs. Public officials wanted Daley to aid their political careers. Because all these people had a personal stake in a Daley victory, they were willing to work hard for his re-election.

People who admired Daley's ability to manage the city were a second source of support. Daley had a reputation as a leader who could get things done. Chicago was called "the city that works." This meant that the city provided public services that citizens expected. Many people believed that Chicago was gov-

William Singer

erned better than any other big city in the United States. Many business leaders supported Daley for this reason. They believed that Daley's leadership was good for Chicago's businesses.

A third important source of support for Daley was Chicago's "blue-collar" workers—people who worked in manufacturing and various trades. These people felt that Daley had values similar to their own. Daley had grown up in a "blue collar" Chicago neighborhood. He had lived there all his life. He felt at ease with the great mass of Chicago working people, and they felt comfortable with him as well.

When primary day arrived, Daley's supporters turned out in great numbers. Even with the strong campaign that Singer had waged, Daley won a smashing victory with fifty-eight percent of the vote. Singer won twenty-nine percent of the vote. The other two candidates split the remainder.

Richard Daley was a winner in part because he knew how to use his office to build a strong political party—a party that knew how to get out supporters on election day. But Daley was also a winner for other reasons. His supporters believed that he was personally honest, and most of them shared his values and his goals for the city. Finally, a great many people saw Daley as an effective manager of city government. Because enough people felt that they benefited in some way by having Daley as mayor, he won again and again.

Reviewing the Case Study

1. What was the occasion for decision in this case?
2. What were the alternatives?
3. What goals of Singer's supporters caused them to vote as they did?
4. What goals of Daley's supporters caused them to vote as they did?

Richard Daley

Chapter Thirteen Test and Activities

★★

Vocabulary

Match the following words with their meanings.

1. ballot
2. straight ticket vote
3. propaganda
4. voter registration
5. split ticket vote

a. a procedure that citizens must follow in order to prove that they are qualified to vote
b. voting for all the candidates of one party
c. a public action taken to advance one's own cause or damage someone else's
d. the form that people mark when they vote
e. voting for candidates from two or more parties

Reviewing Chapter Ideas

1. True or false: In 1790 Indians, blacks, and women could not vote.
2. The Constitution says that no person can be denied the right to vote on the basis of _____ .

    a. color
    b. race
    c. sex
    d. all of the above

3. Who is responsible for making election rules?

    a. Congress
    b. the President
    c. the state governments
    d. the federal agencies

4. True or false: All people in every state must register in order to vote.
5. True or false: More people vote in states where it is easy to register.

6. Which of the following is a purpose of election campaigns?

    a. to register voters
    b. to educate voters about the candidates
    c. to nominate a person for office
    d. to educate voters about political parties of the past

7. In recent years _____ have been used more and more in election campaigns.

    a. billboards   c. television ads
    b. speeches   d. newspaper ads

Using Basic Social Studies Skills

Finding Information

Read the table below. Then answer these questions: (1) The table shows the results from what election? (2) Who came in last? (3) About how many more votes did the second place candidate have over the third place candidate?

Results of the Democratic Party Mayoral Primary Election, February 25, 1975

Candidate	Votes	Percent
Richard J. Daley	432,224	58
William Singer	217,764	29
Richard Newhouse	58,548	8
Edward Hanrahan	37,034	5

Comprehending Information

1. On election day you must show that you are a qualified voter in order to vote. Explain what this means.
2. Why do many voters look for candidates (1) with whom they share goals and values (2) who are honest and reliable (3) who are able to get things done?

3. Why might a voter support a candidate who is sure to lose?

Organizing Ideas

Use the section head and subheads to outline the information in Section 2. The outline has been partially completed below:

Title: Deciding How to Vote

I. _____
   A. _____
   B. _____
   C. _____
   D. _____
II. Detecting Propaganda in Campaign Appeals
   A. Name-calling
   B. _____
   C. _____
   D. _____
   E. _____
   F. _____
   G. _____
   H. _____

Evaluating Information

1. Tell why you think this statement is true or not true: The more we insist on learning all sides of an issue, the less likely we are to be influenced by propaganda.

2. Do you think that the government should make it easy or difficult for people to register to vote? Why do you think so?

Communicating Information

Draw two cartoons—one illustrating the use of *transfer* in a campaign appeal.

Using Decision-Making Skills

1. If you had to vote in the Democratic primary described in the case study, would you need more information before making a decision? If so, what information?

2. If you had to vote in that primary based on what you know now, how would you vote? Why would you vote for that candidate?

Activities

1. Find out which members of Congress will be running for re-election in your district in the next election. Try to find out as much as you can about the candidates and the stands they have taken on the issues. Report your findings to the class.

2. Cooperate with others in your class to create a bulletin-board display about propaganda. Cut ads from magazines and label the propaganda techniques used.

3. Cooperate with a small group of students to create a "television ad campaign" for a fictitious politician. Create some ads that are straightforward, that do not make use of propaganda. Create some others that do use propaganda techniques. Perform the ads for the class. Ask the class to determine whether or not propaganda was used in an ad. If it was, ask what type it was.

4. Contact the local branch of a major political party. Ask to interview someone who has worked at a polling place on election day. Compare the job that is described in the interview with those described in the text. Report the results to the class.

5. Students who want to learn more about voting and elections should read *Every Vote Counts: A Teen-age Guide to the Electoral Process,* by James J. O'Donnell (Messner, 1976).

Unit Three Test

★★★

Vocabulary

Write *true* if the underlined word or phrase is used correctly. Write *false* if it is used incorrectly.

1. The time, money, skills, or information needed to help achieve political goals are called <u>political resources</u>.
2. An <u>interest group</u> is an organization that tries to influence government decisions and that is made up of people who share common interests and beliefs.
3. A <u>coalition</u> is a series of statements that tell a political party's position on public issues.
4. People hired by interest groups to try to influence government decision makers are called <u>lobbyists</u>.
5. A <u>polling place</u> is a city office where opinion polls are filled out.
6. A neighborhood election district is often called a <u>precinct</u>.
7. <u>Independent voters</u> are voters who support only minor party candidates.
8. A <u>major party</u> is a party that has a long history of winning many important elections.
9. A group formed to nominate and support candidates for public office is called a <u>political party</u>.
10. In a <u>two-party system</u> only two political parties are allowed to exist.
11. The form that people mark when they vote is called a <u>petition</u>.
12. A preliminary election in which voters choose candidates to represent a political party in a final, or general, election is called a <u>direct primary</u>.
13. A <u>party platform</u> is the place that a person goes to vote.

Vocabulary
1. T	4. T	7. F	10. F	13. F
2. T	5. F	8. T	11. F	
3. F	6. T	9. T	12. T	

Recalling Information

1. The authors suggest that you ask some questions about an interest group before joining it. Which question below is <u>not</u> one of those suggested?
   a. Does the group work toward goals in an honest and legal way?
   b. Do you share the group's goals?
   c. Is the group able to accomplish what it sets out to do?
   d. Has the group received national recognition in a widely read news magazine?
2. Which of the following is one of the "guidelines for effective group action" that were suggested by the authors?
   a. Use resources wisely.
   b. Do not try to do too much at once.
   c. Do not give up easily.
   d. All of the above.
3. Which of the following would the authors tell you to do when writing your senator?
   a. Apologize for writing.
   b. Tell your senator that you will never vote for him or her again if your wishes are not granted.
   c. Impress your senator with information on as many topics as you know about.
   d. Do not use a form letter.
4. True or false: Political parties were formed in the early years of United States history because political leaders had ideas about government that differed from one another.
5. Which of the following is a major political party?
   a. the American Legion
   b. the Republican party
   c. the Progressive party
   d. the Prohibition party

Recalling
1. d	4. T	7. F	10. F	13. a
2. d	5. b	8. T	11. d	14. b
3. d	6. b	9. a	12. a	

6. The main purpose of political parties is to
_____ .
   a. get people to vote
   b. win elections
   c. raise money
   d. get new party members
7. True or false: The Republicans and the Democrats became the two major political parties in the 1930s.
8. True or false: Voter turnout is highest in states where it is relatively easy to register.
9. Which of the following is <u>not</u> one of the ways political parties work after an election?
   a. National committee members operate the Department of the Treasury.
   b. Party members are appointed to some government jobs.
   c. The party out of power plays "watchdog" over the party in power.
   d. Party ties link various levels of government.
10. True or false: In the past, the Republicans have been more likely than the Democrats to urge that the national government try to solve social problems.
11. Which of the following is a way of being nominated for public office?
   a. a party convention
   b. a direct primary
   c. a national committee meeting
   d. *a* and *b*
12. Before a voter can use a voting machine, he or she must _____ .
   a. prove that he or she is qualified to vote
   b. pass a test on the state constitution
   c. insert money into the machine
   d. none of the above

13. When candidates say that they support "love, peace, and justice," but never talk about specific actions they will take if elected, the candidates are using a propaganda technique called _____ .
   a. glittering generality
   b. bandwagon
   c. testimonial
   d. plain folks
14. If candidates distort the truth by presenting only one side (their side) of an argument, the candidates are using a propaganda technique called _____ .
   a. plain folks
   b. card-stacking
   c. glittering generality
   d. name-calling

Building Skills

1. Explain how an interest group could use time, money, information, and skills to influence voters.
2. Write a sample letter to your senator. Try to influence him or her in some way. (You can make up the issue or issues to be discussed.) Follow the directions for writing a good letter that Senator Baker provided.
3. Write a paragraph describing the ideal candidate. Base your description on the "points that many experienced voters consider before selecting a candidate."
4. Make a Decision Tree that shows what is involved in deciding whether or not to join a political party.
5. Assume that you have decided to try to influence government decision making. Name three ways you might be able to do so. After each method, tell what resources you would need.

Making Decisions in State Government

We live in a nation of states. The states and state government existed before we had any real national government. It was delegates from the thirteen states who met in Philadelphia in 1787 "to form a more perfect union." Since 1790, thirty-seven more states have joined the Union. Each has a place in the Union equal to all other states.

As new states entered the Union, they planned their governments after those of the older states. They also borrowed ideas from the federal Constitution. The fifty state governments differ in many details from each other. Yet they are also alike.

The decisions and services of state government are all around you. The largest share of a state budget goes to pay for the public elementary schools, high schools, colleges, and universities in the state. State governments make decisions about what should be taught in schools. They decide how much state money to spend on each student. They often help decide which textbooks will be used. And they decide what kinds of taxes will pay for public schools.

Building and maintaining roads is the second most costly service provided by state governments. There are over 2 million miles of paved roads in the United States. The national government provides less than 30 percent of the money spent on these roads. Most comes from state governments. So they make decisions about where to build new roads, how to keep up old roads, how to police the highways, and how to pay for roads.

State governments operate health care and welfare programs. Most states have orphanages, homes for the aged, state and county hospitals, and homes for the physically and mentally ill. States cooperate with the national government in paying for welfare programs, and they run some national programs.

In this unit you will learn how the decisions of people in state governments affect life in the states and how citizens in turn can affect state government decision makers.

Campus of the University of California at Berkeley.

Chapter 14

States and State Legislatures

★★

Note: Students may be able to find the data for their state.

You must pay a sales tax. When driving, you must observe speed limits. You must have a license to operate a beauty parlor.

Who decides these things? Legislators, the men and women who make up the legislature, the lawmaking body, in your state.

Altogether, voters elect more than 7,500 men and women to serve in state legislatures. Their duties often require hard work and long stays away from home. And in many states the pay is not high, although it has been getting better in recent years.

Why would anyone want the job? Here is what four state legislators had to say about that:

Stanley Sivinski: "They need people down here who will represent the average worker. The state legislature needs people that aren't lawyers, that are for the common man."

Sheila Greenberg: "For eight years I worked in the county treasurer's office. During that time I visited the state legislature often on business, and I provided the legislature with information on several laws affecting county government officials. I decided I had some good experience and that I should run for the legislature."

James Robbins: "I own my own business. Many people asked me to run for the legislature. I didn't want to spend time away from my factory. But my friends convinced me the business point of view needed to be represented in the legislature."

Allen Shepard: "I am a lawyer. I have always been interested in state government. Being a state lawmaker was a good way to expand my knowledge of the law. Also by working here I have met many people who can help me improve my own law office at home."

Discuss: Why are these people interested in being state legislators? Can you think of any other reasons?

As you have read, people serve in state governments for many reasons. In this chapter you will learn more about state government as you read:

1/The Powers of State Government
2/How State Legislatures Work
3/State Lawmakers
Case Study: Decision on a State Tax

298

1/The Powers of State Government

Many countries in the world do not have separate states as we know them. Such countries as France, Sweden, and Great Britain have unitary systems of government. In a **unitary system,** the central government has all the power. Local governments, such as counties, cities, or provinces, merely carry out the decisions of the central government. The central government can change the size of the territory ruled by a local government. It can even abolish the local government.

In contrast, the United States has a **federal system** of government. In our federal system, the powers of government are divided between the national government and the fifty state governments. The Constitution defines the place of state governments in the federal system. The diagram on page 300 shows how powers are divided. The top part shows those powers that only the national government has. The bottom part shows some of the many powers reserved for the states. In the middle are powers shared by both the national government and the states. For example, both levels of government make and collect taxes, borrow money, pay debts, set up courts, protect health and safety, and so on. However, the federal Constitution, laws, and treaties are supreme over state constitutions and laws.

Discuss: What are the pros and cons of a unitary system and a federal system?

Note: Have students locate on a world map examples of countries with each system of government.

Barbara Ackerman, mayor of Cambridge, Massachusetts, explains her city's needs to the state legislature.

State Constitutions

All fifty states have their own constitutions. Each state constitution describes how the government shall be organized. It gives the powers and duties of various officials and agencies. It names the rights of citizens. It deals with voting and elections, the means of making laws, and the way to change the constitution itself.

State constitutions vary a great deal in length. They range from Vermont's 6,600-word document to some that are five or six times longer. The average state constitution is more than three times longer than the federal Constitution with all its amendments. The short constitutions deal only with the basic rules for state government. They give the state legislature the power to make changes in the rules to keep up with the times. Long state constitutions include many details about running state government on a day-to-day basis.

By early 1976 nineteen states were still using their original constitutions. That of Massachusetts dates from 1780, but of course it has been amended many times. Many states have had two or three new constitutions over the years. By 1976 Louisiana had had 11; Georgia, 8; South Carolina, 7; and three other

Discuss: What does your state constitution specify? Is it long or short? Is it the original? If not, how many times has it been changed? Is there any proposal to change it now?

DIVISION OF POWERS IN OUR FEDERAL SYSTEM

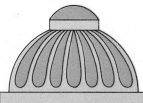

POWERS OF NATIONAL GOVERNMENT
To coin money; regulate foreign and interstate commerce; pass naturalization and immigration laws; establish post offices; grant patents and copyrights; declare war and make peace; admit new states and govern territories; maintain military establishments; fix standards of weights and measures; provide for the common defense; govern the District of Columbia; conduct foreign relations; do anything "necessary and proper" for carrying out the delegated powers.

POWERS COMMON TO BOTH (Concurrent powers)
To tax; borrow money; charter banks; pass bankruptcy laws; establish courts; promote agriculture, industry, and science; protect the health, safety, and morals of the people; take property for public purposes; pay debts.

POWERS OF STATE GOVERNMENTS
To provide for local governments; conduct elections; ratify Constitutional amendments; make laws about wills, contracts and domestic relations; regulate commerce within the states; provide for and supervise schools; care for crippled, handicapped, and mentally ill; assume power not granted to the United States nor prohibited to the states (reserved powers).

300

states, 6 each. Much change has taken place in state constitutions since 1950 as the states seek to modernize their governments.

In spite of how they vary in length, content, and age, all state constitutions have some common features. They all begin with a preamble. Most start out like the federal Constitution, "We the people," and then list purposes that the government is to serve. All state constitutions have a Bill of Rights that lists basic freedoms like those in the federal Constitution. Some go further. That of Illinois, for instance, says that there shall be no discrimination against women or handicapped people.

As with the national government, state constitutions also assign powers and duties of government to three branches. The diagram below shows the basic pattern of organization of state governments. Your state government may be organized a bit differently, but in general it will look like this diagram.

State constitutions give each branch of government power to check the other branches. This is to keep the powers of the three branches in balance. For example, the state legislature has the power to make laws. A governor can check the legislative branch with a veto of any law he or she may oppose.

Discuss: When is it necessary to rewrite a state constitution?

Note: Have students compare this diagram and the pattern of your state government.

STATE GOVERNMENT ORGANIZATION

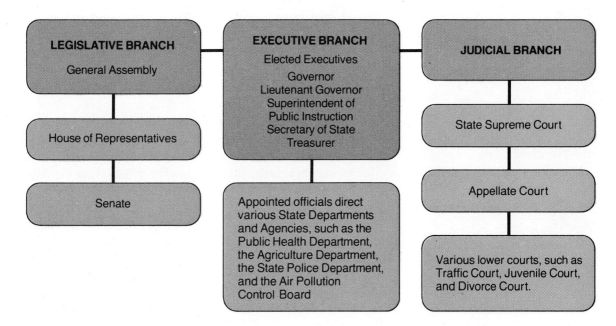

LEGISLATIVE BRANCH

General Assembly

House of Representatives

Senate

EXECUTIVE BRANCH

Elected Executives

Governor
Lieutenant Governor
Superintendent of
Public Instruction
Secretary of State
Treasurer

Appointed officials direct various State Departments and Agencies, such as the Public Health Department, the Agriculture Department, the State Police Department, and the Air Pollution Control Board

JUDICIAL BRANCH

State Supreme Court

Appellate Court

Various lower courts, such as Traffic Court, Juvenile Court, and Divorce Court.

301

State Legislatures

The legislative branch is known as the State Legislature in a little over half the states. It is called the General Assembly or Legislative Assembly in twenty-one of the states. In New Hampshire and Massachusetts it is called the General Court.

Discuss: What are the advantages of a bicameral legislature? Why do you think Nebraska has kept a unicameral legislature?

In all but one of the states, the legislature is **bicameral.** This means that it is divided into two houses: a house of representatives (or assembly) and a senate. Nebraska has a one-house, or **unicameral,** legislature called the Senate.

Regardless of name, a legislature is a state's chief lawmaking body. Legislatures may enact any law that does not conflict with the state constitution, the United States Constitution, or federal laws and treaties.

Every year state legislatures pass thousands of bills having to do with such items as:

gambling	highway speed limits
hunting seasons	crime
taxes	public schools
teachers' minimum pay	advertising
the sale of fireworks	marriage and divorce
rules for jury duty	licenses

Discuss: What are the key roles of state legislatures?

Here are some of the major activities of state legislatures.

State legislatures decide the rules that govern the licensing of motor vehicles. License fees are a source of state revenue.

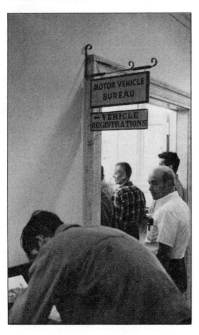

State Legislatures Pass Laws on Taxes and Spending. One of the state legislature's important tasks is to pass laws providing for the collection of money to pay for government. State and local governments use this money to provide for firefighters and police; roads, bridges, and dams; care for the poor; and many other services. Money also goes for state employees' salaries.

Where does a state government get money? Your state gets most of its money from taxes. These include state sales and income taxes, death and gift taxes, sometimes property taxes, and fees for various licenses. States also receive money from the federal government.

Legislatures tax and allot money according to a plan called the state budget, which the governor's office prepares. The budget usually covers a specific period of time, in many states a two-year period.

No money from the state treasury can be spent unless the legislature approves. It does this by passing laws called **appropriations.** For instance, in order for the schools to get the money they need to operate, the state must pass an Education Appropriations bill. Each legislature must appropriate money every year or every other year.

Much conflict arises over how much money to spend on various programs. During legislative sessions, the halls of state capitols are filled with individuals and groups urging legislators to allot money for programs they support.

Discuss: How is money raised in your state? How is it spent?

State Legislatures Pass Laws to Guide Behavior. These laws spell out what people and businesses must and must not do. Many of these laws aim to protect health and safety. All criminal laws are in this category. They set penalties for such acts as theft, murder, arson (setting fire on purpose), and vandalism. Other health and safety laws may require inspection of restaurants. Or they might provide for truck weight inspection or set speed limits on state and county roads.

As times change there is often a need for new laws. Laws regulating nuclear power plants, for example, were not needed until recently. Now state legislatures may make such plants pass safety inspections.

State Legislatures Pass Education Laws. Each state provides for public schools. As a result, a large portion of a state budget goes for education. Legislatures also pass laws affecting school operations. Such laws may set qualifications for school bus drivers as well as for principals. They may require schools to have fire drills twice a month or to teach the metric system in grades seven and eight. Legislatures also provide money for and regulate state colleges and universities.

State laws may set standards for the selection and training of firefighters.

Legislatures Create Local Governments. The power of local governments in a state is set by the state legislature. When a community believes it needs its own government, it asks the state legislature for a charter. All cities, towns, and villages have charters. The charter says where the city boundaries are and what laws it is free to pass. It will say how the city may raise money.

State laws set up districts to provide certain services. These districts are usually run by a local board, either elected or appointed. Thus school districts, park districts, airport districts, hospital districts, urban mass transit districts, and cemetery districts are all examples of local governments.

State lawmakers pass laws that regulate the jobs of such local officials as mayors, sheriffs, police chiefs, fire chiefs, and county engineers. They may also regulate local government operation, for example by requiring county offices to stay open one night each week.

Other Legislative Activities. Usually the legislature, or at least the state senate, must approve many of the governor's appointments to state jobs. In some states, the legislature itself has the power to appoint certain high-ranking officers. Except in Oregon, legislatures can impeach state officials and remove them from office upon conviction. Legislatures also vote on proposed amendments to the United States Constitution.

Section Review

Vocabulary: appropriations, bicameral legislature, federal system, unicameral legislature, unitary system.

Reviewing the Main Ideas

1. Describe how our federal system differs from a unitary system of government.
2. How does a state government get money?
3. Give five examples of different kinds of things state legislatures pass laws about.

Skill Building

1. Read the diagram on page 301 to find out in which branch of government each of these state officials works:
   a. governor
   b. judge of the Appellate Court
   c. state senator
   d. Superintendent of Public Instruction
2. What is the state legislature called in your state?
3. Name five different local governments you come in contact with.
4. Read Article 1, Section 10 of the Constitution and list the powers states do *not* have.
5. How old is your state constitution? When was it last amended?

2/How State Legislatures Work

Once elected to a state legislature, a person becomes part of a large, well-organized group. The new member works with others to make decisions and create laws. The rules of the legislature guide his or her behavior.

Committees

Most of the work of a state legislature is done in committee. There are between twenty and thirty **standing committees.** Each considers a certain area of legislation. The Rules Committee decides on the procedures for submitting bills, when they will come to the floor for a vote, how bills can be amended, under what conditions a roll-call vote is needed, and so on. The Appropriations Committee decides which state projects will get how much money. These two committees are very powerful. The chart opposite shows the senate committees of the Georgia legislature. They are typical of those in most states.

At the beginning of a session, each legislator lets party leaders know which committees he or she is interested in being on. Usually, those who have been in the legislature the longest get their choices first. But leaders try to give each new member at least one of his or her choices.

Committee members read through all the bills proposed in their area. They choose the ones they favor most. Or they may put parts of several together. Or they may work out a bill on their own. Then they put the bill before the house for a vote. If a committee does not approve a legislator's proposed bill, it has no chance of becoming law. So legislators want to be on the committees that matter most to the people in their district.

How a Bill Becomes a Law

A bill becomes a law in a state legislature in much the same way as in Congress. Once a bill is introduced in one house, it goes to a committee. The committee can hold hearings.

If the committee approves the bill, it is then placed on the calendar. At a certain time, the entire house considers it. Members may agree on amendments, and they eventually vote on the bill. If that house passes the bill, it goes to the other house. There the committee, calendar, amendment, consideration, and voting procedure is repeated. If the second house approves a different version of the bill, a **conference committee** of members of both

STANDING COMMITTEES OF THE GEORGIA SENATE

1. Agriculture
2. Appropriations
3. Banking and Finance
4. Business, Trade and Commerce
5. County and Urban Affairs
6. Defense and Veterans Affairs
7. Economy, Reorganization and Efficiency in Government
8. Elementary and Secondary Education
9. Health and Welfare
10. Highways
11. Industry and Labor
12. Institutions and Mental Health
13. Interstate Cooperation
14. Judiciary
15. Natural Resources and Environmental Quality
16. Penal and Correctional Affairs
17. Public Utilities and Transportation
18. Retirement
19. Rules
20. Scientific Research
21. Senate Administrative Affairs
22. Special Judiciary
23. Temperance
24. University System of Georgia
25. Vocational and Technical Education

houses irons out the differences. The bill then goes to the governor. He or she may sign it into law, or veto it. The legislature can override a veto by a two-thirds majority of both houses or, in Nebraska, the one house.

Leaders

Not every legislator has equal influence on what happens in a legislature. Leaders who organize and guide legislative work have the most influence.

Both houses have leaders. In most states the lieutenant governor serves as **president of the senate.** Members of the house elect a leader, usually called the **speaker of the house.** These leaders are a legislature's **presiding officers.** As a rule, they appoint committee members and chairpersons, refer bills to proper committees, and conduct sessions of the two houses. They also help set the legislative calendars and take part in debates. The speaker votes on all bills. The lieutenant governor votes only in case of a tie.

In most legislatures each political party has **floor leaders.** These leaders try to pass bills their political parties want passed. They make certain that all party members know how their leaders want them to vote on key bills. They also remind lawmakers when important bills are coming up for consideration so they can be present. In addition, floor leaders help the presiding officers decide which people to assign to which committees.

Section Review

Vocabulary: conference committee, floor leaders, president of the senate, presiding officers, speaker of the house, standing committees.

Reviewing the Main Ideas
1. What do standing committees do?
2. How do floor leaders help their parties pass legislation?

Skill Building
With classmates, find out the names of your state legislators in both houses. Find their addresses at the state capitol. Then divide into groups to write letters and find out on which committees each serves. Ask for information about the legislation each has introduced in the most recent session.

3/State Lawmakers

Most state legislatures meet for only a few weeks during the year. Some meet only every other year. Therefore, the job of state lawmaker is part-time for many legislators. This means that they must have other jobs. And their jobs must allow them time to attend lawmaking sessions at the state capital.

Discuss: When does your legislature meet?

Legal training is useful to legislative work, and many state lawmakers are lawyers who have their own law practices at home. For some lawyers, service in the legislature is a step toward such other public jobs as judge or attorney general. Many other lawmakers own their own businesses, or are teachers, farmers, or homemakers. See the chart on page 306.

Discuss: How does the background of your legislator compare with those described here?

State lawmakers represent citizens of their districts. They know their people's problems and needs. Most lawmakers come from the district they represent. In a recent year in New Jersey, for example, 83 percent of the legislators were born in the district they represented or had lived there at least thirty years. Even in California, where people change residences frequently, 56 percent of the lawmakers were born or raised in their districts.

Note: Have available a map of legislative districts.

The Job Today

The job of state lawmaker is often a brief one. Many legislators serve only one term of two or four years. Usually this is because

A Wisconsin state legislator testifies at a public hearing about a bill.

they find the job takes too much time from other duties. One legislator put it this way:

"Any way you look at it, the job means a sacrifice to you, your home, your business. Lawmaking duties take time enough. But doing special jobs for the voters also takes time. Why, yesterday my phone rang 68 times. It's a problem of time."

A smaller number of lawmakers stay on year after year. As one said, "I enjoy being a legislator. I am interested in government. I like solving problems with people at home and working on new laws here."

Making Decisions. The primary task of lawmakers is to make decisions about laws. To do this they study bills. They listen to individuals or groups interested in certain legislation. In committees they listen to witnesses. They might testify on bills themselves. They offer amendments. Unlike national legislators, they have small staffs to help with their work. A considerable burden is placed on the individual legislator and his or her time.

A lawmaker may vote on hundreds of bills during a session. Deciding whether to vote "yes" or "no" will be more difficult in some cases than in others.

Many of the bills a lawmaker must consider affect only a few people. For example, a bill might provide special medical benefits for two state workers hurt in an accident. Such bills do not call for great change and usually do not involve great sums of

Like national legislators, state legislators work in committees to study bills and recommend which ones should be passed.

money. Not many people outside the legislature will care about them.

On the other hand, a bill might affect many people's income, property, health care, or education. The lawmaker who must vote on such a bill finds citizens swamping his or her office with letters. Interest groups try to influence legislators' decisions. Then the state legislature becomes an arena of action and pressure. Decisions about such bills can be difficult to make.

Helping Citizens. Another part of the lawmakers' job is to help citizens and groups that come to them with problems. Legislators know that such help may earn them votes in the next election. Many also believe that it is their duty to help. One legislator put it this way: "A good lawmaker should serve as a contact between the voters and the departments of state government. A lawmaker should be a sort of walking directory that can refer citizens to the right person or department when they have a problem with state government."

A legislator might help a builder learn about environmental regulations. He or she might help a trucker get required licenses. A lawmaker might help a set of parents learn about state college scholarships. Examples of legislators aiding people of their districts are endless.

Who Influences Lawmakers?

Many people try to influence lawmakers' decisions. Chief among these are the governor, interest groups, and individuals.

The Governor. Lawmakers and citizens expect the governor to suggest legislation on taxes, pollution, education, health services, and the like. During every session many bills are written in the executive branch of the state government. Lawmakers who belong to the governor's political party introduce these bills and the governor tries to influence their passage.

In addition, the governor prepares the state budget. He or she tries to influence legislators to accept it. Each legislator has an interest in at least certain items in the budget.

The veto power is also a way in which a governor can influence legislation. Every state legislature can override a governor's veto, but in most states this requires a two-thirds majority of both houses. In fact, sometimes the mere threat of a veto can influence legislators' decisions.

Discuss: How are state legislators influenced?

Discuss: Has your state had any special sessions recently? If yes, why?

Governors may also call legislatures into **special session.** This is a series of meetings of the legislature at a time when it usually does not assemble. Many legislators do not like having to return to the capital to consider special problems or bills. Governors sometimes use this dislike for special sessions to force legislators to act on a proposal during a regular session.

Governors can also rely on **prestige.** The news media and citizens pay attention to what a governor says. Governors can command air time more easily than lawmakers. They can use their prestige as the state's highest elected official to build public opinion in support of their legislative programs.

Patronage is another political resource governors have. It is the power to give jobs or favors. A governor can often arrange to have new roads, parks, or hospitals built in a lawmaker's district, or grant state jobs or business to friends of lawmakers. In return, a governor expects the lawmaker's support for his or her programs.

Discuss: What is the role of patronage? Do you know of any examples in your area?

Finally, as leaders of their political party, governors can use party leadership to influence legislators from their own party. As party leader, a governor can appeal to a lawmaker's party loyalty, asking for support of a bill for "the good of the party." At times a governor may offer a lawmaker a good party job in return for support.

Interest Groups. Many different interest groups seek to influence lawmakers' decisions. These groups include such business and labor organizations as chambers of commerce and particular unions. They also include organizations representing teachers, farmers, and government employees.

Groups with an interest in legislation support lobbyists who work in the state capital and attend legislative sessions. Lobbyists provide lawmakers with useful information about bills, and they seek to influence votes just as lobbyists in Congress do. State legislators often depend more on lobbyists for information than do members of Congress. This is because they work only part-time as lawmakers. And, unlike members of Congress, they do not have large staffs to collect information for them.

Consider, for example, this state legislator's comment: "I think lobbyists are usually helpful. They can study issues and present information we have no time to get for ourselves. In ten minutes a lobbyist can explain what it would take you hours to learn by reading bills."

Discuss: What local groups try to influence legislators? How could you get involved?

Individual Citizens. Unless you are a lobbyist, you will not be able to spend much time trying to influence lawmakers. But there are things individual citizens can do to communicate their interests to legislators.

Citizens can contact them. Although few people write or call their lawmakers, this is not hard to do. Legislators like to keep in touch with **constituents.** It is not easy for lawmakers to know what citizens of their district think about proposed legislation.

In addition, citizens can find groups working for goals they are interested in. A person might join an interest group, or at least contribute money to one.

Finally, every citizen has the right to vote and to join a political party. By working with a party, citizens may help elect to state legislatures candidates who support their ideas.

Section Review

Vocabulary: constituents, patronage, prestige, special session.

Reviewing the Main Ideas
1. Why do many state legislators hold other jobs?
2. Describe two key parts of the lawmaker's job.
3. Name the ways citizens might try to influence lawmakers' decisions.

Skill Building
1. Write a paragraph describing what you think is the most important part of a legislator's job. Give your reasons.
2. What political resource is each governor in the stories below using? Be prepared to defend your answers.
   Governor 1: State Senator Alice Irwin answered the phone. The governor was calling. "Alice," the governor said, "you are a loyal party member. I hope you will vote for the new tax bill I want. It's important for our party that we pass that bill."
   Governor 2: Governor Hill was a guest on a TV interview show. The governor answered questions about his legislative program. He explained why the public should support it.
   Governor 3: Representative Ed Kolski had been a loyal supporter of Governor Kauffman for many years. Kolski had almost always voted for the governor's programs. Last week the governor named Kolski to be the state director of public works.

Main Ideas
1. p. 307
2. pp. 308–309
3. p. 311
Skill Building
1. Answers will vary.
2. Governor 1: party leadership, Governor 2: prestige, Governor 3: patronage

Decision on a State Tax

Nearly all states have some sort of general sales tax. This kind of tax is placed on things when they are sold. For example, in states where there is a five percent sales tax, people pay five cents tax on each dollar they spend every time they go to the store. In some states, certain items such as food and medicine are not taxed.

In 1969, Oregon was one of the few states without a sales tax. It was no surprise, then, that some people in the state suggested a sales tax as a way to get more money for increased state expenses. Early in the year, the Oregon House of Representatives, after committee hearings and much debate, passed a bill to have a general sales tax in the state. The bill went to the Senate, where a majority voted for it. Governor McCall signed the bill.

In Oregon, no tax law takes effect until citizens have had ninety days to petition for a referendum. (A referendum is a direct vote by citizens on a bill.) Within this time, any citizen may try to get a certain percent of the voters to sign a petition calling for a referendum on the tax bill. The people opposed to the sales tax did just that. They got enough signatures to get a referendum. Oregon's voters would decide whether or not the state would have a sales tax.

Leaders in the campaign *for* the sales tax were the Association of Oregon Industries, the Farm Bureau, and certain business leaders. They argued that the state needed more money for key services, especially public education. They pointed out that the state depended mainly on income and property taxes for revenue. These taxes were too high already and shouldn't be raised, they said.

Supporters of the sales tax believed that business firms and property owners carried too much of the burden of the income and property tax. Thus, a general sales tax would be a fair way to spread the tax burden among the public.

Labor unions, most newspaper editors, and various consumer groups were leaders in the campaign *against* the sales tax. These people argued that sales taxes are unfair. They said sales taxes make poorer people carry a heavier tax burden than richer people. Richer people may pay more taxes than poorer people, but the sales tax takes a smaller slice from their earnings than from the earnings of the poor.

The opponents of the sales tax agreed that the state needed

As the population in a state grows, the need for services grows, and so does the need for more money to pay for them. Portland, Oregon, in 1860; population including suburbs: 60,000 (this page). Portland today, population over 1,108,000 (facing page).

more money, especially for schools. But they thought that it would be fair to raise the state income tax rather than to have a sales tax.

The voters went to the polls on June 3, 1969, to decide the issue. By a vote of almost eight to one, they voted down the sales tax.

Oregon continued to rely on the income tax as the major source of revenue. A majority of the voters thought that this was the fairest way to get the needed money.

Reviewing the Case Study

1. What was the occasion for decision?
2. What were the alternatives?
3. How did the goals of those backing the different choices differ?
4. The question hung on what seemed the fairest way to raise money for state government. What did the voters decide?
5. Do you agree with the Oregon voters? Give your reasons.

Chapter Fourteen Test and Activities

★★

Vocabulary

Match the following words with their meanings.

1. appropriations
2. bicameral legislature
3. federal system
4. unitary system
5. unicameral legislature
6. constituents
7. patronage
8. prestige
9. special session
10. conference committee

a. influence and reputation
b. a legislature with one house
c. a legislature with two houses
d. a form of government in which all power is concentrated in the central government
e. a form of government in which states agree to set up a central government and keep some powers to themselves
f. laws allowing certain amounts of government money to be spent for specific items
g. a series of meetings of the legislature outside the regular time
h. the power to offer jobs and grant favors
i. a group of legislators from both houses who iron out their differences on a bill
j. the voters a legislator represents

Reviewing Chapter Ideas

1. True or false: After the thirteen states signed the Constitution, there was no need for states to have their own constitutions.
2. True or false: States can pass laws that punish people for crimes.
3. Both the national government and the states have power to _____ .
   a. conduct elections
   b. establish post offices
   c. establish courts
   d. make treaties with foreign governments
4. Which of the following is not a concern of state legislatures?
   a. decisions about foreign policy
   b. decisions about raising and spending money
   c. decisions about education
   d. decisions about local governments
5. True or false: The Appropriations Committee is very powerful because it decides on the rules for the legislature.
6. True or false: A bill becomes a law in a state legislature in much the same ways as in Congress.
7. Name your state legislators.
8. True or false: Many of the bills that come up for a vote in state legislatures are not important to very many people.
9. Which of the following is a way governors influence state lawmakers?
   a. by supporting lobbyists
   b. by suggesting bills
   c. by voting for bills
   d. all of the above
10. True or false: Citizens can influence laws in their states by voting in referendums.

Using Basic Social Studies Skills

Finding Information

1. How could you find out who your state legislator is?
2. Where would you write if you wanted to influence your state senator?

3. Suppose you wanted to know how your state lawmakers had voted on the most recent tax legislation. How would you find out?

Comprehending Information

1. Write a short paragraph on what you think is the most important way a governor can influence legislation.
2. Explain in a short paragraph or diagram how a bill becomes a law in a state legislature.

Organizing Information

For each of the following examples of government powers, write (1) if it is a power the Constitution gives the national government alone, write (2) if it is a power only a state can have, and write (3) if it is a shared power.

a. form an army and navy
b. build high schools in Lake County, Indiana
c. coin money
d. build highways
e. make rules about the purchase of oil from Saudi Arabia
f. deliver the mail
g. issue licenses to drive cars

Evaluating Information

If you were trying to make a judgment about your state legislator before voting to reelect, what questions would you want answered to help you make up your mind? (Give at least three.)

Communicating Ideas

Your legislature is considering a bill to raise the age at which one can get a driver's license to nineteen. Write a letter to your state senator explaining why you are for or against this bill.

Using Decision-Making Skills

1. You are a state legislator. The legislature is considering a bill to require people who ride motorcycles to wear helmets. You oppose this bill. You believe it violates liberties and is unconstitutional. Yet there is much evidence to show that wearing helmets reduces serious injury and death from traffic accidents involving motorcycles. When the bill comes to a vote you will:
   a. _____ vote for it
   b. _____ vote against it
   c. _____ be absent from the legislature that day
   d. _____ abstain from voting
2. Why did you choose your course of action?
3. What do you think will be the consequences of your action?

Activities

1. If your legislature is in session, clip articles from newspapers that tell about legislative activities. Group the articles by subjects that concern the legislature: education, budget, taxes, and so on.
2. Use the *Readers' Guide* to find articles on referendums that have been held in various states. Choose one referendum and write a short report on it, dealing with its background, arguments for and against, and the outcome.
3. For students who want to know more about state government and lawmaking, the following books are recommended:
   (a) *There Ought to Be a Law! How Laws Are Made and Work,* by Ellen Switzer (Atheneum, 1972).
   (b) *State Government,* by Judith Bentley (Watts, 1978).

Chapter 15 Governors and State Agencies

★★

The governor is the highest elected public official of a state. Look over the news flashes below to see some of the powers and duties a governor has:

Jefferson City, MO—Missouri's governor today ordered 3,500 National Guard troops to the state's flood-ravaged areas along the Mississippi River. The troops are stacking sandbags along the river to prevent further flooding.

Austin, TX—Governor Dolph Briscoe told reporters he would not approve a tax increase even if the legislature passes one. "I promised no new taxes. I'm keeping my promise," Briscoe said.

Springfield, IL—Governor Jim Thompson today signed a bill that sets stiff penalties for certain crimes. The governor also announced that the state will build two new prisons.

Along with the governor, the executive branch of state government is made up of many agencies and departments. Here are some examples of their work:

Atlanta, GA—Georgia is going to get a new system of hiking trails in state parks. The state Department of Natural Resources announced it would start building the new trails shortly.

Richmond, VA—The Department of Highways and Transportation said that new markers would be placed on dangerous curves on state roads. It is hoped that the markers will cut down highway accidents.

Columbus, OH—The Department of Education will suggest new objectives for citizenship education in grades eight and twelve. Educators from around the state will be asked to give their advice on the project.

In this chapter you will learn more about governors and state agencies as you read:

1/The State Executive Branch
2/The Governor's Job
3/State Agencies
Case Study: Governor Dukakis's Roadblock

Discuss: What responsibilities does the executive branch of state government have?

1/The State Executive Branch

The executive branch of government enforces laws. This branch includes the governor, six to ten other executive officers such as the lieutenant governor, state treasurer, attorney general, and numerous agencies.

The Office of Governor

Voters in each state elect governors directly. Each state constitution sets the requirements for becoming governor. Generally, a candidate must be an American citizen, a resident of the state for a certain number of years, at least thirty years old (in some states, twenty-five), and a qualified voter in the state.

Discuss: Who can be governor? What is a governor's term in office?

In forty states, governors have four-year terms. The other ten elect them to terms of two years. In twelve states, mostly in the South, governors cannot run for election for a second term in a row. In ten states, the limit is two terms in a row.

Discuss: Has any governor or executive officer been impeached in your state?

Every state except Oregon provides for the impeachment of the governor and other state officials. As a rule, in a case of wrongdoing, the house brings a "bill of impeachment" against the governor, and the senate tries the individual. If found guilty, a governor must leave office and usually cannot hold any public office in the state again.

A well-organized National Guard can respond to emergencies quickly. Here residents get shots to prevent typhoid after a flood has contaminated the community's water supply.

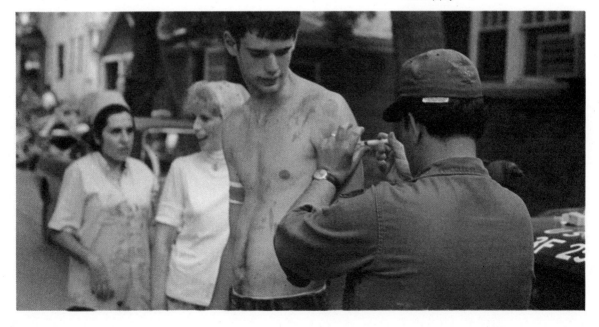

Shared Powers. Some governors can be stronger leaders than others. One reason is that some state constitutions grant governors more power than others. In some plans for state government, the governor can be a strong leader because he or she can appoint the heads of state agencies. This allows governors to choose people loyal to them. Such people are likely to try to carry out the governor's programs.

In other states, voters elect the heads of key state agencies. In addition, appointed officials serve long terms in office. Officials elected by the people or appointed to long terms do not owe as much support to the governor as those a governor can hire and fire at will. The governor has less influence over them.

Many experts believe the governor should have power to appoint and remove state officials who serve in the executive branch. One reason is that voters seldom know much about the different state offices or the candidates seeking those offices. Another reason is governors are unable to tie state activities together if they lack authority over those who carry out the activities.

In any state, a governor's power also will depend a great deal on his or her leadership skills. Strong governors are those who can command support from their political party, citizens, and interest groups in the state. They are leaders who can persuade others to support their decisions.

Discuss: What are the pros and cons of each plan for state government? Which plan do you have in your state?

New York Lieutenant Governor
Mary Ann Krupsak

Personal Background. Who becomes a governor? About half of all governors elected over the past one hundred years have been lawyers. Most governors also have had experience in other state or local elected offices. Some have previously served as congressmen. Many have held such state posts as lieutenant governor or secretary of state. A great number have also been state legislators.

Note: Have students find out about the background of your governor.

Other Executive Officers

No governor alone can carry out the laws of a state. Every state has several other important executive officials. They are responsible for managing the services and duties of the various state agencies. In many states they are elected. In some the governor appoints them.

Lieutenant Governor. Elected directly in thirty-eight states, this official is the "vice president" of state government. It is not uncommon for the lieutenant governor to belong to the opposite party from the governor. The lieutenant governor in most states becomes the governor should the governor be unable to serve. Lieutenant governors also serve as presiding officers of state senates and on many boards and commissions dealing with state services or problems.

Attorney General. This official is elected in forty-two states. The attorney general serves as legal advisor to the governor and other state officials and represents the state in legal proceedings. People expect the state's attorney general to go after serious crime problems by gathering evidence and prosecuting suspects.

Secretary of State. The secretary of state is elected in thirty-nine states. In most states, he or she is in charge of elections, official state records, and various licenses and permits.

State Treasurer. Treasurers are elected in forty-one states. The state treasurer's main duties are to supervise collection of state funds and to pay the state's bills.

State Auditor or Comptroller. Thirty-one states elect a person to this office. This officer serves as a watchdog over state funds. He or she makes sure that money is spent according to law and that state funds are accounted for.

Chief School Officer. This official is called the superintendent of public instruction or the commissioner of education. He or she is the leader in carrying out state laws and providing services related to schools.

Section Review

Vocabulary: governor, secretary of state, state treasurer, lieutenant governor, attorney general, state auditor, chief school officer.

Reviewing the Main Ideas

1. What is the job of the executive branch of state government?
2. Describe the requirements for a governorship.

Skill Building

1. Which state executive official would be responsible for:
   a. Paying a construction company for work on a state building.
   b. Making arrangements for an election in the state.
   c. Serving as the presiding officer in the state senate.
   d. Advising the governor on how a decision would fit state laws.
2. Decide whether the following statements are true or false. Rewrite each false statement to make it true.
   a. The lieutenant governor shares a great deal of power with the governor in most states.
   b. Top state officials are elected rather than appointed in most states.
   c. The secretary of state is mostly busy with keeping official state records and supervising state elections.
3. Find the names of the people in your state who have the jobs of governor, lieutenant governor, attorney general, secretary of state, state treasurer, state auditor or comptroller, and chief school officer. Try to get their pictures from newspapers or their election campaigns and make a display of your state's executive branch for the classroom.

Discuss: How do the executive officers assist the governor?

Main Ideas
1. to enforce laws
2. p. 317
Skill Building
1. a. treasurer, b. secretary of state, c. lieutenant governor, d. attorney general
2. a. T, b. T, c. T
3. Students should use the nearest public library.

2/The Governor's Job

The governor has several different leadership roles. He or she is expected to be (1) a ceremonial leader, (2) the executive leader, (3) the chief legislator, (4) the commander in chief, and (5) the political party leader.

Discuss: What are the roles of the governor? How do they compare to the roles of the President?

Ceremonial Leader. A governor's weekly schedule is filled with ceremonial duties. He or she meets groups of people, leads parades, dedicates new buildings, welcomes official visitors, and travels to make speeches and hand out awards. The governor also represents the state at governors' conferences.

Executive Leader. The governor must work with many other officials in the executive branch to carry out state laws. And as most governors are leaders in shaping state budgets, they can influence the goals and actions of state agencies.

Governors and their staffs prepare a plan for income and spending. This goes to the legislature which, after some changes, usually approves it. The governor then oversees spending by the various agencies, departments, and commissions in the state.

Chief Legislator. Governors can be leaders in lawmaking even though they are not part of the legislative branch. The governor sends messages to the legislature proposing new laws

Governor Bill Clinton of Arkansas

or changes in existing ones. In addition, every governor except North Carolina's has veto power.

Governors can also issue executive orders. An **executive order** is a rule issued by a governor that has the effect of law.

Commander in Chief. The governor is commander in chief of the state's unit of the National Guard. The governor can order the Guard out to help with such disasters as floods. Governors have also used the Guard to put down riots and to keep order.

Political Party Leader. The governor usually is the head of a major political party in the state. As party leaders, governors support and campaign for party candidates. The governor also names key party supporters to some top level state positions. If a state's United States senator dies or resigns, the governor often chooses a party member to fill out the term.

Factors in a Governor's Decision Making

When governors make decisions, they must consider many **factors,** or conditions. Among them are time, legal authority, other decision makers, and public opinion.

When a governor supports a program, it has a good chance of succeeding. Here teenagers get the straight picture on what a convict's life is like—direct from a lifer. It's part of a very successful delinquency-prevention program.

Time. Governors sometimes face such disasters as floods and such emergencies as prison riots. These demand fast action. A governor has life and death decisions to make, and quickly.

Decisions concerning new goals or changes in policies can be made more leisurely. For example, a new state tax plan presented to the legislature will have undergone months of careful consideration by the governor, the state tax collector, and budget officials.

Legal Authority. State constitutions set limits on the appointment and removal powers of governors. They also spell out procedures and rules a governor must follow. State legislatures pass laws concerning what a governor can or cannot do. And state courts further limit governors' powers.

The Constitution and federal laws also affect the power of a governor. He or she is also responsible for enforcing federal laws and the Constitution.

Other Decision Makers. Governors seek advice and support from many other officials. A governor will often consult with agency heads, state legislators, and leaders of his or her political party. He or she will meet with interest groups affected by a decision. Local and federal authorities may need to be contacted in decisions affecting highways or pollution control, for example. Governors who ignore others with an interest in a decision do so at their peril.

Personal Beliefs. No two governors agree exactly on what is best for their state. Some governors want to attract new industries and more people to their states. They believe in growth. Other governors may not want industrial growth or more people as much as they want a high quality of environment.

A few years ago the governor of one eastern state was able to limit the growth of industries and housing along the state's coastline. He said his state needed to preserve some of its natural beauty for future generations. The governor of a western state made a different choice. He urged the building of a huge hydroelectric plant near the state's most scenic parklands. The coal-burning plant would provide much needed jobs and income for the state.

Some governors favor state spending for the poor and needy. They strongly support programs in welfare, education, and health care. Other governors may believe the state government should not try to take on heavy spending programs. They may prefer instead low taxes, low-cost public service programs, and more government activity in creating a climate for business growth. Thus, personal beliefs are an important factor in a governor's decision making.

Public Opinion. Governors gain their position through election. So, before making decisions, they consider the public opinion factor. Governors who ignore public opinion may not be elected again to public office. And governors with strong public support stand a good chance of being able to carry out their programs.

Discuss: How is a governor influenced in the decision-making process?

Section Review

Vocabulary: ceremonial leader, executive leader, executive order, factors, commander in chief, political party leader.

Reviewing the Main Ideas

Main Ideas
1. pp. 321–322
2. pp. 323–324
Skill Building
1. Answers will vary.
2. a. political party leader, b. ceremonial leader, c. chief legislator

1. What are a governor's leadership roles?
2. List and briefly explain the factors that can affect a governor's decision making.

Skill Building

1. Which two factors do you think are the most important in a governor's decision making? Give reasons for your answer.
2. Identify the governor's leadership role in each of the following examples:
   a. Governor Ella Grasso headed the Connecticut delegation to the 1976 Democratic National Convention. She called out the delegation's vote for the presidential nomination when the roll call of the states was read.
   b. New York's Governor Hugh Carey greeted Queen Elizabeth at the pier when the royal yacht docked. The queen began an official visit to New York City.
   c. The governor of Michigan asked the state legislature to approve his new tax program. It called for a state income tax and for cutting the sales tax on such items as food and medicines.

3/State Agencies

A governor works with the many agencies that are a part of the executive branch. A **state agency** is a unit of government that provides a certain service. Agencies are called departments, boards, or commissions. For example, the Public Health Department in Illinois is a state agency that enforces laws concerning health and sanitation. Among its functions, the agency licenses and inspects nursing homes and hospitals, educates the public on health matters, and inspects restaurants and other food service businesses. Other agencies might include the Racing Commission, the Department of Children and Family Services, and the state Library Board.

Among the nearly three million people who work in agencies of the fifty state governments, only a few have top-level executive jobs. These administrators are called **bureaucrats** [byùr'ə-krats]. Bureaucrats are government employees who supervise or carry out government regulations and programs.

Discuss: What services do state agencies provide?

People who work for state agencies often must pass a civil service exam to get their jobs.

State Nutritionist

Marni Miller is public health nutritionist for the State of Wisconsin. She works for the Division of Health in the state's Department of Health and Social Services. Marni's job is to teach others about the foods that people need for good health.

Marni's job takes her from place to place within an eight-county region. She gives talks and demonstrations to many different people. She often works with people who are in charge of local health-care programs, public-health nurses, and people who plan meals in places such as nursing homes. She has also worked with parents of children in early-education programs such as Headstart, people in physical-fitness programs, the elderly, and diabetics.

One project that Marni has worked on is a clinic for migrant workers. People come to the clinic for many different health-care needs. Marni helped set up a nutrition program at the clinic. She worked with public-health nurses such as this man.

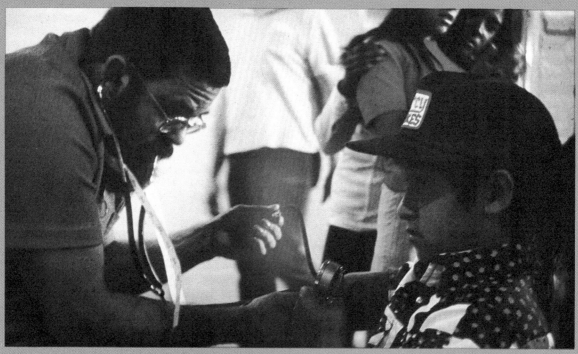

People and Government

Another project that Marni has had a hand in developing is a public health-care clinic for women with infants and small children. In the picture directly below, one of Marni's co-workers interviews a clinic visitor. In the lower picture below she gathers information about a child who has been brought to the clinic.

When Marni gives a talk on nutrition for people such as those who come to the clinic, she often uses pictures of food.

These girls show what they're learning about food at the clinic.

Those who work at the top levels of decision making usually are appointed to their jobs. Some are chosen for certain skills. Others get their positions as a reward for supporting the elected official who named them.

As in the federal government, lower-level state employees often get their jobs through the civil service system. Thirty-three states have civil service. Most of the other seventeen states are moving toward some form of civil service or merit system. You will remember that under a civil service system, government employees are hired and promoted for their ability and length of service. Jobs are filled by people who score highest on tests. Pay is based on levels of employment. The people at higher levels earn higher salaries.

Discuss: How do bureaucrats get their jobs?

Factors in a State Agency Official's Decisions

State agency officials carry out laws. Frequently they interpret laws. The officials in a state environmental protection agency, for example, make rules about how much air or water pollution is acceptable. The state's antipollution laws guide the officials in making rules. State agencies also act like courts. They make decisions to settle disputes about the enforcement of laws.

When state agency officials make decisions, they usually consider the same factors as governors do. These include time, legal authority, other decision-makers, and public opinion.

Features of a Bureaucracy

In addition, state agency officials work in a bureaucracy. A bureaucracy is a collective term for government agencies. All bureaucracies in local, state, and federal government have these same things: (1) a chain of command, (2) formal rules to guide their actions, (3) a division of work, and (4) resources.

Discuss: What is a bureaucracy? How does it work?

Chain of Command. A bureaucracy is organized into ranks or levels. The agency chief holds the top rank, and has the authority to direct those below that position. Department heads usually hold positions just below the agency chief. These leaders rank second in command. They have the authority to give orders to those lower in the organization, and so on down the line.

Conformity to Rules. The chain of command in a bureaucracy works according to written rules. There are rules for hiring and firing workers, for promoting people, for dealing with citizens, and for managing day-to-day business. Bureaucrats and other workers who do not go along with the rules might lose their jobs.

Division of Work. In a bureaucracy, work is divided into different departments. For example, a state department of agriculture deals only with matters related to farming. The state education agency handles educational services and problems.

Each agency hires experts. The department of health hires medical doctors and nurses. Agronomists, experts in farming, work for the state agricultural agency. Lawyers work in the office of the attorney general.

Note: Have students make a chart summarizing the features of your local bureaucracy.

Resources. The resources available to reach a goal will influence state agencies' decisions. An agency cannot accomplish much without money, and without workers having knowledge and skills.

Holding back funds from a state agency checks it. When the governor and the legislature make up the budget, they can help or hurt an agency by giving it more or less money. They often will reward an agency when its officials are doing things they approve. They can cut the funds of agencies doing things they disapprove.

Tips for Influencing State Agencies

Suppose the state insurance commission approved a 45 percent increase in car insurance rates for drivers under twenty-one. Many teenagers would think the state insurance commission's decision was unfair. When they took driver's education they were told that it would help them get less expensive auto insurance. What could they do? How can citizens influence the decisions of state agencies? Here are some ideas that can help citizens act effectively.

Approach the Agency. If you think you've been wronged, tell someone about it. Lower-level bureaucrats are normally quite available to citizens. If you're not happy with the response, move to higher levels of the agency. Try to contact the department chief at the highest level. (Your state publishes a directory, often called a "Blue Book," that lists all the state officers, legislators, agencies, and agency heads. Most public libraries carry it.) Teenage drivers could contact the head of the state insurance commission. Some top officials are easily approached. Others are almost impossible to see. But the citizen owes the agency at least the chance to hear a complaint directly.

Contact an Elected Official. Sometimes the agency or its staff are unable or unwilling to solve a problem. Or the citizen still feels he or she is being treated unfairly. Then the next step is to write or telephone a state senator or representative. They usually will try to be of help if a complaint or problem really deserves a hearing.

Appeal to the Governor's Office. Governors receive hundreds of letters from citizens with complaints or problems. Most appeals are given to staff aides, who then forward the letters to the proper agencies or officials. Sometimes agencies are quicker to act when the request comes by way of the governor's office.

Organize with Others. Citizens who share the same problem or complaint will be more effective if they work together. When a large number of citizens complain, public officials are more willing to listen. Or citizens can contact an interest group concerned with their kind of problem. The interest group may use its resources to help.

Use the Press. Citizens can contact the local newspaper or a television station. They can try to get a reporter interested in their problem. Some newspapers carry regular "hotline" or action columns that seek out such problems. Or citizens may write a letter to the editor with the facts of their problem.

Tell the Ombudsman. An ombudsman [om budz′mən] is a high government official with the power to investigate citizen complaints against public officials. The word *ombudsman* is Swedish. It means *grievance man.* Sweden appointed the first ombudsman in the world in 1809. In 1969, Hawaii became the first state to have an ombudsman. Since then six more states have followed suit. They are Alaska, Oregon, Iowa, Nebraska, South Carolina, and North Carolina.

Discuss: Does your state have an ombudsman? What is the role of your ombudsman?

Five states have ombudsmen for their state penitentiary systems. The officials hear complaints from prisoners about prison guard treatment, food, and medical care.

North Carolina's Department of Transportation and Department of Human Resources each have an ombudsman. They can be called toll free from anywhere in the state.

Discuss: How can state agencies be influenced?

Section Review

Vocabulary: state agency, bureaucrat, bureaucracy, chain of command, ombudsman.

Reviewing the Main Ideas
1. Explain the jobs of three agencies in your state.
2. Describe four factors that affect decision making in agencies.

Skill Building
1. Find information in Section 3 to support this statement: State agency officials cannot make simply any decision they wish.
2. The *Thorndike Barnhart Advanced Dictionary* gives the following as one definition of *bureaucracy:* "excessive insistence on rigid routine, resulting in delay in making decisions or in carrying out requests; red tape." How do the features of a bureaucracy help explain why this has come to be a meaning of the word?

Main Ideas
1. Answers will vary.
2. time, legal authority, other decision-makers, public opinion
Skill Building
1. Answers will vary.
2. Answers should refer to the features of a bureaucracy listed on pp. 328–329.

Governor Dukakis's Roadblock

It was not exactly another Boston Tea Party. But the roar of anger that greeted the governor of Massachusetts's order could be heard all over the Bay State.

Governor Michael Dukakis had ordered a halt to some $57 million worth of highway projects. He called the proposed highway work a "waste of taxpayers' money."

The governor's order meant that the secretary of transportation and the commissioner of public works were not to apply for federal highway grants-in-aid, amounting to around $51 million. The governor said that the planned highway projects did not meet the real transportation needs of Massachusetts. Furthermore, he said, the projects would slow down traffic and cause tie-ups on many sections of the state's interstate system. And, he added, Massachusetts would have to put up $5 million of its own funds to get the federal money. He preferred to spend state money on mass transportation.

Reaction to the governor's decision was swift. "Massachusetts will lose 4,000 construction jobs," said the owner of one of the companies expecting to work on the projects. Another construction official predicted that 4,700 jobs would be lost.

"For a year and a half, the governor has been telling us he wants jobs and federal funds," said an official. "Now at his first opportunity, he puts thousands of construction workers out of jobs and gives away $50 million to other states!"

Labor union officials were also angry. One labor leader said that Massachusetts already had as many as a third of its construction workers unemployed.

In further explaining his refusal to take the federal money and continue the projects, Governor Dukakis said he believed that the projects might damage the state's environment. He also pointed out that he had a duty to see that state and federal tax dollars were "spent wisely and well."

Other state officials did not agree with the governor. One was Lieutenant Governor Thomas P. O'Neill III. Another was the commissioner for public works. He refused to answer any questions. He referred all calls to the governor's office. The transportation secretary was also silent. Environmental Affairs Secretary Evelyn Murphy said she had no objection to the highway projects. Even so, several environmental groups had protested against some of them.

Governor Michael Dukakis

Perhaps the most important opposition came in the Massachusetts legislature. Both Republican and Democratic leaders, in a rare show of unity, proposed a resolution asking the governor to reconsider. Republican leader Francis Hatch said of the governor's decision: "It was just one more example of a long list of things the governor has done to lose our confidence." The lawmakers approved the resolution by a 219 to 1 vote.

Most newspapers opposed the governor's decision. Said one editorial: "The governor's action . . . will not save the taxpayers here or anywhere else a dime. If Massachusetts fails to participate in the program, the federal government will simply give that $51 million to other states where it will be spent for the same purpose, whether or not it is spent 'wisely and well.' "

The angry public reaction and the state legislature's action were consequences Governor Dukakis had not expected when he made his decision. He held a press conference. Said Governor Dukakis, "I have concluded that the economic arguments to proceed with the program outweigh the dubious values of the projects themselves." He ordered the appropriate state agencies to get the federal money and complete the highway construction programs.

House leader McGee said: "I'm pleased with the governor's decision. It means money and jobs for our state. And we need both badly."

The leaders of construction companies scheduled to work on the projects were also happy. They thanked the governor for his decision. They promised to get started quickly on the work in order to provide new summer employment for workers.

Highway construction.

Reviewing the Case Study

1. Draw a decision tree to show the alternatives and consequences involved in the governor's decision to stop the highway projects.
2. What goal moved the governor to halt the projects?
3. What legal authority did the governor appear to have?
4. What groups were affected by the governor's decision to stop the projects? What was their reaction to the decision?
5. What caused the governor to change his mind?
6. Do you think the governor should have changed his mind? Why or why not?

Chapter Fifteen Test and Activities

★★★

Vocabulary

Match the following words with their meanings.

1. lieutenant governor
2. executive order
3. factors
4. state auditor
5. bureaucracy
6. ombudsman

a. an order issued by the governor that has the force of law
b. all the government agencies together
c. the vice-president of state government
d. the agency head who sees that state money is spent according to law
e. the government official who acts as a go-between for the state and its citizens
f. things to consider; parts

Reviewing Chapter Ideas

1. Which of the following is *not* a constitutional requirement for governor in most states?
   a. at least thirty years old
   b. an American citizen
   c. born in the state
   d. a qualified voter
2. When the governor cuts a ribbon opening a new highway, he or she is acting in the role of _____ .
   a. ceremonial leader
   b. executive leader
   c. chief legislator
   d. political party leader
3. When the governor works out a new budget, he or she is acting in the role of _____ .
   a. ceremonial leader
   b. executive leader
   c. chief legislator
   d. political party leader
4. When the governor travels across the state to make a speech urging the reelection of a certain state senator, he or she is acting in the role of _____ .
   a. ceremonial leader
   b. executive leader
   c. chief legislator
   d. political party leader
5. True or false: A state in which the voters elect most state agency heads has a stronger governor than one in which these people are appointed.
6. True or false: A chain of command is a feature of bureaucracies.
7. True or false: In a bureaucracy, workers must go along with the rules.
8. True or false: You can't fight the bureaucracy.
9. In the past one hundred years, over half of all governors elected have been:
   a. clergymen
   b. owners of their own businesses
   c. lawyers
   d. doctors
10. True or false: In a civil service system, most government workers have their jobs as a reward for helping a political party.

Vocabulary
1. c   4. d
2. a   5. b
334   3. f   6. e

Ideas
1. c   4. d   7. T   10. F
2. a   5. F   8. F
3. b   6. T   9. c

★★★

Using Basic Social Studies Skills

Finding Information

1. How can you find the name of the person who heads up a state agency, if you need to contact that person?
2. What state government office would you contact if you had information about serious crime taking place?
3. What state office would you go to to get information about the requirements for a driver's license?

Comprehending Information

Write a short paragraph explaining the various factors a governor considers before making a decision.

Organizing Information

1. Referring to the case study, list the individuals and groups that had an interest in the decision on federal highway money for Massachusetts. Under each individual or group, list the various concerns they expressed.
2. Referring to page 318, list the factors that would tend to make the office of governor strong. In another column, list the factors that would tend to make the office weak.

Evaluating Information

In the case study, what seemed to be the main factor that changed the governor's mind? Do you think this should have been a main factor in the decision? Why or why not?

Communicating Ideas

The governor of your state has vetoed a bill removing food from state sales taxation. Write a letter to the editor of your newspaper explaining why you agree or disagree with the governor's action.

Using Decision-Making Skills

1. Governor Dukakis's alternatives were (a) to spend $5 million and get federal money to work on highways in the state and (b) not to spend the money and work out a mass transit plan. Which alternative did he choose?
2. What did he expect would be the consequence of his decision?
3. What factor did he not pay enough attention to?
4. What happened to cause him to change his decision?

Activities

1. Find newspaper articles telling about the activities of the governor of your state. Group the articles under the various leadership roles of the governor.
2. If your local newspaper has an action or "hotline" column, collect it for a week. Or, if your TV station has one, keep a record of the kinds of problems that come up in a week. Study these columns or notes to see how the paper helps people with their problems. Sort the problems into two groups, (1) those the people could have solved for themselves if they had gone about it right, and (2) those the paper or TV station solved because of their ability to use public attention or official pressure. Which group is larger?
3. The following books are recommended for interested students:

   (a) *Government by the States: A History,* by D. S. Halacy, (The Bobbs-Merrill Company, 1973).

   (b) *Governors of Tennessee,* by Margaret Phillips (Pelican, 1978).

16   # State Courts

★★

Most people do not realize it, but it is the more than 1,200 state and local courts in the nation that settle most of our legal disputes. These courts handle millions of cases each year. The news items below show some of the legal problems they deal with.

Castel Found Innocent—A criminal court jury today found Joe Castel innocent of the armed robbery of a Los Angeles jewelry store. Castel had claimed he was at a movie at the time of the robbery. After the decision, Castel's lawyer said, "The state never had enough evidence to prove Joe guilty."

Court Rules for Resort Owners—A state court today ordered the Drake Chemical Company to stop dumping chemical waste into nearby Moon Lake. The dispute started when resort owners on the lake took the company to court. They claimed that if the dumping continued, the lake would be ruined and they would lose all their business.

State Supreme Court Overturned Suspension Case—The state supreme court ruled today that a lower court decision allowing teachers to suspend students without a hearing violated the state constitution. In other action, the court agreed to review a lower court decision that allowed state police to search a person's house without a warrant. Lawyers for the state say the case involves the Fourth Amendment to the United States Constitution.

The news flashes show that state courts handle cases like Joe Castel's, in which a crime has taken place. State courts settle lawsuits between individuals, such as the dispute between the resort owners on Moon Lake and the chemical company. Some state courts review the meaning of the state constitution, as this one did when it declared teachers could not suspend students without a hearing. Finally, in handling cases state courts may also have to interpret the federal Constitution. In this chapter you will learn more about state courts as you read:

Discuss: What kind of cases are handled in state courts?

1/State Court Systems
2/Criminal and Civil Cases
3/Lawyers
Case Study: You Be the Jury

1/State Court Systems

Each state constitution provides for a state court system. However, the state legislatures spell out the courts' actual organization.

Organization of State Courts

All states have at least four kinds of courts: (1) lower or local courts, (2) general trial courts, (3) appellate courts, and (4) a state supreme court. The chart on page 339 shows how most state court systems are organized.

Discuss: What is each type of court like?

Lower Courts. The lower courts in most states hear only special cases. Usually these are minor violations of state law or lawsuits involving small amounts of money. Some of these courts hear only cases involving traffic violations and are called traffic courts.

General Trial Courts. The job of the general trial courts is to handle all major criminal and civil cases. **Criminal cases** always involve the government as one party to the dispute. The other party is an individual accused of crime. In state courts, the criminal cases involve the breaking of state or local laws. The least

serious crimes are called **misdemeanors.** Driving through a red light is a misdemeanor. More serious crimes are called **felonies.** Armed robbery and murder are felonies. Each state has a criminal code that says what acts are which kinds of crimes and sets out the punishments for them.

Civil cases involve disputes between people over their legal rights and duties. Civil cases often involve a dispute over property, money, or damages of some kind. For example, suppose you buy a bottle of soda pop. When you start to open it, the bottle explodes and injures your eye. You ask the soft-drink company to pay you $50,000 in damages. You claim the injury was their fault. They do not believe you and refuse to pay anything. So, you go into court to try to collect from them. In other words, you sue them. This is a civil case.

Appellate Courts. These courts hear appeals from trial courts. Appeals are made when lawyers think the law was not correctly applied in the original trial, or if they believe illegal procedures were used. Suppose a judge would not allow an important witness to testify, and the accused person was found guilty. His or her lawyer might appeal the case hoping the appeals court judge would agree that the witness's testimony was allowable.

State Supreme Court. This is the highest court in the state. It is made up of three to nine judges. The state supreme court reviews cases appealed from general trial courts and the appellate courts. Unless a case involves some aspect of the United States Constitution, there is no further appeal from the decision of a state supreme court. It is final.

Note: Have students find out how many judges your state supreme court has.

State Courts Are Crowded

Even though many new courts have been set up over the years, cases move slowly. In big cities, criminal **defendants** (people accused of crimes) often must wait a year or more for their cases to be heard. In Massachusetts in 1969, a man charged wtih armed robbery was set free because the state had failed to try his case within the two-year limit the state constitution set.

Long delays have caused riots. One hot August in 1970, around 4,500 prisoners in New York City's five largest jails rioted. The prisoners had many complaints. One of the most important was the long delay in city courts. Many of these prisoners were too poor to afford bail. They were in jail waiting their trials. They had not been found guilty yet. Even so, most had been in jail about ninety days. Some had been waiting six months. Others a year. One prisoner, charged with murder, had been waiting three years for a trial.

Why does it take so long? There are four reasons. First is the huge number of cases that go through state courts. Recently the Florida Supreme Court heard about 1,000 cases a year. Florida Circuit Courts deal with almost 100,000 cases every year. Other trial courts in Florida handle over 400,000 cases in a typical year.

Second, often there are not enough judges. In New York City, for example, each judge may face as many as 200 serious criminal cases each day.

Third, most states do not spend enough money to hire enough clerks, secretaries, and other people to help judges do their work.

Discuss: Why are there long delays in courts?

ORGANIZATION OF STATE COURTS

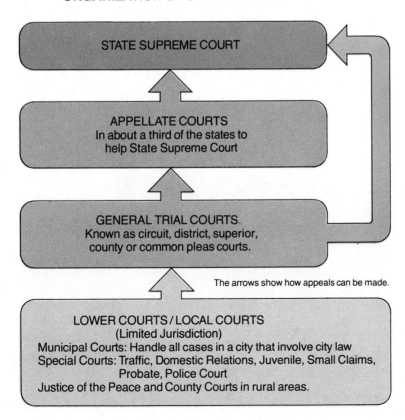

STATE SUPREME COURT

APPELLATE COURTS
In about a third of the states to help State Supreme Court

GENERAL TRIAL COURTS.
Known as circuit, district, superior, county or common pleas courts.

The arrows show how appeals can be made.

LOWER COURTS / LOCAL COURTS
(Limited Jurisdiction)
Municipal Courts: Handle all cases in a city that involve city law
Special Courts: Traffic, Domestic Relations, Juvenile, Small Claims, Probate, Police Court
Justice of the Peace and County Courts in rural areas.

Fourth, there are many steps to follow in legal cases. Many state court systems are not set up to help cases move smoothly and quickly. In some states the defendant is first brought before a judge to plead "guilty" or "not guilty." In another step, a trial date is set. The trial itself is another step. Defendants, lawyers, police and witnesses must return to court six to ten times before a case is completed.

Another thing that causes delays is the number of cases in which lawyers ask for a **continuance.** When a lawyer is not ready to defend a case, he or she goes into court and asks to have the trial date changed. Most judges allow a case to be continued once or twice. Many allow it to be delayed more often than that. Continuances are meant to give lawyers time to gather evidence or prepare a defense. Some lawyers use them to discourage witnesses.

Small Claims Courts

Today every state has small claims courts. These were developed as one answer to overcrowding in other state courts. To ease the workload, small claims courts handle cases involving small amounts of money—a few hundred dollars at most. No lawyers are needed. Suing someone is fairly simple in such courts. See Skills for Life on page 342 for tips on how to use a small claims court.

Although the number of seats is limited, trials are public. What happens in court is a matter of public record.

Section Review

Vocabulary: civil case, continuance, criminal case, defendant, felony, misdemeanor.

Reviewing the Main Ideas

1. List the four types of state courts and describe their jobs.
2. Why are state courts so crowded?
3. In what ways are small claims courts different from other courts?

Skill Building

Which of the following examples would be civil cases and which would be criminal cases?

1. Hal takes a sweater from a local clothing store. As he leaves the store, he is stopped. He is later arrested.
2. Al received a bill from the dentist but refused to pay. He says the dentist charged too much. The dentist disagrees and demands payment. The dentist sues Al.
3. A passenger on a Chicago to Los Angeles flight hijacks the plane. She is caught and brought to trial.
4. Maria starts building a garage on her property. Bob claims part of the garage will be on his land. Maria disagrees. Bob asks a court to stop Maria from finishing the garage.

Using Small Claims Courts

Small claims courts have worked for many people. If you have a problem with a product you bought, if you think someone has cheated you, or if someone owes you money, you can file a suit in the small claims court in your area. You do not need a lawyer.

Suppose that on May 24, 1979, you went to Happy Harry's House of Electronics on West Main Street. There you bought a used color TV for $200. The salesperson told you the TV had been "completely rebuilt and checked out." When you tried it in the store, it worked fine. A big sign in Happy Harry's window said: "Everything We Sell Is Guaranteed for Free."

Your TV worked well the first week. Then the picture turned a bright orange and kept flipping upside down. The only way you could watch your favorite shows was standing on your head wearing sunglasses!

You asked Happy Harry's to fix the TV. They refused because you didn't buy a "TV Service Contract" for $40 from them. It cost you $85 to get the TV fixed at ACME TV Repair. You sent a copy of the $85 bill to Happy Harry's. They refused to pay it. You decide to sue in small claims court. You follow these guidelines.

Guideline 1: Find the right court and the correct procedures. There may be more than one small claims court in your area. Call the clerk of the small claims court closest to you. (Look under "courts" or "government services" in the phone book.)

Ask how and where to file a small claims suit. The clerk's office will want to know where you live, where the person you want to sue lives, where the problem happened, and other information. It is very important to know what the local rules are and to make sure you are dealing with the right court.

Guideline 2: Get all names and addresses straight. Make sure you have the proper name and legal address of the party you want to sue. If the business or organization you are suing is a corporation, call or write the Secretary of State in your state to get the exact corporate name. If the business is not incorporated, you must get the name of the owner or owners.

In this case, you learn that Happy Harry's is incorporated as Harry Hooplesnake Electronics, Inc., 246 West Main Street.

Guideline 3: Get your papers and ideas together. These would be the receipt for $200, to prove you bought the television from Happy Harry's, and the $85 receipt for having the television repaired. The receipts and your testimony are the evidence that support your claim.

Plan your testimony. Because you are bringing suit, it is your job to convince the judge you have a valid claim. But do not go into court thinking you need to be persuasive like the lawyers you have seen on TV shows. Explain your problem in a short, simple statement. Tell what happened and exactly why you believe you have a claim.

Guideline 4: Be at court early. You must not miss your court date. If you're not there but Harry is, the case will be dismissed.

It is a good idea to get to court early. Many cases will be scheduled for every hour. You may be at court for at least several hours. Use your waiting time. Ask people who work in the

342

court anything you want to know about how things work. Listen carefully to other cases so you can learn how the court operates. Get to feel at home. When it is your turn, you want to be as relaxed as possible.

When you file your claim with the clerk's office, you may be asked to fill out a form like the one here and pay a small filing fee. You will need to know a few special terms. You are the *plaintiff*. The person you are suing is the *defendant*. (Defendants have to defend themselves against the suit.) The word *alleged* means "supposed"; yours is an alleged debt because it hasn't been proved yet.

UNITED COUNTY MUNICIPAL COURT
SMALL CLAIMS DIVISION

PLAINTIFF'S STATEMENT

PLEASE PRINT OR TYPE   Date: _____

1. PLAINTIFF (Your name): _____
   ADDRESS (Street and City): _____
   _____ PHONE: _____

2. DEFENDANT (Name of the individual(s) or corporation you
   wish to sue): _____
   ADDRESS (Defendant's residence): _____
   _____ PHONE: _____

3. AMOUNT OF MONEY INVOLVED (Maximum amount is $300.00): _____

4. FACTS (Your complaint): _____
   _____
   _____
   _____

5. DATES (When occasion for complaint occurred): _____
   _____

6. PLACE(S) (Where occasion for complaint occurred): _____
   _____

7. Have you made a demand on the defendant for performance? Yes___ No___
   Have you made such a demand in writing? Yes___ No___

PLEASE RETURN THIS FORM TO THE RECEPTIONIST. DO NOT WRITE BELOW

CONCILIATION DATA

NOTIFY: Plaintiff _____   Defendant _____   Other _____
CLAIM: _____
TIME _____, _____. M. on _____, _____ _____, _____, 19 _____
REMARKS: _____
_____

2/Criminal and Civil Cases

How do state courts handle criminal and civil cases? This section tells what actually happens in court.

Criminal Cases from Arrest to Sentencing

Criminal cases begin with the arrest of a suspect. If the crime is a misdemeanor, the accused is simply brought before a judge. The judge listens to the evidence, decides whether the accused is guilty or innocent, and what penalty to hand out. If a felony is involved, there are many more steps.

Preliminary Hearing. Whenever the arrest takes place, the suspect must be brought before a judge as quickly as possible to hear why he or she is being held. The judge decides whether the person should be released or be "held to answer." At this time, bail may be required. Sometimes a person is released on his or her "own recognizance." This happens when the judge decides that a person is a good risk to return to court for the trial. He or she is released without having to post bail.

A lawyer checks over the facts of the case with her client.

Indictment. After the preliminary hearing, the prosecutor must bring a formal charge called an indictment [in dīt′ mənt] against the accused. In some states, a grand jury of from six to twenty-three persons hears evidence and decides whether the person should be indicted and brought to trial.

Arraignment. After indictment, the accused comes before a judge. The charge is read and the judge asks, "guilty or not guilty?" This step is called the arraignment [ə rān′ mənt]. If the person pleads guilty, the judge pronounces sentence.

Trial. If the accused pleads innocent, then the case goes to trial, usually before a jury. Defense and prosecuting attorneys choose jurors from a large group of people. They try to avoid seating any juror who might be unfavorable to their side. Both lawyers can turn down a certain number of would-be jurors without saying why.

Once a jury is chosen, the prosecutor presents the case against the accused. Witnesses are called, sworn in, and questioned. They may be cross-examined by the other side. Next the defense presents its case. Then the attorneys for both sides sum up their arguments.

Before the jury goes out to arrive at a verdict, the judge gives them instructions in what the law is in this case. Then the jury retires to reach a "guilty" or "innocent" verdict. The vote must be unanimous.

If the verdict is guilty, the judge must decide on a sentence. Usually the law sets minimum and maximum penalties, and the judge chooses a sentence within that range. He or she may choose to suspend the sentence. This means the person does not have to pay any penalty. Usually a person who gets a suspended sentence has never been in trouble with the law before.

Plea Bargaining. Most criminal cases in state courts today do not go through all the steps you have just read about. In fact, 90 percent of all criminal cases never come to trial. Instead, these cases are settled by **plea bargaining.** In plea bargaining, the prosecutor, the defense lawyer, and the police work out an agreement. In many courts, the judge is also a part of the process.

How does it work? Sam Carver was charged with armed robbery. If Carver was found guilty, he could be sentenced to up to twenty years in prison. The prosecutor had hundreds of cases

Note: Students may be able to find examples of cases where juries are being selected. Discuss the problems involved.

Discuss: What is the reason for each step in a criminal case?

to deal with. He thought the evidence showed that Carver was clearly guilty. To avoid the time and money involved in a trial, the prosecutor would agree to reduce the charge to unarmed robbery if Carver would agree to give up his right to a trial and plead guilty to this lesser charge. The lesser charge carries a much lighter sentence. So Sam Carver agreed to plead guilty and was sentenced to ninety days in jail.

People have widely differing views about plea bargaining. Here are the views of two people who are against it:

1. "In the United States, people are supposed to be considered innocent until proven guilty in a fair trial. Plea bargaining treats people as if they were already proven guilty. It encourages people to give up their right to a trial."

2. "It's not a good idea because it lets real criminals get off lightly. People who fully deserve to spend twenty years in jail are back on the streets inside a year. No wonder there's so much crime!"

Here are two opposite views:

3. "The system works well. It gives the defendant a chance to save himself. It allows him to bargain with the court to get a fair break, even if he can't afford a fancy lawyer."

4. "Like it or not, plea bargaining is necessary. If every person charged with a crime were given a full-scale trial, we would need thousands more judges and courts."

The Supreme Court has ruled that plea bargaining is constitutional. That means states who want to do away with it must pass laws making it illegal. Chief Justice Warren Burger has said he believes that when done properly and fairly, plea bargaining is necessary and should be encouraged.

Note: Students may be able to add other arguments for and against plea bargaining.

Civil Cases

Civil cases settle disputes between parties. There are two kinds, lawsuits and equity cases. In a lawsuit, one party believes it has suffered damages at the hands of the other. In an **equity suit,** a person or group of persons is trying to stop some action before it suffers any damages. The news story about the resort owners on Moon Lake at the beginning of the chapter told about an equity suit.

A judge makes the decision in equity cases. No jury is used. In the Moon Lake case, the lawyer for the resort owners tried to show that they would be harmed if the chemical company continued dumping. The company's lawyer tried to show that this

Discuss: How are lawsuits and equity suits the same? How do they differ?

346

was not true. The judge listened to the arguments and finally decided in favor of the resort owners.

The judge ordered the company to stop dumping waste into Moon Lake. This order is called an **injunction.** An injunction orders a person or a group to stop doing something that does or might do harm to others.

As the result of an equity suit, a court may order a person or group to *do* something. This order is called a **writ of mandamus.** For example, Mary, a good tennis player, wants to play on the high-school team. School rules do not allow girls on this team. So Mary goes to court to get a writ of mandamus that forces the school authorities to let her try out for the team.

Note: Have news articles on examples of local court cases that involve a writ of mandamus.

Like criminal cases, a great many civil cases do not end in a trial. Going through a trial is costly and time-consuming. Often the threat of a suit makes both parties work out a deal with each other. For example, Alice Moy suffered a back injury after a traffic accident. She hired a lawyer. Her lawyer contacted the insurance company of the driver of the car that hit Alice. The lawyer threatened to sue the company for $100 thousand. After much bargaining back and forth, Alice's lawyer agreed not to sue if the insurance company paid Alice $10 thousand. So the case was settled out of court.

Section Review

Vocabulary: arraignment, equity suit, indictment, injunction, plea bargaining, preliminary hearing, writ of mandamus.

Reviewing the Main Ideas
1. List and describe the steps in a criminal case.
2. How are equity suits and lawsuits alike? How are they different?

Skill Building
Use decision-making skills to make a judgment about plea bargaining by answering these questions:
1. Is plea bargaining practical?
2. How might plea bargaining affect you?
3. How might it affect others, such as judges, prosecutors, criminals, families of criminals, taxpayers, and citizens who live in high crime areas?
4. Is plea bargaining fair?

Main Ideas
1. pp. 344–345
2. p. 346
Skill Building
1. –4. Answers will vary; they should reflect use of decision-making skills taught on pp. 28–30.

3/Lawyers

Lawyers are important decision makers in the court system. If you should ever find yourself in court, you would be in front of a judge for a short time. You would, however, spend a lot more time with your lawyer.

Lawyers are experts in the legal system. A lawyer's job is protecting, negotiating, and giving advice. In general, you need a lawyer when you are in a fight. You need a lawyer when you are trying to make a business deal, or when you have to be sure exactly where you stand. You need a lawyer when you are thinking of doing something that might cause you trouble.

As life in America gets more complicated, more and more people may find they need a lawyer. You cannot escape lawyers by reading books about law. And it can be very risky to take legal advice from someone who is not a lawyer.

Guidelines for Deciding You Need a Lawyer

Until you are age 18 or older, you will probably not need to call a lawyer for help. Your family may need one from time to time. And throughout your lifetime there are likely to be a number of times when the services of a lawyer will be needed. The following guidelines can't cover every occasion. But they can help you and your family decide about whether or not to get legal help. *You need a lawyer when:*

You're Charged with a Crime. You need legal help immediately. Get a lawyer to help you. You may be completely innocent. But the police don't know that. It is their job to be suspicious. In addition, they may have violated a constitutional right in some way.

You Need a Will. A **will** is a legal document that explains what will happen to all your things when you die. What if there is not a will when you die? Your things will be distributed according to state law. This could mean that your property and money is divided up in ways you wouldn't like.

You Buy a House or Land. A lawyer can make sure you are protected from problems you are not aware of. For example, you could buy land and discover years later that someone else claimed to own it.

You're Bankrupt. Not a pleasant thought, but it can happen. If you really can't pay your bills, and can see no way of ever paying them, you probably should see a lawyer. A lawyer can help complete forms that declare you legally bankrupt. This can help protect you from the people to whom you owe money.

Sometimes the decision about getting a lawyer is more difficult. *You* may *need a lawyer when:*

You're Hurt in a Car Accident or by a Product. You learned that civil cases for personal injury may take years to settle in court. If you are not badly hurt, it may be better to settle directly with an insurance company or the maker of the product.

Most companies will be willing to pay your medical expenses plus a small amount for the pain you suffered. You can collect this yourself and save paying a lawyer one-third or more of what you collect.

However, if you are crippled or if your ability to do your job is affected or if the injury may stay with you for years, you do need a lawyer. The fact is, a lawyer can help you win damage awards much larger than you can win alone.

You Start Your Own Business. You've saved your money for several years. Now you're ready to start your own hot-dog stand. Or you and a friend put your money together. You are going to start an auto repair business. You should probably see a lawyer.

The victim of an automobile accident may need a lawyer.

It might be a good idea for you to form a corporation. But only a lawyer can tell you. If you have a partner, it is much easier to get things straight at the start than to untangle misunderstandings later. Also, you may need special licenses or permits or tax forms. A lawyer can help you with these.

You Buy Something That Doesn't Work. You may not need a lawyer. Many items have guarantees or warranties. You can usually come to an agreement with the business that sold you the product. Sometimes a call to the Better Business Bureau, Chamber of Commerce, or local newspaper will help. If this product cost less than $500, you may be able to use a small-claims court to solve your problem. If all else fails and you paid a lot of money for something you may need a lawyer.

You Have a Problem with the Government. This is a tricky one. If the government needs your house or land for a new road you need a lawyer. A lawyer can help you get a fair settlement. However, when you are fighting with a government bureaucracy, there are people other than lawyers who may be more helpful.

For example, suppose you have been denied a Medicare payment. You feel your claim is fair. A doctor who supports your case may know people in the local Medicare office. The doctor may be able to get your claim paid faster than any lawyer could. And remember, your state and federal lawmakers may be willing to help. And their help costs no more than a stamp for a letter.

Finding a Lawyer

You decide you need a lawyer. Now how do you find one? There are several ways.

You can ask your friends or neighbors if they know a lawyer. This may be a very good way to find a lawyer. Your friends would be able to tell you how well the lawyer helped them. If their lawyer can't help you, he or she can send you to a lawyer who can.

You can call a **lawyer referral service.** There are lawyer referral services in all 50 states. Most big cities have such a service. Look in the Yellow Pages of a telephone book under "Attorney" or "Lawyer Referral Service." If you can pay for a lawyer, a referral service will give you the names of lawyers who specialize in the kind of problem you have.

Discuss: What do you think might be the first time you would need a lawyer?

Discuss: When do people have need for a lawyer?

Discuss: What is the best way to choose a good lawyer?

350

If you cannot afford a private lawyer, you still may be able to get some help. There are about 700 Legal Aid or Public Defender offices in the United States. To get a phone number look under "Legal Aid" or "Public Defender" in the phone book.

Legal Aid lawyers probably won't be able to give you as much help as a lawyer you paid for yourself. Legal Aid lawyers are usually overworked and not well paid. In big cities, a Legal Aid lawyer may have to handle 1,000 cases each year. And Legal Aid offices often have to turn people away because they have too many cases already. But many Legal Aid lawyers are dedicated and hardworking. They will try to help if they can.

Check your local paper. You may find advertisements for **legal clinics.** This is a place that works on everyday legal problems. Legal clinics are usually best for handling simple legal jobs like writing a standard will. Because these clinics serve large numbers of people they may charge lower fees than a private lawyer. However, you may not get personal service for special problems at a clinic.

Section Review

Vocabulary: lawyer referral service, legal clinic, will.

Reviewing the Main Ideas

1. Explain a situation in which a person would need a lawyer.
2. List three ways to find a lawyer.

Skill Building

Read each of the situations below. Use the guidelines in this section to decide: (1) *Yes,* you would need a lawyer, (2) *Maybe* you would need a lawyer, or (3) *No,* you would not need a lawyer. Write your decisions down with brief notes that explain your reasons.

1. You are in an automobile accident. Your car is smashed but can be fixed. Your back is sore but you can still go to work.
2. Your Social Security check does not come in the mail. You call the local Social Security office. They say they have no record of your name.
3. You are at a noisy party. Some other kids have liquor at the party. Someone complains—the police come and you are arrested.

Main Ideas
1. Answers will vary.
2. pp. 350–351
Skill Building
1. –3. accept reasonable answers that are justified by explanation.

You Be the Jury

Joe Hill left his office for home. As he drove his car out of the parking lot, turning left onto Washington Street, another car collided with his. The other driver was Louise Milton.

Not long afterward, Joe developed back trouble. Ms. Milton's insurance company refused to pay the $100,000 damages Joe's lawyer demanded. It said the accident had been Joe's fault. So Joe's lawyer filed a lawsuit against the company.

The trial opened about two years later before a judge and jury. Joe's lawyer first called Joe's doctor. The doctor testified that the accident had caused the back trouble. Joe's lawyer then questioned Joe:

Q. Will you describe the circumstances of the accident, Mr. Hill?
A. Well, it was raining. I was going home from work. I pulled up to the entrance to the parking lot by my office. I intended to turn left onto Washington Street.
Q. Did you clear yourself?
A. Both ways. There was a car approaching from the left. It had the right turn signal blinking. I assumed it would turn into the lot, so I pulled out. The car collided with mine.

On cross-examination Louise Milton's lawyer questioned Joe:

Q. Have you ever had the experience of a car not turning even though a signal was on?
A. Well, once or twice, I guess.
Q. But you still trust turn signals?
A. I certainly did in this case! They're supposed to indicate a driver's intentions.

She then questioned Louise Milton:

Q. Please explain the circumstances of the accident.
A. I turned right from Bush Road onto Washington to go east. I saw a car waiting at the parking lot entrance. As I approached, it suddenly pulled out and we collided.
Q. Did you apply your brakes?
A. Oh yes, but the distance was short and the road was wet.
Q. Was your right turn signal on?
A. No. I'm sure it was not.
Q. Had you used it when you made a right turn from Bush?
A. Yes. I always use signals when making turns.
Q. And the signal was in good working order?
A. Yes, it was.

Joe's attorney then cross-examined Louise:

Q. Have you ever had a turn signal on and not noticed it?

A. Well, yes. I guess everybody does that some time or other.

Q. Might that have happened on the occasion in question?

A. No. I'm sure not.

Q. Would you agree it was possible that the signal malfunctioned, and because of the weather and so on you didn't notice it was on?

A. Well . . . that could have happened, I suppose. But no, I don't think so.

Q. How fast were you going, Ms. Milton?

A. About twenty-five miles per hour.

Q. Did you check your speedometer?

A. I don't remember doing so. But I'm a cautious driver, and it was raining. I'm sure I was not over the speed limit.

Q. And did you try to avoid the accident?

A. Yes. I braked, but it was too late.

When the testimony was over, the judge instructed the jury as to the facts and the law. The judge said:

"You have heard conflicting testimony here as to the facts in the case. Your task is to decide just what the facts are.

"As to the law, this is a negligence case. *Negligence* is carelessness. It means not taking reasonable care to avoid an accident or to avoid causing harm. According to law, if negligence on the part of one party causes harm or injury to another, the negligent party must make amends for the harm done. Mr. Hill claims that Ms. Milton's negligence caused him injury and he asks $100,000 damages as a result.

"You must decide. If you find that Ms. Milton was indeed negligent, then you must award damages to Mr. Hill. If, on the other hand, you find that Ms. Milton was not negligent, then you must deny the award of damages.

"Ladies and gentlemen of the jury, you may now retire to consider your verdict."

Reviewing the Case Study

Suppose you were a member of the jury. Consider the following questions:

1. How would you vote?
2. How did you arrive at your decision?
3. What role did the lawyers play in this case?
4. Was this a civil or a criminal case?

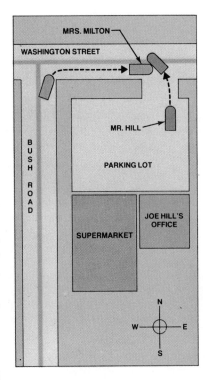

Chapter Sixteen Test and Activities

★★

Vocabulary

Match the following words with their meanings.

1. felony
2. arraignment
3. plea bargaining
4. jury
5. defendant
6. indictment
7. misdemeanor
8. equity suit
9. injunction
10. writ of mandamus

a. a court order to do something
b. a process seeking to prevent harm
c. a serious crime
d. a court order to stop doing something
e. a formal charge of wrongdoing
f. a person accused or sued in a court
g. discussing a reduced charge
h. a minor crime
i. a group of citizens who hear evidence and decide guilt in a trial
j. the step in which a person formally charged with a crime answers "guilty" or "not guilty"

Reviewing Chapter Ideas

1. The four main types of state courts are lower courts, _____ , appellate courts, and the state supreme court.
   a. tax courts
   b. general trial courts
   c. customs courts
   d. federal courts

   Vocabulary
   1. c   4. i   7. h   10. a
   2. j   5. f   8. b
   3. g   6. e   9. d

2. State courts are overcrowded because:
   a. there are not enough judges
   b. states don't spend enough money on courts
   c. there are too many steps in bringing a case to trial
   d. all of the above
3. Number the following steps in a criminal case in the proper order.
   a. sentencing
   b. arraignment
   c. preliminary hearing
   d. presentation of evidence
   e. bail
   f. jury gives a verdict
4. True or false: because of legal requirements, all civil cases eventually come to trial.
5. An equity suit is different from a lawsuit in that _____ .
   a. the government is a party to the case
   b. the party suing has not been damaged yet
   c. a criminal law has been broken
   d. the damages sought are under $500

Using Basic Social Studies Skills

Finding Information

List three ways you could find yourself a lawyer.

Comprehending Information

1. Make up a situation in which a person would try to get a writ of mandamus from a court.
2. Make up a situation in which a person might try to get an injunction from a court.

   Ideas
   1. b   4. F
   2. d   5. b
   3. c, e, b, f, a

★★

Organizing Information

Read over the testimony in the case study. Then list the events that led up to the accident in the order that they happened.

Evaluating Information

You are a member of a jury. The case is a civil case growing out of a two-car accident at a street intersection. Several people are called to testify on how the accident happened. Which person's testimony do you think would be most accurate? Which would be least accurate? Rank the persons on that basis from 1 to 6:

a. policeman called to the scene
b. drivers of the cars
c. a person waiting to cross the street
d. passengers in the cars
e. a person who saw the accident from a block away
f. a person who heard the crash and came out of a store to investigate

Communicating Ideas

Hold a class discussion to discover why members of the class assigned numbers above as they did.

Using Decision-Making Skills

You are accused of grand larceny. In your state this is a theft involving more than $200. It carries a sentence of from three to ten years in prison. At the time of the theft, you were in a movie. But you can find no one who will testify to this. Yet the prosecution has witnesses who will testify that they saw you at the scene of the crime at around the time it was committed. Your attorney says that it is possible to plea-bargain you down to petty larceny if you will plead guilty to that. This crime carries a sentence of from one to three years in prison in your state. Will you accept the offer and plead guilty? Why or why not? What alternatives do you have? What are some of their likely consequences?

Activities

1. Organize a panel discussion on the question of whether judges should be elected or appointed. You can find information on this question in newspapers and articles listed in the *Readers' Guide.*

2. A recent United States Supreme Court decision allows lawyers to advertise. Gather information on the subject from newspapers and from articles listed in the *Readers' Guide* and write an essay upholding or opposing the idea of lawyers advertising.

3. For students who want to know more about our legal system, the following books are recommended:

   (a) *You Can't Eat Peanuts in Church and Other Little-Known Laws,* by Barbara Seuling (Doubleday, 1975).

   (b) *Your Legal Rights as a Minor,* by Robert H. Loeb (Watts, 1978).

   (c) *The Law and You; a handbook for young people,* by Elinor Porter Swiger (Bobbs, 1975).

   (d) *Verdict: The Jury System,* by Morris J. Bloomstein (Dodd, 1972).

   (e) *Crisis in Corrections: The Prison Problem,* by Janet Harris (McGraw, 1973).

Unit Four Test

★★★

Vocabulary

Write *true* if the underlined word or phrase is used correctly. Write *false* if it is not.

1. If state legislators want to be elected again, they should pay attention to the views of their <u>constituents</u>.
2. The United States has a <u>unitary</u> system of government.
3. A governor can use <u>patronage</u> as a political resource.
4. The people in Oregon voted "no" to a state <u>sales tax</u>.
5. <u>Floor leaders</u> help keep order in state courtrooms.
6. In the governor's role of <u>political party leader</u>, the governor may work to get other members of the same party elected.
7. The state's <u>attorney general</u> is the "vice-president" of state government.
8. State agency officials are part of the bureaucratic <u>chain of command</u>.
9. If people in the state have trouble with the <u>bureaucracy</u>, they should elect someone else in the next election.
10. When a governor wants something done, he or she issues a special order called an <u>ombudsman</u>.
11. A <u>civil case</u> is when the crime is not very serious.
12. A <u>felony</u> is a serious crime.
13. If you want a court to make someone stop hurting you, you ask for an <u>injunction</u>.
14. <u>Plea bargaining</u> is a practical solution to overcrowding in state courts.
15. A person guilty of a <u>misdemeanor</u> who had never been in trouble with the law before might get a suspended sentence.

Recalling Information

1. State and federal governments share all of the following powers <u>except</u> _____ .
   a. tax us
   b. set up courts
   c. control health care programs
   d. admit new states
2. Which of the following powers do <u>not</u> belong to state governments?
   a. establish a post office
   b. establish police protection
   c. provide for public health
   d. control education
3. Which of the following services are provided by state government?
   a. schools and grocery stores
   b. police and firefighters
   c. churches and recreation centers
   d. all of the above
4. State legislators can pass laws that regulate all the following <u>except</u> _____ .
   a. jury duty
   b. other states
   c. highway speeds
   d. gambling
5. State legislatures usually have all the following parts <u>except</u> _____ .
   a. a senate
   b. a house of representatives
   c. committees
   d. courts
6. Which of the following influence the decisions a governor makes?
   a. personal values
   b. public opinion
   c. other decision makers
   d. all of the above

Vocabulary

1. T	4. T	7. F	10. F	13. T
2. F	5. F	8. T	11. F	14. T
3. T	6. T	9. F	12. T	15. T

Recalling

1. d	4. b	7. b	10. a
2. a	5. d	8. c	11. d
3. b	6. d	9. F	12. b

7. Which of the following is not a state agency?
   a. board of health
   b. district court
   c. highway commission
   d. state police department

8. Which of the following do not have to do with civil cases?
   a. equity suits
   b. injunction and writ of mandamus
   c. felonies
   d. all of the above

9. True or false: As long as you stay out of trouble, you will never need a lawyer.

10. One of the following ways of getting a lawyer is not as good as the others. Which is it?
    a. pick one from the list of attorneys in the Yellow Pages of the phone book
    b. ask a friend who has used a lawyer
    c. call a Lawyer Referral Service
    d. b and c

11. State governments get money from _____ .
    a. the federal government
    b. state taxes
    c. license fees
    d. all of the above

12. To spend state money, state legislatures must _____ .
    a. amend their constitutions
    b. pass appropriations bills
    c. issue executive orders
    d. ask the national government

13. State legislatures can _____ .
    a. prosecute criminals
    b. set up local governments
    c. appoint ambassadors
    d. none of the above

13. b   16. Vary
14. Vary   17. d
15. Vary   18. d

14. What is the state legislature called in your state?
15. Who are your state legislators?
16. Who is governor of your state?
17. Who influences lawmakers?
    a. the governor
    b. interest groups
    c. individual citizens
    d. all of the above
18. How can you get help dealing with the state bureaucracy?
    a. write a legislator
    b. contact the head of the agency
    c. write your local newspaper
    d. all of the above

Skill Building

1. What are the four guidelines for using a small claims court?
2. Read the graph below to answer these questions.
   a. What does the graph show?
   b. In 1974, what did Texas spend most state money on?
   c. True or false: In 1974, most of the state money went to improve highways.
   d. Does the graph give information to help you judge if Texas spent enough money on state courts?

TEXAS STATE EXPENDITURES IN 1974

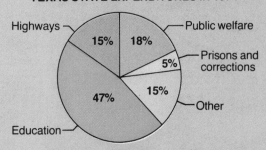

357

Making Decisions in Local Governments

The governments that affect all of us the most are often the ones that are closest to home. Is it safe to walk outside after dark? Are there bad traffic snarls every day at 5 o'clock? Is there a safe place for small children to play outdoors? Can people find employment? Is the city wasting taxpayers' money fighting the county over who has the power to decide about park land? Is it cheaper to buy gasoline in the next county? Is it cheaper to live in another county? The answers to these questions lie in the decisions local government leaders make.

This unit explores the many different local governments we have in the fifty states. You will read what some of these governments are, how they are governed, what services they provide, and what problems they try to solve.

You will learn how local officials deal with state and national officials as well as with officials from nearby local governments.

Mayor Sharon Greene is a good example. Ms. Greene is the mayor of a medium-size city. Recently the city began a project to build bike paths around the city. Mayor Greene worked with national government officials to obtain grants of money from the national government to help build the bike paths. She also worked with state government officials to get permission to build the bike paths next to some state roads. And she bargained with county government officials. County officials wanted some of the new bike paths to go to nearby parks operated by the county.

This Unit also explores how local officials deal with problems facing the cities today. These problems include air and water pollution, crowded streets and highways, and poor housing.

Finally, you will learn that in the United States millions of citizens volunteer their time and efforts to help solve community problems. In a democracy citizens seek to improve community life without government help. Many voluntary groups work to bring services to our communities. Unit 5 covers this aspect of community life as well.

Volunteers help clean the beach after an oil spill.

Discuss: What is local government? How are these people involved?

359

Chapter 17 Local Governments

★★

More than 470,000 people serve as elected officials in local governments. They perform many important services for citizens in cities, towns, counties, and townships across the United States.

Roger Adair has been a county sheriff for ten years. Last year Sheriff Adair and six deputies handled 465 traffic violations, 90 cases of assault, 75 fishing and hunting violations, 69 robberies, and 15 drug violations. "In addition to crime, we deal with lots of other problems," says the sheriff. "This week," he adds with a smile, "we rounded up a bunch of cows that had gotten loose and were blocking the county highway."

Laura Jones is serving her second term on a city council. Recently, the city council had to decide where in the city to build a new trash-burning plant. "Everyone agreed we needed the plant," she recalls, "but no one wanted it in their neighborhood. It was a tough decision."

In addition to elected officials, more than eight million people work for local governments in the United States. These people include clerks, secretaries, construction workers, administrators, and scientists.

Linda Berg, a city sanitation engineer, helps to plan garbage collection services. "And right now," she explains, "I am planning a collection center where people can bring paper, cans, and bottles to be recycled."

Sue Farley is a doctor in a county health department. She wants all children in the county to have physical checkups and the shots that prevent diphtheria, polio, tetanus, and measles.

Such people bring the services of local government directly to citizens.

Discuss: Could any of these people live in your community? Why?

The purpose of this chapter is to introduce local government to you. In the chapter you will read about:

1/Kinds of Local Governments
2/How County Governments Provide Services
3/Paying for Local Government
Case Study: Proposition 13: A Homeowners' Revolt

1/Kinds of Local Governments

Local governments are part of state government. They are created by states to help them carry out laws and provide services. Local governments must operate according to state law. They can do only those jobs authorized by state law or the state constitution.

State government officials influence the decisions of local officials in several ways. They require reports from local governments. They give advice and technical help to local governments. They also issue orders and make rules for local governments. For example, the state can order a local government to build a sewage-treatment plant. They appoint and remove certain local officials. And they can withhold money from local governments if they do not obey state laws or meet state standards.

Local governments are also influenced by officials in the national government. More than one hundred national government agencies supply services to local governments.

The FBI, for example, works with city and county police officers. FBI agents will help local police identify handwriting, fingerprints, tire treads, hairs and fibers, and shoe prints.

What are the main types of local government? Chief units of local government are counties, townships, cities and towns, and

Discuss: How are local governments influenced?

A meeting of the school board in Pleasantville, New York.

special districts. The chart at the left shows how many local governments there are in the United States.

Counties

Each state is divided into parts called counties. In Alaska such units are called **boroughs.** Louisiana calls them **parishes.** The number of counties ranges from three in Delaware and Hawaii to 254 in Texas. Connecticut and Rhode Island have counties but no organized county government. In the other New England states the counties exist chiefly as court districts.

States set up counties to help carry out state law. In the early days it made no sense to try to administer state law from the capital city. Also, from the start, Americans liked the idea of local control. They set up county courts with sheriff, prosecuting attorney, and judge to deal with people breaking state laws or having legal disputes. Other county officials took care of such state duties as issuing marriage licenses, keeping records of property deeds, and collecting taxes.

Over the years the states took on more and more activities. Often the state law would direct the counties to handle the program. Thus aid to poor people might be handled by a county welfare department.

Townships

In twenty states, the counties are divided into townships to handle certain jobs. In horse-and-buggy days even the county seat was too far for getting everyday needs attended to. Thus a township constable and a justice of the peace took care of small problems.

In some states today this unit of local government is losing ground. Most of its jobs have been taken over by other local units, especially the county. But in other places, township government is very much alive.

Municipalities

Cities, towns, villages, and many suburbs are municipalities. This means they operate under a **municipal charter** granted by the state. The charter is a kind of constitution. It tells what form of government the community will have.

Why do states create municipalities when there are already counties (and sometimes townships) to provide public services? The answer is that where many people are crowded close to-

Discuss: What are they called in your state? How many are there?

LOCAL GOVERNMENTS IN THE UNITED STATES

Government	Number
National	**1**
State	**50**
County	3,044
Cities & Suburbs	18,517
Townships & Towns	16,991
Special Districts	23,885
School Districts	15,781
Total	**78,269**

gether in an area they need more services than rural people need. City residents often want extra police protection, fire fighting, garbage collection, public water supply, sewage disposal, parks, playgrounds, libraries, and museums.

When a community reaches a certain size, state governments usually permit it to become a municipality. The city, town, suburb, or village can then make some laws for local use and provide services beyond those required by the state.

Discuss: Why is each unit of local government important? What is the role of each local government unit in your state?

Special Districts

A fourth kind of local government is the special district. It is organized to supply the people of a given area with one or a few special services. See the chart on page 364 for examples of special districts.

The school district is a kind of special district. It usually has the same boundaries as some other local government: county, township, or city. In some places, one or more cities in the county each has its own school district, and the rest of the county makes up another school district. In another case, three or four townships may each have its own school district for operating elementary schools. But the townships set up a separate district to operate a consolidated high school.

Over the past twenty years the number of school districts has dropped sharply because of school consolidations. But there has been a big rise in the number of other special districts. One

Note: Have maps of your state's local government units available. Include a school districts map.

Sewage treatment plant.

363

Discuss: How do the
special districts in your
area compare to those in
the chart below?

Discuss: How is decision
making for special districts
handled where you live?

STATE SPECIAL SERVICE DISTRICTS

Many states set aside particular geographic areas in which they administer a single service. This list includes some of the most common districts.

Air Pollution Control	Port Authority
Alcohol Rehabilitation	Recreation
Ambulance Service	Sanitation
Animal Control	School
Fire Service	Sewer Service
Flood Control	Soil Conservation
Forest Preserve	Street Lighting
Hospital	Transportation
Mental Health	Authority
Mosquito Abatement	Water Pollution
Noise Abatement	Control
Parks	Water Supply

reason is that within a special district, a service can be given only to an area that needs and wants it. Another reason is that local units such as cities or counties can support a service jointly that would be too costly if each had its own department. A third reason is that state law often puts a limit on the amount a local government may tax and borrow. If a city or county is near this limit, people may ask the state to set up a special district to raise money and pay for some needed service.

Decision making for a special district is usually in the hands of a board of three to five members. They make policy, set the tax rate needed to support the service, borrow money, and hire people to run the program.

Section Review

Vocabulary: borough, county, municipal charter, municipality, parish, special district, township.

Reviewing the Main Ideas

1. Give at least three ways that state government officials influence the decisions of local officials.
2. How are local governments affected by the national government?
3. What are four kinds of local governments?

Skill Building

1. Why does a state set up special districts to offer services?
2. How many local governments affect your daily life? Name them.

Main Ideas
1. p. 361
2. p. 361
3. counties, townships,
municipalities, special districts
Skill Building
1. p. 363–364
2. Answers will vary.

2/How County Governments Provide Services

Citizens get more services from local governments than from any other governing unit. This means that the government decisions that affect your daily life are most often made by people close by.

How are local government services provided and who makes the decisions? First we will look at local government in action by visiting a typical county. Second, we will see how local governments are facing the problem of providing services in growing urban areas.

A Visit to Franklin County

Half the states in the nation have a county named after Benjamin Franklin. Franklin is a very popular name for a county. The largest Franklin County is in Ohio. It has more than 800 thousand people living in it. Nebraska's Franklin County is the smallest with 45 hundred people. Most have a population between 10 thousand and 40 thousand—a typical size for American counties. Farming is likely to be a chief source of income in many of the Franklin counties.

Discuss: What size is your county? What is its population? Compare the county you live in and Franklin County.

Discuss: What are the roles of elected officials in local government?

State law says what officials a county shall have and what their powers and duties are. The Franklin County we will visit is governed by a board of five commissioners. They are elected by voters in the county.

The Board of Commissioners. The Franklin County board acts as both legislature and executive. As a legislative body, the board levies taxes, votes how money will be spent, and borrows money—all subject to state limits. Some states let counties pass local laws, called **ordinances.** For example, a board might pass ordinances about waste disposal, land use, or public health. The board may also have power to issue licenses for such things as drive-in movies, eating places, junkyards, and the like.

As an executive body, the county board sees that various state and county programs are put into effect. In most cases the board has the power to appoint certain other county officials and to hire county workers.

During a regular Franklin County board meeting, the members may spend some time going over next year's budget. They might hear a report on plans for the upcoming county fair. At tonight's meeting they appoint a new member to the Board of Health. They approve plans for building an addition to the county nursing home. And they act on requests for road repair.

In most counties, the voters also select six to twelve other county officers. Let's tour the Franklin County Court House and see how some of them bring services to the citizens of the county.

County Judge. Judge Sheila McNabb is winding up a divorce case. This week she has handled three other civil cases. Friday she'll preside at a trial of three persons charged with auto theft. In addition to handling adult criminal cases, McNabb is judge of the juvenile court. A larger county might have a separate person holding this office. In a juvenile court, young offenders get special treatment different from a formal criminal trial.

Prosecuting Attorney. The office of Prosecutor Wayne Bender is next to the judge's chambers. Bender brings formal charges against persons accused of crime. In court, he presents evidence to get such persons convicted.

Bender is also county attorney, which is a separate job in some counties. He gives legal advice to other county officials. He also represents the county whenever it is involved in a court case.

DIRECTORY

FIRST FLOOR

ASSESSOR	EAST HALL
RECORDER	EAST "
SHERIFF OFFICE	EAST "
STATE PROBATION OFFICER	EAST "
AUDITOR	SOUTH "
COLLECTOR	SOUTH "
TREASURER	SOUTH "
COUNTY COURT	WEST HALL
COUNTY CLERK	WEST "
PUBLIC ADMINISTRATOR	WEST "
PROBATE COURT	WEST "
PROSECUTING ATTORNEY	NORTH "
MAGISTRATE SECOND DIST.	NORTH "
MENS REST ROOM	NORTH "

SECOND FLOOR

CIRCUIT CLERK	WEST HALL
CIRCUIT COURT NO.3	WEST "
CIRCUIT COURT NO.1	SOUTH SIDE
CIRCUIT COURT NO.2	EAST HALL
COURT REPORTER NO.2	EAST "
JUDGES CHAMBERS NO.1&2	EAST "
JURY ROOM	NORTH HALL
JUVENILE OFFICE	NORTH "
MENS REST ROOM	NORTH "
LADIES REST ROOM	NORTH "
JUDGES CHAMBERS NO.3	WEST "

BASEMENT

MAGISTRATE FIRST DIST.	EAST HALL
HEALTH UNIT	EAST "
SUPT. OF SCHOOLS	EAST "
BOILER ROOM	NORTH "
COUNTY HIGHWAY ENGINEER	SOUTH HALL
STATE VETERANS OFFICE	SOUTH "
STATE HIGHWAY ENGINEERS	WEST "

Sheriff. Sheriff Roger Adair and his deputies are the county police force. They patrol areas not covered by city police. The sheriff is in charge of the county jail. Adair is also an officer of the court. He delivers court orders. For instance, recently the Brown Hotel won an injunction from the county court. The court ordered the Hanson Construction Company to stop drilling in the lot next door after ten at night. Adair delivered the injunction to Mr. Hanson and got his signature on a receipt.

Coroner. From time to time Dr. Elaine Lydon, the county coroner, gets a call to look into a death if the cause is unknown or foul play is suspected. Lydon works closely with Bender to get the facts on murders and suicides. Then she presents the evidence before a jury to get a decision about the cause of death— murder, suicide, or death by natural causes. In some states this job is done by an appointed medical examiner or the prosecuting attorney.

Treasurer, Auditor, and Assessor. As we go to Treasurer Edgar Cash's office, we see a few people in line to pay their property tax bills. He deposits county income in selected banks and writes checks when money is to be paid out. Before writing any checks, he must have auditor Charles King's approval. To protect against misuse of public money the auditor examines and approves all claims for payment. About a third of the states have county auditors.

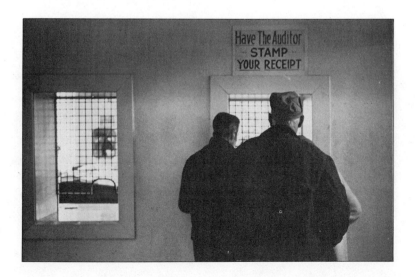

Assessor Jim Drummey's job is to keep track of the value of all property on which property taxes are levied. His office prepares the tax bills.

Clerk and Recorder. As county clerk, Ann Vogel holds one of the top jobs in Franklin County. She is clerk of the county court, keeping all court records. She also serves as secretary for the county board. Clerk Vogel is also chief election officer in charge of registering voters, printing and distributing ballots, and setting up polling places. In addition she issues various licenses and keeps records of births, deaths, marriages, and divorces.

County Recorder Martha Alexander keeps public records of the sale and transfer of real estate. In some states her title would be Register of Deeds.

Appointed Boards and Officials. Other officials in Franklin County are not elected. They get their jobs through the state civil service system or are appointed by the governor, state legislature, or state agency heads. The head of the county board of health and the superintendent of the county highway department are two examples.

In some places an official county surveyor conducts land surveys and determines boundary lines. A county engineer may supervise the building of roads and bridges. In Franklin County, the commissioners simply hire experts for these jobs on a part-time basis.

Discuss: What are the roles of appointed officials in local government?

The county clerk keeps the court records.

Like most counties, Franklin County has a county agricultural agent and a home demonstration agent to give farm people expert advice and to help with 4-H Club work. They are part of the federal-state Agricultural Extension Service.

Providing Services in Urban Counties

Seven out of every ten Americans today live in an **urban area.** The Census Bureau calls cities, suburbs, and all other towns with a population of 25 hundred or more urban areas.

Note: Have students examine a state population map if available. Have them locate urban areas.

People have moved steadily from rural to urban areas. This has meant the growth of urban areas in counties which used to be mostly rural. For example, Howard County, Maryland, had a whopping 70 percent increase in population from 1960 to 1970. Johnson County, Iowa, had a large, but more typical, 34 percent increase in people from 1960 to 1970.

The urban areas in some counties have expanded to the county boundaries. For example, Nashville, Tennessee, just about fills Davidson County with more than 500 thousand people. Some urban areas spill over into two or three counties. Kansas City lies in two states—Missouri and Kansas. The urban area around New York City spreads from the state of New York to parts of New Jersey and Connecticut.

Urban growth has made it hard for local governments to provide services effectively. Within one urban area there may be one large city, several suburbs and parts of two counties, each with its own local government. The entire area, tied together with a network of roads and commuter trains, has the same needs for government services. There can be waste and inefficiency when too many local government units are trying to do the same things.

One answer to the problems of urban counties has been for several communities to cooperate in setting up a special district for one service or another. However, some people believe that special districts merely add to the confusion. They urge **consolidation** to solve the problem of too many local governments in urban counties.

City-County Consolidation. When governments consolidate, they put their different departments together and become just one government. In recent years, several urban areas have consolidated their city and county governments into one. Some examples are the city of Jacksonville and Duvall County, Florida, in 1967; the city of Indianapolis and Marion County, Indiana, in 1969; Carson City and Ormsby County, Nevada, in 1969; the city of Nashville and Davidson County, Tennessee, in 1962; and the city of Lexington and Fayette County, Kentucky, in 1972.

Merging Services. Another way to get some unity in city-county government is to merge only certain public services. For example, the city and county might merge their public health boards or their air pollution control boards. But the governments would not otherwise be merged.

The city of Rochester and Monroe County, New York, have merged to provide nineteen public services. However, the city and county governments are still separate.

Buying Services. Another way to end overlapping is for one unit of government to contract with another to buy a certain service. For example, suburbs may ask the city to provide fire protection. A contract will be made to pay the city for fire protection. Since 1954, Los Angeles County has provided various services to communities by contract.

Section Review

Vocabulary: consolidation, ordinance, urban area.

Reviewing the Main Ideas

1. What official would handle each of the following matters in Franklin County?
   a. a complaint about a tax bill
   b. an application for a marriage license
   c. paying a bill for painting the courthouse
   d. deciding what to do with three youths who admit to vandalism
   e. investigating the death of a body found in the woods
2. What kinds of government problems are caused by urban growth?

Skill Building

1. Name three services which city and county governments might merge to provide.
2. Name three services one government might buy from another.

3/Paying for Local Government

The services provided by local governments cost a lot of money. Recently, local governments spent more than $113 billion a year. Where does the money come from?

Local governments get most money from the **property tax.** They also get money from the national and state governments. And they receive some money from non-tax sources such as parking meters and vehicle stickers.

With few exceptions, local governments have no power to tax on their own. If a city finds its property tax does not bring in enough money, city council members cannot decide to put a tax on liquor sold in the city or to have a city income tax. They must ask the state legislature to let them add a new tax.

Discuss: How do local governments get the money they need? How does your community get the money it needs?

Property Taxes

About 84% of all local tax revenue comes from the property tax. This is a tax on the value of the property a person or business owns. The usual items on which people pay property tax are land, houses, and other buildings. In some states, people also pay a property tax on such things as cars and boats.

The property tax is usually paid to the county treasurer and then given to the various units of local governments. Property owners pay the property tax directly. Others pay it indirectly. Renters pay it as part of the rent, and businesses pass on the cost of property taxes in the prices they charge to customers.

COOK COUNTY COLLECTOR
118 N. CLARK STREET   1500 MAYBROOK SQUARE
CHICAGO, ILLINOIS 60602   MAYWOOD, ILLINOIS 60153
HOURS 9 AM TO 5 PM MONDAY THRU FRIDAY

REAL ESTATE TAX BILL — 1977

| VOLUME 86 | PERMANENT REAL ESTATE INDEX NUMBER 09-07-219-037-0000 | TOWN 22026 MAINE |
| ASSESSED VALUATION 8,058 | EQUALIZED VALUATION 11,404 | |

RATE	AMOUNT OF TAX	TAXING AGENCIES
2.448	279.17	SCHOOL DISTRICT C E #62
		NORTH SUBURBAN MASS TRANSIT DIST
		DES PLAINES MASS TRANSIT DISTRICT
.958	109.25	CITY OF DES PLAINES
.325	37.06	DES PLAINES PARK DISTRICT
.257	29.31	COMMUNITY COLLEGE 535
2.496	284.64	MAINE TOWNSHIP HIGH SCHOOL #207
.016	1.82	NORTHWEST MOSQUITO ABATEMENT DISTRICT
.534	60.90	METROPOLITAN SANITARY DIST OF GREATER CHGO
.012	1.37	GENERAL ASSISTANCE MAINE TOWNSHIP
.034	3.88	ROAD & BRIDGE MAINE TOWNSHIP
.026	2.97	TOWNSHIP OF MAINE
.022	2.51	SUBURBAN T B SANITARIUM
.106	12.09	FOREST PRESERVE DISTRICT OF COOK COUNTY
.401	45.73	COUNTY OF COOK
.203	23.15	HOSPITAL GOVERNING COMMISSION
7.838	893.85	TOTAL 1977 TAX

DO NOT DETACH

A property tax bill shows the portions of the tax that go to different governing bodies.

Other Taxes

The need for more money has led local governments to look for new ways to get money beyond the property tax. States have allowed large cities to tax all kinds of things. If you take a look at a phone bill or bill for gas or electricity, you are likely to see a charge for taxes. This kind of tax is a utility tax. Some cities have city sales taxes—another half percent or so on top of the state sales tax. Cities often tax visitors and tourists. New York and Atlantic City, for example, have a hotel room tax. And Mount Clemens, Michigan, a resort center, taxes every mineral bath taken within the city limits.

State and National Money

State governments prefer to pass money on to local governments rather than letting them create their own taxes. States give money to local governments through **grants** and **shared taxes.** A grant is a direct payment from the state to the local government. Shared taxes means the state creates and collects a tax. Then the state shares part of the revenue from that tax with local governments in the state. The amount each local government gets depends on how much tax is collected. State taxes on gasoline, automobiles, liquor, and income are most often shared with local governments.

Local governments also get money directly from the national government. The amount of national government aid to local governments has been small but is growing. Recently the national government has given more than $11 billion a year directly to local governments.

Money from the national government comes from the federal income tax paid by citizens and businesses. In the national budget, the money given to local governments is called **revenue sharing** and **grants-in-aid.** Grants are usually given for a specific job, like building a health clinic, that national government decision-makers think is important. Grants have become one way these officials influence the decisions of local government leaders.

For example, suppose the national government wants to build low-cost housing for poor families. The national Department of Housing and Urban Development (HUD) will offer grants to local governments to do the job. Local decision-makers may not think the project is very important. But they will do the job because the national government is putting up all or most of the money.

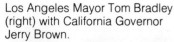

Discuss: How do state and local governments work together?

Los Angeles Mayor Tom Bradley (right) with California Governor Jerry Brown.

Other Sources

Local governments have several other ways to raise small amounts of money. Cities and counties earn money from **licenses** and **fines.** They charge a small amount for marriage licenses, building permits, and traffic tickets. In many counties, lawyers, doctors, plumbers, undertakers, and others have to buy a license to work in the county.

Local governments also borrow money by selling **bonds.** A bond is a certificate stating that the government has borrowed a certain amount of money from the owner of the bond. Bonds are used to raise money for special projects like building a bridge or a school. When people buy bonds, the local government gets the money it needs right away. In return, the government promises to repay the full amount it borrowed plus interest by a certain date.

Some cities and counties also issue **service charges.** Individuals or businesses may get separate bills for water supply, garbage collection, street lighting, snow removal, weed cutting, schoolbook rental, and others. Local governments often use service charges to avoid raising taxes.

Discuss: Are there any other ways your community raises money?

Section Review

Vocabulary: bond, fine, grant, grant-in-aid, license, property tax, revenue sharing, service charge, shared tax.

Reviewing the Main Ideas
1. What is the largest source of money for local governments?
2. How do state governments help support local governments?
3. How does the national government help pay for local services?

Skill Building
1. If your community needed more money to give people the services and protection they want, how would you suggest the money be raised?
2. How would your answer affect yourself?
3. How is your answer fair?
4. How is it a practical solution?

Main Ideas
1. property taxes
2. grants and shared taxes
3. through revenue sharing and grants-in-aid
Skill Building
1. –4. Answers will vary.

Proposition 13:
A Homeowners' Revolt

The problem began in the mid-1970s. At that time, the value of land and houses went up rapidly. This caused property taxes to go up a great deal.

Sheila Washington's case was typical. In 1972 she bought a house near San Francisco for $35,000. Her property taxes were $575 that year. By 1978, the market value of Sheila's home had risen to $65,000 and her property taxes were $1,885. During the same time, Sheila's income did not go up nearly enough to help her pay the new taxes.

By 1978, many homeowners across the country were angry about high property taxes. In Cook County, Illinois, groups of citizens threatened not to pay their taxes. In Maryland, protest groups were organized. In DeKalb County, Georgia, 12,000 angry homeowners forced county officials to stop using computers to figure home values. National news magazines said there was a revolt under way.

In California, groups of property owners took action. They got 1.5 million people to sign petitions forcing a special election on property taxes. To be voted on was Proposition 13, a proposal to limit property taxes to 1 percent of the market value of property. If it won, this proposal would mean that Sheila Washington's taxes would go down to $650 (a savings of $1,235).

Local government officials understood the problem. But, they said, the costs of local government were going up. Trucks

and gasoline cost more. New buildings and parks were more costly to build. Plus, many citizens were asking for better services or new ones—better mental health care, a new sports center. Proposition 13 would mean an enormous cut in revenue provided by the property tax. Where was the money for government services going to come from?

The mayor of San Francisco was clearly worried. "Our police, our fire department, and our schools would be crippled," he said. In Berkeley, the city manager said he might have to lay off seventy-six police officers and fifty firefighters. In Oakland, Alameda County officials warned they could lose $115 million in revenues. And school district officials were telling teachers across the state that many could lose their jobs.

Many property owners did not agree with the government officials' point of view. "It's time we cut back on property taxes," they said. Many believed taxes could be cut and there would still be enough money for important government services. They felt that government officials should look for ways to cut out waste and increase efficiency.

The California State Legislature came up with an alternative. It passed a bill cutting property taxes on homes and apartments by 30 percent. However, this new law would only go into effect if Proposition 13 were turned down by the voters. Governor Jerry Brown signed the bill.

The state legislature's bill would not save homeowners as much money as Proposition 13. In Sheila Washington's case, the savings would be $565 instead of more than $1,200. But the state's plan would leave more money for local governments. However, the legislature's bill was too little too late.

On June 6, 1978, California voters said "yes" to Proposition 13. Immediately, state and local officials in California began to cut expenses and services. And across the nation, government officials looked for ways to cut down the costs of government and head off other homeowners' revolts.

Reviewing the Case Study

1. What caused California homeowners to put Proposition 13 on the ballot?
2. What alternatives for tax relief did California voters face on June 6, 1978?
3. What was the voters' decision?
4. Do you think they made a wise choice? Explain your answer.

Chapter Seventeen Test and Activities

★★

Vocabulary

Match the following words with their meanings.

1. borough
2. municipal charter
3. parish
4. special district
5. consolidation
6. urban area
7. bond
8. fine
9. grant-in-aid
10. property tax

a. a tax on land and houses
b. a certificate of government borrowing
c. money the federal government gives for a specific project
d. money paid as a punishment for breaking a law or ordinance
e. a division—like a county—in Louisiana
f. the "constitution" for a city or town
g. an area in a state set up to provide a single service
h. the combining of two or more governments into one
i. a city, suburb, or town with a population of 25 hundred or more
j. a division—like a county—in Alaska

Reviewing Chapter Ideas

1. True or false: The main role of local government is to help state government by enforcing laws and providing services.
2. True or false: The only rules a local government has to follow are the ones it sets up for itself in its constitution.

3. Townships _____ .
   a. are found in all states
   b. are becoming less popular in all states
   c. are very popular in some states
   d. are larger than counties
4. Which of the following do not have municipal charters?
   a. counties
   b. cities
   c. towns
   d. villages
5. The major source of money for local governments is the _____ .
   a. federal government
   b. state government
   c. property tax
   d. fees for drivers' licenses

Using Basic Social Studies Skills

Finding Information

1. What is the name of the county, parish, or borough in which you live?
2. Do you live in a township? If you do, what is its name?
3. What is the name of your school district?
4. Where is your county (parish or borough) courthouse? Find its address.
5. Where would you write if you needed a copy of your birth certificate? To what official would you address your letter?

★★★

Comprehending Information

1. Look at the property tax bill on page 371. What services are paid for in part by this property tax?
2. Which community service receives the largest amount of this property tax?
3. Are there any services shown here you think should <u>not</u> be paid for out of property taxes? Explain your answer.

Organizing Information

Make a diagram to show how local, state, and national governments are related to each other.

Evaluating Information

1. If you read that your community was trying to get state approval to add a one-half percent sales tax, what would you think? How would such a tax affect you?
2. What in your opinion would be the best way for local governments to get money to provide needed services? Explain your answer.

Communicating Ideas

Write a well-organized paragraph with a topic sentence explaining your judgment of the homeowners' revolt described in the case study in this chapter.

Using Decision-Making Skills

Make a decision tree for the California voters in June, 1978. Show the occasion for decision, the alternatives they faced, some good and bad consequences for each alternative, and the goals they held that influenced their choice.

Activities

1. Arrange to visit your county courthouse. If you go as a class, call ahead to see if a guide could be provided to show you which officials work there and what goes on in the different offices. Perhaps you could visit a courtroom. The judge should be asked in advance.
2. With your parents' permission, bring a property tax bill to class and study it to see what services in your community are paid for with property taxes.
3. As a class project, survey your community to see which taxes, service charges, licenses, and fees bring in money to the local governments.
4. Students who want to know about government in our communities could read: *Local Government* by James A. Eichner (Watts, 1976).

Chapter 18   City Government

★★

In the summer of 1976, people on Myrtle Avenue in Chicago could not agree. Martin Sosin spoke for many when he said, "I want the tree down." Tom Bowler spoke for others when he said, "I've fought for five years to keep that tree."

The cause of this disagreement among neighbors was a giant cottonwood that stood at the edge of an alley. It was more than 135 years old, the largest tree in the northwest part of the city, and experts said it was healthy and had historical value.

The people on Myrtle Avenue had paid a special fee to have the dirt alley behind their houses paved. The city planned to cut the tree down before paving the alley so its growing roots would not crack the new pavement. Many wanted to keep the old giant. Some wondered who would pay for the tree's removal if it died later.

The giant cottonwood was also a decision problem for Alderman Roman Pucinski [pü chin'skē], who represented the Myrtle Avenue area in the Chicago City Council. After considering the alternatives, Pucinski said, "We're going to save that tree." His choice was influenced by the experts who said the tree was healthy.

The mayor and commissioner of streets agreed. They cancelled the order to cut down the tree. They said the city would pay for its removal if the tree died. Nearly everybody was satisfied with the decision.

The daily lives of most citizens are affected by decisions of city government officials like those you have just read about.

There are about 18 thousand towns and cities in the United States. Three out of every four Americans live in a city or town. In this chapter you will learn more about city government as you read:

1/Plans for City Government
2/City Decision Makers
3/Who Influences City Politics?
Case Study: "Who's Going to Put Out the Fires?"

Discuss: What steps were involved in making the decision to save the tree? What city government officials were involved? Could it have happened where you live?

1/Plans for City Government

Cities are not mentioned in the United States Constitution. They are created by state governments. They have only those powers given them by their states. The city or municipal charter granted by the state is the authority for a community to have its own government. No two cities are the same, but most use one of the following plans for government.

Mayor-Council Plan

The diagram on this page shows the **mayor-council plan** for government used by over half of all American cities. All cities with populations over 1 million use this plan.

The **mayor** is the main executive official, and is elected by the citizens of the city. The mayor has the duty of enforcing and carrying out laws.

Discuss: What are the key features of each plan for city government?

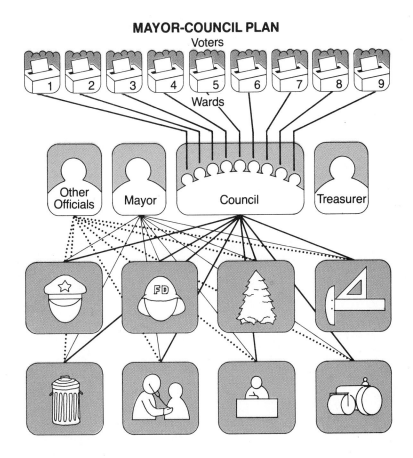

MAYOR-COUNCIL PLAN

379

The **council** is the legislative branch of the government. The city is divided into wards, and each ward is represented in the council by one member. Council members are called councilors, councilmen, aldermen, or supervisors. The council makes ordinances for the city by majority vote. In most states, the mayor can veto bills passed by the council. Often the council can overrule the mayor's veto with a two-thirds majority.

In the mayor-council plan, the voters elect a treasurer and other executive officials such as a clerk and a city attorney. The mayor and other executive officials appoint the heads of the city departments that provide city services—the police department, the fire department, the department of sanitation, the department of public health and others.

Council-Manager Plan

About 43 percent of American cities use the **council-manager plan** shown in the diagram below. The voters elect a council which hires (and can fire) a **manager.** The manager appoints the other executive officials.

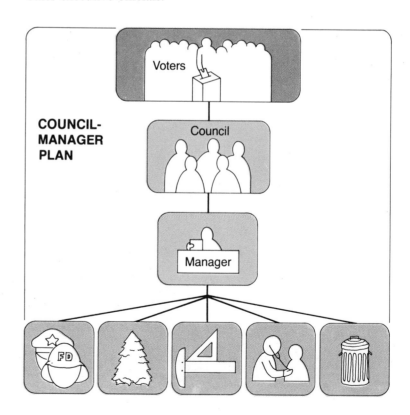

COUNCIL-
MANAGER
PLAN

Voters

Council

Manager

The council's job is to make rules and set goals. The manager's job is to carry out the rules and conduct the day-to-day business of the city. The manager hires the heads of the various city departments. The manager is responsible to the council, and the heads of the city departments are responsible to the manager.

The council-manager form of government was first used in the early 1900s. It was created because many city government officials had become dishonest, and citizens were not getting the services they wanted. People wanted city government taken out of the hands of corrupt political leaders and run instead by people trained in the skills of management. It was thought that a city could be run like a business. Many people called for putting city government on a "business-like" basis.

More and more cities and towns have turned to council-manager government in recent years. Some 28 hundred cities now have city managers. Most rapidly growing cities in the South and Southwest have such a plan.

Commission Plan

The diagram on this page shows the **commission plan.** It is used by only about 6 percent of cities in the United States. The com-

Discuss: Why do you think one plan is more widely used than the others?

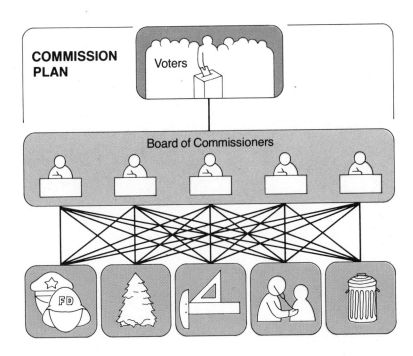

mission is usually a body of five elected officials who make local laws. Each commissioner also heads a city department. A mayor is elected from among the commissioners.

Cities have moved away from the commission plan because often it did not work well. Few commissioners had the skills or training to run city departments. In some cities, commissioners developed separate areas of personal power and influence. As a result, the commission as a body was often unable to agree on decisions. Only a few large cities have a commission form of government today. They include Memphis, Tennessee; St. Paul, Minnesota; Omaha, Nebraska; and Tulsa, Oklahoma.

New England Town Government

In **New England,** colonists settled in small villages and farmed the land nearby. Out of these settlements developed a form of self-government that still exists in towns in the New England states. (The New England states are Maine, New Hampshire, Vermont, Massachusetts, Rhode Island, and Connecticut.) The New England town is governed by all its citizens of voting age. Those interested attend an annual open town meeting. It is chiefly devoted to approving the budget drawn up by the town's elected officials.

Discuss: What plan for city government is most like the plan used where you live?

Note: Have students locate these states.

At the town meeting, all citizens of voting age may vote.

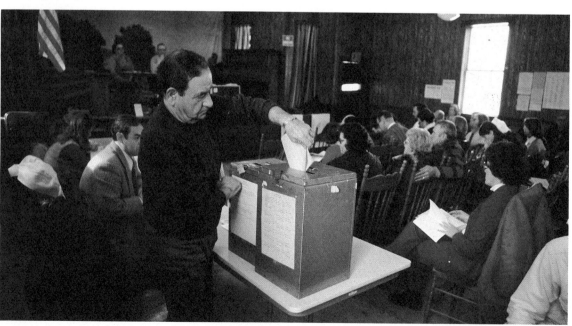

The citizens elect a board of **selectmen** of three to nine members. The board meets regularly and governs the town between annual meetings. The board chooses certain members to be officers, such as treasurer, tax assessor, constable, and overseer of the poor.

The board and town officers have the major responsibility for carrying out policies set at the town meeting. New England towns do not have mayors. A president, or "first selectman," chosen by the board at the town meeting, comes close to acting as the town's chief executive. Like a growing number of cities, many larger New England towns may now hire a professional manager to administer town policies. The manager takes direction from the citizens and their elected town selectmen.

Section Review

Vocabulary: commission plan, council, council-manager plan, manager, mayor, mayor-council plan, New England, selectmen.

Reviewing the Main Ideas
1. List the four plans for city government.
2. For each plan write one sentence that tells how this plan is different from the others.

Skill Building
1. Which plan for city government do you think gives citizens the most voice in their government? Explain your answer.
2. Do you think the New England plan would work well in large cities? Explain your answer.

Main Ideas
1. mayor-council, council-manager, commission, New England town
2. pp. 379–383
Skill Building
1. Answers will vary.
2. Answers will vary.

2/City Decision Makers

Discuss: Who are the city decision makers? What are their roles?

City governments have several key decision makers. The mayor, the city manager, city council members, and other city bureaucrats—all make decisions which affect citizens.

Mayors

President Lyndon Johnson once said, "Things could be worse, I could be a mayor." Mayors are in the "hot seat" of American politics. They must keep important city services working well. They must also deal with such urban problems as housing, racial tension, unemployment, crime, and deteriorating business districts. They must find the money to keep their cities going.

Some mayors have more power to do these jobs than others depending on which of the different plans for government a city or town has. In cities with a council-manager plan, the mayor does not usually have many administrative duties or much power. The job may be mostly ceremonial. A city manager once compared his role to that of the city's mayor in saying, "The mayor cuts ribbons while I cut costs!"

Even in cities with a mayor-council plan, mayors may have to share power with other city officials and the city council. Mayors with little formal power are called **"weak mayors."** They

San Francisco Mayor Dianne Feinstein

have only limited power to appoint or remove officials. They have little formal control over the city council and city budget. Weak mayors have to rely on bargaining and persuasion to influence others to go along with their programs.

Mayors with more formal power, especially those in our largest cities, are known as **"strong mayors."** Strong mayors oversee the operation of most, if not all, city agencies and departments. They can appoint and remove many top city officials. They play an important role in shaping the city budget. They can suggest legislation to the city council. And they have the power to veto bills passed by the council.

In city government, mayors have several leadership roles to play. They handle these roles differently from city to city. It depends on whether the mayor is strong or weak.

Discuss: How does the role of a "weak mayor" compare to the role of a "strong mayor"?

Ceremonial Leader. The mayor leads parades, dedicates new parks, and crowns beauty queens. The mayor digs the first shovelful of dirt at a groundbreaking ceremony for an important new project. The mayor welcomes famous visitors and issues proclamations. Weak or strong, all mayors do these things. The role is important; the mayor stands as the symbol of the city.

Executive Leader. Strong mayors are chief executives. They have power to run the executive branch. Weak mayors have far fewer executive powers and duties.

The mayor's most valuable executive power is to appoint and remove people from important government posts. Strong mayors are able to appoint many city officials. The appointment power gives a mayor control over day-to-day business. If a mayor does not like the way a certain department is being run, or the way a program is being administered, he or she can do much more about it with the power to get rid of the department head.

Legislative Leader. All mayors can recommend legislation to city or town councils. Strong mayors often have a great deal of influence in setting goals for the council.

In cities where the mayor is elected by the other members of the city council, the mayor may propose legislation and vote just like any other council member. In other cities, the mayor may not be on the council but can vote on legislation in case of a tie vote in the council. Strong mayors have the power of veto. About one-third of America's mayors do not have veto power.

Political Leader. The mayor is the head of his or her political party in the city. The mayor has much influence over council members who belong to the same party.

However, city politics in many American cities is **nonpartisan.** This means that people who run for mayor or for city council do not identify themselves to the voters as either Republicans or Democrats. Often they represent local political groups that might have such names as the Good Government party, the Urban Reform movement, or the Independent ticket. As with the major political parties, the mayor elected from a local political group is recognized as the leader of that group.

Promotional Leader. Mayors represent their cities or towns in dealings with business, labor, and government leaders. Most cities want to attract new businesses to the communities both to increase the city's income from taxes and to give jobs to city people. The mayor works with leaders to make the community attractive to business.

Often the mayor must compete with other mayors and public officials for funds from state and federal government. A great deal of today's city budget comes from state and federal programs. The mayor is the city's representative in dealing with these important sources of money.

Discuss: What are the key roles of the mayor?

City Manager

City managers are important decision makers in cities with a council-manager plan of government. They set the agenda for council meetings, prepare the city budget, write reports on city problems, and supervise the heads of city departments. Let's look at how one city manager influences decisions.

Mike Arredondo is a city manager hired by the city council. He works in a city of about 85 thousand people in south Texas. Mike is an expert in administration and management.

One of Mike's first duties after he was hired was to decide whether to keep the heads of the various city departments or to hire new people to work for him. He decided to hire a new police chief and a new city planner. He kept the rest of the city department heads. He fired the police chief because the crime rate was rising, and most city leaders thought police protection needed to be improved. He fired the city planner because she had goals for the future of the city that were quite different from Mike's. He decided they could never agree.

Discuss: How do the roles of mayor and city manager compare?

During his first weeks on the job, Mike developed a smooth working relationship with the council members. He knew that his ability to get things done depended on his being able to work with the city council.

One of Mike's best skills is managing money. He did an outstanding job of preparing the annual city budget. He worked closely with the city budget director and city tax collector to find out how much money the city could take in and what each different department's history of spending was.

Mike influenced the council through his budget management. He knew that his planning determined how the city would distribute its resources to its citizens. When the council approved his budget proposal with next to no change, they let him decide "who gets what" from the city.

Mike also influenced the council's decisions about technical matters. For example, the council was trying to decide whether to allow a nuclear energy plant to be built within city limits. Mike asked technical experts whom he trusted to provide the council with facts about the need, costs, benefits, and possible dangers involved in having the plant within city limits.

Mike Arredondo keeps a low profile. "I'm not running for any public office," he says. "I don't need to shake a lot of voters' hands or make a lot of speeches to civic groups. I leave politics to the politicians." But in his own way Mike is a first-rate politician. He knows how to use influence to gain his goals.

Discuss: How does the city council influence a city or town?

City Council Members

Every city and town in the United States has a legislature. Most are called city councils. They vary greatly in size. Chicago's fifty-member council is the nation's largest. Several small town councils have only two members. Many average between seven and nine members. Terms of office differ from city to city as well. Four-year terms are the most common.

Within the limits of the city charter, councils make ordinances. Two of the most important legislative duties they perform have to do with taxation and spending. Councils decide who is to be taxed and how. They decide how the city government's money is to be spent.

People who serve on city councils are chosen in one of two ways. The **ward system,** once the most common, today is mostly found in larger cities such as Chicago, Philadelphia, Los Angeles, Cleveland, Baltimore, and Houston. Here, the city is divided

Council members consider plans for the city.

into sections called wards. Each ward elects a representative to the council. Each voter chooses only one representative. The other system of choosing city council members is through at-large elections. Here a voter gets to choose for all the council members. If the council has seven members, each voter votes for seven representatives.

Other City Officials

In larger cities, many officials make decisions. Heads of key city departments and the city attorney and city planners all make important decisions that affect citizens' lives.

Many city departments are run by boards or commissions. The city officials who serve on these boards make decisions about important city services. The library board may choose a location for a new library. The city water commission often decides how much people will have to pay for water.

The city attorney handles legal matters affecting the city. The city attorney advises other city officials on what they can and cannot do within their charter.

Thus when the headlines read: "Mayor Announces New Park Program" or "City Council Cracks Down on Gambling," many unnamed officials may be involved in planning and carrying out these decisions.

Discuss: What are the roles of the other city bureaucrats who make major decisions?

Section Review

Vocabulary: nonpartisan, "strong mayor," ward system, "weak mayor."

Reviewing the Main Ideas

1. What is the difference between a "strong mayor" and a "weak mayor"?
2. Compare the manager's role and the mayor's role. Which leadership roles do both play? Which belong only to the mayor? To the manager?
3. Describe the job of city council members.

Skill Building

1. Which form of city government does the nearest city have?
2. What is the name of the mayor? If it has a manager, what is the manager's name? If a first selectman, give that person's name.

Main Ideas
1. pp. 384–385
2. pp. 384–387
3. pp. 387–388
Skill Building
1. Answers will vary.
2. Answers will vary.

3/Who Influences City Politics?

Many groups influence the decisions of city government officials. One city council member put it this way: "Pressure groups are probably more important in local government than they are nationally or in the state because they are right here. You see them and they see you, and what you do affects them."

Discuss: Who are the key influencers of city government in your city or the city nearest you?

Business Groups

People doing business in the city have a big stake in the decisions made by city officials. City government decisions may affect how much money a business makes, what taxes it pays, and how easy it is to conduct business in the city.

In New York, for example the city council passed an ordinance permitting a parade on Fifth Avenue during a regular business day. Store owners tried to influence the mayor to veto the ordinance. They said closing off the street for the parade would cost them $1 million in sales.

Many businesses are concerned with city government decisions. Department stores usually want low taxes, plenty of parking spaces near their stores, and good highways and public transportation to bring customers in. Banks are interested in the growth of the city and in rising property values because they lend money for mortgages. City building codes give rules about how plumbing, electricity, driveways, garages, elevators, and so on have to be put into buildings. These determine business costs for builders.

A crowd watches a parade.

389

Most cities have a **chamber of commerce.** This is an organization of businesses in the city. The chamber of commerce usually supports lower taxes and efficiency in government operations. Chambers of commerce may also support civic improvements such as new street lighting or new playgrounds.

City Employees

Police, firefighters, teachers, street crews, bus drivers, welfare workers, sanitation workers, clerks, and secretaries work for the city government. They all have a personal stake in decisions about their wages, working hours, and working conditions. They frequently try to influence the decisions of city officials.

In larger cities, workers often belong to labor unions. In other cities, city workers do not have unions, but they may form interest groups such as the Fraternal Order of Police.

City workers are **public employees.** They work for a government. Most state laws give public employees the right to organize unions and bargain with city officials about wages and working conditions. But state laws usually make it illegal for public employees to go out on strike.

However, in recent years, many teachers, police, firefighters, garbage collectors, and others have ignored no-strike laws. Strikes by police or firefighters threaten the safety of the city. Strikes by bus drivers or garbage collectors greatly inconvenience citizens. These strikes put great pressure on city officials to meet the city workers' demands. Handling strikes by public employees requires some of the toughest political decisions faced by city government officials.

Newspapers

Newspapers are an important influence in local politics. **News stories** on the front and inside pages tell what's going on around town. These stories give straight facts that tell: Who did something? What happened? Where? When? How? and Why?

In addition to factual news stories, **editorials** interpret and judge the things going on in the city. An editorial might start by stating, "The city council's vote to build a new library is a good idea." It would go on to explain why the editor felt this way. Editorials often support candidates. The day or so before an election, a newspaper prints a list of the candidates it recommends. In communities where there are many elected officials and more names on the ballot than most voters have ever heard of, voters take their favorite newspaper's recommendations into the polling place to help them decide how to vote.

Newspapers in large cities usually favor people and policies that promote business interests. They tend to like such programs as mass transit, urban renewal, or more downtown parking space. They generally do not favor strikes by city employees.

In addition to the official views of the paper given in editorials, newspaper columnists give their personal opinions in the **columns** that usually carry their names and pictures. A local columnist might begin a column with: "There is a rumor around city hall that some members of the council who opposed the new sports arena made a deal with the mayor." The column might then go on to give the columnist's opinion of what happened.

Columnists often are active supporters of one or the other political party. They do not try to be objective. Rather, their columns are interesting because they contain strong views. Columnists, too, are influential with those readers who share their general views.

In the **letters-to-the-editor** section of the paper, citizens have an opportunity to use the newspaper to influence others. If you glance at this part of the paper for a few days, you can get a good idea of what is on people's minds.

Discuss: What are the pros and cons of a paper favoring one political party?

Note: Have students find examples of the various ways newspapers can influence local governments.

Section Review

Vocabulary: chamber of commerce, column, editorial, letters-to-the-editor, news story, public employee.

Reviewing the Main Ideas

1. What three groups influence city decision makers?
2. What are four or five programs that business groups would be interested in seeing their city provide?
3. What are two or three reasons city employees might threaten to strike?

Skill Building

1. Bring in newspapers and look for articles about some issue in your city that is "hot."
2. Find news stories about the issue.
3. Find an editorial about it. What is the newspaper's view of it?
4. Find a columnist who has a viewpoint different from yours. How do you disagree with him or her?

Main Ideas
1. business groups, city employees, newspapers
2. pp. 389–390
3. p. 390
Skill Building
1. –4. Check students' news articles to be sure they can distinguish among the different types.

Reading a Newspaper

A person wishing to keep up with events reads a newspaper. Newspapers are published daily in hundreds of American cities. And most contain not only news stories, but also feature stories, sports stories, editorials, essays by columnists, recipes, advice to the lovelorn, advertisements, and even more. The discussion here is confined to the characteristics of news stories and feature stories.

News Stories

A news story relates what happened, sticking to facts. It might report opinions, but offers none of its own. Read the story on this page.

Now examine the parts of the news story:

A. The headline. This attracts a reader's attention, telling what the story is about. Headline writers usually drop articles and forms of the verb "to be."

B. By-line. This tells who wrote the story. Some stories contain no by-line. Others give credit to a news agency, such as Associated Press or United Press International.

C. Dateline. This gives the story's date and place. If there is no dateline, the story originated locally. The date might be indicated by the words "today" or "yesterday," or by the name of a day of the week.

D. Lead. This first paragraph always answers the questions Who? and What? It might also answer the questions When? and Where? Some leads also yield information as to How? and Why?

E. Subhead. This merely breaks up a story for easier reading.

U.S. SAYS NEW YORK MAY SET ASIDE FUND TO OPERATE HOUSING

By STEVEN R. WEISMAN
Special to The New York Times

WASHINGTON, April 9—In a victory for Mayor Koch, the Carter Administration ruled today that New York City could set aside $100 million in Federal community-development funds to help maintain the vast amount of run-down housing that it owned as a result of foreclosure proceedings.

The ruling, transmitted to Mr. Koch from Vice President Mondale in a telephone call this evening, permits the city to tap a key Federal program to operate the housing. It could thus avoid dipping into its own scarce resources to handle a problem that has exploded in magnitude in recent months.

At present the city owns more than 5,000 buildings containing more than 30,000 apartments throughout the five boroughs. The buildings were taken over for nonpayment of real-estate taxes. An additional 12,000 apartments are expected to fall into the city's hands for the same reason before the year is up, and city officials fear the number will rise to 75,000 by mid-1980.

Some Other Problems Remain

Had the Federal ruling not come through, the city would have had to pay the astronomical cost of running these buildings on its own, at a

Not all news stories are serious, nor do they need to be. Some are humorous, dealing with the day-to-day trials people face. The following story, about a secretary who reached the end of the tether, is one of this kind:

Now try these exercises:
1. Rewrite the headline, using no slang and a complete sentence.
2. What is the story's dateline?
3. When did the event take place?
4. To whom is the story credited?
5. Show how the lead answers Who? What? When? Where? How? and Why?
6. Tell the story in your own words.

Feature Stories

Feature stories are like news stories in that they have headlines and often by-lines and datelines. And feature stories have leads.

A feature story lead, though, is often catchier than that of a news story. It aims to "hook" the reader. It tantalizes, arouses curiosity, and makes the reader want to go on. Feature stories often are humorous. They might offer opinion as well as fact. Here is an example of a feature.

Questions
1. Describe the contents of this story.
2. What makes it a feature instead of a straight news story?

Secretary frosted by duty, fired

MEMPHIS (AP)—A secretary at an advertising agency said she did not mind making coffee or even cleaning the windows in her office in between her other duties. But she drew the line at defrosting the office freezer and now she is out of a job.

Catherine Hayes-Crawford, 22, said she was fired after she refused to defrost the refrigerator in the office of Les Brueck & Associates Advertising.

"I didn't mind taking care of the garbage, cleaning the windows, emptying the ashtrays or making coffee," she said, "but I really put my foot down when he asked me to defrost the refrigerator. That wasn't my job description."

HER FORMER boss, Les Brueck, declined to discuss the matter.

After being fired, Hayes-Crawford said she went to an office of the Equal Employment Opportunity Commission to complain. But she was told that being asked to defrost a refrigerator was not a sex discrimination offense.

TWA pilot feels '400 years old'

LAS VEGAS, Nev. (AP)—Harvey (Hoot) Gibson had to lie about his age when he got his flying license at 14.

Since then, he has logged more than 23,000 flying hours, "probably more than any pilot my age."

It was only a matter of seconds, though, that proved how good Gibson could be in the cockpit.

The Trans World Airlines pilot, a onetime air traffic controller at Midway Airport, regained control of his jetliner with 80 passengers aboard after it did two 360-degree rolls and hurtled into a 5-mile nosedive.

"I FEEL LIKE I'm 400 years old," said Gibson, fatigued from only three hours of sleep in 48 hours.

Federal Aviation Administration officials said it was "miraculous" that the Boeing 727 trijet survived the midair incident Wednesday night. Gibson, 44, was commended by FAA chief Langhorne Bond for averting a crash by lower-

"Who's Going to Put Out the Fires?"

CASE STUDY

One evening in August, 1975, some tourists were dining in a Chinese restaurant in San Francisco. Silence suddenly fell as one of two men with guns shouted, "This is a stick-up! Hand over your money."

The two robbers left the restaurant with their pockets stuffed with money. A few people started to call the police. Then it dawned on them—there were no police to be called!

The day before, San Francisco's police force and firefighters had gone on strike. These public employees were bitter because they put their lives on the line every day for the citizens of San Francisco. They felt they were not being paid enough for the important jobs that they did. They had demanded a 13 percent pay raise. San Francisco's council, the Board of Supervisors, offered only 6.5 percent. So the public employees went out on strike.

After the strike started, several small fires were put out by fire department officers. If a really big fire started, the city would be in deep trouble.

Small bands of youths were breaking shop windows and taking merchandise. There was no way of knowing how much crime was going on. There was no one on duty to report calls from victims.

The strike took place at the busiest time of the tourist season. Many visitors left the city. Others canceled their visits.

Mayor Joseph Alioto said the strike could not go on much longer. But he refused to call in the state police to provide the missing services. That would make the city look like an armed camp. And such action would make it harder to bargain with the striking workers.

Instead the mayor met with strike leaders and arranged a wage settlement. The strikers accepted the mayor's offer.

The Board of Supervisors voted nine to nothing against the mayor's plan. "We do not wish to negotiate with outlaws," argued one supervisor. The strike was illegal. Board members did not want to make any agreement until the strikers went back to work.

Also, board members feared taxes would have to go up sharply to pay for the big raise. They believed the city could not afford the mayor's plan.

Mayor Alioto checked with the city attorney to see what alternatives he had. He learned that the San Francisco city charter clearly gave the mayor power to take action without board approval if he declared an emergency existed in the city.

Mayor Alioto declared a state of emergency. He granted the strikers a 13 percent wage increase. The strikers accepted and began returning to work.

Board members were furious with the mayor's decision. One supervisor called the mayor a "dictator." Another said the mayor's settlement was a "sellout."

Newspaper editorials supported the supervisors saying, "Mayor Alioto's decision to give in to striking firefighters and police ended the strike, but San Francisco residents will be paying for it soon."

A columnist wrote, "Mayor Joseph Alioto was a willing 'fall guy' in the recent strike settlement. As he is not up for reelection in November, he was in a good position to take the heat from city taxpayers. The board, most of whom are facing the election, get to look like public heroes."

Anxious to prevent a mayor from overruling them again, the Board of Supervisors added three propositions to the November ballot: (1) future mayors cannot declare emergencies without board approval, (2) striking by police and firefighters will be grounds for dismissal, and (3) future police and firefighter salaries will be based on the average salaries for those jobs paid in the five largest cities.

On November 6, 1975, San Francisco voters overwhelmingly accepted all three propositions.

Reviewing the Case Study

1. What is your judgment of Mayor Alioto's decision to pay the striking workers the full amount they were demanding?
2. What is your judgment of the way the Board of Supervisors handled the entire situation?
3. If you had voted in the November 6, 1975 election, how would you have voted?

With firefighters off the job, a major fire could be devastating.

Chapter Eighteen Test and Activities

★★

Vocabulary

Match the following words with their meanings.

1. chamber of commerce
2. council
3. mayor
4. manager
5. ward
6. nonpartisan
7. letter-to-the-editor
8. editorial
9. column
10. news story

a. a hired professional who runs a city
b. an elected official who runs a city
c. a division of a city represented by a council member
d. the legislative branch of city government
e. an organization of businesses in the community
f. not controlled by a political party
g. a newspaper article that gives the personal opinion of one who regularly writes under his or her name
h. a newspaper article that gives only facts about what happened
i. a newspaper article that gives the official opinion or judgment of the paper
j. a newspaper article sent to the newspaper to express a citizen's point of view

Reviewing Chapter Ideas

1. What portion of America's people live in cities and towns?
   a. about 25 percent
   b. about half
   c. about 75 percent
   d. nearly 90 percent
2. True or false: City governments are set up in Article III of the Constitution.
3. Most American cities use the _____ form of government.
   a. New England town
   b. commission
   c. council-manager
   d. mayor-council
4. Which form of city government is growing most rapidly?
   a. New England town
   b. commission
   c. council-manager
   d. mayor-council

Using Basic Social Studies Skills

Finding Information

1. The authors say "no two cities are the same." Find two examples in this chapter that show what they mean.
2. Find the section in this chapter that describes New England towns. Find the names of the states that make up New England. What are they?

Comprehending Information

1. In your own words, describe the difference between a "strong mayor" and a "weak mayor." Include at least two differences in their powers.

★★

2. Draw a diagram or cartoon to show what is meant by "mayors are in the 'hot seat' of American politics today."

Organizing Information

1. Diagram the most widely used form of city government.
2. Name two ways the mayor-council plan and the council-manager plan are the same.
3. Name two ways the mayor-council plan and the council-manager plan are different.
4. Make a circle graph showing the percent of cities using each of the four plans for government.

Evaluating Information

Suppose you could interview your mayor or manager about city government in your community. Write up the questions you would ask. Write at least five.

Communicating Ideas

Write a brief summary of the main ideas of this chapter. Include at least five words from the vocabulary section of this test. Underline each vocabulary word you use.

Using Decision-Making Skills

1. What were Mayor Alioto's alternatives when the police and firefighters went on strike in San Francisco?
2. What were the possible good and bad consequences of each alternative?
3. What different goals influenced the decision he made?
4. If you had to make the decision, would you have been influenced by different goals?
5. Do you believe Alioto's decision was a good one? Explain your answer. Include your opinions about how fair and how practical you believe it was.

Activities

1. Use the *Readers' Guide to Periodical Literature* to find out more about the government of cities around the country. List at least five articles you believe would give you information.
2. Use your newspaper to find three articles that might influence city decision-makers—both officials and voters. Choose one news story, one editorial, and one column. Write a brief summary of your findings. Share your report and the articles with other class members.
3. Visit a city or town council meeting. Notice how the agenda controls what things can be discussed. In what ways can citizens make themselves heard at the meeting? Who seems to be in charge? After the meeting, talk over your impressions with classmates.
4. Students who want to read more about cities may enjoy *The Changing City,* by Jorg Muller, McElderry/Atheneum, 1977.

Chapter 19   Urban Problems

★★

Thomas Jefferson once wrote to his good friend James Madison, "When our governments get piled upon one another in large cities, as in Europe, they will become corrupt as in Europe." Jefferson, like many others of his time, thought life on the farm was better than life in the city.

In a recent survey, the national Department of Housing and Urban Development (HUD) asked Americans to compare cities, suburbs, and rural areas. Over 7 thousand citizens across the country took part in the study. Most of them said that cities are great places to visit and to work in but not so good to live in.

People rated cities best for job opportunities and public transportation. They also gave them high marks for culture, education, shopping, and health care.

But the survey also found that people thought cities were the worst places to raise children, that cities had the worst housing, the most crime, the worst public schools, and the highest taxes.

The HUD survey found that many people were planning to leave the city. Thirty-nine percent said they were planning to move to the suburbs or to rural towns in the next few years.

On the other hand, the survey showed that many people in suburbs and rural towns come into the cities to use its services. About a third of all people who live in suburbs work in a nearby city.

In this chapter we look at the quality of life in cities as you read:

1/How Cities Have Grown
2/City Problems
3/Help from Washington?
Case Study: Worms in the Big Apple

Discuss: Given a choice, would you live in a city?

398

1/How Cities Have Grown

When Miami police officer Ed Kezar retired, he thought of the many changes he had seen in the big Florida city.

Expressways now cut through and around the city. A rapid transit system was in the works. Tall new office buildings lit up the skyline at night. The people had changed too. Thousands of immigrants from nearby Cuba had enriched the city's cultural life. And every year, more and more "snow-birds," people from the north, kept moving to the Miami area. In recent years the area's population had jumped by nearly 16 percent. This growth had brought some problems, too. More cars jammed the roads. Housing prices went up. Crime increased.

Like Miami, every American city has seen new people, new buildings, and new problems. Our cities have always been changing.

Discuss: How has your area changed in your lifetime?

The City in Our History

The United States began as a rural nation. At the time of the American Revolution, 95 percent of the colonists were doing farm work. In 1790 the first census showed that New York with

Los Angeles

33 thousand people and Philadelphia with 28 thousand were our biggest cities. Baltimore and Boston were towns with fewer than 20 thousand people each.

In the 1860s, after the Civil War, cities began to grow rapidly. By 1900, New York had over 3 million people. Chicago had 1.5 million people. Boston and Baltimore had more than 300 thousand each.

The growth of factories and industry had brought many people into the cities. There was work in the city for newcomers. By the late 1800s and early 1900s, millions of immigrants from such countries as Ireland, Italy, Germany, Poland, and Russia had arrived.

The cities also offered jobs to Americans from the farms. The invention of new machinery had changed farming, so fewer farmers and farm laborers were needed. Farm workers and younger members of farm families moved to the cities for work.

Cities were exciting places to be. The growing cities had gas lighting and running water. They had new theaters, restaurants, museums, and libraries. There were people to see and know. And fortunes could be made in the city.

By 1920, more Americans were living in the city than in rural areas. During this century, our cities have continued to grow. Now we have nearly 400 cities with more than 50 thousand people. We have over 50 cities with 250 thousand or more people. And 6 cities have populations over 1 million.

A Pattern in City Growth

Most American cities have grown from the inside out. They started as small towns near a river, fort, waterfall, or crossroads. Then they grew out from the center in bigger and bigger circles. If you start at the center of a typical city, you see tall buildings, stores, banks, and theaters. The traffic is heavy. This is the original section of the city. Next you come to a run-down area that surrounds the central city. Here you find old warehouses, vacant lots, junk cars, and slum buildings.

After this is a ring of small homes, grocery stores, and apartment buildings. Most of the houses are old. Many are built side by side with little or no space between them. Signs in foreign languages tell that different ethnic groups are part of this circle.

As the traffic gets lighter, you move into the next circle. Here you'll find newer shops, banks, and a big modern shopping center. If you turn into the smaller, side streets, you'll see larger one-

Discuss: Why were people moving to cities around 1900?

Discuss: How have cities grown?

family homes with yards and garages. There are fewer apartment buildings here than nearer in. The ones you do find are quite new.

Soon you'll be out of the city and into the next community—a suburb. Since the 1950s, many people have been moving from the city to the suburbs. In recent years, nearly 20 million Americans moved to suburbs.

Families moving to suburbs seek to get away from city problems. They want cleaner air, more living space, less traffic and crowding, and better schools. Many businesses, stores, and factories have followed. They too want to go to areas where land is less expensive and big city problems do not exist. Shopping centers and industrial parks dot the suburbs. Two-thirds of all suburban dwellers either work in the suburb where they live or commute to another suburb to work.

Discuss: How do reasons for moving in 1900 compare with reasons for moving today?

Supercities

This pattern of city growth has produced two new kinds of communities that did not exist fifty years ago.

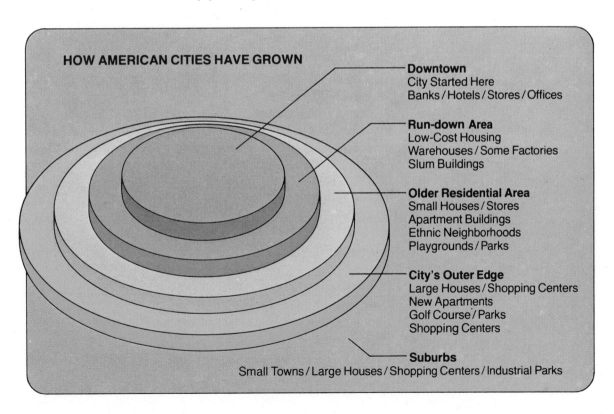

HOW AMERICAN CITIES HAVE GROWN

Downtown
City Started Here
Banks / Hotels / Stores / Offices

Run-down Area
Low-Cost Housing
Warehouses / Some Factories
Slum Buildings

Older Residential Area
Small Houses / Stores
Apartment Buildings
Ethnic Neighborhoods
Playgrounds / Parks

City's Outer Edge
Large Houses / Shopping Centers
New Apartments
Golf Course / Parks
Shopping Centers

Suburbs
Small Towns / Large Houses / Shopping Centers / Industrial Parks

Discuss: Why are
metropolitan areas and the
megalopolis important in
understanding the growth
of cities? How do problems
develop in cities?

Metropolitan Areas. Today, a large city with its nearby suburbs and small towns is called a metropolitan area. The United States Census Bureau calls any area including a city and its suburbs that has a population of 50 thousand or more a **Standard Metropolitan Statistical Area** (SMSA). There are more than 243 such areas in the United States today.

People in metropolitan areas come from different racial and ethnic backgrounds. They have different political and social attitudes from each other. They often have needs for different services from the city and their needs may conflict. The differences among city dwellers are the source of both richness and conflict in city life.

People in metropolitan areas are dependent on each other. People in the city's outer circles and suburbs depend on the center city for food, clothes, newspapers, entertainment, hospitals, jobs, and many other things. The center city looks to the rest of the area for its workers, managers, and customers. Everyone looks to the city government to provide key services.

Note: Contact the United
States Census Bureau in
order to have the latest
census data on cities
available. Also, have maps
of any SMSA in your state.

Megalopolis. As metropolitan areas have grown, the space between gets smaller and smaller. New housing built on the outer edge of the city pushes further and further into the country. An area where large cities have started to overlap is called a **megalopolis.** The word means "very great urban area." We have three in the United States.

One is an area about 100 miles wide and 500 miles long that goes from Boston to Washington, D.C. About one-fifth of the entire United States population, or 40 million people, live in this megalopolis—called Boswash by some, Boshington by others.

Note: Locate these areas
on a map. By studying the
map students may be able
to come up with names for
one of the other areas.

The area along the shores of the Great Lakes from Chicago, Illinois, to Buffalo, New York, is another megalopolis. The third is in southern California, spreading out from Los Angeles.

Section Review

Vocabulary: megalopolis, metropolitan area, SMSA.
Reviewing the Main Ideas
What are some advantages of living in the city?
Skill Building
Draw a diagram showing how cities have grown.

Main Ideas
Answers will vary.
Skill Building
Students should follow the
model on p. 401.

2/City Problems

Juliet Hazen is one of the more than 100 woman mayors in the country. Recently she was interviewed by Allan Hernandez, a local reporter.

Hernandez: In your opinion, has city life been getting better or worse?

Hazen: Most city dwellers today live more comfortably than ever before. Cities are cleaner than, say, in the 1920s. There are more schools and more people go to school. And the treatment of racial and ethnic minorities is better than it was fifty years ago.

Hernandez: What problems face local government leaders today?

Hazen: Major problems include poor housing, slums, crime, traffic problems, and pollution. In addition, many city governments are short of money. New York City almost went broke a few years ago.

Hernandez: Can local governments solve all these problems?

Hazen: They have to try. One of the toughest problems is deciding how much local government can do and how much

Discuss: How would your mayor (if you have one) answer these questions? How would you? Can you add to Hazen's list of problems and solutions?

403

Discuss: How do each of these problems affect cities? How can these problems be solved? Some people say solving old problems only creates new ones. Do you agree?

citizens and private businesses must do for themselves. Governments have an important role to play in solving city problems. But citizens cannot be excused from efforts to improve their own lives.

This section looks at some of the problems Mayor Hazen is talking about.

Poor Housing

Jean lived in Apartment 2W. Forty other families lived in the small building. Most tried to keep the building clean, but it was just no use. The owner did not live there and did not care. The owner only wanted the rent.

The building was a mess. There was no janitor to fix things. The toilets didn't work, the sinks were cracked, windows were broken. The walls had holes in them. Many times the furnace broke and there was no heat.

And there were the big, ugly rats. People set traps for them but most got away. They lived in the walls growing fat and bold.

Slum buildings like Jean Palmer's are one of the toughest problems facing cities. A **slum** is an old, dirty, run-down part of a city. People in slums may live crowded together in a few small rooms. Slums are found mainly in the circle next to the downtown area. But, slums can develop in any area of the city where buildings are neglected and there is overcrowding.

Slum areas have very high crime rates. Alcoholics, drug addicts, and criminals roam the slums.

Slums develop as some people move out to more desirable neighborhoods and poorer people move in. Often the only housing newcomers can find or afford is in already run-down buildings left behind by others. These areas then get worse as landlords take advantage of the poor who need housing. The rents are high. Few, if any, repairs are made on buildings.

City government decision makers have used several programs to fight slums and improve housing. Some have worked better than others. One plan has been to build **public housing projects.** These are apartment buildings built with public money. Slums are torn down to make way for these projects. The rents are kept at a level the families can afford.

Another plan is called **urban renewal.** Slums are torn down, and the land is used for light industry, civic centers, modern hotels, or office buildings. In the past, some urban renewal projects did not create new housing for the people from the slum areas that were torn down. Therefore, urban renewal caused new problems as it solved old ones. But today urban renewal projects usually include housing for the people who are displaced by the building.

Most city governments have special departments that work on slum problems. The federal government has provided much of the money for such projects. The Department of Housing and Urban Development (HUD) grants billions of dollars to cities for urban renewal and housing projects.

All these efforts have helped improve urban life. But most city officials agree that much more needs to be done to solve the housing problem in cities.

Discuss: Are any of these problems found in your community? If so, how are they being handled? Have any been solved? How? Are there other problems? How are they being handled?

Transportation

The auto population in our country is growing faster than the human population. In 1921 there were 20 million cars. Today there are over 110 million.

Automobiles helped cities and suburbs grow. With cars people could live away from the downtown center and still get around the city. But now cities are choking on automobiles.

Most cities were not planned for the automobile. City traffic is a mess. There are not enough parking spaces. And during "rush hours," when people are all going to and from work, traffic moves at a snail's pace.

In addition, giant expressways and parking garages take up valuable space in the city. This space could be used for buildings that pay property taxes. In Los Angeles people were shocked to learn that more than two-thirds of the downtown area was used in one way or another for automobiles.

Urban experts agree that trains are the best way to move people around the city. Such trains are called **rapid transit systems,** or **subways** when they run under the ground. In recent years Atlanta, San Francisco, Baltimore, and Washington have built rapid transit and subway systems. Building such systems is expensive. It also requires planning and cooperation by many local government decision makers.

Miami is an example. By the mid-1970s the city was swamped with cars. Downtown Miami was surrounded by parking lots. U.S. Highway 1, a main north-south road, was designed to carry 1,800 cars an hour; instead it carried 3,000.

To help solve the problem, city and Dade County government officials began planning for a $795 million, 21-mile rapid

BART—Bay Area Rapid Transit—is the system that serves San Francisco.

transit system. The county, which includes Miami, would provide $132 million. The rest would come from the federal government. A Metropolitan Dade County Office of Transportation Administration was set up to design and operate the system. Hundreds of meetings with local residents were held to plan the system. Sometimes the spots for stations were moved when residents objected to them. In 1978 Dade County voters approved the county's plans in a special election, and work on the system started.

City officials hope new, fast, clean rapid transit systems like Miami's will encourage city dwellers to get off the expressways and onto trains.

Pollution

Air and water pollution have been problems for cities for a long time. Dirty air and dirty water can make city life unpleasant.

Dirty Air. Air pollution hurts plants and trees. It makes clothes dirty. It can ruin the paint on cars. And it can and does cause lung disease. Almost every city dweller today has some damage to the lungs as a result of air pollution.

About 60 percent of the air pollution in large cities is caused by fumes from cars, trucks, and buses. A second major cause of air pollution is the smoke and gases from factories. Every year factories spray tons of dirt and gases into the air.

City governments have fought air pollution for many years. The first air pollution law in the United States was an ordinance passed by the Chicago City Council in 1881. The problem is tough to deal with. Even when one city cleans up its air, winds can bring dirty air from a nearby city or factory. And each local government makes its own decisions about air pollution.

In Cuyahoga County, Ohio, for example, there are more than sixty town and city governments including Cleveland. They all suffer from air pollution. But this many local governments rarely cooperate on strong air pollution programs.

Something more than local efforts are needed. In 1955, Congress passed the first federal law on air pollution. Others have followed. Federal laws provide money to help cities and counties clean up their air. They also limit the amount of pollutants factories and autos can put into the air.

Dirty Water. As cities have grown, water pollution has become a serious problem in some areas. One source of water pollution is sewage. Cities have spent over $15 billion on sewers and sewage treatment plants.

A dangerous source of water pollution is waste from factories and from farms. Animal wastes, fertilizers, and farm chemicals drain into nearby rivers and lakes. This pollution, along with sewerage, is carried by rivers past many cities. Each city then adds more pollution to the river. For example, the Cuyahoga River cuts through Akron and Cleveland. So much oil had been dumped in the river that in 1969 part of the river caught fire!

Discuss: What other kinds of pollution are there? How are they being handled? Have any been eliminated?

Planning for the Future

"The Alamo calls upon every friend and member to come to the aid of the Alamo—quickly!" The Daughters of the Republic of Texas were sounding a call for help. Nearly 140 years after the Alamo fell to the Mexican Army, the Daughters thought the old mission was being threatened again, this time by San Antonio city planners.

City Manager Sam Granata had directed the city planners to design a new plaza as a project for America's Bicentennial in 1976. The plan called for paving a large grassy area in front of the Alamo. The Daughters were against the plan because they said it would make the area too hot. They were also against doing away with parking stalls for automobiles that line the street.

Mayor Lila Cockrell persuaded the Daughters and city planners to work on a compromise plan. "Not everyone is going to get what they want but we can get some kind of plan that will help us get this project built," the mayor said.

Like San Antonio, most cities today have official planning agencies. Almost every large city employs full-time, professional planners. In a large city, planners include traffic engineers, population specialists, economists, political scientists, landscape architects, and many other types of scientists.

Many city problems have come from lack of planning. As cities grew no one gave much thought to protecting the environment. Nor were streets, parks, businesses, hospitals, and public transportation planned to best fit people's needs. Instead cities grew by chance.

Today there is a real need for planning. Here are the kinds of problems planners deal with. Where should a new rapid transit system go? How will it affect people who live along the route?

Discuss: How are cities planning for the future? How is your area planning for the future?

Making Plans for a City

City planners work in cities throughout the United States. Some planners work for private companies. Others work in planning departments that are part of city government. Large cities most often have their own planning departments.

The people hired to work in planning departments often have university degrees in planning. Most have studied a broad range of subjects that relate to city growth and city needs.

Before making recommendations, city planners seek information and advice from many people. They work with lawyers, engineers, architects, geographers, political scientists, sociologists, and economists. They also talk to residents of the city. The planners have information from all these sources in mind when they make proposals.

The overall plan that is created for a city is called the *master plan.* The master plan shows what the city is like today and what planners think it should be like in the future. The planners work with diagrams, maps, and small-scale models to show the physical layout of the city.

When planners create a master plan, they recommend changes for the future. They may recommend changes in the city's transportation system. They may recommend new recreational facilities, a new sewer system, increased public health services, an increased or decreased number of public schools, or changes in patterns of new home building. The goal of the planner is to create a city that is pleasant to live in—a city that meets the needs of its residents.

To make all the changes proposed in a master plan may take ten or twenty years. And sometimes the master plan itself is changed as new information comes to the attention of planners, residents, and city officials.

A building comes down to make way for new construction in downtown Atlanta.

Mayor Kevin White (below right) speaks at the opening of Quincy Market, a section of Boston where old buildings have been restored and walkways have been made pleasant for shoppers (below left).

How many newcomers to the city are expected in the next ten years? What kinds of services will they need? Does the city need more parks or more land for factories?

Planners have no legal powers to make other city officials and citizens accept their plans. They report on their plans to the mayor or city manager and to the city council. It is up to these officials to put the plans into action and make them legally binding upon others.

Thus planners may influence the decisions of city officials with their ideas for the future. Real estate developers, builders, property owners, and citizens such as the Daughters of the Republic of Texas also try to influence city officials. They may or may not agree with the planners.

Discuss: Would rezoning of your area be a problem?

One way city officials enforce new plans is through **zoning ordinances.** Zoning divides the city into different "zones," or areas, for industry, homes, apartment buildings, and stores. Owners of land in each zone may use the land only as called for in the ordinance. Planners often help write zoning ordinances for the city council to vote on.

Today the federal government requires cities to develop a plan before it will give federal money for public housing, urban renewal, airports, sewage systems, highways, parks, or even hospitals. This rule has led many cities to set up planning agencies.

Section Review

Vocabulary: public housing project, rapid transit system, slum, subway, urban renewal, zoning ordinance.

Reviewing the Main Ideas

1. What are slums and how do they develop?
2. What problems have automobiles created for cities?
3. How have cities tried to solve the problems caused by automobiles?
4. What are the major causes of pollution in cities?
5. What is the job of a city planning agency?

Skill Building

Using what you know about overlapping local governments, tell why pollution is a hard problem for local governments to deal with.

Main Ideas
1. p. 404
2. p. 405
3. rapid transit systems or subways
4. fumes from cars, trucks, and buses
5. pp. 407–410
Skill Building
Answers will vary; they should include mention of overlapping jurisdiction and lack of coordination.

3/Help from Washington?

Dealing with urban problems takes a lot of money. Many large cities today are short of money. Services such as rapid transit become more and more costly. Controlling pollution is expensive for businesses and for government. And clusters of poor people who need special services place a further burden on city governments.

During the Depression of the 1930s, the national government began granting money to cities for child welfare, public welfare, public housing, and employment programs. After World War II, money from Washington was also available for building schools and expressways.

As their money problems got worse, cities in the 1960s turned to the national government for even more money. Washington responded with many new aid programs. These programs often bypass state governments and give money directly to cities.

Today federal money is a big part of the budget of many cities. In 1978, for example, money from Washington made up 36 percent of Baltimore's budget, 25 percent of Cleveland's budget, and 33 percent of Atlanta's budget.

Discuss: What ways does the federal government help cities? What are the pros and cons of each?

Workers for the Environmental Protection Agency of the national government sample water on the Hudson River.

Today cities get money from Washington in two ways: (1) revenue sharing and (2) federal grants-in-aid.

Revenue Sharing

Discuss: What help is your city getting from the federal government? What additional help is needed?

When the national government takes part of the money it collects from federal taxes and gives it back to city governments, this is revenue sharing. The money comes with few strings attached. It can be spent for nearly anything the city needs. Most cities use this money to help pay for such services as police and fire protection, sewage and garbage disposal, air and water cleanup, and parks.

Many big city mayors think the national government is better at collecting taxes than local governments. But, they say, local officials are closer to the people and better able to spend the money from Washington to meet local problems.

Many national government officials do not like revenue sharing. These officials argue that decisions about spending should be made by the same people who have the burden of collecting the tax money.

Federal Aid

Cities also depend a great deal on grants-in-aid from Washington. There are more than 500 federal aid programs. All are for different purposes and have different requirements. Cities may get federal grants to assist in everything from draining water from swamps to buying school milk.

Rapid transit control center—from this room all the trains are monitored. Special equipment lets the controllers talk directly to a train operator, to various stations on the line, and with police or fire departments when necessary.

Federal Control. City officials have learned that along with federal aid comes a lot of federal control. The national government gives money to cities only if cities are willing to meet conditions set by Congress. For example, Washington may grant a city money for a new library. But city officials must agree to build special ramps for the handicapped, hire members of minority groups to work in the library, and use certain types of building materials. These are all federal regulations.

About thirty-five federal standards apply to most aid programs to cities. These represent things people in Washington think are important. In this way, Washington officials make local government officials go along with national programs.

Red Tape. To get aid from Washington, city officials must find the right program. They must learn how to apply for aid. They must fill out forms correctly. Once they get money, they must make regular reports to federal agencies in Washington.

All the paperwork takes time and costs money. One official figured her city needs 20 percent of the federal aid it gets just to pay for the paperwork.

Discuss: Is it worth it?

Supporters of federal aid point out that it helps cities provide important services they could not afford alone. They add that federal guidelines have helped improve local programs. And these guidelines have helped to ensure that cities do not engage in discrimination.

Section Review

Vocabulary: grant-in-aid, revenue sharing.

Reviewing the Main Ideas

1. Give three reasons cities need money from Washington.
2. What is one argument city officials give for why the money should come from Washington?
3. What is one argument national government officials make against giving money directly to cities?

Main Ideas
1. p. 411
2. p. 412
3. p. 412
Skill Building
pp. 152 and 372

Skill Building

Use your index to look up other places in this book where grants-in-aid and revenue sharing are discussed. Write down those page numbers. Look up the other references to make up a list of programs paid for with these two kinds of federal money.

Worms in the Big Apple

After the national government, New York City is the second largest government in the United States. The giant city spends more than any other state or city in the country. Over 300 thousand people work for the city government.

During the summer of 1975, New York had the worst money crisis ever faced by an American city. The "Big Apple," as New Yorkers call their city, almost went broke.

New York City spends about $13 billion a year. It takes in less than $12 billion a year. To get the extra money it needs, the city sells municipal bonds to banks, investment companies, and individuals. In return, the city promises to pay back the amount of the bond plus interest.

Over the years, the city had built up a huge debt. By 1975, New York owed $13 billion, and each year it needed another $2 billion just to pay the interest on earlier bonds.

How did New York get into such a mess? First, the city had a history of helping the poor and needy. Since the 1800s, the Big Apple had welcomed wave after wave of poor immigrants to America. Over the years, the city created many free programs for its residents. By 1975, New York offered more free services than any other American city. These included libraries, parks, recreation centers, city hospitals, museums, zoos, welfare and public housing programs, drug treatment centers, day-care centers, and a free university.

Second, the city paid high salaries to its public employees. New York had a lot of employees—one for every twenty-four citizens compared to one for fifty-five in Los Angeles and one for seventy-three in Chicago.

Third, like many cities, New York had lost homeowners and businesses to the suburbs. At the same time, more and more poor people kept moving into New York. The need for such expensive services as welfare and police protection increased at the very time that income from taxes was moving out.

In early 1975, New York City banks and other investors refused to lend the city any more money. Mayor Abraham Beame was in a tough spot. The city would go broke if it could not borrow enough money to pay its debts. City services would stop. Investors would lose huge amounts of money. New York's situation was a national warning that other cities might have the same problem.

Mayor Beame asked both the President of the United States and the Governor of New York to help the city. Both answered that the mayor should cut the city's budget by trimming back city services. President Ford especially wanted the Big Apple to solve its own problems. The federal government was already giving the city millions of dollars a year.

Mayor Beame went to work. In July, nearly 3 thousand sanitation workers were fired. More than 5 thousand police officers turned in their badges and pistols. More than 2 thousand firefighters were laid off and twenty-five firehouses closed. Still Beame planned to fire another 20 thousand city workers.

But the city's strong unions struck back. Garbage collectors went out on strike. Garbage began piling up in the streets. Many police and firefighters walked off the job to protest the budget cuts. Police were predicting a big crime wave. Someone said New York should be renamed "Fear City."

Mayor Beame backed down. He began rehiring workers. His plan to cut the budget had failed. The city's debts were coming due. There seemed to be only one place left for the mayor to turn.

Early in the fall of 1975, Mayor Beame went to Washington. Again he asked President Ford for special aid to keep the city from going broke. Again the President said no. He threatened to veto any law Congress might pass to help the city. However, by late fall, the mayor, the President, the unions, the banks, and others realized they could not let the city go broke. The bad economic effect on the rest of the country would be too great.

Finally, everyone involved in the crisis was forced to come to an agreement. The national government agreed to give the city over $2 billion a year in loans. Sales taxes in the city were raised. The banks agreed to delays in repayment. The city made budget cuts, and the unions went along. In addition, the unions loaned money to the city.

Reviewing the Case Study

1. Describe the conditions that led to the crisis in New York City.
2. Could the city government have avoided the crisis?
3. How were the problems faced by New York different from those of other American cities?
4. How were New York's problems similar to those of other cities?

Chapter Nineteen Test and Activities

★★★

Vocabulary

Match the following words with their meanings.

1. metropolitan area
2. megalopolis
3. revenue sharing
4. grants-in-aid
5. rapid transit system
6. slum
7. urban renewal
8. public housing project
9. pollution
10. zoning ordinance

a. returning part of the federal tax collected to the city
b. a large city, its suburbs, and nearby towns
c. trains that move people around in the city
d. a run-down part of the city
e. a very large urban area where cities have started to overlap
f. uncleanness
g. residences for the poor built with public money
h. city law about the kind of houses or businesses allowed in an area
i. federal money set aside for special purposes in cities
j. tearing down slums and building new places to live and work

Reviewing Chapter Ideas

1. True or false: In the HUD survey of over 7,000 people, most people agreed that cities were fine places to live.
2. How many of the people surveyed said they were considering leaving the city?
   a. less than half   c. more than half
   b. about half   d. nearly all

3. Most cities have grown _____ .
   a. from the inside out
   b. from the outside in
   c. only in the middle
   d. with no pattern
4. A Standard Metropolitan Statistical Area is a city and surrounding area with a population of _____ .
   a. 20,000
   b. 30,000
   c. 40,000
   d. 50,000
5. Which of the following is not an example of a megalopolis?
   a. Chicago to Buffalo
   b. Washington, D.C., to Boston
   c. Minneapolis to Chicago
   d. Los Angeles to San Diego
6. True or false: There are about one thousand autos in this country.
7. What do urban experts agree is the best way to move people around a city?
   a. cars
   b. trains
   c. buses
   d. all equally good
8. The largest cause of air pollution in cities is
   a. office buildings
   b. traffic
   c. people
   d. industries
9. True or false: Water pollution has only begun to appear in the past ten years.
10. True or false: City planners have no legal powers.

Vocabulary
1. b   4. i   7. j   10. h
2. e   5. c   8. g
3. a   6. d   9. f

Ideas
1. F   4. d   7. b   10. T
2. a   5. c   8. b
3. a   6. F   9. F

416

★★

Using Basic Social Studies Skills

Finding Information

1. Find the results of a HUD survey about cities at the beginning of this chapter. What are three things people like about cities?
2. Find and name three things people say are bad about cities.

Comprehending Information

1. Explain why cities grew rapidly in the late 1800s.
2. Name three problems most large cities face today.
3. How has the federal government influenced cities to have city planners?

Organizing Information

1. Draw a diagram of the pattern in which most cities grew.
2. Explain what kinds of buildings and city activities you would find in each of the parts of your diagram.

Evaluating Information

Thomas Jefferson felt life on the farm was better than life in the city. Using your own experiences and things you have read and seen, tell whether you agree or disagree and why.

Communicating Ideas

Express your ideas about city problems. You may write a paragraph, compose a song, paint a mural, make a stand-up picture in a box, draw a cartoon, or use any other art form you choose.

Using Decision-Making Skills

1. Of the major problems facing cities, pick one that you could think of ways to solve.
2. If you were a leader in a city, which other leaders and groups would you work with to solve the problem you've picked?
3. When you present your solution to the people whose help you want, you might say, "We have these three alternatives." What would they be?
4. Which of the groups in a city would be most critical of your solution?
5. Why?
6. What outcome would you anticipate from your activities?

Activities

1. Use an atlas. Make a list of the cities in the United States with a population of a million or more.
2. Look up *cities* in the *Readers' Guide to Periodical Literature.* Are there many articles listed or few? Pick one that interests you and that is in a magazine your library carries. Read it and report anything new to the class.
3. Students interested in reading books about cities may enjoy the following:

    (a) *The Cities in Tomorrow's World; Challenges to Urban Survival,* by David Reuben Michelsohn and the Editors of Science Book Associates, Messner, 1973.

    (b) *Central City/Spread City,* by Alvin Schwartz, Macmillan Publishing Company, 1973.

    (c) *Patterns in City Growth,* by Joel Tarr, Scott, Foresman and Company, 1975.

Chapter 20 | Taking Part in Community Life

★★★

The car swung into the parking lot full of Saturday shoppers. As the car came to a halt, Jim Woyack jumped out and raised a loudspeaker.

"Attention," he cried, "there's a killer in the area." Before panic started, Jim explained that the killer was cancer. Jim and four neighbors were collecting donations so a cancer clinic could be built in their community.

Every year more than 37 million citizens like Jim Woyack do volunteer work to help make their communities a better place to live. These Americans volunteer to work in health clinics, little leagues, nursing homes, animal welfare shelters, and many other places. They may be high-school students working to clean up a vacant lot or grandparents teaching nursery-school children or business people giving up weekends to organize a sports program for handicapped children.

Discuss: How are these people helping others?

The United States has always been a nation of volunteers. More than 150 years ago, Alex de Tocqueville, a Frenchman, visited America. He wanted to see how the young country was doing. He was amazed to find Americans volunteering to work on all sorts of problems that government handled in other countries. In this chapter you will learn about voluntary group activity as you read:

1/Voluntary Groups
2/How Voluntary Groups Are Governed
3/How Volunteers Help Make Democracy Work
Case Study: Teen-agers Volunteer

1/Voluntary Groups

"I like the way the kids feel toward me when I come in each day. For weeks I worked really hard with one boy. Then, one day, he put his hand out and shook mine."

Barb Ferris, a high-school junior, was describing her volunteer work with a mentally retarded child at Sonoma State Hospital. Every day, groups of teen-agers visit the hospital to work with patients. These young volunteers spend hours taking patients out for walks, helping with physical therapy, reading to patients, playing with children, starting arts and crafts projects and much more.

Many students also spend part of their summer vacation working at the hospital. The volunteers took over an old barn on the hospital grounds. They fixed it up and turned it into a living quarters they call Volunteer Village.

To **volunteer** is to offer to work or help without pay. Voluntary groups are spare-time organizations whose members are mostly unpaid volunteers. Working with a voluntary group is one important way citizens in America help meet needs in their community.

A college student volunteers her time to work with a patient at Children's Hospital Medical Center in Boston.

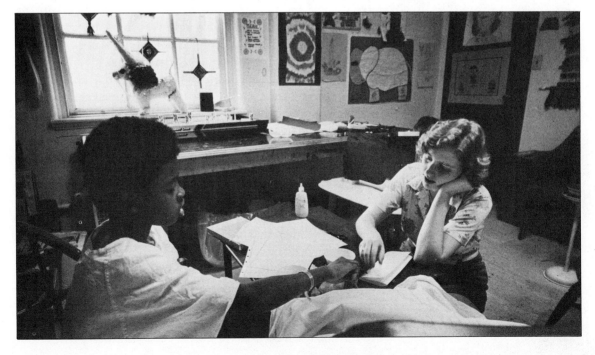

Large Groups

There are many different kinds of voluntary groups working on solving community problems. Some groups may be very large. The American Red Cross, for example, has 30 million members spread across the United States, and the Girl Scouts has over 3 million members. Examples of other large groups are the American Cancer Society, the League of Women Voters, the Kiwanis Clubs, and the General Federation of Women's Clubs. A large group usually works on many different activities. They sponsor sports projects; provide food baskets, cut wood, and give other help to the poor; and support medical clinics and research.

The Lions Club is one very large voluntary group that carries on many important services. The group has more than a million members. These members belong to over 27,500 local Lions Clubs in cities all over the world.

Lions Club members pay $15 in dues each year and go to regular meetings, usually once a week. They use their spare time to work on many local projects. Some attend an annual convention of the entire group.

The motto of the Lions Club is "We Serve." At a 1925 convention, Helen Keller, a great lecturer of the blind, asked the Lions Club to work to help the blind. Since then group members have worked on many projects for the blind. They set up eye clinics and eye banks. They hold workshops and help pay scholarships for blind students. They introduced the white canes used by the blind. They provide guide dogs for many blind people. Some other Lions Clubs projects include repairing hearing aids for the needy who are hard of hearing, sponsoring career night at local high schools, building playgrounds, and starting local clean-up campaigns.

Small Groups

Many voluntary groups are small and locally organized. They often work on one or two projects, such as collecting toys for needy children at Christmas time. Here are two examples.

The Worthington Historical Society is a group of citizens working to preserve the heritage of the city of Worthington, Ohio. Members collect antiques, old pictures, and other items that show what frontier life in the Ohio town was like.

The Orange Johnson House is one of the group's biggest projects. Built in 1816, the house is a good example of early life in Worthington. Hundreds of people each year tour the beautiful

Note: Have a community map available. Locate any places where volunteer work might be done.

Discuss: What are the key roles of volunteer groups? How do large and small groups compare?

420

old house. To raise money for their projects, historical society members hold an annual flea market, an antique show, and a summer concert.

Many high-school students in Fall River, Massachusetts, have volunteered to help their community in another way. They work in the Youth Elderly Services (YES) program. In YES, the student volunteers work with elderly people in Fall River's nursing homes. The students spend one or two hours a week meeting with their elderly friends. They write letters, run errands, help with odd jobs, and provide companionship. The YES program is a way students can help their community. It also gives the elderly a sense that young people care about them.

Discuss: What voluntary community activities are there in your area? What groups have you participated in? What groups would you like to join in the future?

Section Review

Vocabulary: voluntary group, volunteer.
Reviewing the Main Ideas
1. Define *voluntary group*.
2. How are the Lions an example of a voluntary group?
3. How is a voluntary group different from a business?
Skill Building
1. Make a list of as many voluntary groups in your community as you can. Add your list to the lists of classmates, eliminating duplicates.
2. What services are not being provided in your community that could be handled by a voluntary group?

Main Ideas
1. spare-time organizations whose members are mostly unpaid volunteers
2. p. 420
3. It does not have profits as one of its goals.
Skill Building
1. Answers will vary.
2. Answers will vary.

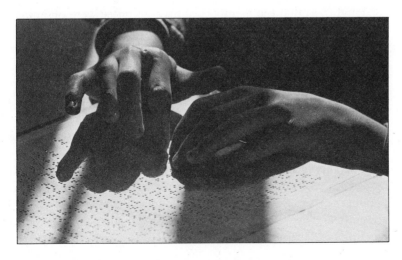

Braille is a system of writing in which the letters of the alphabet are represented by different arrangements of raised dots. The Lions Club provides books in braille for the blind.

2/How Voluntary Groups Are Governed

Discuss: Why are regular meetings and designated leaders important to a voluntary group?

Sheila McCreary was president of the Parent Teacher Association (PTA) at her son's school. As president, it was her job to run the group's business meetings. It was also the president's job to be the leader of the group. "Good evening," Sheila began, "I'm glad everyone could be here. We have some important business to discuss."

Like any group, voluntary groups must govern themselves in order to get things done. This involves making rules, setting goals, and planning projects to meet the goals. Many voluntary groups have **bylaws** which serve as a written constitution for the group.

Let's look closely at the officers. Alan Hartford was the secretary. His job was to keep formal notes of what happened at business meetings. These notes are called the **minutes.** Alan began the meeting by going over the minutes from the last meeting.

Next the group heard from Lucy Shaefer, the treasurer. The treasurer is in charge of the group's money. The treasurer pays the group's bills, collects dues, and deposits the group's money in a bank. Lucy reported that the group had $985 in its account. She also reported that a bill of $20 for printing new membership forms was paid last week.

Children performing in a mime act—part of a PTA sponsored program.

Tony Rossi was the vice-president. The vice-president takes charge of meetings if the president cannot attend. Often he supervises the work of the group's committees. Tony asked Hugh Falbo to report on the membership committee's work.

Hugh said that the members of his committee were planning several projects to get new members. On Monday, for example, all the students were going to bring a membership form home to their parents.

The PTA also had a committee for special projects and a publicity committee. Committees are one way voluntary groups carry on projects.

After hearing reports, the officers of Sheila's PTA group discussed plans for the spring bike safety rodeo. Sheila suggested they set up a new committee to plan the rodeo. The others agreed. Sheila said she would contact Mike Hudson, a PTA member, to see if he would be chairperson of the bike rodeo committee. Then she said, "If there is no further business, the meeting is adjourned."

Group Leaders and Members

How do people become voluntary group officers? In most groups the officers are elected by members. Often there is a **nominating committee** that meets to talk over possible candidates. The nominating committee will talk to the various individuals it wants for offices. The committee wants to make sure these people have the time, energy, and commitment the leadership jobs require. Then they will suggest a **slate** of candidates. Most of the time, candidates for office in voluntary groups are unopposed. However, most group bylaws allow nominations to be added by anyone at election time. Then all the members vote.

In most cases, committee chairpersons are chosen by the president. Members of committees may be selected by the president or by the committee chairperson. Often members may choose which committees to serve on based on their interests.

Voluntary groups need good officers. The officers must act as leaders if the group is to be successful. It is the leader's job to govern the group, to keep projects going, to raise money, to plan and follow through on new projects, and to find new members.

Voluntary groups also need good followers. No group can be successful without members who pay their dues, go to meetings regularly, support the goals of the group, and work hard on group projects. Not every person may have the chance or want to be a group leader. But every group member can have a chance to be a good follower and contribute to the success of the group.

Discuss: What is an ideal volunteer? Can anyone be a volunteer?

Section Review

Vocabulary: bylaws, minutes, nominating committee, slate.

Reviewing the Main Ideas

1. What are the jobs of the different officers in a typical voluntary group?
2. Why do voluntary groups have committees?
3. How are officers chosen in most voluntary groups?

Skill Building

What ways of governing a voluntary group are similar to the ways our other governments are run? Find at least five points of comparison.

Main Ideas
1. president, secretary, treasurer, vice-president, committee chairpersons
2. to divide up the work and accomplish projects
3. p. 423
Skill Building
Answers will vary.

3/How Volunteers Help Make Democracy Work

Volunteer work and voluntary groups make an important contribution to democracy. In every community, citizens working in voluntary groups take responsibility for meeting important community needs that otherwise might have to be taken care of by government.

Here is an example. Every year thousands of voluntary groups in local communities across the country provide useful services for the sick and the poor. Volunteer members of these groups collect money for new medical equipment, run clinics for the deaf and blind, collect food and clothes, run sports programs for handicapped youngsters, help with physical therapy programs and much more. Without these volunteers many of these needs simply would not be met—or the government would have to do the job.

Discuss: What contributions do voluntary groups make to communities?

Volunteers help handicapped children play volleyball.

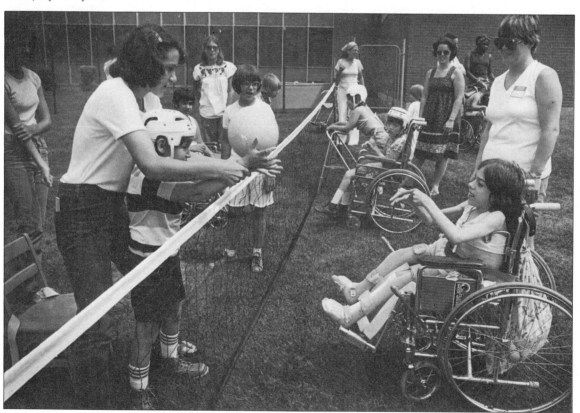

Volunteer groups are one of the most important differences between a democracy and a **totalitarian society.** In totalitarian societies, such as many communist countries, almost all areas of life are controlled by the government. There are no voluntary groups of the kind we have in our society. Instead citizens must look to the government for guidance in meeting all community needs.

Citizen participation in most totalitarian societies is controlled by the government or a communist political party. It is the government, not the individual, who decides how and when citizens should take part in community problems such as building a new well or repairing a school building. In the People's Republic of China, for example, many services are provided by citizens working in their spare time. But this work is planned and controlled by the government. Citizens have little or no freedom to decide for themselves whether or not to participate.

In a free society, the government and citizens share responsibility for meeting the community's needs. For example, we expect the government to provide police service and roads in our communities. But it is up to citizens to volunteer their time to help run the libraries, hospitals, nursing homes, sports programs, historical societies, and museums in their communities. In a democracy, there is a limit to the services a government provides. Thus, along with being a free citizen comes the responsibility of taking part in solving community problems without the government.

One political leader put it this way, "In every community and every state we need a program for voluntary action by the people, not just government action for the people." The idea in a democracy is that many community needs can best be taken care of through local voluntary groups.

Discuss: What is your role as a responsible citizen? What would it be in a totalitarian society?

Section Review

Vocabulary: democracy, totalitarian society.

Reviewing the Main Ideas

1. Why are voluntary groups important in a free society?
2. Why is there little place for voluntary groups in totalitarian society?

Skill Building

Summarize in a paragraph the main idea of section 3.

Main Ideas
1. p. 425
2. because the government decides what people will do with their time
Skill Building
Answers should be in a correctly constructed paragraph.

Teen-agers Volunteer

Adults are not the only ones who do volunteer work in their communities. A national survey in the mid-1970s showed that 22 percent of all volunteers in America were between the ages of 14 and 17.

These teen-agers made the decision to spend some of their time and energy helping meet important needs in their community. Here are several case studies that describe teen-age volunteer work.

In Rockville, Connecticut, a group of high-school students have helped to run the town's volunteer ambulance service during the daytime. The students decided to volunteer because the community was having trouble keeping the service going during the day. Rockville students worked out a plan to help. The plan called for two students and a faculty member to always be available during school study periods to handle emergencies. The Board of Education approved the plan. Students and faculty members then took ten-week advanced first aid courses to prepare for their work. The plan worked well and the students have answered calls for accidents and other emergencies.

In Knoxville, Tennessee, members of the Key Club at Fullerton High helped a voluntary group working with physically

Teen-age volunteers help clean up their community.

426

handicapped children. The Easter Seal Society in Knoxville wanted to organize a bowling league for handicapped youngsters. But the society needed volunteers to help get the program started and keep it going. Fullerton students decided to help. They coached the youngsters and handled the wheelchairs of those who used them. Their volunteer work made sure the new program got off to a good start.

At about the same time, in Geneva, New York, the Senior Girl Scout troop decided to organize a day camp for the children of migrant workers. The scouts planned the camp program with the help of the adults on their Senior Advisory Board. The camp was made up of two one-week sessions for nearly 150 boys and girls ages seven to twelve. The outdoor program included hikes, games, and arts and crafts. In addition, each child received a hot lunch. Overall the camp program was a success. The Girl Scouts planned and carried out a worthy project. The needy children had fun, learned new skills, and enjoyed the benefits of a hot lunch.

Reviewing the Case Study

1. In what ways are the three cases described above similar?
2. Explain how the volunteer work described in the cases help contribute to democracy.

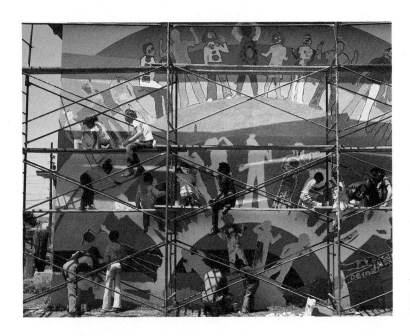

Volunteers paint a wall mural as part of a neighborhood beautification program.

Chapter Twenty Test and Activities

★★★

Vocabulary

Match the following words with their meanings.

1. to volunteer
2. voluntary group
3. bylaws
4. nominating committee
5. minutes
6. totalitarian society
7. slate

a. a group who recommends candidates for election as officers
b. a group that uses members' spare time to provide service to the community
c. a large group in which almost all areas of life are controlled by the government
d. to work without pay
e. formal notes of a group's meeting
f. the "constitution" of a voluntary group
g. a list of recommended candidates

Reviewing Chapter Ideas

1. True or false: Citizens volunteering to help in their communities is a new idea. It has only happened in the last ten or fifteen years.
2. True or false: There are many ways people can volunteer to help.
3. True or false: All voluntary groups are part of large national organizations.
4. Which of the following is not an example of a large voluntary organization?
   a. Boy Scouts
   b. Youth Elderly Services
   c. Red Cross
   d. League of Women Voters

5. The group treasurer does all the following except
   a. pay bills
   b. collect dues
   c. take notes on the meeting
   d. put money in the bank
6. True or false: In most voluntary groups, the officers volunteer for their positions.
7. True or false: In order for any group to work well it needs both leaders and followers.
8. Voluntary groups meet needs that otherwise would have to be met by _____ .
   a. businesses
   b. government
   c. wealthy citizens
   d. students
9. True or false: The United States is a totalitarian society.
10. Approximately what percent of volunteers are in high school?
    a. 5 percent
    b. 20 percent
    c. 50 percent
    d. 70 percent

★★

Using Basic Social Studies Skills

Finding Information

1. Give examples of three large voluntary groups.
2. Name three small groups.
3. Look up *democracy* and *totalitarian system* in the glossary. What is the basic difference between these two ways of life?

Comprehending Information

1. How are voluntary groups like the national government?
2. How are they different?

Organizing Information

Use the section heads and subheads to outline the information in the chapter. The outline has been partially completed below:

Title: Taking Part in Community Life

  I. Voluntary Groups

    A. _____

    B. _____

  II. _____

    A. _____

    B. _____

  III. _____

Case Study: _____

Evaluating Information

1. The authors have said that voluntary groups help a democratic form of government. What reasons do they give?
2. Do you agree or disagree? Give your reasons.

Communicating Ideas

1. Choose a voluntary group in your community whose work you feel is worthwhile. Design a poster to get more people to help.
2. You want to convince a friend to join a voluntary group. List your key arguments.

Using Decision-Making Skills

1. What ways could you volunteer your time to help your community? Choose at least three ways.
2. Which of the voluntary programs in the case study do you feel was most worthwhile? Why?
3. Which of the case study programs would be easiest to have in your community? Why?

Activities

1. Use the card catalogue to find books about Helen Keller. Record the title and author of each book available.
2. Read one of the books listed on Helen Keller. Share a brief summary of the story with class members. How has she made it possible for voluntary groups to help?
3. Invite a member of a community voluntary group to talk to the class about the group's projects. Ask if class members could help with any projects.
4. Suggest a voluntary service your class could provide. How would you govern yourselves to get the job done?

Unit Five Test

★★★

Vocabulary

Write *true* if the underlined word or phrase is used correctly. Write *false* if it is used incorrectly.

1. A <u>municipal charter</u> is a "constitution" for a city or town.
2. In some New England states, <u>counties</u> are mainly court districts.
3. There are large farms in <u>urban areas</u>.
4. The city of Lexington and Fayette County <u>consolidated</u> their governments.
5. In order to get more money to provide services, a city can sell <u>ordinances</u>.
6. California voters did not want to pay high <u>property taxes</u>.
7. The <u>council-manager</u> plan is a way some cities are governed.
8. Politics in many local governments is <u>nonpartisan</u>.
9. One role of a mayor is to act as <u>treasurer</u>.
10. You could expect to read the newspaper's endorsement of candidates in the <u>letters-to-the-editor</u> section.
11. States are divided into sections called <u>wards</u>.
12. A <u>city manager</u> could suggest ordinances.
13. The council voted to begin a <u>megalopolis</u> to help solve the problems of slums in the city.
14. <u>Revenue sharing</u> is a way that county and state governments can merge into one government.
15. A city planner could recommend that a <u>rapid transit system</u> would help solve traffic problems.
16. If the city council did not want to have a bowling alley in a certain district of houses and apartments, it could pass a <u>zoning ordinance</u>.
17. A <u>metropolitan area</u> is a rural area.
18. Thirty-seven million Americans <u>volunteer</u> to help their communities.
19. <u>Bylaws</u> are the way that ordinances are passed.
20. Communist countries are <u>totalitarian societies</u>.

Recalling Information

1. Which governments are <u>not</u> mentioned in the United States Constitution?
   a. local governments
   b. state governments
   c. the federal government
   d. all of the above
2. All states have the following types of local government <u>except</u>
   a. special districts
   b. states
   c. cities
   d. townships
3. Which form of government provides you the most services?
   a. state government
   b. local government
   c. federal government
   d. all of the above equally
4. Which form of city government do most cities over 1 million in population have?
   a. New England town
   b. commission
   c. council-manager
   d. mayor-council
5. True or false: The national government has been able to get many communities to use city planners.

★★★

6. Where in a city would you usually expect to find government offices?
   a. downtown
   b. in the run-down area
   c. in the older residential area
   d. at the outer edge

7. An enclosed shopping mall and a zoo would most likely be found _____ .
   a. downtown
   b. in the run-down area
   c. in the older residential area
   d. at the outer edge

8. The run-down area would most likely include
   a. large homes, golf courses, and new apartments
   b. factories, warehouses, and low-cost housing
   c. banks, hotels, and offices
   d. all of the above

9. Which of the following is <u>not</u> a voluntary organization
   a. Lions Club
   b. Red Cross
   c. League of Women Voters
   d. Franklin County

10. In a democracy, a person has _____ choice than in a totalitarian society.
   a. more
   b. less
   c. about the same
   d. sometimes more and sometimes less

Skill Building

People have many roles. Match the following people to the local government job each performs.

1. sheriff
2. prosecuting attorney
3. county judge
4. coroner
5. treasurer
   a. Mary Ellis made the formal charges in a murder case.
   b. Perez decided a juvenile court case.
   c. Sam Jones delivered a summons for a witness to appear in court.
   d. Sherman is the person to pay property taxes to.
   e. A woman drowned and Johnson was called in.

6. Name three services provided by local government.

7. Name three local officials that are elected. Which job do you feel is most important? Why?

8. What is the main way a local government gets the money it needs? Name two other ways.

9. Divide your paper into two columns. Label one column "mayor-council." Label the other "council-manager." Compare the two forms of city government.

10. Name three leaders in city government. Explain the role of each.

11. Name three groups that try to influence city governments.

12. Name at least three major problems cities are facing today.

13. "Most of the problems facing cities today will be solved by the year 2000." Do you agree? Why?

14. What key officers do most voluntary groups need? Explain one role of each.

Our Free Enterprise System

You must have heard the words "national economy" at least once in the past few months. Few other things get more attention in the national news.

Economy means "making the most of what one has." You'll find out how individuals as well as nations try to make the most of what they have in the chapters that follow. *Economy* also means "a system for managing the production, distribution, and consumption of goods." Some of these words may be new, but they mean something simple. People need certain things in order to live—such things as food, shelter, and clothing. They want other things too—things that they could probably get along without, such as vacation trips and tennis rackets and movies on Saturday night. The system for getting these things produced and into the hands of individual people is called the economy, or the economic system.

It is important for citizens in the United States to know how the economy works because they all take part in it. They make decisions that affect it. Citizens decide what to buy and citizens decide what to produce.

Citizens also take part in the economy as voters, for the government makes decisions that affect the economy too. In the United States, the government makes rules for buying and selling. The rules are mostly concerned with fairness. Government also takes part in the economy as a buyer. You learned the type of things that government buys when you studied government spending.

When citizens understand how the economy works, they can make wiser decisions as buyers, sellers, producers, and voters.

Discuss: Why is it important to understand how the economy works?

Gas firing of bowls in a glass factory.

433

Chapter 21

The Economy

★★★

Mary Ross works in a factory. She earns $250 per week. Mary earns enough money to pay for the things she must have in order to live—food, clothing, and a place to live. But she does not earn enough to pay for everything she would like to have. As a result, Mary has to make choices about what to buy and what to do without.

Last night, Mary went shopping. She saw two items that she wanted very much—a wool coat and a camera. Mary did not have enough money to buy both. She had to decide which one she wanted most.

Mary already had a coat that was warm. It was old, but it would last for another year or two. A camera, on the other hand, was something that would be especially valued in the next few months. Mary would be taking a trip to Canada. Having a camera to take along was beginning to seem important.

Mary decided to buy the camera. She wanted it more than she wanted the coat. Next year, when she really needed one, a coat would top her list of purchases.

In choosing between the coat and the camera, Mary made an economic decision. She had to choose between two things that she wanted because she had a limited amount of money to spend. In this chapter you will learn about the economic problems that nations as well as individuals face. You will also learn various ways that those problems are solved. You will read:

Discuss: Did Mary make the best decision? How is Mary participating in the economy?

1/Making Economic Decisions
2/Economic Systems
3/Judging an Economy's Performance
Case Study: Competing for Survival

1/Making Economic Decisions

People throughout the world use goods and services every day. **Goods** are products such as shoes, automobiles, and food. **Services** are what people do for someone in exchange for something of value. Car dealers sell goods (automobiles). Auto mechanics sell services (car repairs).

In order to produce goods and services, people need resources—natural resources and human resources. **Natural resources** come from the earth. They include water, soil, trees, and minerals. **Human resources** come from people. They are the skills, knowledge, energy, and physical capabilities of human beings.

One thing that is true of almost all resources is that they are scarce; they exist in limited amounts. There are never enough natural and human resources available to produce all the goods and services that the people of a nation could possibly want. As a result, choices must be made. People must decide what goods and services they want most.

As people live with the economic problem of **scarcity**—limited resources and unlimited wants—they make three kinds of

Discuss: What goods and services has your family used recently?

Discuss: What natural resources are found in your state?

Shopping for boots.

435

Discuss: What kinds of decisions are influenced by scarcity? How does each of these questions apply to your community?

decisions. They make decisions about what goods and services to produce, how to produce them, and how to distribute them.

What Should Be Produced?

When a nation is fighting a war, huge amounts of the nation's resources are used in the war effort. Metal resources are used to make weapons instead of pots and pans and soft-drink cans. Farmers are retrained as soldiers and there are far fewer foods to choose from in the stores. Shortages of goods appear, and people get along with their old things. The war forces the nation to make certain choices about what to produce. In peacetime, too, people make choices about what to produce, but it is not so easy to see.

Every decision about what to produce is also a decision *not* to produce something else. For example, the steel used to make autos cannot be used to produce airplanes or railroad cars. Thus, every time an automobile is built, something else made of steel is not built.

Sometimes people decide to do without certain goods and services in the present so that they can prepare for the future. This is what happens when people use resources to produce capital goods. **Capital goods** are any products that are used to make other goods. Tools and machines are capital goods. In contrast, **consumer goods** are products that are made to be used up. Food, clothing, and cosmetics are examples of consumer goods. If a group decides to produce more capital goods, they will have fewer consumer goods in the present. However, these capital goods can be used to produce large amounts of consumer goods in the future.

How Should Goods and Services Be Produced?

A second kind of economic decision is concerned with how things get produced. What resources will be used to produce desired goods and services? Almost everything can be created in more than one way. For example, when a county decides to build a new road, someone must decide which natural resource to use. Should the road be made of gravel, of dirt, of cement? Someone must also decide what human resources and capital goods to use. Should the road be built by seventy people working with hand tools or by eight people working with power machines? The people who must decide try to determine the best possible combination of resources. An important consideration

Painting bowling pins.

will be the cost of each resource. Is cement less costly than gravel? If not, is it needed to do the job right?

For Whom Should Goods and Services Be Produced?

A third kind of economic decision is concerned with the distribution of goods and services. Should everyone get the same amount of everything? Should some get more than others? How will these decisions be made? In the United States, decisions about how products are shared are tied to the incomes people receive. People who make the most money are able to buy the most goods and services.

Section Review

Vocabulary: capital goods, consumer goods, goods, human resources, natural resources, scarcity, services.

Reviewing the Main Ideas
1. What three decisions are made when people are trying to satisfy unlimited wants with limited resources?
2. Why does increased production of capital goods mean decreased production of consumer goods (at least for the present)?

Skill Building
1. If you had to make the three decisions referred to in item *1* above, which would be most difficult for you to make? Why?
2. Each day after school you use your energy, which is a human resource, to do something. In deciding to do that thing, you are also deciding not to do other things. For example, if you decide to play the piano, you are also deciding not to read a book, play baseball, babysit, or clean your room. Make a list of activities that you usually do after school. Next to each activity write another activity that you could have used your energy for but didn't. Tell why you made the choice you did.

Main Ideas
1. what to produce, how to produce goods and services, how to distribute goods and services (for whom to produce them)
2. p. 436
Skill Building
1. Answers will vary.
2. Answers will vary. If a student wishes, this answer should be kept private.

2/Economic Systems

The basic economic questions—what goods and services to produce, how to produce them, and how to distribute them—must be answered in every nation. The way in which these questions get answered is determined by each nation's **economic system.** An economic system is a nation's way of producing and distributing goods and services.

Discuss: What is an economic system?

In any economic system important economic decisions get made by one or more of the following three groups: producers, consumers, and government. **Producers** are those who offer goods and services for sale. Producers include the owners and managers of businesses; people who make goods with their hands and with machines; and people such as teachers, hairdressers, and firefighters, who provide various services. **Consumers** are those who buy the goods and services. They are called consumers because they consume, or use up, the goods and services that have been produced.

One way to compare economic systems is to look for differences in who makes the basic economic decisions. Does the government decide what to produce, how to produce, and for whom? Do producers and consumers decide? Do producers, consumers, and the government share these decisions? Two

In a market system, customers in the marketplace help decide what goods are produced.

kinds of economic systems in which economic decisions are made quite differently are the **market system** and the **command system.**

The Command Economy

In a command economy the government makes all major economic decisions. Government officials decide what to produce, how much of everything to produce, and who will get the goods and services that are produced.

Discuss: How are decisions made in a command economy?

In the past, some countries had strong kings or dictators who made important economic decisions for their nations. These nations had command economies. Today, the command-economy countries that first come to mind are **communist** countries—countries where most natural resources and capital goods are owned by the government. The two largest communist countries are China and the Soviet Union.

In China, producers carry out the orders of central government planners. Government officials tell factory managers what to produce, how much to produce, and at what price to sell. Government planners also decide who will get what goods and services. They do this by directing workers into one job or another and by deciding how much money workers in various jobs will be paid.

Political parties do not compete for office in communist countries. The one political party is the Communist party. Therefore, citizens have no real chance to influence economic decisions with their votes.

There are some countries that use the command system for only a part of their economy. Great Britain, Sweden, Denmark, and India are a part of this group. In these countries the government operates such important industries as mining and transportation. However, it does not operate industries that produce goods such as clothing, food, and household items. Because these countries have free elections and competing political parties, citizens influence the economic decisions that are made by government. Citizens can also vote to increase or decrease the total amount of control that government has over industry.

The Market Economy

In a **market system,** economic decisions are made by consumers and producers. Buyers (consumers) and sellers (producers) meet in the marketplace. Buyers give money to sellers in return for

439

goods and services. The government creates and controls the supply of money in this economic system. The money is used as a measure of the value of economic goods and services.

Discuss: How are decisions made in a market economy?

The first economic question—what to produce—is answered largely by consumers in the market economy. Producers decide what and how much to produce according to what they think consumers will buy. They try to provide goods and services in the amount consumers seem to want and at prices they will pay.

Competition among producers plays an important role in answering the second economic question. Successful producers satisfy consumers by offering the best goods and services at prices consumers can afford. In order to keep prices down, producers use the resources that cost the least. It is producer decisions responding to consumer wants, then, that answer the second economic question—how to produce goods and services.

Competition also plays a role in answering the third economic question—for whom are goods and services produced? In a market economy consumers compete in the marketplace for goods and services. Consumers with the most money can buy the most and best products and services. Consumers get their money by competing too. For example, workers compete to sell their skills and services. They offer their time and skills to those who will pay the highest wage, or fee. Those who compete most successfully get the most money and, thus, get the greatest share of goods and services.

Discuss: What does this statement mean: "Everyone's income comes from someone else's expenses"?

In a market system everyone is at some time a producer and seller and at other times a consumer and buyer of goods and services. Everyone's income comes from someone else's expenses.

Capitalism. People often refer to the United States economic system as capitalistic. One feature of capitalism is the market system of economic decision making, but there are other features too. In a capitalistic system all property, or capital, is privately owned. Citizens in a capitalistic economy are free to begin a business of any kind and use resources as they see fit. This is sometimes called **free enterprise.** People are also free to buy what they want and work where they please.

A Mixed-Market Economy. The United States economy has many capitalistic features. Most property is privately owned. Most economic decisions are made through the market system.

People are free to start their own businesses, buy the goods that they want, and work where they please. However, the United States economy also has features that are not true of pure capitalism. For instance, some United States property is publicly owned. In addition, the national government is involved in making important economic decisions. For example, the government helps determine what will be produced and how it will be produced. Remember how the government's decision not to build the B-1 bomber affected different businesses? Also, through taxes the government affects the way goods and services are distributed. More taxes are collected from those who earn the most. Many government programs redistribute this money to those who have little. Because the United States economy has features that would not exist under pure capitalism, it is sometimes referred to as a **mixed-market economy.**

Discuss: Why is the U.S. referred to as a mixed market economy?

All economic systems are to some degree mixed. Command and market systems, public ownership and private ownership, as well as other factors combine in many ways. Nonetheless, there are great differences among the countries of the world. (See the diagram at right.)

Section Review

Vocabulary: capitalism, command system, communist, competition, consumers, economic system, free enterprise, market system, mixed-market system, producers.

Reviewing the Main Ideas
1. How do most economic decisions get made in the United States—by the command system or the market system?
2. How do most economic decisions get made in China and in the Soviet Union—by the command system or the market system?
3. Why is the United States economy often called a mixed-market economy?

Skill Building
1. Explain how consumer decisions help answer these two economic questions—What should be produced? How should it be produced?
2. What role does competition play in helping decide how goods will be produced and who will receive the most or best goods and services?

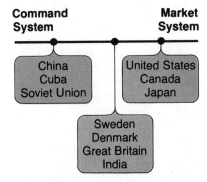

HOW ECONOMIC DECISIONS GET MADE

Command System ———————————— Market System

China
Cuba
Soviet Union

United States
Canada
Japan

Sweden
Denmark
Great Britain
India

Main Ideas
1. market system
2. command system
3. p. 441
Skill Building
1. pp. 439–440
2. p. 440

3/Judging an Economy's Performance

If you could look at newspapers from the past few years, you would see headlines like these: *U.S. Economy Is on the Upswing, U.S. Economy Dips, Inflation Rises 6 Percent.* People read articles with headlines like these because they want to know what's happening with the nation's economy. They know that whatever is going on will affect them sooner or later.

Finding Out Where the Economy Stands

When people want to find out how an economy is doing, these are some of the questions they ask: How productive is the economic system? In other words, how many goods and services does it produce? How much wealth does it provide for each citizen? How well do people live?

Discuss: What do you learn about an economy from these questions?

Discuss: What is the role of GNP in a country?

Productivity. When people want to learn about productivity, they look at **gross national product** (GNP). GNP tells the total value of the goods and services produced in a country during a certain period of time.

When economists add up the gross national product, they count only final goods and services. They count goods that are ready for people to buy, such as bicycles and typewriters. They count services that are provided directly to consumers, such as the services of a doctor or teacher. They do not count goods or services that might be counted twice. For example, an auto manufacturer must buy steel in order to build cars. The steel will not be counted in the gross national product when it is first produced. Instead, the steel will be counted as part of the value of the car once the car is produced. To count the steel before it is made into a car as well as after it is made into a car would be to count it twice.

Once the GNP has been figured out for a period of time, it is used to make comparisons. Sometimes the United States GNP is compared with the GNP of other countries. The table at left shows that the United States had 25 percent of the world's total GNP in 1975 in spite of the fact that it had only 5 percent of the world's population. One reason for this is that the United States has many power machines. These machines help workers produce goods and services in large quantities very quickly. For example, a farmer who uses large farm machines can pick more

POPULATION AND GNP IN 15 MOST POPULOUS COUNTRIES

	Population*	GNP*
China, People's Republic	21%	5%
India	15	2
USSR	6	11
United States	5	25
Indonesia	3	Under 0.5%
Japan	3	8
Brazil	3	2
Bangladesh	2	Under 0.5%
Pakistan	2	Under 0.5%
Nigeria	2	Under 0.5%
Germany, Federal Republic of	2	7
Mexico	1	1
United Kingdom	1	4
Italy	1	3
France	1	5
Rest of world	32	27
Total	100%	100%

*Percent of world's total in 1975.

corn than a farmer who picks by hand. The machine makes the one farmer more productive than the other.

Another fact you should know when looking at GNP is that goods and services which are traded, volunteered, or otherwise given free of charge are not counted in the GNP. This is true in the United States, and it is true in all other countries. In a country like the United States, people buy most goods and services with money. In some countries that is not true. In countries like Nigeria many people grow some of their own food and make some of their own clothing and tools. What they do not make themselves, they may get without using money: they may trade. Because these goods and services are not included in GNP, the GNP makes it look as if the people have fewer goods and services than they really do.

United States GNP figures are also compared with earlier United States figures. The list at right shows that in 1977 GNP in the United States was $1,337.3 billion. This means that, taken together, all the goods and services produced in 1977 were worth that much. The table also shows a steady increase of GNP in the United States over the past thirty years. People like to see the GNP rise, or at least stay about the same, from one year to the next. If the GNP goes steadily down month after month, it means that fewer and fewer goods and services are being produced (at least those that are counted in the GNP). That can mean that more and more people are out of work.

Note: Some students may be able to find news items referring to GNP to share with the class.

GNP from 1947–1977	
	in Billions
1947	$468.3
1966	$981.0
1967	$1,007.7
1968	$1,051.8
1969	$1,078.8
1970	$1,075.3
1971	$1,107.5
1972	$1,171.1
1973	$1,235.0
1974	$1,214.0
1975	$1,191.7
1976	$1,265.0
1977	$1,337.3

Discuss: In a healthy economy which direction should the GNP move?

Productivity is a measure of an economic system. Heavy machinery makes this Indiana farmer more productive.

443

Discuss: What does it mean that "the U.S. ranked third in the world in yearly income per person"?

Income. A second way to judge an economy is to look at **personal income** (PI). Personal income is the money earned by the people who produce and sell goods and services. The graph on this page shows that from 1955 to 1975 there was an increase in the percentage of United States families getting higher incomes. In 1977 the United States ranked third in the world in yearly income per person. Only Sweden and Switzerland scored higher.

Consumption. A third way to judge an economy is to look at consumption—what people actually buy with their money. The graph on page 445 shows the different kinds of goods and services bought by Americans in 1977. The many goods and services enjoyed by Americans suggest that they have a high **standard of living.**

Gross national product, personal income, and consumption figures do not tell everything about an economy. They tell about the quantity, or amount, that is produced, earned, and purchased. However, they cannot tell much about the quality of the goods and services produced. Are goods carefully made? Are services provided with care and thoughtfulness? Neither can GNP, PI, nor consumption figures tell much about the overall quality of life in the economic system. Do people have enough leisure time? Are people happy with the kind of work they do? Is the natural environment being protected from pollution? In the United States, people think that the quality of life is important. Because citizens help make the important economic decisions, they ask these kinds of questions all the time.

The Ups and Downs of a Market System

In the 1930s millions of people throughout the United States were out of work. Many others had had their **wages** cut. People couldn't buy what they wanted and needed. Businesses couldn't sell what they made, and so they stopped producing. The country was in a **depression.** Times were so bad, in fact, that the period is called the Great Depression. It lasted for almost ten years.

A depression is a time of very slow business activity. Producers stop producing and buyers stop buying. A **recession** is also a time of slow business activity. During a recession, however, things aren't as bad as they are during a depression. Recessions sometimes turn into depressions.

THE PERCENTAGE OF FAMILIES IN VARIOUS INCOME GROUPS

Income	1955	1965	1975
$15,000 and Over	15.7	33.2	44.4
$10,000–14,999	26.0		
$5,000–9,999	35.4	27.0	22.3
		24.2	21.1
Under $5,000	22.9	15.6	12.0

Depressions and recessions are the "down" side of what is sometimes called the **business cycle** in a market system. There is also an "up" side of the business cycle. This is when business activity begins to grow—when producers begin to produce more and buyers begin to buy more. The middle 1960s was such a time. In the mid-1960s jobs were easy to get compared to the 1930s. Not many people were out of work. Wages were going up. Businesses were producing many goods and services. They had an easy time selling what they made. A period of rapidly increasing business activity is sometimes called an economic **boom.** The ups and downs of the business cycle happen regularly.

The problems that come with a recession or a depression are easy to understand. People suffer when they lose their jobs or have their wages lowered. They can't buy the things they need. However, people can also suffer in a time of increased business activity, a boom. The suffering is caused by **inflation.**

Inflation is a time of rising prices. One cause of inflation is consumer demand. Consumers want to buy more goods than have been made. When demand is greater than supply, prices go up. When demand is less than supply, prices go down. In economics, this is called the **law of supply and demand.**

Inflation is also a time of rising wages. Sometimes, however, prices begin to rise faster than wages. And some people's wages

Discuss: What is a depression?

Note: Some students may be able to diagram the relationship between depression, recession and inflation (business cycle).

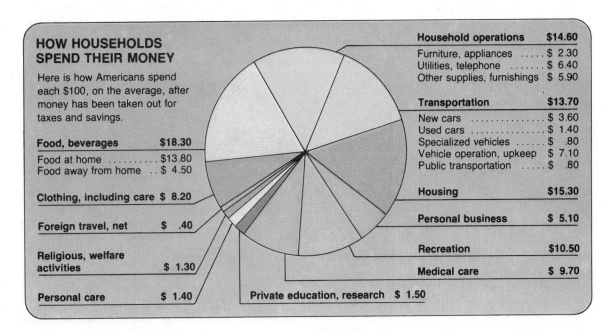

HOW HOUSEHOLDS SPEND THEIR MONEY

Here is how Americans spend each $100, on the average, after money has been taken out for taxes and savings.

Food, beverages	$18.30
Food at home	$13.80
Food away from home	$ 4.50

Clothing, including care	$ 8.20

Foreign travel, net	$ .40

Religious, welfare activities	$ 1.30

Personal care	$ 1.40

Household operations	$14.60
Furniture, appliances	$ 2.30
Utilities, telephone	$ 6.40
Other supplies, furnishings	$ 5.90

Transportation	$13.70
New cars	$ 3.60
Used cars	$ 1.40
Specialized vehicles	$ .80
Vehicle operation, upkeep	$ 7.10
Public transportation	$ .80

Housing	$15.30

Personal business	$ 5.10

Recreation	$10.50

Medical care	$ 9.70

Private education, research $ 1.50

don't go up at all. This is true of retired people who have a limited amount of money to last the rest of their lives. People whose wages don't keep up with prices suffer. They can buy less and less with their money.

Even people whose wages do keep up with inflation feel cheated. For example, prices of many goods and services more than doubled between 1960 and 1975. A worker earning two dollars an hour in 1960 would have to earn more than four dollars an hour in 1975 just to be able to buy the same things. Most people hope that after working fifteen or twenty years, they can afford more things than when they first began. So you see, inflation seems to take away what people work for. It makes people feel like a hamster on a wheel. They work and work and don't get anywhere. The graph on page 447 shows how inflation affected the buying power of wages between 1967 and 1978.

Since the 1930s, the United States government has tried to keep recessions from becoming depressions. One way government does this is by spending money. For example, the Congress may spend money on road repairs. It pays the workers who do the work and it buys the materials that are used. Workers are given jobs and businesses are encouraged to keep producing more goods (in this case, road-building materials). In other words, business activity increases.

Another way that government tries to prevent depression is by making it easy to get loans. When people are able to get loans

Discuss: Is inflation always good?

Photographer Dorothea Lange's unforgettable pictures show what the Great Depression meant to people who lived through it. This one is a bread line in San Francisco in 1933.

easily, they buy more goods than they could without the loans. When people buy goods, businesses are encouraged to keep producing more goods. When businesses are producing goods, they can keep workers on the job.

The national government fights inflation by doing the opposite of what it does when it fights depressions. To fight inflation, Congress spends less money. When Congress stops buying, demand for goods goes down and prices go down. (Remember the law of supply and demand.) The government also fights inflation by making it more difficult to get loans. When people cannot get loans, they buy fewer goods. Once again, as demand goes down, prices go down.

Discuss: How has the government tried to prevent a depression?

The problems of the business cycle have never been completely solved. Slowing down economic activity to fight inflation usually leads to recession and unemployment. Increasing economic activity to fight off unemployment leads eventually to inflation. Government planners try to make decisions that prevent either unemployment or inflation from becoming too severe.

Discuss: Where is the U.S. in the business cycle just now?

Section Review

Vocabulary: boom, business cycle, consumption, depression, gross national product, inflation, law of supply and demand, personal income, recession, standard of living, wages.

Reviewing the Main Ideas
1. How does the government try to prevent the unemployment that comes with a depression?
2. How does the government try to prevent inflation?

Skill Building
1. Which country had the second largest GNP in 1975? Third? (See the table on page 442.)
2. Use the graph on page 445 to answer this question: Did consumers spend more on housing or on food in the year described in the graph?

Main Ideas
1. pp. 446–447
2. p. 447
Skill Building
1. Japan had second largest; Germany was third.
2. food

HOW INFLATION GOBBLES UP YOUR PAYCHECK

Average Married Worker With Two Children

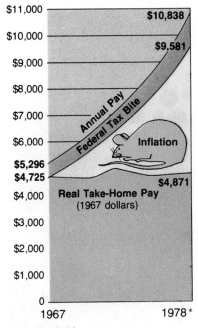

*Annual rate in July

Competing for Survival

Competition is a key part of how things work in a market economy. Increased competition can mean a fight for survival on the part of producers. For consumers, however, it can mean something quite different.

In the early and mid-1960s people who wanted to travel by air from one point in Texas to another used one of two airlines—Braniff International or Texas International. These two airlines competed for the business of local consumers.

In 1968 another airline, Southwest Airlines, joined the competition. It had received permission from the Texas Aeronautics Commission (the state agency that regulated air travel) to provide air service between Houston, Dallas, and San Antonio.

When the two existing airlines learned of their new competition, they reacted. They went to court to try to prevent the change. They said that there was no need for a new airline in Texas. They argued that the Texas Aeronautics Commission had made an error in allowing Southwest to begin operations.

Southwest fought back. It took its case all the way to the United States Supreme Court. In 1971 Southwest won. The Supreme Court decided that it did have the right to operate in Texas.

Once Southwest began operating, its primary goal was to attract enough customers to stay in business. There were two sources of passengers: (1) people who were flying Braniff or Texas International and (2) people who were not using any airline service. Southwest had to find a way to sell its services to these people.

The Southwest owners identified three possible plans of action. One choice would be to charge less for air fare than either Braniff or Texas International. Perhaps customers would come to Southwest to save money. A second choice would be to provide services that the other airlines did not offer. Perhaps customers would come to Southwest to enjoy a more comfortable flight. The owners could survey passengers to find out what services they wanted. Then Southwest might provide them. A third choice would be to offer gifts. Consumers might fly Southwest to get gifts that were not offered by Braniff or Texas International.

Southwest decided to lower the price of air fare. They charged $20 to travel between the cities of Houston, Dallas, and San Antonio. The other airlines charged $27.

At first the decision to cut prices worked. Customers flocked to Southwest.

Braniff and Texas International fought back. Braniff and Texas International also lowered the price of fares to $20. In addition, they offered extra services such as hot towels, free telephone calls at the check-in gate, free beverages, and free newspapers. Most passengers returned to Braniff or Texas International.

After one year Southwest Airlines was in trouble. They could not make a profit by charging only $20 for tickets. As a result the air fare was raised to $26. Braniff and Texas International quickly raised the price of their tickets to $26 too.

Southwest's next move was to offer service to Houston's Hobby Airport instead of to the Houston International Airport. A customer survey had revealed that most passengers wanted the service. This decision attracted many passengers back to Southwest. In response, Braniff also switched its flights to Hobby.

Next Southwest's owners decided to offer gifts. In addition, they offered a bonus plan in which a person could win a free flight after purchasing a certain number of tickets.

Braniff and Texas International continued to compete vigorously against Southwest Airlines, but the new company continued to attract enough passengers to survive. There seemed to be enough customers to support three local airlines. Although increased competition caused those who were producing a service to work harder for customers, it brought benefits to consumers. They had better service and lower prices than they would have had without it.

Reviewing the Case Study

1. What was Southwest's main problem when it first began operating?
2. What decisions did Southwest make in attempting to solve its problem? Why?
3. What were the consequences of Southwest's choices?
4. What is your judgment of the outcomes?
5. What was the role of government in economic decision making in this case?
6. What was the role of consumers?
7. How did competition influence economic decision making?

Chapter Twenty-one Test and Activities

★★★

Vocabulary

Match the following words with their meanings below.

1. goods
2. services
3. natural resources
4. human resources
5. scarcity
6. boom
7. economic system
8. producers
9. consumers
10. market economy
11. command economy
12. capitalism
13. free enterprise
14. gross national product

a. the value of goods and services produced in an economic system during a year
b. a time of increasing economic activity
c. the skills, energy, strength, and knowledge of humans
d. an economic system that includes features such as private ownership of property
e. those who provide goods and services to be sold
f. an economy in which all economic decisions are made by the government
g. the freedom of people in an economy to start and operate their own businesses
h. a nation's way of producing and distributing goods and services
i. those who buy goods and services
j. an economy in which economic decisions are made by consumers and producers
k. products such as shoes and bicycles
l. the basic economic problem of limited resources and unlimited human wants
m. what people do for someone in exchange for something of value
n. materials such as water and minerals that are supplied by nature

Reviewing Chapter Ideas

1. True or false: The basic economic problem of all nations is having too great a supply of resources.
2. True or false: Every time we buy something, we make an economic decision.
3. True or false: Consumer goods are products used to make other products.
4. Which of the following questions has to do with the distribution of goods and services?
   a. How do we decide who gets what?
   b. What resources will be used?
   c. How much should be saved for later?
   d. none of the above
5. True or false: Government involvement in decision making is the same for all countries.
6. During a depression _____ .
   a. many people are out of work
   b. businesses produce more goods
   c. wages go up
   d. buyers buy more goods
7. Which economic system would have the least government involvement in decision making?
   a. a command system
   b. a mixed-market system
   c. a market system
   d. All would be the same.
8. True or false: Inflation is a time of rising prices.

Vocabulary

450   1. k   4. c   7. h   10. j   13. g
      2. m   5. l   8. e   11. f   14. a
      3. n   6. b   9. i   12. d

Ideas

1. F   4. a   7. c
2. T   5. F   8. T
3. F   6. a

★★

Using Basic Social Studies Skills

Finding Information

All countries make economic decisions. In doing so, they answer three important questions. Find the section in which the three questions are named and discussed. What is the section title? What are the three questions? Was it easy or difficult to find the questions? Why?

Comprehending Information

The three economic questions get answered differently in China than they do in the United States. Explain the difference.

Organizing Information

Look at the graph on page 445. List the major categories of goods and services shown on the graph. Begin with the item that people spend the most on. End with the item that they spend the least on.

Evaluating Information

Look back at the decision the government had to make about Southwest Airlines. Did the government make a wise decision? How did you decide?

Communicating Ideas

List two or more questions you would ask to find out what kind of economic system a country has.

Using Decision-Making Skills

Write the name of some item in your house. Then list the different materials that it could possibly be made from. (For example, a wall could be built of bricks, stone, sod, ice, plastic, steel, or wood.) List the methods that could be used to make it. Which materials and methods would you choose? Why?

Activities

1. Look for newspaper and magazine articles about the economy of your country. Make a class booklet of any articles you find.

2. Use the *Readers' Guide to Periodical Literature* to find articles on the United States economy that were written in the past year. Record the name of one article, the magazine it is found in, its date, and its page number.

3. Work with a partner. Choose a country in Europe other than the Soviet Union. Gather information on the country's economic system. Report your findings to the class.

4. Work with three or four other students to make a montage of ads for goods or services in your community.

5. Locate the GNP for the United States last year. Compare it to the GNP for 1977. Report your findings and tell where you located the information.

6. Draw a sequence of cartoonlike pictures that shows what happens in times of depression and boom.

7. For those students who want to learn more about economic systems and economic problems, the following books are recommended.

   (a) *Inflation,* by James D. Forman (Franklin Watts, 1977).

   (b) *Inflation in Action,* by Adrian A. Paradis (Messner, 1974).

   (c) *Capitalism; Economic Individualism to Today's Welfare State,* by James D. Forman (Franklin Watts, 1972).

   (d) *Communism; from Marx's Manifesto to 20th Century Reality,* by James D. Forman (Franklin Watts, 1972).

Chapter 22 Production Decisions

Lee Wong is a great mechanic. His special interest is older cars. He thinks all cars should have a very long life and likes to help people keep them running.

Lee's interest in cars first developed when he was seventeen. He bought an old car himself. Then one part after another had to be replaced or repaired. Lee quickly learned how to "do-it-himself."

By nineteen Lee was getting regular offers of money to work on the cars of friends and relatives. At first Lee said "no." He already had a job in a factory. Finally, Lee decided to give it a couple of hours a night. That is how Lee Wong's car-repair business was born.

During the first six months, Lee worked by himself in his parents' garage. He didn't have to pay for space, but he did have to buy some new tools.

Business was so good from the very first weeks that Lee soon got back every penny he had spent. As word spread of Lee's skill and fair prices, requests for his services became far greater than he could provide. He simply couldn't work faster or work more hours.

Finally, Lee decided to make his part-time business a full-time business. He would give up his factory job, rent a large garage that he knew about, equip it with the necessary tools, and hire one or two people to help him.

First, Lee went to a nearby bank to get a loan. He had some money saved, but not enough to pay for all the equipment he would need. Then Lee hired two helpers. One was a beginner. The other was a skilled mechanic.

Lee took a risk when he opened the business. He couldn't be sure that he would get enough customers to pay his bills and himself. Lee decided to take that risk in order to become a full-time producer and seller of car-repair services. In this chapter you will learn more about the decisions of people who produce goods and services. You will read:

Discuss: Would this be possible in your community?

1/Organizing and Managing Businesses
2/How Labor Unions Affect Business Decisions
Case Study: Mass Produced Meals

452

1/Organizing and Managing Businesses

In a market economy, the owners and managers of businesses make important decisions. They decide what to produce, how to produce it, what price to charge for finished products, how much of the **profits** (money made over and above expenses) to save, and how much to spend on capital goods.

Discuss: What decisions do owners and managers of business make?

Organizing a Business

Anyone who runs a business must first decide how to organize it. There are three main kinds of business organizations: (1) the single proprietorship, (2) the partnership, and (3) the corporation. In addition, cooperatives are sometimes organized to meet special needs.

Single Proprietorship. A business owned by one person is a single proprietorship. This is the most common form of business in the United States. (See "Business in the United States" on page 454.)

Lee Wong's auto-repair business is an example of single proprietorship. Lee is the single owner; he is the only boss. You may know of such businesses in your community. Many drugstores, beauty shops, small grocery stores, shoe-repair shops, and restaurants fit this category.

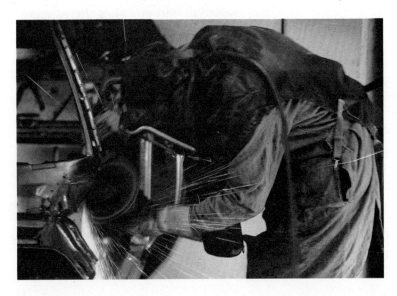

Working on an automobile.

One important advantage of a single proprietorship is that the owner gets all the profits. A second advantage is that the owner does not have to check decisions with anyone else. Thus, the single proprietor has a great deal of freedom to act as he or she thinks best. Finally, the single proprietor can take special pride and satisfaction in business ownership.

Partnership. A business owned by two or more people is a partnership. The partners share the costs, profits, and responsibilities of the business.

A major advantage of the partnership is that it is easier for two or more people to raise the money needed to start or expand a business than it is for one person to do so. Another advantage is that partners can take charge of different parts of the business. One partner might make decisions about production while the other makes decisions about selling. By sharing the responsibilities of management, the partners can often do better together than either could do alone.

The Corporation. The type of business that produces and sells most goods and services in the United States is the corporation. (See the graph on this page.) Corporations sell about 86 percent of all goods and services produced in the country each year.

Ownership in a corporation is divided into **shares of stock.** The people who organize the corporation sell these shares in order to raise the money needed to start operating the business. The number of shares that each person owns represents his or her portion of the ownership. For example, suppose a corporation issues 100,000 shares of stock. A person who buys 10,000 shares owns 10 percent of the company.

People who own stock, **stockholders,** do not operate the business themselves. Instead, they elect a **board of directors** to do so. The board of directors appoints the top managers of the corporation. They include the company's president, vice-presidents, secretary, and treasurer. These top managers direct the day-to-day business of the corporation.

A primary advantage of the corporation is **limited liability.** This means that the owners' risk is strictly limited to the amount of money paid for shares of stock. If the business fails, the stockholders can lose the money they paid for stock, but they do not have to pay the company's debts.

BUSINESS IN THE UNITED STATES

Types of Businesses

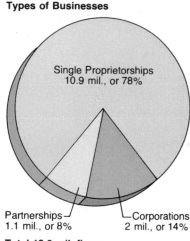

Single Proprietorships
10.9 mil., or 78%

Partnerships
1.1 mil., or 8%

Corporations
2 mil., or 14%

Total 13.9 mil. firms

**Money Received for
Goods and Services**

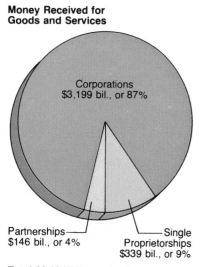

Corporations
$3,199 bil., or 87%

Partnerships
$146 bil., or 4%

Single
Proprietorships
$339 bil., or 9%

Total $3,684 bil. received

A second advantage of the corporation is that a very large sum of money can be raised to set up the organization. Once the corporation is running, it can sell more shares of stock if it needs to raise more money. Some corporations have thousands of stockholders. (See the table on this page.) The money that they have spent on stock can amount to millions of dollars when it is put together.

A third advantage of corporate organization is unlimited life. A single proprietorship ends when the owner dies. Likewise, a partnership dies when one partner dies; it must be reorganized if the business is to continue. However, the life of a corporation is not tied to the lives of stockholders, who are the owners. Upon the death of stockholders, the shares can be willed to other people, or they can be sold. The corporation lives as long as enough people are willing to buy shares of stock in it.

Discuss: What examples of each type of business organization are found in your area?

Discuss: What are the key benefits and drawbacks of each kind of business organization?

Cooperatives. A cooperative is a business association that provides services for its own members. Producer cooperatives help members sell goods that they have produced. Many farmers are members of producer cooperatives. Consumer cooperatives offer savings to members on the purchase of certain goods. Sometimes consumers set up their own grocery stores. By purchasing food in large quantities, the cooperative is able to buy items at a reduced rate. These savings are eventually passed on to members. The **credit union** is another type of consumer cooperative. Credit unions provide banking services to members. Members can deposit money and earn interest on these savings. Often the rate of interest is higher than it would be at a bank. The credit union also offers loans to its members. The rate of interest charged on loans is reasonable.

Note: Have students summarize this table.

Managing the Factors of Production

Anyone who sets up a business must have resources in order to produce goods or services. The person must have natural resources, capital goods, labor, and management skills. (Labor and management skills are, of course, both human resources.) Economists call these four resources the **factors of production.** Without them, production could not happen. Business success depends on how wisely the factors of production are used.

Natural Resources. Natural resources are important to all businesses. Minerals such as oil, coal, and iron ore make up one

COMPANIES WITH THE LARGEST NUMBER OF STOCKHOLDERS

Company	Number of Stockholders
American Telephone and Telegraph	2,897,000
General Motors	1,225,000
Exxon Corporation	684,000
International Business Machines	582,000
General Electric	545,000
General Telephone and Electronics	443,000
Texaco, Inc.	414,000
Gulf Oil	357,000
Ford Motor	335,000
Southern Company	293,000

Discuss: What are the factors of production? How do they influence the business owner?

important group of natural resources. Minerals are used in making most manufactured goods. For example, iron ore is used to produce many of the automobile parts that Lee Wong uses in his car-repair business.

The soil is another natural resource important to the production of manufactured goods. Most important, the soil is used for growing crops. The bread that you ate for breakfast was made from flour that was ground from grains that needed fertile soil in order to grow. The land is also used to provide space on which to put buildings. For example, Lee Wong's auto shop sits on a certain amount of land. The land is a natural resource that Lee Wong needs in order to operate his business.

Because natural resources and the products created from them are scarce, they are costly. One must pay a price to get them. For instance, part of the rent that Lee Wong pays every month is for the land under his building. When Lee moved his business out of his parents' garage into a bigger building, he picked a building located at the edge of town. Land prices are lower there than they are in the center of town. Lee decided that keeping his prices down was more important than locating his business in the most convenient possible place. His customers seem to agree.

All business owners must make decisions that involve the use of natural resources. Like other business decisions, these are important because they help make the business succeed or fail.

Discuss: What is the role of labor in a business?

Labor. People who offer their services in exchange for wages are the labor force. No business can succeed without a capable labor force. The more skilled the work force is, the better off the business will be.

Labor, which is a collection of many human resources, is costly, just as natural resources are. Lee Wong, for instance, must pay his two workers a certain amount of money for each hour they work.

Workers who get the highest wages are often those who have special skills or special knowledge. They can do jobs that most others can't do. Lee Wong hired two people. One is a skilled mechanic. The other is unskilled; he is being trained by Lee. Lee pays the skilled worker higher wages for two reasons: First, the skilled worker can do more jobs and do them faster and better than the other worker can. Therefore, he is more valuable to the business. He helps bring in more income. Second, the supply of skilled mechanics is rather small and the demand for their services is great. This tends to increase the price of their services—their wages. You will recall that when the supply (the amount) of any good or service is small and the demand (by consumers or employers) is great, prices tend to go up. On the other hand, when supply is great and demand is small, prices go down.

Capital Goods. Equipment, machines, and tools needed to produce goods and services are capital goods. For example, the wrenches, jacks, and other tools in Lee Wong's auto shop are capital goods.

Capital goods help workers produce goods and services. Businesses with good equipment and workers who can use it skillfully are likely to be successful. Thus, decisions about which and how many capital goods to buy can also contribute to the success or failure of a business.

Discuss: Why are capital goods crucial to a business?

Management. People who run businesses are called managers. They decide how to produce goods and services. They also decide how to sell their products, what price to charge, and what to do with profits.

Managers need skills in decision making. Lee Wong is one of the mechanics in his own business, but he is also the manager. If he makes the right decisions—decisions such as what workers to hire, what tools to buy, and what prices to charge, he will be successful.

Discuss: How does management influence a business?

Carpenters are skilled workers in the labor force.

Government Regulation of Business

When one company controls all or most of the supply of a particular good or service, a **monopoly** is said to exist. If there were only one company that produced automobile tires, for example, consumers would be forced to deal with that company if they wanted tires for their cars.

Usually consumers are hurt when they can get something in only one place. Monopoly owners know that consumers have no choice but to buy from them. As a result a monopoly may produce goods or services of poor quality, or the monopoly may charge more than it should for its products. In order to keep monopolies from forming, Congress has passed antimonopoly laws.

Antimonopoly Laws. The most important antimonopoly laws have been (1) the Sherman Antitrust Act, (2) The Clayton Antitrust Act, and (3) the Federal Trade Commission Act.

The Sherman Act was passed in 1890 to give government the right to break up businesses that had established monopolies by forming trusts. John D. Rockefeller, head of the Standard Oil Company in the 1800s, formed a trust in the following way: First, he got stockholders from several oil companies to turn over their voting rights to a group of men called trustees. The trustees then acted as a single board of directors to manage all the companies as if they were one. Such a trust could gain enough power to wipe out competition. The Sherman Act said that the government could stop the formation of trusts. Because the language of the law was not absolutely clear, however, it was not easily enforced.

In 1914 both the Clayton Antitrust Act and the Federal Trade Commission Act were passed to strengthen the government's ability to control monopolies. The Clayton Act was easier to enforce than the Sherman Act because it listed a number of specific activities as being monopolistic and, thus, illegal. The Federal Trade Commission Act created a government agency called the Federal Trade Commission (FTC). The Federal Trade Commission was to help enforce antimonopoly laws and protect consumers against other unfair business practices.

Legal Monopolies. Although monopolies are usually bad for consumers, there is one type of monopoly that is considered acceptable. These are monopolies that provide services such as

Discuss: What is the value of government regulation of business?

In this early twentieth-century cartoon, Liberty is covered over by trusts.

water, sewage disposal, electricity, gas, and telephones—services that everyone in the community needs. The companies that provide these services are called **public utilities.**

Discuss: Why are public utilities so important to a community?

Public utilities are allowed to operate as legal monopolies because it saves consumers money to allow them to do so. In order to set up one of these companies, enormous amounts of money must be spent on such capital goods as telephone lines, underground cables and pipes, and power plants. The amount of money is so great that a company needs many customers to pay back the original cost and to pay for upkeep. The more customers there are to share these costs, the lower the cost to each person will be. By being allowed to function as monopolies, (one company for each public service in a community), the public utility companies get the customers they need in order to provide service at reasonable prices.

Like any other monopoly, these companies could take advantage of consumers. To prevent this from happening, government officials have the authority to control, or regulate, the utilities' activities. When important company decisions are made, such as raising prices or changing service, government officials must first give approval.

Section Review

Vocabulary: board of directors, cooperative, corporation, credit union, factors of production, limited liability, monopoly, partnership, profits, public utilities, shares of stock, single proprietorship, stockholders.

Reviewing the Main Ideas

1. What are the advantages of each of these kinds of business organizations: (a) single proprietorship, (b) partnership, (c) corporation, (d) cooperative?
2. What are the four factors of production?
3. Why does the government want to prevent companies from trying to form monopolies?

Skill Building

1. Write a paragraph that summarizes the information in the graphs on page 454.
2. Why do you think Lee Wong paid less rent for a garage at the edge of town than he would have in the center of town?

Main Ideas
1. pp. 454–455
2. natural resources, labor, capital goods, management
3. p. 458
Skill Building
1. Answers should be in a correctly constructed paragraph.
2. Answers will vary.

2/How Labor Unions Affect Business Decisions

Labor unions are an important influence on some business decisions. A **labor union** is an organization of workers. A union's purpose is to get better wages and working conditions for its members. For example, workers in the automobile industry have formed the United Auto Workers Union (UAW). UAW leaders represent union members in dealing with the managers of auto manufacturing companies such as Ford, Chrysler, and General Motors.

Discuss: What are the key roles of unions?

Big labor unions have not always existed in the United States. It was only in the late 1800s that the type of labor union we have today began to develop.

The Growth of Unions

Before 1800, most Americans were self-employed as farmers, shopkeepers, and skilled craftsmen. Very few people worked for wages. Those people who did work for wages usually saw such jobs as short-term work. They planned to work only long enough to save the money they needed to set up households or businesses or to buy farms of their own. After 1800, all that began to change.

(Left) early membership card of the United Mine Workers and (right) members of the Ladies Garment Workers' Union protest laws that prevent them from picketing, 1910.

Courtesy Chicago Historical Society

460

During the nineteenth century, manufacturing developed rapidly in the United States. Factories were built and equipped with expensive machinery. Hundreds of people were hired to help run the machines.

Working conditions in the factories were often unpleasant and dangerous. There were hardly any laws to require safe conditions or to provide money in case of injury or death on the job. The men, women, and children who worked in the factories labored ten to fifteen hours a day and six, sometimes seven, days a week. The wages they earned were very low. Often, all family members had to work.

Most workers could do nothing to improve their situation. Few of them had special skills. Most worked at jobs that required little training, and there were more people who needed these jobs than there were jobs to fill. As a result, workers had no power to bargain with their employers about wages or working conditions. If a worker needed a job, he or she had to take whatever the employer wanted to give.

Several congressional committees looked into working conditions in factories, but little was done to help workers. Government officials such as judges, governors, and senators were generally friendly to the interests of business owners. In addition, it was a widely held view in the late 1800s that government aid for workers was government interference in the economy. Business leaders, as well as government officials, believed that business owners alone had the right to decide about wages and working conditions in factories and mines.

In an attempt to solve their problems, some workers decided to form labor organizations, or unions. Workers knew that business leaders had increased their strength by forming giant corporations and business organizations. Laborers felt that they, too, would have to combine to increase their strength. Once labor was united, employers would have to improve conditions or be faced with worker strikes. When workers **strike,** they stop working. They know that a company cannot make profits during a strike. Workers hope that a loss of profits will influence the employer to give in to their demands. They also hope that making their complaints known to the public will influence the employer.

Most nineteenth-century Americans were opposed to unions. In fact, such union activities as strikes were illegal at that time. Many people thought that individual workers should be able to

A "scab" is a worker who won't join the union but works while others are on strike. These New York girls were sympathetic to a car strike in 1916.

get ahead on their own. They said it was unfair for workers to join together in their demands for change.

The clash between those who supported unions and those who opposed unions was fought with more than words. Between 1880 and 1890 there were over 1000 strikes per year, and many of the strikes ended in bloodshed. The issues were almost always the same. Workers wanted a greater share of profits, better working conditions, and shorter hours.

The union movement grew slowly in the late 1800s and early 1900s. In the 1930s, however, it began to grow quickly. In the early and mid-1930s Congress made it legal for workers to form unions, to strike, and to bargain collectively with employers. The right to **collective bargaining** meant that employers were required to talk to individuals from the workers' union about wages, hours, and working conditions. Employers had to try to come to some decision that would satisfy both sides.

In the late 1930s workers organized unions in the steel and automobile industries. These victories gave a boost to unions in other industries. By the early 1940s, after many strikes, most big manufacturing industries were unionized.

Unions Today

In the United States today about twenty-four percent of all workers belong to labor unions. This number is down from a high of thirty-six percent in 1945. (See "Union Membership in the United States" on page 463.) Workers in the big manufacturing industries such as steel and automobiles usually belong to unions, as do workers in the clothing industry. (See "Today's 10 Biggest Unions" in the margin at left.) Craft workers, such as electricians, plumbers, bricklayers, and carpenters, also tend to belong to unions.

Union goals have been similar from one industry to another. In fact, many unions have joined together in the American Federation of Labor and Congress of Industrial Organizations (AFL-CIO). The AFL-CIO is made up of over 100 different unions. Over seventy-five percent of all union members belong to organizations that are part of the AFL-CIO. Two large unions that are not a part of the AFL-CIO are the United Auto Workers (UAW) and the Teamsters.

Union Goals. One important union goal has always been higher wages. Labor leaders generally have been successful in

Discuss: Why is collective bargaining important?

Discuss: How have labor unions developed?

TODAY'S 10 BIGGEST UNIONS

1.	Teamsters	1,888,895
2.	United Auto Workers	1,358,354
3.	Steelworkers	1,300,000
4.	International Brotherhood of Electrical Workers	923,560
5.	International Association of Machinists and Aerospace Workers	917,266
6.	United Brotherhood of Carpenters and Joiners	820,000
7.	American Federation of State, County and Municipal Employees	750,000
8.	Retail Clerks International	728,200
9.	Laborers International Union	627,406
10.	Service Employees International Union	575,000

reaching this goal. In 1971, for example, the average hourly wage of craft workers who belonged to unions was $4.28. The average hourly wage of craft workers who did not belong to unions was $2.96.

A second union goal has been shorter working hours. Most workers today spend about eight hours per day five days per week on the job. This is many fewer hours per week than workers labored in the late 1800s. In some unions the push for fewer hours has become a more important goal than higher pay.

A third union goal has been job security, or job permanence. Unions have tried to influence businesses to guarantee **seniority rights.** Workers who have held their jobs for the shortest time have the least seniority. Thus, they would be the first to lose their jobs if the company decided to lay off workers. Those who have the most seniority have the most job security.

A fourth union goal has been to protect workers against dangers to health and safety in the work place. Unions have cooperated with managers of businesses to try to create the best possible working conditions.

Finally, unions have tried to get better **fringe benefits** for members. Fringe benefits include medical care plans, life insurance plans, paid vacations, and retirement programs. Companies pay for all or part of these benefits.

Discuss: What are the goals of unions? How have unions helped workers?

UNION MEMBERSHIP IN THE UNITED STATES

Year	Total Workers (Nonagricultural)	Union Members	Percent in Unions
1930	29,424,000	3,401,000	12%
1935	27,053,000	3,584,000	13%
1940	32,376,000	8,717,000	27%
1945	40,394,000	14,322,000	36%
1950	45,222,000	14,267,000	32%
1955	50,675,000	16,802,000	33%
1960	54,234,000	17,049,000	31%
1965	60,815,000	17,299,000	28%
1970	70,920,000	19,381,000	27%
1975	77,051,000	19,473,000	25%
1976	79,443,000	19,432,000	24%

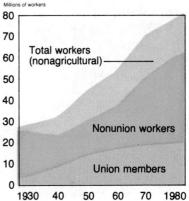

463

Bargaining Power. Most of the goals that unions have worked for have been gained through collective bargaining. The final agreement that results from collective bargaining is called a **labor contract.** If the union and the employer cannot come to an agreement, the union may call a strike.

Union bargaining power is greatest when all workers in a company are union members. When this is so, a strike will cause a complete stop to production, which can hurt a company severely. To increase bargaining power, union leaders try to influence companies to have closed shops or union shops wherever they are legal. In a **closed shop,** the company agrees to hire only union members. In a **union shop,** the company can hire non-union workers, but workers must join the union within a certain period of time. If they do not, they lose their jobs.

In 1947 a national government law called the Taft-Hartley Act banned closed-shop agreements for any company doing business in more than one state. Unions were becoming powerful in the late 1940s; some people thought they had become too powerful. The Taft-Hartley Act was passed to place limits on their power. The Taft-Hartley Act allows the President to stop, for 80 days, any strike that would be a threat to national security or well-being. In addition, the act gives state governments the right to pass **right to work laws.** By 1976, twenty states had passed such laws. If a state has a right to work law, both closed

Auto workers assembling trucks:

shops and union shops are illegal. These states allow only the **open shop.** In an open shop, a worker does not have to join a union in order to keep his or her job. Both union workers and nonunion workers may be employed in the same company. Labor union leaders are against the open shops since it weakens their power during collective bargaining.

Unions are active in many areas today in addition to the bargaining they do with employers. Political activities are a particular interest. At election time, unions may try to influence union members to support candidates who support union goals. Between elections, unions hire lobbyists to try to influence government decision makers. Whatever activities a union takes part in, however, its central purpose remains the same. That purpose is to make sure that workers' interests are represented when economic decisions are made—whether the decisions are made by business owners or by government officials.

Discuss: How do closed and open shops compare?

Discuss: Why is bargaining power so important?

Section Review

Vocabulary: closed shop, collective bargaining, fringe benefits, labor contract, labor union, open shop, right to work laws, seniority rights, strike, union shop.

Reviewing the Main Ideas
1. What conditions in the 1800s led to the development of labor unions?
2. What are five goals that labor unions have worked for?
3. How do labor unions affect the decisions of business owners?

Skill Building
1. Write a paragraph that supports one of these statements:
   a. The union shop should be required by law in every state.
   b. Every state should have a right to work law.
2. Summarize the information given in the margin on page 463 in a few sentences.

Main Ideas
1. p. 461
2. pp. 462–463
3. Answers will vary.
Skill Building
1. Answer should be in a correctly constructed paragraph.
2. Of all workers (not including farm workers), the largest percent were union members in 1955—33%. By 1976, membership had dropped to 24%.

Mass Produced Meals

More than twenty-five years ago, the two McDonald brothers of California went into business for themselves. They put their money into a small restaurant in San Bernardino. They decided to sell only hamburgers, french fries, and milk shakes.

For a time, the McDonald brothers ran a successful small-scale business. Then they met Ray A. Kroc and the McDonalds' restaurant business was never the same.

Ray Kroc owned a small business that made fast-working milk-shake machines. Kroc got together with the McDonalds because he wanted to make some sales.

The McDonalds liked the machines. They bought eight. Kroc liked the McDonalds' restaurant. In fact, it was the restaurant that set Kroc to thinking. Why not a chain of McDonald restaurants—all making use of the special milk-shake mixers?

Kroc presented his ideas to the McDonald brothers. Kroc would put up the money for several new McDonald restaurants. Kroc would manage them, too, and pay a share of the profits to the McDonald brothers. All Kroc wanted in return was the McDonald name. The brothers accepted the offer.

Ray Kroc's goal was to produce the best hamburgers at the lowest price. Kroc believed that efficient production methods would lead to his goal. Efficiency means producing goods as cheaply as possible. By keeping costs low, Kroc could sell hamburgers for the lowest possible price and still make a good profit.

Kroc decided that three keys to efficiency were (1) specialization, (2) standardization, and (3) division of labor.

Specialization meant limiting the menu to only a few items, such as hamburgers, cheeseburgers, and french fries. Kroc could buy large amounts of the raw materials needed to make the few products. By buying large quantities of raw materials, he could save money.

Standardization meant making each product in exactly the same way. For example, each McDonald's hamburger would be a 1.6 ounce patty, .221 inches thick and 3.875 inches wide when uncooked. The patty would fit in a 4.25-inch bun. By standardizing products, waste would be limited. This, too, would help to keep production costs as low as possible.

Division of labor meant that the restaurant work would be divided into several different jobs. Each worker would be re-

Ray Kroc

quired to do only one job. For example, one person would make only french fries. Another would make only shakes. The job of grilling hamburgers would be done by one worker, and so on. A manager would make sure that each job was done efficiently and in harmony with other jobs. Division of labor could result in fast food production. Each worker would have to do only a few tasks and thus should be able to do them quickly and do them well. The end result was to be mass produced meals—the making and selling of very large amounts of each item.

Ray Kroc's production decisions were aimed at keeping costs as low as possible. Savings on production costs could be passed on to customers in the form of lower prices. Prices could be kept low as long as the business attracted a large number of customers. A small amount of profit would be made on each sale, but a very large number of sales would add up to a large profit.

Kroc's mass-production system worked. Customers flocked to the restaurants. In fact, profits were so large that Kroc soon had enough money to build more stores. It wasn't long before the McDonald name had spread across the United States.

Eventually Kroc bought the McDonald brothers' share of the business. Then he went on to expand the business even more.

By 1975, the McDonald's chain had sales of more than two billion dollars, and its symbol, the golden arches, had become familiar around the world. Kroc's business decisions had led to the goal he had hoped for. By carefully managing the factors of production, Kroc was selling more hamburgers each day than anyone else in the world.

Reviewing the Case Study

1. What decisions did Ray Kroc make about the four factors of production?
2. What were the consequences of Kroc's decisions?
3. What values may have led Kroc to make the decisions he made?

Chapter Twenty-two Test and Activities

★★

Vocabulary

Match the following words with their meanings below.

1. single proprietorship
2. corporation
3. partnership
4. cooperative
5. monopoly
6. labor union
7. shares of stock
8. seniority
9. strike
10. profits
11. collective bargaining
12. public utility

a. a business that provides a service such as telephone service
b. a business owned by one person
c. an organization of workers
d. a business owned by its customers
e. a business whose ownership is divided into many shares held by many people
f. a business owned by two people
g. a refusal to continue working
h. portions of ownership in a corporation
i. having to do with the number of years one has worked in a place
j. the right of workers to have formal talks with employers about such issues as wages and hours
k. the one and only source of a good or service
l. money made over and above expenses

Reviewing Chapter Ideas

1. True or false: The most common form of business in the United States is single proprietorship.
2. The type of business that takes in the most money each year is the _____ .
   a. single proprietorship
   b. partnership
   c. corporation
   d. cooperative
3. True or false: There are about as many single proprietorships as partnerships.
4. True or false: A credit union is an example of a cooperative.
5. True or false: There are no monopolies in the United States.
6. Which of the following has <u>not</u> been something that labor unions have worked toward?
   a. higher wages
   b. more hours on the job
   c. safe working conditions
   d. more fringe benefits
7. If a worker decides not to join the company union and is able to keep his or her job anyway, the person must work in a(an) _____ .
   a. open shop
   b. closed shop
   c. union shop
   d. nonunionized shop

Using Basic Social Studies Skills

Finding Information

1. Skim the chapter heads and subheads to find the advantages of organizing a business as a corporation. How were the heads and subheads helpful? What are the three advantages that you were looking for?

★★

2. Use the table below to answer these questions: (a) Which corporation has the largest number of employees? (b) Which corporation had greater sales—General Motors or Chrysler?

TOP TEN CORPORATIONS IN THE UNITED STATES (1977)

	Total Number of Employees	Sales*
1. Exxon	137,000	$48,630,817
2. General Motors	681,000	47,181,000
3. Ford Motor Company	416,120	28,830,600
4. Texaco	75,235	26,451,851
5. Mobil Oil	71,300	26,062,570
6. Standard Oil of California	38,801	19,434,133
7. Gulf Oil Company	52,100	16,451,000
8. IBM	288,647	16,304,333
9. General Electric	375,000	15,697,300
10. Chrysler	217,594	15,537,788

*in billions of dollars

Comprehending Information

Pretend that you are the owner of a bakery. Tell how you would make use of the four factors of production.

Organizing Information

Write the following dates on your paper: 1850, 1890, 1935, 1945. After each date, describe in a general way what, if anything, was happening in the labor union movement at that time.

Evaluating Information

A monopoly is never of value. Do you agree? Why or why not? Use information in the chapter to help support your answer.

Communicating Ideas

Create a questionnaire to be used to interview the owner of a single-proprietorship business in your area. Review what Lee Wong did before you decide what to ask.

Using Decision-Making Skills

Pretend that you are a union member who has to decide whether to vote for or against a union strike. Use a decision tree to illustrate alternatives and possible consequences. Tell how your goals would influence the decision you would make.

Activities

1. Work with a partner. Use the questionnaire you made in "Communicating Ideas." Interview a single-proprietor owner in your area. Compare the responses with what you found out about Lee Wong.

2. Work with several other class members. Choose a major corporation from the table opposite. Use the business section of a large city newspaper to chart the value of one share of that corporation's stock over several weeks. Summarize your findings.

3. Locate an article on the AFL-CIO in the *Readers' Guide to Periodical Literature.* Read the article and summarize its contents for the class.

4. Students who want to learn more about corporation ownership may want to read *The Young Investor's Guide to the Stock Market* by Murray Hoyt (Lippincott, 1972).

5. Students who want to learn more about the United States labor force and about unions should read *The U.S. Department of Labor History of the American Worker,* edited by Richard B. Morris (U.S. Government Printing Office, 1978).

Chapter 23 Consumer Decisions

★★

Nick and Elena Busic are a young married couple with two small children, Joey, 9, and Mary, 6. Nick works at a steel mill. He earns $17,500 a year.

Like most people, the Busics have to plan their spending carefully. Their income is limited. Nick's take-home pay (after money is taken out for taxes and health insurance) is $1,015 per month. Each month, the Busics usually want to buy more than they can afford. Thus, they have to make choices.

Some of the Busics' expenses are the same every month. For example, the Busics use $105 per month for payments on their car. Other expenses vary from one month to another. The Busics must buy food every month, but the amount they spend is different from month to month.

After the Busics have paid for the things they must buy each month, they usually have about $125 left. They try to put a part of that $125, about $75 a month, in their savings account at the company credit union. They use the rest to pay for entertainment or special purchases. They like to go to the movies at least once a month. Last month, Elena and Nick bought a basketball for Joey and a dollhouse for Mary. Nick also bought a pair of earrings for Elena as a birthday gift.

The decisions that the Busics make each month about how to use their income are consumer decisions. Anyone who buys and uses goods and services is a consumer. Thus, anyone with money can make consumer decisions. Consumers decide how much to spend and to save. They make choices about what to buy, how much, and where.

The main purpose of this chapter is to help you learn about consumer decisions. You will read about:

1/Buying Goods and Services
2/Saving and Borrowing
3/Protecting Consumer Rights
Case Study: Consumer Advocate

Discuss: Who can make consumer decisions?

470

1/Buying Goods and Services

American consumers spend billions of dollars each year on various goods and services. The graph on page 445 shows what those goods and services are.

Many consumers tend to be satisfied with their purchases. Others are often disappointed. Careful buying may make the difference. The careful consumer plans ahead, examines products, and knows where to get information about products, producers, and sellers. Careful consumers are likely to get the most for their money.

Plan Before Buying

What do you want? When do you want it? How much money can you spend to get what you want? The consumer who plans before buying thinks carefully about these questions.

Discuss: How should you plan before buying?

Thinking About Wants, Needs, and Values. Wants are tied to needs. You can find out exactly what you need to purchase by taking stock of what you do or do not have. For example, Elena Busic took stock of her children's clothing and decided that each

A careful shopper compares labels to be sure he is getting the best buy.

child needed a new pair of shoes and a winter coat. Elena also takes stock of the family food supply before buying groceries. Thus, she is sure to buy what the family needs. Consumer decisions are also tied to values and goals. Nick Busic revealed certain values and goals when he bought a compact car last year. Nick chose a small, energy-saving car because he wants to cut down on air pollution and fuel waste.

Making a Budget. Consumers have only so much money to spend. Every time the Busics decide to spend money on one thing, they are giving up the chance to spend that money on something else. If the Busics decide to spend more on clothes, they have less to spend on food, on entertainment, or on other expenses.

Consumers can make budgets to help them use their incomes wisely. A **budget** is a plan for spending and saving. It helps consumers make sure that money gets used for the things they need and want most. It also helps them avoid spending more than they have. For example, if you have a budget, a quick look will tell you whether or not you can afford a new record. The budget may show that if you buy the record, you will have no money for a Friday night movie. Whatever it shows, it will help you make choices.

Discuss: What is a budget? How does it work?

Transportation is an item in most people's budgets.

When people make a budget, they try to match expenses and income. They write down the sum of money they expect to receive during a certain period. Then they list all the things they need to buy as well as the amount they need to spend on each item. The amount of money that goes out cannot be greater than the amount that comes in.

The first step in making a budget is to write down **fixed expenses.** Fixed expenses are necessary costs that are known in advance. They stay the same from month to month. For example, the Busic family pays $300 per month to rent an apartment.

The next step is to estimate **flexible expenses.** These are costs that change from month to month. The costs of food and clothing change somewhat from month to month. So do amounts spent on recreation, gifts, medical bills, and household needs.

When the Busics first made a budget, they weren't sure how much they were spending on flexible expenses. To find out, they began to write down everything they bought in a small notebook. At the end of each week they recorded these purchases in a larger notebook. The large notebook had one column for each type of expense—clothing, food, recreation, and so on. At the end of each month the Busics added up the columns. In that way they were able to find out exactly how much they were spending on what.

The final step in making a budget is to balance estimated expenses with income. If expenses are more than income, consumers must decide where to cut down. The consumer will have to ask questions like these: How can I get cheaper transportation to and from work? How can I save money on clothing or on electricity? How much is too much for recreation? (The budget on this page shows how one urban family of four spends its money.)

Look Before Buying

Wise consumers plan ahead. They think, they save, and they budget. They also look before buying.

Looking for a Sleeping Bag. Imagine for the moment that you want to buy a sleeping bag. You know what you want. You want a bag that will keep out the cold when the temperature gets down to freezing. You also know what you can afford to spend.

Now you are ready to get information. Go to your public library. Magazines of all sorts describe and rate products. The

Discuss: What are the key features of this budget?

Budget for March, 1979

Income before taxes	$1,916.00
Taxes	425.00
Income after taxes	$1,491.00

Expenses
Food, household supplies	$420.00
Housing	380.00
Electricity, gas, telephone, water	84.00
Gifts, contributions, insurance	65.00
Reading, recreation, education	70.00
Medical care	80.00
Clothing	80.00
Transportation	205.00
Savings	107.00
	$1,491.00

Note: Have copies on hand.

Discuss: What does a smart shopper do?

Discuss: What does it mean to say: "Wise consumers plan ahead"?

best kind of magazine is a consumer magazine such as *Consumer Reports* or *Consumer Bulletin*. Consumer magazines are published by organizations that test products for quality. When the organization rates a group of products, it tells what the tests showed. If a consumer magazine has rated sleeping bags, it will tell you which type gives the warmth you want for a price you can pay.

Once you have information, begin to shop around. Find the stores that carry the bag you want. Then compare prices. One store may charge less for the bag than other stores. Also, look carefully at the bag itself. Do you fit inside? Is there room for growth? Is it carefully sewn? Finally, make sure that you can return the bag if you find something wrong with it when you get it home.

Tips for Smart Shoppers. The steps to follow in buying other items are much the same as those you followed in buying the sleeping bag.

(1) Plan ahead. Know exactly what you want. Don't buy just because you're in a "buying mood."

(2) When you're buying something expensive, get as much information as you can. Check the consumer magazines.

(3) Shop around. Buy where you get the best price (as long as the dealer is honest, of course.) When you're buying food, check the **unit price.** Check to see how much you are paying for each ounce, each quart, each pound, or each piece.

(4) Examine the item to make sure that all parts are working.

(5) Ask about **warranties** and **guarantees.** These are promises that the seller or producer makes to repair, replace, or refund if a product doesn't do what it's supposed to do. Make sure that warranties and guarantees are put in writing, and make sure that you save them. Also save **sales receipts.** You'll need them if you have a complaint.

(6) Read **labels** on food. Make sure you know what you're eating. Also check the freshness dates. If an item is still on the shelf and the date has passed, don't buy it.

(7) Read the labels on clothing too. Are the pants you just bought likely to shrink? What do you have to do to keep them clean? If it takes great effort or expense to keep the pants looking good, you may decide not to buy them.

(8) Don't give in to salespeople. Most salespeople try to treat customers fairly. But once in a while you'll meet those who do

not. Don't let a salesperson persuade you to do something you don't want to do.

(9) Be a critical watcher and reader of ads. Some advertisements give useful information. Newspaper ads and catalog ads often tell size, price, and so on. Other ads, particularly television ads, do not tell much at all. Instead, they use propaganda techniques to appeal to your emotions. (See pages 284–287 in Chapter 13.)

(10) If you buy records or books through the mail, make sure you know what you're agreeing to do. If you accept a number of almost-free items, you will probably have to follow up with a certain number of purchases. Be sure to read all letters that you get from the seller. Otherwise, you may receive books and records that you didn't order.

Note: Have students bring examples to class.

(11) Beware of **"bait and switch."** If you go into a store to buy an item that has been advertised at a very low cost and the salesperson tries to sell you a more expensive version of the same item, he or she may be doing something illegal. The store has offered "bait" in the form of the ad and you have been "switched" to another item. Such activity is against many state or local laws.

Discuss: How is this handled in your state?

Section Review

Vocabulary: bait and switch, budget, guarantee, fixed expense, flexible expense, label, sales receipt, unit price, warranty.

Reviewing the Main Ideas
1. Describe the main steps in making a budget.
2. Why should consumers make budgets?

Skill Building
1. Look at the budget on page 473. Which three items does this family spend most on?
2. Write instructions for someone who wants to buy a television set. Keep "Tips for Smart Shoppers" in mind as you give advice.

Main Ideas
1. p. 473
2. p. 472
Skill Building
1. food, household supplies; housing; transportation
2. Answers will vary.

2/Saving and Borrowing

Consumers regularly make decisions about saving and borrowing money. When people save, they put money aside for a certain time so that it can be spent later. When people borrow, they use someone else's money with the promise to pay it back at a certain time.

Discuss: Why do people save and borrow money? How do they do it?

When Should Consumers Save or Borrow?

People can always find ways to spend what they earn. Why then, is it wise to save?

Note: Have students write a summary statement of this graph.

Reasons for Saving. Many people save in order to prepare for emergencies such as getting sick or losing a job. People also save for retirement. Finally, people save so that they can buy certain costly items. It almost always takes planning and saving if a person wants to pay cash for such items as pianos and vacation trips.

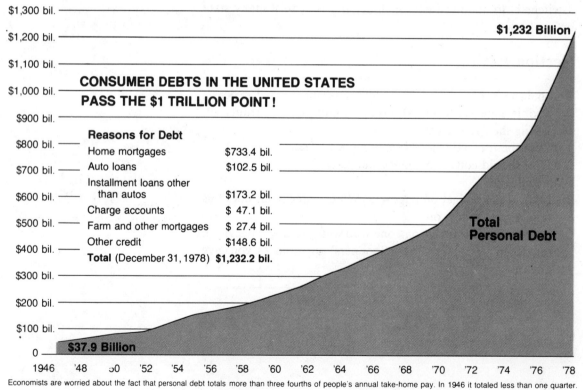

CONSUMER DEBTS IN THE UNITED STATES PASS THE $1 TRILLION POINT!

$1,232 Billion

Reasons for Debt

Home mortgages	$733.4 bil.
Auto loans	$102.5 bil.
Installment loans other than autos	$173.2 bil.
Charge accounts	$ 47.1 bil.
Farm and other mortgages	$ 27.4 bil.
Other credit	$148.6 bil.
Total (December 31, 1978)	**$1,232.2 bil.**

Total Personal Debt

$37.9 Billion

1946 '48 '50 '52 '54 '56 '58 '60 '62 '64 '66 '68 '70 '72 '74 '76 '78

Economists are worried about the fact that personal debt totals more than three fourths of people's annual take-home pay. In 1946 it totaled less than one quarter.

476

Reasons for Borrowing. As the graph on page 476 shows, many consumers borrow money. In 1978, American consumers owed more than one trillion dollars to various lenders. These consumers were buying goods and services on **credit.** To buy on credit means to pay later for what you get now.

The main reason that people use credit is so that they can buy very high-priced items such as cars and houses. Consumers also borrow money during emergencies. Illnesses or accidents can result in unexpected expenses. Loss of a job may leave a person short of money until a new job is found. Because there is always a charge for borrowing money, it is best to save for emergencies in advance.

Where to Go to Save or Borrow

There are various places where a person can save or borrow money. It is useful to know how services differ from one place to another.

Banks. Banks provide services to people who want to save as well as to those who want to borrow. When people save in a bank, the bank pays them interest. The amount of interest earned depends on the amount of money put in the bank and the length of time it is left there. When people borrow, they must pay interest to the bank.

Note: Collect data from banks on the services they provide.

Other Places to Borrow and Save. People also borrow and save at savings and loan associations and at credit unions. **Savings and loan associations** specialize in large loans such as the kind given when people buy houses. Savings and loans also offer savings accounts. Usually they pay a higher rate of interest than banks. Savings and loan associations do not offer checking accounts.

Credit unions, as you will recall, are nonprofit organizations formed to serve members. Interest rates charged for loans often are lower than rates charged elsewhere. Interest rates paid on savings accounts often are higher.

Buying government bonds and buying shares of stock in corporations can also be ways of saving. Even buying insurance can be a form of saving; it helps prepare for emergencies. Some kinds of life insurance policies can be used for borrowing. A policy holder can borrow part of the money he or she has paid in premiums. The interest charged on these loans is low.

Checks

Millions of people do not pay bills with cash. Instead, they pay with checks. They do so because that is convenient.

What is a check? It is a written order to a bank to pay the person presenting the check the amount of money shown on it.

To write checks, a person must have a checking account with a bank. To open one, you fill out a card showing your name, address, and signature. Then you deposit money in the bank. The bank will give you a checkbook full of blank checks or for a small fee you can have ones with your name and address printed on them. Then you can write checks, which can be used as money, to anyone you wish. You can make additional deposits anytime you like, and you may write checks up to the amount you have on deposit.

Check service is a convenience, but banks do not perform it free. Banks offer two kinds of checking accounts. One kind, often called a "special account," charges a small fee for each check you write. This amount is subtracted from your account each month. The other, or "regular account," does not charge a fee, but you must always leave a certain "minimum deposit" (usually $200 or $300) in your account.

Here is an example of a check filled out, with explanations of the various items on it.

Name(s) and address(es) of person(s) authorized to write checks on the account

Date check written

Check number

Payee—to whom payable

Amount in figures

Amount written out

Name and address of bank

Purpose of check

Number assigned bank

Account number

Check number

Authorized signature

FRANK T. FLYNN
BARBARA G. FLYNN
529 WILMETTE AVE.   PH. 211-8108
WILMETTE, ILL.   6009

2021

September 19, 1980   70-1669 / 719

PAY TO THE ORDER OF   *Maria Gutierrez* $15.00

Fifteen and no/100   DOLLARS

The Wilmette Bank
200 Central Avenue, Wilmette, Illinois 6009

MEMO *babysitting*   *Barbara G. Flynn*

⑆0718⑆1669⑆   ⑈875⑆746⑆2⑆   7071

Here are some things to note:

1. The amount of the check must be given in both figures and words. If the amounts are different, the bank accepts the one written in words.
2. If you wish, you may print or type all the information on a check except the signature.
3. If your check reads "Pay to the order of 'Cash,'"—and you may write a check this way if you wish—*anyone* may exchange it for cash by simply placing his or her signature on the back.

Statements and Records

The person to whom one writes a check can, after signing it on the back, exchange it for cash or use it to pay a bill. Eventually, the check returns to the bank of the person who wrote it. The bank then subtracts the amount of the check from that person's account.

Each month the bank sends you a statement. This shows the amount of money in the account at the beginning of the month, called the "balance forward." It shows each check written and each deposit made during the month. If a service charge is made, this will be shown too. The final figure is your "balance" at the end of the month, as far as the bank knows. Included with the statement are all the checks that have returned as of the statement's date. These are called "canceled checks."

Usually, there are some outstanding checks—checks written that have not yet cleared the bank. No record of these will appear on the statement. You should keep a record of all checks you write. Then you tick off the ones that the bank returns. Subtract the outstanding checks from your ending balance to find out how much money you actually have left.

Here is an example of a check record. You get the form with your checkbook.

PLEASE BE SURE TO **DEDUCT** ANY PER CHECK CHARGES OR SERVICE CHARGES THAT MAY APPLY TO YOUR ACCOUNT

CHECK NO.	DATE	CHECKS ISSUED TO OR DESCRIPTION OF DEPOSIT	(−) AMOUNT OF CHECK	√ T	(−) CHECK FEE (IF ANY)	(+) AMOUNT OF DEPOSIT	BALANCE
							237 80
2020	9/5	Schultze Cleaners	10 50				227 30
	9/14					85 00	312 30
2021	9/19	Maria Gutierrez	15 00				297 30

As you can see, there is a space to show a balance and to subtract the amount of each check. There is a space to record deposits made to the account. And there is a column for checking off canceled checks that arrive with the statement.

It is important to keep an up-to-date record of the checks you write. If you forget to record a check, you might accidentally overdraw your account later. There would not be enough money to cover a new check. The bank will not pay out on a check when there are not enough funds in the account; instead, it stamps "insufficient funds" on the back and returns it to the payee. You would hear from the payee and be expected to pay the amount of the check immediately. Overdrawing an account can be embarassing. It is also against the law.

Try These Questions

1. What might happen should you forget to name a payee on a check? (Anyone receiving or finding the check could write a name or the word "Cash" on it and cash it.)

2. What if you should forget to sign a check? (The check would be worthless.)

3. What would happen should you fail to write something after "Memo"? (Nothing. The space is for your record only.)

Other Sources of Credit. There are several other ways to borrow or buy on credit. One source of credit is the finance company. It is sometimes easier to borrow from a finance company than it is from a bank. However, the amount of interest that finance companies charge can be very high.

Some stores provide credit to consumers by offering **charge accounts.** A person with a charge account can buy now and pay later. If a bill is paid very quickly, the store may charge no interest at all. However, if payments are made over months or years, a high rate of interest is charged.

Credit cards, such as Master Charge, Visa, and American Express, also allow consumers to buy now and pay later. **Credit cards,** like other charge cards, offer convenience. The credit-card owner can buy without carrying large amounts of cash. However, interest is charged on over-due accounts.

Buying on credit is sometimes necessary. Few consumers would be able to buy houses if they couldn't get loans. Buying on credit, as you have seen, can also be convenient. However, buying on credit can be expensive. Always find out how much you must pay for the use of someone else's money.

Discuss: What are the pros and cons of charge accounts or credit cards?

Note: Collect applications for various credit cards. Compare the information that is asked for. Read the fine print.

Section Review

Vocabulary: charge account, bank, credit, credit card, savings and loan association.

Reviewing the Main Ideas
1. Why do people save money?
2. Why do people borrow money?
3. Where and how can people save money?
4. Where and how can people borrow money?

Skill Building
1. If Janet wanted to buy a refrigerator, would you suggest that she use cash or credit? Explain your answer.
2. If you had to borrow money, would you go to a credit union, a bank, or a finance company? Why?

Main Ideas
1. p. 476
2. p. 477
3. p. 477
4. pp. 477, 479
Skill Building
1. Answers will vary.
2. Answers will vary.

3/Protecting Consumer Rights

What happens when a consumer buys a product that doesn't work right and the seller won't take the product back? How can consumers protect themselves when a producer makes goods that are a danger to health and safety? What can consumers do if a seller labels products falsely, so that buyers are misled? In other words, what can consumers do when producers or sellers treat them unfairly?

Discuss: How can government agencies help you?

Government Agencies That Help Consumers

There are agencies at all levels of government that aid consumers. The work that some of them do is described below.

Federal Trade Commission (FTC). The FTC hears complaints about false advertising. The commission enforces laws that prohibit misleading or dishonest information in guarantees, warranties, ads, or product labels. Consumers may bring problems to any one of twelve FTC regional offices.

Food and Drug Administration (FDA). The FDA inspects certain food products to make sure that they do not threaten the

Banks provide many services from checking and savings accounts to safe-deposit boxes and advice on financial planning.

Working to Protect Consumers

The main goal of the Consumer Product Safety Commission is to help prevent injuries related to the use of consumer products. The Commission works toward that goal in several ways. It sets and enforces safety standards for many products. It looks into the causes of product-related illnesses and accidents. It tries to find ways of preventing those illnesses and accidents in the future. And it carries out educational programs to make consumers aware of product safety.

People who work for the Commission do many different jobs. Lawyers, writers, scientists, engineers, and field investigators are some of those people. Lawyers help the agency with legal questions that come up when safety rules are set and enforced. Writers help carry out the agency's public-education program. Scientists and engineers test products to see whether or not they are safe. And investigators go "into the field" to gather information from consumers who have complaints and from stores and factories where products are made and sold.

The Commission wants to know whether or not a certain product contains benzene, a liquid that can damage health. This technician prepares a machine to run the test.

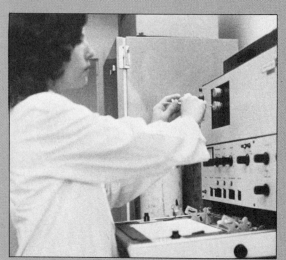

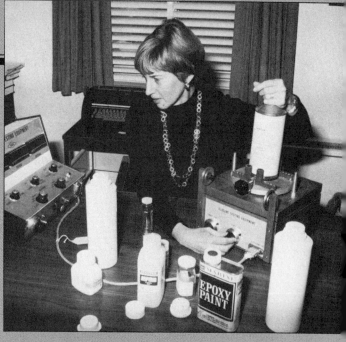

A Commission employee tests safety caps to make sure that small children can't get them off.

A Commission investigator measures the distance between bicycle handle bar ends. This inspection took place at a retail store to make sure that manufacturers were complying with government rules.

People and Government

A chemist checks to see whether or not poisonous chemicals are present in a consumer product.

This television set was destroyed by fire. The fire was caused by faulty construction. A Commission investigator photographed the set in the home of a consumer.

Agency workers have tested many products to see how easily they catch fire. The object of this test is a tent.

health of consumers. For example, the FDA examines chemical additives that are put in food products to preserve or color them. The FDA decides whether these additives are dangerous to health. If so, the FDA has the power to ban them—to say that they cannot be used. The FDA also inspects drugs and cosmetics to make sure they are safe.

Consumer Product Safety Commission (CPSC). The CPSC can investigate and control the sale of all products that might be unsafe. The CPSC requires producers to report information that shows their products might be unsafe.

The Postal Inspection Service. The Postal Service handles complaints about products or advertisements that have been sent through the mail. For example, a consumer may see an ad that tells how to order a product through the mail. The consumer may send money with an order but never receive the product. Or the consumer may receive a product that is different from the one described in the ad. When this sort of thing happens, the consumer should complain to postal inspectors.

State and Local Agencies. Each of the fifty state governments, as well as many local governments, have agencies that protect consumer rights. For example, most states have set up consumer protection agencies within the state attorney general's office. The main purpose of these agencies is to investigate false advertising or misleading claims on product labels. Many state and local governments also have bureaus to deal with complaints about repair shops.

Private Groups That Aid Consumers

Many private groups have been organized to protect consumer rights. The following are only a few examples.

Consumer Interest Groups. Consumer interest groups have been organized at both the national and local levels. Ralph Nader's Public Citizen, Inc., is a widely known national interest group that backs consumer causes. The leader, Ralph Nader, is a well-known **consumer advocate.** He speaks out about consumer problems and tries to correct them.

An example of a group that works at the state level is the Louisiana Consumers' League. This group brings legal action

The FDA provides standards for the safe manufacture of medicines.

against producers and sellers who break consumer-protection laws. The group also lobbies in the Louisiana state legislature on behalf of consumer goals.

Better Business Bureaus. The National Better Business Bureau was founded in 1912 to work for fair business practices and to protect consumer rights. Today, there are local Better Business Bureaus in communities all over the United States. These Bureaus provide shopping tips, information about local businesses, and warnings about dishonest business practices. Bureaus will also investigate written consumer complaints about false or misleading advertising. The Bureau tries to persuade businesses to follow the law. If the Bureau fails to influence a business to change its ways, the Bureau may take the business to court.

Discuss: What groups are available in your community to help consumers?

Section Review

Vocabulary: consumer advocate.

Reviewing the Main Ideas

1. What are some government agencies that aid consumers? Describe the services that one of them provides.
2. What is one private group that aids consumers?

Skill Building

1. Find a newspaper or magazine article about consumer interest group activities. Summarize the article.
2. Find a newspaper or magazine article about work that a government agency is doing to aid consumers. Write a summary of the article.

Main Ideas
1. pp. 481–484
2. pp. 484–485
Skill Building
1. Answers will vary.
2. Answers will vary.

Consumer Advocate

Ralph Nader and his followers try to influence government decision makers to pass laws that defend consumer rights. Several federal laws that protect consumer rights can be traced to Nader's work.

Nader began his work as a consumer advocate in 1963. He had graduated a short time before from Harvard Law School. Nader was practicing law in Hartford, Connecticut. He was specializing in automobile accident cases.

Nader found that unsafe cars, not poor drivers, caused many accidents. He was disturbed. Should he try to inform consumers about his findings? Should he try to influence government officials to do something about auto safety?

Nader was faced with an important decision. He had a promising career as a lawyer. Giving a great deal of time to auto safety might interfere with his job. Furthermore, Nader would be taking a risk. Some important people might become angry if he reported embarrassing facts about the production and sale of unsafe autos. They might try to hurt Nader in some way.

However, Nader believed in assuming citizenship responsibility. He thought that auto companies were not treating consumers fairly and believed that something had to be done. Nader decided to defend consumer rights no matter what the personal risks might be.

Nader continued to study the problem of unsafe autos. The result was a best-selling book, *Unsafe at Any Speed,* which pointed out safety hazards in cars. Members of Congress and federal agency workers read Nader's book. People inside and outside the automobile industry read the book too.

After the book came out, Nader gave many speeches about the need to pass laws requiring safer autos. He was asked to share his ideas with congressional committees.

The auto makers were worried that Nader's activities would hurt car sales. They tried to persuade him to stop his consumer-protection campaign. First, they tried to influence public opinion. They tried to make Nader seem to be an irresponsible troublemaker. When this tactic failed, auto makers hired private detectives to investigate Nader's private life. They hoped to find embarrassing information that could be used against Nader.

The private investigators uncovered no embarrassing facts about Nader. Rather they found that Nader was dedicated to-

Ralph Nader

tally to his work. He sometimes worked as long as sixteen hours a day seven days a week. He spent little money. His friends and neighbors praised him.

The outcome of Nader's auto-safety campaign was a new federal law, The Motor Vehicle Act (1966). The law required auto makers to add seat belts, dashboard padding, and other safety features to their cars.

Nader became a public hero. Many young citizens began to work with him. Together they started new projects to try to improve the way government and businesses serve the public. Nader's career as a consumer advocate had begun.

Nader has achieved many goals, but he does not always win. Nader suffered a big setback in 1978 when Congress voted against a consumer-protection law he had worked for. Despite this loss, Nader continues to work on solutions to consumer problems. His goal is to arouse public opinion so that citizens will ask for and get better products and services from businesses.

Ralph Nader has made a career of acting as a public citizen. His full-time job is keeping a watch on government officials and businesses so that they might do better in serving all citizens.

Reviewing the Case Study

1. An important occasion for decision was described in the early part of this case. What was it?
2. What were Nader's alternatives?
3. What decision did Nader make? Why?
4. What were the consequences of his decision?

An illustration from Nader's book shows independent rear wheel suspension in a 1964 car and improved in 1965.

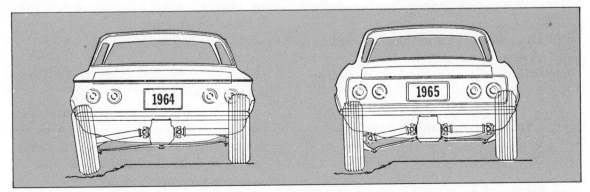

Chapter Twenty-three Test and Activities

★★

Vocabulary

Match the following words with their meanings.

1. budget
2. fixed expense
3. flexible expense
4. consumer advocate
5. guarantee
6. credit

a. a person whose job it is to work for consumer protection
b. a plan for spending and saving money
c. a promise to repair, replace, or refund your money if there is something wrong with a product
d. necessary costs that stay the same each month
e. costs that change somewhat from month to month
f. buy now and pay later

Reviewing Chapter Ideas

1. True or false: A careful consumer tries to get the most for his or her money.
2. True or false: A budget helps consumers make choices about how to use their money.
3. If you were to buy a vacuum cleaner, you would use a consumer magazine in order to find out _____ .
   a. how many people bought vacuum cleaners in the past year
   b. which stores carry the kind of cleaner you want
   c. where you can get your cleaner repaired
   d. how cleaners are rated in terms of quality

4. Bait and switch is _____ .
   a. a method for catching fish
   b. an illegal way of selling goods
   c. a board game similar to chess
   d. none of the above
5. Savings and loan associations specialize in _____ .
   a. checking account services
   b. large loans such as those given to people buying houses
   c. credit-card services
   d. insurance sales
6. True or false: States and local communities almost never have agencies to help consumers.
7. The Better Business Bureau is an organization that _____ .
   a. helps businesses locate in new cities
   b. lobbies in state legislatures on behalf of business interests
   c. works for consumer rights
   d. helps business people sell their products
8. True or false: Public Citizen, Inc., is a government agency that works for consumer rights.
9. The FTC is mostly concerned with _____ .
   a. health
   b. safety
   c. false advertising
   d. loaning consumers money

Using Basic Social Studies Skills

Finding Information

Use your book index to find where budgets are discussed. List all the pages. A budget for an urban family is shown in this chapter. How much does the family spend on transportation each month?

Vocabulary
1. b   4. a
2. d   5. c
3. e   6. f

Ideas
1. T   4. b   7. c
2. T   5. b   8. F
3. d   6. F   9. c

★★★

Comprehending Information

When people buy cars, how do their car choices show something about their values?

Organizing Information

Write the three steps in making a budget in the order that you would do them.

Evaluating Information

1. According to what you have read, is it ever wise to borrow money? Why?

2. Marty must borrow money to buy a car. She can borrow from a bank or a credit union. Which would you recommend? Why? If you wanted to be sure that you were making the right recommendation, what additional information would you need?

Communicating Ideas

Make up a set of instructions to follow when a person makes a major purchase such as a TV, car, or dishwasher.

Using Decision-Making Skills

Pretend that you have just been given $50. Use a decision tree to help you decide what to do with it.

Activities

1. Work with two other people. Identify ten items you like to eat. Check the price of each item in at least three stores. Summarize your findings.

2. As a class, collect brochures from your local banks and savings and loan associations. Make a chart to compare them.

3. The national government's Consumer Product Information Coordinating Center distributes a *Consumer Product Information* catalog. The catalog lists more than two hundred government publications of special interest to consumers. As a class, send for one copy of the catalog. When you receive it, pick out publications that might be of use to you and send for them too.

4. Watch three television commercials. Write down all factual information that was given in each ad. Tell whether or not you think the ads gave useful information about the products. Did the ads make use of propaganda techniques? If so, what were they and how were they used?

5. Keep track of all money you spend for two weeks. Write a paragraph telling whether or not you think you are using your money in the best possible way. If not, tell what changes you might make.

6. Choose an item that you might be interested in buying one day. See if *Consumer Reports* has rated that product in the past two years. If so, read the article and summarize your findings for the class.

7. For students who want to learn more about handling money or about consumer issues in general, the following books are recommended:

   (a) *Money of Your Own,* by Grace W. Weinstein (E. P. Dutton, 1977).

   (b) *The Consumer Movement,* by James S. Haskins (Franklin Watts, 1975).

   (c) *Consumer Protection Labs,* by Melvin Berger (The John Day Company, 1975).

   (d) *The Consumer's Catalog of Economy and Ecology,* by Jeanne and Robert Bendick (McGraw-Hill Book Company, 1974).

   (e) *The New Consumer Survival Kit,* by Richard George (Little, Brown and Company, 1978).

Unit Six Test

★★

Vocabulary

If the underlined word or phrase is defined correctly, write *true*. If it is not defined correctly, write *false*.

1. Goods are products such as cars, refrigerators, and shoes.
2. Food, clothing, houses, buses, tools and books are types of services.
3. Natural resources are the skills and knowledge of human beings.
4. Economic decisions are choices about how to use scarce resources.
5. A nation's economic system determines how economic decisions get made in the country.
6. Inflation is a time of rising prices.
7. After a business boom reaches a peak, a recession begins.
8. Depression is a time of full employment, high personal income, high GNP, and high business profits.
9. GNP stands for gross national product.
10. In a command economy, most economic decisions get made by consumers and producers.
11. In a market economy, most economic decisions are made by government.
12. Consumer goods are never used up.
13. A monopoly exists when only one company makes a product.
14. Single proprietorship is the most common form of business in the United States.
15. In an open shop you don't have to join a union, but in a union shop you do.
16. Corporations usually have one owner.
17. During collective bargaining, employers and workers try to reach decisions that will satisfy both sides.
18. A labor union is an organization of business owners.
19. Flexible expenses may occur each month but the amount spent changes.
20. What a person pays in rent each month is a fixed expense.
21. A budget is a plan for spending and saving money.
22. Credit unions are stores that sell only on credit.

Recalling Information

1. True or false: The problem of scarcity is the problem of too many resources and too few needs.
2. Which of the following provide economic services?
   a. coats
   b. pizzas
   c. dentists
   d. bikes
3. In a capitalistic system _____ .
   a. the government makes all major economic decisions
   b. there is private ownership of property
   c. everyone works for the government
   d. all of the above
4. True or false: Producers who fail to offer what consumers want will probably go out of business.
5. True or false: A communist country usually has free enterprise.
6. In a market system, prices _____ when there is a large supply of some item and a very small demand for the item.
   a. go up
   b. go down
   c. stay the same
   d. none of the above

Vocabulary

1. T	4. T	7. T	10. F	13. T	16. F	19. T	22. F
2. F	5. T	8. F	11. F	14. T	17. T	20. T	
3. F	6. T	9. T	12. F	15. T	18. F	21. T	

★★

7. True or false: In the United States most economic decisions are made by the command system.
8. Gross national product tells _____ .
   a. the value of goods and services produced during a certain period of time
   b. the number of cars built during a certain period of time
   c. the income earned by workers during a certain period of time
   d. the value of services bought by consumers during a certain period of time
9. You and a friend want to form a business. You would most likely form a _____ .
   a. single proprietorship
   b. partnership
   c. corporation
   d. none of the above
10. Could any of the following people be called producers?
    a. the owner of a bakery
    b. a manager of a can company
    c. an assembly worker for Ford
    d. all of the above
11. Capital goods are _____ .
    a. workers
    b. machines and tools
    c. natural resources
    d. all of the above
12. Which of the following has been a goal of labor unions in the past one hundred years?
    a. to improve working conditions
    b. to increase wages
    c. to get more fringe benefits
    d. all of the above

13. Which of the following should a person do when making a budget?
    a. List fixed expenses.
    b. Estimate flexible expenses.
    c. Balance estimated expenses with income.
    d. all of the above
14. True or false: Banks offer checking accounts, savings accounts, and loans.
15. The Food and Drug Administration _____ .
    a. is concerned with the safety of such items as bicycles, cars, and toys
    b. is supposed to make sure that food products are safe to eat
    c. is concerned with false advertising
    d. handles complaints about goods that have been sent through the mail
16. True or false: One of Ralph Nader's goals is to get consumers to demand that they be treated fairly.

Skill Building

1. Explain the difference between producers and consumers.
2. How do consumers influence producers in the United States?
3. Why are people hurt by inflation?
4. Describe conditions in the 1800s that led to the rise of labor unions.
5. In which chapter would you find tips for making wise purchases? How do the heads and subheads help you find the tips? List five that you think are most important when buying an expensive item.
6. Pretend that you see a sign that says "Olson's Finance will loan money for anything." What should you consider before taking advantage of the offer?

Recalling
1. F 4. T 7. F 10. d 13. d 16. T
2. c 5. F 8. a 11. b 14. T
3. b 6. b 9. b 12. d 15. b

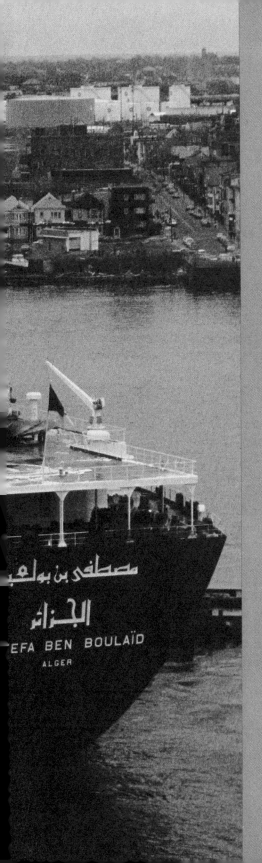

America and the World

The United States is linked to the world in many ways. Government leaders in the United States make decisions about the relationships between our country and others. Some of these decisions involve American troops and weapons. Such decisions can affect millions of lives.

At the same time, our business activities take us all over the world. Americans buy and sell raw materials and finished goods in places as far away as China and Chile. Decisions made by American business people affect other people the world over.

Likewise, our lives are affected by the business decisions of others in the world. The decision by a German company, for example, to sell cameras in the United States gives us new choices as consumers. It also means American companies making cameras will have more competition. Or the decision of Arab states to raise the price of crude oil affects the price of our gasoline and the cost of heating our homes.

Our farmers also link the United States to the world. American technology and know-how have made us some of the best farmers in the world. We can get more food out of an acre of land than any other nation. As a result, private farmers and government officials often make decisions about selling or giving food to others in the world. And many individuals come to the United States to study our farming techniques.

Our students and teachers also link the United States to others in the world. Over fifty thousand American students go to school in other countries. Nearly four times that number of foreign students study in the United States.

In this unit you will learn about foreign policy. You will read about the decisions of national government leaders that affect how the United States behaves toward other nations in the world. And you will learn what some major concerns of our foreign policy have been over the years.

You will also learn about new foreign-policy challenges facing citizens of the United States. And you will learn how the daily lives of ordinary citizens link them to others around the world.

Boston Harbor

Discuss: How are Americans involved around the world?

493

Chapter 24 — Making Foreign Policy

★★

Thousands of United States government officials work full-time on international relations. One of these officials is the Secretary of State. Here's a recent day in the life of a Secretary of State.

7:30 a.m. The Secretary wakes up in his hotel room in Cairo, Egypt; showers, dresses, and has breakfast. While eating, he reads messages from Washington.

8:30 a.m. An assistant enters the room. They discuss the Secretary's plans for the week. The Secretary decides to meet with the Russian foreign minister later in the week.

10:00 a.m. The Secretary meets with the foreign minister of Egypt. The two officials make final plans for an $80 million loan from the United States to Egypt. News reporters take pictures.

11:08 a.m. The Secretary rushes to the airport. His government 707 jet plane is waiting.

1:05 p.m. In Syria, the Secretary and the Syrian president discuss peace in the Middle East.

6:10 p.m. The Secretary is back on his plane and flying to Israel. He talks with American news reporters who are traveling with him.

9:00 p.m. Dinner with the prime minister of Israel and other officials. The Secretary explains why the United States has loaned money to Egypt. The Israeli leaders ask for more military aid for their country.

11:30 p.m. The Secretary returns to his hotel, writes a report to the President, issues orders to his assistants, and goes to bed.

This chapter looks at how the United States government works out plans for dealing with others in the world.

Discuss: How could the events of this day influence foreign policy?

1/What Is Foreign Policy?
2/Who Makes Foreign Policy in the National Government?
3/From Cold War to Coexistence
Case Study: The Panama Canal Treaties

1/What Is Foreign Policy?

The plans a national government makes about how to act toward other nations and groups in the world are called its **foreign policies.** The goals of American foreign policies are to protect the United States and to promote peace and trade. Creating a foreign policy means making decisions about how to behave toward others in the world.

Discuss: What does it mean to have a foreign policy?

Our foreign policies have changed over the years as the nation's needs have changed. In the early 1800s the United States was a small and weak nation. Our foreign policy was aimed at protecting the new nation from the strong European countries. We wanted to avoid becoming involved in European affairs. Thus our foreign policy at this time was called **isolationism.**

By the mid and late 1800s our nation's needs were changing. The nation was growing stronger. Our foreign policies were aimed at adding new territory and at helping protect our growing industries. In 1898 the United States won the Spanish-American War and gained control of Cuba, Puerto Rico, Hawaii, Guam, and the Philippines.

After World Wars I and II, the United States emerged as one of the very strongest nations in the world. We created new foreign policies designed to hold back the spread of communism.

United States Secretary of State Cyrus Vance with Soviet president Leonid Brezhnev and Soviet foreign minister Andrei Gromyko.

These policies involved the United States in wars in Korea and Vietnam.

Today the United States, like any large nation, has many foreign policies. For example, the national government has policies about how much trading American business should do with other countries around the world. It also has policies about which nations can buy American weapons and bombs. And it has policies about which countries the United States will defend if they are attacked.

Some of these foreign policies stay the same for many years. For instance, the United States has promised military support to many Western European countries for many years. And we have given aid to poorer countries since the early 1950s.

Foreign policies change. For example, in late 1945 there was a revolutionary war in China. Communists defeated the Nationalist government led by Chiang Kai-shek [chyäng′ kī′shek′]. Because of America's policy to try to stop the spread of communism, we supported Chiang. For years we did not recognize the communist Chinese government. However, one third of the world's people live in China. Gradually we changed our policy towards China. In 1972, President Nixon visited China to begin friendly relations. In 1979, we took the formal step that gave China full diplomatic recognition.

Discuss: Why is it important to be informed about our foreign policy?

'Like it or not, it's all one world and I'm a leader.'

Section Review

Vocabulary: foreign policy, isolationism.
Reviewing the Main Ideas
1. What is foreign policy? Give an example.
2. Give examples of how our foreign policies have changed.
Skill Building
Study the political cartoon on this page. What is the cartoonist's view of United States foreign policy? How does the cartoonist think the United States should act toward others in the world? Do you agree or disagree? Why?

Main Ideas
1. p. 495
2. p. 495–496
Skill Building
The cartoonist believes the United States must be a leader in solving world problems.

2/Who Makes Foreign Policy in the National Government?

Who decides how the United States should act toward others in the world? Many people and groups in government help make foreign policy.

The President

The President is a very important foreign-policy decision maker. Americans and others in the world look to the President to represent our country in foreign affairs.

The President is the nation's chief **diplomat.** (Diplomats are the officials who manage relations between countries.) The Constitution gives the President the power to: (1) make treaties with other nations (two-thirds of the Senate must approve the treaty), (2) appoint diplomatic officers (subject to Senate approval), and (3) recognize the legal existence of a nation and its government. In addition, as Commander in Chief of the armed forces, Presidents can use troops and weapons to carry out foreign-policy decisions.

Discuss: What foreign-policy roles does the Constitution give the President?

President Ford considers a tough decision as he confers with Secretary of State Kissinger.

The Foreign-Policy Bureaucracy

The President and assistants in the White House do not make foreign-policy decisions alone. They work with a large foreign-policy bureaucracy. This bureaucracy is made up of the Department of State, the Department of Defense, the Central Intelligence Agency, and the National Security Council.

Where did this bureaucracy come from? At the end of World War II (1945) many Americans feared the United States could not stop Russia from taking over other countries. They believed foreign-policy decisions had to be made quickly as problems came up. In 1947, Congress created the Department of Defense, the Central Intelligence Agency, and the National Security Council. It put these agencies in the Executive Branch of government under the authority of the President. The idea was to give a President the information and advisers needed to respond quickly to foreign-policy problems.

These agencies have helped make the President very powerful in foreign affairs. They give the President valuable information. They can carry out presidential decisions around the world. Today key foreign-policy decisions about war and peace, nuclear

Discuss: What is the foreign-policy bureaucracy? What are the key roles of groups in the foreign-policy bureaucracy?

United States Ambassador to Norway Louis A. Lerner (on the right).

weapons, and national defense are made in the Executive Branch by the President and the foreign-policy bureaucracy.

However, the foreign-policy bureaucracy can be hard for a President to control. Many of the people in the bureaucracy have had their jobs from before the President took office and they will be there long after he or she leaves. President Truman once complained, "Those fellows in the State Department, who stay there no matter what happens in elections, can't be trusted to carry out a President's policies."

The Department of State. This is a major agency for government foreign-policy decision making. The Secretary of State heads the Department. The Secretary is the President's official adviser on foreign-policy matters. Most Secretaries of State work closely with the President on foreign-policy decisions.

The State Department's job is to make decisions about how the United States should act toward other countries and toward global problems such as hunger or pollution. The State Department is supposed to carry out decisions made by the President. The Department arranges treaties and other agreements with foreign governments. It helps American citizens who get in trouble in foreign countries. And the State Department gives information about the United States to foreigners.

Discuss: Why is the Department of State said to be the major agency for foreign-policy decision making?

The Department of Defense. The Department of Defense is directed by the Secretary of Defense. The Defense Department shares directly in making foreign-policy decisions. The Secretary of Defense and the Joint Chiefs of Staff advise the President about military aspects of foreign policy and other defense matters. Presidents rarely make important decisions without consulting their military advisers.

In addition, many foreign-policy decisions about military affairs are made in the Defense Department. The Department is in charge of over 320 American military bases in thirty countries. The Department gives military assistance to over fifty countries. The Department also sells American arms (airplanes, tanks, rifles, cannons, bombs, and the like) to many countries around the world.

Discuss: How does the Department of Defense help the President?

The Central Intelligence Agency. This agency finds out what is going on in other countries. The CIA was set up to gather information, evaluate it, and pass it on to the President and other foreign-policy decision makers. It gets its information from its own secret agents, from paid informers, from foreign news sources, and from the information agencies of foreign governments friendly to the United States. All large nations have information-gathering agencies like the CIA.

Discuss: How could you best summarize the roles of the CIA?

Information-gathering agencies are necessary to a country's security. In 1962, when the Soviet Union sent nuclear missiles into Cuba, in striking distance of our nation, we needed to know it. Then our President was able to take action to make the Soviet Union take the missiles away. But information-gathering agencies are troublesome in a democracy just because they work in secret. Americans have always been suspicious of the things a government does in secret. In the mid-1970s, Congress investigated the CIA and called for stricter control of its activities.

The National Security Council. This is an advisory group for the President. The Council brings officials from the foreign-policy bureaucracy together. The Council consists of the President, the Vice-President, the Secretaries of State and Defense, the Chairman of the Joint Chiefs of Staff, and the Director of the Office of Emergency Preparedness. The President can also invite others to be part of this group. The Council can recommend specific policies and decisions to the President. The President makes the final decision whether or not to follow the advice of the Council.

Discuss: Why is the National Security Council said to be only an advisory group?

Other Government Agencies

Almost all government agencies are involved to some degree in foreign affairs. Three of the most important agencies are the Departments of Treasury, Commerce, and Agriculture.

The Treasury Department makes decisions about money problems and international loans. The Department of Commerce makes decisions related to foreign trade. The Department of Agriculture makes decisions related to technical assistance to other countries and selling American food products.

Discuss: What other government agencies influence foreign policy?

Congress and Foreign Policy

Today Congress has little direct control over foreign-policy decisions. The foreign-policy job of Congress has been to review decisions made by the foreign-policy bureaucracy and the President. The Constitution gives Congress various powers to perform this review task.

War Powers. The Constitution (Article 1) gives Congress alone the power to declare war and maintain an army and navy. But from the beginning Presidents have ignored this authority. In 1798 President Adams ordered American warships to fight French ships. Since then Presidents have sent American troops to fight more than 40 times without a declaration of war.

In 1973, Congress passed the War Powers Act over a presidential veto. Congress wanted to limit the President's power. The law requires the President to consult Congress "in every possible instance . . . before introducing U.S. armed forces into hostilities or into situations where . . . involvement" of troops is likely. But in 1975, President Ford did not consult Congress before he sent American troops to attack Cambodians involved in stopping an American ship.

Approval Powers. The Constitution also requires the Senate to approve all treaties the President arranges with other countries. Two-thirds of the Senate must vote in favor of a treaty before it becomes law. Presidents often avoid this step by making executive agreements with other countries. An executive agreement is made directly between the President and the leader of another country.

President Carter with the Joint Chiefs of Staff.

Ambassadors, ministers, consuls—all members of the foreign service—must also be approved by the Senate. The Senate usually accepts the President's choices in these matters.

Money Powers. The President and other government agencies cannot spend money for foreign-policy activities unless Congress gives it to them. When the President submits the national budget every year, committees in the House and Senate must approve his requests for foreign policy and military defense. During the year, the President may submit bills about foreign policy·that call for special funding.

Discuss: What is the role of Congress in foreign policy?

Main Ideas
1. pp. 498–500
2. pp. 500–502
Skill Building
1. T, p. 498
2. F, pp. 498–502
3. F. The Department of Defense does this.
4. F, p. 499
5. T, p. 501

Section Review

Vocabulary: diplomat, Department of State, Department of Defense, Central Intelligence Agency, National Security Council.

Reviewing the Main Ideas

1. Describe the agencies that make up the foreign-policy bureaucracy. What is the relationship of these agencies to the President?

2. How can Congress check the President's foreign-policy actions?

Skill Building

Label each statement below as true or false. Support your choice with evidence from this section.

1. The President has to work with many people when making foreign-policy decisions.

2. Only the President and State Department actually make foreign-policy decisions.

3. The National Security Council sells military equipment to foreign countries.

4. The Department of Defense has little influence on the President's foreign-policy decisions.

5. The President can send American troops into combat without a declaration of war by Congress.

3/From Cold War to Coexistence

The most important concern of American foreign policy since World War II has been our security against the expansion and competition of the communist nations of the Soviet Union and China. The years from 1947 to the 1970s have been called the Cold War. During that time the United States and the Soviet Union never fought each other directly. But they competed in many ways. Each country built many weapons to defend itself against the other. Each country threatened the other. Each country has given aid to either communist or noncommunist groups fighting in other countries. How did the Cold War start?

Discuss: What has been the major foreign-policy concern of the United States since World War II?

Communism and Cold War

Karl Marx (1818–1883) developed the ideas behind communism. Marx, a German writer, believed that workers in all nations were treated unfairly by the capitalists, or factory owners and business leaders. In a book, *Das Kapital,* Marx argued that the workers, called the **proletariat** [prō′lə ter′ē ət], should take over factories and businesses in all nations. Marx called for the proletariat to take control of government by force if necessary. Under commu-

In Berlin, Germany, a wall divided the free world from the communist world. It kept families and friends apart.

nism there would be no private property or businesses. Instead, the government would own everything and run factories in the name of the workers.

In a democracy, individuals are free to own property and seek their fortunes. Under communism, the state owns nearly everything and individuals come to have much less freedom.

In 1917, Russia became the first country to accept communism. Under the leadership of a man called Lenin, workers, soldiers, and peasants overthrew the Russian czar and took over the government. In 1924, Joseph Stalin became the leader of Russia—now called the Union of Soviet Socialist Republics, or the Soviet Union. Stalin made the Soviet Union into a world power. He also created a powerful dictatorship that took complete control of Russian life.

In World War II, the Soviet Union and the United States fought together against Germany. But shortly after the war, they began to disagree. Perhaps neither government ever really trusted the other. The Russians believed they had done most of the fighting against Hitler. Their military casualties were fifteen times those of the United States. Seven-and-one-half million Russian soldiers lost their lives in World War II! Stalin wanted to keep control of Poland and other Eastern European countries to protect Russian borders against future attacks.

So the Russians kept their troops in the countries of Eastern Europe. They did not permit free elections. In each country they created communist governments under their control.

By 1947, President Truman and others were convinced the Russians wanted to take over Europe and then the rest of the world. They believed World War II had started because Hitler was not stopped when he began taking over other countries. They did not want to make the same mistake with the Soviets.

In a 1947 speech before Congress, President Truman announced a new foreign policy toward the Soviet Union. The President said it was necessary for the United States to help countries all over the world fight off the expansion of the Soviet Union and communism.

The policy came to be known as **containment.** The policy of containment meant the United States would use money and military power to contain the Soviet Union, that is, to keep it from expanding the territory it controlled, and to prevent countries from developing governments friendly to communism. This policy has been followed by all Presidents since Truman.

Discuss: How have communism and the Cold War influenced U.S. foreign policy?

504

Tools of Containment

Here are some of the more important foreign-policy tools the government has used to carry out the policy of containment.

Foreign Aid. This involves giving economic or military goods to other countries. Aid has been given to try to strengthen countries against communism. It has included gifts of food, money, technical help, road building, education programs, and weapons. Since the end of World War II, the United States has given more than $160 billion in aid to over ninety countries.

Security Treaties. The United States has made over forty mutual defense treaties with other countries. Under these treaties, countries that sign them promise to protect each other from communist aggression. If a country is attacked, others that have a treaty with it are supposed to come to its aid.

Secret Operations. These involve secret activities in another country. These operations include such things as spying, giving money to political groups, or helping one political party fight another. Some of our secret operations have been aimed at changing the government of another country to get someone in power favorable to our interests.

Using the Armed Forces. Small numbers of American troops have sometimes been sent into other countries to act as police. They may stop rioting or help governments the United States wants to keep in power. For example, in April 1965 rebels attacked the government of the Dominican Republic. This government was supported by the United States. President Lyndon Johnson sent several thousand American troops to keep order and protect the government. Johnson said that the rebels were communists.

Massive Retaliation. This is the threat to use our large and small nuclear weapons. The United States invented the atomic bomb during World War II. Atomic bombs were used in 1945 to end the war with Japan. Since then America has not used such weapons but it could. This threat really stands behind all the other "tools" of containment.

However, the Soviet Union also has enough nuclear weapons to mean that war between our two countries would destroy life

Discuss: What are the tools of containment? How are they used?

Discuss: What is the most dangerous containment tool?

as we know it. The most important goal of foreign policy is to prevent an all-out nuclear war.

Fighting Limited Wars

Discuss: What is a limited war? How have we been influenced by these wars?

American troops have been used to fight **limited wars** against communist-supported armies in Korea and Vietnam. A limited war is fought without the use of major weapons, especially nuclear weapons.

The Korean War. In June, 1950, communist North Korea attacked South Korea, a noncommunist country. President Truman sent many thousands of American troops to fight with the South Korean army. Communist Chinese troops soon entered the war to help North Korea. The goal of the United States was limited to driving the Chinese and North Koreans back into North Korea. When General Eisenhower became President in 1952, he threatened to use nuclear weapons against China to stop the war. In July of 1953 a truce was signed and the fighting stopped. Over 36,000 Americans were killed in Korea and more than 103,000 were wounded. The war cost $54 billion dollars.

The Vietnam War. In the 1950s it looked as if a communist group in North Vietnam was going to take over all of Vietnam. President Eisenhower sent money and a small number of military advisers to help the noncommunist government in South Vietnam. But the communists grew stronger. Under President Kennedy, the United States sent more money, weapons, and military advisers to help South Vietnam. By 1963 there were 15 thousand American advisers helping the South Vietnamese government. Russia and China, in turn, were helping North Vietnam.

There was no formal declaration of war between the United States and North Vietnam. But in 1964, Congress passed the Gulf of Tonkin Resolution giving President Johnson power to take emergency action in Vietnam. During 1964 and 1965, the total numbers of United States troops in Vietnam jumped to 185 thousand. By 1968, one-half million Americans were fighting in Vietnam.

In spite of these large numbers of American helpers, the South Vietnamese were not able to win. The war dragged on for eight more years. Americans became very unhappy with a foreign policy that involved it in a long, drawn-out war. People

American troops land by helicopter to help fight North Vietnamese communists.

questioned if it really was in our interest to be fighting this war. Finally, in 1973, a truce was signed, and President Nixon withdrew all American troops from Vietnam. In April, 1975, the South Vietnamese government surrendered and Vietnam became one communist nation.

The End of Cold War?

In recent years things have begun to change. The Vietnam War may have been one of the last acts in the American policy of containment. Vietnam was a bitter experience for the United States. More than 46 thousand Americans gave their lives in the war. And another 304 thousand were wounded. Between 1965 and 1973, the United States spent more than $107 billion to fight the war.

Discuss: Has the Cold War ended?

In 1970, President Nixon started making changes in American foreign policy toward Russia and China. President Nixon did not give up the policy of containment completely. American foreign-policy decision makers still do not trust Russia or China. But these decision makers think Russia, China, and the United States can live together in the world. They also believe there may be ways for these countries to cooperate on such problems as arms control, international trade, and global energy.

Discuss: What is current U.S. foreign policy regarding these countries?

Section Review

Vocabulary: Cold War, containment, *Das Kapital,* limited war, massive retaliation, proletariat, secret operations.

Reviewing the Main Ideas
1. Explain the term Cold War and describe how the Cold War started.
2. What is the policy of containment?
3. Describe the foreign-policy tools used by America to carry out the policy of containment.

Skill Building
Find information to answer the following questions.
1. What is the name of the current Secretary of State?
2. What foreign-policy problems concern decision makers today?
3. Read a recent news-magazine article about a foreign-policy problem to find out which people and ideas are influencing foreign-policy decision makers.

Main Ideas
1. pp. 503–504
2. p. 504–505
3. p. 505
Skill Building
1. –3. Recent news magazines are a good source for answering these questions.

The Panama Canal Treaties

CASE STUDY

The Panama Canal cuts across the narrow Isthmus of Panama. Before the canal was built, it took many weeks for ships to sail around South America from the Atlantic to the Pacific. American business needed a shorter water route to transport goods. And during the Spanish-American War, when it took an American battleship 68 days to reach Cuba, American interest in building a canal grew even stronger.

At that time the Isthmus was under the control of Colombia. In 1903, the United States Secretary of State and the Colombian representative in Washington negotiated a treaty. The United States Senate ratified the treaty, but the Colombian government did not.

The people in Panama wanted the canal to be built. It would bring much business to their land. They revolted against the Colombian government—some historians say the United States aided their revolution. President Theodore Roosevelt arranged a treaty with the new Panamanian government.

The treaty gave the United States complete authority forever over a ten-mile-wide strip of land across Panama. This was called the Canal Zone. Panama got $10 million and yearly payments.

The Canal was built by the United States from 1903 to 1914. It cost $387 million. More than 6,000 workers died from malaria, yellow fever, and other diseases while working on the canal.

Over the years the people of Panama came to believe the 1903 treaty was unfair. They did not like the idea that the United States would control forever a strip of land that split their country from ocean to ocean. Some Panamanians were angry because the better jobs at the canal went to Americans living in the Canal Zone. For many years young people in Panama were taught that Americans were causing many of their country's problems.

In 1964 anger at the Americans finally boiled over. There was rioting in Panama. Four Americans and 21 Panamanians died. There was fear that the canal might be damaged by even more violence.

President Lyndon Johnson decided it was time to change American foreign policy toward Panama. State Department officials began to work with the Panamanians on a new treaty.

Work on the treaty continued under Presidents Nixon, Ford,

Locks on the Panama Canal.

and Carter. Finally, in 1977, two new treaties were ready. One called for the United States to give Panama control of the canal by the year 2000. The other gave the United States the right to defend the canal even after 2000.

The treaties represented a new foreign policy toward Panama. On September 7, 1977, President Jimmy Carter and General Omar Torrijos [tôr hē′yōs], the leader of Panama, signed the treaties in Washington. President Carter said it was the start of a new era of friendship between the United States and the peoples of Latin America.

Now all eyes turned to the U.S. Senate. Two-thirds of the senators had to vote yes before the treaties would become law. For seven months opponents and supporters of the treaty waged a battle to influence the Senate's decision. The opponents' beliefs were summed up by former California Governor Ronald Reagan who said, "We bought the canal; we paid for it; it's ours."

Opponents said that Panama would not run the canal well, it would be more expensive for us to pay tolls to Panama than to run it ourselves, and Panama might turn communist. They ran ads in newspapers. They urged citizens to write their senators and tell them to vote no. Some formed a "truth squad" that traveled and gave speeches.

At the same time President Carter worked to gain support for the treaties. He sent the Secretary of Defense and the Secretary of State to give speeches to the Senate. He talked personally with many senators.

Supporters of the treaty argued that a no vote on the treaties could cause rioting in Panama and serious damage to the canal. A yes vote would show other Latin American countries that the United States was fair. A no vote would weaken the President's ability to carry out other important foreign-policy decisions.

The Senate debated the treaties for a long time. Finally in the spring of 1978, the Senate approved both treaties by 68 to 32.

Reviewing the Case Study

1. What was the goal of President Johnson's foreign policy toward Panama?
2. What decision did the U.S. Senate have to make about that policy? What alternatives did the Senate have?
3. What consequences did supporters and opponents argue each alternative would have?
4. What is your judgment of the Senate's decision? Why?

Demonstrators (above) in Panama (below) in the United States.

Chapter Twenty-four Test and Activities

★★★

Vocabulary

Match the following words with their meanings.

1. foreign policy
2. isolationism
3. *Das Kapital*
4. CIA
5. Cold War
6. containment
7. foreign aid
8. diplomat
9. massive retaliation

a. relations between the United States and the Soviet Union from 1947 to the 1970s
b. Karl Marx's book that gives the ideas behind communism
c. the plans a government makes about how to relate to other countries
d. a foreign policy of preventing the spread of communism
e. economic or military help to other countries
f. the threat of using nuclear weapons
g. an agency that collects information about other countries
h. a foreign policy of not getting involved in European affairs
i. an official who manages relations between countries

Reviewing the Chapter Ideas

1. True or false: Our foreign policies have changed over the years.
2. True or false: The United States is one of the most powerful nations in the world.

3. The Constitution gives the President power to do which of the following?
   a. appoint diplomatic officers with Senate approval
   b. acknowledge the existence of a nation and its government
   c. make treaties with Senate approval
   d. all of the above
4. True or false: The President makes all foreign-policy decisions alone.
5. True or false: All large nations have groups like the CIA.
6. The State Department
   a. makes decisions about global problems
   b. makes decisions about military affairs
   c. secretly collects information about other countries
   d. is only an advisory group
7. The Department of Defense
   a. arranges treaties with other countries
   b. is in charge of our military bases
   c. gives assistance to United States citizens traveling in other countries
   d. is only an advisory group
8. Which of the following was not a Russian leader?
   a. Lenin
   b. Hitler
   c. Stalin
   d. all of the above
9. True or false: The Cold War has taken place during most of this century.
10. Which President arranged the treaty that allowed the U.S. to build the Panama Canal?
    a. Theodore Roosevelt
    b. John Kennedy
    c. Harry Truman
    d. none of the above

Vocabulary
1. c   4. g   7. e
2. h   5. a   8. i
3. b   6. d   9. f

Ideas
1. T   4. F   7. b   10. a
2. T   5. T   8. b
3. d   6. a   9. F

★★

Using Basic Social Studies Skills

Finding Information

1. What subheads in this chapter help you to find out what the foreign-policy bureaucracy is made up of? Write them down.
2. Where in this chapter does it tell how we have tried to control expansion of Russia?
3. What are the major points of the latest treaties the U.S. signed with Panama?

Comprehending Information

1. Explain the main goals of United States foreign policy.
2. What branch of government makes foreign policy?
3. What checks are there on this branch's foreign-policy decisions?
4. Why does the United States need an information-gathering agency such as the CIA?
5. Explain what it means to be involved in a "cold war."
6. What tools has the United States used to contain the spread of communism?

Organizing Information

Make a time line for the years 1900–1980. Include at least ten important dates and events relating to foreign policy.

Evaluating Information

Since 1903, the people of Panama felt the original treaty was unfair. Were they right? Give evidence to support your answer.

Communicating Ideas

Suppose you were Secretary of State. List 5-10 goals you would have for American foreign policy. Explain which of these goals are the most important and why you have chosen these goals.

Using Decision-Making Skills

In the months before ratification of the 1978 treaties with Panama, there was a controversy in the United States. Many citizens felt strongly about the question and let their senators know how they felt.

1. What is your opinion: Should the Senate have ratified the treaties?
2. Would you have felt it was important to give your senator your opinion?
3. What would be the consequences of trying to influence your senator?
4. What would be the consequences of not trying?
5. Is it a good idea for citizens to get involved in foreign-policy decisions? Explain.

Activities

1. Write ten true-or-false statements about the Panama Canal case. Then exchange your statements with another class member. Answer them. Make all false statements true.
2. Use current magazines and newspapers to look for examples of cooperation between the United States and Russia or China.
3. Students who want a close-up look at some events in the Cold War could read:
   (a) *The U-2 Incident, May, 1960: An American Spy Plane Downed over Russia Intensifies the Cold War,* by Fred J. Cook (Franklin Watts, 1973).
   (b) *The Cuban Missile Crisis, October, 1962: The U.S. and Russia Face a Nuclear Showdown,* by Fred J. Cook (Franklin Watts, 1972).
4. Look up "International Treaties, Agreements, and Organizations" in the *Information Please Almanac* to find which countries the United States has agreements with.

Chapter 25   Into the Future

★★

Discuss: What are other ways our lives are becoming more connected with other people around the world?

Stanley and Helen Carson know very little about Japan. Yet their lives were recently affected by a decision made by some Japanese business leaders.

The Carsons own a small farm in southern Wisconsin. Owning the farm has meant hard work for Stanley and Helen. It also has brought the Carsons into touch with the wider world around them.

Like most of their neighbors the Carsons raise soybeans. Things have gone pretty well for them since Kikkoman Shoyu, a Japanese company, opened a $9 million dollar plant in nearby Walworth, Wisconsin. The Kikkoman plant buys soybeans from local farmers to make soy sauce. The plant has meant the Carsons have a steady customer for their crop.

Stanley and Helen Carson are one example of the many ways our lives are becoming more connected to others around the world. Other examples of our links to the world can be found on almost any airplane flight. Peggy Robinson recently left Cleveland, Ohio, on a business trip. She was traveling to Japan to buy bicycles for a store in Cleveland. Also on the plane were a university president, a group of ministers, and Governor James Rhodes of the State of Ohio. The university president was going to Tokyo to arrange a student exchange program between a Japanese university and her university in Ohio. The ministers were going to represent United States churches at a meeting of the World Council of Churches. Governor Rhodes was going to try to influence the Toyota Motor Company to build a factory in Ohio. A decision by Toyota to build a plant in Ohio could create many new jobs for Ohio citizens.

As our links to the world increase, new foreign-policy problems arise for the United States and for individual citizens. In this chapter you will read about:

1/Our Shrinking World
2/Poor vs. Rich: The New Decisions
3/The United Nations
Case Study: Your Community in the World

1/Our Shrinking World

People today say "the world is growing smaller." By this they mean that there have been many changes in the modern world that are bringing people closer together. Travel, for example, is faster than ever. And through satellites, words and pictures can be flashed around the globe instantly. One of the most important changes is a great increase in interdependence.

Discuss: What does it mean when we say "the world is growing smaller"?

Global Interdependence

The world is becoming more interdependent. This means people and nations all over the world now depend more on one another for goods and services. It also means that what happens in one nation or area of the world affects what happens in other places.

Here is an example of **global interdependence.** Bad weather in the winter of 1971–1972 caused the Soviet Union to lose most of its wheat crop. It gave American farmers the chance to make greater profits by selling wheat to the Soviets. This in turn meant there was less wheat for sale in the United States. Such a shortage led to higher prices for bread in American supermarkets. Some people have felt the national government should decide to make a new foreign policy about selling American wheat to the Soviet Union.

Discuss: What is global interdependence?

A Wisconsin farm.

513

The simple candy bar provides another example of global interdependence. In Hershey, Pennsylvania, many Americans earn their living working in a candy factory. Chocolate, sugar, and nuts go into the candy bars they make. In today's world many things can affect the production of these candy bars and hence people's jobs.

Chocolate comes from cacao seeds. Many of these seeds are grown in Central Africa. A good crop can lower the price of cacao and hence of chocolate. On the other hand, a war in Central Africa could disrupt farming and affect the supply of cacao.

Nuts for the candy bar may come from Brazil. Dock workers in Brazil might strike for higher pay. The strike could prevent the nuts from being shipped to America.

Sugar for the candy bar may come from a Caribbean island. A revolution in such an island could change the government of the island. The United States might not recognize the new government and might refuse to trade with it. The candy factory would have to find a new source of sugar.

The fuel to power our cars, planes, trucks, buses, and factor-

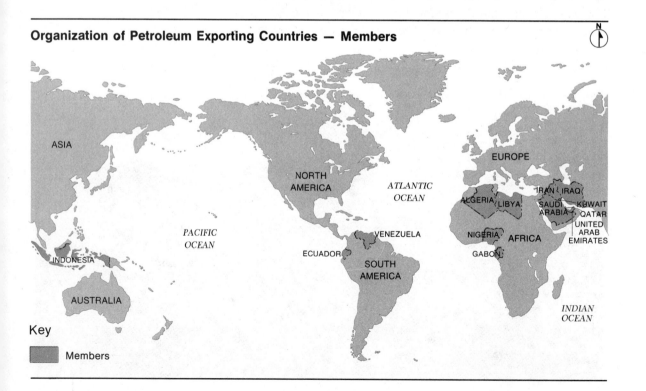

Organization of Petroleum Exporting Countries — Members

N

Key

Members

ies is an important example of growing interdependence. This fuel comes from crude oil. Today the United States uses far more oil than it can produce by itself. As a result we import about 50 percent of the oil we need. One of the important goals of United States foreign policy is to keep friendly relations with the oil-producing countries.

Global interdependence also means that other countries are dependent on the United States. This is especially true of many of the smaller, poorer nations of the world. These nations may depend on the United States for food, technology, or weapons.

Discuss: How are other countries dependent on the U.S.?

The Effects of Interdependence

Growing global interdependence is affecting the way people live. One effect is that new and interesting jobs have opened up. Job advertisements such as these show the effects of global interdependence:

"International executive wanted. Must have solid educational background and experience in international business. Must be able to speak and read Spanish. Duties involve travel."

"Metcalf and Eddy, an international leader in water management, wants candidates to work in the Middle East."

Discuss: How is growing global interdependence affecting the way people live?

INTERDEPENDENCE IS BRINGING PEOPLE TOGETHER

Travel to a Different Country*	1950	1976	Change
Americans visiting other countries	651,000	7,700,000	up 1,083%
Foreigners coming to the U.S.	288,000	4,439,000	up 1, 441%

*Figures do not include land travel between the U.S. and Canada and Mexico.

	1950	1976	
Pieces of Mail Sent Abroad	417 million	933 million	up 124%
Value of Goods Traded in the Free World	$56 billion	$875 billion	up 1,463%
Telephone Calls Overseas*	9,000	50,555,000	up 5,517%

*Figures do not include calls to Canada and Mexico.

Foreign Investments	1950	1975	
U.S. direct investment abroad	$11.8 billion	$133.2 billion	up 1,029%
Foreign direct investment in the U.S.	$3.4 billion	$26.7 billion	up 685%

Foreign Exchange Students	1955–56	1975–76	
U.S. students studying abroad	9,000	50,000	up 405%
Foreign students studying in the U.S.	36,500	179,400	up 392%

Getting Jobs Overseas

With all the governmental, business, and commercial interest in foreign countries, there are ample job opportunities for Americans who wish to work overseas. Opportunities must be carefully weighed in terms of a person's qualifications and jobs available. As a rule, Americans who land jobs overseas are specialists who know their work thoroughly.

Government Positions

The United States government employs around 95,000 American citizens in foreign countries. The jobs range from secretary to nuclear scientist and many of them are covered by the federal Civil Service.

To get on the Civil Service list, you must fill out application forms you got from the nearest Civil Service office or from Washington, D.C. On the form you put down facts about your education and work experience, as well as other information. Some Civil Service positions require an examination, one of which, dealing with simple language, arithmetic, and other problems, covers some two hundred different jobs. For many Civil Service positions, applicants do not take a test; instead they are ranked according to education, experience, and competency.

Getting on the Civil Service list does not guarantee a job. Ordinarily, a government agency with a position open requests the names and qualifications of the top three persons on the appropriate list. After examining their credentials and interviewing the candidates, the agency chooses one of them. The other two names return to the top of the list.

What are some overseas government jobs? In recent years, the Agency for International Development (AID) has been one of the largest government employers for foreign positions. AID grants economic and technical assistance to developing countries. It employs experts in the fields of agriculture, engineering, public health, education, public administration, economics, housing, transportation, auditing and accounting, and communication. AID also hires secretaries and some teachers.

Other government departments that hire for overseas positions are Air Force, Navy, Army, Commerce, Transportation, Interior, and Agriculture. The military services use secretaries, teachers, engineers, scientists, and other specialists. The Department of Commerce, among other activities, operates the U.S. Travel Service (USTS), which serves people of other countries who wish to visit America. The Department of Transportation hires bridge and road engineers and maintenance workers. The Department of the Interior has positions for engineers, geologists, foresters, elementary teachers, and metallurgists. The Department of Agriculture places agronomists, horticulturalists, and veterinarians, among others, in foreign countries.

The Department of State also sends personnel abroad, but most of them have first put in time in the department in this country. Many overseas State Department jobs are filled by rotation. The Central Intelligence Agency employs Americans to work in foreign countries too, often in highly specialized positions.

A number of government agencies and departments employ teachers, as many as 5,000 in some years. Some American teachers work in overseas military bases, where they teach American children. Others teach in private American schools abroad. And some work for American companies that run schools for employees' children. Still others, such as those who join the Peace Corps or belong to religious groups, often mingle at the village level, receiving small pay but learning a great deal about how other people live.

United Nations agencies such as the United Nations Educational, Scientific, and Cultural Organization (UNESCO) also hire American teachers—as well as many other specialists—for overseas positions.

Business and Commercial Firms

American business firms employ thousands of people in overseas jobs, nearly all of which demand some technical skill and work experience. These jobs are in such areas as secretarial, sales, shipping, air transport, insurance, advertising, marketing, engineering, agriculture, geology and other sciences, and construction of all kinds.

To succeed in many overseas jobs a person must know the appropriate language. However, this is not necessarily the case with jobs in business. Usually a person must be willing to learn the language. Often a foreign-job hunter must agree to sign up for a certain length of time, frequently for three years.

There are also jobs available with foreign firms if a person possesses the necessary language ability. As a rule these jobs have lower salaries than do jobs with American firms.

Volunteer Jobs

For a person who wishes to live and work overseas, and does not mind living simply, there are possibilities with many voluntary agencies. The Peace Corps has about 10,000 workers. Other voluntary agencies include the Salvation Army, the American Red Cross, the American Friends Service Committee, the Joint (Jewish) Distribution Committee, and the International Voluntary Services.

Jobs with volunteer organizations are challenging. The people who hold them get a good chance at personal satisfaction. Though they do not earn much money, usually less than $100 a month, they do get enough to eat, although they may have to become accustomed to different foods.

How to Proceed

Suppose you want to find out about overseas jobs, pay scales, and living conditions in other countries, how do you go about it? For government jobs, the best way is to write to the agency or department you are interested in—for example, Agency for International Development, Department of State, Washington, D.C., 20523; or Personnel Division, Foreign Agricultural Service, Department of Agriculture, Washington, D.C., 20520. With respect to jobs with a business or commercial firm or a volunteer group, write the nearest office of the company or agency you have in mind.

Note: Have students look for examples of jobs that are currently available.

"The Solar Energy Research Institute needs men and women with expertise in these areas: thermal conversion; solar data bank; international cooperation."

Today people all over the world communicate with each other, trade with each other, and learn from each other in greater numbers than ever before in history. The chart on page 515 shows the increases in international trade, mail, travel, and communications that are evidence of growing global interdependence.

Interdependence has brought the world directly into our communities. Today we can find many examples of links with other parts of the world in our own towns and cities. We will look more closely at these global links at the end of this chapter.

Finally, interdependence has created many new foreign-policy decisions for the United States. We look at these decisions in the next section.

Section Review

Vocabulary: global interdependence.

Reviewing the Main Ideas:
1. What is meant by the phrase "our shrinking world"?
2. Define *global interdependence* and give two examples.
3. Describe two effects of increasing global interdependence.

Skill Building
1. Summarize the main ideas of this section in a paragraph.
2. Explain in your own words the significance of the chart on page 515.

Main Ideas
1. p. 513
2. pp. 513–515
3. pp. 515–518
Skill Building
1. Answer should be in a correctly constructed paragraph.
2. Answers will vary.

518

2/Poor vs. Rich: The New Decisions

As a result of global interdependence, the United States faces many new foreign-policy decisions. Most of these decisions involve a growing split between the rich and poor nations of the world. On one side are the twenty or so rich, industrial countries including Japan, the United States, West Germany, Canada, and the Soviet Union. These nations are often called **developed countries** because they have used natural resources to develop a way of life based on business and industry.

The developed countries have natural resources such as coal and iron. They have many large industries such as steel, electronics, and automotives. Citizens of these states consume most of the world's resources. They also make most of the goods sold around the world. They enjoy the highest standard of living in history.

On the other side are more than 100 poor nations. Many of their citizens live in the shadow of death by starvation or disease. **Life expectancy** in the poorest of these is only 35 years. Because most of the poor countries of the world are trying to develop industrial economies, they are called **developing countries.**

Discuss: What is "rich"? What is "poor"?

A watering hole in Niger. Over ten years of drought in this region has made it impossible for the population to raise enough food to feed itself.

519

Some of these developing countries, such as Ethiopia, Mali, Peru, and Thailand are very poor. They have few natural resources. They cannot farm enough food to feed their populations. They make few products to sell to others. They have high levels of unemployment, disease, and poverty.

Other developing countries have natural resources. The countries of the Middle East, such as Saudi Arabia and Iran, have oil. Colombia grows coffee. Zaire has copper. But these developing countries have little industry. They do not have the health and educational facilities to develop their human resources. It takes scientists, engineers, business leaders, and designers to develop industry. These countries are dependent on the richer nations.

Obviously, with such differences in the world, the needs of people in the poor countries are very different from those in the rich ones. One leader of an oil-producing country explained his people's point of view: "My people need money from oil for food, schools, and medicine. You use energy to light ballparks at night and to drive large cars to the corner store for a pack of cigarettes." Energy use is only one area of difference. There are others.

The Use of the Oceans

Note: Have students debate, "Who owns the oceans?"

Oceans cover 71 percent of the earth. And the oceans are rich. They contain badly needed food, oil, and scarce minerals. All

Fiji Islanders fishing with nets.

countries of the world need these resources. Who owns the seas?

Until recently the law of the sea has been simple. Each nation had control of its coastal waters up to three miles from shore—the distance a cannonball could be shot. Beyond three miles, the seas were free for all.

Today the rich nations like France, England, Japan, and the Soviet Union want to keep things pretty much that way. They would like each nation to control its own coastal waters. They want to let all countries mine the open sea under the supervision of the International Seabed Authority.

Over seventy of the coastal developing nations like Ecuador and Ghana think that arrangement would be unfair. To them it would let the big, industrial nations "loot" the seabed at the expense of the poor nations. They say the poor nations don't have the technology to mine the deep sea.

The United Nations has sponsored several conferences aimed at writing a new law of the sea. But the issues are complex. It may be years before the more than 138 nations involved will reach an agreement.

One basic foreign-policy decision for the United States here is: Should the United States cooperate with poorer nations to create a new law of the sea or should we start mining the sea on our own no matter what other countries do?

Discuss: Why are oceans an important resource?

Who Will Feed the Hungry?

Every week 10,000 people in Africa die of starvation. Around the world more than 500 million people are starving. And as the world's population grows the problems will get worse.

The United States has plenty of food. But most other nations do not. As a result, food is becoming an important political resource for America. A communist leader recently said: "America has something more powerful than atom bombs. You have protein."

The United States has given food aid to its political allies in the Cold War since 1954. But when our food supply is smaller because of bad harvests, our food prices go up. At such times the United States faces a hard decision. Should we keep giving food to our allies and selling it to other nations or should we cut back on our food aid to keep prices down at home? And what about poor nations that cannot pay for food but need it desperately? Do we have a duty to give them food before we give it or sell it to richer nations?

Discuss: Where are people starving? Are there any starving people in your community?

The Growing Sale of Weapons

The world is arming itself as never before. Today nations of the world spend more than $200 billion a year on military expenditures. And the amount has been going up over the last years. Recently military expenditures were up in the United States by 62 percent, in Denmark by 116 percent, in Greece by 182 percent, in East Germany by 685 percent, and in Brazil by 338 percent.

For years America gave military aid to its allies. But recently the Soviet Union, France, England, and China have been selling weapons too. The biggest buyers have been the Arab states and other developing nations such as Zaire, Guinea, and Nigeria.

The result has been insecurity in the poor countries as each races to have more weapons than its neighbors. United States foreign-policy makers face a choice. Should we continue to sell weapons or should we begin to limit our military sales in an effort to halt the growing arms race among poor countries?

Global Pollution

Another major problem today is worldwide destruction of our natural environment. Some people say the earth is in danger of becoming a global sewer.

Poisonous metals such as mercury and lead have been dumped into the seas and air by the world's industries and automobiles. Giant oil spills from tankers have spread millions of gallons of oil into the oceans and onto beaches. These spills kill fish, sea birds, and important food for marine life.

DDT, a poison, has been spread all over the world. It is found in fish, animals, and humans in the most faraway places—even in Antarctic penguins. And more than 150 species of birds and animals have become extinct because of human actions.

Rich and poor nations have disagreed on what to do about pollution problems. Rich nations want to cut down on new global pollution. Many of the changes they want are expensive. These changes would make it harder to gather natural resources.

Poor nations think anti-pollution regulations are unfair. New rules controlling pollution would make it harder for them to develop their own industries. They argue that the developed nations polluted freely while they were becoming rich, but now they do not want to let the poor countries do the same.

One decision facing the United States is: Should we push for the same pollution-control rules for everyone or should the

Discuss: Why do some people say the earth is in danger of becoming a global sewer?

poorer nations be given the chance to develop their economies without worrying about pollution?

Section Review

Vocabulary: developed countries, developing countries, life expectancy.

Reviewing the Main Ideas
1. What do the developed countries have in common?
2. What do the developing countries have in common?
3. List and briefly explain four foreign-policy issues that divide the developed and developing countries.

Skill Building
1. How are the foreign-policy issues today different from the issues faced during the Cold War?
2. Which of today's foreign-policy problems, if any, do you think are more important than problems of containment and Cold War? Give reasons for your answer.

Main Ideas
1. natural resources, a way of life based on business and industry, a high standard of living
2. much disease and starvation, low life expectancy, few resources, few health and educational facilities
3. pp. 520–523
Skill Building
1. The Cold War issues divided the free world from the communist world, today's issues separate the developed countries from those that are developing their industries.
2. Answers will vary.

3/The United Nations

Many of the new foreign-policy issues between the poor and rich nations are being argued in the United Nations (UN). The UN is an international organization with over 130 nations as members.

The United States and other nations started the planning for the UN during the years of World War II. In 1944, delegates from the United States, Britain, and the Soviet Union drafted a charter for the UN. In 1945, representatives from fifty countries signed it at a meeting in San Francisco. By October of that year, twenty-nine of those countries had ratified it, and the UN was born. Its headquarters are in New York City.

The basic purposes of the UN are: to help maintain international peace and security, to promote friendly relations among all nations, and to work on the solution of global problems.

Organization. The chart on page 525 shows the organization of the UN. The six major parts of the UN are the General Assembly, the Security Council, the Economic and Social Council, the Trusteeship Council, the International Court of Justice, and the Secretariat.

Discuss: What is the role of the UN in world foreign-policy decision making?

The United Nations General Assembly.

The **General Assembly** has been called the "town meeting of the world." Each member-nation is represented in the General Assembly. And each nation has one vote regardless of size or wealth.

The General Assembly may admit, suspend, or expel members. It has many powers. It can recommend actions to the Security Council, other UN agencies, and the member-nations.

The **Security Council** has the power to carry out the UN's peace-keeping purpose. The Security Council decides when to send an international armed force into a country to stop aggression and restore law and order. When North Korea invaded South Korea, the UN sent in troops.

The Security Council has fifteen members. Real power in the Council is held by the five permanent members: the United States, the Soviet Union, China, Great Britain, and France. The ten other members are chosen by the General Assembly for two-year terms. Five are elected each year.

All important decisions in the Security Council must have nine yes votes. All five permanent members must vote yes. This gives any one of them a veto power over actions they oppose.

The UN has been successful in several ways. It has served as a meeting place where decision makers of many nations can

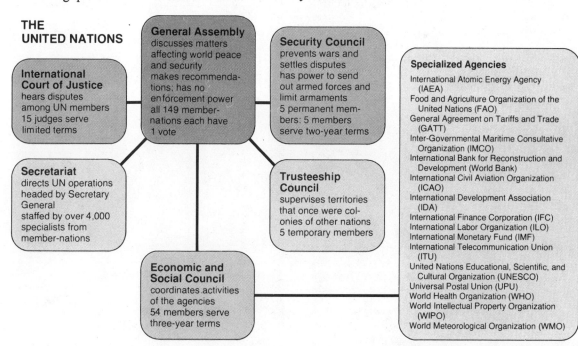

THE UNITED NATIONS

General Assembly
discusses matters affecting world peace and security
makes recommendations; has no enforcement power
all 149 member-nations each have 1 vote

International Court of Justice
hears disputes among UN members
15 judges serve limited terms

Secretariat
directs UN operations headed by Secretary General
staffed by over 4,000 specialists from member-nations

Economic and Social Council
coordinates activities of the agencies
54 members serve three-year terms

Security Council
prevents wars and settles disputes
has power to send out armed forces and limit armaments
5 permanent members: 5 members serve two-year terms

Trusteeship Council
supervises territories that once were colonies of other nations
5 temporary members

Specialized Agencies
International Atomic Energy Agency (IAEA)
Food and Agriculture Organization of the United Nations (FAO)
General Agreement on Tariffs and Trade (GATT)
Inter-Governmental Maritime Consultative Organization (IMCO)
International Bank for Reconstruction and Development (World Bank)
International Civil Aviation Organization (ICAO)
International Development Association (IDA)
International Finance Corporation (IFC)
International Labor Organization (ILO)
International Monetary Fund (IMF)
International Telecommunication Union (ITU)
United Nations Educational, Scientific, and Cultural Organization (UNESCO)
Universal Postal Union (UPU)
World Health Organization (WHO)
World Intellectual Property Organization (WIPO)
World Meteorological Organization (WMO)

Peace Corps Volunteers

The Peace Corps is a volunteer program sponsored by the United States government. It sends United States citizens to work in developing countries around the world.

The work that volunteers do is determined by their skills and by the needs of the areas to which they are sent. Most often those needs are for teachers and farmers. Carpenters, bricklayers, nurses, doctors, businesspeople, and others are needed as well.

Volunteers use their skills in more than one way. They use their skills directly in work, and they teach them to others as well. Nurses teach others to care for the sick. Farmers teach others to farm. In this way the skills of one person can be multiplied many times.

A volunteer (at left) from Kansas works in Fiji in the South Pacific. She works with women's clubs in the islands teaching home economics, health, and sanitation.

A volunteer from Wisconsin works with a Guatamalan farmer.

A volunteer from Oregon (at right) works in Gambia. He has helped local artisans develop a cooperative to market their products.

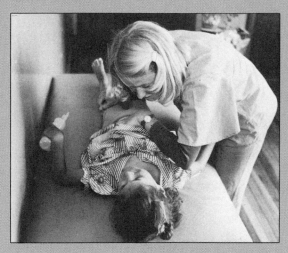

People and Government

This volunteer (at left) is from Vermont. He works in a hospital in Kinshasa, Zaire keeping medical equipment in good repair. He also gives on-the-job training to local workers.

This volunteer works in the library of an agricultural center in Colombia. She is training two assistants.

This volunteer is an occupational therapist from Illinois. She works with children in a hospital for the mentally retarded. The hospital is located in Conocoto, Ecuador.

A volunteer from California teaches English to children in the Galápagos Islands.

discuss mutual problems. It has been able to settle fights between several smaller nations. Some special agencies of the UN (see chart, page 525), like the World Health Organization and UNESCO, have done a great deal to fight sickness, poverty, and ignorance around the world.

Poor vs. Rich in the UN. Until recently the United States and other rich nations were able to control things in the UN. They were able to have things pretty much their own way. But this does not always happen today.

In the mid-1970s, the UN became a truly global organization. Since 1955 over 70 new nations have joined the UN. Most of these new UN members are poor nations.

In recent years the poor nations have pushed for many new programs. They have asked for new trade policies, foreign aid, and money from the rich nations. The poor nations have voted together against some United States foreign policies in the General Assembly. On the other hand, the United States still dominates the Security Council.

Some people say the United States should ignore the UN since the majority of members no longer agree with American foreign policy. These critics say that the UN is not in America's interest.

Others think the rich countries, including the United States, must learn to live with the poor nations of the world. They argue that the United States should try to strengthen the UN, not weaken it.

Section Review

Vocabulary: General Assembly, Security Council, United Nations.

Reviewing the Main Ideas
1. Why and when was the UN created?
2. In what part of the UN are all member nations equally represented?
3. What is the main job of the UN Security Council?

Skill Building
Study the political cartoon on this page. What is this cartoonist's view of the UN? What important job does the cartoonist think the UN is doing?

The Small Society

The UN building is in the background.

Main Ideas
1. p. 524
2. The General Assembly
3. to keep peace in the world

Skill Building
The cartoonist believes that even though the UN seems to accomplish nothing more than talk, the world would be worse off if the nations were not talking to each other.

528

Your Community in the World

Ken Shulman answered the phone. Ken worked in the international division of a bank in Des Moines, Iowa. The caller asked about investing money in a new housing project in Africa. Yes, Ken said, he could arrange an investment without any trouble.

Ken Shulman is one of many millions of people involved in international activity as a result of increasing global interdependence. These people help bring the world into their community and their community into the world.

Most of today's international activity is carried out from cities and towns around the world. Cities and towns provide the many services that people in international activity depend on. These include banks, airports, shipping, travel agencies, convention services, and many more.

Columbus, Ohio, is a good example. In many ways Columbus is a typical, midwestern city. It is located near the center of Ohio. It does not have a seaport. Yet like most communities Columbus is connected to other parts of the world in many ways.

IBM computer alphabet for Japanese.

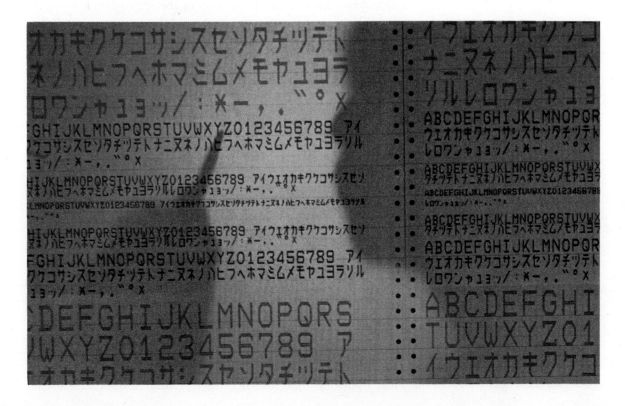

Columbus and the World

Here are some of the ways Columbus is linked to the world.

Travel. At least 29,000 international trips were made out of Columbus in a recent year. Many of the people traveling from Columbus go to Western Europe, Canada, and Mexico. Over one-third go to Africa, Asia, and the Middle East. Many Columbus residents travel for pleasure. Others travel for business.

At the same time Columbus has more than five thousand visitors from other countries each year. Some of these visitors come as students, some come on business, and still others come for a vacation.

Business Connections. The Columbus business community is closely linked with the rest of the world. Banks in Columbus deal with more than 500 foreign banks around the world. Other Columbus businesses export over $140 million worth of machinery, scientific equipment, chemicals, and other goods. At the same time these firms import more than $88 million worth of goods each year. More than 3,000 jobs in the Columbus area result from the international activities of such businesses.

Agriculture. Like any American city today, Columbus shoppers can go into a supermarket and select from more than 70 imported items. These include bananas from Panama, wine from Italy, sausage from Germany, oranges from Japan, and cheese from Denmark.

In addition, a large part of the crops grown in the nearby country side are exported. For example, 60 percent of the wheat crop is sold to other countries. In Columbus, large companies export $53 million worth of corn, soy beans, wheat, and oats. These companies store, sell, and ship the crops for Ohio farmers.

The Arts. As with most cities, the Columbus arts menu has a growing international flavor. Recently, for example, the city welcomes the Vienna Choir Boys from Austria, several British rock groups, opera star Maria Callas from Italy, Israeli violinist Zvi Zeitlin, the Royal Tahitian Dance Company, Romanian dancers, Spanish guitarists, and, just in time for St. Patrick's day, the Irish Rovers.

In addition, the Columbus Gallery of Fine Arts is one of many places people can visit to see pictures and statues from all

Armenian grocery store.

over the world. The Gallery has Chinese vases, Greek statues and many wood carvings from Pacific islands.

Art galleries in cities around the world share art work with each other. So a citizen in Columbus may look at a French painting in August. In December, a person in Tokyo, Japan, may be looking at the same painting.

Ethnic Groups. Many members of the ethnic groups in Columbus—Italians, Germans, Serbians, Irish, Croatians, Greeks and Hungarians—keep up ties with their countries of origin. These ties help link Columbus to the world. Activities in the black and Jewish community also link Columbus to the world. Black churches, for example, send people abroad to teach and to learn from people in Africa, Asia, Latin America, and Europe.

Reviewing the Case Study

You have seen some ways one city is linked with the world. Now here are some ideas for how you can chart the global linkages of your community.

1. Make a list of the items in your own household that come from another country. These could include food, television and stereo sets, furniture and sports equipment. Some of these items will say: "Made in _____ ." Others will be unmarked, such as the rubber from Asia used to make balls and boots.
2. Use the yellow pages of the telephone books to find examples of global links. Look under such headings as: restaurants, automobiles, cameras, churches, travel agencies, manufacturing firms, civic and professional organizations.
3. Collect ads from your local newspapers that describe products or services from another country. Collect articles from the newspaper describing ways your community is linked to the world.
4. Keep a record of the number of stories about other countries, foreign policy, or international problems on the nightly news on television.
5. Keep a record of foreign cars seen in your school parking lot and in nearby parking lots. Do the same thing for bicycles.

Examining a painting in an art gallery.

Chapter Twenty-five Test and Activities

★★

Vocabulary

Match the following words with their meanings.

1. developing countries
2. developed countries
3. global interdependence
4. UN
5. General Assembly
6. Security Council
7. life expectancy

a. rich, industrialized nations
b. an international organization that works to promote world peace
c. the average number of years people can expect to live
d. the part of the United Nations that has the power to send out troops
e. poor countries
f. the "town meeting of the world"
g. people around the world depend on each other

Reviewing Chapter Ideas

1. Developing countries usually have _____ .
   a. a shortage of food
   b. great industries
   c. many natural resources
   d. a high standard of living
2. True or false: Developed nations make many products to sell in other parts of the world.
3. Which of the following are examples of foreign-policy concerns?
   a. feeding the world
   b. sale of weapons
   c. use of oceans
   d. all of the above
4. Which of the following nations does not favor our policy on coastal waters?
   a. Ecuador
   b. France
   c. England
   d. Japan
5. True or false: Planning for the UN began during World War II.

Using Basic Social Studies Skills

Finding Information

1. Name the five permanent members of the UN Security Council.
2. Name three things in your community that give evidence of global interdependence.

Comprehending Information

Use the facts shown on the table opposite to answer the following questions.

1. (a) The United States produces more food than its people eat. What percent of its population works at farming?
   (b) How does that percentage compare with the other nations on the chart?
2. (a) Which four countries have the highest GNP?
   (b) Do these countries have more than half the population engaged in farming?
3. In which country did inflation grow the fastest between 1970 and 1976?
4. (a) Which countries have the highest percentage of adults who can read?
   (b) What else do those countries have in common?

Organizing Information

1. Use the facts on the table to divide the countries into two lists. Head one: Developed Countries. Head the other: Developing Countries.

Vocabulary
1. e   4. b   7. c
2. a   5. f
3. g   6. d

Ideas
1. a   4. a
2. T   5. T
3. d

★★★★★★★★★★★★★★★★★★★★★★★★★★★★★★★★★★★★★★☆★★★★★★★★★★★★★★★★★★★★★★★★★★★★★★★★

2. Add up the populations of the countries in your Developed Countries list.
3. Add up the populations of the countries in your Developing Countries list.
4. Make a bar graph showing the difference in size of these two populations.
5. Which group of countries includes more people?

Evaluating Information

1. From the information on the chart, which three countries have the greatest health problems?
2. Which sets of facts did you use to reach this conclusion?

Communicating Ideas

Explain in your own words why the differences between the United States and the developing countries make for foreign-policy decisions.

Using Decision-Making Skills

Suppose you could influence a government decision about giving food to Nigeria.

1. What are the alternatives involved?

2. What are the consequences of each alternative for the Nigerians?
3. What are the consequences of each alternative for Americans?
4. What decision would you support? Why?

Activities

1. On an outline map of the world, locate the ten countries on the chart. Color the Developed Countries in one color; use another for the Developing Countries.
2. Work with two other people. Prepare a display of some activity of the UN.
3. Make a class bulletin board to show links between your community and the rest of the world. Attach items to a world map with string.
4. Recommended books include:
   (a) *Hunger on Planet Earth* by Jules Archer (Thomas Y. Crowell, 1977).
   (b) *The Twenty-ninth Day: Accommodating Human Needs and Numbers to the Earth's Resources,* by Lester R. Brown (Norton, 1978).

FACTS ABOUT THE WORLD'S TEN MOST POPULOUS COUNTRIES

These ten countries account for 63.5% of the population of the world.

Country	Population	GNP per person (1976)	Annual Inflation Rate (1970–1976)	Percent of Working Population in Farming	Life Expectancy at Birth in 1975	Availability of Doctors	Percent of Adults Who Can Read
Bangladesh	80.0 million	$ 110	20.7%	86%	42 years	1 for every 9,350 people	23%
Brazil	110.0 million	$1,140	26.1%	46%	61 years	1 for every 1,160 people	64%
China	835.8 million	$ 410	not available	68%	62 years	not available	not available
India	620.4 million	$ 150	9.2%	69%	50 years	1 for every 4,160 people	36%
Indonesia	135.2 million	$ 240	22.7%	66%	48 years	1 for every 18,160 people	62%
Japan	112.8 million	$4,910	10.1%	20%	73 years	1 for every 810 people	99%
Nigeria	77.1 million	$ 380	16.1%	62%	41 years	1 for every 25,440 people	not available
Pakistan	71.3 million	$ 170	15.2%	59%	51 years	1 for every 3,970 people	21%
Soviet Union	256.7 million	$2,760	not available	26%	70 years	1 for every 340 people	99%
United States	215.1 million	$7,890	6.8%	4%	71 years	1 for every 610 people	99%

Unit Seven Test

★★★

Vocabulary

Write *true* if the underlined word or phrase is used correctly. Write *false* if it is not used correctly.

1. International relations arc dealings with other countries.
2. Isolationism is becoming involved in foreign affairs.
3. Foreign policy is our plan for how we act toward other nations in the world.
4. The Department of State is the major agency for foreign-policy decision making.
5. The Secretary of State directs the Department of Defense.
6. The Security Council is an advisory group for the Secretary of State.
7. Foreign-policy money powers must be approved by Congress.
8. *Das Kapital* was written by Karl Marx.
9. During the Cold War the Soviet Union and the United States were competing with each other.
10. Our policy of containment meant that the U.S. would try to stop Soviet expansion.
11. Massive retaliation is a most dangerous containment tool.
12. What happens in one part of the world affects what happens in other places. This is global interdependence.
13. Developing countries are very wealthy and have clearly defined goals.
14. Global pollution can be described as worldwide destruction of our natural environment.
15. The developed countries include England, Canada, and the United States.

Recalling Information

1. Goals of our foreign policies include _____ .
   a. promoting peace
   b. protecting the United States
   c. encouraging trade
   d. all of the above
2. The chief diplomat of the United States is
   a. the President
   b. the Vice-President
   c. the Secretary of State
   d. none of the above
3. Our foreign-policy bureaucracy is made up of _____ .
   a. the Department of Defense
   b. the Department of State
   c. the CIA
   d. all of the above
4. The purpose of the CIA is _____ .
   a. to distribute food and money to foreign countries
   b. to gather information about foreign countries for use in foreign-policy decision making
   c. to gather information about American citizens' activities inside the United States
   d. all of the above
5. True or false: The President is able to reject ideas of the National Security Council.
6. True or false: The State Department sells American arms to countries around the world.
7. True or false: Only a few government agencies are involved in foreign affairs.
8. True or false: Congress has a great deal of direct control over foreign policy decisions.

Vocabulary

1. T	4. T	7. T	10. T	13. T
2. F	5. F	8. T	11. T	14. T
3. T	6. F	9. T	12. T	15. T

534

★★★

9. Which of the following can the President do without Congressional approval?
   a. make treaties with other countries
   b. make executive agreements with other countries
   c. appoint ambassadors
   d. spend money for foreign-policy activities

10. Foreign aid involves
    a. making defense treaties
    b. sending troops
    c. giving economic goods
    d. carrying on secret activities

11. Which of the following are examples of the effects of global interdependence?
    a. increased numbers of jobs
    b. more opportunities for trade
    c. more links with other countries in your community
    d. all of the above

12. True or false: Interdependence has created new foreign-policy decisions.

13. Examples of developed countries are:
    a. U.S. and Ethiopia
    b. Japan and Canada
    c. Mexico and Peru
    d. USSR and Zambia

14. Most foreign-policy decisions involve _____ .
    a. young people vs. old people
    b. educated people vs. people who can't read
    c. rich countries vs. poor countries
    d. bad weather

15. True or false: Africa is the only continent faced with a starvation problem.

16. True or false: Food is an important political resource of the United States.

17. The countries of the world are spending about _____ billion a year on military expenditures.
    a. $2
    b. $200
    c. $2,000
    d. $20,000

18. True or false: The Security Council was organized to give the developed nations the most influence.

Skill Building

1. Where would you look in this unit to find the foreign-policy roles of such government agencies as the Treasury Department, Department of Agriculture, or Department of Commerce? Give page numbers.

2. Compare communism and democracy. List three ways they are similar and three ways they are different.

3. Which Presidents were involved in decision-making roles in Vietnam and Korea?

4. You want to summarize this unit for a friend who hasn't read it. Which four pictures or charts would you use? Identify each by page and location (if there is more than one). Explain your choices.

5. Explain how coffee is an example of global interdependence.

6. Give three examples of natural resources found in the oceans.

7. Do you agree that the earth is in danger from worldwide pollution? Explain your viewpoint.

8. List three powers of the UN General Assembly.

9. What is the main responsibility of the Security Council?

Recalling

1. d	4. b	7. F	10. c	13. b	16. T
2. a	5. T	8. F	11. d	14. c	17. b
3. d	6. F	9. b	12. T	15. F	18. T

Resource Section

Presidents of the United States   537
Facts About the States   538
Names of State Legislative Bodies   539
Flag Etiquette   540
Map of the United States   542
How Many Voted in Your State?   543
Declaration of Independence   544
Glossary   546
Index   552

Presidents of the United States

President	Party	State	Term of Office
George Washington (1732–1799)	None	Virginia	1789–1797
John Adams (1735–1826)	Fed.	Massachusetts	1797–1801
Thomas Jefferson (1743–1826)	Rep.[1]	Virginia	1801–1809
James Madison (1751–1836)	Rep.[1]	Virginia	1809–1817
James Monroe (1758–1831)	Rep.[1]	Virginia	1817–1825
John Quincy Adams (1767–1848)	Rep.[1]	Massachusetts	1825–1829
Andrew Jackson (1767–1845)	Dem.	Tennessee (S.C.)	1829–1837
Martin Van Buren (1782–1862)	Dem.	New York	1837–1841
William Henry Harrison (1773–1841)	Whig	Ohio (Va.)	1841
John Tyler (1790–1862)	Whig	Virginia	1841–1845
James K. Polk (1795–1849)	Dem.	Tennessee (N.C.)	1845–1849
Zachary Taylor (1784–1850)	Whig	Louisiana (Va.)	1849–1850
Millard Fillmore (1800–1874)	Whig	New York	1850–1853
Franklin Pierce (1804–1869)	Dem.	New Hampshire	1853–1857
James Buchanan (1791–1868)	Dem.	Pennsylvania	1857–1861
Abraham Lincoln (1809–1865)	Rep.	Illinois (Ky.)	1861–1865
Andrew Johnson (1808–1875)	Rep.	Tennessee (N.C.)	1865–1869
Ulysses S. Grant (1822–1885)	Rep.	Illinois (Ohio)	1869–1877
Rutherford B. Hayes (1822–1893)	Rep.	Ohio	1877–1881
James A. Garfield (1831–1881)	Rep.	Ohio	1881
Chester A. Arthur (1829–1886)	Rep.	New York (Vt.)	1881–1885
Grover Cleveland (1837–1908)	Dem.	New York (N.J.)	1885–1889
Benjamin Harrison (1833–1901)	Rep.	Indiana (Ohio)	1889–1893
Grover Cleveland (1837–1908)	Dem.	New York (N.J.)	1893–1897
William McKinley (1843–1901)	Rep.	Ohio	1897–1901
Theodore Roosevelt (1858–1919)	Rep.	New York	1901–1909
William H. Taft (1857–1930)	Rep.	Ohio	1909–1913
Woodrow Wilson (1856–1924)	Dem.	New Jersey (Va.)	1913–1921
Warren G. Harding (1865–1923)	Rep.	Ohio	1921–1923
Calvin Coolidge (1872–1933)	Rep.	Massachusetts (Vt.)	1923–1929
Herbert C. Hoover (1874–1964)	Rep.	California (Iowa)	1929–1933
Franklin D. Roosevelt (1882–1945)	Dem.	New York	1933–1945
Harry S. Truman (1884–1972)	Dem.	Missouri	1945–1953
Dwight D. Eisenhower (1890–1969)	Rep.	New York (Tex.) Pennsylvania	1953–1961
John F. Kennedy (1917–1963)	Dem.	Massachusetts	1961–1963
Lyndon B. Johnson (1908–1973)	Dem.	Texas	1963–1969
Richard M. Nixon (1913–	Rep.	New York (Calif.)	1969–1974
Gerald R. Ford (1913–	Rep.	Michigan (Neb.)	1974–1977
James Earl Carter (1924–	Dem.	Georgia	1977–

[1]The party is often called the Democratic-Republican party because in the 1820s it became the Democratic party.

[2]State of residence at time of election. If state of birth is different, it is shown in parentheses.

Facts About the States

Order of admission to the Union[1]	State name	Year admitted to the Union[1]	Area in square miles	Population[2]	Number of Representatives in Congress
22	Alabama	1819	51,609	3,614,000	7
49	Alaska	1959	586,412	352,000	1
48	Arizona	1912	113,909	2,224,000	4
25	Arkansas	1836	53,104	2,116,000	4
31	California	1850	158,693	21,185,000	43
38	Colorado	1876	104,247	2,534,000	5
5	Connecticut	1788	5,009	3,095,000	6
1	Delaware	1787	2,057	579,000	1
27	Florida	1845	58,560	8,357,000	15
4	Georgia	1788	58,876	4,926,000	10
50	Hawaii	1959	6,450	865,000	2
43	Idaho	1890	83,557	820,000	2
21	Illinois	1818	56,400	11,145,000	24
19	Indiana	1816	36,291	5,311,000	11
29	Iowa	1846	56,290	2,870,000	6
34	Kansas	1861	82,264	2,267,000	5
15	Kentucky	1792	40,395	3,396,000	7
18	Louisiana	1812	48,523	3,791,000	8
23	Maine	1820	33,215	1,059,000	2
7	Maryland	1788	10,577	4,098,000	8
6	Massachusetts	1788	8,257	5,828,000	12
26	Michigan	1837	58,216	9,157,000	19
32	Minnesota	1858	84,068	3,926,000	8
20	Mississippi	1817	47,716	2,346,000	5
24	Missouri	1821	69,686	4,763,000	10
41	Montana	1889	147,138	748,000	2
37	Nebraska	1867	77,227	1,546,000	3
36	Nevada	1864	110,540	592,000	1
9	New Hampshire	1788	9,304	818,000	2
3	New Jersey	1787	7,836	7,316,000	15
47	New Mexico	1912	121,666	1,147,000	2
11	New York	1788	49,576	18,120,000	39
12	North Carolina	1789	52,586	5,451,000	11
39	North Dakota	1889	70,665	635,000	1
17	Ohio	1803	41,222	10,759,000	23
46	Oklahoma	1907	69,919	2,712,000	6
33	Oregon	1859	96,981	2,288,000	4
2	Pennsylvania	1787	45,333	11,827,000	25
13	Rhode Island	1790	1,214	927,000	2
8	South Carolina	1788	31,055	2,818,000	6
40	South Dakota	1889	77,047	683,000	2
16	Tennessee	1796	42,244	4,188,000	8
28	Texas	1845	267,339	12,237,000	24
45	Utah	1896	84,916	1,206,000	2
14	Vermont	1791	9,609	471,000	1
10	Virginia	1788	40,817	4,967,000	10
42	Washington	1889	68,192	3,544,000	7
35	West Virginia	1863	24,181	1,803,000	4
30	Wisconsin	1848	56,154	4,607,000	9
44	Wyoming	1890	97,914	374,000	1
	District of Columbia	1791	67	716,000	

Total number of representatives[3]   435

1. For the thirteen original states, the order of admission and year of admission represent their ratification of the Constitution.
2. United States Bureau of the Census population estimates for 1975.
3. The total number of representatives in Congress does not include the representative from the District of Columbia, who does not vote.

Names of State Legislative Bodies

State or other jurisdiction	Both bodies	Upper house	Lower house
Alabama	Legislature	Senate	House of Representatives
Alaska	Legislature	Senate	House of Representatives
Arizona	Legislature	Senate	House of Representatives
Arkansas	General Assembly	Senate	House of Representatives
California	Legislature	Senate	Assembly
Colorado	General Assembly	Senate	House of Representatives
Connecticut	General Assembly	Senate	House of Representatives
Delaware	General Assembly	Senate	House of Representatives
Florida	Legislature	Senate	House of Representatives
Georgia	General Assembly	Senate	House of Representatives
Hawaii	Legislature	Senate	House of Representatives
Idaho	Legislature	Senate	House of Representatives
Illinois	General Assembly	Senate	House of Representatives
Indiana	General Assembly	Senate	House of Representatives
Iowa	General Assembly	Senate	House of Representatives
Kansas	Legislature	Senate	House of Representatives
Kentucky	General Assembly	Senate	House of Representatives
Louisiana	Legislature	Senate	House of Representatives
Maine	Legislature	Senate	House of Representatives
Maryland	General Assembly	Senate	House of Delegates
Massachusetts	General Court	Senate	House of Representatives
Michigan	Legislature	Senate	House of Representatives
Minnesota	Legislature	Senate	House of Representatives
Mississippi	Legislature	Senate	House of Representatives
Missouri	General Assembly	Senate	House of Representatives
Montana	Legislature	Senate	House of Representatives
Nebraska	Legislature	(a)	. . .
Nevada	Legislature	Senate	Assembly
New Hampshire	General Court	Senate	House of Representatives
New Jersey	Legislature	Senate	General Assembly
New Mexico	Legislature	Senate	House of Representatives
New York	Legislature	Senate	Assembly
North Carolina	General Assembly	Senate	House of Representatives
North Dakota	Legislative Assembly	Senate	House of Representatives
Ohio	General Assembly	Senate	House of Representatives
Oklahoma	Legislature	Senate	House of Representatives
Oregon	Legislative Assembly	Senate	House of Representatives
Pennsylvania	General Assembly	Senate	House of Representatives
Rhode Island	General Assembly	Senate	House of Representatives
South Carolina	General Assembly	Senate	House of Representatives
South Dakota	Legislature	Senate	House of Representatives
Tennessee	General Assembly	Senate	House of Representatives
Texas	Legislature	Senate	House of Representatives
Utah	Legislature	Senate	House of Representatives
Vermont	General Assembly	Senate	House of Representatives
Virginia	General Assembly	Senate	House of Delegates
Washington	Legislature	Senate	House of Representatives
West Virginia	Legislature	Senate	House of Delegates
Wisconsin	Legislature	Senate	Assembly (b)
Wyoming	Legislature	Senate	House of Representatives
American Samoa	Legislature	Senate	House of Representatives
Guam	Legislature	(a)	. . .
Northern Mariana Is.	Legislature	Senate	House of Representatives
Puerto Rico	Legislative Assembly	Senate	House of Representatives
Trust Territory of the Pacific	Congress of Micronesia	Senate	House of Representatives
Virgin Islands	Legislature	(a)	. . .

(a) Unicameral legislature. Members go by the title Senator. (b) Members of the lower house go by the title Representative.

Flag Etiquette

The proper way to honor and display the flag has been set forth in Public Law 829. This is a summary of the main ideas of that law.

In a group of state and local flags.

With other flags on a halyard.

1. On buildings and stationary flagstaffs in the open, the flag should be displayed only from sunrise to sunset. However, when a special patriotic effect is desired, the flag may be displayed for twenty-four hours a day if it is properly lighted. It should not be displayed on days when the weather is bad unless an all-weather flag is used.

2. The flag should be displayed on or near the main building of all public institutions. It should be displayed in or near every polling place on election days. It should be displayed during school days in or near every school.

3. There are certain correct ways to display the flag. The blue field, called the union, must always be at the top. The union hangs from the peak of a flagstaff. It is on the observer's left, the flag's right, if the flag is hung on a wall. In a group of state and local flags, the United States flag is in the center and at the highest point. When they are flown from the same halyard, the United States flag is at the peak. The United States flag is hoisted first and lowered last. No other flag should fly higher or be placed to the United States flag's right. When flags of two or more nations are displayed, they are to be flown from separate staffs of the same height.

4. When the flag is displayed over the middle of the street, it should be suspended vertically with the union to the north in an east and west street or to the east in a north and south street.

5. The flag, when flown at half-staff, should first be hoisted to the peak for an instant and then lowered to the half-staff position. It should again be raised to the peak before it is lowered for the day.

6. When the flag is used to cover a casket, it should be placed so the union is at the head and over the left shoulder. The flag should not be lowered into the grave or allowed to touch the ground.

7. When the flag hangs across a corridor or lobby in a building it should hang vertically with the union to the observer's left upon entering. If the building has more than one

With another flag with crossed staffs.

entrance, the flag should hang near the center of the corridor with the union to the north when entrances are to the east and west or to the east when entrances are to the north and south. If there are entrances in more than two directions, the union should be to the east.

Horizontally on a wall.

8. No disrespect should be shown to the flag. It should not be dipped to honor any person or thing. It should never be displayed union down, except as a signal of dire distress. It should never touch anything beneath it. It should never be carried flat or horizontally, but always aloft and free. It should never be used as wearing apparel, drapery, bedding, nor to cover a ceiling. Nothing should be placed on it, drawn on it, or attached to it. It should not be used for advertising purposes, and should not be printed, sewn, or embroidered on anything disposable, like paper napkins. A flag patch may be put on uniforms, and should be worn on the left lapel, near the heart.

9. When the flag is raised or lowered and during the national anthem, all present should face the flag and stand at attention with the right hand over the heart. People in military uniform should give a military salute. Men wearing a hat should remove it with the right hand and hold the hat at the left shoulder, the hand being over the heart. The same rules apply while saying the Pledge of Allegiance:

Vertically on a wall.

> "I pledge allegiance to the Flag of the United States of America, and to the Republic for which it stands, one Nation under God, indivisible, with liberty and justice for all."

10. When the flag is in such condition that it is no longer a fitting emblem for display, it should be destroyed in a dignified way, preferably by burning.

In an auditorium or meeting place.

From a staff projecting from a window or wall.

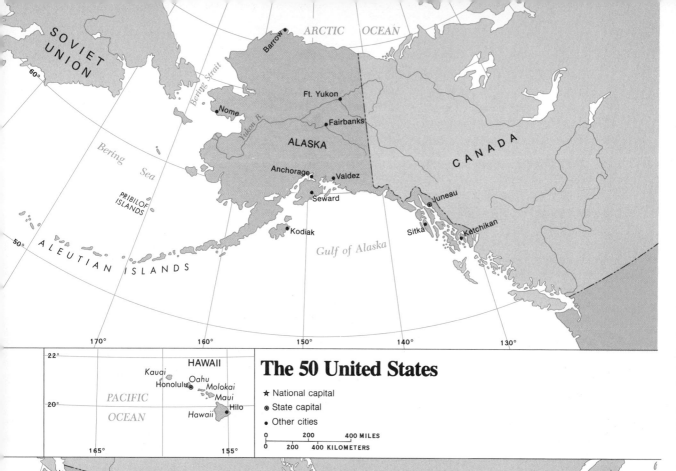

ARCTIC OCEAN

SOVIET UNION

60°

Barrow

Ft. Yukon

Nome

Yukon R.

Fairbanks

Bering Strait

ALASKA

CANADA

Bering Sea

Anchorage

Valdez

PRIBILOF ISLANDS

Seward

Juneau

50°

Kodiak

Sitka

Ketchikan

Gulf of Alaska

ALEUTIAN ISLANDS

170°   160°   150°   140°   130°

22°

HAWAII

The 50 United States

Kauai

Oahu

Honolulu

Molokai

PACIFIC

Maui

20°

OCEAN

Hilo

Hawaii

★ National capital

⊛ State capital

● Other cities

0   200   400 MILES

0   200   400 KILOMETERS

165°   155°

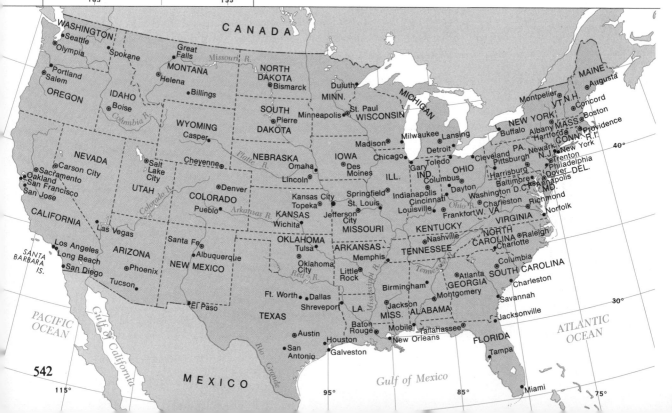

CANADA

WASHINGTON
Seattle
Olympia
Spokane
Great Falls
Missouri R.
NORTH DAKOTA
Bismarck
MAINE
Augusta

Portland
Salem
OREGON
MONTANA
Helena
Billings
Duluth
MINN.
St. Paul
Minneapolis
MICHIGAN
Montpelier
VT. N.H.
Concord

IDAHO
Boise
Columbia R.
WYOMING
Casper
SOUTH DAKOTA
Pierre
WISCONSIN
Madison
Milwaukee
Lansing
Detroit
Buffalo
Albany MASS. Boston
NEW YORK
Hartford
CONN. R.I.
Providence

NEVADA
Carson City
Sacramento
Oakland
San Francisco
San Jose
Salt Lake City
UTAH
Cheyenne
NEBRASKA
Platte R.
Omaha
Lincoln
IOWA
Des Moines
Chicago
ILL.
Toledo
OHIO
Cleveland
PA.
Pittsburgh
Newark N.J. New York
Trenton
Philadelphia
Dover DEL.
40°

Denver
COLORADO
Kansas City
Topeka
Springfield
St. Louis
Indianapolis
IND.
Columbus
Dayton
Cincinnati
Harrisburg
Baltimore
Washington D.C.
Annapolis MD.
Charleston
Richmond

CALIFORNIA
Las Vegas
Pueblo
Arkansas R.
KANSAS
Wichita
Jefferson City
MISSOURI
Louisville
KENTUCKY
Frankfort W. VA.
Ohio R.
Norfolk
VIRGINIA

SANTA BARBARA IS.
Los Angeles
Long Beach
San Diego
ARIZONA
Phoenix
Santa Fe
Albuquerque
NEW MEXICO
OKLAHOMA
Tulsa
Oklahoma City
Little Rock
ARKANSAS
Memphis
Nashville
TENNESSEE
Tennessee R.
NORTH CAROLINA
Raleigh
Charlotte
Columbia
SOUTH CAROLINA
Charleston

Tucson
El Paso
Ft. Worth
Dallas
Shreveport
LA.
MISS.
Jackson
Birmingham
Montgomery
ALABAMA
GEORGIA
Atlanta
Savannah
Jacksonville

PACIFIC OCEAN
TEXAS
Austin
San Antonio
Galveston
Houston
Baton Rouge
New Orleans
Mobile
Tallahassee
FLORIDA
ATLANTIC OCEAN
30°

542

MEXICO

Rio Grande

Gulf of California

Gulf of Mexico

Tampa

Miami

115°   95°   85°   75°

How Many Voted in Your State?

	Voting Age Population	Turnout for Statewide Elections —Percent of Voting Age Population			
	1978	1966	1970	1974	1978
Alabama	2,604,000	35.8	36.3	23.4	28.4
Alaska	272,000	41.7	45.0	45.0	38.3
Arizona	1,642,000	39.7	38.1	37.7	31.9
Arkansas	1,535,000	26.1	14.7	29.8	34.6
California	16,052,000	54.8	51.1	39.9	42.6
Colorado	1,900,000	54.7	48.0	45.5	42.7
Connecticut	2,279,000	56.6	56.8	50.2	45.3
Delaware	418,000	54.2	49.2	41.1	38.8
Florida	6,502,000	27.5	28.1	18.1	38.0
Georgia	3,543,000	31.3	29.5	25.3	18.7
Hawaii	637,000	49.9	44.0	45.2	44.2
Idaho	597,000	64.6	56.1	47.4	48.1
Illinois	7,975,000	57.1	51.4	37.3	38.8
Indiana	3,752,000	57.6	55.7	48.4	—
Iowa	2,057,000	53.6	45.5	46.1	40.4
Kansas	1,694,000	50.2	52.2	49.1	42.5
Kentucky	2,457,000	33.9	22.2	29.7	19.3
Louisiana	2,674,000	28.0	17.6	22.4	—
Maine	776,000	53.1	52.9	49.5	47.6
Maryland	2,991,000	35.2	37.3	31.4	33.0
Massachusetts	4,230,000	53.4	50.9	41.9	46.8
Michigan	6,405,000	48.5	49.3	41.5	44.6
Minnesota	2,828,000	58.6	59.6	46.3	55.2
Mississippi	1,612,000	31.5	24.9	20.3	36.1
Missouri	3,471,000	38.0	41.1	36.6	45.0
Montana	538,000	64.3	60.3	51.5	53.5
Nebraska	1,117,000	54.6	49.5	42.4	43.3
Nevada	461,000	47.7	45.4	43.1	40.1
New Hampshire	614,000	56.1	47.3	39.8	43.9
New Jersey	5,305,000	49.6	46.6	41.1	40.0
New Mexico	815,000	50.2	50.9	44.1	42.0
New York	12,967,000	49.3	47.2	38.5	34.7
North Carolina	3,964,000	32.8	30.6	26.9	28.5
North Dakota	461,000	55.2	58.4	55.0	—
Ohio	7,589,000	46.0	47.4	40.4	37.4
Oklahoma	2,043,000	42.7	35.1	27.1	38.1
Oregon	1,750,000	56.1	49.9	47.6	51.7
Pennsylvania	8,611,000	55.5	48.8	40.6	41.9
Rhode Island	678,000	58.1	54.6	46.5	44.7
South Carolina	2,011,000	26.5	28.7	28.1	31.4
South Dakota	484,000	58.5	60.4	59.4	53.6
Tennessee	3,107,000	35.5	41.0	31.5	38.2
Texas	9,063,000	20.9	27.5	18.4	25.0
Utah	827,000	58.0	64.0	55.7	—
Vermont	344,000	56.6	57.6	44.6	36.1
Virginia	3,736,000	26.2	32.1	27.4	32.7
Washington	2,651,000	51.3	49.2	40.6	—
West Virginia	1,341,000	47.1	40.9	33.5	36.7
Wisconsin	3,319,000	46.5	50.7	38.7	44.6
Wyoming	290,000	64.9	58.7	51.8	47.4

— = no election

The Declaration of Independence—1776

IN CONGRESS, JULY 4, 1776. THE UNANIMOUS DECLA-RATION OF THE THIRTEEN UNITED STATES OF AMERICA—When in the Course of human events, it becomes necessary for one people to dissolve the political bands which have connected them with another, and to assume among the Powers of the earth, the separate and equal station to which the Laws of Nature and of Nature's God entitle them, a decent respect to the opinions of mankind requires that they should declare the causes which impel them to the separation.

We hold these truths to be self-evident, that all men are created equal, that they are endowed by their Creator with certain unalienable Rights, that among these are Life, Liberty and the pursuit of Happiness.

That to secure these rights, Governments are instituted among Men, deriving their just powers from the consent of the governed,

That whenever any Form of Government becomes destructive of these ends, it is the Right of the People to alter or to abolish it, and to institute new Government, laying its foundation on such principles and organizing its powers in such form, as to them shall seem most likely to effect their Safety and Happiness. Prudence, indeed, will dictate that Governments long established should not be changed for light and transient causes; and accordingly all experience hath shown, that mankind are more disposed to suffer, while evils are sufferable, than to right themselves by abolishing the forms to which they are accustomed. But when a long train of abuses and usurpations, pursuing invariably the same Object evinces a design to reduce them under absolute Despotism, it is their right, it is their duty, to throw off such Government, and to provide new Guards for their future security.

Such has been the patient sufferance of these Colonies; and such is now the necessity which constrains them to alter their former Systems of Government.

The history of the present King of Great Britain is a history of repeated injuries and usurpations, all having in direct object the establishment of an absolute Tyranny over these States. To prove this, let Facts be submitted to a candid world.

He has refused his Assent to Laws, the most wholesome and necessary for the public good.

He has forbidden his Governors to pass Laws of immediate and pressing importance, unless suspended in their operation till his Assent should be obtained; and when so suspended, he has utterly neglected to attend to them.

He has refused to pass other Laws for the accommodation of large districts of people, unless those people would relinquish the right of Representation in the Legislature, a right inestimable to them and formidable to tyrants only.

He has called together legislative bodies at places unusual, uncomfortable, and distant from the depository of their Public Records, for the sole purpose of fatiguing them into compliance with his measures.

He has dissolved Representative Houses repeatedly, for opposing with manly firmness his invasions on the rights of the people.

He has refused for a long time, after such dissolutions, to cause others to be elected; whereby the Legislative Powers, incapable of Annihilation, have returned to the People at large for their exercise; the State remaining in the mean time exposed to all the dangers of invasion from without, and convulsions within.

He has endeavoured to prevent the population of these States; for that purpose obstructing the Laws of Naturalization of Foreigners; refusing to pass others to encourage their migration hither, and raising the conditions of new Appropriations of Lands.

He has obstructed the Administration of Justice, by refusing his Assent to Laws for establishing Judiciary Powers.

He has made Judges dependent on his Will alone, for the tenure of their offices, and the amount and payment of their salaries.

He has erected a multitude of New Offices, and sent hither swarms of Officers to harass our People, and eat out their substance.

He has kept among us, in times of peace, Standing Armies without the Consent of our legislature.

He has affected to render the Military independent of and superior to the Civil Power.

He has combined with others to subject us to a jurisdiction foreign to our constitution, and unacknowledged by our laws giving his Assent to their acts of pretended legislation:

For quartering large bodies of armed troops among us:

For protecting them, by a mock Trial, from

Punishment for any Murders which they should commit on the Inhabitants of these States:

For cutting off our Trade with all parts of the world:

For imposing taxes on us without our Consent:

For depriving us in many cases, of the benefits of Trial by jury:

For transporting us beyond Seas to be tried for pretended offences:

For abolishing the free System of English Laws in a neighboring Province, establishing therein an Arbitrary government, and enlarging its Boundaries so as to render it at once an example and fit instrument for introducing the same absolute rule into these Colonies:

For taking away our Charters, abolishing our most valuable Laws, and altering fundamentally the Forms of our Governments:

For suspending our own Legislature, and declaring themselves invested with Power to legislate for us in all cases whatsoever.

He has abdicated Government here, by declaring us out of his Protection and waging War against us.

He has plundered our seas, ravaged our Coasts, burnt our towns, and destroyed the lives of our people.

He is at this time transporting large armies of foreign mercenaries to compleat the works of death, desolation and tyranny, already begun with circumstances of Cruelty & perfidy scarcely paralleled in the most barbarous ages, and totally unworthy the Head of a civilized nation.

He has constrained our fellow Citizens taken Captive on the high Seas to bear Arms against their Country, to become the executioners of their friends and Brethren, or to fall themselves by their Hands.

He has excited domestic insurrections amongst us, and has endeavoured to bring on the inhabitants of our frontiers, the merciless Indian Savages, whose known rule of warfare, is an undistinguished destruction of all ages, sexes and conditions.

In every stage of these Oppressions We have Petitioned for Redress in the most humble terms: Our repeated Petitions have been answered only by repeated injury. A Prince, whose character is thus marked by every act which may define a Tyrant, is unfit to be the ruler of a free People.

Nor have We been wanting in attention to our Brittish brethren. We have warned them from time to time of attempts by their legislature to extend an unwarrantable jurisdiction over us. We have reminded them of the circumstances of our emigration and settlement here. We have appealed to their native justice and magnanimity, and we have conjured them by the ties of our common kindred to disavow these usurpations, which, would inevitably interrupt our connections and correspondence. They too have been deaf to the voice of justice and of consanguinity. We must, therefore, acquiesce in the necessity, which denounces our Separation, and hold them, as we hold the rest of mankind, Enemies in War, in Peace Friends.

We, therefore, the Representatives of the united States of America, in General Congress, Assembled, appealing to the Supreme Judge of the world for the rectitude of our intentions, do, in the Name, and by Authority of the good People of these Colonies, solemnly publish and declare, That these United Colonies are, and of Right ought to be Free and Independent States; that they are Absolved from all Allegiance to the British Crown, and that all political connection between them and the State of Great Britain, is and ought to be totally dissolved; and that as Free and Independent States, they have full Power to levy War, conclude Peace, contract Alliances, establish Commerce, and to do all other Acts and Things which Independent States may of right do. And for the support of this Declaration, with a firm reliance on the Protection of Divine Providence, we mutually pledge to each other our Lives, our Fortunes and our sacred Honor.

John Hancock

Button Gwinnett	Carter Braxton	Abraham Clark
Lyman Hall	Robert Morris	Josiah Bartlett
George Walton	Benjamin Rush	William Whipple
William Hooper	Benjamin Franklin	Samuel Adams
Joseph Hewes	John Morton	John Adams
John Penn	George Clymer	Robert Treat Payne
Edward Rutledge	James Smith	Elbridge Gerry
Thomas Heyward, Junior	George Taylor	Stephen Hopkins
Thomas Lynch, Junior	James Wilson	William Ellery
Arthur Middleton	George Ross	Roger Sherman
Samuel Chase	Caesar Rodney	Samuel Huntington
William Paca	George Read	William Williams
Thomas Stone	Thomas McKean	Oliver Wolcott
Charles Carroll of Carrollton	William Floyd	Matthew Thornton
George Wythe	Philip Livingston	
Richard Henry Lee	Francis Lewis	
Thomas Jefferson	Lewis Morris	
Benjamin Harrison	Richard Stockton	
Thomas Nelson, Junior	John Witherspoon	
Francis Lightfoot Lee	Francis Hopkinson	
	John Hart	

Glossary

Pronunciation Key

hat, āge, fär; let, ēqual, tèrm; it, īce; hot, ōpen, ôrder; oil, out; cup, pùt, rüle;

ə represents *a* in about, *e* in taken, *i* in pencil, *o* in lemon, *u* in circus.

A

administrative law   law made by a government agency.

adviser   (ad vī′zər), *n.*   person who gives advice.

agenda   (ə jen′də), *n.*   list of items of business brought before a meeting to be dealt with.

alien   (ā′lyən, ā′lē ən), *n.*   person living in a country but remaining a citizen of another country.

alternative   (ôl tér′nə tiv), *n.*   one of two or more choices faced when making a decision.

amendment   (ə mend′mənt), *n.*   change offered or made in a law.

Anti-Federalist   (an′ti fed′ər ə list), *n.*   opponent of the new Constitution and supporter of individual liberties and rights under state governments.

appropriation   (ə prō′prē ā′shən), *n.*   the setting aside of money for a stated purpose.

arraignment   (ə rān′mənt), *n.*   the stage in a criminal proceeding in which the accused person comes before a judge, hears the charges, and pleads guilty or not guilty.

attorney general   chief law officer of a state or country. In the President's cabinet, the Attorney General is head of the Department of Justice. Forty-two states elect an attorney general to fight crime.

B

bail   (bāl), *n.*   money or property an accused person gives the court to hold as a guarantee of returning for trial, so he or she may stay out of jail in the meantime.

bait and switch   to advertise an item at a low price to attract customers with the intention of selling them, instead, a higher priced item.

balanced budget   a budget in which income is equal to expenses.

ballot   (bal′ət), *n.*   piece of paper, ticket, or other object used in secret voting.

bandwagon   (band′wag′ən), *n.*   propaganda technique of persuading others to join what appears to be the winning candidate or group.

bank   (bank), *n.*   an institution in the business of lending, protecting, and handling money.

benefit   (ben′ə fit), *n.*   anything that is for a person's good; advantage.

bicameral   (bī kam′ər əl), *adj.*   having two legislative chambers. The U.S. Congress is bicameral; it has the Senate and the House of Representatives.

bicameral legislature   a legislature divided into two houses.

bill of rights   a statement of the rights of individuals that their government can't take away. The American Bill of Rights is made up of the first ten amendments to the Constitution.

binding commitment   a promise with the force of an order. In some states, the delegates to a national nominating convention must vote for the candidate who won in the primary election. This commitment is binding for the first ballot only.

board of directors   people elected by stockholders to run a corporation.

bond   (bond), *n.*   a certificate stating that the government has borrowed a certain amount of money from the owner of the bond.

boom   (büm), *n., v.* —*n.*   a period of rapidly increasing business activity. —*v.*   burst into sudden activity.

borough   (bér′ō), *n.*   in Alaska, a district similar to a county. In some states a borough is an unincorporated town, and in New York City there are five divisions called boroughs.

brief   (brēf), *n.*   written document that explains one side's position in a legal case.

budget   (buj′it), *n., v.*   plan for gathering, spending, and saving money.

bureaucracy   (byù rok′rə sē), *n., pl.* **-cies.**   the departments, divisions, and commissions in the executive branch of government.

bureaucrat   (byùr′ə krat), *n.*   government official in the executive branch who administers a government program or supervises the carrying out of regulations.

business cycle   business activity seen as periods of growth alternating with periods of recession.

bylaws   (bī′lôz′), *n.*   the written constitution for a company, club, city, or other group.

C

Cabinet   (kab′ə nit), *n.*   group of advisers to the President, each of whom heads a department of government.

Cabinet department   an executive agency of the national government, headed by a member of the President's Cabinet and responsible for a special area of activity.

canvass   (kan′vəs), *v., n.* —*v.*   to contact the people of a district systematically in support of a candidate, asking for votes and counting supporters and opponents. —*n.*   a systematic coverage of a district to measure support. A person conducting a canvass may be supporting a candidate or may be attempting to predict results of a coming election.

capital goods   products that can be used to make other goods.

capitalism   (kap′ə tə liz′əm), *n.*   an economic system in which property and the means of production are privately owned and in which the market system is the means of economic decision making.

card-stacking   (kärd′stak′ing), *n.*   propaganda technique of presenting only one-sided facts favorable to a candidate or issue.

career worker   permanent employee.

ceremonial leader   head of state, such as President or governor, who greets official visitors, delivers awards and speeches, and lends dignity to special occasions by participating in them.

chain of command   system of authority in government or business, through which the person holding top responsibility directs those just below, who direct the next level below, and so on, down the line.

chamber of commerce group of business people organized to protect and promote the business interests of a city, state, or country.

charge account system of buying on credit.

chief executive person in charge of seeing that the laws passed by the legislature are carried out.

chief legislator the person with the largest role in proposing new laws. In the role of chief legislator, the President suggests most of the new laws that Congress considers.

chief school officer superintendent or commissioner who directs the state department of education in carrying out state laws and providing service related to schools.

CIA Central Intelligence Agency; group that helps the National Security Council by secretly gathering, weighing, and sharing information to aid in decision making.

circuit (sėr′kit), *n.* area served by one of the eleven federal appellate courts.

citizenship (sit′ə zən ship, sit′ə-sən ship), *n.* membership in a state or nation, with all the duties, rights, privileges, and responsibilities that go with being a member.

civics (siv′iks), *n.* the study of the duties, rights, privileges, and responsibilities of citizenship.

civil case court case involving a dispute between people over property, money, or damages of some kind.

civil service system a plan for hiring and promoting government workers in which people pass examinations to get jobs.

client group the group of citizens an agency serves. Farmers are a client group of the Department of Agriculture.

closed primary an election in which only declared party members are allowed to choose the party's nominees.

closed shop union-employer contract providing that only union members may be hired.

coalition (kō′ə lish′ən), *n.* combined pool of two or more interest groups working together to reach a goal.

Cold War the contest for power after World War II between communist nations, headed by the Soviet Union, and western nations, headed by the United States.

collective bargaining negotiation between an employer and a union representing the employees.

column (kol′əm), *n.* part of a newspaper or magazine used for a special subject or written by a special writer.

commander in chief person in charge of all the armed forces. In national government, the President is commander in chief of the armed forces. In state government, the governor is commander in chief of the National Guard.

command system an economy in which the government makes all major economic decisions.

commission plan a plan of city government in which a small group of elected commissioners, each heading a city department, make and carry out the laws.

common law law that has developed from custom, common practice, or previous decisions judges have made in similar cases.

communicate (kə myü′nə kāt), *v.* share ideas; give or exchange information or news.

communist (kom′yə nist), *adj.*, *n.* —*adj.* having to do with an economic system in which the land and the means of production are owned by the community or government. In a communist country, the government can control the distribution of goods and the use of individuals' labor. —*n.* person who supports communism.

competition (kom′pə tish′ən), *n.* rivalry; effort to obtain something wanted by others.

concurring opinion an opinion of one or more judges who agree with the decision of the court but for reasons that are different from those given in the majority opinion.

compromise (kom′prə mīz), *n.*, *v.* —*n.* settlement of a dispute in which each side gives up something so agreement can be reached. —*v.* settle a difference by having each side give up part of what is wanted.

confederation (kən fed′ə-rā′shən), *n.* a group of independent states joined together for a special purpose. A confederation may not make laws that apply directly to individuals without agreement of the member states. Some people say the United Nations is a confederation.

conference committee group of legislators from both houses who work out a compromise version of a bill when both houses have passed different versions of the bill.

conflict (kon′flikt), *n.* disagreement between people; a fight, struggle, or clash.

congressional district area in a state from which a representative is elected to Congress as a member of the House of Representatives.

consequence (kon′sə kwens), *n.* outcome or result of a decision; effect.

consolidation (kən sol′ə-da′shən), *n.* a joining to form one unit. In several urban areas, people have combined the government departments of city and county to make a city-county consolidation.

constituent (kən stich′ü ənt), *n.* a voter in a legislator's district.

constitution (kon′stə tü′shən, kon′stə tyü′shən), *n.* the basic plan of government that sets up the government's framework, lists the powers and duties of its sections or parts, and describes the connection between the people and their government.

constitutional law law based on the Constitution or an interpretation of the Constitution described in a Supreme Court decision.

consumer (kən sü′mər), *n.* person or group that uses goods and services.

consumer advocate person who works on getting consumer problems corrected.

consumer goods items produced to be used up, such as food or clothing.

consumption (kən sump′shən), *n.* the total money value of goods and services a group or nation buys in a given period of time.

containment (kən tān′mənt), *n.* the confinement of a possibly hostile political force in existing geographical boundaries; American policy, 1947 to the 1970's, of limiting expansion and influence of the Soviet Union.

continuance (kən tin′yü əns), *n.* postponement of a court date to allow lawyers time to gather evidence and prepare their case.

convention (kən ven′shən), *n.* a meeting or gathering of people representing the sections of an organization; an assembly of delegates.

cooperative (kō op′ər ə tiv), *n.* a business association that is set up to provide services for its own members.

corporate income tax a tax on a corporation's profits.

corporation (kôr′pə rā′shən), *n.* a business owned by its stockholders. Those who own stock in a corporation elect a board of directors who pick top management people to run the business.

council (koun′səl), *n.* the legislative branch of most city governments.

council-manager plan a plan of city government in which voters elect a council which hires, and can fire, a manager to carry out the laws.

county (koun′tē) *n., pl.* **-ties.** a division of a state set up to help carry out state law.

court of appeals in the national court system, the court below the Supreme Court. The United States court of appeals reviews cases from lower courts or from federal regulatory commissions. The losing party in a lawsuit can generally ask the court of appeals to check on errors in the lower court's decision.

credit (kred′it), *n.* payment later for what you buy now.

credit card a card that identifies its holder as entitled to charge goods and services.

credit union a consumer cooperative that provides banking services.

criminal case court case in which the government charges someone with a crime.

customs duty tax on a product brought into the United States.

D

decision (di sizh′n), *n.* choosing among alternatives; making up one's mind.

deduction (di duk′shən), *n.* an amount subtracted from the income tax a person has to pay, based on an allowable expense of some kind.

defendant (di fen′dənt), *n.* a person accused of a crime or sued in a court of law.

deficit (def′ə sit), *n.* shortage; the difference between income and greater expenses.

delegate (del′ə gāt, del′ə git), *n.* person sent to a convention to represent the people from one place; person with power to act for others.

democracy (di mok′rə sē), *n., pl.* **-cies.** government run by the people who live under it.

denaturalization (dē nach′ər ə lə zā′shən), *n.* loss of naturalized citizenship through proof that the citizenship was falsely obtained.

Department of Defense the largest department in the executive branch of government in money spent and in civilians employed. The department helps form military policies and maintains the armed forces.

Department of State department in the executive branch of government headed by the Secretary of State and responsible for advising the President on foreign policy.

depression (di presh′ən), *n.* a time when business activity slows down and many people are out of work.

developed country one of the twenty or so built-up nations of the world having a comparatively high standard of living based on business and industry.

developing country one of the 100 or so poor nations that are trying to increase industry and business to raise the standard of living of their people.

diplomat (dip′lə mat), *n.* person skilled in managing relations between nations. A nation's diplomats include its ambassadors, envoys, and chargés d'affaires.

direct primary a preliminary election in which voters choose candidates to represent a political party in the general election.

dissenting opinion an opinion of one or more judges who disagree with the court's decision.

district court federal court where most federal cases are tried. Every state has at least one United States district court.

Domestic Council group of advisers to the President whose job is to recommend policy on matters within the country.

domestic tranquility peace in all the states, with people's health, safety, and property free from threat.

due process lawful treatment. A person is entitled to the protection of due process of law, with all the standard legal steps and no shortcuts, anytime government threatens his or her life, freedom, or property.

E

economic leader person who guards the welfare of the people as a whole in their requirements for working, earning, and surviving.

economic system a nation's way of producing and distributing goods and services.

editorial (ed′ə tôr′ē əl, ed′ə tōr′ē əl), *n.* article in a newspaper or magazine giving the editor's or publisher's opinion on some subject; radio or television broadcast expressing the opinion of the program station or network.

electoral college group of people chosen by the voters to elect the President and Vice-President of the United States.

equal justice an ideal on which the legal system of the United States is based, that every person is treated the same under the law.

equity suit a civil case in which a person or group seeks to prevent some kind of damaging action by another person or group.

estate tax a tax on money, property, and other valuables left by a person who has died.

excise tax a federal tax collected on certain luxury goods or services.

executive branch the branch of government that enforces laws. The executive branch of the national government is headed by the President.

executive leader head of the branch of government that carries out the laws passed by the legislature.

Executive Office of the President large general staff who help the President carry out the duties of being President. Many agencies are part of the Executive Office of the President.

executive order rule issued by the President, a governor, or an administrative authority, that has the effect of law.

expatriate (*n.,* ek spā′trē it, ek-spā′trē āt; *v.,* ek spā′trē āt), —*n.* person who loses citizenship by becoming a citizen of another country; exile. —*v.* withdraw from citizenship by becoming a citizen of another country.

extradition (ek′strə dish′ən), *n.* return by one state to another of a person accused of a crime; surrender of a fugitive or prisoner to another state or nation for trial or punishment.

F

factor (fak′tər), *n.* a condition that must be considered in making a decision.

factors of production the resources required to produce goods or services: natural resources, capital goods, labor, and management skills.

fair (fer, far), *adj.* not putting undue hardship on anyone; just; honest; giving equal consideration to all sides.

favorite son candidate for President supported chiefly by his own state delegation.

federal agency a unit set up in the executive branch of government to carry out laws by running a government program, making rules, and settling disputes.

federal judge a chief decision maker in the judicial branch of government.

federal system plan of government in which powers are divided between national and state governments.

Federalist (fed′ər ə list), *n.* supporter of the new Constitution and of strong central or national government.

felony (fel′ə nē) *n., pl.* **-nies** crime more serious than a misdemeanor. Armed robbery is a felony.

FICA Federal Insurance Contribution Act; social security.

fine (fīn) *n., v.* —*n.* money paid as a penalty for breaking a law. —*v.* made to pay a fine.

fiscal year year-long period set up for budget purposes.

fixed expense a necessary cost that stays the same from month to month.

flexible expense a cost that changes from month to month.

floor leader member of House of Representatives (national or state), elected by members in his or her political party, who times the introduction of bills and organizes the voting of party members.

foreign policy the plans a national government makes about how to act toward other nations and groups.

foreign-policy leader person who directs the country's relations with other nations.

free enterprise the right of private business to select and run a business for profit with little government regulation.

fringe benefits benefits received by an employee in addition to pay, such as insurance plans, retirement plans, and paid vacations.

G

General Assembly central body of the United Nations, in which every member-nation has one vote. The General Assembly is sometimes described as the "town meeting of the world."

general welfare good living conditions for all; people's health, happiness and prosperity.

gift tax a tax on any gift, including cash, that is worth more than a certain amount set by law.

glittering generality propaganda technique of using broad, vague statements in support of one's views, avoiding specific ideas that can be debated or corrected.

global interdependence the need of people around the earth for each other. Foreign interchanges of products, services, and information are indications of global interdependence.

goal (gōl), *n.* something a person or group tries to reach; something desired.

goods (gùdz), *n. pl.* things for sale, products.

government (guv′ərn mənt), *n.* group that has power to make and enforce laws. In the United States, governments (local, state, and national) have the power and duty to furnish public services, settle conflicts, keep order, and

provide security against outside threats.

government corporation a business run by the government, such as the Federal Deposit Insurance Corporation which insures bank deposits.

governor (guv′ər nər, guv′nər), *n.* chief executive officer in state government.

grant (grant), *n., v.* —*n.* a direct payment from the state to the local government; something given, such as money, or a right or privilege. —*v.* give or transfer.

grant-in-aid a contribution from the national government to a state or local government for a specific program. States also issue grants-in-aid to local governments.

grass roots neighborhood level; the ordinary citizens.

gross national product the GNP; the total value of goods and services produced for money in a country during a certain period.

guarantee (gar′ən tē′) *n., v.* —*n.* a pledge to replace or repair a purchased product or return the money if the product is not as represented. —*v.* to stand behind one's merchandise.

H

head of state person who represents all the people of the country in greeting people, awarding honors, and filling other ceremonial requirements.

hearing (hir′ing), *n.* a public information-gathering session of a legislative committee; a formal listening to evidence.

human resources the skills, knowledge, energy, and physical capabilities of people.

I

ideal (ī dē′əl), *n.* belief about the way something should be; a perfect type, model to be imitated, or goal.

immigrant (im′ə grənt), *n.* person from a foreign country who comes into a country to stay.

independent agency unit of the executive branch of government set up to do a special job not covered by any Cabinet department.

independent voter person who votes for a person or an issue, regardless of political party.

indictment (in dīt′mənt), *n.* formal charge against an accused person, made by the prosecutor or by the grand jury.

inflation (in flā′shən), *n.* a time of rapidly rising prices.

injunction (in jungk′shən), *n.* a judge's order to a person or group to stop doing something that might do harm to others.

interest (in′tər ist), *n.* money paid for the use of money.

interest group organization of people who share common beliefs and interests, and who try to influence government decisions.

isolationism (ī′sə lā′shə niz′əm, is′ə lā′shə niz′əm), *n.* principle or policy of avoiding political and economic relations with other nations.

J

joint committee a committee with members from both houses of the legislature, selected to consider problems and bills in a particular field.

judgment (juj′mənt), *n.* opinion about the worth of an action, object, idea, or person.

judicial branch the branch of government that judges laws and decides legal cases. The courts are in the judicial branch of government.

judicial review the power of the courts to declare acts of the legislative or executive branches unconstitutional.

jurisdiction (jūr′is dik′shən), *n.* authority to judge and administer the law.

L

label (lā′bəl), *n.* a tag attached to anything and marked with information about the item.

labor contract a recorded agreement between employees, represented by their union, and the employer listing pay rates, benefits, and conditions of employment.

labor union an organization of workers that seek to improve working conditions and pay through collective bargaining.

law (lô), *n.* rule made by government.

law of supply and demand in economics, the principle that prices go up when demand for a product is greater than the supply and down when the supply is greater than the demand.

lawyer referral service a service that supplies, on request, the names of private lawyers who specialize in handling any specific kind of problem.

legal clinic group of lawyers who handle simple legal jobs, at reduced fees, for large numbers of people.

legislative branch the branch of government that makes laws. Congress is the legislative branch of the national government.

legislative program the group of bills a President, governor, or legislator will introduce and work to get passed.

letters-to-the-editor a section of a newspaper containing letters of opinion by people not connected with the paper.

license (lī′sns) *n., v.* —*n.* a certificate, from a government agency, of permission to do something. People get licenses to do such things as drive a car, get married, open a radio station, or practice medicine. —*v.* to give a license to; to permit by law.

lieutenant governor public official next in rank to the governor of a state.

life expectancy average number of years a group of people live.

limited liability having only certain obligations and no others. Limited liability is one of the advantages of organizing a business as a corporation.

limited war a war fought without the use of nuclear weapons and for objectives other than complete defeat of the enemy.

lobbyist (lob′ē ist), *n.* person hired by a special interest group to influence government decision makers.

loyalty (loi′əl tē), *n., pl.* **-ties.** a feeling of faithfulness to a friend, group, or country. Loyalty to a friend can make a person defend that friend, even against heavy odds.

M

magistrate (maj′ə strāt, maj′ə-strit), *n.* a minor judicial officer with power to try cases for lesser offenses. A federal magistrate holds preliminary hearings in federal criminal cases and helps with the work of the federal district court.

major party one of the two main political parties; Republican Party or Democratic Party.

majority party in either legislative chamber, the political party having the most members.

manager (man′ə jər), *n.* director; person who runs such a thing as a business, a department, an institution, or a city.

market system an economy in which consumers and producers make all major economic decisions.

marshal (mär′shəl), *n.* the official who performs police duties in connection with a federal district court. The United States marshal is in the Department of Justice.

massive retaliation the use of all one's weapons, especially nuclear weapons, upon provocation.

maturity (mə chúr′ə tē, mə-tûr′ə tē, mə tyúr′ə tē), *n.* time a note or debt is payable.

Mayflower Compact the agreement to form a government, signed by men on the Pilgrim ship *Mayflower* before landing at Plymouth.

mayor (mā′ər, mer), *n.* the main executive official in most American cities.

mayor-council plan a plan of city government with an elected mayor for executive officer and elected council members for a law-making body.

megalopolis (meg′ə lop′ə lis), *n.* an area where large metropolitan areas have started to overlap; a large metropolitan area, often including several cities.

metropolitan area a large city with its nearby suburbs and small towns.

minor party a political party with few supporters compaed to the major parties.

minority party in either legislative chamber, the major political party having fewer members than the other party.

minutes (min′its), *n.* the formal notes of what happens at a meeting of a club, board, committee, or other group.

misdemeanor (mis′di mē′nər), *n.* least serious crime or breaking of a law, such as a minor traffic offense.

mixed-market system an econ-

550

omy in which most economic decisions are made by the market system and some decisions are made by the command system.

monopoly (mə nop′ə lē), *n.*, *pl.* **-lies.** a business with no competition; exclusive control of a product or service people want to buy.

municipal charter a local constitution granted by the state to a heavily populated community.

municipality (myü nis′ə pal′ə-tē), *n.*, *pl.* **-ties.** city, town, or other district having local self-government under a charter granted by the state.

N

name-calling (nām′kô′ling) *n.* propaganda technique of labeling an opponent in a bad way.

National Security Council President's advisory group on foreign policy.

national supremacy the constitutional principle that national government is the highest law in the land, and that no state can pass a law that goes against the Constitution.

natural resources the supplies that come from nature, or from the earth, such as soil, water, and minerals.

naturalization (nach′ər ə lə zā′-shən), *n.* the steps an alien takes to become a citizen.

New England section of the United States that includes Maine, New Hampshire, Vermont, Massachusetts, Rhode Island, and Connecticut.

news story factual article in a newspaper.

nominate (nom′ə nāt), *v.* to name as candidate for an office.

nominating committee group of people who select candidates for office.

nomination (nom′ə nā′shən), *n.* selection of candidates for the ballots in an election.

nonpartisan (non pär′tə zən), *adj.* not identified with either major political party.

O

Office of Personnel Management the central personnel agency of the national government, charged with impartially selecting among job applicants and with carrying out laws about fairness in government employment.

OMB Office of Management and Budget, in the executive branch of the national government.

ombudsman (om budz′mən), *n.* a government official with the power to investigate a citizen's complaint against a public official.

open primary a nominating election in which qualified voters may take part without telling their party preference.

open shop contract allowing each worker to join the union or not.

opinion (ə pin′yən), *n.* statement by a judge or jury of the reasons for a decision made by the court.

ordinance (ord′n əns), *n.* a local law.

P

parish (par′ish), *n.* in Louisiana, a district similar to a county.

partnership (pärt′nər ship), *n.* a business owned by two or more people who share the costs, profits, and responsibilities of the business.

party chief leader of his or her political party.

party convention method of nomination in which party members pick delegates in all parts of the state, then the delegates meet and select candidates; meeting at which candidates are chosen.

party platform written series of statements on election issues that a particular party stands for.

party whip member of Senate or House of Representatives whose job it is to keep after members of the same political party to get their votes registered when a bill is on the floor.

patriotism (pā′trē ə tiz′əm), *n.* loyalty to a country or nation; love and support of one's country.

patronage (pā′trə nij, pat′rə nij), *n.* power to give jobs or favors.

personal income the total money earned by all individuals, measured before taxes; the PI.

personal income tax tax charged on the income each person earns in a year.

petition (pə tish′ən), *n.*, *v.* —*n.* a request signed by qualified voters asking that a wrong be corrected or that a particular candidate or issue be on the ballot. —*v.* to ask the government for a corrective action, a right guaranteed by the First and Fourteenth Amendments.

plain folks propaganda technique of influencing people to think one is just like them—a worker among workers, a farmer among farmers, etc.

plank (plangk), *n.* a position statement from a party platform giving the party view on an election issue. Support for federal aid to education is often a plank in both parties' platforms.

plea bargaining arrangement between a prosecutor and an accused person (or the defense lawyer) to exchange a guilty plea from the accused for a reduced charge or promise of leniency.

pocket veto a special way the President can veto a bill. The pocket veto is only possible with bills the President receives in the last ten days of a legislative session. If the President does not sign the bill (carries it around in a pocket is the implication), it is as good as a veto.

political appointee person named by a public official to a job in government; a person whose job does not come under civil service.

political party an association of voters who organize to elect members to public office, operate government, and determine public policy.

political party leader the person with the highest political office or most political influence in the party.

political resource time, money, skill, or information available to influence government decisions.

polling place a location where voting takes place.

popular vote the votes cast by the voters as a whole.

practical (prak′tə kəl), *adj.* useful; having strong possibility that results wanted will be achieved.

Preamble (prē′am′bəl), *n.* preface or introduction to the Constitution, naming goals for the United States.

precedent (pres′ə dənt), *n.* legal decision in a preceding case; action or case that serves as a pattern in future cases that are similar.

precinct (prē′singkt), *n.* neighborhood election district; district in certain boundaries, such as a police precinct.

preliminary hearing a procedure in a criminal case to protect an accused person from being held if there is not sufficient cause. The judge examines the accused and decides whether or not the person should be held for trial.

preside (pri zīd′), *v.* have charge of a meeting, seeing that speakers have a chance to be heard, keeping order, and urging the group to finish its business.

president of the senate leader and presiding officer of the state senate, often the lieutenant governor.

president pro tempore officer elected by the Senate to be chairperson in the absence of the Vice-President of the United States.

presiding officer person in charge of a meeting.

prestige (pre stēzh′, pre stēj′), *n.* reputation, influence, or distinction.

priority (prī ôr′ə tē, prī or′ə tē), *n.* what comes first; preference in order of importance.

producer (prə dü′sər, prə-dyü′sər), *n.* a person or group that grows things, manufactures goods, or performs a service used by others.

profit (prof′it), *n.* the money left over after the cost of doing business has been subtracted from a company's income.

proletariat (prō′lə ter′ē ət), *n.* in socialist and communist writing, a word that means: working-class people.

propaganda technique a means used to carry out a plan for spreading opinions or beliefs.

property tax local tax on the value of property a person or business owns.

protective tariff a customs tax that protects an American product from competition with foreign-made goods. The tariff raises the price of the foreign-made goods.

public employee person employed by a government.

public housing project apartment buildings built with public money.

public interest group an interest group that works to influence government on issues it believes are good for most citizens.

public opinion what people think; citizens' views, attitudes, or beliefs.

public service action of government carried on for people's health, safety, employment, or other common benefit.

public utility a legal monopoly regulated by government officials that provides an essential service.

rapid transit system trains used to move people around a city.

ratify (rat′ə fī), *v.* approve; confirm in a formal way, as by a vote.

real case rule a requirement of the Supreme Court in deciding whether a law agrees with the Constitution. The Supreme Court will not consider a case unless a law has been broken or a person has claimed injury from the carrying out of a law.

recession (ri sesh′ən), *n.* a period of slow business activity that is less serious than a depression.

regulatory commission a board, usually of three or more people, chosen to direct a particular government function. The Federal Communications Commission, for example, regulates interstate and foreign radio, television, telephone, telegraph, and cable communications.

respect (ri spekt′), *n., v.* —*n.* high regard, honor, or esteem for someone or something of recognized worth. —*v.* feel or show honor or esteem for.

responsibility (ri spon′sə bil′ə-tē), *n., pl.* **-ties.** duty or obligation.

revenue sharing a turning over of tax money by the national government to state and local governments, with little restriction on its use. States also issue revenue sharing money to local governments.

right to work laws laws that prohibit both closed shops and union shops.

role (rōl), *n.* job; part one plays; position.

Rules Committee powerful committee in the House of Representatives that decides on the rules for debate on bills.

sales receipt a written record, showing the amount of a sale.

savings and loan association a banklike institution that specializes in large loans such as the kind given when people buy houses.

scarcity (sker′sə tē, skar′sə tē), *n., pl.* **-ties.** the basic economic problem of limited resources and unlimited wants; too small a supply to meet the demand or satisfy the need.

search warrant court order or legal paper allowing police to search a place where there is good reason to believe evidence of a crime will be found.

secret operations government actions in another country that are kept under cover.

secretary (sek′rə ter′ē), *n., pl.* **-taries.** person in charge of a department of government or similar organization, such as the Secretary of Commerce.

secretary of state an executive officer in the national government or in one of thirty-nine state governments. The President's Secretary of State advises on foreign affairs. In most states, the secretary of state manages elections, official records, licenses, and permits.

security (si kyur′ə tē), *n., pl.* **-ties.** freedom from danger; feeling of being safe. —*usually pl.* bond or stock certificates.

Security Council a major body within the United Nations, having five permanent member-nations and ten members elected for two-year terms. The Security Council has the power to send out troops.

selectmen (si lekt′mən), *n.* members of a board of town officers in New England, elected to govern the town between annual meetings of the voters.

self-nomination (self′nom′ə nā′-shən), *n.* announcement by a person not on the ballot that he or she is a candidate requesting a write-in vote.

seniority rights job security based on length of service. In case of a layoff, those on the job the most years would be the last to be laid off.

seniority rule custom of making

the majority party member with the most years on a committee the chairperson.

service charge a bill from a government agency for a certain kind of service, such as water supply or garbage collection.

services (sėr′vis əz), *n.* what people do in exchange for something of value; work done in the service of others rather than in the production of goods.

shared tax a tax created and collected by a state, with part of the money going to local governments and part to the state government.

shares of stock certificates of ownership of a corporation.

single proprietorship a business owned by one person.

slate (slāt), *n., v.* —*n.* list of candidates to be considered for appointment, nomination, or election. —*v.* to list for an office, a promotion, or other event. She is slated for the club presidency next year.

slum (slum), *n.* an old, dirty, run-down part of a city.

social security tax money people pay as tax, most of which is used to provide income for retired persons, their dependents, and survivors.

speaker of the house the presiding officer and most powerful leader in the national or a state house of representatives, a member of the majority party.

special committee a committee set up to do a special job, disbanding when the job is done.

special district a local government set up to supply one or a few special services. A school district is a kind of special district.

special interest group organization of people who have some common interest and who try to influence the decisions of government officials.

special session an extra series of meetings of the legislature called at a time when it usually does not assemble.

split ticket a vote for some candidates from one party and some candidates from another.

staff (staf), *n., adj.* a group of employees. Congressional staff members run offices, gather information, arrange for meetings, and help their boss get reelected.

Standard Metropolitan Statistical Area (SMSA) any area including city and suburbs that has a population of 50,000 or more.

standard of living the level of comfort a person or community enjoys through available goods and services.

standing committee a permanent legislative committee that continues its work from session to session.

state agency a department, board, or commission in a state government.

state auditor person elected to watch over state funds and make sure all money is accounted for. Thirty-one states have a person in this job.

state treasurer person elected to be in charge of collecting state funds and paying the state's bills. Forty-one states elect treasurers.

statutory law law made by a law-making body such as Congress, a state legislature, or a city council.

stockholder (stok′hōl′dər), *n.* person owning shares of stock in a company.

straight ticket a vote for all the candidates in one party.

strike (strīk), *n., v.* —*n.* a stopping of work by employees to force agreement of the employer to improved pay or conditions of employment. —*v.* to stop work to get better pay or working conditions.

strong mayor a mayor who has broad powers to appoint, to shape the budget, to suggest laws, and to veto bills from the council.

subcommittee (sub′kə mit′ē), *n.* a small committee chosen from and acting under a larger general committee for some special duty.

subway (sub′wā′), *n.* parts of rapid transit systems that run under ground; an electric railroad running beneath the surface of streets in a city.

T

tax (taks), *n., v.* —*n.* fee that people must pay to support the government. —*v.* to put a fee or charge on, for government support.

taxable income amount of a person's income that is taxed.

testify (tes′tə fī), *v.* give opinions and facts about a bill being considered; give evidence.

third party an independent political party, often organized as a protest movement, that succeeds in becoming a temporary challenger to the two major parties.

title of nobility name showing high rank or position of honor such as countess, prince, or duke. The United States government may not grant titles of nobility.

totalitarian society people governed by one political group which controls many aspects of citizens' lives and suppresses opposition.

township (toun′ship), *n.* part of a county, having certain powers of government.

transfer (*n.* tran′sfėr′; *v.* tran sfėr′, tran′sfėr′). —*n.* propaganda technique of associating something everyone thinks is good with a candidate (or idea or product). —*v.* to give approval to someone because of his or her association with something one thinks is good.

treason (trē′zn), *n.* most serious crime against a government; in the United States, carrying on war against the United States or helping its enemies.

treaty (trē′tē), *n., pl.* **-ties.** agreement between governments of two or more countries, signed and approved by each nation.

two-party system political order in which two major parties generally compete at election time with one of the two winning.

U

unanimous (yü nan′ə məs), *adj.* agreed on by all.

uncommitted (un′kə mit′əd), *adj.* not pledged to support a particular candidate or cause.

unconstitutional (un′kon stə tü′shə nəl, un′kon stə tyü′shə nəl), *adj.* contrary to the constitution.

unicameral legislature a legislature with one house.

union shop union-employer contract that says workers who are hired must join the union within a certain period of time.

unit price the cost of one part—one ounce, one quart, one inch, one meter, etc.

unitary system plan of government in which the central government has all the power.

United Nations an international organization of about 150 nations working to promote peace, friendly relations between nations, and the solving of global problems.

United States attorney the lawyer for the Department of Justice who prosecutes violations of federal law in each federal district court.

urban area a center of population and business activity having 2500 people or more.

urban renewal the tearing down of slums to replace them with new buildings.

V

values (val′yüz), n., pl., v. —n. things people think are important or good. —v. regards highly.

veto (vē′tō), v., n., pl. -toes. —v. reject; refuse to consent to. —n. rejection; right or power of a president, governor, or such officer, to reject bills passed by a lawmaking body.

voluntary group a group of people who work together for no pay to help others.

volunteer (vol′ən tir′), n., v. —n. a person who gives time and effort, without pay, for the benefit of others. —v. offer one's services.

W

wages (wā′jəs), n., pl. money paid regularly, at a fixed rate, for work done or for hours worked.

ward system a way of choosing members of a city council by electing one representative from each ward or section of the city.

warranty (wôr′ən tē, wor′ən tē), n., pl. -ties. a pledge that something is what it is claimed to be.

watchdog agency a government regulatory commission, responsible for protecting the public by setting up and enforcing rules within an industry that carry out the law.

weak mayor a mayor who has limited power, power being with the council and other officials.

White House Office group of people close to the daily work of the President, who help him or her to use time only on important matters others cannot handle. The White House Office is part of the Executive Office of the President.

will (wil), n. a legal document that explains what will happen to all your things when you die.

winner-take-all unit system by which the party winning the most popular votes in a state receives all of the state's electoral votes.

writ of mandamus a judge's order to a person or group to do what someone has a legal right to expect will be done.

write-in (rīt′in′), adj., n. —adj. having to do with voting for a candidate not on the ballot. —n. a vote for someone not on the ballot, or a candidate voted for in this way.

Z

zoning ordinance a law about how land may be used in a particular area.

★★★

Index

A

Ackerman, Barbara, *illus.* 299
Adams, John Q., 42, 121, 501
Adams, Samuel, 50
Administrative law, 209
Agenda, 122
Alabama, 9, 120, 538, 539, 543
  Senator John Sparkman, 136
Alamo, 407
Alaska, 110, 120, 264, 331, 362, 538, 539, 543
  pipeline, *illus.* 195
Amendments, 51, 66–67, 95–102. *See also* Amendments by number
  bill of rights, 95–100
  fifteenth, 275
  fourteenth, 101, 225
  nineteenth, 275
  sixteenth, 66
  twenty-sixth, 111, 275
American Association of Retired Persons, 234
American Cancer Society, 420

American Conservative Union, 282
American Farm Bureau Federation, 235
AFL-CIO, 235, 242, 282, 462
American Legion, 235
American Medical Association, 235
American Red Cross, 420
Americans for Constitutional Action, 282
Americans for Democratic Action, 282
American territories, 495, 539
  Territorial Courts, 215
American Tobacco Institute, 241
Anti-Federalists, 50, 256
Antimonopoly laws, 458
  cartoon in support of, *illus.* 458
Appellate courts, 338
Appointees, in county government, 368.
  presidential, 172, 175–77, 195–96, 215–216
  in state government, 318–319, 322, 328
  See also Political appointees

Arguments, in Supreme Court, 220–221
Arizona, 120, 220, 538, 539, 543
  Congressman John Rhodes, *illus.* 121
  Navajo reservation in, 33–35
Arkansas, 120, 538, 539, 543
  Governor Bill Clinton, *illus.* 321
"Armband rule," 223
Arms, 522
Arraignment, 345
Articles of Confederation, 39–41
  and constitutional convention, 43
Atlanta, Georgia, 411, 413
Atlantic City, New Jersey, 372
Atomic bomb, 505
Attorney general, 176
  in state government, 319

B

B-1 bomber, 181–183, *illus.* 181
  manufacture halted, *illus.* 183
  opposition to, *illus.* 182
Bail, 100
"Bait and Switch," 475
Baker, Howard, 245, 246

Balanced budget, 155, 156
Ballot, 276, 278–279
Baltimore, Maryland, 400, 411, *illus.* 143
Bandwagon, 286–287
Banks, 477, *illus.* 481
BART, *illus.* 405
Beame, Abraham, 414–415
Begin, Menahem, *illus.* 173
Benefits, 10
Berkeley, California, *illus.* 139, 296–297
Berlin, Germany, *illus.* 503
Bernstein, Carl, 68
Better business bureaus, 485
Bicameral, 119, 302
Bill of Rights, 50, 95–100
in state constitutions, 301
Bills, 132–135, 305–306, 308–309
process to become laws, *chart* 133
Binding commitment, 167
Black, Hugo, 224
Black Mesa Mine Decision, 33–35
Board of Commissioners, 366
Board of Directors, 454
Bonds, 150, 373
Boroughs, 362
Boston, Massachusetts, 400, *illus.* 16, 65, 96, 148, 493
Boycotts, *illus.* 245
Bradley, Tom, *illus.* 372
Brezhnev, Leonid, *illus.* 495
Brief, 220
Briscoe, Dolph, 316
Brown, Jerry, *illus.* 372
Brown v. Board of Education of Topeka, Kansas, 225–227, *illus.* 227
segregated schools, *illus.* 225
Budget, national, 154–158. *See also* Government spending
Budget, personal, 472–473, *chart* 473
Buffalo, New York, *illus.* 65
Bureaucracy, 186
features of, 328–329
Bureaucrats, 325
Burger, Warren, 346
Business, and the Democratic party, 258
Business cycle, 445
Businesses, 452–465, *chart* 454, *illus.* 464
case study of, 466–467
factors of production, 455–457
government regulation of, 458–459
and labor unions, 460–465, *illus.* 460
with largest numbers of stockholders, *chart* 455
organization of, 453–455, *illus.* 453, 457

Bylaws, 422
Byrd, Harry, 216
Byrne, Jane, *illus.* 263

C

Cabinet, 176
Carter cabinet, *illus.* 175
Cabinet departments, 188–192, *chart* 177
California, 120, 167, 169, 538, 539, 543
Berkeley, *illus.* 139, 296–297
Congressman Ronald Dellums, *illus.* 281
Dianne Feinstein, *illus.* 384
Governor Jerry Brown, *illus.* 372
Los Angeles, 370, 395, 399, 405, 414
Proposition 5, 241
Proposition 13, 374–375
San Francisco, 394–395, *illus.* 108, 257, 394, 405, 446
Senator John Tunney, *illus.* 271
Tom Bradley, *illus.* 372
California Frontlash, 270–271
Callaghan, James, *illus.* 204
Cambodia, 501
Campaign for Clean Indoor Air, 241
Campaigning, 168, 265–268, *illus.* 255, 257, 259, 268
Candidates
choosing between, 281–287
nomination of, 166–167, 263–265
Canvass, 265
Capitalism, 440
Capital goods, 436
as factor of production, 457
Capitol, *illus.* 127, 130
Card-stacking, 286
Carter, Jimmy, 166, 167, 179, 215–216, *illus.* 168, 173, 501
and B-1 bomber, 181–183
cabinet officers, *illus.* 175
and national budget, 154, 155, 156
and Panama Canal, 509
and retirement law, 234
Carey, Hugh, 324
Case studies
B-1 bomber, 181–182
Black Mesa Mine Decision, 33–35
bottle litter controversy, 248–249
California frontlash, 270–271
city government at work, 394–395
Concorde controversy, 202–205
economic competition, 448–449
global interdependence, 529–531
government spending, 159–161
jury, 352–353

lowering the voting age, 110–111
McDonalds, 466–467
New York City, 414–415
Panama Canal, 508–509
Proposition 13, 374–375
Ralph Nader, 486–487
Richard Daley, 289–291
state government, 332–333
state tax, 312–313
Supreme Court case, 225–227
teenagers volunteer, 426–427
territorial waters, 16–17
timber cutting bill, 136–139
Watergate, 68–71
Whiskey Rebellion, 52–53
CIA, 179, 193, 499–500
Chain of command, in a bureaucracy, 328
Chairpersons, 124–125
Chamber of Commerce, 390
Charge accounts, 480
Checking accounts, 478–479
Chiang Kai-shek, 496
Chicago, Illinois, 378, 400, 406, 414, *illus.* 13
Chief executive, 172
Chief school officer, 320
China, 425, 496, *illus.* 171
communism in, 506, 507
economy of, 439
Church, Frank, *illus.* 235
Circuit, 214
Cities. *See also* cities by name
case studies, 394–395, 414–415
growth of, 399–402, *chart* 401
help for, 411–413
planning, 407–410
pollution, 406–407
poor housing, 404–405
problems of, 403–410
transportation, 405–406
See also city government
Citizenship, 5, 7
by birth, 103
and Constitution, 57–58
loss of, 104–105
by naturalization, 103–104, *chart* 103
rights and responsibilities of, 94–109, *chart* 107
City councils, 387–388, *illus.* 387
City government, 378–391
decision makers in, 384–388
and influence groups, 389–391
plans for, 379–383
See also Cities
City managers, 386–387
City planning, 407–410
Civics, 5
Civil cases, 338
Civil Service Commission, 196–197
taking the exam, *illus.* 325

Clark, Dick, 233
Clayton Antitrust Act, 458
Cleveland, Ohio, 411
Client groups, 199–200
Closed primary, 264
Closed shop, 464
Coalition, 244
Coast Guard, *illus.* 16, 17
Cockrell, Lila, 407
Cold War, 503–504
Coleman, William, 202–205
Collective bargaining, 462
Colorado, 10, 120, 538, 539, 543
Columbus, Ohio, 529–531
Commander in Chief, 171
Command system, 439
Commission plan, 381–382
Committee on Political Education, 282
Committees, 122–125
  in political parties, 256–257
  power of over bills, 132–134
  in state legislatures, 305–306
  of volunteer groups, 422
Common Cause, 237
Common law, 209
Communism, 495
  and economy, 439
  and U.S. foreign policy, 503–507
  See also Cold War, Wars
Competition, 440
Comprehensive Employment and Training Act
  use of funds, *illus.* 157
Compromise, 46
Concorde, controversy over, 202–205, *illus.* 203
Confederation, 40
  Articles of, 39–41
Conference committee, 135, 305–306
Congress, 118–135, *chart* 60
  characteristics of the 95th, *chart* 126, 141
  decision making in, 118
  and federal agencies, 198
  and foreign policy, 500–502
  growth of staff, *chart* 131
  jobs of, 127–130
  leaders of, 121–122
  making laws in, 132–135
  members of, 126–127
  organization of, 119–125
  and presidential decisions, 179
  standing committees of, *chart* 122
  See also Legislation
Congressional districts, 120
Congressional hearings, 130
Congressional staff, 130–131
Connecticut, 40, 46, 50, 120, 369, 538, 539, 543
  Governor Ella Grasso, 324

local government in, 362
  teenage volunteers in, 426
Consequences, 22–23
Consolidation, 369
Constituents, 311
Constitution (United States), 3, 56–93
  amending, 66–67
  approval of, 49–51, *chart* 50
  Bill of Rights, 95–100
  branches of government, 60–64
  copy of, 74–93
  in federal courts, 211
  preamble, 58–59
  and presidential power, 170
  purpose of, 57–60
  and right to vote, 275
  on state and national government, 65–67
  text of, 74–93
  and war powers, 501
  See also Bill of Rights, Amendments
Constitutional convention
  background of, 39–42
  decision making at, 43–47
Constitutional law, 209
  and Supreme Court, 219
Constitutions, state, 300–301
Consumer Bulletin, 474
Consumer goods, 436
Consumer interest groups, 484–485
Consumer Product Safety Commission, 484
Consumer Reports, 474
Consumers, 438, 439, 470–485
  buying goods and services, 471–475, *illus.* 471
  case study, Ralph Nader, 486–487
  growth of debt, *chart* 476
  making a budget, 472–473
  protecting rights of, 481–485
  saving and borrowing, 476–480
Consumption, 444
Containment, 504–506
Continuance, 340
Conventions, 167
Coolidge, Calvin, 166
Cooperatives, 455
Coroner, 367
Corporate income tax, 145, 148
Corporations, 454–455
  ten largest, *chart* 469
Council-Manager plan, 380–381
Counties, 362
County assessor, 367, 368
County auditor, 367
County clerk, 368, *illus.* 368
County government, example of, 405–406
County judge, 366
County recorder, 368

Court system, 211–216. *See also* Supreme Court
  federal, 213–216
  and interest groups, 242–243
  jobs of people at court, *illus.* 209
  reporting in, *illus.* 97
  schooling of lawyers, *illus.* 212
  small claims, 340, 342–343
  state, 336–351
  videotaped evidence, *illus.* 210
Cox v. Louisiana, 224
Credit, 477, 480
Credit unions, 455, 477, *illus.* 149
Crime prevention, *illus.* 322
Criminal cases, 344–346
Criminal courts, 337
Cuba, 495, 500
Currency, in states before Constitution, 40–41
Customs duty, 148
Cuyahoga County, Ohio, pollution in, 406, 407

D
Dade County, Florida, 405–406
Daley, Richard J., 289–291, *illus.* 291
  election victory celebration, *illus.* 289
Das Kapital, 503
Davis, John W., 226
Dean, John, *illus.* 70
Debs, Eugene, *illus.* 254
Decision making, 7, 9–10, 20–26
  judging decisions, 27–30
Decision tree, *chart* 31
Declaration of Independence, 94
Defendants, 338
Defense department, 177, 189
  and B-1 bomber debate, 181–183
  and foreign policy, 498, 499
  Joint Chiefs of Staff, *illus.* 501
Deficit, 155
Delaware, 44, 45, 50, 120, 226, 362, 538, 539, 543
Delegates, 167
  to constitutional convention, 41–42
  to nominating conventions, 167, 265
Democracy
  and communism, 504
  and totalitarian societies, 425
  and volunteer groups, 424–425
  See also Bill of Rights, Constitution, Government, Mayflower Compact, Rights
Democratic-Republican Party, 256, 537
Democrats, 253–257
  and California frontlash, 270–271

and Richard J. Daley, 289–291
See also Political Parties
Denaturalization, 104–105
Department of Agriculture, 177, 188, 192
Department of Commerce, 177, 188, 192
Department of Defense, 177, 188, 189, 499
  and B-1 bomber debate, 181–183
Department of Energy, 177, 188, 192
Department of Health Education and Welfare, 177, 188, 189
Department of Housing and Urban Development, 177, 186, 188, 192, 372, 398
Department of the Interior, 177, 188, 192
Department of Justice, 177, 186, 188, 189
Department of Labor, 177, 188, 192
Department of State, 177, 188, 189, 499. *See also* Secretary of State
Department of Transportation, 177, 188, 192
Department of the Treasury, 177, 188, 189, *illus.* 189
Depression, 411, 444
  preventing, 446, 447
Des Moines, Iowa, 529
DeTocqueville, Alexis, 418
Developed countries, 519
Developing countries, 519–520
Diplomat, 497
Direct primaries, 263–264
Division of federal system powers, *chart* 300
Domestic Council, 175
Domestic tranquility, 59
Due process, 97
Dukakis, Michael, 332–333, *illus.* 332

E
Economy, 433, 434–437
  case study, 448–449
  economic decisions, 435–437, *chart* 441
  economic systems, 438–441
  judging performance of, 442–447
  See also Businesses
Eighteenth Amendment, 91
Eighth Amendment, 88, 100
Eisenhower, Dwight D., 166, 178, 506
Election judges, 277
Elections, 109
  campaign of 1916, *illus.* 255
  canvassing, *illus.* 270

counting of votes, *illus.* 275
example of close, 233
1976, *chart* 111
1960–1976, *chart* 260
nominating convention, *illus.* 253
primary, 263–264
See also Campaigning, Candidates, Conventions, Voting
Electoral College, 168–169
Eleventh Amendment, 88
Ellender, Allan, 137
Energy
  conservation, *illus.* 172
  new sources, *illus.* 172
Environmental Protection Agency, 187
  and Concorde controversy, 203, 204
  workers, *illus.* 411
Equal justice, 210
ERA, 66
  opponents of, *illus.* 66
  supporters of, *illus.* 67
Equity suits, 346–347
Ervin, Sam, 69, *illus.* 69
Estate tax, 149
Excise Law of 1791, 52
Excise taxes, 148
Executive branch, 61–63, *chart* 188
  and court system, 216
  watched by Congress, 129–130
  See also Presidency, State executive branch
Executive Office of the President, 175–177
Expatriates, 104–105
Extradition, 65

F
Factors of production, 455–457
Favorite son, 167
Federal agencies, 186–201
  career workers in, 196–197
  client groups and, 199–200
  Congress and, 198
  decision making in, 186–201
  political appointees in, 195–196
  President and, 199
  work and organization of, 187–194
FBI, 189
Federal courts, 211–212
  decision making in, 208–224
  judges in, 215–216
  organization of, 213–215
  serving the people, 209–212
  See also Supreme Court
Federal government, *chart* 60, 62
  aid to cities, 411–413, 415
  number of workers, *chart* 196
  regulation of business, 458–459

See also Government spending
Federal judges, 215–216
Federalists, 49–50, 256
FICA, 145
Federal system of government, 299
Federal Trade Commission, 481
Federal Trade Commission Act, 458
Feinstein, Dianne, *illus.* 384
Felonies, 338
Fifteenth Amendment, 90, 100, 101, 275
Fifth Amendment, 87, 97
Fines, 373
First Amendment, 86, 95–96, *chart* 96
Fiscal year, 154
Fisheries and Conservation Act enforcement, *illus.* 16
Fixed expenses, 473
Flexible expenses, 473
Floor leader, 122, 306
Florida, 120, 339, 369, 538, 539, 543
  Miami, 399, 405
  Senator Edward Gurney, *illus.* 68
Food, as political resource, 521
Food and Drug Administration, 481, 484
  services, *illus.* 484
Ford, Gerald, 71, 166, 169, 415, 501, *illus.* 168, 497
  and B-1 bomber decision, 182
  and Panama Canal, 508
Foreign Aid, 505
Foreign policy, 493
  bureaucracy, 498–500
  case study of Panama Canal, 508–509
  and communism, 503–507
  and congress, 500–502
  defined, 495–496
  and global interdependence, 519–523
  and President, 171, 497
Fortas, Abe, 223
Fourteenth Amendment, 89–90, 100, 101, 225
Fourth Amendment, 87, 97
Franklin, Benjamin, 41, 47
Freedom of speech, 95–96
Free enterprise, 440, *illus.* 432–433, 435, 436, 438
Fringe benefits, 463

G
Gardner, John, 237
General Assembly, UN, 525
General Federation of Women's Clubs, 420
General trial courts, 337
General welfare, 59

Georgia, 50, 110, 120, 226, 316, 374, 538, 539, 543
  Atlanta, 411, 413
  Senate committees, *chart* 305
  state government, 300, 305
Gerry, Elbridge, 42, 44
Gettysburg Address, 108
Gift tax, 149
Girl Scouts, 420, 427
Glittering generality, 285
Global interdependence, 513–515
  case study of, 529–531
  effects of, 515–518
  and foreign policy, 519–523
GNP, 442–443, 444
  and population, *chart* 442
  United States growth of, *chart* 443
Goods, 435
Government, 9–11
  need for, 12–15
  See also Government spending, Federal government, Local government, State government
Government Affairs Committee, *illus.* 129
Government bonds, 477
Government corporations, 193
Government spending, 151–158, *chart* 151, 153, 154
  case study of, 159–161
  and the economy, 446, 447
  by state legislatures, 302–303
  See also Federal government
Governors, 317–319, 321–324
  and state legislators, 309–310
Granata, Sam, 407
Grants, 372
Grants-in-Aid, 152, 372, 412–413
"Grass roots," 257
Grasso, Ella, 324
Gray Panthers, 234, *illus.* 235
Great Compromise, 46–47
Great Depression, 444
Gromyko, Andrei, *illus.* 495
Gross National Product, 442–443
Guam, 495, 539
Guarantees, 474
Gulf of Tonkin Resolution, 506

H

Hamilton, Alexander, 41, 49, 255, 256
Hancock, John, 41
Hanrahan, Edward, 290
Harding, Warren, 166
Hartke, Vance, 240
Hawaii, 110, 120, 331, 362, 495, 538, 539, 543
  Congressman Daniel Akaka, *illus.* 123
  Senator Spark Matsunaga, *illus.* 123

Head of state, 173
Henry, Patrick, 42, 50
Highway construction, *illus.* 333
Hoover, Herbert, 166
House Judiciary Committee, 69–70, *illus.* 117
House of Representatives, 45, 46, 119–121
  leaders of, 121–122
  See also Congress
Howlett, Michael, 240
Human resources, 435
Humphrey, Hubert, 130–131, *illus.* 176

I

Idaho, 120, 538, 539, 543
  Senator Frank Church, *illus.* 235
Ideal, 94
Illinois, 120, 167, 316, 374, 538, 539, 543
  Governor James Thompson, 240, 241, 316
  Senator Stevenson, 167
  state constitution, 301
Illinois Education Association, 240–241
Immigrants, 103
Immigration hearing, *illus.* 63
Impeachment, 70, 120–121, 317
Income, 444
  in family groups, *chart* 444
  national government sources of, *chart* 143, 154
Income tax, 143–144
Independents, 258, 260–261
Indiana, 120, 282, 370, 538, 539, 543
  farming in, *illus.* 443
  Senator Bayh, 282
  Senator Hartke, 282
  Senator Lugar, 240
  Representative Myers, 282
Indictment, 345
Independent agencies, 192–193
Inflation, 445
  effect of, *chart* 447
  preventing, 447
Injunction, 347
Interest, 150
Interest groups, 234–248
  case study of, 248–249
  and city government, 389–391
  and the courts, 242–243
  deciding which to support, 237
  and government decision makers, 242
  political resources of, 239–240
  rating of Congress, *chart* 282
  and state legislation, 310
  taking part in, 244–245
  and voters, 240–241, 282
  why citizens join, 235–237
Interest rates, 477

Interstate Commerce Commission, 187
Iowa, 120, 331, 369, 538, 539, 543
  elections in, 233
  Senator Dick Clark, 233
Isolationism, 495

J

Jackson, Andrew, 178, 256
Jails, crowded, 338–339
Javits, Jacob, 129
Jefferson, Thomas, 41, 42, 50, 121, 398
  and history of Democratic Party, 253, 255, 256
Jepsen, Roger, 233
Johnson, Lyndon, 166, 171, 505, *illus.* 61
  and Panama Canal debate, 508
  and Vietnam, 506
Joint committees, 124
Joint Chiefs of Staff, *illus.* 501
Judges, 215–216
  county, 366
  in equity cases, 346–347
Judgments, 27–28
Judicial branch, 63–64, 208–227, *chart* 213
  and national budget, 158
Judicial review, 219
Judiciary Act of 1789, 219
Jurisdiction, 211
Jury trials, 346
  case study, 352–353

K

Kansas, 120, 226, 538, 539, 543
  Senator Nancy Kassenbaum, *illus.* 128
Kansas City, 369
Kennedy, John F., 7, 124, 155, 165, 166
  and Vietnam, 506
Kentucky, 110, 120, 282, 370, 538, 539, 543
  Senator Walter Huddleston, 282
  Senator Wendell Ford, 282
  Representative Gene Snyder, 282
Kentucky Mountain Housing Development Corporation, 160–161, *illus.* 161
Kerr, Robert, 129
King, Martin Luther, Jr., 124
  assassination committee, *illus.* 124
Kissinger, Henry, *illus.* 497
  and Concorde controversy, 204, *illus.* 204
Kiwanis Clubs, 420
Korean War, 506
Kroc, Ray A., 466–467, *illus.* 466
Krupsak, Mary Ann, *illus.* 318
Kuhn, Maggie, 234

L

Labor
  and Democratic party, 258
  as factor of production, 456–457
Labor contract, 464
Labor unions, 460–465
  bargaining power of, 464–465
  goals of, 462–463
  growth of, 460–462, *illus.* 460,
    461
  membership, *chart* 463
  supporters of, *illus.* 236
  ten largest, *chart* 462
Ladies Garment Workers Union,
  illus. 460
Laws, 9
  carried out by state agencies,
    328
  from Constitution, 57–58
  enforcing, 13
  made by state legislatures,
    302–303, 305–306
  making, 127
  and presidential decisions, 179
  respect for, 106
  and Supreme Court, 222–223
  See also Legislative branch,
    Legislation
Lawyers, 348–351, *illus.* 344
League of Women Voters, 237,
  420
Lee, Richard Henry, 50
Legislation, 120, 132–135
  case study of, 136–139
  and President, 172–173
Legislative branch
  at national level, 60–61
  at state level, 301–311, *illus.*
    307, 308
Lenin, Nikolai, 504
Lerner, Louis A., *illus.* 498
Letters to the editor, 391
Letter writing, effective, 245, 246
Licenes, 373
Lieutenant Governor, 106, 319
Life expectancy, 519
Limited liability, 454
Lincoln, Abraham, 108, 256
Lions Club, 420
  services, *illus.* 421
Lobbyists, 199, 242, 310
Local government
  case study of, 374–375
  kinds of, 361–364
  paying for, 371–373
  services of, 365–370
  See also City government,
    County government
Longley, James, 265
Los Angeles, California, 405, 414,
  illus. 395, 399
Los Angeles County, 370
Louisiana, 120, 300, 362, 538, 539,
  543

Senator Allan Ellender, 137
Lugar, Richard, 240

M

McCall, Tom, 312
MacDonald, Peter, 33
McDonalds, 466–467. *See also*
  Ray A. Kroc
McGovern, George, *illus.* 283
McMillan, John, 137
Madison, James, 41, 42, 49, 51,
  219, 398
Magistrates, 216
Maine, 120, 265, 538, 539, 543
  Governor James Longley, 265
Majority party, 121
Major parties, arguments
  for and against, 260–261
Management, as factor of
  production, 457
Marbury v *Madison,* 219
Market system, 439–440
  ups and downs of, 444–447
  See also Businesses
Marshall, John, 219
Marshall, Thurgood, 219, 226,
  illus. 227
Marx, Karl, 503
Maryland, 46, 50, 120, 369, 374,
  538, 539, 543
  Baltimore, 400, 411, *illus.* 143
Massachusetts, 41, 45, 50, 120,
  338
  Blackstone River, *illus.* 198
  Boston, 400, *illus.* 16, 65, 96,
    493
  case study, 332–333
  Congressman Thomas O'Neill,
    illus. 121
  constitution, 300
  Fall River, 421
  Governor Michael Dukakis,
    332–333, *illus.* 332
  Senator Lowell Weicker, *illus.*
    68
Mayflower Compact, 4
Mayor-council plan, 379–380
Mayors, 384–386. *See also* by
  name
Medicaid, 152
Medicare, 152
  supporter of, *illus.* 134
Megalopolis, 402
Metropolitan area, 402
Miami, Florida, 399, 405
Michigan, 120, 324, 538, 539, 543,
  illus. 10
  Senator Don Riegle, *illus.* 127
Mifflin, Thomas, 52
Minnesota, 120, 538, 539, 543
  Senator Hubert Humphrey,
    130–131
Minority party, 122

Minutes, 422
Misdemeanors, 338
Mississippi, 120, 538, 539, 543
Missouri, 120, 316, 369, 538, 539,
  543
Mixed-market economy, 440–441
Monopoly, 458, 459
Montana, 120, 538, 539, 543, *illus.*
  137, 138
Motor Vehicle Act, 487
Municipal charter, 362
Municipalities, 362
Murphy, Evelyn, 332

N

Nader, Ralph, 484–485, 486–487,
  illus. 486
Name-calling, 284
Nashville, Tennessee, 369
National Aeronautics and Space
  Administration, 193
  astronauts, *illus.* 187
  moon walk, *illus.* 155
National American Woman
  Suffrage Association, 245
National Association for the
  Advancement of Colored
  People, 226, 243
National Association of
  Manufacturers, 235
National borrowing, 149–150
National Bureau of Standards
  international cooperation, *illus.*
    200
  responsibilities, *illus.* 193
National debt, *chart* 156
National Education Association,
  235
National Farmers Union, 282
National Guard, 79, *illus.* 317
National Health Insurance bill
  supporters of, *illus.* 127
National Organization for Women
  rally, *illus.* 102
National Priorities, 154
National Rifle Association, 240
National Security Council, 500
National supremacy, 65–66
National Urban League, 234
National Woman's Conference,
  illus. 102
Naturalization, 103
Natural resources, 435
  in developed countries, 519
  as factor of production, 455–456
  ocean as, 520–521
  in territorial waters, 16–17
  See also Pollution
Navajos, 33–34
Nebraska, 120, 331, 365, 538, 539,
  543
Negligence, 353
Nevada, 120, 370, 538, 539, 543

Neville, John, 53
New England town government, 382–383
New Hampshire, 50, 120, 167, 538, 539, 543
Newhouse, Richard, 290
New Jersey, 40, 44, 50, 120, 167, 369, 538, 539, 543
New Jersey Plan, 45–46
New Mexico, 120, 538, 539, 543
Newspapers
  influence on local politics, 390–391
  reading a, 392–393
New York, 40, 50, 120, 370, *illus.* 361, 411
  Governor Hugh Carey, 324
  Lieutenant Governor Mary Ann Krupsak, *illus.* 318
  opposition to SST, *illus.* 202, 205
  Senator Daniel Moynihan, *illus.* 121
  teenage volunteers, 427
New York City, New York, 51, 338, 339, 369, 372, 389, 399–400, 414–415
Niger, *illus.* 519
Nineteenth Amendment, 91, 102, 275
Ninth Amendment, 88, 100
Nixon, Richard, 10, 121, 166, 171, 178, 496, *illus.* 70, 71, 171
  and Panama Canal controversy, 508
  and Vietnam, 507
  and Watergate, 68–71
Nobility, title of, 61
Nominating committees, for volunteer groups, 423
Nomination, 166–167, 263–265
Non-partisan, 386
North Carolina, 41, 50, 120, 322, 331, 538, 539, 543, *illus.* 137
  1976 election results, *chart* 167
  Senator Sam Ervin, 69, *illus.* 69
North Dakota, 120, 538, 539, 543

O

Oceans, use of, 520–521
Office of Management and Budget, 156–157
Ohio, 53, 111, 120, 167, 316, 365, 420
  Cleveland, 411
  Columbus, 529–531
  Cuyahoga County, 406, 407
Oil spill, *illus.* 358–359
Oklahoma, 120, 129, 538, 539, 543
Ombudsman, 331
O'Neill, Thomas P., III, 332
Open primary, 264
Open shop, 465
Opinions, 214, 221

Order, keeping, 13
Ordinances, 366
Oregon, 120, 312, 317, 331, 538, 539, 543, *illus.* 312–313
  Governor Tom McCall, 312
Overseas jobs, 516, 517

P

Panama Canal Treaties, 508–509
Parishes, 362
Partnership, 454
Party chief, 174
Party conventions, 265
Party leaders, 310
  governor as, 322
Party platforms, 259
Party whip, 122
Party workers, 265–268
Paterson, William, 46
Patriotism, 7, 540–541
Patronage, 310
Pay check deductions, *chart* 145
Peace Corps, 526–527
Pennsylvania, 40, 44, 45, 50, 52, 53, 120, 538, 539, 543
Personal income, 444
Petition, 265
Philadelphia, Pennsylvania, 41, 43, 400
Philippines, 495, 539
Pilgrims, 4
Plain folks, 285–286
Plea bargaining, 345–346
Plessy v *Ferguson,* 225
Pocket veto, 135
Political appointees, 268
Political parties, 252–269
  case study of, 270–271
  choosing between, 258–262
  leaders, 310, 322
  major, 253–254
  majority, 121
  minor, 254
  minority, 122
  1971–1978 preferences, *chart* 254
  organization of, 256–257
  origins of, 255–256
  role of, 263–269
  and state legislation, 310
  third, 254–255
  workers for, 265–267
Political resources, of interest groups, 239–240
Polling place, 264, 276
Pollution, 406–407, 522–523
Popular vote, 168
Population, 538
  ten most populous countries, *chart* 533
Populists, 254
Portland, Oregon, *illus.* 312–313
Postal Inspection Service, 484
Preamble

of U.S. Constitution, 58
of state constitution, 301
Precedents, 219, 223–224
Precincts, 257
Preliminary hearings, 344
Preside, 43
Presidency, 164–180
  advisors to, 175–177
  decision making in, 178–180
  getting elected to, 165–169
  job of, 170–174
President, 47
  approval of bills, 135
  in executive branch, 61–63
  and federal agencies, 199
  and foreign policy, 497
  statistics about, 165–166
  and Supreme Court, 218–219
  in twentieth century, *chart* 166
  See also by name
President of the senate
  at national level, 122
  at state level, 306
President pro tempore, 122
Presiding officers, of state legislature, 306
Prestige, 310
Producers, 435, 439
Productivity, 442–443
Profits, 145, 453
Progressive party, 254, 255
Prohibitionist party, 254
Proletariat, 503
Propaganda, 284–287
Property taxes, 371
Proposition 5, 241
Proposition 13, 374–375
Prosecuting attorney, 366
Protective tariff, 148–149
Public employees, 390
  case study, 394
Public housing projects, 404
Public interest groups, 237. *See also* by name
Public opinion, 179
Public services, 12–13
Public utilities, 459
Pucinski, Roman, 378
Puerto Rico, 495, 539

R

Randolph, Edmund, 44
Rapid transit systems, 405
Ratify, 49
Reagan, Ronald, 169, *illus.* 259
Real case rule, 220
Recession, 444
Referendum, 312
Regulatory commissions, 193–194, 200
Representation in Congress, 119–120, 538
  after 1970 census, *chart* 120
Republicans, 253–257, 258–260.

See also Political parties
Retirement, 234
Revenue sharing, 152, 372, 412
Rhode Island, 41, 50, 120, 362, 538, 539, 543
Rights
  defending, 107–108
  knowing and respecting, 106
  Bill of, 95–100
Right to work laws, 464
Rockefeller, John D., 458
Rockefeller, Nelson, 71
Roles
  of President, 170
  of governors, 321–322
Rome, 5
Roosevelt, Franklin D., 66, 166, 175, 178
Roosevelt, Theodore, 56, 166, 255, 508, *illus.* 57
Rules committee, 134

S
Sadat, Anwar, *illus.* 173
Sales receipts, 474
San Antonio, Texas, 407
San Francisco, California, 394–395, *illus.* 108, 257, 394
  BART, *illus.* 405
  Dianne Feinstein, *illus.* 384
  during Great Depression, *illus.* 446
Savings and loan associations, 477
Scarcity, 435
Schools, 297, 303, 320, 357, 362–364
  and the Supreme Court, 222–224, 225–227
Search warrants, 97
Second Amendment, 86, 96
Secretary of State, 319
  typical day for, 494
  See also by name
Secret operations, 505
Securities, 150
Security, providing, 14
Security treaties, 505
Segregation, and *Brown* v *Board of Education,* 225–227
Self-nomination, 265
Senate, 46, 121
  leaders of, 122
  See also Congress
Seniority rule, 125
Service charges, 373
Services, 435
Seventeenth Amendment, 90, 101
Seventh Amendment, 87, 100
Sewage, 407
  treatment, *illus.* 363
Shared taxes, 372
Shares of stock, 454, 477
Shays, Daniel, 41
Sheriff, 367

Sherman Antitrust Act, 458
Sherman, Roger, 46
Shopping, tips for careful, 474–475
Singer, William, 289–291, *illus.* 290
Single proprietorship, 453–454
Sixteenth Amendment, 66, 90
Sixth Amendment, 87, 97
Slums, 404
Small claims courts, 340, 342–343
Socialist party, 254
Social security benefits, 151
Social security tax, 144–145
South Carolina, 50, 120, 226, 300, 331, 538, 539, 543
  Congressman John McMillan, 137
South Dakota, 120, 538, 539, 543
Soviet Union, 500, 503–504, 506, 507
Sparkman, John, 136
Speaker of the House
  at national level, 121
  at state level, 306
Special committees, 124
Special district, 362, 363–364
Special interest groups, 132
Special sessions, 310
Spending
  by households, *chart* 445
  See also Government spending
Split ticket, 277
SST
  Concorde, illus. 203
  opposition to, *illus.* 202, 205
Stalin, Joseph, 504
Standard of living, 444
Standard Metropolitan Statistical Area, 402
Standard Oil, 458
Standing committees, 123, 305
State auditor or comptroller, 319
State constitutions, 300–301
State courts, 336–351
  case study of, 352–353
  civil cases, 346–347
  criminal cases, 344–346
  lawyers in, 348–351
  organization of, 337–338
State executive branch, 317–331
  executive officers, 319–320
  governors, 317–319, 321–324
  state agencies, 325–331
State government
  agencies, 325–331
  case study of, 332–333
  court system, 336–351
  executive branch, 317–324
  lawmakers, 307–311
  legislatures, 302–306
  occupations of lawmakers, *chart* 306
  power of, 299–304
  responsibility of, 297

standards set by law, *illus.* 303
state tax, 312–313
See also Local government
State legislatures, 302–311, 539
  legislators in, 307–311
  what they do, 302–304
  workings of, 305–306
States
  facts about, *chart* 538, 539
  power of, 100
  under Articles of Confederation, 40–41
  under constitution, 65–67
State supreme courts, 338
State treasurer, 319
Statutory laws, 209
Stevenson, Adlai, 167
Stock holders, 454
Straight ticket, 277
Strikes, 461, *illus.* 463
  by public employees, 390, 394–395
Subcommittees, 123
Suburbs, move to, 401
Subways, 405
Supercities, 401–402
Supply and demand, 445
Supreme Court, 47, 63–64, 214, 218–224, *illus.* 214, 218, 221
  case study of, 225–226
  how cases reach, 220
  influences on, 222–224
  judicial review, 219
  justices of, 218–219, *illus.* 221
  at state level, 338
  steps in review by, 220–222, *illus.* 221
  work load, *illus.* 220
  See also cases by name, Federal courts

T
Taft, William, 166, 255
Taft-Hartley Act, 464
Taxable income, 144
Taxes, 143–149, 372
  income, 146–147
  property, 371
  sales, 312–313
  sample tax bill, *illus.* 371
  and state legislatures, 302
Teamsters, 462
Tennessee, 120, 370, 538, 539, 543
  Nashville, 369
  Senator Howard Baker, *illus.* 69
  teenage volunteers in, 426–427
Territorial Courts, 215
Territorial waters, 16–17
Territories, *See* American territories
Testimonial, 285
Texas, 120, 316, 362, 538, 539, 543
  airline competition in, 448–449
  Congressman Jim Wright, 245

Congresswoman Barbara
Jordan, *illus.* 132
Governor Dolph Briscoe, 316
1974 expenditures, *chart* 357
Third Amendment, 86–87, 96
Third parties, 254–255
Thirteenth Amendment, 89,
100–101
Thompson, James, 240, 241, 316
Torrijos, Omar, 509
Totalitarian society, 425
Town government, *See* New
England town government
Town meeting, *illus.* 382
Townships, 362
Transfer, 285
Transportation, in cities, 405–406,
illus. 472
Treason, 64, 104–105
Treasurer, 367
Treaty, 66, 497, 501, 505
Panama Canal Treaties, 508–509
Trial by jury, 97, 100
Trials, 345, 347, *illus.* 340
Truman, Harry, 56, 166, 504, 506,
illus. 57
Tunney, John, 271
Twelfth Amendment, 88–89
Twentieth Amendment, 91
Twenty-Fifth Amendment, 67, 93
Twenty-First Amendment, 92
Twenty-Fourth Amendment,
92–93, 102
Twenty-Second Amendment,
66–67, 92
Twenty-Sixth Amendment, 93,
102, 111, 275
Twenty-Third Amendment, 92,
102
Two-party system, 253
deciding between parties,
258–262
roots of, 255–256
See also Democrats and
Republicans

U
Union shop, 464
United Auto Workers, 460, 462
United Mine Workers, *illus.* 460
United Nations, 524–528, *illus.*
528
General Assembly, 524, 525,
illus. 524
organization of, *chart* 525
Security Council, 524, 525
UNESCO, 528
U.S. Attorneys, 216
U.S. Chamber of Commerce, 282
U.S. Court of Appeals, 214
U.S. District Courts, 213
U.S. Postal Service, 193
Unitary system of government,
299

Unit pricing, 474
Upheld, 214
Urban areas, 369–370
Urban problems, 403–413
case study, 414–415
and city planners, 407–410
federal help for, 411–413
housing, 404–405
pollution, 406–407
transportation, 405–406
Urban renewal, 404–405
Utah, 120, 538, 539, 543

V
Values, 23–24
Vance, Cyrus, *illus.* 495
Vermont, 120, 300, 538, 539, 543
Vice President, 61, 62, 67, 121,
122, 176–177
Vietnam, 171, 506
American veterans, *illus.* 10
war in, *illus.* 506
Virginia, 4, 40, 41, 44, 45, 50, 120,
215–216, 226, 316, 538, 539,
543
Senator Harry Byrd, 216
Virginia Plan, 44–45
Volunteers, 109, 418, 419, *illus.*
109, 358–359, 422, 424, 426,
427
case study of, 426–427
contribution of, to democracy,
424–425
governing, 422–423
groups, 420–421
Voter registration, 276, *illus.* 101
Voting, 20, 274–288, *illus.* 21, 101
affected by interest groups,
240–241
case study of, 289–291
deciding how to, 281–287
for President, 168
rules for, 275–279
See also Elections
Voting age, lowering of, 110–111
Voting machines, 264, *illus.* 3, 101

W
Wages, 445, 446, 463
Wallace, George, 285
War Powers Act, 179, 501
Warranties, 474
Wars
American Revolution, 38, 40
communist revolution in China,
496
communist revolution in Russia,
504
cost of, 156
Korean, 496, 506
limited, 506–507
and presidential power, 171
Spanish-American, 495, 508
Vietnam, 496, 506–507

See also World Wars
Washington, 120, 264, 538, 539,
543, *illus.* 136
Washington, D.C., 226
Washington, George, 16, 52, 117,
143, 255
at constitutional convention, 38,
39, 41, 42, 43
Washington Post, 68
Watchdog agencies, 200
Watchdog, political parties' role
as, 269
Watergate, 68–71
Weapons, 522, *illus.* 14
West Point, *illus.* 22
West Virginia, 120, 538, 539, 543
*West Virginia State Board of
Education* v *Barnette,*
223–224
Whig party, 256
Whiskey Rebellion, 52–53
White House, *illus.* 165
White House Office, 175–176
Wills, 348
Wilson, Woodrow, 56, 166, 255,
illus. 57
Winner-takes-all, 169
Wisconsin, 10, 120, 538, 539, 543,
illus. 513
Senator William Proxmire, *illus.*
182
state legislator, *illus.* 307
Woodward, Bob, 68
World Health Organization, 528
World Wars, and foreign policy,
495, 498, 503, 504, 505
World War II, 504
and United Nations, 524
Worthington, Ohio, 420–421
Wright, Jim, 245
Write-in vote, 277
Writ of mandamus, 347
Wyoming, 120, 538, 539, 543

Y
Yochelson, Ellis, 248, 249
Youth Ederly Service, 421

Z
Zoning ordinances, 410

Acknowledgments

Quoted Material

392 From "U.S. Says New York May Set Aside Fund to Operate Housing," by Steven R. Weisman from *The New York Times*, April 10, 1979. Copyright © 1979 by The New York Times Company. Reprinted by permission. **393** *Chicago Sun-Times,* April 8, 1979. Copyright © 1979 by The Associated Press. Reprinted by permission of The Associated Press.

Illustrations

The abbreviations indicate the position of illustrations on the page: *t* is top, *b* is bottom, *l* is left, *r* is right, *c* is center.

2-3 Jim Anderson/Woodfin Camp Assoc. 5 Courtesy Pilgrim Hall Museum 8 Wide World 10 (r) Wide World (l) Clif Garboden/Stock Boston 12 Rose Skytta/Jeroboam 14 Chicago Tribune Photo 16 (l) UPI (r) Arthur Grace/Sygma 17 UPI 21 (l) Erik Anderson/Stock Boston (t) Bohdan Hrynewych/Stock Boston (b) Jacques Jangoux/Peter Arnold, Inc. 22 (t) Wide World (b) Owen Franken/Stock Boston (r) Costa Manos/Magnum 27 (l) Frederich D. Bodin/Stock Boston (lc) Stephen Pardon/Taurus Photos (rc) Donald Dietz/Stock Boston (r) David Huff/Taurus Photos 29 (t) Charles Gatewood (b) Donald Dietz/Stock Boston 32 MISS PEACH by Mell Lazarus Courtesy of Mell Lazarus and Field Newspaper Syndicate 33 John Running/Black Star 34-35 Alan Copeland/ © 1976 John Day Co. 39 National Geographic Photographer, George F. Mobley, Courtesy U.S. Capitol Historical Society 40 The Chase Manhattan Bank Museum of Moneys of the World 41 painting by Rembrandt Peale, The Historical Society of Pennsylvania 41 painting by Charles Wilson Peale, The Historical Society of Pennsylvania 42 John Trumbull, Art Commission of New York 42 painting by John Vanderlyn, James Monroe Memorial Library 44 (l) painting by John Singleton Copley, The Historical Society of Pennsylvania (r) painting by Marston, The Massachusetts Historical Society 45 (l) The New Haven Colony Historical Society (t) The Metropolitan Museum of Art, Gift of Mrs. John Sylvester, 1936 (b) John Work Garrett Library, The John Hopkins University 46 (l) The Metropolitan Museum of Art, photograph by Robert S. Crandall (r) Courtesy of The New York Historical Society 47 (l) Both: The New York Public Library, Astor, Lenox and

Tilden Foundations (r) painting by William Birch, The Historical Society of Pennsylvania 48 (l) painting by John Singleton Copley, Courtesy Museum of Fine Arts, Boston, The Edgar Ingersoll Browne Fund, 1774 (r) engraving by William Birch, The Historical Society of Pennsylvania 49 (l) The New York Public Library, Rare Book Division (t) The New York Public Library, Arents Collection (b) Courtesy American Antiquarian Society 51 Courtesy of The New York Historical Society 52 Culver Pictures 53 painting by James Peale, The Metropolitan Museum of Art, Collection of Edgar William and Bernice Chrysler Garbisch 57 (l) The Bettman Archive (c) Brown Brothers (r) Tom Henle/Photo Researchers 59 (l) Tom Pix/Peter Arnold, Inc. 61 Capt. Cecil Stoughton/UPI 63 Edward Grazda/Magnum 65 (t) Cary Wolinsky/Stock Boston (b) John DeVisser/Black Star 66 (t) Owen Franken/Sygma (b) UPI 67 (t) Ginger Chih/Peter Arnold, Inc. (b) Sam C. Pierson, Jr./Photo Researchers 68 Mark Godfrey/Magnum 69 (l) Wide World (r) Owen Franken/Stock Boston 70 (l) Wide World (r) Leo Choplin/Black Star 71 Alex Webb/Magnum 95 Ellis Herwig/Stock Boston 96 Owen Franken/Stock Boston 97 Verna Sadock, NBC/WMAQ-TV 98-99 Robert Ipcar 101 (l) Ebony Magazine, Johnson Publishing Co. (t) Owen Franken/Stock Boston (b) Wide World 102 (t) Owen Franken/Sygma (c) Ginger Chih/Peter Arnold, Inc. (b) Oliver Rebbot/Stock Boston 104 (b) Karen Engstrom/Chicago Tribune Photo (t) mural by Ben Shahn/EPA-Scala 106 (t) Cecile Bunswick/Peter Arnold, Inc. (b) John Sotomayor/New York Times Pictures 108 Rose Skytta/Jeroboam 109 Christopher Morrow/Stock Boston 110 (t) Dirck Halstead/Sygma (c) Eric Kroll/Taurus Photos (b) Lawrence Cameron/Jeroboam 116-117 J. P. Laffont/Sygma 119 Arthur Grace/Sygma 121 Mark Godfrey/Magnum 123 Courtesy, Office of Congressman Daniel K. Akaka 124 Dennis Brack/Black Star 125 Tom Darcy/Newsday, Inc. 127 Paul S. Conklin 128 Courtesy, Office of Sen. Nancy Kassenbaum 129 Ken Hawkins/Sygma 130 Paul S. Conklin 132 Dennis Brack/Black Star 134 Karen R. Preuss/Jeroboam 136 John Running/Black Star 137 (l) Harvey Lloyd/Peter Arnold, Inc. (r) Frank J. Miller/Photo Researchers 138 (l) Dirck Halstead/Sygma (r) Harvey Lloyd/Peter Arnold, Inc. 139 Ron Partridge 143 UPI 148 Ellis Herwig/Stock Boston 149 George Gardner 152 (l) John Launois/Black

Star (r) Wide World 155 NASA 157 Paul S. Conklin 158 Lou Grant/*Oakland Tribune* 165 Wolf Von Dem Bussche/Photo Researchers 168 (l) Peter Southwick/Stock Boston (r) Wide World 171 Tashi/Black Star 172 (l) Cary Wolinsky/Stock Boston (r) Richard Choy/Peter Arnold, Inc. 173 Courtesy The White House/Bill Fitz-Patrick, photographer 175 UPI 176 Richard Kalvar/Magnum 179 Owen Franken/Stock Boston 181 U.S. Air Force Photo 182-183 UPI 187 NASA 189 Fred Ward/Black Star 190-191 William Holman/U.S. Forest Service 193 Smithsonian Institution Photo 195 Alyeska Pipeline Service Co. 198 Jack Swedberg 200 Smithsonian Institution Photo 201 Scrawls/*Palm Beach Post* 202-204 UPI 205 Wide World 210 Larry Nighswander 212 Ellis Herwig/Stock Boston 214 Yoichi Okamoto/Photo Researchers 218 Susan McCartney/Photo Researchers 220 Yoichi Okamoto/Photo Researchers 221 (t) Fred J. Maroon; (c, b) Yoichi Okamoto/Photo Researchers 224 (t) Crawford Neat © 1967/NEA (b) Engelhardt in the *St. Louis Post-Dispatch* 225 Library of Congress 226 (t) Library of Congress (c) Danny Lyon/Magnum (b) Elliott Erwitt/Magnum 227 UPI 232-233 Mark Godfrey/Magnum 235 UPI 236 C. Templin/Jeroboam 237 League of Women Voters Education Fund 241 Dirck Halstead 245 Mark Godfrey/Magnum 246 Courtesy, Office of Sen. Howard Baker 248 Engelhardt in the *St. Louis Post-Dispatch* 249 Andrew Sacks/Editorial Photocolor Archives 253 Paul S. Conklin 254 Brown Brothers 255 Culver Pictures 257 Hank Lebo/Jeroboam 258 Don Hesse, © 1970, *St. Louis Globe-Democrat.* Reprinted with permission, Los Angeles Times Syndicate 259 Paul Sequeira 263 UPI 268 George Gardner 270 Alex Webb/Magnum 271 Bob Clay/Jeroboam 275 Cornell Capa/Magnum 277 Brickman/Washington Star Syndicate, Inc. 278 Computer Election Systems, Inc. 281 Roger Lubin/Jeroboam 283 Hank Lebo/Jeroboam 289-291 UPI 296-297 Jeff Albertson/Stock Boston 299 Ellis Herwig/Stock Boston 302 George Gardner 303 Owen Franken/Stock Boston 307-308 Daniel S. Brody/Stock Boston 312 Library of Congress 313 Courtesy Oregon Chamber of Commerce 317 Leonard Freed/Magnum 318 UPI 321 Steve Roberts, New York Times Pictures 322 Neal Boenzi/New York Times Pictures 325 U.S. Office of Personnel Management 326-327 Marni T. Miller 330 Fischetti © 1978 *Chicago Sun-Times* 332 Owen Franken/Stock

Boston **333** Ellis Herwig/Stock Boston **337** Michael D. Sullivan **340** Verna Sadock, NBC/WMAQ-TV **344** John Running/Stock Boston **349** Bennett/FPG **358–359** Richard Choy/Peter Arnold, Inc. **361** Cary Wolinsky/Stock Boston **363** Daniel S. Brody/Stock Boston **365** J. P. Laffont/Sygma **366–368** George Gardner **372** Wide World **374** Chris Springman/Black Star **375** Matt Herron/Black Star **382** Arthur Grace/Sygma **384** Courtesy, Office of Mayor Diane Feinstein **387** J. Zimmer/FPG **389** Owen Franken/Stock Boston **394** Donald Deitz/Stock Boston **395** Lawrence Moorhouse/Stock Boston **399** Spence Air Photos **405** Daniel S. Brody/Stock Boston **408** (t) Burt Glinn/Magnum (b) Costa Manos/Magnum **409** (tl) Wm. R. Wright/Taurus Photos (tr) Mark Godfrey/Magnum (b) Ellis Herwig/Stock Boston **411** Ronald F. Thomas/Taurus Photos **412** Peter Menzel/Stock Boston **415** Dirck Halstead/Sygma **419** Christopher Morrow/Stock Boston **421** Isaiah Karlinsky/FPG **422** Hennepin County Public Affairs **424** Anestis N. Diakopoulous/Stock Boston **426** (l) Judith Aronson/Peter Arnold, Inc. (r) Richard Choy/Peter Arnold, Inc. **427** Karen R. Preuss/Jeroboam **432–433** George Hunter/FPG **435** J. P. Laffont/Sygma **436** Cary Wolinsky/Stock Boston **438** (l) Bill Stanton/Magnum (r) Abigail Heyman/Magnum **443** Mike Wannemacher/Taurus Photos **446** Dorothea Lange/The Oakland Museum **448–449** Southwest Airlines **453** Burk Uzzle/Magnum **457** Tony Korody/Sygma **458** cartoon by Thomas Nast/The New York Public Library, Astor, Lenox and Tilden Foundations **460** (l) Courtesy of The New York Historical Society, photograph by Robert S. Crandall **461** Culver Pictures **463** Dave Healey/Sygma **464** Burt Glinn/Magnum **466–467** Courtesy McDonald's Systems, Inc. **472** Donald Dietz/Stock Boston **481** J. P. Laffont/Sygma **482** (b) U.S. Consumer Product Safety Commission (t) U.S. Office of Personnel Mngmt. **483** U.S. Consumer Product Safety Commission **484** T. Moore/FPG **486** Arthur Grace/Sygma **487** Ralph Nader, *Unsafe at Any Speed* © 1965, Grossman Publishers **492–493** Wyman/Sygma **495** Hatami/Sipa Press/Black Star **496** Jack McLeod in the *Buffalo Evening News* **497** David Kennerly/FPG **498** Courtesy, Office of Ambassador Louis Lerner **501** Ken Hawkins/Sygma **503–506** UPI **508** Olivier Rebbot/Stock Boston **509** (t) Wide World (b) Ken Hawkins/Sygma **513** Daniel S. Brody/Stock Boston **517** ACTION/Peace Corps Photo **519** .

Victor Englebert **520** Jack Fields/Photo Researchers **524** UN Photo Library **526–527** ACTION/Peace Corps Photos **528** Brickman/The Washington Star Syndicate, Inc. **529** IBM **530** Ellis Herwig/Stock Boston **531** Magnum

Charts, Diagrams, Graphs, and Tables 126 *U.S. News and World Report,* Vol. LXXXII No. 1. "What a Congressman Must Do for the Folks Back Home," p. 28, Washington, D.C. **167** *U.S. News and World Report* Vol. LXXX No. 14. "North Carolina Results in Brief," p. 18. Washington, D.C. **254** *The Chicago Tribune,* 2-23-78. "Political Party Preference." Chicago, Ill.: Chicago Tribune, Inc. **260** *The Gallup Opinion Index* Report No. 137. "Vote By Groups In Presidential Elections Since 1952," pp. 16–17. Princeton, N. J.: The Gallup Poll, Dec. 1976. **282** *The Louisville Courier Journal.* "Interest Groups Rate Members of Congress." Louisville, Ky. **306** *U.S. News and World Report* Vol. LXXXII No. 1. "Occupations of State Lawmakers," p. 64. Washington, D.C. **442** Chamber of Commerce of the U.S.A., *The Years of Change: An Almanac of American Progress.* "Percentage of World Population and World GNP in 15 Most Populous Countries," tbl. 9.1, p. 65. Washington, D.C.: Nation's Business, 1978. **447** *U.S. News and World Report* Vol. LXXXV No. 13. "How Inflation Gobbles Up Your Paycheck," p. 30. Washington, D.C. **455** *The New York Stock Exchange Facts Book.* "Companies with the Largest Number of Stockholders." New York: The New York Stock Exchange, Inc., 1978. **463** *World Book Encyclopedia* L Vol. 12. "Union Membership in the United States," p. 11. Chicago, Ill.: World Book-Childcraft International, Inc., 1979. **469** Hodgetts, Richard & Smart, Terry L., *Fundamentals of the American Free Enterprise System.* "The Top Ten Corporations in the U.S.," p. 57. Reading, Mass.: Addison Wesley, 1978. **533** *Information Please: Almanac.* "Quality of Life: Selected National Development Statistics," pp. 134–35. New York: The Viking Press, 1978. **543** Cook, Rhodes, *Congressional Quarterly Weekly Reports,* resp: Nov. 4, 1978 and March 31, 1979. "Voting Age Population and Midterm Turnout," p. 3178; "Voter Turnout: Lowest Midterm Turnout Since 1942," p. 574. Washington, D.C.: Congressional Quarterly, Inc., 1978.